CREATING INCLUSIVE CLASSROOMS
Effective and Reflective Practices

CREATING INCLUSIVE CLASSROOMS
Effective and Reflective Practices

Fourth Edition

Spencer J. Salend
State University of New York at New Paltz

Merrill
Prentice Hall

Upper Saddle River, New Jersey
Columbus, Ohio

Library of Congress Cataloging in Publication Data

Salend, Spencer J.
   Creating inclusive classrooms : effective and reflective practices / Spencer J. Salend.—
4th ed.
      p. cm.
   Rev. ed. of: Effective mainstreaming. 3rd ed. c1998.
   Includes bibliographical references and index.
   ISBN 0-13-019073-X (pbk.)
      1. Inclusive education—United States. 2. Mainstreaming in education—United States. 3.
Curriculum planning—United States. 4. Classroom management—United States. 5.
Handicapped children—Education—United States. I. Salend, Spencer J. Effective
mainstreaming. II. Title
LC1201 .S24 2001
371.9′046—dc21   99-089661

Vice President and Publisher: Jeffery W. Johnston
Executive Editor: Ann Castel Davis
Development Editor: Gianna Marsella
Editorial Assistant: Pat Grogg
Production Editor: Sheryl Glicker Langner
Design Coordinator: Karrie Converse-Jones
Cover Designer: Ceri Fitzgerald
Cover art: Artville
Photo Coordinator: Sandy Lenahan
Electronic Text Management: Karen L. Bretz
Production Manager: Laura Messerly
Director of Marketing: Kevin Flanagan
Marketing Manager: Amy June
Marketing Services Manager: Krista Groshong

This book was set in New Caledonia by Carlisle Communications, Ltd. It was printed and bound
by Von Hoffmann Press, Inc. The cover was printed by Von Hoffmann Press, Inc.

PHOTO CREDITS

pp. 1, 2, 6, 28, 34, 76, 88, 93, 100, 117, 123, 125, 130, 158, 169, 171, 182, 200, 217, 223, 226, 240,
270, 277, 282, 316, 320, 325, 334, 344, 347, 350, 379, 390, 399, 412, 416, 422, 441 by Scott Cun-
ningham/Merrill; p. 11 by James L Shaffer; pp. 16, 196, 287, 291, 367 by Anthony Magnacca/Mer-
rill; pp. 20, 249, 255, 303, 310 by Larry Hamill/Merrill; p. 40 by Laura Dwight/Laura Dwight Photography; p. 51 by Corbis Digital Stock; p. 58 by PH College; pp. 61, 404 by David
Young-Wolff/PhotoEdit; pp. 72, 142, 435 by Tom Watson/Merrill; p, 83 by Richard Abarno/The
Stock Market; p. 107 by John Paul Endress/Silver Burdett Ginn; pp. 118, 174, 190 by Todd Yarring-
ton/Merrill; p. 155 by Nancy Acevedo/Monkmeyer; p. 176 by Pearson Education; pp. 208, 376 by
Michael Newman/Photo Edit; p. 232 by David Buffington/Photo Disc, Inc.; p. 261 by PhotoDisc,
Inc.; p. 269 by Mike Peters/Silver Burdett Ginn; p. 329 by Richard Hutchings/Photo Researchers,
Inc.; p. 358 by Corbis Digital Stock; pp. 363, 411 by Grantpix/Monkmeyer; p. 409 by SuperStock,
Inc.; p. 429 by Gail Meese/Meese Photo Research.

Merrill
Prentice Hall

10 9 8 7 6 5 4 3 2 1
ISBN 0-13-019073-X

PREFACE

As reflections of society, our nation's schools have historically been challenged to respond to various societal changes and mandates. In 1954 the Supreme Court, in its decision in the case of *Brown* v. *Board of Education,* mandated that schools stop segregating students based on race. With passage of the Education for All Handicapped Children Act of 1975 (PL 94-142), now called the Individuals with Disabilities Education Act (IDEA), Congress required our nation's educational system to include students with disabilities. Within the last 20 years, demographic shifts, economic conditions, and changes in the structure of families have challenged schools to meet the needs of a diverse group of students.

The inclusion movement has developed to meet these educational mandates and challenges. However, there is still a considerable gap between theory and practice. This book is intended to fill that gap by keeping the perspectives of teachers, students, and families in mind, and translating current research on inclusion into effective and reflective classroom practices that address and expand the realities of the classroom setting. Within each chapter are numerous classroom-based examples and case studies of real situations that educators, students, and family members encounter in inclusive classrooms as well as guidelines, strategies, and procedures that have been used to address these situations to educate *all students* successfully in inclusive classrooms.

The book is designed to serve as a text for undergraduate, graduate, and in-service courses for teachers, ancillary support personnel, and administrators interested in teaching and providing services to students with diverse learning needs. Because of its focus on instructional procedures and collaboration, the book also can serve as a supplementary text for a course on methods or consultation.

ORGANIZATION AND APPROACH

The book is organized into four parts. Part One includes Chapters 1, 2, and 3 and introduces you to the foundations and fundamentals of inclusion and the challenges of its implementation. Part Two includes Chapters 4, 5, 6, and 7 and provides you with strategies for creating an inclusive environment that supports learning for *all students.* Part Three includes Chapters 8, 9, 10, and 11 and offers you strategies to differentiate instruction to promote the learning of *all students* within inclusive educational settings. Part Four consists of Chapter 12 which offers a framework and specific strategies and resources for evaluating inclusion programs in terms of individual and programmatic progress.

A Principled Philosophy

The following principles of effective inclusion also provide a framework for this book. These four principles—*diversity, individual needs, reflective practice,* and *collaboration*—are integrated into each chapter of the book and demonstrate that inclusion is not just a government mandate but a principled philosophy of reflective, effective teaching.

Principle #1: Effective inclusion improves the educational system for all students by placing them together in general education classrooms—regardless of their learning ability, race, linguistic ability, economic status, gender, learning style, ethnicity, cultural background, religion, family structure, and sexual orientation. Inherent in the concept of inclusion is the recognition of the need to individualize the educational system for *all students.* The result can be an educational system that is more able to accommodate and respond to the individual needs of *all students.* Thus, changes in the educational system designed to facilitate effective inclusion also benefit *all students,* teachers, families, ancillary support personnel, and administrators.

Principle #2: Effective inclusion involves sensitivity to and acceptance of individual needs and differences. Educators cannot teach students without looking at the various factors that have shaped and will continue to shape their students and make them unique. Therefore, since race, linguistic ability, gender, economic status, and learning ability interact to create a complex amalgam that affects academic performance and socialization, educators, students, and family members must be sensitive to and accepting of individual needs and differences. Educators also must be willing to modify attitudes, instructional techniques, curriculum, and models of family involvement to address and accommodate these needs. Our ability to redefine the mainstream to include the unique needs and differences of students and their families, as well as incorporate their varied visions, voices, and contributions, is critical in expanding the educational, social, and cultural base of our educational system and promoting effective inclusion programs.

Principle # 3: Effective inclusion requires reflective educators to modify their attitudes, teaching and classroom management practices, and curricula to accommodate individual needs. Success at creating inclusive classrooms depends on the ability of educators to become effective and reflective practitioners who are able to think critically about their values, beliefs, and practices. They continually engage in self-improvement by reflecting upon and evaluating the impact of their actions on students, families, and other professionals and refining their teaching practices and curricula to facilitate the learning of all students. Therefore, in addition to providing you with effective practices and examples of their use in inclusive settings, the book contains several innovative pedagogical features designed to help you develop your skill as a reflective practitioner.

Principle # 4: Effective inclusion is a group effort which involves collaboration among educators, other professionals, students, families, and community agencies. When these groups work together, the likelihood for effective inclusion is increased. Thus, the book outlines the roles and responsibilities of educators, families, students with disabilities and their peers, and community agencies to promote effective inclusion programs, and offers strategies for integrating these roles so that individuals work collaboratively and communicate regularly.

These four principles, along with the incorporation of instructional technology into each chapter, make the book consistent with professional standards for preparing teachers to work in today's diverse classrooms.

A Non-Categorical Approach

The book is also organized to the serve as a model for creating inclusive classrooms for *all students.* It is meant to facilitate your development of a holistic approach to educating students while focusing on individual needs rather than on global disability characteristics. Thus, it is not separated into chapters by disability category or cultural and linguistic background that imply and focus on the differences that have been used to segregate students from one another. Rather, the book approaches inclusion as an ongoing, dynamic process for *all students*. Chapter titles and content relate to and address the key factors that contribute to effective and reflective practices for educating *all students* in inclusive settings. Instead of separate chapters on students with various disabilities or students from culturally and linguistically diverse backgrounds, information and classroom-based examples related to these students as well as other students are integrated and embedded in each chapter. It is also important to note that strategies appropriate for one group of students also can be used with other groups of students.

New Additions and Special Features

Content Coverage

Each chapter has been significantly revised to reflect not only what is happening in the field but also how these changes are affecting educators, students, and families, and the delivery of effective instructional programs to *all students*. Among the changes you will see are:

- A new chapter (Chapter 12: Evaluating Student Progress and the Effectiveness of Your Inclusion Program) that offers you *guidelines and sample assessment devices to evaluate the success of your inclusion program.* In addition, this chapter also provides you with new information on *authentic and portfolio assessment, testing accommodations,* and *test-taking skills* which can assist you in helping students perform at their optimal levels on standardized and high stakes testing.
- New content related to *diversity, collaboration,* and *technology* integrated into each chapter.
- Two new sections in Chapter 1—the first includes *the latest information on the Individuals with Disabilities Education Act (IDEA)* and the second provides you with a summary of the *latest research on the impact of inclusion on teachers, students, and family members.*
- A broader and more detailed discussion of the IEP in Chapter 2, including *guidelines for developing IEPs and implementing them in inclusive settings.* Chapter 2 also includes current information about the *educational needs of students with low-incidence disabilities,* and strategies for educating them in inclusive settings.
- In Chapter 3, additional information and examples related to *differentiating cultural and language differences from learning problems* as well as the latest research and programs addressing the *needs of students from culturally and linguistically diverse backgrounds.*
- An expanded discussion of *cooperative teaching, working with paraeducators,* and *communicating with families* in Chapter 4.
- Expanded coverage on strategies and resources *for facilitating an acceptance of individual differences and friendships* between your students, including specific activities teachers can implement, in Chapter 5.
- Chapter 6 now contains expanded coverage on *helping students make the transition to inclusive settings.*

❖ New sections on *how to conduct a functional assessment* and *how to prevent students from harming others* in Chapter 7.
❖ Revisions to Chapters 8, 9, 10, and 11 to include the latest information on *differentiating instruction, using technology to support and modify instruction,* and *using research-based inclusion strategies.*

Pedagogical Elements and Special Features

Within each chapter are innovative features designed to help you understand, personalize, and reflect upon the content presented in the book. These features include:

❖ *Chapter-opening focus questions* that serve as advance organizers and provide a structure for the material presented;
❖ *Summaries* at the end of each chapter that address the chapter heading questions and are designed to help you review the main points of each chapter;
❖ *Informational margin notes* that provide you with additional information and resources related to the material in the book;
❖ *Classroom-based examples and case studies* of teachers implementing effective inclusive educational practices in their classrooms;
❖ *Chapter opening vignettes* of a student or teacher, or both, that depict the issues discussed within the chapter;
❖ *Ideas for Implementation* that offer practical examples of the application of techniques in the book that are effective for *all students* educated in inclusive classrooms; and
❖ Examples of effective practices within the text of each chapter.

Each chapter also contains several new features designed to prompt you to reflect upon and interact with the material presented in the book, including:

❖ *Reflecting on Professional Practices*—vignettes describing a classroom experience from the teacher's point of view followed by reflective questions
❖ *Reflecting on Your Practices*—checklists designed to assist you in examining your practices, behaviors, and beliefs
❖ *What Would You Do in Today's Diverse Classroom*—descriptions of classroom situations followed by a set of reflective questions
❖ *Reflective Margin Notes*—questions that ask you to reflect on your personal experiences related to the material in the book.

This textbook also contains several new features designed to introduce you to content about technology and foster your use of technology, including:

❖ *Set Your Sites margin notes* in every chapter link you to websites that offer additional information and resources related to specific topics in the book. These sites can also be accessed via hot links from the companion website, located at *http://www.prenhall.com/salend.*
❖ *Video Insights,* which appear in Chapters 1, 7, 8, and 12, link chapter content to the video segments included in the ABC News/Prentice Hall video library and to the streaming video that can be downloaded from the companion website, located at *http://www.prenhall.com/salend.*
❖ The *Developing Quality IEPs: A Case-Based Tutorial CD-ROM* will walk you through the development of IEPs and the criteria necessary to assess their quality. One of the tutorials is based on the case of Marty, featured in Chapter 2. The CD-ROM is also integrated into Chapter 2 via margin notes.

ANCILLARIES

The ancillaries and supplements package for the fourth edition has been expanded considerably. Several new, exciting supplements are now available for students and instructors, and the high-quality supplements that have always been offered with the text have been thoroughly revised and expanded.

- *Instructor's Manual*—The fourth edition includes an Instructor's Manual to assist students and instructors in using the text. Chapters in the manual parallel the organization and content of the text. Each chapter of the manual includes chapter objectives, chapter overview, transparency masters *(NEW!)*, learning activities, as well as a comprehensive test bank containing both short-answer and essay questions.

- *Computerized Testbank Software*—The computerized testbank software gives instructors electronic access to the test questions printed in the Instructor's Manual, allowing them to create and customize exams on their computer. The software can help professors manage their courses and gain insight into their students' progress and performance. Computerized testbank software is available in both Macintosh and PC/Windows versions.

- *Video Library (NEW!)*—The ABC/Prentice Hall video library contains 3 compelling programs: *Sean's Story,* a video about one boy's experiences becoming a part of an inclusive classroom; *Survival Lessons,* an examination of school-based mental health programs; and *Common Miracles,* an in-depth look at new strategies for teaching and learning, such as cooperative learning and multiple intelligences. *Evaluating the Effectiveness of Inclusion: A Video Case Study of Memorial High School* includes interviews with a mix of students with and without disabilities, and is available as streaming video on the companion website. The Video Insights boxes throughout the text can be used to link the video programming to the text and to promote lively, thoughtful classroom discussion of critical—and sometimes controversial—issues in education.

- *Companion Website (NEW!)*—Located at *http://www. prenhall.com/salend*, the companion website for this text includes a wealth of resources for both students and professors. The *Syllabus Manager* enables professors to create and maintain the class syllabus online while also allowing the student access to the syllabus at any time from any computer on the Internet. *Focus Questions* and *Chapter Summaries* help students review chapter content. Students can test their knowledge by taking interactive *Self-Tests*—multiple-choice quizzes that provide immediate feedback with a percentage score and correct answers—or responding to *Essay Questions* that can be submitted to instructors or study partners via e-mail. The *Set Your Sites* feature contains hot links to all the websites mentioned in the margins of the text and assists students in using the Web to do additional research on chapter topics and key issues. In the *Video Case Study* module, students can watch streaming video online and then respond to reflective questions. Both the *Message Board* and *Live Chat* features encourage student interaction outside of the classroom. Finally, the *Resources* module houses a special education resources supersite and a variety of forms and checklists that can be downloaded.

- *Developing Quality IEPs: A Case-based Tutorial (NEW!)*—The CD-ROM packaged with this text will walk you through the development of IEPs and the criteria necessary to assess their quality. To help you learn more about developing quality IEPs, the CD-ROM provides two interactive tutorials, six case studies with related exercises, and a variety of additional resources to help you implement IEPs in general education settings. These resources include web links, journal articles, assessment and year-end review evaluation forms, checklists, tips, and guidelines.

◆ *Student Study Guide (NEW!)*—The Student Study Guide provides students with additional opportunities to review chapter content as well as offering many support mechanisms to help them learn and study more effectively. These include chapter outlines and summaries, key terms, application and reflective exercises, and self-tests.

ACKNOWLEDGMENTS

This book is a result of the collaborative efforts of my students, colleagues, friends, and relatives. The book is an outgrowth of many ideas I learned from students at Woodlawn Junior High School (Buffalo, New York) and Public School 76 (Bronx, New York), colleagues from PS 76—George Bonnici, Nydia Figueroa-Torres, Jean Gee, and Jean Barber—and colleagues at the University of Kentucky, and the State University of New York at New Paltz. Much of the information in this book was learned through interactions with teachers, administrators, and students in the Easton (Pennsylvania) Area School District and the New Paltz (New York) School District, who both welcomed me and shared their experiences. Many of the examples and vignettes are based on the experiences of my students at the State University of New York at New Paltz. I truly value my colleagues and students, who continue to educate me and add to my appreciation of the remarkable dedication and skill of teachers.

I also want to acknowledge my students, colleagues, and friends who provided support and guidance throughout all stages of the book. I especially want to recognize Lee Bell, John Boyd, Meenakshi Gajria, Judy Dorney, Luis Garrido, Charleen Gottschalk, Margaret Gutierrez, Karen Giek, Mark Metzger, Bob Michael, Jean Mumper, Helen Musumeci, Kathy Pike, Sarah Ryan, Robin Smith, Lorraine Taylor, Margaret Wade-Lewis, Halee Vang, and Catharine Whittaker for supporting and inspiring me throughout the process. My deepest appreciation also goes to Laurel Garrick Duhaney for preparing the innovative instructor's manual that accompanies this book and to Connie D'Alessandro for her invaluable assistance in coordinating various aspects of the book.

This book would not have been possible without the efforts and skills of Gianna Marsella, who provided me with the professional and emotional support needed to enhance many aspects of the book. Her subtle and at times direct prodding helped me to create a more readable, practically-oriented, and pedagogically sound book. I also appreciate the work of Ann Davis, Pat Grogg, Helen Greenberg, and Sheryl Langner. I also am grateful to the following reviewers: Marie Brand, New York University; Frederick J. Bartelheim, University of Northern Colorado; Jim Burns, The College of St. Rose (NY); Moon K. Chang, Alabama State University; Younghee M. Kim, Oregon State University; Rori R. Carson, Eastern Illinois University; Robert J. Evans, Marshall University; Robert W. Ortiz, New Mexico State University; Colleen Shea Stump, San Francisco State University; and Qaisar Sultana, Eastern Kentucky University. Their thoughtful and professional comments helped to shape and improve the book.

I want to dedicate this book to Suzanne Salend, my collaborator in life, Jack Salend, my son, and Madison Salend, my granddaughter, in recognition of their love, spirit, intelligence, encouragement, strength, and passion. They have taught me how to accept and grow from a challenge. I hope that this book will help you accept and grow from the challenge of creating inclusive classrooms for *all students*.

DISCOVER THE COMPANION WEBSITE ACCOMPANYING THIS BOOK

The Prentice Hall Companion Website: A Virtual Learning Environment

Technology is a constantly growing and changing aspect of our field that is creating a need for content and resources. To address this emerging need, Prentice Hall has developed an online learning environment for students and professors alike—Companion Websites—to support our textbooks.

In creating a Companion Website, our goal is to build on and enhance what the textbook already offers. For this reason, the content for each user-friendly website is organized by chapter and provides the professor and student with a variety of meaningful resources. Common features of a Companion Website include:

For the Professor—

Every Companion Website integrates **Syllabus Manager™,** an online syllabus creation and management utility.

- ◈ **Syllabus Manager™** provides you, the instructor, with an easy, step-by-step process to create and revise syllabi, with direct links into Companion Website and other online content without having to learn HTML.
- ◈ Students may logon to your syllabus during any study session. All they need to know is the web address for the Companion Website and the password you've assigned to your syllabus.
- ◈ After you have created a syllabus using **Syllabus Manager™,** students may enter the syllabus for their course section from any point in the Companion Website.
- ◈ Class dates are highlighted in white and assignment due dates appear in blue. Clicking on a date, the student is shown the list of activities for the assignment. The activities for each assignment are linked directly to actual content, saving time for students.
- ◈ Adding assignments consists of clicking on the desired due date, then filling in the details of the assignment—name of the assignment, instructions, and whether or not it is a one-time or repeating assignment.
- ◈ In addition, links to other activities can be created easily. If the activity is online, a URL can be entered in the space provided, and it will be linked automatically in the final syllabus.
- ◈ Your completed syllabus is hosted on our servers, allowing convenient updates from any computer on the Internet. Changes you make to your syllabus are immediately available to your students at their next logon.

For the Student—

- ◈ **Chapter Objectives**—outline key concepts from the text
- ◈ **Interactive Self-quizzes**—complete with hints and automatic grading that provide immediate feedback for students
- ◈ After students submit their answers for the interactive self-quizzes, the Companion Website **Results Reporter** computes a percentage grade, provides a

graphic representation of how many questions were answered correctly and incorrectly, and gives a question by question analysis of the quiz. Students are given the option to send their quiz to up to four email addresses (professor, teaching assistant, study partner, etc.).

◆ **Message Board**—serves as a virtual bulletin board to post—or respond to—questions or comments to/from a national audience

◆ **Net Searches**—offer links by key terms from each chapter to related Internet content

◆ **Web Destinations**—links to www sites that relate to chapter content

To take advantage of these and other resources, please visit the *Creating Inclusive Classrooms: Effective and Reflective Practices* Companion Website at

www.prenhall.com/salend

CONTENTS

PART II
Creating an Inclusive Environment That Supports Learning for All Students 117

CHAPTER 4

Creating Collaborative Relationships and Fostering Communication 118

CHAPTER 5

Creating an Environment That Fosters Acceptance and Friendship 158

CHAPTER 6

Creating Successful Transitions to Inclusive Settings   190

CHAPTER 7

Creating a Classroom Environment That Promotes Positive Behavior   226

PART III
Differentiating Instruction for All Students   269

CHAPTER 8
Differentiating Instruction for Diverse Learners   270

CHAPTER 9
Differentiating Large- and Small-Group Instruction for Diverse Learners   310

SPECIAL FEATURES

IDEAS FOR IMPLEMENTATION

VIDEO INSIGHTS

PART I

Understanding the Foundations and Fundamentals of Inclusion

Part One of this book, which includes Chapters 1, 2, and 3, introduces the concept of inclusion and the challenges of its implementation. The information presented in Part One also is designed to provide a framework for creating learning environments that support the learning and socialization of *all students;* differentiating your instruction to accommodate *all students;* and evaluating the success of your inclusion program for *all students, their families, and professionals.* Chapter 1 introduces the concept of inclusion, the philosophical principles that guide this book, the factors that contributed to the growth of inclusion, and the current research on the impact of inclusion on students, teachers, and families. Chapter 2 introduces the prereferral and placement system for students with disabilities, the Individualized Education Program, and the various special education categories. Chapter 3 discusses societal changes and their impact on students and schools, and explains alternative philosophies for structuring schools to address these changes.

CHAPTER 1

UNDERSTANDING INCLUSION

Marie and Mary

Marie was born in 1949. By age 3, her parents felt that she was developing slowly—speaking little and walking late. Marie's pediatrician told them not to worry; Marie would grow out of it. After another year of no noticeable progress, Marie's parents took her to other doctors. One said she had an iron deficiency, and another thought she had a tumor.

By the time Marie was old enough to start school, she was diagnosed as having mental retardation and was placed in a separate school for children with disabilities. She was doing well at the school when the school district informed her parents that the school was being closed and that the district had no place for Marie and the other students. Marie's parents protested to school officials and their state legislator, but the school district was not required by law to educate children like Marie.

Concerned about her future, Marie's parents sent her to a large state-run program about 200 miles from their home. During visits, they found that Marie was often disheveled, disoriented, and uncommunicative. Once she even had bruises on her arms and legs. After much debate, Marie's parents decided to bring her home to live with them. Although now an adult, Marie cannot perform activities of daily living, and her parents are worried about what will happen to her when they are no longer able to care for her.

Mary, born in 1987, also was diagnosed as having mental retardation. Soon after birth, Mary and her parents enrolled in an early intervention program that included home visits by a professional and parent training sessions. Mary's parents joined a local parent group that was advocating for services. When Mary was 4, she attended a preschool program with other children from her neighborhood. The school worked with Mary's parents to develop an Individualized Family Service Plan to meet Mary's educational needs and assist her family in planning for the transition to public school. After preschool, Mary moved with the other children to the local elementary school. At that time, her parents met with the school district's comprehensive planning team to develop an Individualized Education Program (IEP) for Mary. The team recommended that Mary be educated in a self-contained special education class. However, her parents felt that she should be in a setting that allowed her to interact with her peers who were not disabled. As a result of a due process hearing, Mary was placed in a general education setting for the majority of her school day. She also received the services of a collaboration teacher and a speech/language therapist. Mary had some teachers who understood her needs and others who did not, but she and her parents persevered. Occasionally, other students made fun of Mary, but she learned to ignore them and participated in many afterschool programs.

When Mary was ready to move to junior high school, the teachers and her parents worked together to help Mary make the transition. She was taught to change classes, use a combination lock and locker, and use different textbooks. Her IEP was revised to include grading and testing modifications, as well as the use of word processing to help her develop written communication skills. Mary participated in the science club and volunteer activities after school and went to the movies with her friends on Saturdays.

Mary graduated from junior high school and entered high school, where her favorite subjects are social studies and science. She also enjoys socializing with her friends during lunch. A peer helps Mary by sharing notes with her, and Mary's teachers have modified the curriculum for her. She uses a laptop computer with large print, a talking word processor, and a word prediction program. She is also taking a course called "Introduction to Occupations" and participates in a work-study program. Mary hopes to work in a store or office in town when she graduates.

What factors and events led Marie and Mary and their families to have such different experiences in school and society? After reading this chapter, you should be able to answer this as well as the following questions.

◆ What is inclusion?
◆ What is the least restrictive environment?
◆ What factors contributed to the movement to educate students in inclusive classrooms?

❖ What are the laws that affect special education?
 ❖ What is the impact of inclusion?

Whereas Marie's life was characterized by frustration, isolation, and lack of understanding, Mary's experiences were much more positive. Although Marie was initially placed in a separate school for students with disabilities, no laws existed that required states to educate children with special needs. When the school closed, Marie's parents had few options, and Marie was forced into an even more restrictive environment, a state-run institution. Conditioned to live a life fully dependent on others, Marie was limited at the time by society's restrictive perceptions of individuals with disabilities.

Mary, on the other hand, benefited from early diagnosis and intervention. She was mainstreamed into preschool and included in classes with students from her neighborhood throughout her educational career. Mary's full rights of citizenship, including the right to a free and appropriate education, were ensured by special laws that help protect and empower individuals with disabilities; these laws also granted Mary's parents the right to advocate for her when they disagreed with the school's decisions. Mary's teachers had high expectations of what she could accomplish, and they worked together to individualize her instruction and capitalize on her strengths. Upon graduation from high school, Mary was prepared to act on her own choices, lead a more independent life, and make positive contributions to her community. Born nearly four decades later than Marie, Mary benefited from a totally changed societal perception of what individuals with disabilities can accomplish when supported by their peers, families, teachers, and community.

INFORMATIONAL

The July–August issue of *Remedial and Special Education* (*19*[4], 1998) presents a history of the treatment and education of children and adults with disabilities.

SET YOUR SITES

The Disability Social History Project maintains a Web site on the history of individuals with disabilities in the United States (www.disabilityhistory.org).

WHAT IS INCLUSION?

Inclusion

Whereas Marie attended schools and institutional settings that segregated students with disabilities, Mary's educational experiences were based on *inclusion,* a philosophy that brings students, families, educators, and community members together to create schools and other social institutions based on acceptance, belonging, and community (Bloom, Perlmutter, & Burrell, 1999). Inclusion seeks to establish collaborative, supportive, and nurturing communities of learners that are based on giving *all students* the services and accommodations they need to learn, as well as respecting and learning from each other's individual differences. Rather than segregating students, as in the school Marie briefly attended before being placed in an institution, advocates of inclusion work collaboratively to create a unified educational system like Mary's. While inclusion has focused on individuals with disabilities, it is designed to alter the educational system so that it is more able to accommodate and respond to the needs of *all students.* The following principles, which provide a framework for this textbook, summarize the philosophies on which inclusive practices are based.

Principles of Effective Inclusion

Diversity

Principle 1

Effective inclusion *improves the educational system for* all students *by placing them together in general education classrooms— regardless of their learning ability, race, linguistic ability, economic status, gender, learning style, ethnicity, cultural background, religion, family structure, and sexual orientation.* Inclusionary schools welcome, acknowledge, affirm, and celebrate the value of *all learners* by educating them together in high-quality, age-appropriate general education classrooms in their neighborhood schools. *All students* have opportunities to learn and play together, and participate in educational, social, and recreational activities. These inclusionary practices, which promote acceptance, equity, and collaboration, are responsive to individual needs and embrace diversity.

Individual Needs

Effective inclusion *involves sensitivity to and acceptance of individual needs and differences.* Educators cannot teach students without taking into account the factors that shape their students and make them unique. Forces such as disability, race, linguistic background, gender, and economic status interact and affect academic performance and socialization; therefore, educators, students, and family members must be sensitive to individual needs and differences. In inclusive classrooms, *all students* are valued as individuals capable of learning and contributing to society. They are taught to appreciate diversity and to value and learn from each other's similarities and differences.

Reflective Practice

Effective inclusion *requires reflective educators to modify their attitudes, teaching and classroom management practices, and curricula to accommodate individual needs.* In inclusive classrooms, teachers are reflective practitioners who are flexible, responsive, and aware of students' needs. They think critically about their values and beliefs and routinely examine their own practices for self-improvement and to ensure that *all students'* needs are met. Educators individualize education for *all students* in terms of assessment techniques, curriculum accessibility, teaching strategies, technology, physical design adaptations, and a wide array of related services based on their needs. Students are given a multilevel and multimodality curriculum, as well as challenging educational and social experiences that are consistent with their abilities and needs.

Collaboration

Effective inclusion *is a group effort; it involves collaboration among educators, other professionals, students, families, and community agencies.* The support and services that students need are provided in the general education classroom. People work cooperatively and reflectively, sharing resources, responsibilities, skills, decisions, and advocacy for the students' benefit. School districts provide support, training, time, and resources to restructure their programs to support individuals in working collaboratively to address students' needs.

REFLECTING ON PROFESSIONAL PRACTICES

Implementing Inclusion

7:45 a.m.: Ms. Williams enters the school's office, greets the school secretary, and reviews her mail, which includes a message from one of her student's parents that her son will be late because he has a doctor's appointment.

7:52 a.m.: Ms. Williams enters her classroom. While she sips some tea, she boots up one of the computers in the room and checks her e-mail. She reads a message from a parent whose child will be absent and would like her to send today's homework assignment via e-mail. She starts to review a children's book about the school experiences of a student who does not speak English.

8:01 a.m.: As Ms. Silver enters her classroom, she greets Ms. Williams and thanks her for making tea. She sees Ms. Williams reviewing the book. "What do you think of it?" she asks. "I think it will be a good book to use. We can tie it in to our social studies unit on immigration and our community meetings on friendships." Ms. Williams nods and says, "How's your Spanish? Maybe we can have students work in math by using numbers in Spanish."

8:45 a.m.: Ms. Williams' and Ms. Silver's 23 students start entering the classroom. Amid the chatter, the students organize themselves for the day. While the students socialize, several students perform class jobs. They take the attendance, water the plants, perform the lunch count, and boot up the computers. The class is made up of 12 girls and 11 boys and includes 7 students with disabilities: 4 students with learning disabilities, 1 student with an emotional/behavioral disorder, 1 student with multiple disabilities, and 1 student who has a health impairment. The class also includes three African American students, two Hispanic students, and one who recently arrived in the United States from Eastern Europe.

9:00 a.m.: Ms. Silver rings a bell and the students go to their desks, which are arranged in groups of five or six. Each group contains a mixture of students by gender, ability, and cultural and linguistic background. One student from each group serves as a homework checker, verifying which students have completed their homework and what help students need. Half of the homework checkers report to Ms. Williams and half report to Ms. Silver, who record their findings. Before the reading groups assemble, a group of students select a song and lead the class in singing it.

9:10 a.m.: The students go to their reading groups. Ms. Williams works with one group, while Ms. Silver works with another. Several students also work independently. James works with Mr. Thomas, the paraeducator. First, James listens to and reads along with an audiocassette of a passage from a book; then he reads the section without the audiocassette and answers questions about what he has read and heard. Felicia is using the Internet to find another book written by her favorite author, which her teachers said she could read next.

After each student has had a chance to read, the teachers give them a choice of activities concerning the book. Some students choose to design a book cover reflecting important elements of the book; others choose to write about what they think will happen next; several students work together to role play the part of the story they just read; and some create a Venn diagram comparing themselves to a character in the book.

9:55 a.m.: While Ms. Williams prepares the materials for science class, Ms. Silver and Mr. Thomas remind the students that they have 5 minutes to finish their work and get ready for science. They show the students some rocks they will be working with in science class. Ms. Silver asks Lewis to help Sandy clean up and get ready for the next activity.

10:05 a.m.: The students go back to their desks and get ready for science class. While Ms. Williams reviews the concepts covered in the previous science class, Ms. Silver moves around the room to make sure that all of the students are ready for science and paying attention. Ms. Williams tells the students that "Today, we are going to learn more about different types of rocks." She shows them the flowchart that they had previously developed to identify and classify rocks. After Ms. Williams reviews the flowchart with the students and demonstrates how to use it to categorize a rock, the teachers place the students in groups. Each group is given six rocks and told to use the flowchart to identify the types of rocks they have and the reasons for their classifications. Ms. Williams, Ms. Silver, and Mr. Thomas circulate to assist the groups, monitor their cooperative skills, and make sure that each group member is participating. Near the end of the time period, each group shares its findings. The teachers note the different ways the rocks can be categorized and tell the students that they will continue to work on other rocks tomorrow.

11:10 a.m.: Mr. Thomas announces that it is free time. He shows the students a board game, and several students start playing it. Several other students have brought their yo-yos to school and show each other different tricks they can perform. Other students play with various toys, musical instruments, and computers.

11:30 a.m.: Ms. Williams tells the students that they have 5 minutes left and to start thinking about mathematics.

11:35 a.m.: Ms. Silver asks the students to go to their desks and get ready for math. Several students are still on the floor by the cabinet near the teachers' desks. One student yells, "Geneviere's pen is under the cabinet, and we can't reach it." Ms. Silver again tells the students to go to their desks as Ms. Williams tries to help Geneviere retrieve her pen.

11:38 a.m.: The pen has been retrieved, and the teachers and Mr. Thomas work with the students in math groups. Some students are using Base Ten Blocks to understand place value, while others are using them to work on multidigit addition, subtraction, and multiplication. Near the end of the period, the groups come together to play a math game. Throughout the game, students are rotated from team to team, and the answers to the game's math questions require the input of more than one member of each team.

12:20 p.m.: Ms. Williams asks the students to get ready for lunch, and Ms. Silver takes them to lunch.

12:40 p.m.: The students finish lunch and go outside to play. Milton is playing with a group of students and gets a little too rough. Several of the students call Milton a name.

1:01 p.m.: The students return to class, and Mr. Thomas tells Ms. Williams and Ms. Silver about the name calling that occurred during recess. The teachers take turns reading aloud while students go to the bathroom or for a drink of water.

1:15 p.m.: Ms. Williams and Ms. Silver announce, "We are going to have a community meeting." Without mentioning names, Mr. Thomas describes the name-calling incident. Ms. Williams and Ms. Silver then ask a series of questions. "What does it mean to call someone a name?", "Why does one person call another person a name?", "How does it feel when someone calls you a name?", and "What can be done to prevent name calling?" Students share their responses and brainstorm solutions to the problem. The teachers summarize the students' responses and end the community meeting by role playing a conflict between students and asking the students to identify ways in which the conflict could be handled without name calling.

1:58 p.m.: Ms. Silver asks the students to line up, and Mr. Thomas takes them to music class. Meanwhile, the educators begin assembling a bulletin board. They start discussing the students' reactions to the community meeting, as well as additional activities they could use to counter name calling and to foster a cooperative spirit in the group. They also discuss potential items related to the unit on rocks that students could include in their portfolios, and they put notes to families in students' homework folders.

2:22 p.m.: Ms. Cameron, the speech and language teacher, stops by to talk with the teachers about tomorrow's Writers' Workshop activity. She talks about how she plans to work on expanding

(continued)

sentences with her Writers' Workshop group and says that she will need to use the overhead projector in the classroom. The teachers also discuss the roles family volunteers will play during the Writers' Workshop.

2:40 p.m.: The students return from music class. While one student reads the homework assignment from the chalkboard, Ms. Williams, Ms. Silver, and Mr. Thomas move around the room to make sure that all the students have their colored homework folders and notebooks. The students perform end-of-the-day jobs such as shutting down the computers, washing the chalkboard, and organizing materials.

3:05 p.m.: The teachers praise the students for their good work and remind them of the discussion in the community meeting. While Ms. Silver walks the students to their busses, Ms. Williams sends the day's homework assignment by e-mail to the family that had requested it in the morning.

3:15 p.m.: Ms. Silver and Ms. Williams meet to copy and prepare materials, plan activities, and discuss report grades and testing accommodations for individual students.

4:30 p.m.: Ms. Silver and Ms. Williams wish each other good night and leave the school.

What aspects of their school day and program make you believe that Ms. Silver, Mr. Thomas, and Ms. Williams work in an inclusion classroom? What roles did Ms. Silver, Mr. Thomas, Ms. Williams, and their students play in their classroom? How did Ms. Silver, Mr. Thomas, and Ms. Williams address the educational, social, and behavioral needs of their students? What types of support services do Ms. Silver and Ms. Williams receive to help them implement their program? What types of support do educators need to implement an inclusion program?

Mainstreaming

Because the concept of inclusion grew out of mainstreaming and shares many of its philosophical goals, the terms *mainstreaming* and *inclusion* mean different things to different people. Therefore, you may hear some people use them interchangeably, while others see them as very different concepts.

Following the passage in 1975 of PL 94-142 (an important law we'll discuss later in this chapter), the term *mainstreaming* referred to partial and full-time programs that educated students with disabilities with their peers who were not disabled. Thus, the definition and scope of mainstreaming varied greatly, from any interactions between students who did and did not have disabilities to more specific integration of students with disabilities into the social and instructional activities of the general education classroom. Often, the decision to place a student in a mainstreamed setting was based on educators' assessment of his or her readiness; thus, it was implied that students had to *earn the right* to be educated full-time in an age-appropriate general education classroom. Because the concept of mainstreaming was broadly interpreted and implemented, the practice of mainstreaming involved many different service delivery models, including pull-out programs in which students left the general education setting for supportive services such as resource room programs and speech and language services.

The least restrictive environment (LRE) requires educational agencies to educate students with disabilities as much as possible with their peers who do not have disabilities.

WHAT IS THE LEAST RESTRICTIVE ENVIRONMENT?

Least Restrictive Environment

Both inclusion and mainstreaming are rooted in the concept of the *least restrictive environment (LRE)*. The LRE requires schools to educate students with disabilities as much as possible with their peers who do not have disabilities. The LRE is determined individually, based on the student's educational needs rather than the student's disability. The LRE concept promotes the placement of students with disabilities in general education classrooms. It also means that students can be shifted to self-contained special education classes, specialized schools, and residential programs only when their school performance indicates that even with supplementary aids and services, they cannot be educated satisfactorily in a general education classroom.

The LRE also prefers to allow students to attend school as close as possible to their homes and to interact with other students from the neighborhood. The participation of students with disabilities in all parts of the school program, including extracurricular activities, also is an important aspect of the LRE (Mills, 1998). The LRE also relates to the principle of *natural proportions,* according to which the ratio of students with and without disabilities in a classroom reflects the ratio of the larger population.

Continuum of Educational Placements

To implement the LRE and organize the delivery of special education services, school districts use a continuum of educational placements ranging from the highly *integrated* setting of the general education classroom to the highly *segregated* setting where instruction is delivered in hospitals and institutions (Deno, 1970; Thomas & Rapport, 1998). Figure 1.1

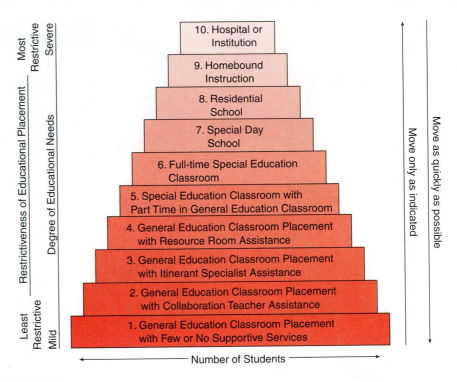

FIGURE 1.1 Continuum of educational services.

presents the range from most to least restrictive educational placements for students, although variation exists within and among agencies. A student is placed in the LRE based on his or her needs, skills, abilities, and motivation. A student moves to a less restrictive environment as quickly as possible and moves to a more segregated one only when necessary. The placement options presented in Figure 1.1 will now be described.

Option 1. General education classroom placement with few or no supportive services. The LRE is the general education classroom with few or no supportive services. The student is educated in the general education classroom, with the general education classroom teacher having the primary responsibility for designing and teaching the instructional program. The instructional program is adapted to the needs of the student, who may use adaptive devices and alternative learning strategies. Indirect services such as teacher inservice training to adapt the instructional program for students with disabilities may be offered.

Option 2. General education classroom placement with collaboration teacher assistance. This placement option is similar to option 1. However, the general education classroom teacher and the student receive collaborative services from ancillary support personnel in the general education classroom. We refer to this type of program as a *push-in program.* The collaborative services will vary, depending on the nature and level of the student's needs as well as those of the teacher. Guidelines for implementing collaborative services are provided in Chapter 4.

Option 3. General education classroom placement with itinerant specialist assistance. Teaching takes place in the general education classroom, and the student also receives supportive services from itinerant teachers. Depending on the school district's arrangement, the itinerant teacher may deliver services to students either inside or outside the general education classroom.

Option 4. General education classroom placement with resource room assistance. Resource room teachers offer direct services to students with disabilities, usually in a separate resource room within the school. They provide individualized remedial instruction in specific skills (such as note taking, study skills, and so on) to small groups of students. In addition, resource teachers often provide supplemental instruction that supports and parallels the instruction given in the general education classroom. Since these teachers typically work in a location outside of the general education classroom, we refer to this type of program as a *pull-out program.* The resource room teacher also can help general classroom teachers plan and implement instructional adaptations for students.

Option 5. Special education classroom placement with part time in the general education classroom. In this option, the student's primary placement is in a special education classroom within the same school building as peers who are not disabled. The student's academic program is supervised by a special educator. The amount of time spent in the general education setting for academic instruction and socialization varies.

Option 6. Full-time special education classroom. This placement alternative is similar to option 5. However, contact with peers who are not disabled typically is exclusively social; teaching takes place in a separate classroom. Students in option 6 share common experiences with other students on school buses, at lunch or recess, and during schoolwide activities (assemblies, plays, dances, sporting events, and so on).

Option 7. Special day school. Students in this placement alternative attend a school different from that of their neighborhood peers. Placement in a special school allows school districts to centralize services. This option is highly restrictive and is sometimes used with students with more severe emotional, physical, and cognitive disabilities.

Option 8. Residential school. Residential programs also are designed to serve students with more severe disabilities. Students attending residential schools live at the school and participate in a 24-hour program. In addition to providing education, these programs offer the comprehensive medical and psychological services that students may need.

Option 9. Homebound instruction. Some students, such as those who are recovering from surgery or an illness or who have been suspended from school, may require homebound instruction. In this alternative, a teacher teaches the student at home. Technological advances such as distance learning now allow students who are homebound to interact and take classes with their peers at school.

Option 10. Hospital or institution. Placing individuals with severe disabilities in hospitals and institutions has been reduced by the deinstitutionalization movement, but it still exists. As with the other placement options, education must be part of any hospital or institutional program. These placements should be viewed as short term, and an emphasis should be placed on moving these individuals to a less restrictive environment.

Judicial decisions in *Daniel R.R.* v. *State Board of Education* (1989), *Greer* v. *Rome City School District* (1991), *Oberti* v. *Board of Education of the Borough of Clementon School District* (1993), *Sacramento City Unified School District, Board of Education* v. *Holland,* (1994), *Clyde K. and Sheila K.* v. *Puyallup School District* (1994), *Poolaw* v. *Bishop* (1995), and *Seattle School District No. 1* v. *B.S.*(1996) have established guidelines that you must consider when implementing the LRE concept for your students (Thomas & Rapport, 1998; Yell, 1998). Taken together, these cases suggest that your students have a right to be educated in general education settings, and that in placing a student in the LRE, your school district should consider:

REFLECTIVE

Some advocates of inclusion see the use of options 1 to 10 as a deterrent to educating students in general education classrooms because it helps to maintain a dual system of general and special education. Others think that these placements recognize the diverse needs of students and the different environments that can be used to address these needs. What is your view?

INFORMATIONAL

McLeskey, Henry, and Hodges (1998, 1999) analyzed the most recent data collected by the U.S. Department of Education on educational placements for students with disabilities. They found a gradual and significant increase in general education placements, a gradual decrease in resource room placements, and a 5 percent increase in separate-class placements.

◈ the anticipated educational benefits in the general education setting with appropriate supplementary aids and services compared with the benefits of the special education classroom;

◈ the noneducational, social, and self-concept benefits that are likely to occur in the general education setting, including interactions with classmates;

◈ the impact of the student with a disability on the education of classmates without disabilities;

◈ the effect of the student with a disability on teachers and their instructional time; and

◈ the cost of educating the student in the general education setting with supplementary aids and services, and the effect of these costs on the district's resources for educating other students.

WHAT FACTORS CONTRIBUTED TO THE MOVEMENT TO EDUCATE STUDENTS IN INCLUSIVE CLASSROOMS?

The number of school districts implementing inclusion for their students with disabilities has increased significantly (McLeskey et al., 1999). Several factors contributing to this movement are discussed in the following sections. (Societal changes have also occurred, and inclusion has proved to be effective for educating diverse learners in general education classrooms. These societal changes are discussed in greater detail in Chapter 3.)

Normalization

Inclusion is rooted in the principle of *normalization,* which originated in Scandinavia and was later brought to the United States (Wolfensberger, 1972). Normalization seeks to provide social interactions and experiences that parallel those of society to adults and children with disabilities. Thus the philosophy of educating students with disabilities in general education settings rests on the principle that educational, housing, employment, social, and leisure opportunities for individuals with disabilities should resemble as closely as possible the opportunities and activities enjoyed by their peers who are not disabled.

Deinstitutionalization

Up to very recently, individuals with disabilities were feared, ridiculed, abandoned, or placed in institutions that isolated them from the general public. Think back to the chapter-opening case study. Whereas Marie spent some time in an institution, this option was never considered for Mary, in part, because of the movement toward deinstitutionalization. Because of the terrible conditions found in many institutions, as well as a growing awareness of the negative effects of institutionalization, smaller, community-based independent living arrangements were developed for individuals with disabilities. Unfortunately, few funds have been earmarked for services to support these arrangements, limiting the impact of the deinstitutionalization movement.

Early Intervention and Early Childhood Programs

The effectiveness of early intervention and early childhood programs (like the one in which Mary participated) has promoted the placement of students with disabilities in general education settings (Hammond, 1999; Udell, Peters, & Templeman, 1998). These programs have increased the physical, motor, cognitive, language, speech, socialization, and self help skills of many children from birth through age 6. They have also reduced the likelihood that secondary disabilities will occur; empowered families to promote their child's development; and decreased the probability that children with disabilities will be socially dependent and institutionalized as adults. In a follow-up study comparing adults who received early childhood services with adults who did not, Schweinhart and Weikart (1993) found that those who received early childhood services made more money, attained a higher level of education, and used fewer social services than those who did not.

SET YOUR SITES

The National Association for the Education of Young Children (NAEYC) maintains a Website that offers information, research, and resources on early intervention and early childhood programs (http://www.naeyc.org).

Technological Advances

Mary's placement in inclusive settings also was fostered by technology that was not available when Marie was growing up. These technological advances have changed the quality of life for many individuals, helping them to gain access, independence, and achievement. Assistive and instructional technology allows individuals with communication, physical, learning, and sensory disabilities to gain more control over their lives and environment, as well as greater access to society and general education classrooms (Behrmann, 1994; Bryant, Bryant, & Raskind, 1998). While these devices were developed for individuals with disabilities, they have consequences and benefits for *all members of society.*

The Technology-Related Assistance for Individuals with Disabilities Act (PL 103-218) (Tech Act), which was passed in 1988, is designed to help states develop and enact programs to give high-quality technology-related assistance to individuals with disabilities and their families (Bryant & Seay, 1998). The Tech Act delineates two aspects of assistive technology: devices and services. An *assistive technology device* is defined as any item, equipment, or product system, whether bought, modified, or customized, that is used to increase, maintain, or improve the functional capabilities of an individual with a disability. An *assistive technology service* is defined as any service that directly assists an individual with a disability to select, acquire, or use an assistive technology device.

As a result of the Tech Act, many state education departments have established programs to link individuals with the devices they need. For example, the Tracer R & D Center at the University of Wisconsin at Madison (608-262-6966, www.trace.wisc.edu) has developed a CD ROM that contains descriptions and ordering information on over 20,000 assistive devices. Additional information on assistive and instructional technology is presented in Chapters 3 and 8.

SET YOUR SITES

Resources to help individuals with disabilities obtain the assistive technology they need include ABLEDATA (www.abledata.com, 800-227-0216), Accent on Information (www.blvd.com/accent, 309-378-2961), Alliance for Technology Access (www.ataccess.org, 415-455-4575), and RESNA (www.resna.org, 703-524-6686).

REFLECTIVE

Technological and medical advances have had an impact on *all members of society.* For example, Alexander Graham Bell's attempts to amplify his voice so that he could communicate more effectively with his wife, who had a hearing impairment, led to the invention of the telephone (Blanck, 1994). What technological devices do you use?

Civil Rights Movement and Resulting Litigation

Separate educational facilities are inherently unequal. This inherent inequality stems from the stigma created by purposeful segregation which generates a feeling of inferiority that may affect their hearts and minds in a way unlikely ever to be undone." (Earl Warren, Chief Justice of the Supreme Court, *Brown* v. *Board of Education*)

Medical and assistive technology devices have promoted the inclusion movement.

. . . [T]here was no equality of treatment merely by providing students with the same facilities, textbooks, teachers, and curriculum, for students who do not understand English are effectively foreclosed from any meaningful education. (The Supreme Court in *Lau* v. *Nichols*, 1974)

The impetus toward educating students like Mary in inclusive, general education settings was also aided by the civil rights movement. The precedent for much special education–related litigation was established by *Brown* v. *Topeka Board of Education* (1954). The decision in this landmark civil rights case determined that segregating students in schools based on race, even if other educational variables appear to be equal, is unconstitutional. This refutation of the doctrine of "separate but equal" served as the underlying argument in court actions brought by families to ensure that their children with disabilities received a free, appropriate public education.

One example of such a court action is *Pennsylvania Association for Retarded Children* v. *Commonwealth of Pennsylvania* (1972). The families of children like Marie questioned the Pennsylvania School Code that was being used to justify the education of students with disabilities in environments that segregated them from their peers without disabilities. In a consent agreement approved by the court, the Commonwealth of Pennsylvania agreed that all students with mental retardation had a right to a free public education. The agreement further stated that placement in a general education public school classroom is preferable to more segregated placements and that families have the right to be informed of any changes in their children's educational program. A second case, *Mills* v. *Board of Education of the District of Columbia* (1972), extended the right to a free public education for students with disabilities. The judge also ruled that the cost of educational services was not a justifiable reason for denying special education services to students who needed them. Both of these cases were catalysts for change in the way individuals with disabilities were educated in the public school system. Figure 1.2 summarizes other cases that influenced the educa-

Since the *Brown* v. *Topeka Board of Education* case (1954), several cases have dealt with the educational rights of students with disabilities and students from diverse cultural and linguistic backgrounds, as well as the schools' responsibility to educate them. These cases also helped establish the importance of giving students a general education in an inclusive setting.

Hobson v. *Hansen* (1967). The federal district court for the District of Columbia ruled that tracking was unconstitutional and should be abolished, as it segregated students on the basis of race and/or economic status.

Diana v. *California State Board of Education* (1970). The California State Board of Education agreed to modify its assessment practices for identifying Mexican American students referred to special education, including testing students in their primary language, eliminating culturally biased test items, using nonverbal tests, and creating alternative intelligence tests (Baca, 1998).

Lau v. *Nichols* (1974). The U.S. Supreme Court extended the concept of equal educational opportunity to include special language programs for students who speak languages other than English. The *Lau* decision, coupled with PL 94-142, also mandated bilingual special education services and set the precedent for other laws and lawsuits relating to meeting the educational needs of students who speak languages other than English (Baca, 1998).

Larry P. v. *Riles* (1979). The federal district court in California ruled that the intelligence tests used to determine whether African American students were eligible for special education classes for students with mental retardation were racially and culturally biased, and ordered California to develop nondiscriminatory procedures for placing students in special education classes. In 1986, the *Larry P.* ruling was extended to question the use of intelligence testing to place African American students in all types of special education categories (Yell, 1998).

Board of Education of the Hendrick Hudson School District v. *Rowley* (1982). The Supreme Court ruled that PL 94-142 was designed to provide students with disabilities reasonable opportunities to learn but that it did not require school districts to help them reach their maximum potential.

Irving Independent School District v. *Tatro* (1984). The Supreme Court stated that whether a medical service is a related service depends on who provides it, rather than on the service itself. This decision also depends on the extent to which the procedure or service must be delivered during the school day for the student to participate in the educational program (Rapport, 1996).

Timothy W. v. *Rochester, N.H. School District* (1989). The Supreme Court let stand a U.S. Court of Appeals ruling that no matter how severe a student's disability is or how little a student may benefit, the school must educate the student.

Agostini v. *Felton* (1997). The Supreme Court ruled that school districts may provide on-site special education and related services to students attending religious schools (Osborne, Dimattia, & Russo, 1998).

Cedar Rapids Community School District v. *Garret F.* (1999). The Supreme Court ruled that the IDEA entitles students with disabilities to necessary nonmedical services, regardless of their cost to the school district.

FIGURE 1.2   Court cases related to special and inclusive educational practices.

tion of children with disabilities, as well as children with culturally and linguistically diverse backgrounds.°

Advocacy Groups

Fueled by the momentum of civil rights campaigns, advocacy groups of family members, professionals, and individuals with disabilities banded together to seek civil rights and greater societal acceptance for individuals with disabilities. Besides alerting the public to issues related to individuals with disabilities, advocacy groups lobbied state and federal legislators, brought lawsuits, and protested polices of exclusion and segregation. The result was greater societal acceptance and rights for individuals with disabilities.

Various economic, political, and environmental factors have increased the number of individuals with disabilities, fueling the growth of the disability rights movement. Individuals with disabilities have transformed themselves from invisible and passive recipients of sympathy to visible and active advocates of their rights as full members of society. These advocacy groups also have created a disability culture that celebrates and affirms disability, fosters community among individuals with disabilities, promotes disability awareness, and challenges society's conventional notions of disability (Martin, 1997).

°For the purposes of this text, culturally and linguistically diverse students are defined as those who are not native members of the Euro-Caucasian culture base currently dominant in the United States and/or those whose native or primary language is not English.

INFORMATIONAL

Many individuals become disabled after birth, and anyone can join this group at any time.

REFLECTIVE

Think of a relative, friend, or neighbor who has a disability. How has that individual affected you and others in your family and neighborhood?

SET YOUR SITES

CEC, the largest professional organization addressing issues related to individuals with disabilities, maintains a Website offering information, research, and resources on special education programs (http://www.cec.sped.org/, 703-620-3660).

Segregated Nature of Special Schools and Classes

As the institutionalization of individuals with disabilities declined, the number of special schools and special classes within public schools for students with disabilities rose. However, educators eventually questioned the segregation of these students. In 1968, Lloyd Dunn argued that special education classes for students with mild disabilities were unjustifiable because they served as a form of homogeneous grouping and tracking. He cited studies showing that students labeled as mildly disabled "made as much or more progress in the regular grades as they do in special classes" (p. 8), as well as studies showing that labeling reduces the student's self-concept and the teacher's expectations for success in school.

SET YOUR SITES

You can obtain more information on programs to help your students graduate by contacting the National Center for Parents in Dropout Prevention (800-638-9675) and the National Dropout Prevention Center (www.dropoutprevention.org, 800-443-6392).

Studies on the effectiveness of special education programs also revealed that, progress aside, students with disabilities have high dropout and incarceration rates and low employment rates (Collet-Klingenberg, 1998; Levine & Nourse, 1998). Several factors promote dropping out of school (Kortering & Braziel, 1999; Razeghi, 1998): being poor, being nonwhite, having very low academic skills, having a disability, speaking a language other than English, being retained in school and separated from one's peer group, being a child of a single parent, holding a job, being pregnant, being a substance abuser, and being bored in or alienated from school. Attending schools with few resources and programs for motivating students and encouraging family participation is another major contributor to school dropout. As a teacher, you can work with others to develop programs that help students complete school (Cantrell & Cantrell, 1995; Kortering & Braziel, 1999; Razeghi, 1998; Sinclair, Christenson, Evelo, & Hurley, 1998).

Disproportionate Representation

Dunn (1968) also raised concerns about the *disproportionate representation* of students from culturally and linguistically diverse backgrounds in special education classes that segregated these students, and saw inclusive placements as a way to counter this segregation. Yates (1998) defines *disproportionate representation,* also referred to as *disproportionality,* as the presence of students from a specific group in an educational program that is higher or lower than one would expect based on their representation in the general population of students. Unfortunately, Dunn's concerns 30 years earlier about disproportionate representation are now a reality. Students from culturally and linguistically diverse backgrounds tend to be overrepresented in special education programs and underrepresented in programs for gifted and talented students (Ford, 1998; Oswald, Coutinho, Best, & Singh, 1999).

REFLECTIVE

Can you think of other examples of disparate treatment and disparate impact in schools? in society?

Since issues of disproportionality are multifaceted and shaped by the cultural experiences of students and professionals (Artiles & Zamora-Duran, 1997), educators need to examine whether their policies, practices, attitudes, and behaviors result in disparate treatment and disparate impact for students from culturally and linguistically diverse backgrounds (Smaile, 1998; Voltz, 1998). *Disparate treatment* refers to treating students differently because of their characteristics and membership in a group such as their racial and linguistic background. An example would be disciplining such students differently from other students for the same offense. While *disparate impact* means treating all students similarly, it also examines whether this similar treatment has different outcomes for members of different groups. For example, sending a letter written in English inviting families to attend a meeting may result in few families who do not speak English attending the meeting.

REFLECTING ON YOUR PRACTICES

Examining Disproportionate Representation

As specified in the new reauthorization of the Individuals with Disabilities Education Act (IDEA), school districts and state departments of education must determine if the problems of overrepresentation and underrepresentation exist, as well as the nature of these problems. You can evaluate the extent to which students in your school district are disproportionately represented by addressing the following questions:

◇ Does the school district maintain a complete data base on issues of disproportionate representation?
◇ Are many students from culturally and linguistically diverse backgrounds being referred for and placed in special education?
◇ Do the reasons for referral for special education differ based on the cultural or linguistic background of the students?
◇ Do patterns of placement differ by race or ethnicity, and are many students from diverse backgrounds identified as having a specific special education disability such as emotional disturbance or mental retardation?
◇ Are students from diverse backgrounds underrepresented in certain special education disability categories and programs for gifted and talented students?
◇ Does the restrictiveness of educational placements vary based on the cultural or linguistic backgrounds of students?
◇ Are placement teams considering the impact of cultural and linguistic backgrounds when assessing

students' educational needs, and are they using assessment practices that account for test bias and assessment bias?
◇ Do students from diverse backgrounds have equal access to the school's supportive services, prereferral intervention programs, transitional services, and extracurricular and community activities?
◇ Do the curriculum, teaching strategies, and instructional materials address the experiences and needs of a diverse student population?
◇ Are families and community members from diverse backgrounds involved in all aspects of the school?
◇ Are a disproportionately large number of students from diverse backgrounds suspended from school or disciplined differently?
◇ Does the school district have policies and procedures to foster the recruitment, hiring, and retention of educators from diverse backgrounds?
◇ Does the school district offer training to all staff members on effective practices in meeting the needs of students and their families from diverse backgrounds?

How would you rate the extent to which disproportionate representation exists in your school district? ( ) Doesn't Exist ( ) Exists to Some Extent ( ) Exists Extensively

What are some goals and steps your school district can adopt to address disproportionate representation?

Educational Reform

The challenge to reform our educational system means that schools must restructure their programs to help *all students*—including those with disabilities—meet higher learning standards (Burnette, 1996). *All students* must be included in high-stakes assessments aligned with the higher standards; this makes schools accountable for educating *all students*. Thus, rather than segregating students with disabilities based on their performance on standardized achievement tests, many schools are unifying general and special education into one service delivery system to provide *all students* with a general education.

INFORMATIONAL

Levine and Nourse (1998) summarize the research on postschool outcomes, postsecondary education, and employment for males and females with learning disabilities, and Heal, Khoju, and Rusch (1997) examine quality-of-life issues for students after they leave special education high school programs.

Students from culturally and linguistically diverse backgrounds, particularly males, tend to be overrepresented in special education programs and underrepresented in programs for gifted and talented students.

WHAT ARE THE LAWS THAT SHAPED SPECIAL EDUCATION?

The factors just discussed helped shape several education and civil rights laws designed primarily to include individuals with disabilities like Marie and Mary in the mainstream of society. The most important of these laws is the Individuals with Disabilities Education Act, also known as the IDEA.

The Individuals with Disabilities Education Act (IDEA)

More than any other law, the IDEA has affected the educational system in this country. Initially known as the Education for All Handicapped Children Act (PL 94-142), it has been amended four times since its passage in 1975 and was renamed the Individuals with Disabilities Education Act in 1990. The IDEA mandates that a free and appropriate education be provided to all students with disabilities, regardless of the nature and severity of their disability. It affirms that disability is "a natural part of the human experience" and asserts that individuals with disabilities have the right to "enjoy full inclusion and integration into the economic, political, social, cultural, and educational mainstream of society" (House of Representatives Report 103-208, 1993, p. 6). The IDEA is the culmination of many efforts to ensure the rights of full citizenship and equal access for individuals with disabilities.

According to Turnbull, Turnbull, Shank, and Leal (1999), the IDEA is based on six fundamental principles that govern the education of students with disabilities. Under the first principle, *zero reject,* schools cannot exclude any student with a disability and each state must locate children who may be entitled to special education services. Under the second principle, *nondiscriminatory evaluation,* schools must evaluate students fairly to see if they have a disability, and provide guidelines for identifying the special education and related services they will receive if they do. The principle of a *free and appropriate education* requires schools to follow individually tailored education for each student defined in an Individualized Education Plan (IEP). The principle of the *least restrictive environment* (LRE) requires schools to educate students with disabilities with their peers who are not disabled to the maximum extent appropriate. The *procedural due process* principle provides safeguards against schools' actions, including the right to sue if schools do not carry out the other principles. The final principle requires *family and student participation* in designing and delivering special education programs and IEPs, which are explained in greater detail in Chapter 2.

An Overview of IDEA from 1975 to the Present

Since IDEA was first passed in 1975, it has been amended several times. This section will outline the key concepts of each law, as well as introduce several other laws affecting special education.

VIDEO INSIGHT

Sean's Story: A Lesson in Life

In this ABC News video segment, we meet Sean Begg, a first-grader with Down Syndrome. Sean's story is the story of inclusion: how his parents had to fight for his right to be educated in a general education classroom, how the teachers and students at the Baltimore public school reacted, how Sean has adjusted to the new environment, and how all of the individuals involved measured the success of the inclusion program.

With your classmates or in your teaching journal, reflect on these questions:

1. What role does each of the four principles of inclusion (diversity, individual needs, reflective practice, and collaboration) play in *Sean's Story*?
2. Explain how the IDEA protects Sean's right to an education in the least restrictive environment.
3. As Sean's teacher in an inclusive classroom, what concerns would you have? What resources would be helpful to you?

PL 94-142: Education for All Handicapped Children Act   Passed in 1975, this act mandates that a free and appropriate education be provided to all students with disabilities, regardless of the nature and severity of their disability. It outlines the IEP and states that students with disabilities will be educated in the LRE with their peers who are not disabled to the maximum extent appropriate. It also guarantees that students with disabilities and their families have the right to nondiscriminatory testing, confidentiality, and due process.

❖ A statement of the infant's or toddler's present level of development
❖ An assessment of the family's strengths and needs for enhancing the child's development, including the resources, priorities, and concerns of the family
❖ A statement of the outcomes to be achieved for the child and family
❖ A list of the criteria, techniques, and timelines for evaluating progress
❖ A statement of the early education services that will be delivered to meet the child's and family's unique needs, including their intensity and frequency
❖ A statement of the natural environments where the early education services will be delivered, as well as why other environments will be used if necessary
❖ The dates for starting services and their duration
❖ The name of the family's service coordinator, who will supervise the implementation of the program
❖ The procedures for moving the child from early intervention to preschool
❖ Annual evaluation of the IFSP, with a review every 6 months or more often if necessary

FIGURE 1.3   Components of the IFSP.

PL 99-457: Education for All Handicapped Children Act Amendments of 1986   PL 99-457 extended many of the rights and safeguards of PL 94-142 to children with disabilities from birth to 5 years of age and encouraged early intervention services and special assistance to students who are at risk. It also included provisions for developing an Individualized Family Service Plan (IFSP) for each child. The components of an IFSP are presented in Figure 1.3.

REFLECTIVE

By replacing the term *handicapped* with the term *disabilities* in the IDEA, Congress recognized the importance of language. What do the terms *regular, normal,* and *special* imply? How do these terms affect the ways we view students with disabilities and the programs designed to meet their needs? Do these terms foster inclusion or segregation?

PL 101-476: Individuals with Disabilities Education Act   In 1990, PL 101-476 changed the title of PL 94-142 from the Education for All Handicapped Children Act to the Individuals with Disabilities Education Act (IDEA), reflecting "individuals first" language. Additionally, all uses of the term *handicapped* were replaced by the term *disabilities.* IDEA continued the basic provisions outlined in PL 94-142 and made the following changes: the category of children with disabilities was expanded to include autism and brain injury; related services were expanded to include rehabilitation counseling and social work services; and the commitment to address the needs of linguistically and culturally diverse youth with disabilities was increased.

PL 105-17: The IDEA Amendments of 1997   PL 105-17 included several provisions to improve the educational performance of students with disabilities by having high expectations for them, giving them a general education and including them in local and state assessments, and making general and special educators and administrators members of the team that writes students' IEPs. PL 105-17 also seeks to strengthen the role of families in their children's education and to prevent the disproportionate representation of students from diverse backgrounds in special education programs. The major provisions of PL 105-17 are presented in Figure 1.4.

Other Laws Affecting Special Education

While many students have unique needs, they may not be eligible for special education services under the IDEA. However, they may qualify for special and general education services under other laws.

ELIGIBILITY AND EVALUATION

Students may not be identified as having a disability if eligibility is based on lack of instruction in reading or mathematics or limited proficiency in English.

The requirement for a complete reevaluation every 3 years was modified so that existing relevant assessment data can be used to assist the IEP team in making decisions about a student's educational program.

THE LRE

States must use placement-neutral funding formulas and revise their funding to ensure that they do not violate the requirement for the LRE.

DISPROPORTIONATE REPRESENTATION

States must collect and examine data to determine if students from culturally and linguistically diverse backgrounds are overrepresented or underrepresented in special education.

THE IEP

The IEP must include both the student's general education and special education teachers, a representative of the school district who is knowledgeable about the general education curriculum and district resources, and an individual who can identify the instructional implications of the evaluation data.

The IEP must include several new factors concerning the student's access to, participation in, and progress in general education, as well as in extracurricular and nonacademic activities with other students. (See Chapter 2 for specific information on these changes.)

The IEP team must consider behavioral interventions, language needs, communication needs, instruction in Braille, and assistive technology when developing a student's IEP.

IEP TRANSITION SERVICES

The IEP must include, beginning at age 14 and updated annually, a statement of transition needs that focuses on the student's course of study (e.g., enrolling in advanced placement courses or vocational education programs) and, beginning at age 16 or younger, a statement of the needed transition services and, when appropriate, a statement of interagency responsibilities or needed linkages.

EARLY INTERVENTION SERVICES AND THE IFSP

States are required to develop policies and procedures to ensure that early intervention services occur in natural environments.

The IFSP must include a statement on the delivery of early intervention services in natural environments with same-age peers without disabilities, including a justification of the use of other environments.

Students aged 3–9 can be identified as developmentally delayed.

PARTICIPATION IN ASSESSMENTS

States must include students with disabilities in state and district assessments of student progress with individualized accommodations and adaptations as determined by the IEP team, and must develop alternate assessments for students who cannot participate in such assessments. States also must report the results of the testing of students with disabilities while protecting their identity, including those students tested by alternate means.

DISCIPLINE

The IEP must include strategies, including positive behavioral interventions and supports, for students whose behavior impedes their learning or that of others.

School district personnel are authorized to discipline a student with disabilities in the same ways in which they discipline students without disabilities. However, students with disabilities cannot be suspended or placed in an alternative setting for more than 10 days unless the disciplinary action is related to carrying a weapon to school or possessing, using, or selling illegal drugs at school. In these cases, the IEP team can place a student for up to 45 days in an alternative setting that must offer a general education and the special education services outlined in the student's IEP. In making this decision, the IEP team also must determine if there is a relationship between the student's disability and misbehavior. (See Chapter 7 for specific information on these provisions).

FIGURE 1.4 Major provisions of the IDEA Amendments of 1997 (PL 105-17). (continued)

FAMILY INVOLVEMENT

The IEP must include a statement of how often the student's family will be regularly informed of their child's progress. This should occur at least as often as families of children without disabilities are informed of their progress.

States must ensure that families of children with a disability are members of any group that makes decisions about the child's educational placement.

MEDIATION

States must offer mediation services for families and school districts to resolve their differences voluntarily. The cost of mediation is paid by the state, and either party may request an impartial hearing if the mediation is unsuccessful.

INCIDENTAL BENEFITS TO STUDENTS WITHOUT DISABILITIES

Students without disabilities can benefit from special education and related services that are provided to students with disabilities in accordance with a student's IEP.

FIGURE 1.4   (continued)

INFORMATIONAL

Blazer (1999) offers tips for developing Section 504 classroom accommodation plans.

Section 504 of the Rehabilitation Act

Section 504 of the Rehabilitation Act (PL 93-112), passed by Congress in 1973, serves as a civil rights law for individuals with disabilities and forbids all institutions receiving U.S. Department of Education funds from discriminating against individuals with disabilities in education, employment, housing, and access to public programs and facilities. It also requires these institutions to make their buildings physically accessible to individuals with disabilities. Section 504 provides students with the right to a general education, extracurricular activities in their local schools, and instructional and curriculum adaptations.

Section 504 has both similarities to and differences from the IDEA. Like the IDEA, Section 504 requires schools to provide eligible students with a free, appropriate public education, which is defined as general or special education that includes related services and reasonable accommodations. Both the IDEA and Section 504 also require that families be notified of the identification, evaluation, and placement of their children. However, because Section 504 is based on a broader definition of disabilities than the IDEA, far more students qualify for special education services under Section 504 than under the IDEA. As a result, potential recipients of services under Section 504 include students with attention deficit disorders, temporary and long-term health conditions, communicable diseases, AIDS, and eating disorders. Individuals who abuse substances are eligible for services under Section 504 as long as they are in rehabilitation or recovery programs. However, if they begin to abuse substances again, they are no longer eligible until they return to a rehabilitation or recovery program.

Under Section 504, educators must make accommodations to meet the learning needs of all students with disabilities covered under Section 504 (Fossey, Hosie, Soniat, & Zirkel, 1995; Marson, 1995). If a student needs special or related services or reasonable accommodations, it is often a good idea for a planning team that knows the student, the assessment data, and the available services, placements, and modifications to develop a written accommodation plan. A sample Section 504 accommodation plan is presented in Figure 1.5.

REFLECTIVE

While the IDEA provides funding to schools for eligible students, money for students eligible under Section 504 comes from the school district's general education funds. As a school administrator, would you prefer a student to be eligible under the IDEA or Section 504? As a parent of a child with special needs, what would you prefer?

Americans with Disabilities Act

In 1990, Congress enacted PL 101-336, the Americans with Disabilities Act (ADA), to integrate individuals with disabilities into the social and economic mainstream of society.

General Education Accommodation Plan

Name: Joshua Green

Date: 6/5/95

School / Grade: Platte Valley Elementary, 3rd

Teacher: Myrna Mae (lead teacher)

Participants in Development of Accommodation Plan

Mr. and Mrs. Walter Green	Julie Hartson	Myrna Mae, Teacher	Arlo Wachal, Teacher
parents(s)/guardian(s)	principal	teacher(s)	

Joel Schaeffer, Counselor	Violette Schelldorf, Nurse		

Building Person responsible for monitoring plan: Joel Schaeffer, Counselor   Follow-up Date: 6/5/96

Currently on Medication   X   Yes   ____ No   Physician Eveard Ewing, M.D.   Type Ritalin   Dosage 15 mg. twice daily

Area of Concern	Intervention or Teaching Strategies	Person Responsible for Accommodation
1. Assignment Completion	1. Daily assignment sheet sent home with Josh 2. Contract system initiated for assignment completion in math and social studies	Myrna Mae Parents will initial daily, and Josh will return the form Myrna Mae, Arlo Wachal
2. Behavior / Distractibility	1. Preferential seating—study carrel or near teacher, as needed 2. Daily behavior card sent home with Josh	Myrna Mae, Arlo Wachal Parents will initial daily; and Josh will return the form
3. Consistency of Medication	1. Medication to be administered in private by school nurse daily at noon	Violette Schelldorf

Comments:

Josh will remain in the general education classroom with the accommodations noted above.

Mr. & Mrs. Walter Green

Parental Authorization for 504 Plan

I agree with the accommodations described in the 504 plan.

I do not agree with the accommodations described in the 504 plan. I understand I have the right to appeal.

FIGURE 1.5 Sample 504 accommodation plan.

Source: "Section 504 accommodation plans" by G. Conderman and A. Katsiyannis, 1995, *Intervention in School and Clinic, 31,* 44. Copyright 1995 by PRO-ED, Inc. Reprinted by permission.

Under the ADA, these individuals have access to public facilities including schools, restaurants, shops, and transportation. Employers and service providers in the public and private sectors cannot discriminate against them. The ADA requires employers to make reasonable accommodations for individuals with disabilities unless the accommodations would present an undue hardship. Under Title III of the ADA, concerning the educational implications of the ADA, schools must make their facilities accessible to students with disabilities.

WHAT IS THE IMPACT OF INCLUSION?
Impact of Inclusion on Students with Disabilities

INFORMATIONAL

Salend and Duhaney (1999) summarize the research on inclusion programs, on students with and without disabilities, and on their teachers.

Several studies have examined the effect of general education placement on students with and without disabilities. Their findings reveal a varied impact on academic and social performance and on the attitude toward placement of students with disabilities.

Academic Performance

There are several studies and school reports on the impact of inclusion on the academic performance of students with disabilities. Some studies show that for students with mild disabilities, inclusion results in better outcomes, including improved standardized test scores, reading performance, mastery of IEP goals, grades, on-task behavior, motivation to learn, and attitudes toward school and learning (Banerji & Dailey, 1995; Malian & Love, 1998; National Center for Educational Restructuring and Inclusion, 1995; Shinn, Powell-Smith, Good, & Baker, 1997; Waldron & McLeskey, 1998a,b). Research also reveals that students with severe disabilities in inclusion programs learned targeted skills, had more engaged and instructional time, and had greater exposure to academic activities than students with severe disabilities educated in special education settings (Helmstetter, Curry, Brennan, & Sampson-Saul, 1998; Hunt, Farron-Davis, Beckstead, Curtis, & Goetz, 1994). Time spent in general education classes may improve students' chances of completing high school, going to college, getting a job, earning a higher salary, and living independently (Malian & Love, 1998; SRI International, 1993; U.S. Department of Education, 1995).

However, some research also questions the effectiveness of inclusion on the academic performance of students with disabilities. Some studies indicate that certain students with mild disabilities are not given "specially designed instruction" to meet their academic needs in inclusion programs and perform better academically in pull-out resource programs (Baker & Zigmond, 1995; Fuchs, Deshler, & Zigmond, 1994; Manset & Semmel, 1997; Marston, 1996; Zigmond et al., 1995). Some studies also suggest that higher-functioning preschoolers and elementary students with disabilities benefit more from placement in inclusion programs than their lower-functioning counterparts (Klingner, Vaughn, Hughes, Schumm, & Elbaum, 1998b; Mills, Cole, Jenkins, & Dale, 1998).

Social Performance

> Like most people, I don't remember much about my first years in school. Most of my memories are from the last 2 years in special education. I remember becoming unhappy about school then. I think I was at the age when I began to realize I was separated from the "regular kids." I can remember that during lunch the special ed kids and the "regular" kids ate at separate tables, and all the special ed kids were herded onto the G-12 bus. The incident that sticks out in my mind involved a kid named Jimmy, who was in another special education classroom but lived in my neighborhood. One morning at the bus stop, Jimmy told me that he was going to start going to the neighborhood school with the "regular" kids. I can remember the sadness I felt that it was not me. (Stussman, 1996, p. 15)

Certain studies have examined the social and self-concept outcomes for students with disabilities educated in inclusive settings. These studies suggest that students with severe disabilities in inclusion programs interact with others more often, receive and offer increased social support, and develop more long-lasting and richer friendships with their general education peers (Hunt et al., 1994; Kennedy & Itkonen, 1994; Kennedy, Shukla, & Fryxell, 1997). However, interactions between these students and those without disabilities are often initiated by the latter, are often assistive, and tend to decline over the school year (Evans, Salisbury, Palombaro, Berryman, & Hollowood, 1992). In addition, students with mild disabilities in inclusion classes develop friendships with other students, have self-concept scores similar to those of their classmates without disabilities, and are rated as equal to their general education peers in terms of disruptive behavior (Banerji & Dailey, 1995; Vaughn, Elbaum, & Schumm, 1996), but they are less often accepted and more often rejected by those without disabilities, and they have lower self-perceptions than their general education peers (Bear, Clever, & Proctor, 1991; Roberts & Zubrick, 1992; Sale & Carey, 1995).

Attitudes Toward Placement

I hated high school. Whether I was in the regular or special education class, it was bad. I was often lost in the regular class, and sometimes other kids would tease me. It was terrible for me when I had to read out loud. Sometimes, I made like I was sick or had to go to the bathroom. Anything to avoid having to read in front of my classmates.

I blamed the teachers. If they spent more time with me, I could have learned more. But they didn't have the time, and it was embarrassing to be helped by the teacher in front of the other kids. Nobody wanted that.

Then, it got worse. I was placed in a special education class. I didn't want anyone to know I was in that class. I knew eventually they would find out, and my friends would not like me anymore, and think I was stupid. No one would date me. Even the kids in the special education class avoided each other and made a special effort to be seen with their friends in the regular classes.

I know I was supposed to learn more in the special education class and I think I did. But I still didn't learn anything important. We kept learning this easy, boring stuff over and over again. You just sit there and get bored, and angry. (A high school student with a learning disability)

The personal accounts of students with disabilities about their experiences in general education settings also present a mixed picture. Some students reported that life in the mainstream was characterized by fear, frustration, ridicule, and isolation (Conaty, 1993), while others saw placement in general education as the defining moment in their lives in terms of friendships, intellectual challenges, self-esteem, and success in their careers (Walsh, 1994).

Several studies have surveyed and interviewed students with and without disabilities about their educational placement preferences, as well as their experiences in general and special education settings. Some studies indicate that although many elementary students with disabilities prefer to leave the general education classroom to receive individualized services that help them academically, they also believe that the general education classroom is best for meeting their academic and social needs. They also worry about the recreational and academic activities they are missing when they are being pulled out of their general education classrooms (Jenkins & Heinen, 1989; Klingner, Vaughn, Schumm, Cohen, & Forgan, 1998a; Padeliadu & Zigmond, 1996; Vaughn & Klingner, 1998). Elementary students also reported that leaving the general education classroom for specialized services was embarrassing, and provoked name-calling and ridicule from their peers (Reid & Button, 1995). Gibb, Allred, Ingram, Young, and Egan (1999) found that the majority of junior high school students with emotional and behavioral disorders enjoyed being educated with all other students in the school, and felt that inclusion helped them socially and academically.

Secondary students with disabilities report having mixed and mostly negative experiences in both general and special education (Guterman, 1995; Lovitt, Plavins, & Cushing, 1999). In terms of social development, despite some name-calling, students tended to prefer placement in general education because their friends were in those classes and

REFLECTIVE

If you were a student with a disability, would you prefer a general or a special education setting?

Research indicates that inclusion results in general education students developing positive attitudes toward, meaningful friendships with, and sensitivity to the needs of students with disabilities.

they were treated like other students. Students also worried that their special education placement would cause them to lose their friends and to feel stigmatized and deficient. Academically, while some students preferred special education classes because they received more help, liked the smaller class size, and believed the work was easier, other students viewed special education as low level, irrelevant and repetitive, and not helping them learn very much. Although some students preferred the general education setting because it was more challenging and "cooler," and resulted in more learning, others reported that it was not reasonable for their general education teachers to accommodate their learning needs and that such accommodations would lead to increased academic stigma.

Impact of Inclusion on Students Without Disabilities

Academic Performance

The impact of inclusive education on the academic performance of students without disabilities has also been studied. The findings indicated that their academic performance was equal to or better than that of general education students educated in noninclusive classrooms (Saint-Laurent et al., 1998; Sharpe, York, & Knight, 1994); these positive academic outcomes were usually reported for high-achieving students (Klingner et al., 1998b). Also, inclusion of students with severe disabilities did not significantly reduce the teaching time for their peers without disabilities or cause many interruptions in teaching (Hollowood, Salisbury, Rainforth, & Palombaro, 1994).

Social Performance

Research has also addressed the social impact of inclusion programs on students without disabilities. Elementary students without disabilities felt that inclusion programs helped them to understand individual differences in physical appearance and behavior, the connection between their experiences and the feelings of students with disabilities, and the worth of their peers (Biklen, Corrigan, & Quick, 1989). Friendships between elementary students without disabilities and students with moderate and severe disabilities did develop in inclusive classrooms. However, these friendships began during noninstructional activities, and as the friendships developed, the majority of the students without disabilities assumed a caretaking role (Staub, Schwartz, Gallucci, & Peck, 1994).

Middle school students educated in an inclusive setting showed reduced fear of human differences and greater understanding and tolerance of others, including their peers with disabilities. Those who attended a noninclusive school were more prone to stereotyping and held more negative characterizations of peers with disabilities and diverse backgrounds (Capper & Pickett, 1994). Furthermore, middle and high school students in inclusive classrooms had positive views of inclusion and believed that it helped them understand individual differences, the needs of others, their ability to understand and deal with disability in their own lives, and their ability to make friends with students with disabilities (Helmstetter, Peck, & Giangreco, 1994; Hendrickson, Shokoohi-Yekta, Hamre-Nietupski, & Gable, 1996; Murray-Seegert, 1989; York, Vandercook, Macdonald, Heise-Neff, & Caughey, 1992).

Students without disabilities in an inclusive classroom were concerned about the noise level, about the physical and behavioral characteristics of some of the students with disabilities, and about being asked to be caretakers (Peck, Donaldson, & Pezzoli, 1990). However, this discomfort tended to decrease over the school year.

Impact of Inclusion on Educators

Because the cooperation of educators is critical to the success of inclusion programs, several studies have investigated the attitudes of general and special educators toward inclusive education and their concerns about program implementation. These studies and their findings are summarized below. More information on the experiences of general and special education teachers working collaboratively to implement inclusion is presented in Chapter 4.

Attitudes Toward Inclusion

> I'm a fourth-grade "Regular Ed" teacher who was very reluctantly drafted to have a child with severe disabilities in my room. It didn't take me long to be genuinely glad to have Sandy in my class. I can support inclusion. But please tell me who is going to watch out for people like me? Who will make sure administrators give us smaller class loads to compensate? Who will keep the curriculum people off my back when I don't cover the already overwhelming amount the state expects us to cover? After all, to properly achieve inclusion my time will now be more pressed than ever. Who will ensure that I receive the time I need to meet with the rest of the team (special educator, physical therapist, occupational therapist, etc.)? Who will watch over us? (Giangreco, Baumgart, & Doyle, 1995, p. 23)

Teachers have complex and varying attitudes and reactions to inclusion. Educators tend to agree with the principle of placing students with disabilities in general education classrooms, although some controversy still exists. Although some teachers and administrators support inclusion (Downing, Eichinger & Williams, 1997; Villa, Thousand, Myers, & Nevin, 1996; Waldron, McLeskey, & Pacchiano, 1999), others are satisfied with a pull-out system for delivering special education services and believe that full-time inclusion of students with mild disabilities would not be academically or socially beneficial (Coates, 1989; Semmel, Abernathy, Butera, & Lesar, 1991).

In general, middle and high school teachers appear to favor inclusion less than elementary teachers (Cole & McLeskey, 1997; Thousand, Rosenberg, Bishop, & Villa, 1997)

REFLECTIVE
Why do you think this is the case?

The factors affecting their attitudes include the effectiveness of the program for students with disabilities and their general education classmates, the availability of administrative support, and the adequacy of the support services and training they receive (Giangreco, Dennis, Cloninger, Edelman, and Schattman, 1993; Idol, 1997; Villa et al., 1996; Werts, Wolery, Snyder, Caldwell, & Salisbury, 1996). Soodak, Podell, and Lehman (1998) found that teachers' responses to inclusion are related to their teaching effectiveness, teaching experience, use of differentiated teaching practices, perceptions of the various student disability categories, and school-based conditions such as the use of teacher collaboration and the size of classes.

Outcomes for General Educators

Positive outcomes for general educators included increased confidence in their teaching efficacy, greater awareness of themselves as positive role models for *all students,* more skill in meeting the needs of *all students* with and without disabilities, and acquaintance with new colleagues (Giangreco, Dennis, et al., 1993; Siegel-Causey, McMorris, Mc-Gowen, & Sands-Buss, 1998; Stanovich, 1999). Concerns included the negative attitudes of others; insufficient support, training, and time to collaborate with others; the large size of their classes; and the difficulty in meeting the medical needs and behavioral challenges of students with disabilities and in designing and implementing appropriate instructional accommodations (Coots, Bishop, & Grenot-Scheyer, 1998; D'Alonzo, Giordano, & Vanleeuwen, 1997; Downing, Eichinger, & Williams, 1997; York & Tundidor, 1995). In light of these concerns, educators frequently have questions regarding the implementation of inclusion (see Figure 1.6).

Based on research, the following are some questions that you and other teachers may have about inclusion. As you read this book, you will be able to answer these questions.

◆ What is inclusion? What are the goals of the inclusion program?
◆ Is inclusion for all students with disabilities or just for certain ones?
◆ Do students with disabilities want to be in my class? Do they have the skills to be successful?
◆ What instructional and ancillary support services will students with disabilities receive? Can these services be used to help other students?
◆ Will my class size be adjusted?
◆ Will the education of my students without disabilities suffer?
◆ What do I tell the students without disabilities about the students with disabilities?
◆ How do I handle name calling?
◆ What do I tell families about the inclusion program? What do I do if families complain about the program or don't want their child to be in my class?
◆ What roles will families play to assist me and their child?
◆ Do I decide whether I work in an inclusion program?
◆ Am I expected to teach the general education curriculum to everyone? How can I do that?
◆ What instructional modifications and classroom management strategies do I need to use?
◆ How am I supposed to evaluate and grade my students with disabilities?
◆ What instructional and ancillary support services will I receive?
◆ How can I address the health, medical, and behavioral needs of students with disabilities?
◆ What does it mean to work collaboratively with other professionals in my classroom? Will I be able to work collaboratively with others?
◆ Will I receive enough time to collaborate and communicate with others?
◆ What type of training and administrative support will I receive to help me implement inclusion successfully?
◆ Who will monitor the program? How do I know if the inclusion program is working? How will I be evaluated?

FIGURE 1.6 Questions teachers have about inclusion.

Outcomes for Special Educators

Special educators working in inclusion programs reported having a greater sense of being an important part of the school community, an enriched view of education, greater knowledge of the general education system, and greater enjoyment of teaching that was related to working with students without disabilities and observing the successful functioning of their students with disabilities (York et al., 1992). Their concerns were related to their fear that inclusion will result in the loss of specialized services to students with disabilities and their jobs (Cook, Semmel, & Gerber, 1999; Downing, et al., 1997). Some special education teachers also were worried that their subordinate role in the general education classroom would cause students to view them as a teacher's aide rather than a teacher.

Impact of Inclusion on Families

An important factor in effective inclusion programs is the involvement of families of children with and without disabilities. Studies suggest that families of children with disabilities have different perspectives on inclusion (Palmer, Borthwick-Duffy, & Widaman, 1998).

Families of Children with Disabilities

> He shouldn't be segregated from the rest of the world because it can't be that way for his whole lifetime. And people have to accept him and realize he is part of the community and accept him for what he is and what he isn't. And I don't think segregating him or keeping him away from other children is going to be better for him or for the other children. (A parent of a child with a disability; Erwin & Soodak, 1995, p. 140)

> I have a 12-year-old daughter named Brooke. . . . She has beautiful blue eyes and braces on her teeth. She has a smile from ear to ear and loves to have a friend over to spend the night.
>
> School is hard for Brooke. She is academically and developmentally delayed. She was slower than her peers in learning to talk. She had difficulty learning to read.
>
> Next year Brooke will be entering intermediate school. We will attempt to place her in the regular classroom. . . . Do you know how I feel as her mother? Scared to death. What if she can't do it? . . . What if she can't keep up with her assignments? . . . What if the teachers and principal don't take care of Brooke? What if no one looks out for my little girl? (Wilmore, 1995, pp. 60, 61)

Some families of children with disabilities believe that inclusive education benefited their children, providing them with increased friendships, higher academic achievement, and better preparation for the real world, as well as an improved self-concept and better language and motor skills (Bennett, Deluca, & Bruns, 1997; Davern, 1999; Freeman, Alkin, & Kasari, 1999; Gibb et al., 1997; Grove & Fisher, 1999; Ryndak, Downing, Jacqueline, & Morrison, 1995). Family members' concerns about inclusive education include the loss of individualized special education services, instructional adaptations, and community-based instruction delivered by trained professionals (Fisher, Pumpian, & Sax, 1998; Green & Shinn, 1995), as well as the fear that their children will be targets of verbal abuse and ridicule, which will lower their self-esteem (Freeman et al., 1999; Guralnick, Connor, & Hammond, 1995; Lovitt & Cushing, 1999).

Families of Children Without Disabilities

Several studies have also explored the reactions and experiences of families of children without disabilities in inclusive and integrated educational programs. Family members felt that an inclusive classroom did not prevent their children from receiving a good education, appropriate services, and teacher attention. It also led to improved feelings of self-worth related to helping others, an increased sense of personal development, and a greater tolerance

REFLECTIVE

Some educators propose that teachers should be allowed to decide whether or not to work in a setting that includes students with disabilities. Do you think teachers should have this choice? Should they be allowed to choose the students in terms of the academic levels, ethnic, linguistic, and religious backgrounds, socioeconomic status, gender, and sexual orientation they want to teach? If you were given such a choice, what types of students would you include? Exclude?

REFLECTIVE

If your child had a disability, would you prefer a general or special education setting? If your child did not have a disability, which class would you prefer?

of human differences (Giangreco, Edelman, & Cloninger, & Dennis, 1993; Lowenbraun, Madge, & Affleck, 1990; Peck, Carlson, & Helmstetter, 1992). Family members also felt that inclusion benefits children with disabilities; it promotes their acceptance, improves their self-concept, and exposes them to the real world (Bailey & Winton, 1987; Staub et al., 1994).

Some family members initially had doubts about inclusion. They worried about the effectiveness of the instruction, whether their children would receive less teacher attention, and whether their children would pick up the inappropriate behaviors of children with disabilities (Reichart et al., 1989). However, they found that their fears of inappropriate behaviors were groundless (Peck et al., 1992). Some families of children with and without disabilities felt that their children would receive less teacher attention, harming their children's education (Peck et al., 1992; Reichart et al., 1989). In general, family members expressed less concern about their children being educated with children with physical and sensory disabilities than about children with severe disabilities and children with behavior disorders (Green & Stoneman, 1989).

Research indicates that inclusion is a complex undertaking that can have a positive impact on students, their teachers, and their families. However, this impact appears to be related to educators' willingness to accommodate the diverse needs of students and their families. This, in turn, depends on the administrative support, resources, and training that educators receive to implement effective inclusion programs.

Given these findings, and the continued commitment to educating students with disabilities in general education classrooms, this book is intended to provide you with the skills to develop and implement effective inclusion programs and create learning environments that promote the academic and social performance of *all of your students*. Toward these ends, the book offers you strategies to promote the sensitivity to and acceptance of your students' individual needs and differences; to help you work collaboratively with your colleagues, families, students, and community agencies; and to assist you in reflecting upon and adapting your teaching and curriculum to meet the academic and social needs of *all of your students*.

SUMMARY

This chapter has presented some of the foundations of inclusion as a philosophy for educating students with disabilities in general education settings. Some of the challenges associated with inclusion and its implementation have also been discussed. As you review the chapter, consider the following questions and remember the following points.

What Is Inclusion?

Inclusion is a philosophy that brings students, families, educators, and community members together to create schools based on acceptance, belonging, and community. Inclusionary schools welcome, acknowledge, affirm, and celebrate the value of all learners by educating them together in high-quality, age-appropriate general education classrooms in their neighborhood schools. Whereas mainstreaming can be viewed as either part-time or full-time placement based on a student's readiness for placement in the general education setting, inclusion is thought of as full-time placement in the general education setting based on the belief that all students have the right to be educated in general education classrooms.

What Is the LRE?

The LRE requires that students with disabilities be educated as much as possible with their peers without disabilities. The LRE tells us to look at and consider the general education setting as the first option, not the last, and to move to a more restrictive setting cautiously and only as needed.

What Factors Contributed to the Movement to Educate Students in Inclusive Classrooms?

Contributing factors include normalization, deinstitutionalization, early intervention and early childhood programs, technological advances, the civil rights movement and its resulting litigation, advocacy groups, the segregated nature of special schools and classes, disproportionate representation, and the educational reform movement.

What Are the Laws that Affect Special Education?

Several laws have had a broad impact on students with disabilities, including PL 94-142, the Education for All Handicapped Children Act; PL 99-457, the Education for All Handicapped Children Act Amendments of 1986; PL 101-476, the Individuals with Disabilities Education Act; PL 105-17, the IDEA Amendments of 1997; PL 93-112, the Rehabilitation Act and Section 504; and PL 101-336, the Americans with Disabilities Act.

What Is the Impact of Inclusion?

Research on the impact of inclusion is inconclusive and offers a variety of perspectives. Some studies suggest that inclusion often results in positive academic and social outcomes for students with disabilities; other studies indicate that some students with disabilities do not receive the instructional modifications they need to benefit from inclusion. Studies suggest that students without disabilities are not harmed academically by an inclusive education and that they benefit socially.

General and special educators have mixed reactions to inclusion. Their attitudes are related to their efficacy in implementing inclusion, which in turn depends on the administrative support, resources, time, and training they receive to implement effective inclusion programs. The attitudes and reactions of families of children with and without disabilities to inclusion appear to be complex, multidimensional, and affected by many interacting variables.

What Would You Do in Today's Diverse Classroom?

Ms. Carr, a general education teacher, and Ms. Stevens, a special education teacher, had just started cooperative teaching in an inclusion program. Things were going well, and they were ready to meet with their children's families at the first open school night.

There was a good turnout of family members. Ms. Carr and Ms. Stevens started talking about the program and the "new arrangement." They discussed the philosophy and goals of the program, the day's schedule, communications with families, and various aspects of the program. Family members asked questions like "Do we have computers?" and "How does the teaming work?" Then one parent asked, "If there are two teachers in a class, which one is my son's 'real' teacher?" Ms. Carr and Ms. Stevens explained that they both teach all the students. Sometimes one of them leads a lesson while the other helps students to participate, and sometimes they both work with small groups at the same time. Then one family member said, "I'm all for having a variety of students in the class, but won't students with special needs take time away from the other kids?"

1. As a teacher, how would you answer such a question?

2. What other questions do you think families might have about inclusion programs?

3. What can teachers do to help family members understand inclusion programs and build support among families for inclusion?

CHAPTER 2

Understanding the Diverse Educational Needs of Students with Disabilities

Marty

Ms. Tupper, a fifth-grade teacher, was concerned about Marty's inconsistent performance in school. He knew a lot about many different topics and liked to share his knowledge with others. He picked things up quickly when he heard them explained or watched them demonstrated. He loved it when the class did science activities and experiments. However, although he was quite intelligent, Marty's performance in reading and math was poor. Despite having highly developed verbal skills, he also had difficulties with writing assignments.

Ms. Tupper noticed that Marty had trouble starting and completing his assignments. Sometimes he began a task before receiving all the directions; at other times, he ignored the directions and played with objects in the room or at his desk. He frequently worked on an assignment for only a short period of time and then switched to another assignment. When he completed assignments, his work was usually of high quality. Marty's parents also were concerned. They felt he was smart but lazy and capable of doing better work.

Marty also worried about his difficulties in school. He wondered why he was not like others. He thought he was "dumb" and that reading, writing, and math would always be hard. Sometimes, out of frustration, he acted like the class clown. At other times, he was quiet and withdrawn to avoid drawing attention to his difficulties.

Marty loved to talk and joke with others. He was fun to be with but sometimes he got carried away, which bothered some of his friends. Marty was the best student in the class at fixing things. When other students needed assistance with mechanical things, they came to Marty. Marty loved to take things apart and put them back together. In his neighborhood, he was famous for fixing bicycles and other toys.

Ms. Tupper liked Marty and felt frustrated by her inability to help him learn. She decided that she needed assistance to help address Marty's needs and contacted the school's Child Study Prereferral Team. The team met with Ms. Tupper and Marty's parents to discuss Marty, including his strengths, weaknesses, interests, and hobbies, as well as effective instructional techniques to use. They also gathered information by observing Marty in several school settings and talking with him. The team then met with Ms. Tupper and Marty's parents to plan some interventions to address Marty's needs. They talked about and agreed to try several environmental and curricular adaptations. To improve Marty's on-task behavior and the communication between Ms. Tupper and Marty's parents, a daily report card system was used. Ms. Tupper also moved Marty's seat closer to the front of the room to improve her monitoring of his ability to pay attention and understand directions. To help Marty with reading and writing, Ms. Tupper tried storyboards, story frames and story maps, and peer tutoring. In math, she attempted to increase her use of manipulatives and cooperative learning groups.

The CD-Rom packaged with this text contains a case-based tutorial that will walk you through the development of IEPs and the criteria necessary to assess their quality. To help you learn more about developing quality IEPs, the CD-ROM provides two interactive tutorials, six case studies with related exercises, and a variety of additional resources.

Members of the Child Study Prereferral Team worked with Ms. Tupper to implement and evaluate the effectiveness of these interventions. The team met periodically to review Marty's progress through observations, interviews, and an analysis of work samples. While the interventions improved Marty's ability to complete his work, Marty failed to make significant progress in reading, writing, and math.

As a result, the Child Study Prereferral Team referred Marty to the school district's Comprehensive Planning Team to determine if he would benefit from special education and related services. With the consent of Marty's parents, the Comprehensive Planning Team conducted a comprehensive assessment of Marty's performance in a variety of areas. The school psychologist gave him an intelligence test and found that Marty had above-average intelligence and strong verbal skills. Tests of fine motor and gross motor abilities as part of a physical exam conducted by the school physician also revealed Marty's strengths in these areas. An interview with Marty and the observations of his parents also led the team to believe that Marty's learning difficulties were lowering his self-esteem.

The special education teacher assessed Marty's skills in reading and math using several achievement and criterion-referenced tests. Marty's reading showed weaknesses in word recognition, oral reading, and reading comprehension. In decoding, he had trouble sounding out words and relied on contextual cues. In reading comprehension, Marty had trouble responding to questions related to large amounts of information and interpreting abstractions.

Marty's math performance revealed both strengths and weaknesses. He performed well in the areas of geometry, measurement, time, and money. However, he had difficulty in solving word problems, working with fractions, and performing multistep computations in multiplication and division.

After all the data were collected, the team met to determine Marty's eligibility for special education. They reviewed the data and listened to the views of the various team members. Some members felt that Marty had a learning disability. Others felt that he had an attention deficit disorder and should be served under Section 504. Several members also believed that Marty needed a program for gifted and talented students. After some discussion and debate, the team concluded that Marty's inability to perform academic tasks at a level in line with his potential showed that he had a learning disability. The team also decided that Marty should remain in Ms. Tupper's class and that an Individualized Educational Program to meet his needs there should be developed. They also agreed to recommend Marty for inclusion in the district's gifted and talented program.

To learn more about how you can use information about individual students' present level of performance to create quality IEPs, complete the *Developing Individualized Education Plans Tutorial* on the CD-ROM, which uses the profile of Marty that you have just read as its basis.

What factors should educators consider in designing an appropriate educational program for Marty? Does Marty qualify for special education services? After reading this chapter, you should be able to answer these as well as the following questions.

◆ How does the special education identification process work?
◆ What are the educational needs of students with high-incidence disabilities?
◆ What are the educational needs of students with low-incidence disabilities?

How Does the Special Education Identification Process Work?

Comprehensive Planning Team

The IDEA requires that a comprehensive team of professionals and family members, with the student when appropriate, make important decisions concerning the education of students like Marty. As we saw, the team initially worked with Ms. Tupper to address Marty's needs in her class. Once it was determined that he needed additional services, the team assessed his eligibility for special education and developed an IEP based on his strengths and needs, current assessment data, and the concerns of Marty's family.

For additional information about the comprehensive planning team, access the *Understanding the Parts of Individualized Education Plans* portion of the CD-ROM.

As the student's general education or special education teacher, you are a member of the team. The other members of the team are the family members of the child, a representative of the school district who is knowledgeable about the general education curriculum and the availability of resources, an individual who can determine the instructional implications of the evaluation results, other individuals selected at the discretion of the family or the school district who have knowledge or special expertise regarding the child, and the student when appropriate. When developing IEPs for students from culturally and linguistically diverse backgrounds, it is recommended, although not mandated, that the IEP team include an individual with expertise in the student's language and culture and an understanding of how second language acquisition affects student performance and behavior (Ochoa, Rivera, & Powell, 1997; Ortiz, 1997). These individuals can help the team understand the cultural and linguistic factors that may affect and explain student performance and behavior (see Chapters 3 and 7), and can help the family and student become involved in the decision-making process. The diverse perspectives and experiences of the members of the team and the ways in which the team functions to make decisions collaboratively are described in Chapter 4.

Prereferral System

INFORMATIONAL

Whitten and Dieker (1995) offer guidelines for using prereferral interventions in schools, and Craig, Hull, Haggart and Perez-Selles (2000), Baca and de Valenzuela (1998), and Ortiz and Wilkinson (1991) describe effective prereferral models for use with students from culturally and linguistically diverse backgrounds.

Like many school districts, Marty's school district employed a *prereferral system,* sometimes referred to as a *teacher assistance team,* to assist classroom teachers like Ms. Tupper before considering a referral for a special education placement (Kovaleski, Gickling, Morrow, & Swank, 1999). The team helps teachers to gather information about students and to develop and use methods to keep students in the general education classroom. Prereferral interventions are determined based on the individual student's strengths and needs; educational, social, and medical history; language and cultural background, as well as the teacher's concerns and the nature of the learning environment (Murdick & Petch-Hogan, 1996). The effectiveness of these methods is then assessed before formally evaluating the student for placement in special education.

Prereferral strategies are especially important in addressing the disproportionate representation of students from diverse backgrounds (Baca & de Valenzuela, 1998; Ortiz, 1997). Effective prereferral interventions with students from diverse backgrounds include embedding students' culture and language in the curriculum, establishing collaborative school and community relationships, offering meaningful and relevant academic programs, understanding how cultural and linguistic backgrounds affect learning, and involving families in all school and classroom activities (Craig, et al., 2000; McCarty, 1998).

When prereferral strategies are not effective, the planning team, with the consent of the student's family, determines if a student is eligible for special education based on various assessment procedures. Although problems with labeling students have been noted, state and federal funding formulas require the use of labels and definitions. However, no two students are alike; therefore, each educational program must be based on individual needs rather than on a label.

Individualized Education Program

If the comprehensive planning team determines that a student's needs require special education services, an IEP is developed for the student. Although the 1997 amendments to the IDEA retain many of the traditional components of the IEP, they also mandate several changes, which are outlined below. (Later in this chapter, you will learn about specific disabilities and the educational needs of students with these disabilities.)

IEP Components

To review additional information about IEP components, access the *Understanding the Parts of Individualized Education Plans* portion of the CD-ROM.

The IEP developed by the team must include the following components:

1. A statement of the student's present level of functioning in terms of academic, socialization, behavioral, and communication skills. This statement also should

REFLECTING ON YOUR PRACTICES

Implementing a Prereferral System

Prereferral interventions have reduced the number of students placed in special education. You can evaluate your school's prereferral system by addressing the following questions:

- Are administrators, educators, and family members committed to implementing and promoting a prereferral system?
- Are there criteria for the selection of educators to serve on the prereferral support team?
- Does the prereferral support team include educators who have a range of backgrounds, experiences, expertise, and training and who perform a variety of functions?
- Are family members and community agencies involved in the prereferral process?
- Does the prereferral support team have the resources and time to perform its activities?
- Is there a system to help teachers access the services of the prereferral team?
- Do the forms and procedures employed in the prereferral system facilitate the process?
- Do prereferral support teams have adequate and reasonable procedures for determining the goals and types of prereferral systems based on students' strengths; needs; educational, social, and medical history; language and cultural background, as well as the teacher's concerns and the learning environment?
- Does the prereferral support team consider and suggest a range of reasonable instructional and family involvement strategies, curricular and classroom design adaptations, alternative assessment procedures, testing modifications, culturally relevant instructional and classroom management techniques, adaptive devices, teacher training and collaboration activities, and school-based and community-based supportive services to address the referral problems?
- Are prereferral interventions suggested by the prereferral support team implemented as intended and for a sufficient period of time?
- Does the prereferral support team collect data to examine the effectiveness of the prereferral interventions and the prereferral process and to make revisions based on these data?

How would you rate your school's prereferral system?
( ) Excellent ( ) Good ( ) Needs Improvement
( ) Needs Much Improvement
What are some goals and steps you could adopt to improve your school's prereferral system?

---

address how the disability affects the student's involvement and progress in the general education curriculum.

2. A list of annual goals, including benchmarks or short-term objectives to address the student's needs and progress in the general education curriculum, as well as other educational needs.

3. A statement of the special education and related services, as well as supplementary aids and services, to help the student reach the annual goals, be involved and progress in the general education curriculum, and participate in extracurricular and nonacademic activities with other students. This statement also should address the program modifications and support for school personnel, such as general educators or receiving consultation services or training related to specific issues.

4. An explanation of the extent, if any, to which the student will *not* participate in the general education classroom and in other activities with students without disabilities.

5. A statement of any testing accommodations that the student will need to participate in state or districtwide assessments. If the IEP team determines that a

To learn more about the role of annual goals and how you can write meaningful ones, complete the case-based *Writing Long-term Goals & Short-term Objectives for IEPs Tutorial* portion of the CD-ROM.

The comprehensive planning team works with family members to design a student's IEP.

INFORMATIONAL

Campbell, Campbell, and Brady (1998) and Roberts and Baumberger (1999) offer guidelines for selecting goals and objectives for IEPs, and Etscheidt and Bartlett (1999) present a model for determining supplementary aids and services for IEPs.

The CD-ROM contains blank electronic IEP forms you can use for additional practice in developing IEPs.

student will not participate in a particular assessment, the IEP must include an explanation and state what alternative methods will be used to assess the student's learning and progress. (See Chapter 12 for specific information about testing accommodations and alternative assessment techniques.)

6. A statement of how the student's progress toward the goals and objectives in the IEP will be measured and how the student's family will be regularly informed of their child's progress. Student progress reports must be as frequent as the progress reports sent to families of general education students. This statement also should state what the student must do to achieve the goals in the IEP by the end of the school year.

7. A projected date for the initiation of services and modifications, as well as their anticipated frequency, location, and duration.

A sample IEP for Marty, the student we met at the beginning of this chapter, is presented in Figure 2.1.

Special Considerations in Developing IEPs

In addition to the components of the IEP outlined above, the IEP team also must consider several special factors related to the unique needs of students, which are outlined below.

◈ For a student whose behavior interferes with his or her learning or that of others, the IEP team must consider behavioral strategies, including positive behavior interventions, strategies, and supports. To address behaviors that interfere with learning and socialization, some teams include a functional behavioral

Unified School District
Individualized Education Program

Student: Marty Glick

School: Hudson Elementary

Placement: General Education Classroom

Date of IEP Meeting: 12/17/2000

Date of Initiation of Services: 1/3/2001

Dominant Language of Student: English

DOB: 8/5/90

Grade: 5

Disability Classification: LD

Notification to Family: 11/28/2000

Review date: 1/3/2002

PRESENT LEVEL OF PERFORMANCE IN THE GENERAL EDUCATION CURRICULUM
ACADEMIC/EDUCATIONAL ACHIEVEMENT

Mathematics

Marty's strongest areas include geometry, measurement, time, and money. He has difficulty with multiplication, division, fractions, and word problems. He especially had difficulty solving problems that contained nonessential information.

Reading

Marty's reading is characterized by weaknesses in word recognition, oral reading, and comprehension. Marty had difficulty with the passages that were written at a third-grade level. His oral reading of the passages revealed difficulties sounding out words and a reliance on contextual cues. He had particular problems with comprehension questions related to large amounts of information and interpreting abstractions.

Written Language

Marty's writing portfolio reveals that he has many ideas to write about in a broad range of genres. However, Marty avoids using prewriting tools such as semantic webs or outlines to organize his thoughts. Consequently, his stories don't usually follow a chronological sequence, and his reports do not fully develop the topic. He uses a variety of sentence patterns but frequently ignores the need for punctuation. Marty has difficulty editing his own work but will make mechanical changes pointed out by the teacher. He rarely revises the content or organization of his writing in a substantial manner. Marty's teacher has observed that Marty enjoys working on the computer and performs better on writing tasks when he uses a talking work processor.

SOCIAL DEVELOPMENT

Level of Social Development

Marty shows attention difficulties when attempting some academic tasks. He has a good sense of humor and seems to relate fairly well to his peers.

Interest Inventory

Marty likes working with peers and using computers. He prefers projects to tests. He likes working with his hands and fixing things.

PHYSICAL DEVELOPMENT

Marty is physically healthy and has no difficulties with his hearing and vision. He has had no major illnesses or surgeries, and he is not taking any medications.

BEHAVIORAL DEVELOPMENT

A functional assessment of Marty's classroom behavior indicates that Marty is frequently off-task and has difficulty completing his assignments. He often works on assignments for a short period of time and then works on another assignment, engages in an off-task activity such as playing with objects, leaves his work area, or seeks attention from his teacher or his peers. His behavior also appears to be affected by other activities in the classroom, the placement of his work area near certain students, and the type and difficulty of the activity.

FIGURE 2.1 Sample IEP.

(continued)

RELATED SERVICES

Service	Frequency	Location
Group counseling	Once/week	Social worker's office

SUPPLEMENTARY AIDS AND SERVICES

Service	Frequency	Location
Collaboration teacher	2 hours/day	General education classroom
Paraprofessional	3 hours/day	General education classroom

PROGRAM MODIFICATION AND SUPPORT FOR SCHOOL PERSONNEL

Marty and his teacher will receive the services of a collaborative teacher and a paraeducator. Marty's teacher will be given time to meet with the collaboration teacher, who also will modify materials, locate resources, administer assessments, and coteach lessons. Marty's teacher also will receive training related to differentiated instruction, classroom management, and assessment alternatives and accommodations.

EXTENT OF PARTICIPATION IN GENERAL EDUCATION PROGRAMS AND WITH PEERS WITHOUT DISABILITIES

Marty will remain in his fifth-grade classroom full-time. The collaboration teacher and the paraeducator will provide direct service to Marty in the general education classroom.

RATIONALE FOR PLACEMENT

It is anticipated that Marty's educational needs can best be met in the general education classroom. He will benefit from being exposed to the general education curriculum with the additional assistance of the collaboration teacher and the paraeducator. The use of testing modifications and computers with talking word processors also should help Marty benefit from his general education program. Marty's social skills and self-concept also will be improved by exposure to his general education peers. Counseling will provide him with the prosocial skills necessary to interact with his peers and complete his work.

ANNUAL GOALS AND SHORT-TERM OBJECTIVES

Annual Goal: Marty will read, write, listen, and speak for information and understanding. (State Learning Standard 1 for English Language Arts)

Short-Term Objectives and Evaluation Criteria	Evaluation Procedures
1. Given the choice of a narrative trade book at his instructional level, Marty will be able to retell the story, including major characters, the setting, and major events of the plot sequence.	Teacher-made story grammar checklist
2. Given a passage from his social studies or science textbook, Marty will develop three questions that require inferential or critical thinking.	Teacher evaluation of student response
3. Using a prewriting structure to organize his ideas, Marty will write a paragraph describing a process that shows logical development and has a minimum of five sentences.	Writing rubric

Annual Goal: Marty will read, write, listen, and speak for literary response and expression. (State Learning Standard 2 for English Language Arts)

Short-Term Objectives and Evaluation Criteria	Evaluation Procedures
1. After choosing a favorite poem to read to his peers, Marty will memorize it and recite it with fluency and intonation.	Peer and teacher feedback
2. Given the choice of texts with multi-syllabic words, Marty will read with 90% accuracy.	Teacher analysis of running record
3. Given a choice of biographies, Marty will reflect upon the events and experiences which relate to his own life.	Teacher evaluation of dialogue journal

FIGURE 2.1   (continued)

Annual Goal: Marty will understand mathematics and become mathematically confident by communicating and reasoning mathematically. (State Learning Standard 3 for Mathematics, Science, and Technology)

Short-Term Objectives and Evaluation Criteria	Evaluation Procedures
1. Given a one-step word problem with a distractor, Marty will write the relevant information and operation needed to solve it 90 percent of the time.	Teacher-made worksheet
2. Given the task of writing five one-step word problems with a distractor, Marty will write four that are clear enough for his classmates to solve.	Teacher evaluation of student response

Annual Goal: Marty will demonstrate mastery of the foundation skills and competencies essential for success in the workplace. (State Learning Standard 3a for Career Development and Occupational Studies)

Short-Term Objectives and Evaluation Criteria	Evaluation Procedures
1. When working independently on an academic task, Marty will improve his time on task by 100 percent.	Self-recording
2. When working in small groups, Marty will listen to peers and take turns speaking 80 percent of the time.	Teacher observation or group evaluation

TRANSITION PROGRAM

Marty is very interested in and skilled at working with his hands to make and fix things. In addition to using these skills as part of the educational program, Marty will participate in a career awareness program designed to explore his career interests.

This program will expose Marty to a variety of careers and allow him to experience work settings and meet professionals who are involved in careers related to Marty's interests. This program also will aid Marty in understanding his learning style, strengths and weaknesses, interests, and preferences.

Annual Goal: Marty will be knowledgeable about the world of work, explore career options, and relate personal skills, aptitudes, and abilities to future career decisions. (State Learning Standard 1 for Career Development and Occupational Studies)

Short-Term Objectives and Evaluation Criteria	Evaluation Procedures
1. Marty will identify three careers in which he may be interested and explain why he is interested in each one.	Self-report
2. Marty will research and explain the training and experiential requirements for the three careers he has identified.	Interview
3. Marty will evaluate his skills and characteristics with respect to these careers by identifying his related strengths and needs.	Self-report
4. Marty will follow and observe individuals involved in these three careers as they perform their jobs.	Student-maintained log

ASSISTIVE TECHNOLOGY AND COMMUNICATION NEEDS

Marty will be given a computer and talking word processing system with word prediction capabilities and a talking calculator to assist him with classroom activities and tests.

PARTICIPATION IN STATEWIDE AND DISTRICTWIDE ASSESSMENTS, AS WELL AS TESTING ACCOMMODATIONS AND ALTERNATIVES

Marty will participate in all statewide and districtwide assessments. He will take these tests individually in a separate location, with extended time and breaks every 30 minutes. Tests that last for more than 2 hours will be administered over several days, with no more than 2 hours of testing each day. Marty will be allowed to use a computer with a talking word processing program and word prediction capabilities. For math tests that do not involve mental computation, he will be allowed to use a talking calculator.

When possible and appropriate, Marty will demonstrate his mastery of classroom content through projects and cooperative learning activities rather than teacher-made tests. When Marty must take teacher-made tests, they will be administered in a separate location by his collaboration teacher with extended time limits. A mastery level grading system will be employed.

FIGURE 2.1 (continued)

METHOD AND FREQUENCY OF COMMUNICATION WITH FAMILY

Marty's family will be regularly informed through IEP progress reports, curriculum-based assessments, and Marty's general education report cards. In addition, feedback on Marty's performance and progress will be shared with his family through quarterly scheduled family-teacher meetings, results of state and district assessments, and portfolio reviews.

Committee Participants	Relationship/Role
Ms. Rachel Tupper	5th grade teacher
Mr. Terry Feaster	Special Ed. teacher
Mr. Kris Brady	Sp. Ed. administrator
Ms. Jessica Amatura	Educational evaluator

Signature(s)

If family members were not members of the committee, please indicate:

I agree with the Individualized Education Program   _____
I disagree with the Individualized Education Program   _____

Harry Glick, Agnes Glick

Parent/Guardian Signature

I participated in this meeting. I agree with the goals and services of the Individualized Educational Program.

Marty Glick

Student's Signature

FIGURE 2.1   (continued)

assessment and an individualized behavioral plan as part of the IEP process (see Chapter 7).

◈ For a student who is developing English proficiency, the IEP team must consider the student's language needs as they relate to the IEP (see Chapter 3).

◈ For a student who is blind or visually impaired, the IEP must provide for instruction in Braille and the use of Braille unless the IEP team determines otherwise.

◈ For a student who is deaf or hard of hearing, the IEP team must consider the language and communication needs of the student, the student's academic level, the full range of needs (including the student's social, emotional, and cultural needs), and the student's opportunities for direct communication with peers and professionals in his or her language and communication mode.

Recommendations for designing IEPs for students with medical needs, with sensory impairments, and from diverse backgrounds are presented in Figure 2.2.

SPECIAL CONSIDERATIONS FOR STUDENTS WITH MEDICAL NEEDS

The IEPs for students with medical needs should identify and address their unique needs and be developed collaboratively with medical professionals. Therefore, IEPs for these students should contain a health plan and include:

◇ the findings of medical and therapy evaluations
◇ appropriate health related goals
◇ suggestions for placement, related services and supports, scheduling, and classroom adaptations
◇ medical treatments and medication requirements, including potential side effects
◇ equipment requirements
◇ vocational, social, and psychosocial needs
◇ training for students so that they can perform or direct others to perform or direct others to perform specialized health care procedures
◇ training for professionals and families
◇ procedures for dealing with emergencies (American Federation of Teachers, 1993; Heller, et al., 2000; Hill, 1999; Phelps, 1995; Prendergast, 1995)

SPECIAL CONSIDERATIONS FOR STUDENTS WITH SENSORY IMPAIRMENTS

The IEPs for students with sensory impairments can address their unique needs and focus on helping them succeed in the LRE. Therefore, IEPs for these students should address:

◇ the skills and instructional strategies necessary to develop reading and writing
◇ the skills and technological devices needed to access information
◇ orientation and mobility instruction
◇ socialization skills
◇ transitional, recreational, and career education needs (Heumann & Hehir, 1995)

SPECIAL CONSIDERATIONS FOR STUDENTS FROM LINGUISTICALLY AND CULTURALLY DIVERSE BACKGROUNDS

The IEPs for students from diverse backgrounds should give teachers additional information to guide the educational program for these students. IEPs for these students should include:

◇ a summary of assessment results, including the student's language skills in her or his native language and English and in social and academic interactions, as well as information about the student's life outside of school
◇ the language(s) of instruction matched to specific goals and objectives
◇ the goals and objectives related to maintaining the student's native language and cultural identity and learning English
◇ teaching strategies relating to the student's linguistic ability, academic skill, cultural and socioeconomic background, and learning style
◇ teaching materials and curricula that address the student's linguistic and cultural background
◇ motivation strategies and reinforcers that are compatible with the student's cultural and experiential background
◇ related services that reflect the student's educational, medical, psychological, linguistic, and cultural needs
◇ bilingual and culturally sensitive educators, paraeducators, community volunteers, and other district resources available to meet the student's needs (Garcia & Malkin, 1993; Ortiz, 1997; Ortiz & Wilkinson, 1989)

FIGURE 2.2 Special considerations in designing IEPs.

Assistive Technology The IEP team also must determine whether the student needs assistive technology devices and services. This decision is based on an individualized technology evaluation that usually includes (1) identification of the student's strengths, weaknesses, preferences, age, gender, cultural perspectives, level of and desire for independence, educational and community-based goals, and ability and willingness to use the device; (2) the needs and cultural values of the family, including the sociocultural factors that affect the family's and the student's opinion,

INFORMATIONAL

Galvin and Scherer (1996) offer guidelines on evaluating and choosing assistive technology and enlisting the help of individuals with disabilities.

Technology
Is the AT functional and appropriate for the child?
Does the device provide for greater opportunities for choice and control?
Does it match the needs of the child?
Does the device physically fit into the child's environments?

Service System
What is the most appropriate AT needed by the child and family?
How can we provide case coordination to secure services for you and your child?
How can we support you in meeting your priority AT goals?

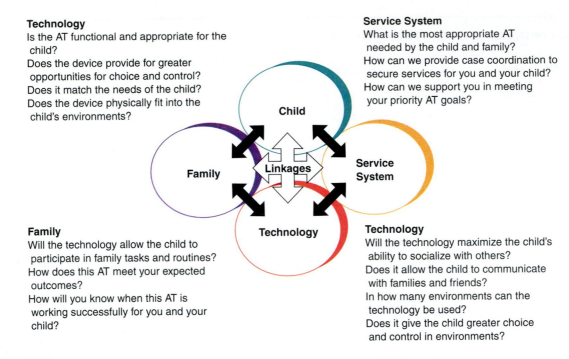

Family
Will the technology allow the child to participate in family tasks and routines?
How does this AT meet your expected outcomes?
How will you know when this AT is working successfully for you and your child?

Technology
Will the technology maximize the child's ability to socialize with others?
Does it allow the child to communicate with families and friends?
In how many environments can the technology be used?
Does it give the child greater choice and control in environments?

FIGURE 2.3 A comprehensive approach to selecting assistive technology (AT) for students.

Source: H. P. Parrette and M. J. Brotherson, *Education and Training in Mental Retardation and Developmental Disabilities*, vol. 31, 1996, p. 32. Copyright 1996 by The Council for Exceptional Children. Reprinted by permission.

acceptance, and motivation to use the device, as well as the impact of the device on the family; (3) the needs of the student in his or her customary environments, such as the classroom, school, home, and work setting; (4) the nature of the technology, including its potential effectiveness, ease of use, features, obtrusiveness and noticeability, comfort level, dependability, adaptability, durability, transportability, safety, cost, impact on peers, and comparability to other devices; and (5) a statement of the advantages and disadvantages of the alternative strategies and technologies for meeting the student's identified technology needs (Bryant & Bryant, 1998; Parette, 1997). In addition, the IEP team should consider whether the device allows the student to function at a higher level and/or more efficiently, as well as the training that the student, family members, and teachers need to ensure that the device has maximum benefit for the student (Bryant, 1998; Summers, Mikell, Redmond, Roberts, & Hampton, 1997).

Additional guidelines for determining appropriate technology to meet the needs of students and their families are presented in Figure 2.3. Information on assistive technology is also presented in Chapters 1 and 8.

For additional information about transition services and IEPs, access the *Understanding the Parts of Individualized Education Plans* portion of the CD-ROM.

Transition Services   IEPs for all students who are 14 years of age or older must include an annual statement of the transition services that will assist these students as they leave high school. Beginning at the age of 16, or younger if determined by the IEP team, the IEP also must include a statement of the transition services for the student, including, when appropriate, a statement of interagency responsibilities or any needed linkages.

The transition services component of the IEP can address a variety of areas related to transition. For example, for students who will go to college after graduation, the transition services component may relate to learning study skills and advocating for one's needs. For students who will go to work, the transition services component may focus on developing important job-seeking and job performance skills, finding recreational opportunities, and preparing for independent living. Some schools meet the transition services requirement by developing an Individualized Transition Plan (ITP) that is included as part of the IEP. Issues related to transitional planning and a sample ITP are presented in Chapter 6.

Student Involvement

The IDEA supports the involvement of students with disabilities in the IEP process. Students can offer a unique perspective on their own strengths and needs, preferences, interests, hobbies, talents, and career goals, as well as successful teaching strategies and materials. Involving students in the team and the IEP process can help the team focus on positive aspects of the student's performance and ensure that practical, functional, and relevant goals are included in the IEP and enhance the effectiveness of the instructional program (Nahmias, 1995; Snyder & Shapiro, 1997).

You and your colleagues and family members can use various strategies to help students participate in the team process (Kroeger, Leibold, & Ryan, 1999). Before the meeting you can outline the purpose of the meeting, including who will attend, what will go on, and how to participate. You also can provide students with copies of their current IEPs, review IEPs and relevant vocabulary with students, give students inventories and checklists to help them identify their needs and feelings about the issues to be discussed, and help students rehearse their comments before the meeting. At the meeting, you can help students participate by allowing them to discuss their past and future goals, and to ask and answer questions regarding their strengths, challenges, aspirations, and opinions. You also can give students a visual representation of the IEP on the chalkboard or overhead projector, give them time to formulate and present their responses, listen and pay attention to their comments, ask them for input and opinions, and incorporate their comments into the educational program. Following the meeting, you can give students a copy of their IEP and encourage them to review it periodically and to work toward meeting the goals and objectives listed there.

Implementing IEPs in General Education Settings

You also will need to work on ways to implement the IEP in the general education classroom (Etscheidt & Bartlett, 1999; Thousand et al., 1997). First, you can work with the IEP team to create a matrix that links the student's IEP goals and services with the student's general education program (see Figure 2.4). In creating the matrix, you need to integrate the objectives, related services, adaptive devices, and special accommodations outlined in the student's IEP with the critical components of the classroom

MATRIX OF DAVID'S IEP OBJECTIVES AND THE SCHEDULE

Name *David Sebastian*   Grade/Age *Sophomore/15*   School Year *1996-1997*

IEP Objectives	World Civics	Geometry	English	P.E.	Biology	Counseling	Lunch	Assemblies	Club Mtgs.	Passing Periods	Peer Support Groups	After School
1. Self-regulate impulsive behaviors	X	X	X	X	X	X	X	X	X	X	X	X
2. Type out a message for emotional support						X						X
3. Self-regulate to make changes	X	X	X	X	X	X	X	X	X	X	X	X
4. Eye contact with persons	X	X	X		X	X	X		X		X	X
5. Functional math	X	X	X	X	X	X	X	X	X	X	X	X
6. Initiate conversation	X		X	X		X	X		X	X	X	
7. Vocational awareness exploration	X	X	X	X		X	X			X		X
8. Active member of class discussions	X	X	X	X	X							
9. Participate in a peer support group											X	
10. Public transportation skills												X

FIGURE 2.4 Sample IEP matrix.

Source: The evolution of secondary inclusion by J. Thousand, R. L. Rosenberg, K. D. Bishop, and R. A. Villa, 1997, *Remedial and Special Education,* vol. 18, p. 281. Copyright 1997 by PRO-ED, Inc. Reprinted by permission.

schedule, curriculum, and routines. The goals and objectives of the IEP are then implemented by all professionals in the general education classroom as part of the class's ongoing instructional activities. You also can develop a Program-at-a-Glance form that gives the student's teachers and supportive service personnel essential aspects of the student's IEP (see Figure 2.5). Finally, an Inclusive IEP Adaptation Checklist, a list of the instructional modifications for addressing the student's needs, can be shared with those who work with the student.

Student's Name: *David Sebastian*

Age __17__   Disability   Down Syndrome, Communication Support

	Staff	Rm.
1	Coppes	SC 123
2	Hubbard	A 206
3	Eshilian	Study Skills
4	Bove	L 123
5	Lablin	Vocational Skills
6	Miller	Study Skills

Lives with: Mother and father. (Sister and brother have moved out)

Positive Student Profile:	**IEP Objectives:**
Friendly	Self-regulate for behaviors
Stays with a task	Type or say messages/communication
Good sense of humor	Deal with change
Very motivated	Eye contact with students and adults
Very artistic	Functional math
	Initiate conversations
	Vocational awareness
	Class participation
	Attend and participate in support group
	Self-advocacy
	Utilization of mass transportation

Management Needs:
Needs support to maintain attention
Needs support to maintain behaviors in class
If it is necessary, have David leave class and not interrupt others while he goes to the Study Skills room or the Guidance Office

Medical Needs: Has had 1 to 2 seizures per year. Knows when they are coming.

Grading Accommodations: May need more time, large print, support from other students for note taking, or support at times from staff and students.

Other Comments:
    Service Coordinator   Ellen North   Extension   123
    Parent/Guardian   Adele and Robert   Phone   888-555-1234

FIGURE 2.5   Sample Program-at-a-Glance.

Source: The evolution of secondary inclusion by J. Thousand, R. L. Rosenberg, K. D. Bishop, and R. A. Villa, 1997, *Remedial and Special Education,* vol. 18, p. 280. Copyright 1997 by PRO-ED, Inc. Reprinted by permission.

WHAT ARE THE EDUCATIONAL NEEDS OF STUDENTS WITH HIGH-INCIDENCE DISABILITIES?

Students like Marty are referred to as having *high-incidence* disabilities or mild disabilities that include such disability categories as learning disabilities, educable mental retardation, mild emotional/behavioral disorders, and speech/language impairments. Students with high-incidence disabilities make up 94 percent of the students with disabilities. As we saw in the case of Marty, educators often have trouble differentiating these disability categories because their characteristics overlap. (Later in the chapter, we will learn about students with low-incidence disabilities, which include students with physical, sensory, and severe disabilities.)

Students with Learning Disabilities

Slightly more than half of the students receiving special education services have *learning disabilities,* making them the largest and fastest-growing group of students with disabilities (Fuchs & Fuchs, 1998; MacMillan, Gresham, & Bocian, 1998). This growing prevalence rate is due to several factors, including the social acceptability of the learning disabilities label. In most cases, the cause of a student's learning disability is not known (Mercer, 1997).

The U.S. Department of Education defines a specific learning disability as

> a disorder in one or more of the basic psychological processes involved in understanding or using spoken or written language, which may appear as an impaired ability to listen, think, speak, read, write, spell, or do mathematical calculations. The term *learning disability* includes such conditions as perceptual handicaps, brain injury, minimal brain dysfunction, dyslexia, and developmental aphasia. It does not include learning problems that are primarily the result of visual, hearing, or motor handicaps, mental retardation, emotional disturbance, or environmental, cultural, or economic disadvantage.

Many students with learning disabilities have average or above-average intelligence, although they often fail to perform academically in line with their potential as well as their peers. The characteristics and behaviors of these students vary; some have difficulties in only one area, while others have difficulties in a variety of areas, such as learning, language, perceptual, motor, social, and behavioral difficulties. Because of the wide range of characteristics associated with learning disabilities, these students present many challenges for educators.

Learning Difficulties

Many students with learning disabilities have memory, attention, and organizational difficulties that hinder their ability to learn and master academic content (Mercer, 1997). Many of these students also experience reading difficulties (Roberts & Mather, 1997). These difficulties appear as the failure to recall letters, their sounds, and words; overreliance on whole-word, phonological, and contextual reading strategies; a slow reading rate; and poor listening and reading comprehension ability.

Although most students with learning disabilities have reading problems, they may be proficient in some content areas and below-average in others. However, large numbers of students with learning disabilities also experience difficulty with mathematics, such as lack of knowledge of basic facts and problems in performing more complex procedures. They also may have trouble writing, with problems in the areas of idea generation and text organization. Students with learning disabilities also tend to use inefficient and ineffective learning strategies.

Language and Communication Difficulties

Language difficulties are a common characteristic of many students with learning disabilities (Schoenbrodt, Kumin, & Sloan, 1997). As a result, some of these students may use immature speech patterns, experience language comprehension difficulties, and have trouble expressing themselves.

Students with disabilities have a variety of needs, and no two students are alike.

Recently, increased attention has focused on the needs of students with nonverbal learning disabilities who have a hard time processing nonverbal communications such as body language, gestures, and the context of linguistic interactions (Matte & Bolaski, 1998). These students employ rote behavior, are repetitive and verbose, and rely on spoken language to communicate, often interpreting language literally. You can aid these students by helping them develop accurate and flexible interpretations of words, verbal analogies, body language, and facial expressions; by fostering their verbal expressive and reasoning skills; and by teaching them to decrease their use of irrelevant verbiage.

Perceptual and Motor Difficulties

Even though it appears that their senses are not impaired, many students with learning disabilities may have difficulty recognizing, discriminating, and interpreting visual and auditory stimuli. For example, some of these students may have trouble discriminating shapes and letters, copying from the blackboard, following multiple-step directions, associating sounds with letters, paying attention to relevant stimuli, and working on a task for a sustained period of time.

Students with learning disabilities also may have gross and fine motor difficulties. Gross motor deficits include awkward gaits, clumsiness, and an inability to catch or kick balls, skip, and follow a rhythmic sequence of movements. Fine motor problems include difficulty cutting, pasting, drawing, and holding a pencil. Another motor problem found in some students with learning disabilities is hyperactivity, which results in constant movement and difficulty staying seated.

Social-Emotional and Behavioral Difficulties

Students with learning disabilities may have social and behavioral difficulties and may show signs of a poor self-concept, task avoidance, social withdrawal, frustration, and anxiety (Gorman, 1999). Research also indicates that because of their poor social perceptions and social skills, these students have problems relating to and being accepted by their peers (Nabuzoka & Smith, 1995; Tur-Kaspa & Bryan, 1994).

SET YOUR SITES

You can obtain resources and information on students with learning disabilities from the Learning Disabilities Association of America (www.ldanatl.org, 888-300-6710).

Students with Emotional and Behavioral Disorders

Several terms are used to refer to students with emotional and behavior disorders. Although an estimated 3 to 5 percent of students have emotional disorders, only 1 percent are identified as such, with boys significantly outnumbering girls. The IDEA defines emotional disturbance as exhibiting one or more of the following characteristics over a long period of time and to a marked degree, which adversely affects educational performance:

1. Inability to learn that cannot be explained by intellectual, sensory, or health factors;
2. Inability to build or maintain good relationships with peers and teachers;
3. Inappropriate behaviors or feelings under normal circumstances;
4. A general, pervasive mood of unhappiness or depression; or
5. A tendency to develop physical symptoms or fears associated with personal or school problems.

The term *emotional and behavior disorders* includes children who have schizophrenia. It does not include children who are socially maladjusted unless they are emotionally disturbed.

Students with emotional and behavior disorders also include those with obsessions and compulsions. While many of us exhibit some type of compulsive behavior, students with obsessive-compulsive disorders feel compelled to think about or perform repeatedly an action that appears to be meaningless and irrational and is against their own will.

Several biological and sociocultural factors interact to affect an individual's behavior. Biological factors are thought to make an individual more vulnerable to emotional and behavioral disorders. Environmental factors such as family considerations, experiential background, economic condition, and school experience also can influence the development of a behavior disorder.

These students are often categorized as mildly or severely disturbed, depending on their behaviors and the nature of their condition. Students who are *mildly emotionally disturbed* may resemble students with learning disabilities and mild retardation in terms of their academic and social needs. Although the intellectual and cognitive abilities of students with mild behavior disorders vary, in the classroom they often have learning and behavior problems that result in poor academic performance and self-control, little on-task behavior, reduced frustration tolerance, poor self-concept, and low social skills (Abrams & Segal, 1998; Rock, Fessler, & Church, 1997). While inappropriate behaviors may mark all students to some degree, those with emotional disturbance may often use inappropriate and noncompliant behavior. They thus run the risk of performing poorly in all academic areas, being rejected by their teachers and classmates, and having high dropout, absenteeism, and suspension rates (Lago-Dellelo, 1998). However, with instructional and classroom management adaptations tailored to their needs, their academic work and behavior can improve significantly.

Depression and Suicide

About 25 percent of all adolescents consider committing suicide, and more suicides are succeeding because of the availability and use of guns (Leary, 1995a). Students with emotional and behavioral disorders may be particularly vulnerable to depression and suicide. Although not all individuals who are depressed attempt suicide, there is a high correlation between depression and suicide. Therefore, you should be aware of the following warning signs:

◆ Overwhelming sadness, apathy, and hopelessness, along with a persistent loss of interest and enjoyment in everyday pleasurable activities
◆ A change in appetite, weight, sleep pattern, or energy level
◆ Pervasive difficulty in concentrating, remembering, or making decisions

◆ Anger, rage, and overreaction to criticism

◆ A sense of inappropriate guilt, worthlessness, or helplessness and a decrease in self-esteem

◆ Recurrent thoughts of death or suicide

◆ Inability to get over the death of a relative or friend and the breakup of friendships

◆ Noticeable neglect of personal hygiene, dress, and health care

◆ An increase in giving valued items to others or engaging in risky behaviors

◆ A dramatic change in school performance characterized by a drop in grades and an increase in inappropriate behaviors

◆ A radical change in personality or increased use of drugs or alcohol

If you suspect that a student is depressed or suicidal, you can work with other professionals and family members to help the student receive the services of mental health professionals. You also should be aware of school policies dealing with depressed and suicidal students, provide adequate supervision, and document and report changes in students' behavior. If you encounter a student who is threatening suicide, you can respond in the following manner:

◆ Introduce yourself to the student (if you are not known) and tell the student that you are there to help.

◆ Stay with the student, remaining calm and speaking in a clear, gentle, and non-threatening manner.

◆ Show concern for the student.

◆ Ask the student to give up any objects or substances that can cause harm.

◆ Encourage the student to talk and acknowledge the student's comments.

◆ Avoid being judgmental and pressuring the student.

◆ Reinforce positive statements and comments on alternatives to suicide.

◆ Remind the student that there are others who care and are available to help (Guetzloe, 1989).

Guetzloe (1989) provides excellent guidelines that can help educators develop programs to counter suicide, including assessing a student's suicide potential, counseling suicidal students, working with families, and dealing with the aftermath of suicide. Wright-Strawderman, Lindsey, Navarrete, and Flippo (1996) offer formal and informal strategies for identifying the needs of students who are depressed, as well as school-based strategies for meeting the needs of these students.

Students with Attention Deficit Disorders

Recently, there has been a growing recognition of the needs of students with attention deficit disorders (ADD) who also have specific learning problems, low self-esteem, and poor socialization with peers (Landau, Milich, & Diener, 1998; Maag & Reid, 1998). The term *attention deficit disorder* defines the most prevalent childhood psychiatric disorder: a "persistent pattern of inattention, impulsivity, and/or hyperactivity-impulsivity that is more frequent and severe than is typically observed in individuals at a comparable level of development" (American Psychiatric Association, 1994, p. 78). These behavioral patterns must have been present before the age of 7 years and must interfere with the individual's social, academic, or occupational functioning in two or more settings (e.g., home, school, or work).

The diagnosis recognizes three subtypes of ADD: students with hyperactivity (ADDH or ADHD), students without hyperactivity (ADD/WO or ADD/noH), and students with a combination of inattention and hyperactivity (ADHD-C) (Nolan, Volpe, Gadow, & Sprafkin, 1999). Students with ADHD have poor attention, impulsive behavior, and overactivity. They

SET YOUR SITES

More information and resources on depression, suicide, and other mental health issues can be obtained from the National Mental Health Association (www.nmha.org, 800-969-6642) or by visiting the website Ask Noah About: Mental Health (www.noah.cuny.edu/illness/mental health/mental.html).

INFORMATIONAL

Stough and Baker (1999) provide information that can help you identify and treat depression in students.

INFORMATIONAL

Anderegg and Vergason (1992) outline the legal decisions that define a teacher's responsibilities when dealing with suicidal students, and Poland (1995) offers policies that schools should establish regarding suicide.

INFORMATIONAL

ADD is often diagnosed in students with learning disabilities, emotional disturbance, and reading problems (Forness, Keogh, Macmillan, Kavale, & Gresham, 1998; Riccio & Jemison, 1998).

INFORMATIONAL

DuPaul and Eckert (1998) review the academic interventions for students with ADD, and Kemp, Fister, and McLaughlin (1995) offer strategies for teaching academic skills to students with ADD, including materials to guide and evaluate teaching.

SET YOUR SITES

You can obtain more information about students with ADD by contacting the National Attention Deficit Disorder Association (ADDA) (www.add.org, 847-432-ADDA) and Children and Adults with Attention-Deficit/Hyperactivity Disorder (CHADD) (www.chadd.org, 800-233-4050).

may have difficulty controlling motor activity, staying in their work areas, refraining from calling out, playing with others, and completing tasks because they shift from one activity to another. Students with ADD/WO, also referred to as *undifferentiated attention deficit disorder (UADD),* have poor attention and impulsivity; they can appear to be distracted, disorganized, lethargic, anxious, withdrawn, and restless (Marshall, Hynd, Handwerk, & Hall, 1997). Students with ADHD-C have many of the characteristics of ADHD and ADD/WO.

Although ADD tends to occur at the same rate in all student groups, regardless of socioeconomic status and ethnicity, boys are four to nine times more likely to be diagnosed than girls, in part because ADD is more likely not to be detected or treated in female students (Katisyannis, Landrum, & Vinton, 1997). However, these behavior patterns also may be found in children suffering from depression, living in chaotic homes, and experiencing health and nutrition problems and auditory processing difficulties. ADD may also affect gifted and talented students who are bored by school. Because of the differing cultural values and expectations of teachers and students, and because of acculturation issues, many students from culturally and linguistically diverse backgrounds are overidentified or underidentified as having ADD (Burcham & DeMers, 1995).

While ADD is a psychiatric diagnosis and is not recognized as a separate disability under the IDEA, school districts must provide special education and related services to students with ADD if these students are otherwise health impaired, learning disabled, or emotionally disturbed. Students with ADD who do not qualify for services under the IDEA can be eligible for these services under Section 504. Whether students with ADD qualify for services under Section 504 or the IDEA, they will probably be educated in the general education classroom, requiring you to use effective educational interventions. Because these students may be taking medication, you must also collaborate with family members, the student's physician, and the school nurse to manage, monitor, and evaluate their response to these medications (Riccio & Jemison, 1998). (Later, we will discuss how you can monitor students who are taking medications.)

Students with Mental Retardation

The significant increase in students with learning disabilities has been paralleled by a decrease in students with mental retardation to approximately 1 percent (U.S. Department of Education, 1997). The IDEA defines students with mental retardation as having "significantly subaverage general intellectual functioning, existing concurrently with deficits in adaptive behavior and manifested during the developmental period, which adversely affects a child's educational performance."

The main cause of mental retardation, particularly mild retardation, is thought to be social-environmental factors. These factors, which can affect a student's intellectual functioning and adaptive behavior, include socioeconomic status, parenting style, health care and nutrition, and educational opportunities.

Under the IDEA's definition of mental retardation, students are classified as having mild, moderate, or severe/profound mental retardation. Students with *mild retardation* have IQs that range from above 50 to below 75 and exhibit many of the behaviors of their counterparts with learning disabilities. However, while students with learning disabilities may have an uneven learning profile, with strengths and weaknesses in different areas, students with mild retardation typically show a steady learning profile in all areas. The frustration of repeated school failure may lead in turn to low self-esteem, an inability to work independently, and an expectancy of failure. Many students with mild retardation may also have poor social and behavioral skills, making it hard to interact with their peers.

IDEAS FOR IMPLEMENTATION

Teaching Students with ADD

Ms. Postell liked Lewis but found him difficult to teach. No matter how hard Lewis tried, he was never able to pay attention and complete his work. He was frequently out of his seat asking her for help, looking out of the window, or bothering another student.

To help Lewis, Ms. Postell varied the types of activities, as well as the locations where students performed them. She followed a teacher-directed activity with a learning game or instructional activity that involved movement. She also adapted assignments by breaking them into smaller chunks, having students work for shorter periods of time, and providing short breaks between activities so that they could move around. When she noticed that Lewis was getting restless, she gave him an excuse to leave his seat for a short time, such as taking a message to the office or sharpening a pencil for her.

Here are some other strategies you can use to create an inclusive and supportive classroom for students with ADD:

❖ Vary the types of learning activities, minimize schedule changes, and limit distractions.

❖ Establish the right learning environment by placing students in work areas with no distracting features and clutter; away from stimulating areas such as doors, bulletin boards, and windows; and near positive role models and the teacher.

❖ Offer a structured program; set reasonable limits and boundaries; establish, post, and review schedules and rules; follow classroom routines; help students make transitions; and inform students in advance of deviations from the classroom routines and schedule.

❖ Give clear, concise, step-by-step written and verbal directions for assignments that include examples. Provide students with daily assignment sheets, and encourage students to show all their work when completing assignments.

❖ Use visuals such as graphic organizers and lists, provide note takers or copies of notes to support oral instruction and directions, and adjust the presentation rate of material according to the students' needs.

❖ Increase the motivational aspects of the curriculum and lessons and the attentional value of the materials as part of the lesson. For example, you can add novelty to lessons and tasks by using color, variation in size, movement, and games. You can also structure learning activities so that students are active and learn by doing.

❖ Break lessons into parts, allow students extra time to work on assignments, and give students one assignment at a time.

❖ Use a multimodality approach to learning that provides opportunities for active responding and prompt, frequent feedback. Employ self-paced instruction such as peer tutoring and computer-assisted instruction.

❖ Give students choices concerning instructional activities. For example, offer students two or three activities and allow them to select one of them.

❖ Offer students outlets for their energy such as hands-on learning activities, instructional games, class jobs, or the opportunity to squeeze a ball. Employ technology (such as computers and calculators) and media (such as audiocassettes and videocassettes) to help students learn and to maintain their interest.

❖ Teach learning strategies, self-management techniques, meditation, and organizational and study skills. Help students to organize their classwork and homework assignments. For example, you can encourage and prompt students to use daily assignment notebooks, different-colored notebooks for each class, and daily and weekly schedules. You can also suggest that they wear a hip or back pack to carry important information and items.

(continued)

- ◆ Monitor students' performance frequently, individualize homework assignments, and offer students alternative ways to show their mastery of content.
- ◆ Pay attention to the students' self-esteem and social-emotional development. Recognize and use students' strengths, special interests, and talents, and involve students in afterschool activities.
- ◆ Teach students with ADD and their classmates about ADD. For example, you can introduce

students to ADD by bringing in books such as *First Star I See* (Caffrey, 1997) and *Zipper: The Kid With ADHD* (Janover, 1997).

Specific guidelines for implementing these recommendations are presented in subsequent chapters.

Sources: Bender and Mathes (1995), DuPaul and Eckert (1998), Loechler (1999), Raza (1997), Welton (1999), and Yehle and Wambold (1998).

SET YOUR SITES

You can obtain resources and information on students with mental retardation by contacting the American Association on Mental Retardation (www.aamr.org, 800-424-3688), and the Association for Retarded Citizens (www.TheArc.org, 800-433-5255).

Students with *moderate retardation* have IQ scores that range from 30 to 50. Educational programs for these students often focus on the development of communication and on vocational, daily living, and functional academic skills. Students with *severe and profound retardation* have IQ scores below 30 and may have behavioral, physical, speech/language, perceptual, and medical needs. Educational programs for these students help them to live independently, contribute to and participate in society, and develop functional living and communication skills. While these students are often educated in self-contained classrooms or specialized schools, successful programs and instructional methods to integrate them into the mainstream of the school exist (Wolery & Schuster, 1997).

Students with Speech and Language Disorders

According to the IDEA, a student with a speech/language impairment has "a communication disorder such as stuttering, impaired articulation, a language impairment, or a voice impairment, that adversely affects a child's educational performance." Although the cause of most communication disorders is difficult to identify, environmental factors such as vocal misuse, inappropriate language models, lack of language stimulation, and emotional trauma may contribute to a speech or language impairment. Also, students from various ethnic backgrounds and geographic regions may have limited experience with English or speak with a different dialect, so you should be careful in identifying these students as speech or language impaired.

Students with language disorders have receptive and expressive language disorders that make it difficult to receive, understand, and express verbal messages in the classroom. *Receptive language* refers to the ability to understand spoken language. Students with receptive language problems may have difficulty following directions and understanding content presented orally.

Expressive language refers to the ability to express one's ideas in words and sentences. Students with expressive language disorders may be reluctant to join in verbal activities. This can impair both their academic performance and their social-emotional development. Expressive language problems may be due to speech disorders that include articulation, voice, and fluency disorders. Articulation problems include omissions (e.g., the student says *ird* instead of *bird*), substitutions (the student says *wove* instead of *love*),

SET YOUR SITES

You can obtain additional information and resources about students with speech and language disorders by contacting the American Speech-Language-Hearing Association (www.asha.org, 800-638-8255).

IDEAS FOR IMPLEMENTATION

Teaching Students with Expressive Language Disorders

Mr. Lombardi's class includes Jessie, a student who stutters. Mr. Lombardi finds it uncomfortable to watch Jessie struggle to express his thoughts, and he avoids asking him to respond. When Jessie does speak, Mr. Lombardi occasionally interrupts him and completes his sentences.

Mr. Lombardi approached Ms. Goldsmith, the speech and language therapist who works with Jessie in his class, for some suggestions. Ms. Goldsmith said, "Why don't you start by asking Jessie to respond to questions that can be answered with relatively few words, such as 'yes' or 'no' questions? Once he adjusts to that, you can ask him to respond to questions that require a more in-depth response. This way, you control the difficulty of the response, and you can help Jessie succeed and develop his confidence. If he struggles with a word or a sentence, be patient, don't speak for him or interrupt him, and encourage him to relax or slow down. In this way, you will serve as a model for the other students, who also will benefit from your teaching them how to respond to Jessie and other students who have difficulty expressing themselves. Let's make some time to talk about how we can teach the other students how to respond to Jessie."

Here are some other strategies you can use to create an inclusive and supportive classroom for students who have difficulty responding orally:

◇ Respond to what the students say rather than how they say it.
◇ Make typical eye contact with students, and pause a few seconds before responding to show them how to relax.
◇ Do not hurry students when they speak, criticize or correct their speech, or force them to speak in front of others.
◇ Collaborate with families and speech/language clinicians to learn about their concerns and expectations and to get their suggestions.
◇ Teach students to monitor and think positively about their speech.
◇ Serve as a good speech model by reducing your speech rate, pausing at appropriate times when speaking, and using simplified language and grammatical structures.

Sources: Conture and Fraser (1990) and LaBlance, Steckol, and Smith (1994).

distortions (the student may distort a sound so that it sounds like another sound), and additions (the student says *ruhace* for *race*).

Voice disorders relate to deviations in the pitch, volume, and quality of sounds produced. Breathiness, hoarseness, and harshness, as well as problems in resonation, are all indications of possible voice quality disorders. Fluency disorders relate to the rate and rhythm of an individual's speech. Stuttering is the most prevalent fluency disorder.

You can help students with speech and language disorders by creating a classroom that fosters language learning (Schoenbrodt et al., 1997). You can create this type of environment by giving students opportunities to hear language and to speak; using concrete materials and hands-on learning activities that promote language; offering students academic and social activities that allow them to work, interact, and communicate with other students; asking students to relate classroom material to their lives; and designing the classroom to promote interactions and language (e.g., posting photographs and other visuals that promote discussion, and placing students' desks in groups rather than in rows).

WHAT ARE THE EDUCATIONAL NEEDS OF STUDENTS WITH LOW-INCIDENCE DISABILITIES?

Students with physical, sensory, and multiple disabilities are sometimes referred to as having *low-incidence disabilities* because they make up only 6 percent of the students with disabilities. While designing and using programs to meet the needs of these students is a challenge, you will find that teaching these students can be a rewarding, enjoyable, and fulfilling experience. When you collaborate with other professionals and family members to deliver appropriate services to these students and help other students understand their needs, they can learn and participate in inclusive classrooms.

Students with Physical and Health Needs

The IDEA recognizes two types of students with physical disabilities: students with orthopedic impairments and with other health impairments. Students with *orthopedic impairments* are defined as having "[a] severe orthopedic impairment which adversely affects a child's educational performance. The term includes impairments caused by congenital conditions (e.g., clubfoot, absence of some member, etc.), impairments caused by disease (e.g., poliomyelitis, bone tuberculosis, etc.), and impairments from other causes (e.g., cerebral palsy, amputations, and fractures or burns which cause contractures)." Students with *other health impairments* are defined as having "limited strength, vitality, or alertness, due to chronic or acute health problems such as attention deficit disorder or attention deficit hyperactivity disorder, a heart condition, tuberculosis, rheumatic fever, nephritis, asthma, sickle cell anemia, hemophilia, epilepsy, lead poisoning, leukemia, or diabetes, which adversely affects a child's educational performance." The term *other health impaired* can also include students who are medically fragile or those who may be dependent on technological devices for ventilation, oxygen, and tube feeding (Heller, Fredrick, Dykes, Best, & Cohen, 1999).

Students with special physical and health needs can learn to perform their routine health-care procedures independently, like this student with diabetes who is giving herself an insulin injection.

Because of the many conditions included in this category, its specific characteristics are hard to define and vary greatly from student to student (Wadsworth & Knight, 1999). Students with physical and health conditions tend to have IQ scores within the normal range, and have numerous educational, social, technological, and health care needs. When developing education programs for these students, you need to be aware of several factors (Heller, Fredrick, Best, Dykes, & Cohen, 2000; Hill, 1999). Because of their conditions, these students may be absent frequently or may have limited exposure to certain experiences that we take for granted. It also is important to remember that these students and their families have social-emotional needs that you should address. Be aware of the importance of your communication and collaboration with the student's family and medical providers, as well as the educational rights of students with special health care needs (Rapport, 1996; Thomas & Hawke, 1999). Finally, professional organizations can provide information and resources, and can offer support groups for students and their families.

The progress of some students, particularly those with sensory and physical disabilities, also depends on the use of adaptive and prosthetic devices. The failure of these devices to work properly can limit the likelihood of success for students who need them; therefore, you will need to monitor their working condition. If there are problems, you should contact students' families or appropriate medical personnel.

Students with Cerebral Palsy

Cerebral palsy, which affects voluntary motor functions, is caused by damage to the central nervous system. It is not hereditary, contagious, progressive, or curable (Hill, 1999). Students with cerebral palsy may have seizures, perceptual difficulties, and motor, sensory, and speech impairments. There are four primary types of cerebral palsy: hypertonia, hypotonia, athetosis, and ataxia.

- *Hypertonia* (also referred to as *spasticity*)—movements that are jerky, exaggerated, and poorly coordinated
- *Hypotonia*—loose, flaccid musculature and sometimes difficulty maintaining balance
- *Athetosis*—uncontrolled and irregular movements
- *Ataxia*—difficulties in balancing and using the hands.

Students with Spina Bifida (Myelomeningocele)

Another group of students with unique physical and medical needs are those with spina bifida (myelomeningocele). Spina bifida is caused by a problem in the vertebrae of the spinal cord that usually results in paralysis of the lower limbs, as well as loss of control over bladder function. Students with spina bifida often have good control over the upper body but may need to use a prosthetic device for mobility such as a walker, braces, or crutches. They also may need a catheter or bag to minimize bladder control difficulty and a shunt for hydrocephalus. In addition to designing and implementing programs that meet their academic and social needs, you can help these students by working with the school nurse to (1) monitor shunts for blockages (some of the signs of blockage are headaches, fatigue, visual or coordination difficulties, repetitive vomiting, and seizures); (2) ensure that the student's bladder, bowel, and catheterization needs are being addressed properly and privately; (3) be aware of the signs of urinary infections (the indicators of bladder infections include a change in urine color or odor, increased frequency of urination with a reduction in urine volume, and fever or chills); (4) prevent sores and

INFORMATIONAL

Wadsworth and Knight (1999) developed the Classroom Ecological Preparation Inventory (CEPI) to help comprehensive planning teams collect information to place students with physical and health needs in general education classrooms.

INFORMATIONAL

Best, Bigge, and Sirvis (1994) offer guidelines for adapting classroom materials and writing utensils to students with physical disabilities.

SET YOUR SITES

You can obtain information and resources about students with cerebral palsy by contacting the United Cerebral Palsy Association (www.ucpa.org, 800-872-5827).

INFORMATIONAL

Rowley-Kelley and Reigel (1993) offer guidelines for preventing skin breakdown in students who use wheelchairs, including making sure that students are positioned properly and moved periodically so that they shift their body weight; giving students opportunities to leave their wheelchairs and use prone standers, braces, and crutches; and examining students' skin for redness and swelling.

IDEAS FOR IMPLEMENTATION

Teaching Students with Cerebral Palsy

As the school year was coming to an end, Mr. Lewis thought about his first interactions with Linda, a student with cerebral palsy. At first he was too protective, and he underestimated her abilities and limited her participation in certain activities. He remembered that the turning point for him was seeing Linda during recess playing with the other students. Although her movements were limited, she was every bit as playful as the other students. From that moment on, he began to treat Linda like other students. He assigned her classroom jobs, reprimanded her when she misbehaved, and encouraged her to participate in all classroom and school activities. Rather than excusing her from assignments, he gave her more time to complete them, reduced the amount of boardwork and textbook copying she had to do, placed rubber bands or plastic tubing around the shaft of her writing utensil, and gave her felt-tipped pens and soft lead pencils so that she could write with less pressure.

Here are some other strategies you can use to create an inclusive and supportive classroom for students with cerebral palsy:

❖ Understand that students may need more time to complete a task, and give them more time to respond verbally.

❖ Do not hesitate to ask students to repeat themselves if others do not understand their comments.

❖ Learn how to position, reposition, and transfer students who use wheelchairs, teach students to reposition themselves, and learn how to push wheelchairs (see Parette and Hourcade [1986], Ricci-Balich and Behm [1996], and Summers et al. [1997]).

❖ Let students use computers, calculators, talking books, and audiocassettes.

❖ Give students two copies of books: one set for use in school and the other set for use at home.

❖ Give students easy access to personal and classroom supplies.

❖ Give students copies of class notes and assignments.

❖ Plan students' schedules so that they move from class to class when the hallways are less crowded.

Source: Knight and Wadsworth (1993).

SET YOUR SITES

You can obtain resources and information about students with spina bifida impairments by contacting the Spina Bifida Association (www.sbaa.org, 800-621-3141).

other forms of skin breakdown; and (5) determine the extent to which students should participate in physical activities (Hill, 1999; Rowley-Kelley & Reigel, 1993).

Students with Asthma

Asthma is an incurable respiratory ailment causing difficulty in breathing due to constriction and inflammation of the airways. It is the most common childhood chronic illness and the leading cause of absence from school (Getch & Neuharth-Pritchett, 1999). The symptoms of asthma vary and include repeated episodes of wheezing, sneezing, and coughing, shortness of breath, and tightness of the chest. The conditions that trigger an asthma attack also vary and include stress, respiratory viruses, exertion and exercise, certain weather conditions, strong emotions, pollens, pet dander, and airborne irritants such as smoke, strong odors, and chemical sprays.

By being aware of the stimuli that trigger students' asthma, you can create learning conditions and activities that minimize the likelihood of an attack. In working with these

Asthma is the most common childhood chronic illness.

students, you may need to observe their reactions, and learn about each student's asthma management plan and your school's policies for dealing with asthma and emergency medical treatments. You also may need to deal with frequent absences; collaborate with families and medical personnel; understand the side effects of medications on behavior and learning; keep the classroom free of dust, plants, perfumes, strong smells, cold or dry air, and other materials that trigger reactions; and understand the students' capacity for physical activities (Getch & Neuharth-Pritchett, 1999; McLoughlin & Nall, 1995). You also can teach *all of your students* about asthma and allergies, using children's books such as *So You Have Asthma Too!* (Sander, 1993), *All About Asthma* (Ostrow & Ostrow, 1989), *Taking Asthma to School* (Gosselin, 1998a), and *ZooAllergy* (Gosselin, 1996a).

Students with Tourette Syndrome

Your classroom also may include students with Tourette syndrome (TS), an inherited neurological disorder whose symptoms appear in childhood. These symptoms include involuntary multiple tics and uncontrolled, repeated verbal responses such as noises (laughing, coughing, throat clearing), words, or phrases. The symptoms appear and disappear at various times and change over time (Bronheim, n.d.). Students with TS also may have learning disabilities, language disorders, obsessive-compulsive behaviors, and difficulty paying attention and controlling impulses, which may result in academic and social difficulties (Packer, 1995).

Students with Diabetes

At some point, you will have a student with diabetes. These students lack enough insulin and therefore have trouble gaining energy from food. Be aware of the symptoms of diabetes, including frequent requests for liquids, repeated trips to the bathroom,

SET YOUR SIGHTS

You can obtain additional information and resources about asthma by contacting the Asthma and Allergy Foundation of America (www.aafa.org, 800-727-8462), the Allergy and Asthma Network–Mothers of Asthmatics (www.aanma.org, 800-878-4403), and the National Asthma Education and Prevention Program Information Center (www.mediconsult.com/asthma, 301-496-5717).

INFORMATIONAL

Getch and Neuharth-Pritchett (1999), Hill (1999), and McLoughlin and Nall (1995) offer guidelines and strategies that can be used when working with students who have asthma and allergies.

SET YOUR SITES

Obtain additional information about Tourette Syndrome and materials to teach your students about TS by contacting the Tourette Syndrome Association (http://tsa.mgh.harvard.edu, 800-237-0717).

IDEAS FOR IMPLEMENTATION

Teaching Students with TS

You could see the signs of anguish on Ms. Dean's face as her principal told her that Frank, a student with Tourette Syndrome (TS), would be joining her class next week. Ms. Dean prided herself on how well behaved her students were, and as she read about Frank's periodic episodes of uncontrolled verbal responses, she was worried about how they would affect her students and her ability to manage their behavior.

Ms. Dean's principal suggested that she talk to Mr. Lopez, a special education teacher who had worked with Frank in the past. Mr. Lopez told her, "Frank is really a neat kid. He works hard, and he's got a wonderful sense of humor. You're going to like him." Ms. Dean said, "I'm sure he's a nice kid. But what do you do when he starts having his episodes?" Mr. Lopez said, "I spoke to Frank and his family about my concerns. They were worried about it as well. We came up with the following system. Before Frank's verbalizations became uncontrollable and distracting, we created a situation that allowed him to leave the room for short periods of time. I would ask him to take a message to the office or return a book to the library. Sometimes, when Frank sensed an episode coming on, he signaled me and he left the room. It worked pretty well. I also helped the other students learn about and understand the needs of students with TS. I showed the class the video *Stop It! I Can't*, which showed several students with TS achieving in school and dealing with ridicule from their peers. The students were very supportive and understanding of Frank."

Here are some other strategies you can use to create an inclusive and supportive classroom for students with TS:

◈ Be patient, and react to students' involuntary inappropriate behavior with tolerance rather than anger.

◈ Provide students with a quiet location to take tests.

◈ Use alternative assignments to minimize the stress on students with TS.

◈ Seek assistance from others such as counselors, school nurses, school psychologists, and families.

---

unhealthy skin color, headaches, vomiting and nausea, failure of cuts and sores to heal, loss of weight despite adequate food intake, poor circulation, as indicated by complaints about cold hands and feet, and abdominal pain. When a student has some of these symptoms, contact the student's family, the school nurse, or another medical professional.

For diabetic students, be aware of the signs of *hyperglycemia* (high blood sugar) and *hypoglycemia* (low blood sugar) and be able to act in an emergency (Rosenthal-Malek & Greenspan, 1999). Students with hyperglycemia are thirsty, tired, and lethargic and have dry, hot skin, loss of appetite, difficulty breathing, and breath that has a sweet, fruity odor. Those with hypoglycemia are confused, drowsy, inattentive, irritable and dizzy, perspiring, shaking, and hungry, with headaches and a pale complexion. When these conditions occur, you must be prepared to act and contact medical personnel immediately. In the case of hyperglycemia, it may be appropriate to have the student drink water or diet soda. For hypoglycemia, it may be appropriate to give the student a source of sugar immediately, such as a half cup of fruit juice, two large sugar cubes, or a can of regular soda. Therefore, you should keep these supplies in your classroom so that they are readily available in case of an emergency.

You can take certain actions to help students with diabetes succeed in school (Rosenthal-Malek & Greenspan, 1999). You can limit hyperglycemia or hypoglycemia by making sure that students eat at the right times. Observe students after physical education class and recess and make sure that their blood sugar levels are measured. You also may need to modify your rules so that students with diabetes can eat snacks and leave the classroom as needed, as well as refrain from penalizing them for frequent absences and lateness. It also may be necessary to reschedule tests or other high-stakes activities for students with diabetes if their performance is affected by their condition. Finally, you can work with the school nurse, family members, certified diabetes educators, and students with diabetes, if they are willing, to educate *all students* about diabetes. For example, you can conduct health science lessons about diabetes and introduce diabetes to students via children's books such as *Taking Diabetes to School* (Gosselin, 1998b) and *Sugar Was My Best Food: Diabetes and Me* (Peacock & Gregory, 1998).

Students with Seizure Disorders

Many students, including those with physical disabilities and other health impairments, may have seizures (Brown, 1997). When these seizures occur on a regular basis, the individual is said to be suffering from a *convulsive disorder* or *epilepsy* (Hill, 1999). There are several types of seizures: tonic-clonic, tonic, absence, and complex and simple partial seizures (Michael, 1995; Spiegel, Cutler, & Yetter, 1996).

Tonic-Clonic Seizure   Also referred to as *grand mal,* this type of seizure is marked by loss of consciousness and bladder control, stiff muscles, saliva drooling out of the mouth, and violent body shaking. After a brief period, the individual may fall asleep or regain consciousness and experience confusion.

Tonic Seizure   A tonic seizure involves sudden stiffening of the muscles. Because the individual becomes rigid and may fall to the ground, these seizures often cause injuries.

Absence Seizure   Also referred to as *petit mal,* this type of seizure is characterized by a brief period in which the individual loses consciousness, appears to be daydreaming, looks pale, and drops any objects he or she is holding.

Complex and Simple Partial Seizures   When a seizure affects only a limited part of the brain, it is called a *partial seizure.* Also referred to as a *psychomotor seizure,* a complex partial seizure is characterized by a short period in which the individual remains conscious but engages in inappropriate and bizarre behaviors. After 2 to 5 minutes, the individual regains control and often does not remember what happened. During a partial seizure, the individual also remains conscious and may twitch and experience a feeling of deja vu. Prior to these seizures, students may experience an *aura* or a *prodrome,* a sensation and a symptom indicating that a seizure is imminent.

Guidelines for dealing with seizures in your classroom are presented in Figure 2.6.

Students Treated for Cancer

A growing number of students treated for cancer are attending school, which can provide a normalizing experience for them and enhance their quality of life. The type and length

SET YOUR SITES

You can obtain more information and resources about diabetes by contacting the American Diabetes Association (www.diabetes.org, 800-232-3472), and the Juvenile Diabetes Foundation International (www.jdfcure.org, 800-223-1138).

INFORMATIONAL

Michael (1995) and Spiegel et al. (1996) offer guidelines for working with students who have seizure disorders.

SET YOUR SITES

Videos, books, films, and pamphlets that provide information about epilepsy and seizures are available from the Epilepsy Foundation of America (www.efa.org, 800-332-1000). This website also offers the EpilepsyRap chatrooms that allow young people with epilepsy to communicate and share information with others.

Students who have seizures need few modifications in the general education setting, but you can minimize the potentially harmful effects of a seizure by carefully structuring the classroom environment and considering the following guidelines before, during, and after a seizure occurs.

BEFORE THE SEIZURE

❖ Be aware of the warning signs that indicate an impending seizure, and encourage the student to speak to you immediately if he or she is able to recognize the aura or prodrome. In these cases, if time allows, remove the student to a private and safe location.

❖ Encourage the student with epilepsy to wear a Medic-Alert bracelet or necklace or carry a wallet card.

❖ Teach students about epilepsy and what to do when a classmate has a seizure. With the student's permission, you, the school nurse, the student, and family members can talk with the class about epilepsy and how to respond to seizures. Children's books such as *Taking Seizure Disorders to School* (Gosselin, 1996b) can be used to introduce students to these issues.

DURING THE SEIZURE

❖ Prevent the student from being injured during a seizure by staying composed and keeping the other students calm (it often helps to remind the class that the seizure is painless).

❖ Do not restrain the student, place fingers or objects in the student's mouth, or give the student anything to eat or drink.

❖ Make the student as comfortable as possible by helping him or her to lie down and loosening tight clothing.

❖ Protect the student by placing a soft, cushioned object under the head, ensuring that the space around the student's work area is large enough to thrash around in, and keeping the area around the student's desk free of objects that could harm the student during the seizure.

AFTER THE SEIZURE

❖ Help the student by positioning the student's head to one side to allow the discharge of saliva that may have built up in the mouth; briefly discussing the seizure with the class, encouraging acceptance rather than fear or pity; providing the student with a rest area in which to sleep; and documenting the seizure.

❖ Contact other necessary school and medical personnel and the student's family.

❖ Document and share with others relevant information regarding a student's seizure. Kuhn, Allen, and Shriver (1995) and Michael (1992) have developed a Seizure Observation Form that can help you record the student's behavior before the seizure, initial seizure behavior, behavior during the seizure, behavior after the seizure, actions taken by you, the student's reaction to the seizure, peer reactions to the seizure, and your comments.

FIGURE 2.6   Guidelines for dealing with seizures.

Source: Hill (1999), Michael (1995), and Spiegel et al. (1996).

SET YOUR SITES

You can obtain additional information and resources on students with cancer by contacting the American Cancer Society (www.cancer.org, 800-227-2345), the Candlelighters Childhood Cancer Foundation (www.candle-lighters.org, 800-366-2223), and the National Children's Cancer Society (www.children-cancer.org, 800–532-6459). Grief Net (www.rivendell.org) offers links to other websites dealing with the grieving process, including resources for grievers and information on support networks.

of cancer therapy vary. However, many treatments are toxic and can affect the student's cognitive, gross and fine motor, language, sensory, and social-emotional development, as well as resulting in life-threatening health problems (Karl, 1992). Frequent or lengthy hospitalizations resulting in erratic school attendance also can hinder learning and socialization. On returning to school, students with cancer may experience many physical and psychological challenges (Hill, 1999).

Students with cancer may also be embarrassed by their appearance and worried about losing their friends and being teased by their peers (Peckham, 1993). You can collaborate with the student, family members, other educators, and medical professionals to address these concerns by using interactive activities that help the student's peers understand the student's illness, including the fact that cancer is not contagious and that radiation treatments don't make the individual "radioactive." Peers also may benefit from understanding the side effects of chemotherapy. In addition, you may need to handle issues related to dying and death (Peckham, 1993). Guidelines to help you deal with these issues with students and families and to understand the grieving process are available (Anderegg, Vergason, & Smith, 1992; Hill, 1999; Kelker, Hecimovic, & LeRoy, 1994; Laufenberg & Perry, 1993; Macciomei, 1996; Peckham, 1993; Thornton & Krajewski, 1993).

Medically Fragile Students

School districts are serving an increasing number of students who are medically fragile (Wadsworth, Knight, & Balser, 1993). The Council for Exceptional Children's Task Force on Medically Fragile Students defines this group of students as those who "require specialized technological health care procedures for life support and/or health support during the school day. These students may or may not require special education" (Sirvis, 1988, p. 40).

Medically fragile students have a variety of chronic and progressive conditions, including cystic fibrosis, congenital malformations, and neurological or muscular diseases such as muscular dystrophy (Prendergast, 1995). While the developmental needs of these students and the extent and nature of their disabilities may vary, these students have comprehensive medical needs and important socialization needs (Strong & Sandoval, 1999). In classroom situations, these students may have limited vitality and mobility, fatigue, and attention problems. Decisions on their educational program and placement should be based on their medical and educational needs and should be made in conjunction with families and support personnel such as physical, occupational, and respiratory therapists, doctors, and nurses who can work with you to develop health care plans for these students and make instructional accommodations to address their needs (Summers et al., 1997). The health plan may need to address such issues as giving students rest periods, help in the lunchroom (e.g., carrying their tray, special dietary considerations), assistive technology, electric devices (e.g., electric pencil sharpener), locker assistance, modified physical activity, early release to help them move from class to class, and schedule adjustments (e.g., shortened day, periods, and bus routes). You can help these students by allowing them to use assistive and instructional technology to obtain, retain, and present information and have an extra set of books for use at home. You can also minimize their fatigue by limiting the number of motor responses you ask them to make. For example, you can limit boardwork and textbook copying by providing them with peer note takers, as well as written copies of directions and other important information.

The social and emotional needs of the student must also be considered. Their problems include embarrassment related to the side effects of treatment on their appearance and behavior, dependence on medical devices, difficulty in accepting their illness, withdrawal and depression, and the need for friendships. Create opportunities for these students to participate in social activities with peers. For example, you can encourage social interactions with others by teaching adults and other students to talk directly to the student rather than to the student's aide or nurse.

When working with these students, become familiar with their equipment, ventilation management, cardiopulmonary resuscitation, universal precautions, and other necessary procedures. It is necessary to understand the warning signs indicating that equipment needs repair; make sure that replacement equipment is readily available; and establish procedures for dealing with health emergencies, equipment problems, and power failures, as well as minimizing interruptions due to medical interventions that the student may need.

Students with Traumatic Brain Injury

Another group of students who have diverse medical needs are those with traumatic brain injury (TBI) (Witte, 1998). Between 1 and 5 million children sustain some type of TBI each year, with the vast majority of these injuries categorized as mild (Doelling, Bryde, & Parette, 1997; Hux & Hacksley, 1996). The IDEA defines TBI as "an acquired injury to the brain caused by an external physical force, resulting in total or partial functional disability or psychosocial impairment, or both, that adversely affects a child's educational performance. The term applies to open or closed head injuries resulting in impairments in one or more areas, such as cognition; language; memory; attention; reasoning; abstract thinking; judgment; problem-solving; sensory, perceptual, and motor abilities; psychosocial behavior; physical functions; information processing; and speech. The term does not apply to brain injuries that are congenital or degenerative, or brain injuries induced by birth trauma."

TBI may be categorized as mild, moderate, or severe, depending on how long one loses consciousness, whether or not there is a skull fracture, and the extent and nature of the aftereffects (D'Amato & Rothlisberg, 1996). The characteristics of students with TBI depend on the nature of the injury and the age at which it occurred. Table 2.1 describes the effects of TBI on students and strategies for helping them in your classroom. For example, because students with TBI may have trouble remembering things, you can show them how to use memory aids such as paging systems, electronic watches and organizers, memory notebooks, checklists, and daily logs (Mateer, Kerns, & Eso, 1996). In addition, you can help students recognize what they can do rather than only what they are no longer able to do. It also is helpful to remain calm and redirect students when their behavior is inappropriate.

It is important to be aware of the differences between students with TBI and those with learning and behavioral problems (Doelling et al., 1997). The performance and behavior of students with TBI tend to be more variable than those of students with learning and behavioral disabilities. Students with TBI also are more likely to tire easily, have headaches, and feel overwhelmed and frustrated. It also is important to keep in mind that students with TBI and their family members, friends, and teachers remember successful experiences before the trauma occurred, which can cause psychosocial problems for everyone involved. In particular, adolescents with a brain injury may have trouble coping with the reality of their new condition (Hill, 1999). Because these students have probably been treated in hospitals, they also may need help in making the transition back to school.

It also is important to (1) establish and maintain communication with families, (2) obtain information about the student's injuries and their consequences from families and medical personnel, and (3) be sensitive to families and understand the pressures associated with having a child with TBI. Conoley and Sheridan (1996) provide strategies for helping families of children with TBI, including education, family support and advocacy, family counseling, and home-school collaboration.

Students with Autism

Autism usually involves a severe disorder in communication and behavior that occurs at birth or within the first 2½ years of life. Students with autism may have trouble dealing with others; engage in repetitive, stereotypic behavior; exhibit various inappropriate behaviors; and have learning and language problems.

INFORMATIONAL

Stuart and Goodsitt (1996), Doelling and Bryde (1995), Phelps (1995), and Clark (1996) offer guidelines for helping students who have been hospitalized make the transition to school.

SET YOUR SITES

You can obtain more information and resources about students with TBI by contacting the Brain Injury Association (www.biausa.org, 800-444-6443).

TABLE 2.1   Characteristics of and Strategies for Accommodating Students with TBI

Effects of TBI:	Provide Student With:	Teach By:
Cognitive and Academic Skill Impacts • Memory • Problem-solving and planning • Attention and concentration • Reading recognition and comprehension • Mathematics calculation and reasoning	• Diagrams, maps, charts, or other graphic cues • Cognitive organizers • Opportunities for problem-solving in functional settings • Preferential seating, proximity to visual or auditory aids and instructional assistance • Personal work space free from distracting stimuli • Individual peer tutor or opportunities to participate in structured collaborative groups	• Using strategies for problem-solving and coping (self-talk, verbal rehearsal, self-questioning, reflection) • Memory aids (visualization, mnemonic devices, paraphrasing, and retelling) • Using survey and preview techniques • Providing practice in guided reading activities • Task analyzing academic requirements • Using a variety of prompts and fading as self-regulation improves
Language Impacts • Expressive • Receptive • Written language	• Support from related services personnel • Assistive technology to communicate and process information and to accommodate motor and sensory deficits • Age-appropriate language models • Opportunities for structured and unstructured communication exchange • Visual aids in conjunction with auditory input • Functional materials and experiential learning opportunities	• Modeling questioning techniques • Providing appropriate wait time to formulate and respond to questions • Teaching note-taking formats and practice during guided lectures • Stressing previewing, active listening, brainstorming, and review from notes and graphic aids • Checking comprehension regularly • Conducting frequent cumulative review • Teaching specific spelling and production strategies • Matching complexity of instructional language to student's PLP (Present Level of Performance) • Modifying writing requirements based on PLP

(continued)

TABLE 2.1 (continued)

Effects of TBI:	Provide Student With:	Teach By:
Social Impacts • Peer/adult interactions • Labile mood • Self-concept • Verbal outbursts or aggressive episodes • Response to stress/demands • Pragmatic language	• Support from related services personnel having expertise in social communication skill development • Support from peer buddy and cooperative learning partners • Strategies and skills for dealing with anger and frustration • Systems for self-monitoring behavior and charting progress • Varied schedules of reinforcement • Structured environment • External cues (charts, contracts, graphs, posted rules, timers, etc.) • Opportunity to remove self and place to go when overwhelmed by stimuli and demands of environment • Opportunities for success with activities appropriate to PLP • System to alert student to problems and cues for redirection to desired target behaviors	• Conducting ecological analysis prior to programming • Identifying TBI-related behaviors and collaboratively developing consistent, positive support plans • Conducting an analysis of the communicative intent of behaviors and teaching skills appropriate to individual needs • Targeting behaviors of greatest concern and implementing behavioral changes gradually • Using direct instruction, modeling, role playing, and scripting to teach specific social and communication skills • Encouraging practice across natural environments • Teaching skills in small group & structured settings • Generalizing skills to larger, less structured contexts
Organizational Skill Impacts • Assignment completion • Arrangement and retrieval of materials • Organization of personal work space • Time management • Orientation and direction	• Group, class, or individual schedule • Daily or weekly calendar and materials checklist corresponding to schedule demands • Individual work area with provision for materials and completed tasks • Notebooks with dividers, colored folders, plastic bins, or portfolio containers • Reduced assignments and/or additional time • Opportunities to practice transition routes (e.g., classroom to cafeteria)	• Using consistent routine, introducing gradual changes in routine • Teaching organizational skills directly related to planning, material organization, and schedule completion • Implementing schedule systems and other organizational cues that transfer across settings and individuals (e.g., resource room to general education settings) • Clearly delineating areas of the classroom by purpose (personal space, leisure areas, centers for instruction) • Collaborating with personnel to consistently provide organizational cues

One form of autism is known as *Asperger's syndrome* (O'Neil, 1999). Students with Asperger's syndrome have good verbal skills and great interest in esoteric subjects, which weakens their social functioning. These students also have difficulties understanding social nonverbal cues and therefore do not make friends of the same age.

Many teaching and classroom management strategies and adaptations can be used to promote the learning and prosocial behaviors of students with autism in general education classrooms (Clark & Smith, 1999). You can post word and symbol cards, posters, and photographs that prompt these students to use prosocial behaviors. You can also use social skill training programs to help them learn to take turns, initiate interactions with others, ask for help from others, and work and play cooperatively with others. In addition, you can work with families to learn more about the student's strengths, skills, and communication patterns and to make sure that students continue to use prosocial behaviors in a variety of situations (Bennett, Rowe, & DeLuca, 1996).

You can also teach your students to support each other and to serve as good role models by teaching them about autism, the importance and value of making friends with all types of students, and other ways to communicate. For example, videos, children's books, and/or guest speakers can be used to teach students about communicating in different ways, responding to attention seeking and unusual behaviors, beginning and maintaining interactions, including others in play and learning activities, and using appropriate behaviors (English, Goldstein, Kaczmarek, & Shafer, 1996).

Students with Severe and Multiple Disabilities

The term *individuals with severe and multiple disabilities* often refers to individuals with profound mental retardation and sensory, communication, medical, motor, and emotional disabilities. Because of the many medical, cognitive, and social needs of students with severe and multiple disabilities, there is no one set of traits that characterizes this group. As a result, they also need many different levels of support to perform life activities (Turnbull et al., 1999). However, students with severe and multiple disabilities may have some of the following: (1) impaired cognitive and intellectual functioning, which causes them to learn at a slower rate, with difficulty maintaining new skills and using them in other situations; (2) delayed use of receptive and expressive language; (3) impaired physical and motor abilities; and (4) few socialization, self-help, and behavioral skills. These students also can be a joy to have in your classroom, as many of them display and model warmth, self-determination, humor, and other positive traits (Heward, 2000).

Inclusive educational programs for students with severe and multiple disabilities have increased their cognitive functioning and social interaction skills (Kennedy et al., 1997; Salisbury, Evans, & Palombaro, 1997). You can help them learn in your inclusive classroom by:

- giving them a developmentally appropriate, community-based curriculum that teaches them the functional skills they need to be more independent and succeed in inclusive settings. For example, you can include functional skills such as coin identification and making purchases in your mathematics curriculum;
- using age-appropriate activities and materials with them;
- giving them opportunities to socialize with others and to work in cooperative learning groups;
- encouraging them to make choices;
- giving them useful technology and assistive devices;

SET YOUR SITES

You can get information about students with autism and students with Asperger's syndrome by contacting The Autism Society of America (www.autism-society.org), Aspen of America (www.asperger.org, 904-745-6741) and Aspen Inc. (www.aspennj.org, 732-906-8043).

INFORMATIONAL

Marks et al. (1999) provides guidelines for educating students with Asperger's syndrome in inclusive classrooms.

INFORMATIONAL

Giangreco, Cloninger, and Iverson (1998) have developed the *Choosing Options and Accommodations for Children (C.O.A.C.H.)*. It offers assessment, a curriculum, and teaching and communication strategies for use with students with severe disabilities in inclusive settings.

SET YOUR SITES

You can obtain resources and information about students with multiple and severe disabilities by contacting the TASH (www.tash.org, 410-828-8274), and for students who are deaf-blind you can visit the website www.eng.dmu.ac.uk/ ~hgs/deafblind.

INFORMATIONAL

Engleman, Griffin, Griffin, and Maddox (1999) and Haring and Romer (1995) provide guidelines for helping students who are deaf-blind in inclusive classrooms.

❖ working collaboratively with families and other professionals;

❖ using physical, pictorial, and oral prompts; and

❖ making sure that you promote the maintenance and generalization of skills taught to students (Heward, 2000).

Medication Monitoring

INFORMATIONAL

An estimated 2 to 3 percent of all students and 15 to 20 percent of students receiving special education are taking medications to treat learning and behavioral disorders (Sweeney, Forness, Kavale, & Levitt, 1997).

INFORMATIONAL

Pancheri and Prater (1999), Sweeney et al. (1997), and Schulz and Edwards (1997) provide overviews and summaries of the potentially positive effects and negative side effects of the most commonly prescribed drugs for students.

Some students, particularly those with medical needs, epilepsy, or ADD, may be taking prescription drugs to improve their school experience and performance. The use of drugs with students is very controversial. Some believe that drugs can improve academic, behavioral, and social performance; others believe that they are ineffective or have only short-term benefits and can have adverse side effects. Some educators suggest that the decision to use drugs should be based on the student's behavior rather than the student's label or diagnosis. Further, they believe, drug use should be considered only after appropriate teaching and classroom management techniques have been used correctly, for a reasonable amount of time, and proved ineffective (Howell, Evans, & Gardiner, 1997).

Ultimately, the decision to use drugs is made by the families and physicians of students. Once that decision is made, it is important for you to (1) know the school district's policies on drug management; (2) learn about the type of medication: dosage, frequency, schedule, and duration; benefits, symptoms, and side effects (e.g., changes in appetite and energy level, aches and pains, irritability, repetitive movements or sounds); (3) use a multimodal approach that includes academic, behavioral/social, and family-based methods; and (4) work collaboratively with families, medical personnel, and other professionals to develop a plan to monitor students' progress and behavior while taking the drug and maintain communication with families and medical professionals (Katisyannis et al., 1997). Because many medications have side effects, you should keep a record of students' behavior in school, including their academic performance, social skills, notable changes in behavior, and possible drug symptoms (Schulz & Edwards, 1997). This record should be shared with families and medical personnel to assist them in evaluating the efficacy of and need for continued use of the medication.

Students with Sensory Disabilities

Students with Hearing Impairments

Students with hearing impairments include students who are deaf and hearing impaired (Easterbrookes, 1999; Schirmer, 1999). According to the IDEA, students are considered *deaf* when they have "a hearing impairment that is so severe that the child is impaired in processing linguistic information through hearing, with or without amplification, which adversely affects educational performance." *Hearing impairment* is defined as "an impairment in hearing, whether permanent or fluctuating, that adversely affects a child's educational performance but that is not included under the definition of deafness."

The degree of hearing loss is assessed by giving the student an audiometric test, which measures the intensity and frequency of sound that the student can hear. The intensity of the sound is defined in terms of decibel (db) levels; the frequency is measured in hertz (Hz). Based on the audiometric evaluation, the hearing loss is classified as ranging from mild to profound.

Some hearing losses may not be detected before the student goes to school. Many students with hearing losses are identified by teachers. Figure 2.7 presents some of the

REFLECTING ON PROFESSIONAL PRACTICES

Students on Medications

Ms. Cheng is proud of her ability to work with challenging students, so it was a blow when Ms. White, a student's mother, called to tell her that the family had decided to place Shaun on medication. Ms. Cheng had tried several teaching and classroom management strategies with Shaun, but they had not been very effective. She knew that the White family was considering the use of drugs. She gave them information about drugs but expressed her concerns about their potential side effects and their effectiveness. However, the Whites decided to try them.

Ms. Cheng realized that regardless of her beliefs, it was now her job to work with the family and the medical staff to manage and evaluate the use of drugs with Shaun. Ms. Cheng researched her district's policies, which included a statement on who can give drugs to students; forms for obtaining the physician's approval, including the name of the drug, dosage, frequency, duration, and possible side effects; a format for maintaining records of drugs given to students; procedures for receiving, labeling, storing, dispensing, and disposing of drugs; and guidelines for students administering drugs to themselves.

Next, Ms. Cheng met with the Whites, their physician, and the school nurse. First, they discussed the potential benefits and adverse side effects of the medication, and the school nurse gave everyone information and a list of references about the medication. They also reviewed procedures on who would administer the drug, when, how, and where. It was agreed that Mr. Schubert, the school nurse, would be the only one to handle and give the drug to Shaun in his office.

Mr. Schubert explained that he stored all medications together in a secured location, clearly labeled each student's medication, and maintained a record of the medications dispensed. He also discussed the importance of maintaining confidentially, and of not attributing the student's good and bad behavior to the drug, such as asking "Have you taken your medication yet?" after a student misbehaves. He also planned to talk with Shaun about the drug's possible side effects, and how Shaun can handle comments from other students about taking it.

Finally, the group developed a plan for monitoring the drug's impact on Shaun. They agreed that Ms. Cheng and the other professionals would use observations, checklists, and interview Shaun to collect data on the drug's effects and side effects on Shaun's academic skills, classroom behavior, and social interactions. The family also agreed to talk with him and keep a diary on Shaun at home and on their feelings about his behavior, friendships, and schoolwork. Ms. Cheng was happy that they also talked about the importance of individualized teaching and classroom management techniques for Shaun, as well as a plan and criteria for phasing out the use of the drug. They ended the meeting by setting up procedures for communicating with each other and setting a date and a time for their next meeting. While still concerned, Ms. Cheng left the meeting feeling somewhat better.

Why was Ms. Cheng concerned about the decision to place Shaun on a drug? As a teacher, how do you feel about this issue? How do you think the White family felt about their decision? How do you feel about the school district's response to their decision? What are the roles of families, teachers, doctors, school nurses, and students in drug use with students? Why did Ms. Cheng feel better at the end of the meeting?

Students with a hearing loss may do some or all of the following:

- ❖ Have trouble following directions and paying attention to messages presented orally
- ❖ Speak poorly and have a limited vocabulary
- ❖ Ask the speaker or peers to repeat statements or instructions
- ❖ Avoid oral activities and withdraw from those that require listening
- ❖ Respond inconsistently and inappropriately to verbal statements from others
- ❖ Mimic the behavior of others
- ❖ Rely heavily on gestures and appear to be confused
- ❖ Turn up the volume when listening to audiovisual aids such as televisions, radios, and cassette recorders
- ❖ Speak with a loud voice
- ❖ Cock the head to one side
- ❖ Complain of earaches, head noise, and stuffiness in the ears

FIGURE 2.7 Warning signs of a possible hearing loss.

Students with hearing loss may have difficulty following directions or remaining engaged in activities requiring listening.

warning signs of a possible hearing loss. If you suspect that a student may have a hearing loss, refer the student to the school nurse or physician for an audiometric evaluation and contact the family.

The intellectual abilities of students with hearing impairments parallel those of students with hearing. However, the student with a hearing impairment experiences communication problems in learning an oral language system. These problems can create difficulties in gaining experience and information that hinder the academic performance and social-emotional development of these students. Depending on their hearing levels, students with hearing impairments may use the following methods to communicate:

◆ oral/aural: use of speaking, speech reading, and residual hearing to communicate with others
◆ manual: use of some form of visual-gestural language to communicate with others
◆ bilingual-bicultural: use of some form of visual-gestural language such as American Sign Language and the written form of English, with no use of spoken English
◆ total communication: use of a combination of approaches, including manual and oral/aural methods (Schirmer, 1999)

An estimated 80 percent of the students with hearing impairments are served in public schools, about a third of them in general education classrooms. As their teacher, you can use experiential and hands-on learning that allows these students to experience a concept; provide a context for understanding language, reading, and writing; use visual aids and cues to support instruction; and act out and role play important principles, concepts, and information (Schirmer, 1999). You also can promote learning by connecting new learning to students' prior knowledge about the topic, using cooperative learning, and adapting the classroom for them. Socially, these students should be encouraged to take part in all school and community activities, and these activities should be adapted to help them participate. Specific teaching, technological, and classroom design factors for educating these students in general education classrooms are discussed in Chapters 7 and 8.

In designing educational programs for students with hearing impairments, you should also be aware of the deaf culture movement. These groups view individuals with hearing impairments as a distinct cultural group whose language, needs, values, behaviors, customs, social interaction patterns, folklore, and arts are quite different from those of hearing individuals who communicate through spoken language (Humphries, 1993). Thus, students with hearing impairments need to be exposed to the deaf culture, and you should view deafness as a cultural issue and explore ways of promoting the bilingual and bicultural abilities of these students.

Students with Visual Impairments

Your classroom also may include students with visual impairments. The IDEA defines a *visual disability* as "an impairment in vision that, even with correction, adversely affects a child's educational performance. The term includes both partial sight and blindness."

Students with visual impairments are classified into three types based on their ability to use their vision: low vision, functionally blind, and totally blind (Lewis, 1999). Students who have *low vision* can see nearby objects but have trouble seeing them at a distance. They usually can read print with some type of optical aid or print enlargement. Students who are *functionally blind* need Braille for effective reading and writing; they can use their vision to move through the classroom and classify objects by color. Students who are totally blind have no vision or limited light perception and do not respond to visual input. Like students who are functionally blind, these students need tactile and auditory teaching activities.

Since visual impairments can hinder a student's cognitive, language, motor, and social development, early detection is important. Figure 2.8 presents some of the warning signs that a student may be experiencing visual problems. If you suspect that a student may have a visual problem, refer the student to the school nurse or physician for an evaluation and contact the family.

Students with visual impairments are a varied group. Most of these students have IQ scores within the normal range. However, their cognitive, language, and social development may be affected because of their limited ability to obtain, experience, and understand visual information, move around their environment, and learn by observing others (Lewis, 1999). For example, these students may have problems learning spatial concepts or vocabulary that describes objects. Their language may rely on verbalisms, or words or phrases that are inconsistent with sensory experiences. Also, because of limited mobility, some students with visual impairments may have delayed motor development.

Eighty-five percent of the students with visual impairments are served in public schools, and about half of them are taught in general education classrooms. As their teacher, you can pair visually presented information with tactile- and auditory-based learning activities. You also will need to adapt your teaching materials by using Braille and audiocassettes, as well as an enlarging machine to prepare large-print materials. You

SET YOUR SITES

You can get resources and information about students with hearing impairments by contacting Info to Go (www.gallaudet.edu/~nicd), the National Association of the Deaf (www.nad.org, 301-587-1788), the National Institute on Deafness and Other Communication Disorders (www.nih.gov/nidcd, 800-241-1044), and the Alexander Graham Bell Association for the Deaf (www.agbell.org, 202-337-5220).

SET YOUR SITES

You can get resources and information about students with visual impairments by contacting the American Foundation for the Blind (www.afb.org, 800-232-3044), the National Federation of the Blind (www.nfb.org, 410-659-9314), the National Association of the Visually Handicapped (www.navh.org, 212-889-3141), and Resources for Parents and Teachers of Blind Kids (www.az.com/~dday/blindkids.html).

Visual problems are indicated when the student does any or all of the following:

- Holds reading material close to the eyes
- Has trouble seeing things from a distance and/or performing close-up tasks
- Reads slowly and has immature handwriting
- Rests the head on the desk when writing or coloring
- Has poorly organized notebooks
- Frequently skips lines, loses place, needs breaks, uses a finger as a guide, and uses head movements when reading
- Blinks, squints, rubs the eyes, or tilts the head frequently
- Covers or closes one eye
- Frequently has swollen eyelids and inflamed or watery eyes
- Complains of seeing double or seeing halos around lights and having headaches
- Exhibits irregular eye movements
- Appears clumsy, trips over and bumps into things, walks hesitantly, and has difficulty negotiating stairs and drop-offs

FIGURE 2.8 Warning signs of a possible visual impairment.
Source: (Hill, 1999).

INFORMATIONAL

"Sources of Braille Reading Materials," a list of organizations that offer Braille reading materials, is available from the National Library Service for the Blind and Physically Handicapped (www.loc.gov/nls/reference/circ-sources.html 202-707-9275).

also can foster learning by letting students work with real objects, linking new material to students' prior knowledge, using cooperative learning, and giving students many activities to practice new skills. Socially, these students should be encouraged to participate in all school and community activities, and these activities should be adapted to help them take part. Specific teaching, technological, and classroom design factors in teaching students with visual impairments in the general education classroom are presented in Chapters 7 and 8.

SUMMARY

This chapter has provided information to help you understand the educational needs of students with disabilities and how you can meet these needs in inclusive classrooms. Other strategies to address these needs are presented in later chapters. As you review the questions asked in this chapter, consider the following questions and remember the following points.

How Does the Special Education Identification Process Work?

The IDEA requires that a planning team composed of professionals and family members, and the student when appropriate, make important decisions about the education of the student with disabilities.

Before considering a referral for special education placement, the planning team uses a *prereferral system.* That is, a team of educators work together to help classroom teachers develop and use methods to keep students in the general education classroom.

If the planning team determines that a student needs special education and related services, an IEP is developed.

What Are the Educational Needs of Students with High-Incidence Disabilities?

Students with high-incidence, or mild, disabilities include those with learning disabilities, mild emotional and behavioral disorders, speech/language impairments, and ADD.

The characteristics and behaviors of these students vary; some have difficulties in only one area, others in several areas. These challenges may occur as learning, language and communication, perceptual, motor, social, and behavioral difficulties.

What Are the Educational Needs of Students with Low-Incidence Disabilities?

Students with physical, sensory, and multiple disabilities are sometimes referred to as having low-incidence disabilities. These students have a range of characteristics. No two students are alike, and each educational program must be based on individual needs rather than disability categories.

What Would You Do in Today's Diverse Classroom?

As a member of your school district's comprehensive planning team, you are asked to address the educational needs of the following students:

◈ Samuel is a sixth grader who is not working up to his potential. He rarely does his work, and when he does, it is either incomplete or incorrect. He shows little self-control, is frequently off-task, gets angry easily, and often seems withdrawn. He annoys other students and has trouble making friends. He frequently calls out, leaves his seat, and refuses to comply with his teacher's requests. He needs more and more of his teacher's time.

◈ Ethel was recently in a serious car accident. Although she was wearing a seat belt, her skull was cracked and there was considerable swelling of her brain. She lapsed into a coma for several days and had surgery to repair the damage to her skull. She has had several seizures since the accident and is currently taking medication to control them. Since she returned to school several months ago, her academic performance has slipped and she seems to be a different person. She has trouble controlling her impulses, organizing her work, socializing with others, and maintaining attention.

◈ Tony is uneasy with visual tasks and usually performs poorly on them. When reading, he holds the book close to his eyes and frequently skips lines, loses his place, needs breaks, and uses his finger as a guide. He often rests his head on the desk when working, and his notebook is poorly organized. He appears clumsy, trips over and bumps into things, and walks hesitantly.

◈ Sadie has severe learning difficulties. She knows her name, basic colors, and some functional words, and she can follow simple commands. Although she can say single words, only a few of her words are understandable. She likes being with others and attempts to participate in all activities.

1. What prereferral strategies might be appropriate for Samuel, Ethel, Tony, and Sadie?

2. Do you think that these students qualify for special education services? If so, under which disability category do they qualify? If not, why not?

3. What goals should their IEPs address, and what services should they receive to meet those goals?

4. How would placement in a general education classroom benefit these students?

5. As their teacher, what concerns would you have about having Samuel, Ethel, Tony, and Sadie in your class?

6. What resources would be helpful to you in meeting their educational needs?

CHAPTER 3

Understanding the Diverse Educational Needs of Learners Who Challenge Schools

Carol

I arrived from Jamaica when I was 7 years old, and my mother enrolled me in first grade. Although the work wasn't that hard, I had a difficult time adjusting. Even though I spoke English, there were many different ways of saying and doing things. One time we had a writing assignment, and I made a mistake and wanted to use an eraser to correct it. Not knowing the word for eraser, I used the Jamaican term and asked the teacher and other students for a "rubber." No one responded to me, so I asked for a rubber again, and again I was ignored. Finally, I took an eraser (rubber) from a student's desk. He got upset and told the teacher, who scolded me. She never told me the correct word. Several months later, I learned the correct word when the teacher asked me to erase the board.

I could tell that the teacher thought I was slow. As a result, she treated me differently, which made me feel different. For example, she always asked me to read more than the other students because she said she liked to hear my accent. This made me withdraw from her and the rest of the class. However, my withdrawal was interpreted as being slow. The teacher would give directions to me by talking very slowly and down to me. Each question was followed by the statement "Do (pause) you (pause) understand?" The teacher also asked peers to show me how to do everything. I was so embarrassed that I stopped talking completely and lost all interest in school.

The teacher must have referred me for special education or something. I remember being tested by several people. I asked my mother to talk to someone at the school, but she couldn't afford to take time off from work. After the testing, they put me in another class. It wasn't a special education class, but I knew it was a slower math and reading class. The work was so easy that I soon became bored. Again, I felt embarrassed and isolated. They also decided that I needed speech therapy to help change my pronunciation. I was proud of my accent and wanted to keep it.

What factors led to some of the difficulties that Carol had in school? Should Carol have been placed in a special education class? How does inclusion affect students like Carol? After reading this chapter, you should be able to answer these as well as the following questions.

◆ How have economic changes affected students and schools?
◆ How have demographic shifts affected students and schools?
◆ What are the needs of students from culturally and linguistically diverse backgrounds?
◆ How can I differentiate cultural and language differences from learning problems?
◆ What are the educational needs of students who are gifted and talented?
◆ What is the impact of discrimination and bias on students and schools?
◆ How have family changes affected students and schools?
◆ What are some alternative philosophies for structuring schools to address societal changes?

The United States continues to undergo major changes that have a tremendous impact on schools and the students they seek to educate. Society has been reshaped as a result of changing economic conditions, demographic shifts, racism and sexism, changes in the structure of families, and increases in substance abuse, and child abuse. As Figure 3.1 suggests, these factors have contributed to a society that jeopardizes the physical and mental health of its children. These factors also make it more likely that students like Carol and the other students you will meet in this chapter, who are not disabled, may experience difficulties in school, be referred for and placed in special education settings, and drop out of school. For students with identified disabilities, these factors often interact with their disability to place students in double jeopardy.

Schools must now respond to these societal changes and meet the needs of increasingly diverse groups of students who challenge the school structure. Inclusive educational practices have focused on the needs of students with disabilities, but it is important to remember that inclusion programs seek to restructure schools so that they address the needs of *all students,* regardless of their race, linguistic ability, economic status, gender, age, learning ability, ethnicity, religion, family structure, and sexual orientation. Like students with disabilities, *all students* benefit from educators who modify their attitudes, teaching techniques, curriculum, and family involvement strategies to reflect and accommodate the needs of students and their families; promote sensitivity to and acceptance of individual differences; and work collaboratively with other professionals, families, students, and community agencies.

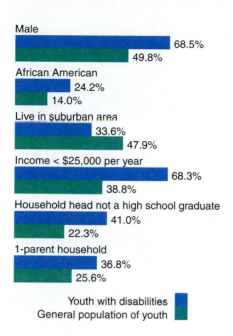

FIGURE 3.1   A demographic comparison of secondary students with disabilities and the general secondary student population.
Source: SRI International (1993).

HOW HAVE ECONOMIC CHANGES AFFECTED STUDENTS AND SCHOOLS?

A Nation of Rich and Poor

In the United States today, there is a growing disparity between wealthy and poor, old and young, and a shrinking middle class (Schwarz, 1995). As a result, the United States is becoming a rich nation with poor children who are worse off than their poor counterparts in other Western industrialized nations (Bradsher, 1995b).

The gap between rich and poor keeps widening, helping to make the United States an economically stratified nation rather than an egalitarian one (Bradsher, 1995a). These economic changes have had a profound effect on children, who represent the fastest-growing poverty group in the United States. Nearly 20 percent of U.S. children live in poverty (Pear, 1998). While the media present childhood poverty as a function of broken families or adults' unwillingness to work, the data show a different picture. For example, about two-thirds of poor children live in families that have at least one working adult.

Brantlinger (1995) interviewed poor and rich students to identify and understand their views on how socioeconomic status affects schooling. She found that the two groups were socially isolated from each other—living in different neighborhoods and attending different elementary schools. The elementary schools of poor children were older buildings with small, poorly equipped playgrounds, higher student-teacher ratios, and less experienced teachers and other professionals. When poor and wealthy students attended the same schools at the secondary level, the social class associated with their elementary school had a strong impact on how they were perceived socially and tracked educationally. Poorer students were more likely to be placed in full-time special education classes or lower tracks within the general education program. They were also more likely to receive more frequent and severe punishment. Wealthy students were educated in the higher-track classes and had little experience with special education. This resegregation often resulted in limited contact between rich and poor students, with both groups holding stereotypic, negative, and unrealistic views of each other.

Poverty

Poverty in the United States continues to grow rapidly, affecting a wide range of children and adults. The majority of poor children in America are white, although African American, Hispanic American, Native American, and Asian American children are more likely to live in poverty than are their white counterparts. When families are both poor and members of nondominant linguistic and ethnic groups, the harmful effects of poverty tend to be greater and long-lasting.

> The child in a poor family who is malnourished and living in an unheated apartment is more susceptible to ear infection; once the ear infection takes hold, inaccessible or inattentive health care may mean it will not be properly treated; hearing loss in the midst of economic stress may go undetected at home, in day care, and by the health system; undetected hearing loss will do long-term damage to a child who needs all the help he can get to cope with a world more complicated than the world of most middle-class children. When this child enters school, his chances of being in an overcrowded classroom with an overwhelmed teacher further compromise his chances of successful learning. Thus risk factors join to shorten the odds of favorable long-term outcomes. (Schorr, 1988, p. 30)

As Schorr indicates, the harmful effects of poverty often interact to affect all aspects of a child's life, including school performance. The mothers of poor children often do not receive early prenatal care. From birth through adolescence, poor children also are more likely to suffer from illnesses and diseases and less likely to receive appropriate medical care. Poor children often have substandard housing; lack health insurance; are victims of hunger, lead poisoning, child abuse, and neglect; usually enter school with fewer skills than their peers; and often attend schools that have limited funds (Slavin, 1998). As a result, they are more likely to fail in school, to be recommended for and placed in remedial and special education programs, and to drop out of school than their middle- and upper-income peers.

The effects of the depth, timing, and duration of poverty on students are also important factors (Brooks-Gunn & Duncan, 1997). Students who live in extreme poverty for a long time are particularly likely to suffer. Students who experience poverty earlier in their lives are more likely to be harmed than students who experience poverty only in their later years.

Urban Poverty

Poverty is prevalent in American cities, where about 30 percent of all students live in poverty (U.S. Department of Education, 1996). Poor urban children often live in crowded, rundown apartments; are more likely to have lead poisoning, which can cause learning and behavioral difficulties, stunted growth, and hearing loss; encounter violence and crime; have limited access to health care; suffer malnutrition; and attend underfunded, dilapidated schools. Poor children in our nation's cities are also less likely to receive immunization against diseases.

SET YOUR SITES

The Children's Defense Fund (www.childrensdefense.org, 202-628-8787), National Center for Children in Poverty (http://cpmcnet.columbia.edu/dept/nccp, 212-304-7100), and Children Now (www.childrennow.org, 510-763-2444, 212-682-1896 in New York City) provide information and resources addressing issues and needs related to poor students.

Homelessness   The growing gap between rich and poor has led to a dramatic increase in homelessness in urban areas, particularly among families with children. The Stewart B. McKinney Homeless Assistance Act is a federal law that guarantees homeless children the right to a free, appropriate public education in a mainstream school environment. But in spite of this law, many homeless students in this country are not attending school. Many of these students cannot attend school because of transportation needs, inappropriate class placement, lack of school supplies and clothes, poor health, hunger, and residency and immunization requirements. In addition, many of them cannot produce birth certificates, school files, and other important records and forms. Homeless students also may have few recreational opportunities, little privacy, and limited access to meals, books, materials, and toys.

Students who are homeless may perform poorly in school; may develop behavioral, socialization, language, motor, health, nutritional, psychological, and self-esteem problems; and are often held over (Rafferty, 1998). Because they may lack washing facilities and adequate clothing, homeless students may have health care needs and may be ridiculed by peers. Zima, Forness, Bussing, and Benjamin (1998) found that about 45 percent of the homeless students living in shelters had a disability and required special education services. However, because of their frequent movement from place to place and their high absenteeism rates, many homeless students who are eligible for supportive services do not receive them.

Several school districts have developed strategies for educating homeless students (Rafferty, 1998; Yamaguchi, Strawser, & Higgins, 1997). These strategies include providing transportation, remediation, and tutoring; school materials and clothes; counseling and other supportive services; and afterschool and full-year programs to meet these students' basic and recreational needs. These school districts also have employed an interagency approach, and have designed and implemented their services in collaboration with shelters and other community agencies.

Rural Poverty

Rural school districts serve more students living in poverty than nonrural school districts and for longer periods of time; many of these students live in "extreme poverty" (U.S. Department of Education, 1995). Rural school districts also serve more students with disabilities in general education classrooms than do nonrural school districts, as well as a growing number of students who are in the process of learning English (U.S. Department of Education, 1995). Educators in rural areas have identified a variety of concerns that affect the teaching of students, including crime, violence, drug abuse, teacher recruitment and retention, limited opportunities for inservice and preservice training, and limited course offerings.

Children of Migrant Workers

My name is Erika Garcia. My parents work very hard in the pickles. Sometimes my sister and I go to help my parents. We have seen my parents work many times, and just by looking, we see it is hard. First, you have to wake up at 5:45 A.M. because everyone goes to the field at 6:00 A.M. Picking pickles is like cracking your back. Some people hang the basket on their waist, and some drag it along.

After work we go home, and my mom and dad take a shower and my mom makes a lot of tortillas. Then we take a nap, and then we go back to the fields at 6:00 P.M. and

SET YOUR SITES

You can obtain more information and resources about working with and addressing the needs of homeless youth by visiting the website of the National Coalition for the Homeless (http://nch.ari.net, 202-737-6444) or by contacting the National Center for Homeless Education (www.serve.org/nche, 800-755-3277).

SET YOUR SITES

The ERIC Clearinghouse on Rural Education and Small Schools provides a directory of agencies and programs serving rural students, as well as a database of educational materials that can be obtained by contacting the Clearinghouse at www.ael.org/eric, 304-347-0419.

REFLECTIVE

Teaching in a rural area presents many unique professional and personal challenges. Could you teach and live in a rural setting? Why or why not?

IDEAS FOR IMPLEMENTATION

Assisting Homeless and Poor Students

Ms. Charles has several students in her classroom from poor households, including one student, Thomas, who is homeless. She started a supply closet to help Thomas, but it has helped other students as well.

Ms. Charles contacted several groups about the supply closet and asked them to donate to it. The local grocery store contributed snacks, the local social service agency gave her clothes, and the Student Association at the local college provided school supplies. Ms. Charles kept these items in a closet, and when students like Thomas don't have something they need, she supplies it quickly and quietly.

"I think it's really working," she notes. "I've noticed that Thomas is coming to school more, feeling better about himself, and interacting with others more, particularly at snack time." Ms. Charles shared these insights with her principal, who said that the school district would pay for Thomas to go on field trips.

Here are some other ideas you can use to create an inclusive and supportive classroom for homeless and poor students:

◈ Help students and their families to complete forms, such as those necessary for the student to receive school breakfast and school lunch.

◈ Collaborate and communicate with personnel from shelters and local agencies.

◈ Provide students with a personal study space in the classroom that is labeled with the student's name, decorated by the student, or personalized by a special symbol selected by the student.

◈ Give students a feeling of accomplishment by breaking assignments into smaller, more manageable segments.

◈ Give students some control over their learning. For example, allow students to choose the order in which they complete assignments.

◈ Understand that students may have particular problems completing homework, and offer help and alternatives such as doing the work in school with a peer or under your supervision.

◈ Encourage students to be involved in extracurricular activities.

Source: Yamaguchi et al. (1997)

---

do more rows of pickles to get a good start in the morning. My parents sent me to summer school but my parents needed some help, and so I only went to school for 3 weeks because I needed to help my parents. Then when the pickles finished, my mom and dad worked in the tomatoes. When the tomatoes are done, my dad works in the sugarbeets. My mom stays home, and my sisters and I go to school. My dad works at 5:00 A.M. and comes home at 1:00 A.M. Sometimes I don't get to see him for up to 4 days. Then when the sugarbeets finish, we go back to Texas and return to Ohio around May 1, and start the season all over again. It's very hard work.

One group of culturally and linguistically diverse students who live in rural areas are the children of migrant workers. Because of the migrant lifestyle, these students experience many difficulties in school. Entering new schools, learning a new language, making new friends, adjusting to new cultural and school expectations, being taught with different instructional techniques and materials, and meeting different graduation requirements are some of these difficulties. As they move from location to location, migrant students face isolation and economic, cultural, and social discrimination. Poor sanitation in

INFORMATIONAL

A national migrant hotline (800-234-8848) is available to help migrant families access education, health, housing, and other supportive services.

Children represent the fastest growing poverty group in the United States.

the fields and work camp facilities; overcrowded, substandard housing and poor diets; exposure to pesticides and other hazards of agricultural work (particularly to pregnant women and young children); limited health care; and low wages make migrant youth particularly vulnerable to poor performance in schools (Strong & Maralani, 1998). Migrant students often work in the fields to help support their families, watch their younger siblings while their parents are working, and serve as the link between their families and societal institutions such as schools (Davis, 1997).

You can help improve the school adjustment and performance of migrant students in a variety of ways. You can welcome and orient them to your class, and assign classroom buddies and mentors to help them. You can also acknowledge their strengths and unique experiences, promote their self-esteem, reach out to their families, and involve them in extracurricular activities. Educationally, you can assess their academic, health, and social adjustment needs, collaborate with migrant and bilingual educators to address these needs, and include their experiences and cultural backgrounds in the curriculum (Kindler, 1995; Menchaca & Ruiz-Escalante, 1995). For example, some teachers incorporate the experiences of migrant workers into their math lessons by using word problems that ask students to calculate the miles traveled by migrant families or to estimate a fair wage based on the number of buckets of produce they have picked (Johanneson, 1999).

Because migrant families travel within and between states, you also need to be aware of the programs available to address the needs of migrant students and promote cooperation among teachers (Perritt, 1997). For example, migrant High School Equivalency Programs (HEP) provide a variety of services to help migrant teenagers graduate from high school. The Portable Assisted Study Sequence (PASS) addresses the high dropout rate among migrant students related to the loss of credits because of frequent travel and high absenteeism; it allows them to complete self-directed courses with teacher monitoring as they travel with their families. You can obtain more information about these and other programs for migrant students by contacting your local migrant education center or your state director of migrant education.

SET YOUR SITES

You can obtain additional information about migrant students and resources to help you meet their needs by contacting the Interstate Migrant Education Council (www.ccsso.org/imec.html 202-408-5505), the National Center for Farmworker Health (www.ncfh.org, 800-377-9968), the Eastern Stream Center on Resources and Training (www.oneonta.edu/~thomasrl, 800-451-8058).

Native Americans   Many of the more than 1.5 million Native Americans reside in remote rural areas. Because of their high unemployment and poverty rates and limited access to health care, Native American youth often experience difficulties in school (Swisher, 1997). You can assist these students by understanding their cultural background and how it affects their learning styles. For example, you can employ flexible timing for completing assignments; offer activities that ask students to work cooperatively; understand that some students may not feel comfortable being "spotlighted" in front of the class; and allow students time to practice a task, skill, or activity.

Suburban Poverty

Even though we often think that the suburbs are affluent, many poor people also live there. Suburban areas are struggling to deal with increased poverty, crime, racial divisions, acquired immunodeficiency syndrome, infant mortality, homelessness, and unemployment (Schemo, 1994a). The suburbs also are segregated, with Hispanics and blacks often forced to live in the least desirable neighborhoods (Schemo, 1994b).

Wealthy Children   Educators also are examining the effects of affluence on children. Baldwin (1989) uses the term *cornucopia kids* to describe wealthy children "who grow up with expectations (based on years of experience in the home) that the good life will always be available for the asking whether they develop personal accountability and achievement motivation or not" (p. 31). Baldwin notes that these children expect the best and the most expensive, demand constant stimulation, have difficulty completing projects, often form superficial relationships, fail to develop a sense of compassion for others, take little responsibility for personal property, mislead others when confronted with a demanding situation, and are present and pleasure oriented. As a result of being insulated from challenge, risk, and consequence, these youth may be underachievers in school, may suffer from boredom, low self-esteem, and a lack of motivation, and may be susceptible to poor school performance, teenage sex, and substance abuse.

HOW HAVE DEMOGRAPHIC SHIFTS AFFECTED STUDENTS AND SCHOOLS?

There have been dramatic changes in the population of the United States, which has become a far more culturally and linguistically diverse country. Since 1980, the U.S. population has grown at the rate of approximately 9 percent per year, with a significant increase in the Asian and Pacific Islander, Hispanic, and Native American populations (Holmes, 1998).

While many of these groups share common traits, variety characterizes the U.S. population. For instance, there are more than 300 independent Native American groups, with different beliefs, customs, traditions, and languages. Similarly, although some Asian and Pacific Islander groups may hold some common beliefs, they come from more than 25 different countries with unique languages, religions, and customs. Hispanic groups speak different dialects of a common language, and each group's identity is based on separate beliefs, traditions, histories, and social institutions.

Population projections suggest that school-age children of color and native speakers of languages other than English now comprise 30 percent of U.S. students, with 37 percent expected in 2010 and 46 percent in 2020. Currently, these students either make up or approach the majority of students in many urban school districts. Schools today are structured to serve students who speak standard English and have cultural perspectives that allow them to feel comfortable in schools and classrooms. As a result, culturally and linguistically diverse students are likely to experience conflicts because schools are not sensitive to their culture, language, family background, and learning styles (Baca & Cervantes, 1998).

Immigration

A significant factor in the U.S. population changes and the makeup of American schools is immigration (Obiakor & Utley, 1997; Sileo & Prater, 1998). Children of immigrants make up approximately 20 percent of the children in the United States (Dugger, 1998). Many immigrants go through a series of stages as they struggle to adjust to their new country (Collier, 1996; Igoa, 1995). Initially, they may be curious as they encounter a new language and culture. Afterward, however, many immigrants may experience shock, depression, and confusion or may show signs of anxiety, withdrawal, fatigue, distractibility, and disorientation. In the final stage, they either assimilate and give up the cultural values of their homeland to become part of the mainstream culture or they become part of the dominant culture while maintaining their own cultural values and traditions.

Students Who Are Immigrants

My mother told me that I was born during the war, which continued for the first ten years of my life. Between ages 2 and 10, I lived on and off with my grandmother so that I could provide her with some companionship. No matter where I lived, the bombing seemed to follow me. Several times a week, the bombing would start, and we would have to leave our homes and hide in the forest.

Finally, when I was 7, the bombing stopped and the war ended. My family was airlifted to an internment camp in a neighboring country, but I was left behind with my grandmother. Three months later, my father returned to get me and smuggled me into the camp. While I was happy to be reunited with my family, I missed my grandmother, who did not come with us.

Although we moved several times from one camp to another, each of the camps was the same. We lived in a small area surrounded by barbed wire, and we had no privacy or toilet facilities. Our camp was frequently raided by the locals, and we were often targets of burglaries, rape, and murders.

I didn't get to go to school because I was a girl. My responsibilities were to help my mother take care of my brothers and sisters. However, I did hear about how life would be wonderful and full of riches for us if we could get to the United States.

After living in the camps for 3 years, we came to the United States. When our plane landed at the airport, I saw a man putting garbage in a clean and shiny plastic bag and thought that the United States really was a wealthy country. However, this view was short-lived, as we were placed in a small apartment in the poorest section of the city.

Soon after settling in, I started school. When I got off the bus with my sister, the teachers were pointing here and there, and I went wherever they pointed. Though I was old enough to be in the fifth grade, I was assigned to a third-grade class. I was scared and very cautious. I looked around to try to understand my environment and mimicked the behaviors of the other students.

I didn't understand or speak much English. When teachers and students spoke to me, I felt overwhelmed, as I didn't understand what they were saying. They would repeat themselves over and over again or talk very slowly, as if that would make me understand them. I still didn't understand and wanted to run away to escape their bombarding me, but there was no forest to run to for safety.

While I struggled academically, I really felt confused by the social interactions and the behaviors of my classmates. At home, I was supposed to be passive and obedient. However, in school, all the other kids were very verbal and physically expressive. One time, we went to a swimming pool and I didn't know that I was supposed to bring a bathing suit. In fact, I didn't know what a bathing suit was. When we arrived at the pool, someone gave me a bathing suit. I put it on over my underwear and was very embarrassed when everyone laughed at me. (Halee Vang)

A growing number of students are immigrants who left their countries to escape political, religious, economic, or racial repression. To reach their new country, many of these students endure a long, difficult, and life-threatening journey characterized by malnutrition, disease, torture, and fear. Once they arrive, they must cope with a type of posttraumatic stress disorder as a result of witnessing atrocities and torture, experiencing losses, and attempting to adjust to a new society. In school, they often encounter racial tension and rejection from peers that takes the form of physical attacks (fights, robberies, and so on), mimicking, and verbal harassment. Immigrant youth also may fear authority figures such as the principal because the child or a family member has an undocumented status. As a result, these youth may be reluctant to make friends with others, to seek help from and interactions with professionals, to attempt to gain recognition or excel in programs, or to draw attention to themselves.

Students who are immigrants face myriad problems as they enter and progress through school (see Figure 3.2). As a result, they are often placed in special education by mistake or not promoted (National Coalition of Advocates for Students, 1993).

Students who are immigrants are likely to encounter several problems, including the following:

◇ Learning a new language that differs from their native language in terms of articulation, syntax, and graphic features
◇ Adjusting to a new culture that values and interprets behavior in different ways
◇ Obtaining access to health care that addresses their needs, such as mental health services to help them deal with their experiences of being tortured or seeing their relatives and friends tortured, raped, and executed
◇ Experiencing guilt as a result of their survival and concern about leaving others behind
◇ Facing economic pressures to work to support their family in the United States and family members in their native country
◇ Coping with sociocultural and peer expectations, such as self-hatred and youth gangs
◇ Dealing with cross-cultural and intergenerational conflicts and posttraumatic stress disorder
◇ Being targets of racism, violence, and harassment
◇ Developing a positive identity and self-concept
◇ Entering school with little, occasional, or no schooling in their native countries
◇ Being unfamiliar with schools in America
◇ Lacking school records and hiding relevant facts in order to avoid embarrassment, seek peer acceptance, and promote self-esteem
◇ Having to serve as cultural and language interpreters for their families

FIGURE 3.2 Problems facing students who are immigrants.
Source: Harris (1991).

You can promote the education of students who are immigrants in a variety of ways (Harris, 1991; Nahme Huang, 1989). You can bring their culture and experiences into your classroom by giving them opportunities to tell their stories through narratives, role playing, and bibliotherapy, using media in their native language, and encouraging them to do projects using materials in their native language. You can also help these students adjust to their new culture and language by offering them language enrichment programs, using nonverbal teaching methods such as music, dance, and art, and teaching them about their new culture. Socially, you can assist these students by using peers and community members as a resource, encouraging these students to participate in culturally sensitive in-school and extracurricular activities, and inviting them to join peer discussion and support groups related to their interests and experiences. It is also important to involve parents, extended family members, and knowledgeable community members in the student's educational program. Finally, you can provide students and their families with materials containing information about the school and about their rights written in their own language.

Educational Rights of Students Who Are Immigrants

It is also important for you to be aware of the educational rights of students who are immigrants. As a result of the Supreme Court decision in *Plyler* v. *Doe* (1982), all undocumented students have the same right as U.S. citizens to attend public schools. School personnel cannot take actions or establish policies that deny students access to public schools, and they have no legal obligation to implement immigration laws. Schools cannot prevent these students from attending school based on their undocumented status, nor can they treat these students in a different way when identifying their residency. School personnel cannot engage in activities that may intimidate or threaten students and their families based on their immigration status, such as allowing Immigration and Naturalization Service (INS) personnel to enter or remain near the school or requiring students or their families to identify their immigration status. They may not inquire about the immigration status of students or their families; ask students to provide Social Security numbers, which may indicate their immigration status; or give the immigration status information contained in a student's school file to outside agencies without the parents' permission (Rosenthal, 1998).

Bilingual Education

Bilingual education employs both the native and the new language and culture of students to teach them. As students acquire English language skills, more and more of the curriculum is taught in English. Many students who are immigrants may be eligible for bilingual education services under PL 90-247, the Bilingual Education Act, enacted in 1968. This act, also referred to as Title VII of the Elementary and Secondary Education Act, established guidelines and funding to encourage school districts to employ bilingual education practices, techniques, and methods to teach students who speak languages other than English.

Research indicates that many second language learners improve their cognitive and sociocultural development, academic progress, and learning of English in bilingual education programs (Genesee & Cloud, 1998). When students are taught in their first language, they develop essential background knowledge. This makes it easier for them to learn a second language and read, write, and perform academically in English. In comprehensive longitudinal studies, Thomas and Collier (1997) and Ramirez (1992) found

REFLECTIVE

Rosibel and her family arrived in the United States several months ago. After Rosibel applied for free lunch, the principal asked you to obtain her Social Security number. As Rosibel's teacher, what would you do? (Developed by Elizabeth Sealey)

SET YOUR SITES

You can obtain additional information about model school programs and organizations, teacher-made materials, relevant research, and resource lists addressing the needs of immigrant students and their families from the National Coalition of Advocates for Students (www.ncas1.org, 617-357-8507).

Research indicates that many second language learners will benefit in terms of academic progress and acquisition of English skills from bilingual education programs.

REFLECTIVE

If you moved to another country that had a different language and culture when you were in fourth grade, what aspects of school would be difficult for you? Would you want to receive your academic instruction in English or the language of your new country?

SET YOUR SITES

Information, resources, and research on programs and issues related to second language learners can be obtained from the National Association for Bilingual Education (www.nabe.org, 202-898-1829), the Center for Applied Linguistics (www.cal.org, 800-276-9834), the National Clearinghouse for Bilingual Education (www.ncbe.gwu.edu, 202-467-0867), the ERIC Clearinghouse on Languages and Linguistics (www.cal.org/ericcll, 202-362-0700), and Multilingual Links (www.multilinguals.com.au/links.html).

that bilingual education does not prevent students from learning English language skills, and it helps students catch up to their English-speaking counterparts in English and other areas of the curriculum. These studies also show that students who received English-only instruction may lag behind their English-speaking peers. Bilingual education also allows second language learners to keep up with their English-speaking peers in learning the content of the general education curriculum (science, social studies, mathematics, etc.). Finally, with bilingual education, these students can continue to communicate with their family and community members in their native language (McLeod, 1994).

Second language learning also has personal, cognitive, and societal benefits (Genesee & Cloud, 1998; Marcos, 1998). Personally, second language learning offers students greater access to other individuals, resources, and employment opportunities, as well as a greater understanding of human experience and cultural diversity. Cognitively, learning a second language helps students improve their problem-solving skills and promotes their creativity. In terms of societal benefits, individuals who speak more than one language can increase the economic competitiveness of the United States.

Two-Way Bilingual Education Programs   One integrated example of a bilingual education program is a *two-way program* that mixes students who speak languages other than English with students who speak English (Thomas & Collier, 1998). These programs seek to help students develop proficiency in both languages, as well as an understanding of different cultures. One language at a time is used to deliver instruction, but content is taught in each language approximately 50 percent of the time.

English as a Second Language   A basic component of bilingual programs is instruction in English as a second language (ESL), sometimes referred to as English to Speakers of Other Languages (ESOL). ESL uses the students' native culture and language to develop their skills in understanding, speaking, reading, and writing English. In ESL programs, content instruction and communication occur only in English. Additional information about ESL techniques is provided in Chapters 4 and 8.

WHAT ARE THE NEEDS OF STUDENTS FROM CULTURALLY AND LINGUISTICALLY DIVERSE BACKGROUNDS?

The IDEA requires assessment materials and procedures to be selected and used so that they do not discriminate racially and culturally and so that a student is not found to have a disability due to language difficulties. However, research indicates that standardized tests *are* culturally and socially biased. As a result, a disproportionate number of students from culturally and linguistically diverse backgrounds are misclassified as having disabilities. Because of this problem in the past, some school districts are now underidentifying these students in terms of their needs for special education (Gersten & Woodward, 1994). Therefore, when designing programs targeting the academic and behavioral needs of students, educators need to be aware of the cultural, linguistic, and economic factors that affect both themselves and their students.

INFORMATIONAL

Garcia and Malkin (1993) offer educators a variety of strategies for enhancing intercultural understanding.

Cultural Considerations

Our schools—and therefore the academic and social expectations for our students—are based on mainstream, middle-class culture. It is important to be aware of this potential cultural mismatch and bias, and adjust your teaching behaviors and curricula to reflect the different cultures, experiences, and languages of your students. You also need to examine how cultural assumptions and values influence your own expectations, beliefs, and behaviors, as well as those of your students, other professionals, families, and community members. In addition, it is important to develop cultural competence and intercultural communication skills.

Learning Style

Cultural differences also affect the way individuals process, organize, and learn material. Hilliard (in Hale-Benson, 1986) believes that in organizing learning, most schools use an analytic approach based on learning through rules, limited movement, convergent thinking, deductive reasoning, and an emphasis on objects. However, Irvine (1991) notes that many students from nondominant cultures use a learning style based on variation, movement, divergent thinking, inductive reasoning, and an emphasis on people. Gilbert and Gay (1989) provide the following example to show how the stage-setting behaviors of some African American students may be misinterpreted by teachers:

> Stage setting behaviors may include such activities as looking over the assignment in its entirety; rearranging posture; elaborately checking pencils, paper, and writing space; asking teachers to repeat directions that have just been given; and checking perceptions of neighboring students. To the black student these are necessary maneuvers in preparing for performance; to the teacher they may appear to be avoidance tactics, inattentiveness, disruptions, or evidence of not being prepared to do the assigned task. (p. 277)

Another factor that affects how classrooms are structured and how students function is the way activities and classroom interactions are ordered (Cloud & Landurand, n.d.).

In polychronic cultures, individuals engage in many different activities at the same time. For example, students from polychronic cultures may talk with others while doing seatwork, whereas those from monochronic cultures may prefer to work without talking.

REFLECTIVE

How has your cultural background affected your learning style? Your teaching and communication style?

Researchers also have found cross-cultural differences in movement (Cloud & Landurand, n.d.). Students who are used to being active may have difficulties in classrooms where movement is limited. These differences also can influence the teacher's perception of a student's academic and behavioral performance. Other cultural factors that may affect classroom behavior are discussed in Chapter 7.

Linguistic Considerations

Students' ability to use language has a great impact on their educational performance. The number of students who are learning English is growing much faster than the overall student population. Because these students often have the usual problems associated with learning a second language, such as poor understanding, limited vocabulary, grammatical and syntactical mistakes, and articulation difficulties, they tend to be over-referred for special education. If they are placed in special education classes, these students often receive little support in their native language, which can hurt their linguistic and academic development. Therefore, to comply with the IDEA, which states that students may not be identified as having a disability based on limited English proficiency, you and other members of the comprehensive planning team must be able to understand the behaviors of second language learners that resemble those of students with learning, speech, and language disabilities so that second language learners are not inappropriately placed in special education. These behaviors are presented in Table 3.1.

TABLE 3.1   Characteristics of Second Language Learners Resembling Those of Students with Learning Disabilities

Characteristics of Students with Learning Disabilities	Characteristics of Second Language Learners
Significant difference between the student's performance on verbal and nonverbal tasks and test items	May have more success in completing nonverbal tasks than verbal tasks
Difficulty mastering academic material	May have difficulty learning academic material that is taken out of context and abstract
Language difficulties	May have language difficulties that are a normal part of second language learning, such as poor comprehension, limited vocabulary, articulation problems, and grammatical and syntactical errors
Perceptual difficulties	May have perceptual difficulties related to learning a new language and adjusting to a new culture
Social, behavior, and emotional difficulties	May experience social, behavioral, and emotional difficulties as part of the frustration of learning a new language and adjusting to a new culture
Attention and memory difficulties	May have attention and memory problems because it is difficult to concentrate for long periods of time when teaching is done in a new language

Source: Fradd and Weismantel (1989) and Mercer (1987).

How Can I Try to Differentiate Cultural and Language Differences from Learning Problems?

Understand Second Language Acquisition

Learning a second language is a complex developmental process (Collier, 1995). Therefore, you and other members of the comprehensive planning team need to understand the stages students go through in learning social and academic language, and how the behaviors associated with this process often parallel many of the learning and behavioral indicators associated with learning difficulties. The stages of second language acquisition are presented in Figure 3.3.

Gaining proficiency in the second language is a long-term process that involves two distinct types of skills (Cummins, 1981, 1984). *Basic interpersonal communication skills (BICS)*, or social language skills, are the language skills necessary to guide students in developing social relationships and engaging in casual face-to-face conversations. BICS are context-embedded and cognitively less demanding, and typically take up to 2 years to develop in a second language. *Cognitive/academic language proficiency (CALP)* refers to the language skills related to literacy, cognitive development, and academic development in the classroom. Because CALP skills are context-reduced and cognitively demanding,

---

In learning a second language, some students may go through the following stages:

◆ *Preproduction or Silent period.* Students focus on processing and understanding what they hear but avoid verbal responses. They often rely on modeling, visual stimuli, context clues, and key words, and use listening strategies to understand meaning. They often communicate by pointing and physical gestures. They may benefit from classroom activities that allow them to respond by imitating, drawing, pointing, and matching.

◆ *Telegraphic or Early Production period.* Students begin to use two- or three-word sentences and show limited comprehension. They usually have a receptive vocabulary of approximately 1,000 words and an expressive vocabulary of approximately 100 words. They may benefit from classroom activities that employ language they can understand; require them to name, label, and group objects; ask them to respond to simple questions and use vocabulary they already understand; and offer praise and encouragement for their attempts to use their new language.

◆ *Interlanguage and Intermediate Fluency period.* Students use longer phrases and start to use complete sentences. They often mix basic phrases and sentences in both languages. They may benefit from classroom activities that encourage them to experiment with language and develop and expand their vocabulary.

◆ *Extensions and Expansions period.* Students expand on their basic sentences and extend their language abilities to synonyms and synonymous expressions. At this stage, they are developing good comprehension skills, using more complex sentence structures, and making fewer errors when speaking. They may benefit from classroom reading and writing activities, as well as from instruction that expands on their vocabulary and knowledge of grammar.

◆ *Enrichment period.* Students are taught learning strategies to assist them in making the transition to the new language.

◆ *Independent Learning period.* Students begin to work on activities at various levels of difficulty with different groups.

FIGURE 3.3   Stages of second language learning.

Source: Maldonado-Colon (1995).

they often take up to 7 years to develop. CALP skills developed in one's first language foster the development of CALP in one's second language.

In learning a new language, second language learners' understanding of the new language is usually greater than their production. Many second language learners also go through a *silent period* in which they process what they hear but avoid verbal responses (Maldonado-Colon, 1990). However, many teachers often misinterpret this silent period as indicating lack of interest or shyness. When students are ready to attempt to speak a new language, their verbalizations are usually single words such as "yes" or "no" or recurring phrases such as "How are you?" and "Thank you." You can help students who are ready to speak by creating a risk-free environment, focusing on communication rather than grammar, providing visual cues and physical gestures that offer students a context for understanding verbal comments, and acknowledging and responding to their attempts to communicate (Fueyo, 1997). Additional suggestions for teaching second language learners are provided in Chapter 8.

Assess the Language Skills of Second Language Learners

You and other members of the comprehensive planning team should assess the academic language skill development of your students who are second language learners (Ortiz, 1997). This evaluation can focus on the students' academic performance and language proficiency in each language spoken by the students, language dominance, language preference, and code switching, as well as the languages and dialects spoken at home and in the students' community. The evaluation also can cover students' learning of surface structures, receptive and expressive language skills, pragmatics, and level of second language learning (Garcia & Malkin, 1993).

Language *proficiency* is the degree of skill exhibited in speaking the language(s), including receptive and expressive language skills. Proficiency in one language does not mean lack of proficiency in another language. Once language proficiency is determined, planning teams can use this information in identifying the student's language *dominance*—that is, the language in which the student is most fluent. Language *preference* refers to the language the individual prefers to use. *Code switching* involves "injecting or substituting phrases, sentences, or expressions from another language" (Harris, 1991, p. 28). Many second language learners make consistent mistakes when they learn English because they often try to apply the rules of their first language to English (Tiedt & Tiedt, 1995). These differences can affect students' pronunciation (e.g., students say *share* for *chair*), syntax (e.g., in Spanish, adjectives follow the noun and agree with the gender and number of the noun), and spelling.

Assessment data can be used to differentiate a language disorder that makes it difficult to learn any language from a bilingual or cross-cultural difference that temporarily affects a student's proficiency in English. This is done by comparing the student's performance in both the primary and secondary languages (Langdon, 1989; Schiff-Myers, Djukic, McGovern-Lawler, & Perez, 1993). In making this distinction, keep in mind that as students begin to learn a new language, they can experience arrested development or language loss in their native language (Schiff-Myers et al., 1993). Damico (1991) developed the following questions that planning teams can use when assessing whether a second language learner or a student from a different culture may have a disability:

It is important for educators to understand the stages students go through in learning a second language and adjusting to a new culture.

1. Are there any factors and conditions that explain the student's learning and/or language difficulties (e.g., lack of opportunity to learn, acculturation, experiences, cultural differences, stressful life events)?
2. Does the student have the same learning and/or language difficulties in community settings and in the primary language? For example, does the student have difficulty communicating in his or her native language when interacting with others from the neighborhood?
3. Is there evidence that the student's learning and/or language difficulties are due to normal second-language acquisition or dialectal factors?
4. Is there evidence that the student's learning and/or language difficulties are related to cross-cultural interference or related cultural factors?
5. Is there evidence that the student's learning and/or language difficulties are related to bias that existed before, during, and after assessment, such as the type and nature of the data collection instruments and tests?
6. How were the student's culture, language, and experiences considered in collecting and analyzing the data?

Data on students' language performance can be collected from standardized tests, language samples, observations, questionnaires, and interviews (Baca & Cervantes, 1998). You can use these methods to address the factors and questions presented in Figure 3.4 to determine if a student's problems are due to language difficulties, a disability, or lack of exposure to effective instruction.

Comprehensive planning teams frequently encounter two types of second language learners who are referred for possible placement in special education (Rice & Ortiz, 1994). One type of second language learner tends to have some proficiency in their native language. However, their skills in and difficulty in learning their new language are

LENGTH OF RESIDENCE IN THE UNITED STATES

❖ How long and for what periods of time has the student lived in the United States?
❖ What were the conditions and events associated with the student's migration?
❖ If the student was born in the United States, what has been the student's exposure to English?

Students may have limited or interrupted exposure to English, resulting in poor vocabulary, slow naming speed, and minimal verbal participation. Being born and raised in the United States does not guarantee that students have developed English skills and have had significant exposure to English and the U.S. culture.

SCHOOL ATTENDANCE PATTERNS

❖ How long has the student been in school?
❖ What is the student's attendance pattern? Have there been any disruptions in school?

Students may fail to learn language skills because they do not attend school.

SCHOOL INSTRUCTIONAL HISTORY

❖ How many years of schooling did the student complete in the native country?
❖ What language(s) were used to guide teaching in the native country?
❖ What types of classrooms has the student attended (bilingual education, English as a second language, general education, speech/language therapy services, special education)?
❖ What has been the language of instruction in these classes?
❖ How proficient is the student in reading, writing, and speaking in the native language?
❖ What strategies and teaching materials have been successful?
❖ What were the outcomes of these educational placements?
❖ What language does the student prefer to use in informal situations with adults? In formal situations with adults?

Students may not have had access to appropriate instruction and curriculums, resulting in problems in language learning, reading, and mathematics.

CULTURAL BACKGROUND

❖ How does the student's cultural background affect second language learning?
❖ Has the student had enough time to adjust to the new culture?
❖ What is the student's acculturation level?
❖ Does the student want to learn English?

Since culture and language are closely linked, lack of progress in learning a second language can be due to cultural and communication differences and/or lack of exposure to the new culture. For example, some cultures rely on body language as a substitute for verbal communication. Various cultures also have different perspectives on color, time, gender, distance, and space that affect language.

PERFORMANCE IN COMPARISON TO PEERS

❖ Does the student's language skill, learning rate, and learning style differ from those of other students from similar experiential, cultural, and language backgrounds?
❖ Does the student interact with peers in the primary language and/or English?
❖ Does the student have difficulty following directions, understanding language, and expressing thoughts in the primary language? In the second language?

The student's performance can be compared to that of students who have similar traits rather than to that of students whose experiences in learning a second language are very different.

FIGURE 3.4 Factors and questions to consider in assessing second language learners.   (continued)

Source: Langdon (1989).

HOME LIFE

◇ What language(s) or dialect(s) are spoken at home by each of the family members?
◇ What language(s) are spoken by the student's siblings?
◇ When did the student start to speak?
◇ Is the student's performance at home different from that of siblings?
◇ What language(s) or dialect(s) are spoken in the family's community?
◇ Is a distinction made among the uses of the primary language or dialect and English? If so, how is that distinction made? (For example, the non-English language is used at home, but children speak English when playing with peers.)
◇ What are the attitudes of the family and the community toward schooling, learning English, and bilingual education?
◇ In what language(s) does the family watch television, listen to the radio, and read newspapers, books, and magazines?
◇ What language does the student prefer to use at home and in the community?
◇ To what extent does the family interact with the dominant culture and in what ways?
◇ How comfortable are the student and the family in interacting with the dominant culture?

Important information on the student's language proficiency, dominance, and preference can be obtained by getting data from family members. The student's language learning can be improved by involving family members in the educational program.

HEALTH AND DEVELOPMENTAL HISTORY

◇ What health, medical, sensory, and developmental factors have affected the student's learning and language development?

A student's difficulty in learning language may be related to various health and developmental problems.

FIGURE 3.4 (continued)

Teachers can tell when a student from a linguistically and culturally diverse background might need special education services for a language-learning disability when some of the following behaviors are manifested in comparison to similar peers:

1. Nonverbal aspects of language are culturally inappropriate.
2. Student does not express basic needs adequately.
3. Student rarely initiates verbal interaction with peers.
4. When peers initiate interaction, student responds sporadically/inappropriately.
5. Student replaces speech with gestures, communicates nonverbally when talking would be appropriate and expected.
6. Peers give indications that they have difficulty understanding the student.
7. Student often gives inappropriate responses.
8. Student has difficulty conveying thoughts in an organized, sequential manner that is understandable to listeners.
9. Student shows poor topic maintenance ("skips around").
10. Student has word-finding difficulties that go beyond normal second language acquisition patterns.
11. Student fails to provide significant information to the listener, leaving the listener confused.
12. Student has difficulty with conversational turn-taking skills (may be too passive or may interrupt inappropriately).
13. Student perseverates (remains too long) on a topic even after the topic has changed.
14. Student fails to ask and answer questions appropriately.
15. Student needs to hear things repeated, even when they are stated simply and comprehensibly.
16. Student often echoes what she or he hears.

If a student manifests a number of the above behaviors, even in comparison to similar peers, then there is a good chance that the student has an underlying language-learning disability and will need a referral to special education.

FIGURE 3.5 Student behaviors to observe when distinguishing a language difference from a language disorder.
Source: C. Roseberry-McKibbin, *Multicultural Education,* Summer 1995, p. 14. Reprinted by permission.

REFLECTING ON PROFESSIONAL PRACTICES

Assessing Second Language Learners

Blanca, a 10-year-old girl, moved to the United States from Chile and was placed in Ms. Ruger's fourth-grade class. She sat quietly in the back of the room and kept to herself. Whenever directions were given, she seemed lost and had difficulty completing tasks and participating in class discussions. During teacher-directed activities, Blanca often looked around at other students or played with materials at her desk.

Ms. Ruger was concerned about Blanca's inability to pay attention and complete her work. She would watch Blanca talk "a lot" (for Blanca) at recess with the other students but be quiet in class during academic instruction. Ms. Ruger felt that as a teacher she was doing something wrong, that she was intimidating Blanca.

She thought Blanca might have a learning problem and referred Blanca to the school's prereferral team. The prereferral team, which included Ms. Nilo, a bilingual special educator, began to gather information about Blanca. Though Blanca's school records were minimal and dated, Ms. Nilo was able to interpret them for the team and Ms. Ruger.

Ms. Nilo assessed Blanca's skills in Spanish. She reported that Blanca grasped concepts quickly when they were explained in Spanish and figured out grammatical patterns in English exercises when directions were explained to her. Blanca told Ms. Nilo that she hadn't read in Spanish for a long time. When she read in Spanish with Ms. Nilo, she was able to decode and comprehend what she read. Blanca could retell stories in her own words, predict sequences in stories, and answer comprehension questions accurately.

Ms. Nilo was also able to obtain information about Blanca's past by speaking to Blanca's mother in Spanish. Ms. Nilo reported that Blanca had not had an easy life. Her mother came to the United States 10 years ago and left Blanca as an infant with her grandmother. Ten years later, Blanca was finally reunited with her mother. Blanca joined her mother and a family of strangers, as Blanca's mother had remarried and had a second daughter, who was now 6 years old.

Other members of the prereferral team collected data on Blanca's English skills. One team member observed Blanca in her classroom, in the cafeteria, and during recess. The team met to share their findings and concluded that Blanca was beginning to learn English. They noted that Blanca was a smart student who was having many of the difficulties second language learners experience in learning a new language and adjusting to a new culture.

The team also discussed and identified ways to assist Ms. Ruger in understanding and meeting Blanca's needs. They helped Ms. Ruger understand that it is not uncommon for students like Blanca to appear to lose their concentration after about 10 minutes of instruction. They explained to Ms. Ruger that instruction delivered in the student's second language requires intense concentration, which is difficult for a second language learner to sustain for long periods of time. They said that Blanca's behavior was not a disability but rather an indication that her "system was shutting down" and that she needed a break. They also talked about learning a second language and how social language develops first, as well as the difficulties in learning the academic language used in the classroom.

Ms. Ruger seemed to understand and to feel better. Knowledge of Blanca's past gave her insights into the emotional side of Blanca. She worked with Ms. Nilo and others on the prereferral team to make instructional, content, and testing adaptations to address Blanca's needs.

Why did Ms. Ruger refer Blanca for assessment? What strategies did the prereferral team use to collect information about Blanca? Why did the team conclude that Blanca did not qualify for special education services? What role did Ms. Nilo play? Why was it important for the prereferral team to include her? If you had a student like Blanca, what services do you think she would need to succeed in your class? What services would you need to help Blanca?

consistent with the typical stages of second language acquisition, and they need help to develop their skills in their new language. Thus, rather than being placed inappropriately in special education classrooms, these students may benefit from a bilingual education and an ESL program.

The other type of second language learner has language, academic, and social behaviors in the first and second languages that are significantly below those of peers who have similar linguistic, cultural, and experiential backgrounds (Ortiz, 1997). In addition, these students may show some of the behaviors listed in Figure 3.5 both in school and at home. Further, assessment may show that they have not made satisfactory progress even with an appropriate curriculum and teaching provided by qualified educators for a long period of time. These students may have a disability and may benefit from a special education program that addresses their unique linguistic, cultural, and experiential learning needs.

WHAT ARE THE EDUCATIONAL NEEDS OF STUDENTS WHO ARE GIFTED AND TALENTED?

Another group of students whose special needs are often overlooked are those who are gifted and talented (Stephens & Karnes, 2000). According to the Gifted and Talented Children's Act of 1988, the federal government defines gifted and talented children as those "who give evidence of high performance capability in areas such as intellectual, creative, artistic, or leadership capacity, or in specific academic fields, and who require special services or activities not ordinarily provided by the school."

Traditional methods used to identify students who are gifted and talented have relied primarily on intelligence testing; however, many educators are now broadening the concept of intelligence. For example, Gardner (1993) uses the framework of *multiple intelligences* to outline at least eight areas in which individuals may exhibit their intelligence and talent (Campbell, 1997). These areas are as follows:

Verbal-linguistic. Sensitivity to the sounds and functions of language and an ability to use language and express oneself verbally or in writing.

Logical-mathematical. Ability to organize and solve numerical patterns, use logic, understand the principles of causal systems, and deal with the abstract.

Visual-spatial. Ability to perceive the visual-spatial world accurately and to create and interpret visual experiences.

Musical. Ability to produce, recognize, remember, and appreciate various forms of musical expression and a sense of rhythm, pitch, and melody.

Bodily-kinesthetic. Ability to control one's physical movements and work skillfully with objects to solve problems, make something, or participate in a production.

Interpersonal. Ability to understand and respond to the feelings, moods, and behaviors of others and to get along and work with others.

Intrapersonal. Ability to understand one's own feelings, reactions, needs, and motivations, as well as one's strengths and weaknesses.

Naturalistic. Ability to understand the environment and other parts of the natural environment.

Educators also are examining the concept of emotional intelligence, which involves understanding one's feelings and the feelings of others (Goleman, 1995).

Although educators tend to focus more often on the academic needs of students who are gifted and talented, these students often have unique social and emotional needs that should be addressed. Some of these students have problems such as uneven development, resentment from peers, perfectionism and self-criticism, pressure to conform, avoiding risks, and difficulty finding peers who have similar interests and abilities (Webb, 1995). Currently, the vast majority of students identified as gifted and talented

INFORMATIONAL

Hertzog (1998a) outlines the roles of gifted education specialists in creating inclusive gifted education programs that address the needs of *all students,* and Sternberg (1996) offers strategies to promote creativity in the classroom.

are educated in general education classrooms. Like *all students,* these students can benefit from the use of the strategies and principles for creating inclusive classrooms presented in this book.

You can adapt your teaching program for gifted and talented students by presenting activities that actively engage students in directing their learning (Belcher & Fletcher-Carter, 1999). To do this, give students opportunities to select what they want to learn, the ways in which they want to learn it, and how they will demonstrate their learning. For example, students can be asked to select their own topics for cooperative learning groups, papers, and presentations. They also can be given choices about whether to present their learning by telling a story, participating in a debate, writing a poem, story, or play, creating a video, song, artwork, or photo album, teaching another student, or reporting on a community-based project. In addition, you can create a learning environment that encourages students to be creative, develop their strengths, take risks, and extend their learning. For example, when learning to solve word problems, you can ask students to create their own word problems. In social studies, students can write journal entries from individuals who have opposite points of view on a specific issue or event.

Students with Special Needs Who Are Gifted and Talented

Although we often think of students with disabilities as having learning difficulties, students with special needs, like Marty, the students we met at the beginning of Chapter 2, may also be identified as being gifted and talented (Reis, Neu, & McGuire, 1997; Robinson, 1999). Unfortunately, like other students who are gifted and talented, students with special needs who are gifted and talented are often overlooked (Willard-Holt, 1998).

The traditional method of defining and identifying students who are gifted and talented underidentifies and underserves gifted and talented students who are from culturally and linguistically diverse backgrounds, poor, disabled, and female (Cohen, 1994; Ford, 1998). To counter this potential basis, you can work with others in your school district to adopt an inclusive and culturally relevant concept of giftedness and use many different forms of assessment. Finally, consider several perspectives when assessing and identifying the unique talents and learning needs of *all students* (Belcher & Fletcher-Carter, 1999; Cunningham, Callahan, Plucker, Roberson, & Rapkin, 1998; Sarouphim, 1999).

SET YOUR SITES

You can obtain information and resources on gifted and talented students from the National Association for Gifted Children (www.nagc.org, (202-785-4268) and the Gifted Development Center (www.gifteddevelopment.com, (303-837-8378).

WHAT IS THE IMPACT OF DISCRIMINATION AND BIAS ON STUDENTS AND SCHOOLS?

Racial Discrimination

Students from specific racial, linguistic, and religious backgrounds face racial discrimination in society and school (Nieto, 1996). While this discrimination is displayed openly in verbal harassment and physical violence in society, it is more subtle in institutions such as schools. Kozol (1991) compared schools that serve students who are poor and predominantly African American and Hispanic with schools that serve students who are wealthy and predominantly white. In addition to almost complete segregation, he found severe inequalities in funding, preschool opportunities, class sizes, physical facilities, resources, remedial services, instructional materials, textbooks, licensed teachers, technology, and expectations of student performance. These inequalities, he concluded, reveal that poor students and students from nondominant groups are seen as inferior, and unworthy of being challenged and of attending well-funded schools. This perceived inferiority is the basis for different treatment and expectations in the classroom based on race and language background (Nieto, 1996).

Through subtle experiences at school, students internalize perceptions of themselves that educators and other members of society hold. Positive perceptions about an individual's race and identity can promote increased self-esteem and success in school, whereas negative attitudes can achieve the opposite results. Unfortunately, school curricula, teacher behaviors, assessment instruments, teaching materials and textbooks, family involvement procedures, and peer relationships usually address only the academic and socialization needs of white middle-class students (Nieto, 1996). As a result, poor students and students from nondominant groups suffer both hidden and overt discrimination in schools. This can cause underachievement and loss of cultural identity, leading eventually to placement in special education classes (Slavin, 1998). Schools and teachers need to challenge racism and offer education programs that promote the identity and academic performance of *all students.*

Multiracial Students

Because of the changing demographics in the United States, teachers will be serving an increasing number of students from multiracial families (Lind, 1998). Multiracial students who grow up appreciating their rich multiracial identity are able to function well in many cultures, and to understand and adjust to a variety of perspectives (Leyva, 1998). However, these students and their families face racial discrimination and many challenges, such as being forced to choose one racial identity over the other, describing themselves to others, and making friends and participating in social groups that are generally based on racial and ethnic similarities (Chiong, 1998). The result can be cultural and racial identification problems, self-concept difficulties, the feeling of being an outsider in two or more cultures, and pressures to cope with conflicting cultural perspectives and demands (Kerwin, Ponterotto, Jackson, & Harris, 1993).

Gender Bias

Teachers also have been exploring differences in the way schools respond to female and male students and the outcomes of this different treatment (Lichtenstein, 1995). Schools tend to treat girls differently from boys and inadvertently reinforce stereotyped views of girls in terms of behavior, personality, aspirations, and achievement, which may stunt their academic and social development (American Association of University Women, 1992; Sadker & Sadker, 1994). Boys and girls generally enter school with equal academic abilities and self-concepts, but girls usually lag behind boys in both areas when they graduate from high school. Although the gap has narrowed in most areas in recent years, girls' access to technology and training in

REFLECTIVE

Because mainstream schools do not educate African American students effectively, several urban school districts have proposed separate schools for African American boys. Do you think this separation by gender and race is appropriate?

INFORMATIONAL

Kerwin and Ponterotto (1994) offer a list of resources for multiracial students and their families and educators, including support groups, correspondence clubs, publications, recommended readings, and books.

computer sciences is still a troubling issue (American Association of University Women, 1998).

In mainly white, middle-class classrooms, many elementary and secondary classrooms have been found to be structured unequally:

◆ Boys talk and are called upon more, are listened to more carefully, and are interrupted less than are girls.
◆ Boys are given more feedback, asked to respond to higher-level questions, and take more intellectual risks than are girls.
◆ Boys are more likely to believe that their poor academic performance is due to lack of effort and can be corrected by greater effort, whereas girls tend to believe that their poor performance is an indication of their inability.
◆ Boys who are enrolled in programs for the gifted and talented in elementary school are more likely to continue in these programs in secondary school than are girls (American Association of University Women, 1992, 1998; Sadker & Sadker, 1994).

These studies were conducted mainly in white, middle-class classrooms. However, gender and race interact, making African American and Hispanic girls even more susceptible to bias in society and in school. In addition, many female students from nondominant cultural backgrounds face conflicts between the cultural values of mainstream U.S. society, which emphasizes independence and ambition, and their own culture, which may promote traditional roles for women. Females from culturally and linguistically diverse backgrounds and poor families also may have to assume responsibilities at home or work to help support their families.

There also appears to be a self-esteem gap in the ways society and schools respond to girls and boys. Girls are taught by society to base their self-esteem on physical appearance and popularity, while boys are encouraged to do so in school and in sports. Girls, particularly in adolescence, may be vulnerable to peer pressure that encourages social success at the expense of high marks. This fear of rejection, and of being smart

Because girls generally don't act out and attract as much attention as boys, their unique and special needs are sometimes overlooked.

but not popular, can cause girls to underachieve, to attempt to hide their success, to not enroll in advanced and challenging courses, and to select careers that are not commensurate with their skills. Frequently, when girls do achieve at high levels or show an interest in a math or science career, they are counseled by advisors who ask them questions that they would not ask boys, such as "How will you handle your family if you're a doctor?" (Smithson, 1990, p. 2). Because girls generally don't act out and attract as much attention as boys, their unique and specialized needs are often overlooked, and therefore programs to address these needs are not funded. Biased tests, curricula, and textbooks also hinder the school performance and reduce the self-esteem of female students. As these students leave school and start to work, they continue to encounter different treatment. As a result, they become overrepresented in low-paying and low-status occupations that offer fewer benefits and training opportunities and less job security (U.S. Department of Education, 1998).

The pressures on girls via advertising, fashion, and entertainment that promote an idealized view of the female body and the need to be the "perfect girl" contribute to eating disorders such as bulimia and anorexia. Bulimia involves binging on food followed by attempts to purge oneself of the excess calories by vomiting, taking laxatives, or exercising. Anorexia, which is less prevalent than bulimia, involves refusal

SET YOUR SITES

You can obtain additional information and resources about these eating disorders from the National Eating Disorders Organization (www.laureate.com/eating/infoschl. asp, 800-322-5173) and the National Association of Anorexia Nervosa and Associated Disorders at (www.anad.org, 847-831-3438).

REFLECTIVE

A disproportionate number of male students are placed in special education classes. Is this an example of discrimination in school?

REFLECTING ON YOUR PRACTICES

Examining Equity in the Classroom

You can evaluate how well your own classroom practices promote equity for *all students* by addressing the following questions:

◈ Do I avoid grouping students based on gender and race, such as by forming separate lines, separate teams, separate seating arrangements, and separate academic learning groups, and comparing students across gender and racial variables?

◈ Do I assign students of both sexes and *all races* to class and school jobs on a rotating basis?

◈ Do I use textbooks and teaching materials that include the contributions of both sexes and *all races?*

◈ Do I use gender/race-inclusive and gender-neutral language?

◈ Do I provide male and female students with same-sex and same-race models and mentors who represent a variety of perspectives and professions?

◈ Do I encourage *all students* to explore various careers, as well as academic, extracurricular, and recreational activities?

◈ Do I decorate the classroom with pictures of males and females from *all races* performing a variety of activities?

◈ Do I use cooperative learning groups and cross-sex and cross-race seating arrangements?

◈ Do I encourage and teach students to examine and discuss books, stories, movies, and other materials in terms of stereotypes and across-race and across-gender perspectives?

◈ Do I identify and eliminate gender and racial bias in the curriculum and standardized tests?

◈ Do I encourage female and male students of *all races* to take risks, make decisions, and seek challenges?

◈ Do I affirm efforts and attributes that contribute to success in *all students?*

How would you rate how well you create a classroom environment that promotes equity for *all of your students?*
( ) Excellent ( ) Good ( ) Needs Improvement
( ) Needs Much Improvement
What are some goals and steps you could adopt to promote equity in your classroom?

to eat, which results in a skeletal thinness and loss of weight that is denied by the individual.

Gay and Lesbian Youth

SET YOUR SITES

You can learn more about the needs of gay and lesbian youth, and the available resources, community agencies, and professionals, by contacting the Gay, Lesbian, and Straight Education Network (www.glsen.org, 212-727-0135), Parents, Families, and Friends of Lesbians and Gays (PFLAG) (www.pflag.org, 202-638-4200), the National Advocacy Coalition of Youth and Sexual Orientation (www.advocatesforyouth.org, 202-783-4165), the National Gay and Lesbian Task Force (www.ngltf.org, 202-467-8180), and Project 10 (www.project10.org, 310-815-1744).

INFORMATIONAL

Lipkin (1992) has developed a high school curriculum offering teachers and counselors guidelines, strategies, and resources for designing and implementing classroom lessons on gay, lesbian, and bisexual issues.

SET YOUR SITES

You can obtain additional information about AIDS from the Centers for Disease Control and Prevention (www.cdc.gov, 404-302-2473).

SET YOUR SITES

The Occupational Safety and Health Administration (www.osha.gov, 202-523-9667) has developed guidelines and universal precautions that you can follow when dealing with blood and body fluids containing visible blood.

Late last semester, I walked into the boys' locker room after gym, and my eyes fell upon a new sign. On the side of a blue locker, somebody had scribbled, "KILL THE FAGGOT" in deodorant. I stopped dead in my tracks, and stared at the sign in anger and disappointment. But what I noticed next was even worse. My friends, my classmates, walked by the sign barely noticing. Nobody noticed, and nobody reacted, because nobody cared. I felt like I would explode, like I would cry, but I didn't say anything. I went on with my day. I went on pretending. . . . I'm sick of it. I'm sick of hearing my friends, my classmates, my teachers say faggot, fairy, and dyke. I'm sick of hearing homophobic jokes in the cafeteria, and being forced to either laugh along, or get looked at funny for speaking up against them. I'm sick of living the fear that if I were discovered, I would be ostracized, tormented, and probably beaten up. I can't stand watching students and teachers snicker, say "Eww," or turn away every time they hear about a gay person.

And it isn't only cafeteria jokes that contribute to the homophobia. It seems that homosexuals have been crossed out of history. (Students for Social Justice, n.d., p. 3)

As this student's comments indicate, gay and lesbian youth and youth who are questioning and exploring their sexual identity face homophobia and discrimination in schools and society that often take the form of ridicule or bias-related physical assaults (Anderson, 1997; Hunt, 1997). Furthermore, when these events occur, very few teachers intervene. As a result, many gay and lesbian youth attempt to hide their sexual orientation, while others are disciplined and referred for placement in special education programs for students with emotional and behavioral disorders (Raymond, 1997).

Because of the pressure to grow up "differently" and because of the homophobia in society, gay and lesbian youth are at greater risk for poor school performance, substance abuse, leaving school, and suicide (Edwards, 1997). They also frequently encounter rejection and abuse from their families, which results in high rates of homelessness. As a result of their isolation and victimization, gay and lesbian youth are particularly susceptible to suicide; the attempted suicide rate of homosexual adolescents is three times higher than that of their heterosexual peers (Bennett, 1997).

Students with HIV/AIDS

Another group of students who have encountered bias are those with acquired immune deficiency syndrome (AIDS), a viral condition that destroys an individual's defenses against infections. Human immunodeficiency virus (HIV), which causes AIDS, is passed from one person to another through the exchange of infected body fluids. Most children with HIV acquire the disease at birth. It is growing most rapidly among heterosexual men and women, infants, teenagers, and young adults in small metropolitan, suburban, and rural areas (Stolberg, 1998; Stuart, Markey, & Sweet, 1995).

IDEAS FOR IMPLEMENTATION

Supporting Gay and Lesbian Students

Mr. Rivers read the flyer inviting him to attend a meeting of the Gay, Lesbian, and Straight Teachers Network. As a junior high school teacher for 5 years, Mr. Rivers had witnessed his share of homophobic comments and actions from students and colleagues, and it bothered him that he had not confronted these biased individuals. At the meeting, the group viewed *It's Elementary: Talking About Gay Issues in School* (415-641-4616), a video that shows elementary and middle school students learning and talking about homophobia. Mr. Rivers thought the video was informative; it gave him some ideas on how to include antihomophobia education in his classroom and school. However, he was still not convinced that it was the school's role to do this. He was concerned that others would view providing support for gay and lesbian youth as promoting sexuality and homosexuality.

At the next meeting, he heard others talk about how they implemented anti–gay bias activities in their schools. One educator noted that "invisibility was a major issue for their school. We all assume everyone is heterosexual, and it's as if these kids don't exist. We decided to make gay and lesbian issues visible and used our language, the school environment, and the curriculum to achieve that goal. We started by using the terms *gay, lesbian,* and *bisexual* in school and in positive ways. We also tried to use gender-neutral language such as *partner* or *significant other* rather than *boyfriend* or *girl friend.* We sought to promote visibility and support by displaying posters and stickers that are sensitive to gay and lesbian issues and by wearing gay-positive symbols. We got other teachers to put a pink or rainbow triangle on their classroom doors to indicate that everyone is safe in their rooms. We also placed books, magazines, and newspapers dealing with issues of sexual orientation on our bookshelves, offices, and common areas. We used the curriculum to make gay and lesbian issues more visible. To counter the bias and exclusion in the curriculum regarding gay

and lesbian issues and individuals, we expanded the curriculum to include these issues and individuals in positive ways. For instance, some teachers mention the sexual orientation of famous gay and lesbian historical figures, authors, musicians, scientists, and poets, which helps establish positive role models for students. We also promoted a discussion of gay and lesbian issues by inviting gay and lesbian guest speakers to talk to classes, assemblies, and faculty and family meetings and by structuring class projects around these issues. It has really helped."

Another group of teachers spoke about their efforts to respond immediately and sincerely to incidents of homophobia, heterosexism, and stereotyping in school. They talked about the need to establish and enforce sexual harassment, antiviolence, and antidiscrimination policies in the schools. They told the audience that "you need to make it clear that language has power, and that abusive language has harmful effects and will not be tolerated. Persons who make derogatory comments, and jokes, and use harassment focusing on an individual's sexuality or other personal characteristics, should be quickly informed that their behavior is inappropriate and will not be tolerated."

Mr. Rivers left the meeting determined to counter homophobic behavior in his school. He spoke to his principal, and to several teachers and students, and shared some materials and resources with them. Together they formed the Gay/Straight School Alliance, an afterschool club that welcomed all members of the school and the local community who were interested in learning more about issues of sexual orientation in a safe environment. The group used various activities that promoted an accepting, safe, nondiscriminatory, and supportive environment in which all students are valued.

Here are some other ideas you can use to create an inclusive and supportive classroom for gay and lesbian youth and youth who are questioning and exploring their sexual identity:

(continued)

◆ Use teaching materials that address issues related to sexual orientation and provide accurate information. For example, you can show videos that allow students to see and hear gay youth talking about their lives, such as *Setting the Record Straight* (212-727-0135), *Homoteens* (415-703-8560), and *Gay Youth* (800-321-4407). You also can make books available to students, such as *Free Your Mind: The Book for Gay, Lesbian, and Bisexual Youth—and their Allies* (Bass & Kaufman, 1996), *The Journey Out: A Guide for and About Lesbian, Gay, and Bisexual Teens* (Pollack & Schwartz, 1995), and *Children of the Horizons: How Gay and Lesbian Teens Are Leading a New Way Out of the Closet* (Herdt & Boxer, 1993). You can work with the school librarian to diversify the school's library and media holdings. For example, Alyson Publications (213-871-1225) and Tapestry Books (800-765-2367) offer an extensive list of books related to gay and lesbian issues for K-12 students and adults. The school library can make these materials available to students, faculty, and family members.

◆ Include a discussion of issues related to gays and lesbians in the school district's plan to address student diversity.

◆ Provide *all students* with confidential access to materials that address their unique needs and concerns.

◆ Help students and their families obtain appropriate services from agencies and professionals who are sensitive and trained to deal with gay, lesbian, and bisexual issues. For example, you can work with others to develop and distribute a list of resources available in the community, regionally, and nationally.

◆ Acknowledge the concerns of gay and lesbian students publicly. For example, you and your students can write an article for the school or community newspaper or the PTA newsletter.

Sources: Edwards (1997), Friends of Project 10 (1993), Guetzloe and Ammer (1995), Raymond (1997), Students for Social Justice (n.d.), and The Governor's Commission on Gay and Lesbian Youth (1993).

While there are no known incidents of the transmission of AIDS in school, teaching students with AIDS continues to be debated. In *School Board of Nassau County, Florida et al.* v. *Arline* (1987), the Supreme Court ruled that individuals with infectious diseases, including AIDS, are covered under Section 504 of the Rehabilitation Act. Similarly, while special education is not required for all students with AIDS, such students who also have special educational needs may be eligible for services under the IDEA. Thus, students with AIDS should have the same rights, privileges, and services as other students and should not be excluded from school unless they represent a direct health danger to others (e.g., engage in biting or scratching others, practice self-abuse, have open sores). Decisions on how to educate students with AIDS should be made by an interdisciplinary team based on the students' educational needs and social behaviors, as well as the judgments of medical personnel. Teachers must also obtain written informed consent before disclosing HIV-related information (Stuart et al., 1995).

IDEAS FOR IMPLEMENTATION

Teaching Students Who Have AIDS

Mr. Ball was recently informed that Mary, one of his students, had AIDS. Not knowing too much about AIDS, Mr. Ball decided that he needed to know more. He used the Internet and found websites that provided information about students with AIDS. Through the Internet, he "spoke" with other teachers who had taught students like Mary. They told him that he needed to follow and maintain the legal guidelines for confidentiality contained in the IDEA and the Family Educational Rights and Privacy Act, which meant that he could not share information about Mary's medical condition with others. They also encouraged him to remember that Mary's social needs might be greater than her academic needs. With that advice, Mr. Ball was determined to encourage and assist Mary in participating in as many classroom and extracurricular activities as possible. Only if necessary would he limit Mary's participation in sports or other activities.

Here are some other ideas you can use to create an inclusive and supportive classroom for students with AIDS:

◆ Collaborate with others to deliver sensitive, nonjudgmental, and compassionate services to students and their families.

◆ Work closely with medical personnel. Because of their condition, students with AIDS may be more susceptible to common childhood infections and serious contagious diseases (e.g., hepatitis or tuberculosis).

◆ Pay attention to quality-of-life issues including relationships with friends and families, enjoying learning, broadening perspectives, and achieving independence and self-determination.

◆ Take universal precautions to protect one's health and safety, as well as the health and safety of the student with AIDS and other students. Methods include using disposable surgical gloves when providing personal or health care to the student, covering wounds, using punctureproof containers, cleaning surfaces with blood spills using a disinfectant, having access to facilities for washing hands, and disposing of all items (i.e., gloves, bandages) that may be exposed.

◆ Educate *all students* and families about AIDS, about the school district's policies and procedures, and about the use of universal precautions that protect *all students*.

Sources: Kelker, Hecimovic, and LeRoy (1994) and LeRoy, Powell, and Kelker (1994).

HOW HAVE FAMILY CHANGES AFFECTED STUDENTS AND SCHOOLS?

Changing Definition of Family

During the last two decades, the structure of the U.S. family has undergone compelling changes. High divorce rates, economic pressures requiring both parents to work, and increases in out-of-wedlock births have brought dramatic changes in the composition, structure, and function of families. As a result, the definition of family in the United States has changed dramatically, and you are likely to have students who live with both parents, one parent, family members, friends, two mothers, two fathers, or foster parents. Regardless of the family's composition, it is important for you to recognize that while these families may have unique needs, they also share the same joys, frustrations, and needs as other families.

Set Your Sites

Resources concerning problems faced by two-parent and single-parent families can be obtained at the websites maintained by The National Parent Information Network (www.npin.org, 800-583-4135) and Parentsplace.com: Single Parenting (www.parentsplace.com/family/singleparent), respectively.

Single-Parent Families

One result of the changes in families is the growing number of children living in single-parent homes. Currently, less than 50 percent of the children in the United States live with both biological parents, and it is estimated that 59 percent of all children will live in a single-parent household before they reach the age of 18. The growing number of children born to unwed mothers also has increased the number of single-parent families; 27 percent of children under the age of 18 live with a single parent who had never married (Holmes, 1994).

Divorce

I was 4 at the time. I was not aware of the divorce exactly, but I was aware that something was out of the ordinary and I didn't like it. Dad was gone. There was a lot of anger, and I had to listen to my mom constantly try to get me to agree with her that he was rotten to leave us. I didn't know what to think. I knew that I wanted him to come back. I'd ask her, "Where is Dad?" and she'd say, "Go ask him!" If I saw him, I'd say, "How come you don't live with us anymore?" and he'd say, "Go ask your mother." I couldn't bring my folks back together no matter how hard I tried. I just didn't know how. I thought if I just wished it, that wishing would be enough. (Michael, age 19)

Divorce has increased the number of children living in single-parent homes, which means that you, as a teacher, are likely to have students like Michael in your class (Frieman, 1997). Approximately 90 percent of these children live with their mothers, who face many burdens as they assume many of the economic and social roles necessary to sustain the family. Divorce also can be hard for nonresidential parents, frequently fathers, who may find that their role in the child's life is decreased.

The effects of divorce tend to vary from child to child; however, the effects on boys seem to be more profound and persistent. Initially, children whose parents have divorced may exhibit anger, anxiety, depression, noncompliance, and poor school performance. While some researchers note that the negative effects of divorce are short-lived, others believe that they are long-lasting (Wallerstein & Blakeslee, 1989). For some children, divorce may have positive effects. Children raised in two-parent families where the parents are in conflict have more difficulty adjusting than children raised in supportive, conflict-free, single-parent homes. The effects of a single divorce or multiple divorces on children depend on several factors, including the amount and nature of the conflict between the parents, the continuity parents provide for their children after the divorce, how much help parents can give their children, and the need to move (Chira, 1995).

As a result of conflicts between divorced parents, you may be put in a difficult situation. Some teachers deal with these conflicts by sending copies of all communications and assignments to both parents, as well as giving both parents the opportunity to attend conferences, either jointly or separately, depending on their preferences (Frieman, 1997). School districts may have different policies regarding communication with family members, and the legal situations between family members may be complex, so consult your principal regarding contacts with both parents. For example, at the beginning of the school year, you can request a list of adults who may interact with your students at school. Since many children live in blended families, in which one of their parents has married someone who also has children, you should also seek clarification regarding the roles of these parents.

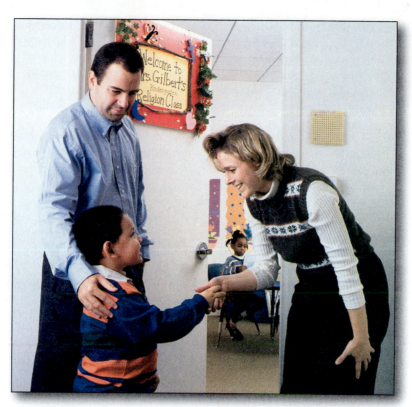

What can teachers do to help students from single-parent households?

Extended Families

There also has been a dramatic increase in the number of children who live in extended families or in households headed by family members other than their parents. Since many children live with their grandparents (Bell & Smith, 1996; D'Errico, 1998), you will probably also have children in your class who live in such a family. In addition to adapting your family involvement strategies to address their needs (see Chapter 4), you can help grandparent-headed households by linking them to groups that offer services to them, such as Grandparents As Second Parents or the American Association of Retired Persons (AARP) Grandparent Information Center.

Families Headed by Gay and Lesbian Parents

An estimated 6 to 14 million children live in families headed by gay and lesbian family members. These families are structured in a variety of ways, including two-adult families, single-parent families, joint parenting arrangements, and extended families. Although some studies suggest that children raised by gay and lesbian parents are well adjusted, these children also may have unique difficulties (Russo, 1997). Because their families may attract prejudice, these children may try to hide their family relationships from others.

SET YOUR SITES

The Family Pride Coalition (www.familypride.org, 619-296-0199) offers advocacy and support for gay and lesbian parents and resources to assist you in interacting with these families.

Adopted Children

Between 1 and 2 percent of the children in the United States have been adopted. Whether children are adopted soon after birth or later, they may face numerous adjustments (Meese, 1999). Early on, they must adjust to their new family and environment and deal with the separation from former caregivers, relatives, and friends. They may feel that they caused others to "give them away because they are bad," which can make them depressed or afraid that they may be abandoned again. As they reach adolescence, adopted children may again experience grief as they seek to develop their identities and try to understand their biological past. Their behavior also may be shaped by the extent to which they were victims of abuse and neglect, and by whether they have lived with many families (Kirby, 1997).

It is important to be sensitive to the unique needs of the child and the child's family (Kirby, 1997; Meese, 1999; Stroud, Stroud, & Staley, 1997). You can help *all children* appreciate the various ways families are formed and model positive attitudes toward adoption. For example, rather than using the terms *real* or *natural parent* and *adoptive parent,* you can use the terms *birth* or *biological parent* and *parent,* respectively. You also can give students alternatives to assignments that assume that students live with their biological parents or family members, and incorporate representations of adoptive families in classroom activities and discussions. For instance, rather than asking students to create a family tree or share baby pictures with the class, you can allow students to chronicle an important time in their lives or share a favorite picture of themselves. When working with students who were adopted after infancy, be aware of anniversaries (e.g., birthdays of relatives and the date they were removed from their birth home) that may cause unexplained or unusual behaviors. In addition, be sensitive to the feelings of adopted parents, understand your role in the telling process, and become aware of adoption services and agencies that can assist you in working with students and their families.

Foster Families

An estimated 500,000 children and youth live with foster families (Noble, 1997). Many of these students blame themselves for their removal from their families and may move from one household to another. Thus they may be secretive about their home life, may be picked on by other students, and may need special services. To help these students, you can establish a good relationship with their foster families, establish reasonable social, behavioral, and academic goals, and implement strategies for enhancing self-esteem. It also is important to work collaboratively with other professionals such as the social worker and guidance counselor and with community agencies.

Child Abuse

A growing number of families, particularly those with children with disabilities, are engaging in child abuse (Waldron, 1996). Because of the rise of child abuse and its harmful effects on children, states have passed laws that require you and other professionals who work with children to identify (see Figure 3.6 for the physical and behavioral indicators of child abuse) and report suspected cases of child abuse. When reporting child abuse, familiarize yourself with your school's policies and document the data that led you to suspect child abuse. It may be helpful to talk with other professionals concerning their views and knowledge of the child and the family, and with your principal to discuss the components of a complete report, how to deal with the family's reactions to the report, and the administrative support you will receive. Since it is an emotionally upsetting experience, you should also seek out educators, family members, and community members who can provide emotional support (Cates, Markell, & Bettenhausen, 1995).

In cases of suspected abuse of children from culturally and linguistically diverse backgrounds, you also need to consider the family's cultural background. In many cul-

SET YOUR SITES

You can obtain additional information and resources on adoptive children and their families from the National Adoption Information Clearinghouse (NAIC) (www.calib.com/naic, 888-251-0075) and Adoptive Families of America (www.adoptivefam.org, 800-372-3300).

INFORMATIONAL

Stroud et al. (1997) offer guidelines for working with adoptive parents and their children, as well as a list of children's books about adoption.

INFORMATIONAL

Bryde (1998) and McCarty and Chalmers (1997) have compiled a list of children's literature on differences in family structures.

INFORMATIONAL

Bryde (1998) has compiled a list of children's books that deal with child abuse.

REFLECTIVE

Kevin, a student in your class, has been misbehaving and failing to complete his homework. Your principal tells you to talk to his family. You are concerned about their reaction, as they frequently use physical punishment to discipline Kevin. What would you do? What professionals might assist you?

IDEAS FOR IMPLEMENTATION

Working with Students Whose Families Are Undergoing Changes

As Ms. Dorney's fourth graders were writing in their journals, Felicia started to cry and Ms. Dorney took her aside and asked, "What's the matter?" Felicia said, "Last night, my parents told me that my father was going to move." Ms. Dorney then asked, "How does it make you feel?" Felicia said, "Sad. I miss my daddy. I want him back." Ms. Dorney said, "I know it's hard for you. Would you like to talk more with me about this?" Felicia said, "No, not now. Can I work on the computer now and do my work later? I just want to be alone." Ms. Dorney agreed and reminded Felicia that she was available to talk with her. As she had done with many of her other students who were having family difficulties, Ms. Dorney also referred Felicia to the school's counseling service, which offered students an opportunity to talk with a counselor and peers about their feelings.

Here are some other ideas you can use to create an inclusive and supportive classroom for students whose families are undergoing changes:

◆ Encourage students to attend and participate in counseling.

◆ Teach students how to express their feelings in appropriate ways.
◆ Communicate with the student's family concerning the child's social and academic adjustment.
◆ Lessen sources of stress in school and make exceptions where possible.
◆ Encourage students to differentiate between events that they can control (e.g., working hard in school, performing a class job) and events that are beyond their control.
◆ Provide alternatives to projects that are based on traditional assumptions of families.
◆ Use books and teaching materials that deal with children in a wider range of family arrangements. For example, the book *Who's in the Family?* (Skutch, 1995) uses a lighthearted approach to introduce students to all types of family arrangements in the human and animal worlds.

Source: Frieman (1997) and Noble (1997).

tures, medical and spiritual cures may require marking the child's body, leaving bruises, and leaving other marks that may be considered abuse. For example, the custom of rubbing hot coins on the forehead to alleviate pain may result in a bruise and may therefore be interpreted by professionals as child abuse. In some cases, confronting family members with information or concerns about their treatment of their child can lead to further difficulties for the child. Therefore, it is important to understand the family's cultural perspective and select the most beneficial outcomes for their students, as well as the most appropriate course of action to comply with laws on child abuse.

Substance Abuse

Although alcohol and drug use among students has declined slightly, many families from all economic backgrounds, ethnic backgrounds, and geographic regions are dealing with the problem of substance abuse (Wren, 1998). While substance abuse rates are roughly equal for boys and girls, it is more widespread among whites than among

SET YOUR SITES

The National Committee to Prevent Child Abuse maintains a website that offers statistics and information on child abuse and resources to support prevention efforts (www.childabuse.org). Reviews of childhood injury prevention interventions can be obtained by visiting the website www.depts.washington.edu/hlprlc.

PHYSICAL ABUSE

Physical Signs

- Bruises, welts, and bite marks
- Lacerations and abrasions
- Burns
- Fractures
- Head injuries
- Parentally induced or fabricated illnesses
- Unexplained injuries

Behavioral Signs

- Avoidance of interactions with parents and other adults
- Anxiety when other children are injured or crying
- Aggressiveness, shyness, and mood changes
- Frequent attempts to run away from home
- Fear of parents or of going home
- Talking about excessive parental punishment
- Blaming self for reactions of parents
- Habit disorders such as self-injurious behavior, phobias, and obsessions
- Wearing inappropriate clothing to conceal injuries
- Low self-image
- Suicide attempts

NEGLECT

Physical Signs

- Physical and emotional needs
- Symptoms of substance withdrawal
- Delayed physical, cognitive, and emotional development
- Attending school hungry or fatigued
- Poor hygiene and inappropriate dress
- Speech/language problems
- Limited supervision
- Medical needs that go unattended for extended periods of time
- Frequent absence from school

Behavioral Signs

- Begging and stealing
- Early arrival to and late departure from school
- Frequent fatigue and falling asleep in class
- Substance abuse
- Thefts and other delinquent acts
- Wearing dirty clothing, wearing clothing that is not appropriate for the weather, wearing the same clothing several days in a row
- Talk about lack of supervision
- Frequent attempts to run away from home
- Stereotypic behaviors such as sucking, biting, and rocking
- Antisocial behavior
- Habit disorders such as phobias, obsession, and hypochondria
- Extreme changes in behavior
- Suicide attempts

FIGURE 3.6 Physical and behavioral signs of child abuse. (continued)

Source: New York State Department of Education, *The Identification and Reporting of Child Abuse and Maltreatment* (n.d.).

SEXUAL ABUSE

Physical Signs

- ◇ Problems in walking or sitting
- ◇ Bloody, stained, or ripped clothing
- ◇ Pain in or scratching of genital area
- ◇ Bruises or bleeding in genital area
- ◇ Evidence of sexually transmitted diseases
- ◇ Pregnancy
- ◇ Painful discharges
- ◇ Frequent urinary infections
- ◇ Foreign materials in body parts

Behavioral Signs

- ◇ Avoiding changing clothes for or engaging in activities during physical education class
- ◇ Engaging in withdrawn, fantasy, or infantile actions
- ◇ Talking about bizarre, sophisticated, or unusual sexual acts
- ◇ Difficulty making friends
- ◇ Delinquent behavior
- ◇ Running away from home
- ◇ Forcing other students to engage in sexual acts
- ◇ Engaging in seductive behaviors with others
- ◇ Fear of being touched by others
- ◇ Absent from school frequently
- ◇ Expressing negative feelings about self
- ◇ Frequent self-injurious acts and suicide attempts

FIGURE 3.6   (continued)

African Americans or Hispanics and more widespread among suburban and rural students than among urban students. Students with disabilities also have significant substance abuse problems.

Because of the harmful effects of substance abuse, you should be aware of some of the signs of possible substance abuse (see Figure 3.7). You also can help prevent problems by learning more about substance abuse, including its effects, prevention strategies, and treatment programs. It also is important to work collaboratively with family and community members, agencies, students, and other professionals to design and implement substance abuse prevention programs (Genaux, Morgan, & Friedman, 1995).

Substance-Abused Newborns

Substance abuse among all socioeconomic groups has increased the number of substance-abused newborns (Sinclair, 1998). Many of these infants are small and underweight, are born prematurely, have birth defects, show neurological damage, exhibit irritability, and have trouble relating to and forming attachments to others. In classrooms, they may have difficulty learning and socializing with others, can be easily frustrated or overwhelmed by the many sights and sounds, and may withdraw or

SET YOUR SITES

You can obtain resources and information on substance abuse, including prevention programs, from the National Clearinghouse for Alcohol and Drug Information (www.health.org/pubs/catalog/health. htm, 800-729-6686), the National Institute on Drug Abuse (www.nida.nih.gov, 888-NIH-NIDA), and the National Council on Alcoholism and Drug Dependence (www.ncadd.org, 800-NCA-CALL). You also can help students whose family members abuse substances by contacting the National Association for Children of Alcoholics (www.health.org/nacoa/interest.htm, 888-554-2627).

Signs of alcohol and other drug (AOD) use vary, but there are some common indicators of AOD problems. Look for changes in performance, appearance, and behavior. These signs may indicate AOD use, but they may also reflect normal teenage growing pains. Therefore, look for a series of changes, not isolated single behaviors. Several changes together indicate a pattern associated with use.

CHANGES IN PERFORMANCE

◇ Distinct downward turn in grades—not just from Cs to Fs, but from As to Bs and Cs
◇ Assignments not completed
◇ A loss of interest in school; in extracurricular activities
◇ Poor classroom behavior such as inattentiveness, sleeping in class, hostility
◇ Missing school for unknown reasons
◇ In trouble with school, at work, or with the police
◇ Increased discipline problems
◇ Memory loss

CHANGES IN BEHAVIOR

◇ Decrease in energy and endurance
◇ Changes in friends (secrecy about new friends, new friends with different lifestyles)
◇ Secrecy about activities (lies or avoids talking about activities)
◇ Borrows lots of money, or has too much cash
◇ Mood swings; excessive anger, irritability
◇ Preferred style of music changes (pop rock to heavy metal)
◇ Starts pulling away from the family, old friends, and school
◇ Chronic lying, stealing, or dishonesty
◇ Hostile or argumentative attitude; extremely negative, unmotivated, defensive
◇ Refusal or hostility when asked to talk about possible alcohol or other drug use

CHANGES IN APPEARANCE AND PHYSICAL CHANGES

◇ Weight loss or gain
◇ Uncoordinated
◇ Poor physical appearance or unusually neat. A striking change in personal habits
◇ New interest in the drug culture (drug-related posters, clothes, magazines)
◇ Smells of alcohol, tobacco, marijuana
◇ Frequent use of eye drops and breath mints
◇ Bloodshot eyes
◇ Persistent cough or cold symptoms (e.g., runny nose)
◇ Always thirsty, increased or decreased appetite, rapid speech
◇ AOD paraphernalia (empty alcohol containers, cigarettes, pipes, rolling papers, plastic bags, paper packets, roach clips, razor blades, straws, glass or plastic vials, pill bottles, tablets and capsules, colored stoppers, syringes, spoons, matches or lighters, needles, medicine droppers, toy balloons, tin foil, cleaning rags, spray cans, glue containers, household products)

FIGURE 3.7 Signs of alcohol and other drug use.

Source: "School-based alcohol and other drug prevention programs: Guidelines for the special educator" by D. L. Elmquist, 1991, *Intervention in School and Clinic, 27,* 10–19. Copyright 1991 by PRO-ED, Inc. Reprinted by permission.

become aggressive and difficult to manage. They also may have communication and motor delays, organizational and processing problems, and difficulties in socializing and playing with others. Early intervention programs that offer medical care, nutritional counseling, instruction in parenting skills and obtaining community services, and a structured and supportive learning environment are needed for these children and their families.

WHAT ARE SOME ALTERNATIVE PHILOSOPHIES FOR STRUCTURING SCHOOLS TO ADDRESS SOCIETAL CHANGES?

Changes in American society have significantly increased the number of students like those discussed in this chapter, whose needs challenge schools and whose academic profiles resemble those of students with mild disabilities; however, these students are not disabled. Unfortunately, the vague definitions of disabilities, imprecise and discriminatory identification methods, and limited funding resulting in a lack of appropriate services, all increase the chances that these students will be identified incorrectly as needing special education. Several alternative viewpoints, such as multicultural education and inclusion, have been proposed for structuring schools to meet the needs of *all students* without labeling and separating them (Wang, Reynolds, & Walberg, 1995). These philosophies challenge schools to reorganize their curriculum, teaching, staff allocation, and resources into a unified system that pursues both equity and excellence by asserting that *all students* can learn at high levels in general education programs. They also seek to transform schooling for *all students* by celebrating diversity, acknowledging the importance of social relationships, establishing a sense of community in schools and classrooms, and fostering the involvement of families, community members, and groups in schools (Schrag & Burnette, 1994).

Multicultural Education

One important educational philosophy for restructuring schools is *multicultural education*. This term originated in the post–civil rights efforts of various ethnic and language groups to have their previously neglected experiences included in the structures and curricula of schools (Nieto, 1996). Multicultural education seeks to help teachers acknowledge and understand the increasing diversity in society and in the classroom. For many, multicultural education has expanded to include concerns about socioeconomic status, disability, gender, and sexual orientation.

Definitions of multicultural education range from an emphasis on human relations and harmony to a focus on social democracy and empowerment. Suzuki (1984) offers the following inclusive definition of multicultural education:

> [It is] a multidisciplinary educational program that provides multiple learning environments matching the academic, social and linguistic needs of students. . . . In addition to enhancing the development of their basic academic skills, the program should help students develop a better understanding of their own backgrounds and of other groups that compose society. . . . Finally, it should help them conceptualize a vision of a better society and acquire the necessary knowledge . . . to enable them to move the society toward greater equality and freedom. . . . (p. 305)

Proponents of multicultural education also try to change the language of schools (Nieto, 1996). Terms such as *culturally disadvantaged, linguistically limited, at risk, slow learners, handicapped,* and *dropouts* locate problems within students rather than within the educational system (Freire, 1970). These labels present a view of students that often

REFLECTIVE

We refer to students who have needs that challenge the school system as *at risk, handicapped, culturally disadvantaged,* or *linguistically limited.* How might things be different if we referred to schools as *risky, disabling, disadvantaging,* and *limiting?*

contradicts the way these students view themselves. These conflicting views can disable students academically and prevent the development of self-esteem.

Multicultural Education and Inclusion

Multicultural education and inclusion are inextricably linked. Many of the challenges confronting advocates for multicultural education are also faced by those who support inclusion. As seekers of educational reform, the multicultural education and inclusion movements have the same goals and seek to provide equity and excellence for *all students*. Both movements also have common academic and affective goals for students. These goals include promoting challenging learning environments that focus on students' needs, experiences, and strengths; developing positive attitudes toward oneself, one's culture, and the cultures and experiences of others; understanding and accepting individual differences; and appreciating the interdependence among various groups and individuals.

Many of the key elements of multicultural education are also those of inclusion. The best practices in terms of assessment, teaching adaptations, culturally responsive teaching, curriculum reform, and an appreciation of individual differences are common to both movements. The empowerment and support of families and communities, and the collaborative efforts of teachers, are other important components of both philosophies. By recognizing their common aims, those who support inclusion and multicultural education seek to create a unified school system in which *all students* are welcomed and affirmed in their classrooms. The inclusion and multicultural education movements mean that increasing numbers of these students will be educated in general education settings. Therefore, educators must be trained and willing to create inclusive classrooms that address their diverse educational, cultural, and linguistic needs.

SUMMARY

This chapter offered information on how societal changes have helped to make inclusive education necessary to meet the needs of increasingly diverse groups of students who challenge the existing school structure. As you review the chapter, consider the following questions and remember the following points.

How Have Economic Changes Affected Students and Schools?

The United States has experienced dramatic economic changes marked by a growing gulf between wealthy and poor, old and young, as well as a shrinking middle class. As a result of these changes, schools are being challenged to meet the educational needs of a growing number of students who live in urban, rural, and suburban poverty.

How Have Demographic Shifts Affected Students and Schools?

The makeup of the U.S. population has also changed dramatically, making the United States a more linguistically and culturally diverse country. As a result, schools will need to structure their programs and services to address a more diverse student population.

What Are the Needs of Students from Culturally and Linguistically Diverse Backgrounds?

In addressing the needs of your students from culturally and linguistically diverse backgrounds, be sensitive to and adapt your services to take into account the cultural, linguistic, and economic factors that affect you and your students. It is important to develop cultural competence and intercultural communication skills. You must also adjust your teaching behaviors and curricula to reflect your students' differing cultural backgrounds, learning styles, economic and experiential backgrounds, and linguistic abilities.

How Can I Try to Differentiate Cultural and Language Differences from Learning Problems?

You can try to differentiate cultural and language differences from learning problems by understanding the stages students go through in learning a second language and by assessing your students' performance in both their primary and secondary languages. Students whose linguistic, academic, and social behaviors in both languages are well below those of peers who have similar linguistic, cultural, and experiential backgrounds may have a learning problem.

What Are the Educational Needs of Students Who Are Gifted and Talented?

Teachers tend to focus on the academic needs of students who are gifted and talented, but these students often have unique social and emotional needs as well. You can address these needs by using Gardner's framework of multiple intelligences and by creating a learning environment that encourages students to be creative, develop their strengths, take risks, and direct their learning.

What Is the Impact of Discrimination and Bias on Students and Schools?

Students from specific racial, linguistic, and religious backgrounds, female students, gay and lesbian students, and students with HIV/AIDS can be victims of discrimination in society and schools. This discrimination harms their school performance, socialization, self-esteem, and outcome in later life. You must use a variety of strategies to foster the academic performance and self-esteem of these students.

How Have Family Changes Affected Students and Schools?

Because of the dramatic changes in the composition, structure, and function of families, you will probably have students who live with both parents, one parent, family members, friends, two mothers, two fathers, or foster parents. You also may be called on to help families deal with child abuse or substance abuse. Regardless of the family's composition, it is important to recognize that while these families may have unique needs, they also have the same joys, frustrations, and needs as other families.

What Are Some Alternative Philosophies for Structuring Schools to Address Societal Changes?

Inclusion and multicultural education are philosophical movements that challenge schools to restructure their services and resources into a unified system that addresses societal changes. Multicultural education and inclusion have the same goals and seek to provide equity and excellence for *all students*.

What Would You Do in Today's Diverse Classroom?

It is August, and you read the following reports about your students:

❖ Carl's family is homeless. He is absent frequently and often comes to school tired and hungry. The other students avoid Carl, and he appears to be a loner. He loses school materials whenever he takes things home and rarely completes his homework.

❖ Erica has good skills, and her family gives her everything she needs. However, she has trouble completing projects, lacks motivation, needs constant attention, and has few friends.

❖ Zoltan arrived in the United States last year after escaping his war-torn country with his uncle's family. He lives with his uncle's family, and misses and worries about his parents and family members who still live in their country. He speaks and understands very little English and often gets into trouble because he doesn't understand and follow the rules.

❖ Julia's parents recently separated, and it was a surprise to everyone. Her parents had been very active in school and in other aspects of Julia's life. Her behavior is now very erratic. Sometimes she withdraws, and at other times she gets angry for no apparent reason. She often complains of headaches that prevent her from completing her work.

1. How would placement in a general education class benefit Carl, Erica, Zoltan, and Julia?

2. What concerns would you have about having these students in your class?

3. What are the educational needs of Carl, Erica, Zoltan, and Julia? What would be your goals for them?

4. What strategies could you use to address their educational needs?

5. What resources would be helpful to you in meeting their educational needs?

PART II

Creating an Inclusive Environment That Supports Learning for All Students

P art II of the book, which includes Chapters 4, 5, 6, and 7, provides strategies for creating an inclusive environment that supports learning for *all students*. Chapter 4 introduces the members of the comprehensive planning team and provides strategies for establishing collaborative relationships and fostering communication with professionals and family members. Chapter 5 offers strategies that support learning by fostering acceptance of individual differences related to disability, culture, language, gender, and socioeconomic status and promoting friendships among your students. Chapter 6 provides a framework for helping students make the transition to inclusive learning environments and from school to adulthood. It also offers strategies for helping your students develop self-determination. Chapter 7 discusses ways in which you can plan and implement strategies to promote positive behaviors that foster learning and prevent students from harming each other. It also provides guidelines for designing your classroom to accommodate students' learning, social, and physical needs.

CHAPTER
4

CREATING
COLLABORATIVE
RELATIONSHIPS AND
FOSTERING
COMMUNICATION

The Smith Family

We knew it would be another rough year. Last year, Paul's teacher told us that he wasn't doing as well as the other students. Now after only 2 months, Paul's new teacher, Mr. Rodl, called and said, "Paul is falling behind, and we need to do something." Mr. Rodl asked us to come to a meeting with a team of professionals to discuss Paul's progress. He said we could schedule the meeting at a time that was convenient for us.

Going into the meeting was scary. There sat Paul's teacher, the principal, the school psychologist, and several other people we didn't know. Mr. Rodl started the meeting by introducing us to the others in the room. Then he said, "Since I work closely with Paul, I'll lead the meeting and coordinate the decisions we'll make about Paul's program. We call that being the service coordinator." He asked each person in the room to talk about Paul. As different people spoke, others asked questions. When several people used words we didn't understand, Mr. Rodl asked them to explain the words to us. When our turn came, Mr. Rodl asked us to talk about what was happening with Paul at home, what we thought was happening with him at school, and what we would like to see happen at school. At first, we felt very nervous. As people in the room listened to and discussed our comments, we became more relaxed. The group discussed several ways to help Paul. In the end, we all came up with a plan to help Paul learn better. Mr. Rodl summarized the plan and the roles each person would play to make it successful. We left the meeting feeling really good about being part of a team that was trying to help our son.

What factors made this meeting successful? What strategies could professionals and families employ to help students such as Paul learn better? After reading this chapter, you should be able to answer these as well as the following questions:

◆ Who are the members of the comprehensive planning team?
◆ How can members of the comprehensive planning team work collaboratively?
◆ How can I foster communication and collaboration with families?

Effective inclusion programs involve good collaboration and communication among teachers, families, and community resources. Educational programming for students with disabilities, once the task of the special educator, is now shared by educators, family members, and community members. This chapter offers strategies for creating collaborative relationships and fostering communication with other professionals, families, and community members to support the learning of *all students*.

WHO ARE THE MEMBERS OF THE COMPREHENSIVE PLANNING TEAM?

INFORMATIONAL

Fradd (1993) offers guidelines for creating teams and communication networks to meet the needs of students from culturally and linguistically diverse backgrounds.

As we saw in Chapter 2, the comprehensive planning team, including the student, makes collaborative decisions about the educational needs of students. The team also provides appropriate services to students and their families to promote the inclusion of students in general education classrooms (Williams & Fox, 1996). The team solves problems, coordinates the services available to students, families, educators, and schools, and shares the responsibility for implementing inclusion.

In addition to students (see Chapter 2), the team may consist of general and special educators, administrators, support personnel such as speech and language therapists, bilingual educators, paraeducators, volunteers, family members, peers, local community resources, and professional and family-based organizations, as shown in Figure 4.1. The members of the team vary, depending on the needs of students, families, and educators. The roles and responsibilities of the different team members are described in the following sections.

Family Members

Family members are key members of the planning team, and communication and collaboration with them are essential (Grigal, 1998). They can provide various types of information on the student's adaptive behavior and medical, social, and psychological history. Family members also can help the team design and implement educational programs and determine appropriate related services.

School Administrators

A school administrator who supervises the districtwide services usually serves as the chairperson of the team. The chairperson is responsible for coordinating meetings and delivering services to students and their families. The chairperson also ensures that all le-

FIGURE 4.1   Members of the comprehensive planning team.

gal guidelines for due process, family involvement, assessment, and confidentiality have been followed. Through their leadership and support, school administrators also can foster acceptance of and commitment to the concept of inclusion.

General Educators

The team must include a general education teacher who has worked with the student and who can offer information on the student's strengths and weaknesses, as well as data on the effectiveness of specific teaching methods. General educators can provide a perspective on the academic and social rigors of the general education curriculum and classroom. Involving the general educator in the process also can allay the fears of general education classroom teachers and promote their commitment to helping the student succeed in an inclusive setting.

Special Educators

The special educator provides information on the student's academic and social skills and the student's responses to different teaching techniques and materials. When a student is to be placed in an inclusive setting, the special educator can work with general education classroom teachers on teaching modifications, classroom management strategies, testing accommodations, grading alternatives, adaptive devices, and peer acceptance.

Paraeducators and Volunteers

Paraeducators and volunteers can perform many important roles (see Figure 4.2) to help you promote the educational performance of *all students* in inclusive settings (French, 1999; Freschi, 1999). In particular, paraeducators and volunteers who are trained in or have experience with students' languages and cultures can play an important role in educating students who are second language learners.

Paraeducators can be invaluable in helping you and your students, but if used improperly, they can hurt the academic, social, and behavioral performance of students with disabilities (Marks, Schrader, & Levine, 1999). Giangreco, Edelman, Luiselli and Mac-Farland (1997) found that when paraeducators work too closely with students with disabilities, they can impede effective inclusion programs by:

◆ Allowing general educators to avoid assuming responsibility for educating students with disabilities (e.g., saying, "She is so good with Mitchell that I just let her handle it");

◆ Fostering the separation of students with disabilities from the rest of the class (e.g., working with a student with disabilities in a separate location);

◆ Creating dependence on adults (e.g., prompting and assisting students when it is not necessary);

◆ Limiting interactions with peers (e.g., being near the student can intimidate peers and reduce socialization);

◆ Teaching ineffectively (e.g., not adjusting an unsuccessful activity);

◆ Causing the loss of personal control (e.g., making decisions for students with significant communication, physical, and/or sensory difficulties);

◆ Causing the loss of gender identity (e.g., taking students to the bathroom based on the gender of the paraeducator, not the student);

◆ Interfering with the teaching of other students (e.g., using behaviors that distract other students).

INFORMATIONAL

Doyle (1997) provides guidelines, resources, and activities that you and your paraeducators can use to work collaboratively in inclusive settings.

Therefore, you should carefully interview potential paraeducators to determine their suitability for the job, give them a job description, and offer to train them (Hilton & Gerlach, 1997; Parsons & Reid, 1999). You can orient them by providing a tour of the school, introducing them to key school personnel, describing relevant programs, and reviewing the dress code and other standards of decorum. In the orientation program you can also

---

◆ Preparing individualized learning materials and modifying materials
◆ Providing individualized and small-group instruction and reinforcing concepts taught previously
◆ Administering teacher-made tests and correcting papers
◆ Helping students with motor and mobility problems, and with health and physical needs, and providing emotional support
◆ Reading to students and playing educational games with them
◆ Serving as a translator
◆ Completing paperwork and performing clerical duties
◆ Supervising students during activities outside the classroom
◆ Observing and recording behavior and helping to manage students' behavior

FIGURE 4.2 Roles of paraeducators and volunteers in inclusive settings.

Paraeducators and volunteers can promote the educational performance of students in inclusive classrooms.

explain the need for and rules on confidentiality, and discuss scheduling, handling emergencies, and other school procedures. In addition, you can offer paraeducators a training program. Such a program includes many different types of information. It explains the roles of paraeducators inside and outside the classroom, as well as their legal and ethical responsibilities. It identifies the special medical, social, and academic needs of students and the equipment they use. It provides an overview of teaching and behavior management techniques and reviews the communication system you will be using. Finally, the program demonstrates how to operate adaptive devices, media, and other necessary equipment. Paraeducators and volunteers also can learn skills by attending workshops and inservice presentations and by reading relevant articles and books.

As you work with paraeducators and volunteers, it is important to communicate regularly with them to jointly plan and coordinate activities, monitor student performance, and solve problems. It is also important to give them feedback on their performance and acknowledge their contributions. Feedback can include job performance, rapport with students and other school personnel, and information on how to work more effectively. You can also ask paraeducators and volunteers for their point of view about their roles in the school, and you can acknowledge their contributions with notes from students and teachers, graphs or other records of student progress, certificates of appreciation, and verbal comments.

School Psychologists

The school psychologist is an expert in the administration and interpretation of standardized tests. In addition to testing, school psychologists collect data on students by observing them in their classrooms and by interviewing other professionals who work with the students. School psychologists also sometimes counsel students and family members,

SET YOUR SITES

Information and resources for working with paraeducators are available from the National Clearinghouse for Paraeducator Resources (www.usc.edu/dept/education/CMMR/Clearinghouse.html) and the National Resource Center for Paraprofessionals in Education and Related Services (www.web.gc.cuny.edu/dept/case/nrcp).

SET YOUR SITES

The University of Nebraska maintains a website (http://para.unl.edu/para/TrainingIntro.html) that offers training to paraeducators.

SET YOUR SITES

You can obtain information and resources on school psychology from the National Association of School Psychologists (www.naspweb.org, 301-657-0270).

and assist classroom teachers in designing teaching and classroom management strategies (Habel & Bernard, 1999).

Speech and Language Clinicians

Information on students' communication abilities can be provided by the speech and language clinician. To rule out or confirm a language disability, these clinicians are often the first persons to whom students learning English are referred. They can also help you improve the communication skills and academic success of students in the classroom (Harn, Bradshaw, & Ogletree, 1999).

Social Workers

The social worker serves as a liaison between the home and the school and community agencies. The social worker counsels students and families, assesses the effect of the student's home life on school performance, and assists families during emergencies. In addition, the social worker can help families obtain services from community agencies, contact agencies concerning the needs of students and their families, and evaluate the impact of services on the family. Social workers also may offer counseling and support groups for students and their families.

School Counselors

The school counselor can provide information on the student's social and emotional development, including self-concept, attitude toward school, and social interactions with others (Deck, Scarborough, Sferrazza, & Estill, 1999). In schools that don't have a social worker, the counselor may assume those roles.

Frequently, counselors coordinate, assess, and monitor the student's program, as well as reporting the student's progress to members of the team. The counselor also may counsel students and their families. For example, during the transition period, the student may need counseling to adjust socially and emotionally to the general education classroom.

SET YOUR SITES

You can obtain information and resources on school counseling from the American School Counselor Association (www.school counselor.org, 703-683-2722).

Vocational Educators

Vocational educators offer valuable information on the student's work experiences and career goals. They can help the team develop the transitional services component of students' IEPs. Vocational educators also provide students with vocational and career education experiences. This involves collaboration with families and employers in the community.

School Physicians and Nurses

School physicians can aid the team by performing diagnostic tests to assess the student's physical development, sensory abilities, medical problems, and central nervous system functioning. They can provide information on nutrition, allergies, chronic illnesses, and somatic symptoms. In addition, they can plan and monitor medical interventions and discuss the potential side effects of any drugs used. Since physicians' services are costly, many medically related services may be provided by school nurses.

Speech and language clinicians help students develop their communication skills.

Physical and Occupational Therapists

Students with fine and gross motor needs may need the help of physical and occupational therapists. These therapists can recommend various types of adaptive equipment and suggest how to adapt teaching materials and classroom environments. The physical therapist usually focuses on the assessment and training of the lower extremities and large muscles; the occupational therapist deals with the upper extremities and fine motor abilities. The physical therapist helps students strengthen muscles, improve posture, and increase motor function and range. The occupational therapist works with students to prevent, restore, or adapt to impaired or lost motor functions. This therapist also helps students develop the necessary fine motor skills to perform everyday actions independently.

Staff from Community Agencies

For many students, the team will need to work collaboratively with staff from community agencies. For example, if a student with a visual impairment must have an adaptive device, a community agency can be contacted to help purchase it. In working with community organizations, the team should consider the unique medical, behavioral, and social needs of each student, as well as the financial resources of the student's family. Since many students may require similar services from agencies, teams can maintain a file of community agencies and the services they provide.

Professionals for Students Who Are Second Language Learners

In addition to the professionals described above, teams for students who are learning English and who are referred for special education services should include personnel who are fluent in the student's native language and bicultural in the student's home culture. Therefore, planning teams working with these students should include such professionals as ESL teachers, bilingual educators, and migrant educators.

ESL Teachers

ESL teachers instruct students in English. They build on students' existing language skills and experiences to enhance their learning of English. They can offer many effective strategies for teaching second language learners (see Chapter 8).

Bilingual Educators

Many students come from backgrounds where English is not spoken and need the help of a bilingual educator (Baca & Cervantes, 1998). This educator performs a variety of roles. These include assessing and teaching students in their native language and in English, involving families and community members in the educational program, helping students maintain their native culture and adjust to their new culture, and working with general educators.

Migrant Educators

To help educate migrant students, the federal government funds migrant education programs through the states. Typically, when a migrant family moves to a new area, it is certified as being eligible for migrant status and services by a recruiter from a local migrant education agency. Then a migrant educator helps the family enroll the children in school. The migrant educator also contacts local agencies, organizations, businesses, and other community resources that can assist migrant families. Once the migrant students are in school, the migrant educator often gives them supplementary individualized instruction in small groups.

HOW CAN MEMBERS OF THE COMPREHENSIVE PLANNING TEAM WORK COLLABORATIVELY?

Employ Collaborative and Interactive Teaming

Successful comprehensive planning teams are collaborative and interactive. All members work together to achieve a common goal, and share their expertise and perceptions with others. A key member of the team is the case manager, service coordinator, or support facilitator. This person promotes the team process, coordinates the services for students and their families, and provides follow-up to ensure that goals are being met (Chase Thomas et al., 1995).

In addition, effective collaborative and interactive teams have the following characteristics:

1. *Legitimacy and autonomy.* Effective teams have a recognized and supported function and are free to operate independently.
2. *Purposes and objectives.* Effective teams have identified goals and work together, sharing information and expertise to achieve these goals. The team members have a common set of norms and values that guide the team's functioning.

SET YOUR SITES

You can obtain information and resources on ESL by contacting Teachers of English Speakers of Other Languages (www.Tesol.org, 703-836-0774).

INFORMATIONAL

Salend, Dorney, and Mazo (1997) describe the roles of bilingual special educators in creating inclusive classrooms.

3. *Competencies of team members and clarity of their roles.* The members of effective teams are skilled not only in their own disciplines but also in collaborative problem solving, communication, and cultural diversity.

4. *Role release and role transitions.* Effective teams consist of members who can share their expertise with others, implement programs, use strategies from other disciplines, learn from others, and seek assistance and feedback.

5. *Awareness of the individuality of others.* Effective teams consist of members who recognize and accept the perspectives, skills, and experiences of others.

6. *Process of team building.* Effective teams are committed to the process of working together and functioning as a team. Conflicts between team members are resolved through problem solving, communication, and negotiation.

7. *Attention to factors that affect team functioning.* Effective teams use cooperative goal structures, create a supportive communication climate, share roles, and reach decisions through consensus.

8. *Leadership styles.* Effective teams rotate leadership responsibilities. Leaders are expected to solicit all points of view and involve all members in the decision-making process.

9. *Implementation procedures.* Effective teams consider a variety of factors when designing and implementing interventions.

10. *Commitment to common goals.* Effective teams are committed to collaborative goals and problem-solving techniques (Thomas, Correa, & Morsink, 1995).

Successful teams also develop good interpersonal and communication skills. Garmston and Wellman (1998) and Landerholm (1990) summarized the roles that team members can perform to help the team function efficiently and establish a positive, trusting working environment:

1. *Initiating.* All members identify problems and issues to be considered by the team.
2. *Information gathering and sharing.* All members collect and share relevant information.
3. *Clarifying and elaborating.* All members seek clarification, probe for specific facts and details, and provide elaboration.
4. *Summarizing.* All members review and paraphrase key points discussed by the team.
5. *Consensus building.* All members participate in decision making.
6. *Encouraging.* All members encourage others to participate in the process and pay attention to the contributions of others.
7. *Harmonizing and compromising.* All members assume that others have good intentions, and seek to resolve conflict and compromise.
8. *Reflecting.* All members reflect upon their own feelings, comments, and behaviors, as well as those of others.
9. *Balancing.* All members try to balance advocacy and inquiry.

To help the team develop these skills, individual team members can be assigned roles such as facilitator, recorder, timekeeper, observer, and summarizer.

Use the Map Action Planning System

The team can coordinate students' inclusion programs by using the Map Action Planning System (MAPS), a systems approach to designing a plan for students (Forest & Lusthaus, 1990). MAPS also can be used to help the team develop IEPs. In MAPS, team members,

INFORMATIONAL

Williams and Fox (1996) offer a model that comprehensive planning teams can use to foster inclusion for students.

INFORMATIONAL

Davern, Ford, Marusa, and Schnorr (1993) offer a framework that you can use to evaluate teams working in inclusive settings.

REFLECTIVE

Think about a situation in which you worked collaboratively with a team. How was the outcome affected by the collaboration? What problems did the team have in working collaboratively? How did the team resolve these problems?

including students with disabilities, their families, and peers, meet to develop an inclusion plan by first responding to the following questions:

1. *What is a map?* This question allows participants to think about the characteristics of a map.
2. *What is (the student's name) story?* This question helps the team understand the events that have shaped the student's life and family.
3. *What is your (our) dream for (the student's name)?* This question allows team members to share their visions and goals for the student's future.
4. *What is your (our) nightmare?* This question helps the team understand the student's and family's fears.
5. *Who is (the student's name)?* This question gives all team members the opportunity to describe their perceptions of the student.
6. *What are (the student's name) strengths, gifts, and talents?* This question helps the team focus on and identify the student's positive attributes.
7. *What are (the student's name) needs? What can we do to meet these needs?* These questions help the team define the student's needs in a variety of areas.
8. *What would be an ideal day for (the student's name)? What do we need to do to make this ideal real?* These questions help the team plan the student's program by listing the student's activities, modifications needed for these activities, and individuals responsible for implementing the modifications.

Work in Cooperative Teaching Arrangements

Many school districts are using cooperative teaching to educate *all students* in general education classrooms. In cooperative teaching, general education teachers and supportive service personnel such as special educators and speech/language therapists collaborate to teach students in inclusive settings (Bauwens & Hourcade, 1997). Teachers involved in cooperative teaching share responsibility and accountability for planning and delivering instruction, evaluating, grading, and disciplining students. Students are not removed from the classroom for supportive services. Instead, academic instruction and supportive services are provided where the need exists: in the general education classroom.

Cooperative teaching teams can use many different instructional arrangements based on the purpose of the lesson, the nature of the material covered, and the needs of students. Examples of these instructional arrangements are described below and in Figure 4.3.

◆ One teacher instructs the whole class while the other teacher circulates to collect information on students' performance or to offer help to students (see Figure 4.3a). This arrangement is also used to take advantage of the expertise of one teacher in a specific subject area.
◆ When it is necessary to lower the student:teacher ratio in order to teach new material or to review and practice material previously taught, both teachers can teach the same material at the same time to two equal groups of students (see Figure 4.3b).
◆ When teaching material that is difficult but not sequential or when several different topics are important, both teachers can teach different content at the same time to two equal groups of students, and then switch groups and repeat the lesson (see Figure 4.3c).
◆ When teachers need to individualize instruction, remediate skills, promote mastery, or offer enrichment based on students' needs, one teacher can work with

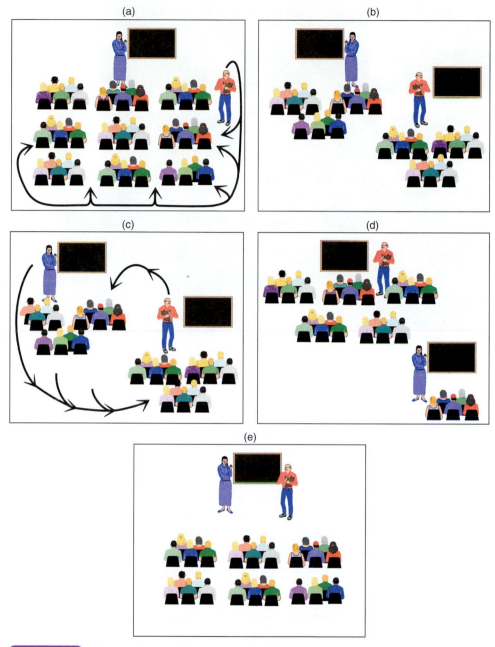

FIGURE 4.3 Cooperative teaching arrangements.

a smaller group or individual students while the other teacher works with a larger group (see Figure 4.3d).

◇ When it is important to blend the talents and expertise of teachers, both teachers can plan and teach a lesson together (see Figure 4.3e).

There are moments when things happen in the classroom that the kids do that are really funny. And you want to share that. And when she's in here, we just laugh hysterically. It's really more enjoyable because you've got another person there to share that with. If you

In cooperative teaching, both teachers should perform meaningful roles that facilitate student learning.

try to save it until you get home to your spouse, you nearly forget it with everything else going on. But we'll just hoot at some of the things that happen. Like, I don't think I'll ever forget one of our little boys, he calls us Miss McSmith. He combined the beginning of her name with the end of mine—and so we're both Ms. McSmith. It doesn't matter which one of us he tries to talk to, that's what he'll call us. (From a member of a cooperative teaching team) (Phillips, Sapona, & Lubic, 1995, pp. 266–267)

Cooperative teaching is designed to minimize some of the problems of pull-out programs, such as students missing academic instruction, insufficient communication and coordination between professionals, scheduling problems, and fragmentation of the curriculum. It also allows supportive services and modified teaching for students with academic difficulties without labeling them (Pugach & Johnson, 1995a). In addition to helping students with disabilities, cooperative teaching gives *all students* the assistance and expertise of at least two professionals rather than just one (Gerber & Popp, 1999; Siegel-Causey et al., 1998). Teachers working in cooperative teams also note that these programs help make teaching more enjoyable and stimulating, give them new insights and experiences regarding teaching strategies, and prevent the isolation that sometimes occurs when teachers work alone (Brownell, Yeager, Rennells, & Riley, 1997; Salend et al., 1997; Walther-Thomas, 1997).

At first, I was nervous, because you're not used to having another teacher in the class-room and all of a sudden you've got another person. I'm like, "am I doing this right? Does she think this is okay?" Even though I knew her and I really liked her personally, I still thought, "What if she doesn't like my style of teaching? What if she thinks I'm lazy? What if she doesn't like this or that?" That sounds terrible but, the most difficult adjustment wasn't really pointed towards the kids, it was what she thought of me. (From a member of a cooperative teaching team) (Phillips et al., 1995, pp. 266–267)

Cooperative teaching teams may encounter several problems that can limit their effectiveness (Dyck, Sundbye, & Pemberton, 1997). Lack of time to plan and implement programs, no administrative support, resistance from colleagues, concerns about grading, increased workloads, and increased responsibilities are major obstacles to successful cooperative teaching (Bauwens & Hourcade, 1995; Walther-Thomas, 1997). Teachers also report that they need to learn to work and teach together so that both members of the team assume responsibility for *all students* and perform relevant and meaningful tasks that promote student learning (Trent, 1998). For instance, if one teacher is always the instructional leader and the other teacher is relegated to the role of assistant or aide for a few students, the team may not be effective. Team teaching takes time and requires teachers to deal with philosophical, pedagogical, historical, logistical, and territorial issues, as well as concerns about working with and being observed by another professional (Phillips et al., 1995; Salend et al., 1997; Wood, 1998). You can address these issues by:

- ◆ Discussing why you want to work together and agreeing on the goals you have for your classroom. It is also important to discuss what you expect of each other, as well as your concerns and fears about working cooperatively (Stump & Wilson, 1996).
- ◆ Learning about each other's abilities, beliefs, routines, teaching and classroom management approaches, communication systems, and assessment strategies. Walther-Thomas, Bryant, and Land (1996) present discussion questions that cooperative teaching teams can address to become familiar with each other's skills, interests, teaching styles, and educational philosophies.
- ◆ Understanding and coordinating each other's responsibilities, as well as the roles of others. Frederico, Herrold, and Venn (1999) developed a checklist to use in coordinating the roles and responsibilities of teachers, support service personnel, administrators, family and community members, and the school district (see Figure 4.4).
- ◆ Being sensitive to cross-cultural perspectives and interactions. Understand and accept multiple perspectives, and work toward accepting and responding appropriately to each other's cultural beliefs and communication style (Jairrels, 1999).
- ◆ Establishing and agreeing on a common set of expectations for judging and grading students' academic, behavioral, and social performance.
- ◆ Working toward thinking and communicating in terms of "we" and "our" rather than "I" and "my."
- ◆ Being prepared to encounter problems at first. Successful cooperative teaching involves taking time to adjust to working with another person to resolve logistical and territorial issues, to determine roles and responsibilities, and to blend skills.
- ◆ Working toward establishing an equal status relationship. Share the workload, vary responsibilities, and don't relegate one person to a lesser role.

RESPONSIBILITIES	General Education Teacher	Special Education Teacher	Principal	Support Services	Parents & Community	School District
General Responsibilities						
Describe the school's position on inclusion						
Prepare the teaching staff for inclusion						
Offer teachers a choice of inclusion teaching						
Describe the inclusion program to parents						
Provide full support services in the general class						
Establish an inclusion support group						
Explain the inclusion program to school personnel						
Specific Professional Responsibilities						
Ensure compliance with state and federal guidelines						
Provide student information to the inclusion team						
Supervise the teaching assistant(s)						
Serve as the student case manager						
Monitor individualized education program (IEP) standards						
Maintain cumulative folders						
Participate in parent conferences						
Assign grades on report cards each semester						
Learning to Be an Inclusion Team Teacher						
Attend inclusion inservice						
Function as part of the inclusion team						
Respect the role of each school inclusion team member						
Teacher-Student Interaction						
Adapt curricular activities for students with disabilities						
Teach student peers to assist students with disabilities						
Use adaptations in classroom activities						
Develop daily lesson plans						
Work one-on-one with students as needed						
Design interaction activities for students						
Assign "buddies" to students with disabilities						

FIGURE 4.4 Checklist for planning inclusive cooperative teaching arrangements. (continued)

Source: Frederico, M. A., Herrold, W. G., & Venn, J. (1999). Helpful tips for successful inclusion: A checklist for educators. *Teaching Exceptional Children, 32*(1), 76–82.

RESPONSIBILITIES	General Education Teacher	Special Education Teacher	Principal	Support Services	Parents & Community	School District
Beliefs About Teaching Inclusion						
Maintain a sense of humor						
Treat the inclusion class as "Our Class," not "My Class"						
Become a community of inclusion learners						
Avoid labeling children in the inclusion program						
Treat all students as equals						
Use appropriate behavior management						
End-of-Year Responsibilities						
Administer end-of-year standardized testing						
Assign final grades on report cards						
Determine student promotions						
Determine inclusion program successes						
Identify inclusion program failures						
Invite others to join the inclusion team						
Select teachers for the next year's inclusion classroom(s)						

FIGURE 4.4   (continued)

◈ Varying the arrangements used to teach students. Use a range of activities that allow both team members to take a leadership role and to feel comfortable. A format for planning cooperative teaching lessons is presented in Figure 4.5.

◈ Meeting periodically with families to explain the program and to share information on students' progress.

◈ Communicating regularly to reevaluate goals, solve problems, plan instruction, divide responsibilities, share instructional roles and administrative tasks, brainstorm new ideas and approaches, and talk about students' progress.

◈ Seeking feedback from families and other professionals.

◈ Engaging in self-evaluation and reflection to examine the team's success and the ways the team can improve. Continually examine shared values and goals, as well as concerns, problems, misunderstandings, expectations, and plans for the future.

◈ Addressing philosophical, pedagogical, and interpersonal differences directly and immediately. Be willing to listen to the other person's perspective and to compromise.

General Educator _____   Special Educator _____

Date	What are we going to teach?	Which co-teaching technique will we use?	What are the specific tasks of both teachers?	What materials are needed?	How will we evaluate learning?	Information about students who need follow-up work

FIGURE 4.5   Cooperative teaching lesson plan format.

Source: Vaughn, S., Schumm, J. S., & Arguelles, M. E. (1997). The ABCDEs of co-teaching. *Teaching Exceptional Children,* *30*(2), 4–10.

◆ Assessing the impact of the program on *all students*.
◆ Acknowledging and celebrating success. Enjoy, share, attribute, and reflect on your accomplishments as a team (Stump & Wilson, 1996).

Employ Collaborative Consultation

Teachers may also use *collaborative consultation*. This involves working together to implement mutually agreed-upon solutions to prevent and address learning and behavioral problems and to coordinate instructional programs for *all students*. Collaborative consultation is designed to address students' needs and to give general education teachers improved knowledge and skills to deal with similar situations in the future.

The "consultant," usually a special, bilingual, or multicultural educator or an ancillary staff member (a school psychologist, speech and language therapist, or physical therapist), works collaboratively with the general education teacher, who has primary

REFLECTING ON PROFESSIONAL PRACTICES

Working as a Cooperative Teaching Team

Cathy, a general education teacher, and Sarah, a special educator, were asked by their principal to work together as a cooperative teaching team. Their class, located in Cathy's former classroom, included 24 students, 7 of whom had been identified as having a disability. Though they had worked together before to reintegrate students with disabilities into the general education classroom for specific subject areas and activities, they were both anxious and excited about working as a cooperative teaching team.

Initially, Cathy and Sarah experienced some difficulties. Sarah felt out of place in Cathy's classroom. She was frustrated because she didn't know where the supplies and materials were located and frequently had to ask Cathy. She also worried that Cathy would have all the responsibility and be the "real" teacher and that she would function like a teacher's aide. Cathy sensed Sarah's concern and was also worried about their differences in terms of roles, teaching style, and philosophy. Sometimes she wondered if Sarah felt that she was too controlling, and disapproved of her concern about getting students ready for the statewide tests. Both Cathy and Sarah were also concerned that the students and their families viewed one of them as the teacher and the other one as a teacher's assistant.

At first, Sarah and Cathy had some difficulty determining their responsibilities and blending their skills. They struggled as they attempted to teach lessons together and coordinate their instructional activities. Sometimes, while Cathy led a lesson, Sarah seemed lost and felt like a helper rather than a teacher. They also had different opinions about the abilities of the students with disabilities. Sarah worried that "her" students would not be able to keep up with Cathy's plans for all the students, and that they were not receiving the services they needed. At the first family meeting their roles were clearly delineated, with Sarah speaking to the classified students' families separately. They quickly realized that this was a mistake and were determined to work on blending their skills.

As they worked together, they began to notice and respect each other's skills, perspectives, experiences, and areas of expertise. Cathy was impressed with Sarah's effectiveness in dealing with behavior problems, and Sarah was excited about the way Cathy made whole language activities come alive. They both wanted to learn from each other. They also started to improve in planning and teaching lessons together and performing administrative tasks. In teaching together, they began to anticipate each other's styles. Their principal observed them teaching a lesson and noticed that they were starting to teach together in a natural way even though their perspectives were different. When they completed the students' report cards together, they were amazed at how close they were in assessing students' needs and progress.

As they got to know each other, Cathy and Sarah began to experiment with new teaching methods, and both seemed to have a renewed enjoyment of teaching. They used role plays, puppets, and sometimes spontaneously acted out stories and lessons. Both teachers were surprised by how much more fun they and their students were having in class.

Though things were going well, Cathy and Sarah's concerns about teaming and their philosophical differences surfaced periodically. Sarah, who was trained in a skills-based approach, was concerned that Cathy's whole language approach was not effective with some of the students. Sarah discussed this with Cathy, who was very understanding, and they decided to do skills work too.

Their commitment to teaming was sustained by the positive changes they saw in their students. Sarah and Cathy were pleased that all the students had progressed developmentally, academically, and socially. They were particularly surprised and motivated by the influence of their collaboration on the sense of community in the classroom, which was seen in the students' unusual sensitivity to their peers.

Cathy and Sarah also were pleased with the support they received from their principal. The principal met periodically with them to discuss problems and solutions, to acknowledge their efforts and growth, and to offer assistance, support, and resources. The principal also rearranged their schedules to give them planning time together and encouraged them to visit schools with model programs.

Looking back on their experiences as a cooperative teaching team, Sarah and Cathy felt that it has been a successful year. Sarah noted, "What an incredible year! After so many years as a special education teacher, it was refreshing to interact with a greater variety of children. It was a great learning year for me. I don't think teachers know how enjoyable teaching can be when you share it." Cathy said, "This is the end of a wonderful year. The children and we as teachers became a close-knit community of learners. We all did learn and grow this year. It was like dancing with someone; sometimes you lead and sometimes you follow. We began with a lot of apprehension and ended with much enthusiasm."

Why do you think Cathy and Sarah were initially both anxious and excited about working together as a cooperative teaching team? What problems and concerns did they have? How did working together benefit Cathy and Sarah and their students? What factors helped to make this a successful school year? How would you feel if you were asked to be part of a cooperative teaching team?

September 7: *I can only be in one place at a time! Juggling teacher schedules and getting to students for assistance in their academic areas of need will be a feat worthy of a gold medal. And on top of that, time has to be set aside to conference with classroom teachers. I'm frustrated!!*

September 8: *I've worried about how junior high students would accept my presence in the classroom. . . . I discussed this with Mr. T, the building principal. During the grade level orientations, Mr. T introduced me as a teacher who would be in several different classes to assist students.*

September 13: *I did it! Schedules typed, all academic areas covered. I even managed to schedule time to conference with teachers (and it's not during lunch!). Mrs. C is not too keen on meeting with me on a regular basis and voiced a great concern about how much work this would add to her already overloaded schedule. Copies of all schedules have been sent to teachers, administrators, and parents. I have contacted every parent by phone and explained the service.*

September 14: *Mrs. M came to see me. She blurted out to me that she didn't know if she could go through with having me work in her room. She indicated to me that she felt extremely intimidated and was worried about what I would think. My first reaction was, "Don't be silly." Thank goodness I didn't say that. It really wasn't silly, because, I, too, was very nervous. I told Mrs. M that I understood what she meant, and explained my own nervousness.*

September 18: *A pleasant surprise. Mr. K introduced me as a co-teacher. He told his students that if they had any questions they could ask either himself or me. . . . I was wondering exactly how this would work out, when several different students raised their hands for assistance. In the end, I put together a small group of children to work with at the back table. How nice to see that the students I expected to work with, along with other students, accepted my presence and wanted my help.*

September 20: *I met with Mrs. E today. Together we worked on J's IEP, reviewed her entire curriculum, and decided on goals which should be included. It was wonderful having her input.*

October 12: *Mrs. C asked me if I would be willing to take a group of students for the social studies lesson and work on latitude and longitude. . . . We discussed the format and objectives of the lesson. During the class, we divided the room into groups and each taught a group. After the lesson, we were able to meet and discuss the results.*

November 16: *Ms. D, a first grade teacher, approached me and asked if I could speak with her about one of her students. I do not have a student in her room. We met after school and discussed the difficulties this child was having. Ms. D then asked if I would sit in on a parent conference. I guess there is a lot more to this job than just working with my assigned students.*

November 20: *Today's consultation with Mrs. K centered on getting her feedback on a study guide I created. We went over all the points, and at the end of the conversation she asked me if I would mind if she duplicated the guide and gave it to all her students.*

December 5: *Mrs. M indicated that the whole class was having difficulty getting the concept of contractions. We discussed some strategies, and she asked if I would like to teach the lesson the following morning. At the end of the consultation session, she turned to me and said, "You know, I am still a little nervous, but I really do like this collaborative consultation."*

FIGURE 4.6   Diary of a collaborative consultation teacher.

Source: K. Giek, Diary of a consulting teacher, *The Forum,* 16(1) (New York State Federation of Chapters of the Council for Exceptional Children, 1990), 5–6. Copyright 1990. Reprinted by permission.

responsibility (Kampwirth, 1999). Figure 4.6, a diary of the experiences of a collaborative consultation teacher, presents some of the services provided.

Steps in Collaborative Consultation

The steps in effective collaborative consultation are (1) goal and problem identification, (2) goal and problem analysis, (3) plan implementation, and (4) plan evaluation.

Goal and Problem Identification   The first step in the consultation process is to identify goals and problems, using who, what, and where questions that help teachers to clarify their goals and concerns (Pugach & Johnson, 1995b). For example, consultation teams can address such questions as: What challenges will students have in this class? What goals do we have for students? What can we do to address these challenges and

ASSISTANCE NEEDED

Teacher _____   Today's Date

Student _____   _____

Other _____

- [ ] There's a problem. Let's put our heads together.
- [ ] I need your help in the classroom.
- [ ] Develop alternative assignment or activity.
- [ ] Arrange cooperative learning groups & activities.
- [ ] Implement peer tutoring or peer partners.
- [ ] Produce alternative materials or locate resources.
- [ ] Develop a modified grading system.
- [ ] Create a study guide.   [ ] Plan a lesson.
- [ ] Modify materials.   [ ] Team teaching.
- [ ] Modify a test.   [ ] Classroom management.
- [ ] Develop guided notes.   [ ] Instructional strategies.

When? _____

Additional information:

_____

_____

_____

_____

FIGURE 4.7 Consultation assistance request form.

Source: E. A. Knackendoffel, Collaborative teaching in the secondary school, in D. D. Deshler, E. S. Ellis, & B. K. Lenz (Eds.), *Teaching adolescents with learning disabilities* (2nd ed.) (Denver, CO: Love Publishing, 1996), p. 585. Copyright 1996. Reprinted with permission.

help students achieve our goals? (Vargo, 1998). Goals and problems also can be identified by examining students' IEPs and observing students in their classrooms.

Often it is best for the consultation to focus on one situation at a time. If several problem areas must be handled simultaneously, it is advisable to set priorities and deal with the most important ones first. A consultation assistance request form that can be used to identify goals and problems is presented in Figure 4.7.

Goal and Problem Analysis   In the second phase of the consultation process, educators analyze the features that appear to be related to the identified goals and problems. These may include the curriculum, the physical environment of the room, teaching strategies, grouping arrangements, teaching and learning styles, peer relationships, student ability levels, family, and the school's policies and procedures. This analysis helps educators to plan appropriate intervention strategies.

INFORMATIONAL

Vargo (1998) and Kirschbaum and Flanders (1995) provide questions and forms, respectively, that allow educators to plan teaching adaptations. This is done by sharing information on topics to be covered, dates on which topics and lessons will be taught, and potential teaching adaptations.

Plan Implementation   During this phase, educators decide which interventions to use to address the identified goals and difficulties. They brainstorm and share their expertise, considering such factors as practicality, effectiveness, resources needed, and effects on others. Once the interventions have been selected, they can be outlined in detail, and responsibilities and timelines can be determined.

Plan Evaluation   Once the intervention has been implemented, its effectiveness should be checked periodically. This can be done by direct observation, curriculum-based assessments, analysis of student work samples, and other techniques that assess student progress (see Chapter 12).

Follow-up evaluation can also examine how the intervention has been implemented and identify any problem areas that need to be solved. Feedback should be an ongoing, interactive process focused on the intervention plan rather than on the individuals involved.

Even though consultation is effective, professionals may resist its use. This attitude is often associated with frustration, professional pride, and different views of the process. Other major barriers include insufficient time for team members to meet and overwhelming caseloads (Voltz, Elliott, & Harris, 1995). Successful consultation programs give classroom teachers and support staff time to consult with one another, and offer educators reasonable caseloads and schedules.

Promote Congruence

Successful collaboration requires *congruence,* a logical relationship among the curriculum, learning goals, teaching materials, strategies used in the general education classroom, and supportive services programs (Allington & Broikou, 1988). A congruent program is one based on common assessment results, goals and objectives, teaching strategies, and materials.

Ideally, remedial teaching should parallel the general education curriculum. Unfortunately, many of these programs are fragmented, based on different, and conflicting, curricula and teaching approaches. These incompatible and conflicting programs confuse students rather than help them learn. For instance, confusion can occur when students receive reading instruction using a phonetic approach in the resource room and a whole language approach in the general education classroom.

Allington and Shake (1986) propose two remedial models for coordinating teaching so that the ancillary program supplements learning in the general education classroom: an a priori model and a post hoc model. In the *a priori* model, supportive services educators teach content that supports the content to be learned in the general education classroom. This instruction lays the foundation for instruction in the general education classroom. For example, the ESL educator might introduce on Monday the spelling words that will be introduced on Friday in the general education classroom.

In the *post hoc* model, supportive instruction reinforces skills previously introduced in the general education classroom. Thus, rather than introducing new content, the supportive services educator reviews and reteaches content previously covered in the general education classroom. For example, while a student is learning how to add fractions in the general educating classroom, the resource teacher helps the student understand the process and develop automatic methods of responding to similar items.

Meetings

Meetings such as IEP conferences also can be used to establish congruence by involving general and supportive services educators in planning and implementing teaching programs. They can agree on common objectives, teaching methods and materials, and evaluation procedures to assess student learning. As students master the objectives, additional meetings can be held to revise the instructional program and evaluate congruence.

Student Interviews

You also can use student interviews to ensure and evaluate congruence. Specifically, you can ask students, "What things are you learning in (class)?" "What type of activities do you do in (class)?" "What materials do you use in (class)?" and "Does (class) help you in other classes?" (Johnston, Allington, & Afflerbach, 1985).

Notecard Systems

Congruence and communication between professionals can be fostered by the use of a notecard system. Each professional working with the student completes a notecard that serves as an ongoing record of the student's performance in that class for a specified period of time. The information on the card could include a rating of the student's progress, a list of the skills mastered and not mastered, upcoming assignments and tests, successful strategies, teaching materials being used, and skills other teachers can attempt to foster. One educator can be asked to categorize the information and share it with others to ensure the continuity of instruction. A sample notecard is presented in Figure 4.8.

Safran and Safran (1985b) have developed the Something's Out of Sync (SOS) form to promote communication between general and special education teachers. The general education teacher completes this form when a student is having a problem in a specific content area. The teacher can then request that the student receive additional work in that area or that a meeting be held to discuss the problem.

SET YOUR SITES

You can use the Internet as a resource for lesson plans by contacting Classroom Connect (www.classroom.net), Teacher's Edition Online (www.teachnet.com), and the Education Place (www.eduplace.com).

Online Services

You and other members of the team can obtain information and communicate with others via online services such as electronic mail (e-mail) and the Internet. E-mail allows

---

Student's Name: Time Period:
Class/Supportive Service: Educator:
Skills taught:
Instructional strategies and materials used:
Upcoming assignments/tests:

Assignment/Test Date Due

Skills to be reinforced in other settings:
Suggested activities to reinforce skills:
Comments:

FIGURE 4.8 Sample notecard.

SET YOUR SITES

You can identify available listservs on a wide range of topics and issues by visiting the website www.liszt.com.

SET YOUR SITES

You can communicate with other teachers via such websites as the Beginning Teachers' Tool Box (www.inspiringteachers.com), Teachers Helping Teachers (www.pacificnet.net/~mandel), and I Love Teaching.com (www.iloveteaching.com).

individuals to "talk to" and distribute communications to others. Online services give professionals, families, and students access to a wide range of resources (e.g., databases, documents, reports, materials) from around the world and opportunities to exchange information and ideas with colleagues. Online discussion groups offer interactions with others who are working in model programs and are interested in similar issues. For example, you can be part of a listserv, an e-mail list that lets you correspond with others on common interests. For students, online services offer exciting, challenging, and novel learning experiences (see Chapter 8 for more information on using online services for teaching purposes).

Most professional organizations or clearinghouses maintain a list of online computer networks and resources, including discussion and support groups. For example, the Educational Resources Information Center (ERIC), through its *AskERIC* service (http://ericir.syr.edu), offers electronic lists and databases with information on curricula, professional development, pedagogy, and teaching materials. Special education sites on the World Wide Web can be located through the use of *SERI—Special Education Resources on the Internet* (www.hood.edu/seri/serihome.htm).

IDEAS FOR IMPLEMENTATION

Promoting Congruence

Ms. Rivera is concerned about Elisa, a migrant student, who leaves her classroom several times a day for supplemental education. To alleviate her concerns, Ms. Rivera meets with Mr. D'Alessandro, Elisa's ESL teacher, to coordinate their activities. They discuss how to plan their programs so that Mr. D'Alessandro's sessions will reinforce what Ms. Rivera is teaching in the classroom.

They decide that Mr. D'Alessandro will preview stories with Elisa before they are read in Ms. Rivera's classroom. Also, Mr. D'Alessandro will review new words from the story and read the story again with Elisa. To coordinate these activities and check on Elisa's progress, Ms. Rivera and Mr. D'Alessandro meet weekly. With this planning, Ms. Rivera feels better and Elisa is better able to participate in class.

Here are some other strategies you can use to establish congruence:

◇ Work with supportive services educators so that their assessment procedures, curriculum, and teaching strategies are aligned with those used in the general education classroom.

◇ Find time for general education and supportive service teachers to share lesson plans and materials and observe each other's classrooms.

◇ Schedule time for teachers to collaborate in planning the student's instructional program.

◇ Use flexible scheduling that gives educators planning time to collaborate and coordinate their teaching.

◇ Have supportive services personnel such as special and bilingual education teachers give presentations at faculty meetings or on inservice days, and conduct a faculty meeting in the classrooms of these personnel.

◇ Maintain a file in which staff members list the areas of expertise they would be willing to share with others.

◇ Encourage all staff members to visit and observe each other's teaching activities. Ask faculty members to switch roles for a day.

◇ Designate an area of the teachers' lounge as a "materials table" where teachers leave certain materials that they think would be of value to others, or set up a lending library.

◇ Teach study skills and learning strategies using the textbooks of the general education program.

How Can I Foster Communication and Collaboration with Families?

A key component of a collaborative planning team is communication with the student's family (Alper, Schloss, & Schloss, 1996). As well as being educationally sound, involving family members in the education of students with disabilities is mandated by the IDEA. Unfortunately, the practices used in some school districts reduce family involvement and empowerment (Ford, Obiakor, & Patton, 1995).

Harry, Allen, and McLaughlin (1995) examined the experiences of family members after their children were placed in special education. They found that the attitudes and involvement of family members changed over time. At first, family members supported their children's schooling and acted as advocates on behalf of their children. Later, they became disillusioned with the special education program and the lack of opportunities for family advocacy. The authors concluded that these changes were related to five practices used by the professionals at the school:

1. Late notices and inflexible scheduling of conferences.
2. Limited time for conferences.
3. Emphasis on compliance and completion of paperwork rather than family participation, information sharing, and problem solving.
4. The use of professional jargon that was not explained to family members.
5. The emphasis on professionals' power and authority over family members. The authority of professionals was established through the following powers:
   a. *Power of structure.* Professionals reported and family members listened.
   b. *Power of need.* Family members' need for professional help and services made it difficult for them to disagree or express dissatisfaction.
   c. *Power of kindness.* The apparent kindness of professionals made it hard for family members to disagree.
   d. *Power of group.* The opinions and consensus of professionals overpowered the family's perspectives and disagreement.
   e. *Power of manipulation.* Experiences and expertise of professionals were used to gain agreement from family members.

Gain the Trust of Families

Family involvement and empowerment are based largely on the trust established between families and educators (Davern, 1999). If families and school personnel distrust or feel uncomfortable with each other, the family's involvement and therefore the student's performance may be harmed. You can involve and empower families by working with them using methods that are based on collaboration, mutual trust, and respect and that recognize the strengths of each family. Trust also can be established when schools collaborate with families to offer and coordinate a broad range of flexible, usable, and understandable services that address the many changing needs of families (Hanson & Carta, 1996). For example, a child with serious health problems creates stress and time demands, which can be reduced through the use of respite services.

When the experiences and expertise of family and community members are incorporated into school programs, the result is mutual respect and trust among schools, families, and the community. Students see their families and community actively engaged in

INFORMATIONAL

Dennis and Giangreco (1996) offer suggestions for interacting with families in culturally sensitive ways.

Incorporating the expertise of family members into schools can promote mutual trust and respect.

schools and classrooms. In the process, families and the community become empowered, positive partners in the educational process. Families and community members can be part of an ongoing program that allows them to share their experiences and knowledge in schools. For example, they can be asked to read to students, make and display artwork, lead extracurricular activities, and teach games. They can also organize field trips into the community, plan community service projects, and help schools communicate with other families and community members.

You also can gain the trust of families by learning about the experiences, cultures, and attitudes of families and students and then interacting with them in ways that respect their cultural values (Harry, Rueda, & Kalyanpur, 1999). In addition, you can examine your own viewpoints, attitudes, and behaviors related to your cultural background and diversity. It is important to recognize how your cultural beliefs may conflict with those of your students and their families and to interact with students and families in culturally sensitive ways (Obiakor, 1999; Thorp, 1997). Figure 4.9 presents some activities you can use to increase your cultural awareness.

Ensure Confidentiality

You can gain the trust of families by ensuring their right to *confidentiality*, which is specified in the Family Educational Rights and Privacy Act and the IDEA. Educators directly involved in teaching a student may have access to his or her records, but before a school district can allow other persons to review these records, it must obtain consent from the family.

Confidentiality also guarantees the family the opportunity to obtain, review, and challenge their child's educational records. The family can obtain their child's records by

SET YOUR SITES

The Helen A. Kellar Institute for Human disAbilities (www.gse.gmu.edu/depart/chd/chd.htm, 800-333-7958) offers resources and training to promote collaboration between professionals and culturally and linguistically diverse families.

REFLECTIVE

Given families' and students' right to confidentiality, what would you do in the following situations? (1) Teachers are discussing students and their families during lunch in the teachers' lounge. (2) You notice that the students' records in your school are kept in an unsupervised area.

- ◇ Talk to your students and their families about their experiences and culture.
- ◇ Learn about your students' communities.
- ◇ Read books, articles, poetry, short stories, and magazine articles about different cultures.
- ◇ View films, videocassettes, and television shows, and listen to radio shows about different cultures.
- ◇ Attend classes and workshops on different cultures, and visit museums focused on different cultures.
- ◇ Use the Internet to obtain information about and interact with others from different cultures.
- ◇ Travel to places inside and outside the United States that reflect cultural diversity.
- ◇ Learn from knowledgeable community members from different cultures.
- ◇ Work with colleagues, students, and community members from different cultures.
- ◇ Socialize with friends and neighbors from different cultures.
- ◇ Volunteer to work in a community agency that serves individuals from different cultures.
- ◇ Participate in community events, celebrations, and festivals of different cultures.
- ◇ Join professional organizations that are committed to meeting the needs of individuals from different cultures.

FIGURE 4.9 Activities to promote cultural awareness.
Source: Fradd (1993), Garcia and Malkin (1993), and Hyun and Fowler (1995)

requesting a copy, which the school district must provide. However, the family may have to pay the expenses incurred in duplicating the records. If the family disagrees with these records, the family can challenge them by asking school officials to correct or delete the information or by writing a response to be included in the records.

Meet Regularly with Families

You can foster communication with families and increase their involvement by improving the quality of family–teacher conferences. These steps are discussed here.

Plan the Meeting

Plan carefully for the meeting by identifying the reasons for the meeting and developing an appropriate agenda. The agenda should allow enough time to discuss and resolve issues and address concerns of families and other educators. These issues and concerns can be determined by contacting others *before* the meeting. Share the agenda with families and other participants, and give them the necessary background information to take part in the meeting (Wilson, 1995). Materials such as work samples, test results, and other teachers' comments related to agenda items and student performance can be organized and sent to participants beforehand. Give family members a list of questions or suggestions to help them participate in the meeting, and tell them which school personnel will also be there. For example, before the meeting, you can ask family members to be prepared to discuss their perceptions of their child's feelings about school, interests, hobbies, strengths and weaknesses, as well as the questions they have.

Good planning also ensures that the meeting time is convenient for families and professionals. Families can be contacted early on to determine what times and dates are best for them, to encourage them to invite persons who are important to them, and to determine if they need help with transportation or child care (Hyun & Fowler, 1995). Once the meeting has been scheduled, you can contact families and professionals in advance to give them the time, place, purpose, and duration of the meeting and to confirm that

SET YOUR SITES

Family and school–family partnership organizations such as the PTA (www.pta.org, 312-670-6782) and the National Network of Partnership Schools (www.csos.jhu.edu/p2000, 410-516-8818) offer resources to help family members and educators work collaboratively.

they will be there. Follow-up reminders to families via mail, e-mail, or telephone will make them more likely to attend.

Structure the Environment to Promote Communication

The setting for the conference can be organized for sharing information (Jordan, Reyes-Blanes, Peel, Peel, & Lane, 1998). Comfortable, same-size furniture can be used by all participants and arranged to promote communication. Barriers such as desks and chairs should not be placed between families and teachers. Chairs can be placed around a table or positioned so that all persons can see each other.

Welcome family members and other participants, engage in pleasant, informal conversation before the meeting starts, and offer refreshments. This will help participants feel comfortable and establish rapport (Perl, 1995). To improve participation and follow-up, you can ask the participants if they would like pads and pencils to take notes and give them name tags.

To make sure that the meeting is not interrupted, post a note on the door indicating that a conference is in session. Distractions caused by the telephone can be minimized by taking the phone off the hook, asking the office to hold all calls, or using a room that does not have a phone.

Conduct the Conference

You should conduct the conference in a way that encourages understanding and participation. Ask participants to introduce themselves, and review the agenda and the purpose of the meeting. The meeting can start on a positive note, with participants discussing the strong points of the student's performance. Next, participants can review any concerns they have about the student. They should present information in a way that is understandable to all and share materials such as work samples, test results, and anecdotal records to support and illustrate their comments.

You can ask families to discuss the issues or situations from their perspective or to respond to open-ended questions. Family sharing at meetings can be increased by listening attentively; by being empathetic; by acknowledging and reinforcing participation ("That's a good point"; "I'll try to incorporate that"); by avoiding asking questions that have yes/no or implied answers; by asking questions that encourage family members to respond rather than waiting for them to ask questions or spontaneously speak their minds; by informing them that there may be several solutions to a problem; by not criticizing family members; by using language that is understandable but not condescending; by checking periodically for understanding; by paraphrasing and summarizing the comments of family members; and by showing respect for families and their feelings (Cronin, Slade, Bechtel, & Anderson, 1992; Wilson, 1995).

You can adjust the structure of the meeting, depending on how the family prefers to communicate (Linan-Thompson & Jean, 1997). For families that value personal relationships, you can create a friendly, open, and personal environment by demonstrating concern for family members, sitting close by, and using self-disclosure, humor, and casual conversation (Ramirez, 1989). Other families may be goal-oriented and respond to professionals they perceive as competent and organized (Nagata, 1989). These families may expect you to structure the meeting, set goals, define roles, and ask questions of family members.

End the meeting on a positive note by summarizing the issues discussed, points of agreement and disagreement, strategies to be used to resolve problems, and roles to be played by family members and educators. At the end of the meeting, participants can

1. Welcome participants.
2. Introduce parents and professionals, including an explanation of the roles of each professional and the services they provide to the student.
3. Discuss the purpose of the meeting and review the agenda.
4. Review relevant information from prior meetings.
5. Discuss student's needs and performance from the perspective of the professionals. Educators support their statements with work samples, test results, and anecdotal records.
6. Give family members the opportunity to discuss their view of their child's progress and needs.
7. Discuss comments of family members and professionals attempting to achieve a consensus.
8. Determine a plan of action.
9. Summarize and review the results of the meeting.
10. Determine an appropriate date for the next meeting.
11. Adjourn the meeting.
12. Evaluate the meeting.

FIGURE 4.10   Sample schedule for a family–educators' conference.

agree on a plan of action, establish ongoing communications systems, and set a date for the next meeting. A sample schedule of activities for a family–educators' conference is presented in Figure 4.10.

Teleconferencing

Recent technological advances now allow school districts to conduct meetings via telecommunications that allow families to participate without leaving work or their homes. When using telecommunications, you should ensure that the technology gives all participants immediate access to all the information presented and allows them to interact directly and actively throughout the meeting. Before the meeting, all participants should receive copies of the materials that will be discussed and referred to at the meeting.

Address the Diverse Needs, Backgrounds, and Experiences of Families

Families, like students, have diverse needs, backgrounds, and experiences. In communicating and collaborating with families, be aware of these factors and adapt your style and services accordingly to promote family involvement.

Cultural Factors

Families are interested in their children's education, but different cultural perspectives often make it hard to establish traditional school–family interactions (Bailey, Skinner, Rodriguez, Gut, & Correa, 1999; Sileo & Prater, 1998). In designing culturally sensitive programs to involve and empower families, you should adjust to the family's level of acculturation, beliefs about schooling, prior experience with discrimination, structure, child-rearing practices, developmental expectations, perceptions of disability, emotional responses, and communication patterns. These factors will now be discussed.

Level of Acculturation   The level of *acculturation,* the extent to which members of one culture adapt to a new culture, will affect a family's cultural perspective. Because children tend to acculturate faster than adults, children may perform some roles in the

REFLECTING ON YOUR PRACTICES

Evaluating Meetings with Families

You can evaluate your meetings with families by considering the following questions:

◆ Was I prepared, and did I help others prepare for the meeting?
◆ Did I schedule the meetings at a time and place that was convenient for the family members and other participants?
◆ Did I allow enough time for the meeting?
◆ Did I ask for suggestions from the family and other participants about the agenda?
◆ Did I create a welcoming, respectful, and comfortable environment that encouraged participants to share their perspectives and work collaboratively?
◆ Did the meeting occur without interruptions?
◆ Did the meeting address the issues participants wanted to discuss?
◆ Did all participants have enough opportunities and time to present their opinions?
◆ Did participants discuss the strong points of the student's performance?

◆ Did I use student work samples to support my comments?
◆ Did I listen attentively, and acknowledge and encourage participation?
◆ Did I communicate in a clear, nonthreatening manner using language that others could understand?
◆ Did I adjust the content, structure, tone, and interaction patterns of the meeting to be consistent with the family's cultural background?
◆ Did I end the meeting effectively?
◆ Was the family's confidentiality protected?
◆ Which aspects of the meeting did I like the best? Which did I like the least?
◆ Was I and the family satisfied with the outcome(s) of the meeting?

How would you rate the quality of your meetings with families? ( ) Excellent ( ) Good ( ) Needs Improvement ( ) Needs Much Improvement

What steps could you take to improve your meetings with families?

---

new culture that adults assumed in their native country, such as interacting with social institutions like schools (Nahme-Huang & Ying, 1989). These roles involve time and stress and the dependence of adult family members on children. This can have a significant impact on adult–child relationships and the student's academic performance.

Beliefs About Schooling   Family members' beliefs about schooling and their own experiences in schools as students also can affect their involvement in school (Thorp, 1997). Family members with limited schooling or negative experiences as students may not feel comfortable participating in family–school activities. These beliefs and experiences also can influence what they expect of schools.

Prior Experience with Discrimination   Many families may have suffered discrimination, which can influence their behavior and attitudes. These families may not want to attend meetings at the school if they or others have been discriminated against or treated with disrespect there. You can increase the family's comfort in attending school-related events and establish trust by doing the following:

◆ Inviting important extended family members to school events
◆ Addressing elders first
◆ Referring to family members by their titles, such as Mr., Mrs., Ms., Dr., or Reverend (unless the family indicates not to do so)

⬧ Making school facilities available for community activities
⬧ Speaking to families in a respectful and sincere manner
⬧ Responding in a warm and caring way
⬧ Decorating the school and classrooms with icons from various cultures

Family Structure   Most school-based strategies for involving families focus on the needs of the nuclear family. However, many cultures emphasize the value of the extended family (Cartledge, Kea, & Ida, 2000). For example, many families live in a framework of collective interdependence and kinship interactions. They share resources and services, and offer emotional and social support (Ramirez, 1989). Rather than asking for help from schools in dealing with educational issues, these families may feel more comfortable relying on community members or agencies. Therefore, you need to identify and involve the informal systems that support families.

In many extended families, elders may play an important role in decision making and child care. When working with families that value and rely on extended family members, you can involve all family members in the school program. For example, in writing to families, you could say that all family members are welcome at educational meetings.

Child-rearing Practices, Developmental Expectations and Perceptions of Disability   Families also have different perspectives on child rearing, appropriate behavior, and developmental milestones. For example, many white, middle-class families may stress the importance of children reaching developmental milestones at appropriate ages, but other families may not (LaFromboise & Graff-Low, 1989). Similarly, for some families, independence is a goal for their child, but others may prefer that their child remain a part of the family (Harry et al., 1999). Since the behavioral and developmental expectations of schools and families may conflict, you must work cooperatively with families to develop a culturally sensitive and relevant teaching program. The program should include agreed-on bicultural behaviors, appropriate cultural settings for these behaviors, and cross-cultural criteria for measuring progress.

Families also may have different attitudes toward the meaning of disability and its impact on the family (Craig, Hull, Haggart, & Perez-Selles, 2000). For example, Harry (1995) found that culturally and linguistically diverse families use a broader idea of disability that is often related to the child's ability to function at home and the family's beliefs about the child's future. The family's feelings about the causes of their child's problems may also have a cultural and religious basis (Gonzalez-Alvarez, 1998). They may believe that the child's difficulties are caused by reprisals for rule violations by family members, spirits, failure to avoid taboos, fate, choice, and lifestyle imbalances (Locust, 1994; Nagata, 1989). Families also may not accept Western views of medicine and technology. Therefore, you may have to address these issues before families accept and respond to traditional educational strategies.

Emotional Responses   Because families also have different emotional responses related to having a child with a disability, you need to understand these responses and adjust your services accordingly (Bedard, 1995; Gonzalez-Alvarez, 1998). Healey (1996) and Smith (1997) noted that families may go through several stages of adjustment as they learn to accept their child's disability. These stages, which vary from family to family based on experience, culture, and socioeconomic level, include:

Stage 1: Families may be shocked and dejected, and experience grief and fear.
Stage 2: Families may be confused, deny their child's disability, reject their child, or avoid dealing with the issue/situation by looking for other explanations.

INFORMATIONAL

Locust (1994) offers information about the cultural beliefs and traditional behaviors of Native Americans that may affect the teaching of Native American students with disabilities.

Stage 3: Families may experience anger, self-pity, disappointment, guilt, and a sense of powerlessness that may be expressed as rage or withdrawal.

Stage 4: Families may start to understand and accept their child's disability and its impact on the family.

Stage 5: Families may accept, love, and appreciate their child unconditionally.

Stage 6: Families may begin to focus on living, on the future, and on working with others to teach and provide support services to their child.

SET YOUR SITES

The National Information Center for Children and Youth with Disabilities (www.nichcy.org, 800-695-0285) provides information, resources, and a directory of organizations that help families of children with special needs.

In addition to helping families as they go through these stages, be aware of the coping strategies that families use and consider these strategies when designing and delivering services. You also can aid families by being honest with them, showing compassion, and encouraging them to obtain supportive services, communicate with other family members and other important persons in their lives, join family-support groups, ask questions, and express their emotions.

Cross-Cultural Communication Patterns   Communication patterns that differ from one culture to another can make it hard to develop trusting relationships between you and your students' families (Bruns & Fowler, 1999). Be sensitive to differences in communication styles, and interpret verbal and nonverbal behaviors within a social and cultural context. For example, eye contact, wait time, word meanings, facial and physical gestures, voice quality, personal space, and physical contact have different meanings in various cultures. You also need to understand that communications between cultures are affected by turn taking, by physical closeness or distance, and by spoken and unspoken rules of conversation. For example, in some cultures "yes" connotes "I heard you" rather than agreement. Similarly, individuals from some cultures may interpret laughter as a sign of embarrassment rather than enjoyment.

REFLECTIVE

Think about several persons you talk to regularly. How do their communication styles differ in terms of eye contact, wait time, word meanings, facial and physical gestures, voice quality, personal space, and physical contact? How do these differences affect you? How do you adjust your communication style to accommodate these differences?

Cultural differences also may affect communication, the discussion of certain issues, and the ways in which families view, seek, and receive assistance (Thorp, 1997). Nagata (1989) noted that some Japanese American families may not feel comfortable discussing personal problems and concerns, viewing that behavior as being self-centered or as losing face. Locust (1994) reported that some Native American groups who accept the idea of "holding the future" may not discuss a person's future because they believe that negative or limiting comments about the person's future can cause those bad situations to happen. Some families may not want to interact with the school staff because they believe that teachers know what is best for their children and that it is not appropriate for them to question the authority of teachers. Community members who understand the family's needs, emotional responses, and culture can help break down these communication barriers by helping you to understand and interpret the family's communication behaviors; serving as liaisons among schools, families, and communities; and orienting new families to the school (Halford, 1996).

Linguistic Factors

INFORMATIONAL

Many school districts are establishing multilingual hot lines to communicate school-related information to families in their native languages.

Language factors also may block communication between schools and families (Zetlin, Padron, & Wilson, 1996). Communication difficulties may be compounded by problems in understanding educational jargon and practices that may not exist in the families' language and culture. For example, some families from different cultural and language backgrounds believe that special education implies a program that is better than general education. You can correct this misconception by giving these families forms, lists of key educational terms, and information about their rights in their native languages. Learning greetings and words in the family's native language also can create a positive environment that promotes communication and respect.

Interpreters can be used to promote communication between English-speaking educators and families who speak other languages (Plata, 1993). Interpreters should speak the same dialect as the family; maintain confidentiality; avoid giving personal opinions; seek clarification from families and professionals when they have problems communicating certain information; use reverse translation when exact translations are not possible; show respect for families and professionals; and encourage family members and professionals to speak to each other rather than directing their comments to interpreters (Fradd, 1993). The interpreter will be more effective if you discuss the topics and terminology with the interpreter before the meeting, use nonverbal communication as well as speech, are aware of the nonverbal behaviors of family members, and ask for the interpreter's feedback about the meeting.

While many families may rely on their child to interpret for them in general, the child or other students should not interpret during meetings. Children serving as an interpreter for their family can have a negative impact on the family, as this situation reverses the traditional adult–child relationship (Alvarez, 1995). For children, interpreting places them in the adult role in the family, which can make them anxious and frightened. For adults, being dependent on their child as their interpreter can be considered demeaning. It also may be awkward for family members to share information about their child when the child is interpreting.

Socioeconomic Factors

Many socioeconomic factors also can affect the family's participation in their child's education. Long work schedules, time conflicts, transportation problems, and child care needs can be serious barriers. These barriers can be reduced by the use of home visits. However, many families may consider a home visit intrusive, so you should ask for the family's permission before visiting their home.

IDEAS FOR IMPLEMENTATION

Overcoming Economic Barriers to Family Participation

Ms. Saavedra was concerned that several of her students' families were not able to attend open school night. She contacted several of the families and found that some had transportation problems and others couldn't find a sitter to watch their children. For the next meeting, Ms. Saavedra contacted families in advance to determine if they needed a ride to school. She then organized carpools so that all family members could attend. She also notified families that they could bring their children with them; child care would be provided by students from the high school.

Here are some other strategies you can use to overcome economic barriers to family participation:

- ◆ Conduct activities and meetings at locations in the community.
- ◆ Ask for the support and assistance of persons, groups, and agencies from the community.
- ◆ Structure sessions so that adults and their children are not separated.
- ◆ Schedule meetings at times that are convenient for family members.
- ◆ Use community organizations to share information with families.

Source: Lucas, Henze, and Donato (1990) and Rhodes (1996).

Use Written Communication

INFORMATIONAL

Boone et al. (1999) provide guidelines for preparing written communications to families.

You can use letters and notes to establish ongoing communication with families (Boone, Wolfe & Schaufler, 1999; Williams & Cartledge, 1997). Written communication is often used to share information on students, schedule meetings, and obtain informed consent from families. Look at Figure 4.11, and note how the letters to fam-

---

LETTER A

To Whom It May Concern:

The school district has scheduled a meeting to review your child's educational program. The meeting will be held on March 15, 2001, in the conference room at the administrative offices.

The following members of the school district will be in attendance:

Mrs. Lorraine Hamilton	School Social Worker
Mrs. Constance Franks	Special Education Teacher
Mr. Patrick Hardees	General Education Teacher
Mr. Donald Fein	School Psychologist
Mrs. Joanne Frederick	Principal

If you would like the school physician to be at the meeting, please contact my office at least three days prior to the meeting.

Please contact my office if you plan to attend the meeting. My office will be able to tell you approximately what time your child will be discussed. If you are unable to attend the meeting in person, you may participate by telephone.

The meeting will take place as scheduled unless you request otherwise. I will send the results in writing after the meeting is over. Feel free to contact me with any questions or concerns related to your child's education.

Yours truly,

Donald Smith,

Director of Pupil Personnel Services

LETTER B

Dear Truman Family:

Hello. My name is Donald Smith, and I am the Director of Pupil Personnel Services for the Bellville School District. It is my job to assist you in understanding the educational system and to work with you in creating an educational program that meets the needs of your child.

Your child's teachers would like to schedule a meeting with you to discuss your child's educational program. It is important that you attend this meeting. You know your child better than anyone and can provide important information concerning your child's school performance. You may also wish to bring others with you to attend the meeting. It is also possible for you to request that the school physician attend this meeting.

If you have time, you can do several things to prepare for the meeting. You can talk to your child and his/her teachers about his/her performance in school and the ways to improve his/her learning. You also can visit your child's classroom. It also will be helpful if you bring materials to the meeting such as your child's schoolwork, school records, and reports, as well as medical information. At the meeting, we will talk about the goals for your child's education, the way your child learns best, and his/her favorite activities and interests.

I will be calling you to schedule the meeting at a time that is most convenient for your family and to answer any questions you may have. We also can assist you in attending the meeting by providing you with transportation, child care, and the services of an interpreter. I look forward to speaking with you and working with you to meet the educational needs of your child.

Yours truly,

Donald Smith,

Director of Pupil Personnel Services

FIGURE 4.11   Samples of written correspondence to families.

ily members are different. Which letter is more likely to result in family members attending the meeting? Letter A is impersonal, uses technical terms, places the school's needs above the needs of family members, can intimidate the family, and does little to encourage family participation. Letter B is welcoming and less formal, tries to establish rapport, and respects the family, their scheduling needs, and their contributions to the education of their child. It also avoids professional jargon, encourages participation and collaboration, and gives the family suggestions for preparing for the meeting. You also can increase the effectiveness of your written communication with families by emphasizing positive aspects of students and their families, providing examples, using cultural referents, and monitoring the response rate from family members.

Informative Notice

You can share information with families by using an informative notice (Sicley, 1993). This is a brief written communication that alerts families to various school and classroom activities, student progress, and the materials students will need to complete their assignments. At the beginning of the school year, the informative notice can take two forms: (1) postcards to students welcoming them to your class and (2) letters to families to introduce yourself and various aspects of your classroom, to explain your expectations, and to ask for their support and collaboration (Williams & Cartledge, 1997).

Newsletters

Another form of written communication with families is a newsletter, which can tell them about school and classroom events, extracurricular activities, meetings, school policies, and menus. Family education also can be provided in a newsletter. Students can also produce their own newsletters (Sicley, 1993).

INFORMATIONAL

Translators who help to prepare written communications and community members can help educators develop culturally relevant and sensitively written documents (Fradd & Wilen, 1990).

Daily Note

The *daily note* is a brief note that alerts families to the accomplishments and improvements in their children and other issues of interest or concern (Sicley, 1993). The value of daily notes can be increased by providing a space for family members to write their own messages to you. Daily notes can be made more effective by pairing them with praise from family members. Therefore, when family members receive these positive notes from you, they will be encouraged to read the notes promptly; praise their child in the presence of others; put the note in a prominent location (such as on the refrigerator door) where their child and others are likely to see it; and share their desire to receive additional notes of praise.

Two-Way Notebooks

You also can communicate with families by using two-way notebooks and assignment folders (Wilson, 1995). Two-way notebooks, carried to and from school by students, allow you and family members to exchange comments and information and ask questions. The notebook can have the student's name on it, as well as a place for family members' signatures, the date, and the number of assignments included.

Daily Report Cards

The *daily report card*, a written record of the student's performance in school, is effective in communicating with families. Its content and format will vary, depending on the needs of students, and could include information on academic performance, preparedness for class, effort, behavior, peer relationships, and homework completion. The format should be easy for you to complete and easy for families to interpret. As students demonstrate success over a period of time, the report card can be shared with families weekly, biweekly, and then monthly. A sample daily report card is presented in Figure 4.12.

Student _____   *Date _____

Teacher _____   Class _____

*Please return report on the next school day

Behaviors	Rating					
1. Follows instructions cooperatively.	0	1	2	3	4	5
2. Stays on task.	0	1	2	3	4	5
3. Works quietly.	0	1	2	3	4	5
4. Completes assignments.	0	1	2	3	4	5
5. Remains in assigned area.	0	1	2	3	4	5

Rating Keys:
    0 = very poor
    1 = poor
    2 = fair
    3 = good
    4 = very good
    5 = EXCELLENT!

Teacher Comments   Signature _____   Date _____

_____
_____
_____
_____

Student Comments   Signature _____   Date _____

_____
_____
_____
_____

Parent Comments   Signature _____   Date _____

_____
_____
_____
_____

FIGURE 4.12 Sample daily report card.

Source: Battle, D. A., Dickens-Wright, L. L., & Murphy, S. (1998). How to empower adolescents: Guidelines for effective self-advocacy. *Teaching Exceptional Children, 30*(3), 28–32.

Home-School Contracts

The daily report system also has been used as part of a home-school contract. *Home-school contracts* allow families to reinforce their children's improved academic performance or behavior in school. You observe students in school and report your observations to families, who then deliver reinforcers to their children. These reinforcers take many different forms. Tangible reinforcers include making special foods; buying clothes, music, or software programs; providing money toward the purchase of a desired item; or getting a pet. Families can also use activity reinforcers such as fewer chores, a family activity, trips, a party at the house, a rented video, or a special privilege.

Before using a home-school contract, you can discuss the specifics of the program with the family. This discussion gives both parties an understanding of the behavior to be changed, details of the communication system between home and school, potential reinforcers, and when and how to deliver the reinforcers. Once the system is in place, follow-up communication is critical to talk about the implementation and impact of the system.

Employ Technology-Based Communications

Technological innovations are changing the ways in which schools and families communicate. Many schools and families use websites, e-mail, and telephone answering machines to receive and send messages. For example, families can use these systems to view their children's work online, see what the school is serving for lunch, check on their child's attendance record, or find out what homework has been assigned. You can use technology to provide families with suggestions for teaching specific skills to their children; report on student performance in school; give families information on their rights and specific programs; offer information on local events of interest to students and their families; encourage family members to attend conferences; and recommend books and other learning materials to families. If family members cannot attend a meeting, an e-conference can be conducted with the professional(s). When using technology-based communication systems, you need to protect the confidentiality of students and their families.

The Internet also gives family members access to information, programs, and resources related to their children's needs. For example, *Our Kids* (www.our-kids.org) is an online discussion group for families of children with disabilities, and *Parents Helping Parents* (www.php.com) offers families a database of organizations addressing the needs of students with disabilities.

Encourage Family Observations

Communication between the home and the school can be improved by encouraging family members to observe in the classroom. This experience allows family members to see and understand different aspects of the school environment and student behavior. It gives families the background information needed to discuss school-related concerns with you.

Family members can be prepared for the observation if you review ways to enter the room unobtrusively; locations in the room to sit; suitable times to observe; appropriate reactions to their child and other students; and the need to maintain confidentiality. Before the observation, you can discuss with family members the purpose of the observation and the unique aspects of the educational setting, such as behavior management systems and reading programs. After the observation, you can meet with family members again to discuss what they saw.

REFLECTIVE

Have you used e-mail, the Internet, or a telephone answering machine to communicate with others? What were the advantages and disadvantages? How do these systems affect the communications and the information shared? What skills do teachers and family members need to use these systems effectively and efficiently?

Offer Training to Families

Because family members may need training to perform various roles in the educational process, many schools offer family training as part of their delivery of services to students and their families (Donley & Williams, 1997). When setting up and evaluating family training programs, you, your colleagues, and your students' families can consider the following issues.

Who Should Receive Training?

INFORMATIONAL

Cramer et al. (1997) and Meyer and Vadasy (1994) provide guidelines on offering workshops and activities for siblings of children with special needs.

SET YOUR SITES

Information on resources for siblings of children with disabilities is available from the Sibling Support Project (www.chmc.org/departmt/sibsupp, 206-368-4911) and the Sibling Information Network (www.parentsoup.com/library/organizations/bdfa009.html 203-344-7500).

REFLECTIVE

Do you or someone else have a family member with a disability? How has this individual affected other family members? What types of training would benefit the family?

INFORMATION

Alper, Schloss, and Schloss (1994), McDonald, Kysela, Martin, and Wheaton (1996), and Miller and Hudson (1994) offer guidelines for improving family information sessions, using family support groups, and helping families learn to be advocates for their children, respectively.

SET YOUR SITES

Family-based centers like the Technical Assistance for Parent Programs (www.fcsn.org/tapp/home.htm, 617-482-2915) and the PACER Center (http://pacer.org, 800-53-PACER) offer training, resources, and information for families.

Although most programs train mothers, training should be available to all family members, including fathers, grandparents, and siblings (Sandler, 1998; Seligman, Goodwin, Paschal, Applegate, & Lehman, 1997). For example, training and support can help siblings understand the nature of their brother's or sister's disability and deal with the impact of having a brother or sister with special needs (Cramer et al., 1997; Powell & Gallagher, 1993). Training for siblings can focus on helping them understand the causes of various disabilities; dispelling myths and misconceptions about disabilities; discussing ways of interacting with and assisting their sibling; dealing with unequal treatment and excessive demands; responding to the reactions and questions of their friends and other persons; understanding human differences; and understanding the long-term needs and future of their sibling (Meyer, Vadasy, & Fewell, 1996; Turnbull & Ruef, 1997). Training also can address the concerns siblings may have about their own children being born with a disability.

What Is the Content of the Training Program?

The training program should focus on the needs of family members. Generally, training should give family members the skills to teach their child at home; the ability to communicate and collaborate with professionals serving their child; information on how the child will be taught; the ability to serve as advocates for their child; the counseling and emotional support they need; the information they need to obtain services for their child; and the ways to plan for their child's future. Families of younger children may want training in child care and development, early intervention, discipline, the school's expectations, legal rights of families and children, and finding community resources. Families of adolescents may prefer information on services and agencies that can help them and their children make the transition to the adult world and find employment. Family members who speak languages other than English may benefit from family-based ESL and literacy programs, as well as instruction in the policies and practices of the school district.

Where Will Training Occur?

Training can occur in the home or in the school. Home-based training, which occurs in the family's and child's natural environment, can promote the ability to maintain the skills learned and to use them in many different settings. Home-based training programs are especially appropriate for families who have trouble attending school meetings because of transportation problems or work schedules. School-based training allows many families to be trained as a group, making it easy to share information and experiences. School-based programs also give families the opportunity to meet and interact with many different professionals and families. In some cases, it may be im-

Having a child with a disability may affect the whole family—siblings as well as parents.

portant to conduct the training in nonintimidating, community-based locations such as religious establishments, social clubs, community centers, restaurants, and shopping malls.

How Do You Train Families?

You can use a variety of strategies to train families, including lectures, group discussion, role playing, simulations, presentations by service providers and other family members, and demonstrations. Videocassettes are excellent because they provide a visual image and a model; allow family members and educators to stop the video at any time to discuss, review, or replay the content; and can be viewed in school or at home. Print materials and training programs for families are also available from state education departments, as well as from local groups serving families and professional organizations. Family training programs and materials can be previewed by contacting various family-based organizations.

Experienced, skilled, and highly respected family members can be a valuable resource for training other families. These individuals can share their knowledge and experience with other family members, and provide emotional support and information on the services available in the community.

INFORMATIONAL

Searcy, Lee-Lawson, and Trombino (1995) offer guidelines for using family members as mentors to help educate other family members.

SUMMARY

This chapter provided guidelines for establishing an inclusive environment that supports the learning of *all students* by creating collaborative relationships and fostering communication among professionals, families, and community members. As you review the questions posed in this chapter, remember the following points.

Who Are the Members of the Comprehensive Planning Team?

The comprehensive planning team may consist of general and special educators, administrators, support personnel such as speech and language therapists, bilingual educators, paraeducators, volunteers, family members, peers, local community resources, and professional and family-based organizations. The members of the team vary, depending on the needs of students, families, and educators.

How Can Members of the Comprehensive Planning Team Work Collaboratively?

Members of the comprehensive planning team can work collaboratively by using collaborative and interactive teaming, MAPS, cooperative teaching, and collaborative consultation, as well as by promoting congruence.

How Can I Foster Communication and Collaboration with Families?

You can foster communication and collaboration with families by gaining their trust, ensuring confidentiality, meeting regularly with families, addressing their needs, backgrounds, and experiences, using written and technology-based communication, encouraging family members to observe at the school, and offering training to families.

 ## What Would You Do in Today's Diverse Classroom?

As a teacher in an inclusion classroom, you encounter the following situations:

◇ Ms. Singer, your paraeducator, and Billy, one of your students with disabilities, have developed a comfortable working relationship. It's become so comfortable that they are both reluctant to work with others. You also notice that Ms. Singer anticipates Billy's needs before he expresses himself.

◇ When you volunteered to work in a cooperative teaching team, you and your partner were excited about the possibility of using a variety of teaching arrangements. However, you find that your team is using the same format, with the same teacher taking the lead while the other teacher monitors individual students.

◇ You have held several meetings and provided activities for families. You notice that the same people keep attending these sessions and that many families of color are not able to attend.

◇ One of your students has been acting as the class clown and fails to complete his schoolwork. His family is concerned and believes that he should receive special education services. Although you are also concerned about the student, you do not believe he needs special education services.

1. What problem(s) are you encountering in each situation?
2. What would you do to address the situation?
3. What strategies, resources, and support services could help you in addressing the situation?

CHAPTER 5

CREATING AN ENVIRONMENT THAT FOSTERS ACCEPTANCE AND FRIENDSHIP

Mr. Monroig

One of Mr. Monroig's goals is to teach his students how to interact with, understand, and accept others. In his teaching, Mr. Monroig uses Easy or Hard? That's a Good Question *(Tobias, 1977), a children's book that makes the point that all people are similar in some ways and different in other ways, and that certain things are easy for some people and hard for others.*

Mr. Monroig begins the lesson by asking his students to identify two things that are easy and two things that are hard for them to do. He then divides the classroom in half, with one side of the room labeled the easy side (he puts an "EZ" sign on that side of the room) and the other side the hard side (he puts a sign with a rock on that side of the room). After reading each "easy" or "hard" sequence in the book, he has students indicate whether the behavior or task mentioned in the book is easy or hard for them by moving to the easy or hard side of the classroom. Periodically, he notes the similarities and differences between the students' responses and records them on a "same/different" chart.

After completing the book, Mr. Monroig asks students to identify aloud two things they feel were easy and the two things that were hard to do. Again, he notes the similarities and differences in their responses. He then discusses with the class some of the factors that affect the ease with which one can perform a task. He asks them to identify things that would be easy or hard to do if they:

had difficulty reading
used a wheelchair
didn't understand English
couldn't hold a pencil

couldn't see
couldn't hear

Mr. Monroig then has the students perform various tasks with and without a simulated difficulty. He has students watch a television show in Spanish and walk around the classroom blindfolded. As follow-up activities, he asked students, "What was hard for you?" and "How did it feel?" He concludes by asking students, "If you knew someone who found something hard to do, what could you do to show that person that you understand that some things are hard?"

What other strategies can Mr. Monroig use to help his students understand and accept individual differences and develop friendships? After reading this chapter, you should be able to answer these as well as the following questions:

◆ How do attitudes toward individual differences develop?
◆ How can I assess attitudes toward individual differences?
◆ How can I teach acceptance of individual differences related to disability?
◆ How can I teach acceptance of individual differences related to culture, language, gender, and socioeconomic status?
◆ How can I facilitate friendships?

Like Mr. Monroig's classroom, today's classrooms include students with a variety of individual differences. These differences can be a rich source of learning for *all students,* but they also can create divisions and conflicts between students that you will need to address. Therefore, rather than assuming that your students respect and accept one another, an important goal of your inclusive classroom is to teach *all students* to appreciate diversity, and to value and learn from each other's similarities and differences.

Teaching students to accept and appreciate the value of individual differences can be integrated into your curriculum. This will facilitate the acceptance of *all students* and establish a sense of community in the classroom (Coots et al., 1998). It can also help your students understand that they are more similar to each other than different, and can identify their unique strengths and weaknesses, likes and dislikes. Finally, it can help reduce name-calling, staring, and the formation of exclusive cliques and make it easier for students to develop friendships.

How Do Attitudes Toward Individual Differences Develop?

REFLECTIVE

When you were growing up, did you have opportunities to interact with children and adults with disabilities? How did these experiences help you understand and accept individual differences?

Research shows that by the age of 4, students are aware of and curious about cultural and physical differences. Unfortunately, because of the environment in which they are raised, many students enter school holding misconceptions and stereotypic views about persons they perceive as different (Pang, 1991).

Most studies show that students who do not have disabilities have negative attitudes toward their peers who do, and this often causes them to reject students with disabilities (Roberts & Zubrick, 1992). For example, Reid and Button (1995) studied narratives written by students with disabilities. At school these students experienced isolation ("I [had] nobody to play with . . . I had almost no friends . . . I mean nobody really cared about how I felt" [p. 609]) and victimization ("They always called me names. . . . People call us retarded . . . or tell lies about you [and] it makes you feel mad" [p. 608]).

Factors such as cultural background, gender, age, and socioeconomic status may interact with disability to influence the acceptance of students. General education students tend to be more accepting of students with sensory and physical disabilities and less accepting of students with learning and emotional problems. Wealthy students with disabilities are viewed more positively by their classmates than those who are poor, and girls with learning disabilities are more likely than boys with learning disabilities to be rejected by their peers. However, female and younger students tend to have more favorable attitudes toward students with disabilities.

Many factors lead to the development of negative attitudes toward students with individual differences. The way children are raised limits interactions between them based on disability, race, and language abilities. Attitudes toward persons who have disabilities, speak different languages, and have different cultures also are shaped by the media, which tend to portray these groups negatively.

REFLECTIVE

How are persons with disabilities and those from various cultural and linguistic backgrounds pictured in books, television shows, movies, and cartoons? How do these portrayals affect your and your students' understanding and acceptance of individual differences?

HOW CAN I ASSESS ATTITUDES TOWARD INDIVIDUAL DIFFERENCES?

It is important to understand your students' attitudes toward and knowledge of individual differences so that you can plan appropriate activities. In addition to using observations and sociograms to assess your students' social interactions (see Chapter 12), you can use the techniques described below to determine your students' knowledge and acceptance of individual differences.

Attitude Assessment Instruments

Several instruments have been developed to assess attitudes toward individuals with disabilities. One of them is the *Acceptance Scale*, which includes elementary and secondary versions (Antonak & Livneh, 1988). Students indicate their agreement with ("Yes, I agree"), disagreement with ("No, I disagree"), or uncertainty about ("Maybe, I'm not sure") negatively ("I wouldn't spend my recess with a kid with a disability") and positively ("I believe I could become close friends with a special education student") phrased items. The *Personal Attribute Inventory for Children (PAIC)* (Parish, Ohlsen, & Parish, 1978) is an alphabetically arranged checklist consisting of 24 negative and 24 positive adjectives that asks students to select 15 adjectives that best describe a particular student or group of students. Billings (1963) developed a two-step procedure that uses pictures to measure attitudes. First, students view a picture; then they write a story about the child in the picture. In the second step, students again write a story, but this time they are told that the child in the picture has a disability.

These instruments can be adapted to assess attitudes toward persons with other types of individual differences by modifying the directions. For example, the Acceptance Scale can be adapted by asking students to complete each item with respect to individuals who speak a language other than English. You also can adapt these instruments by simplifying the language, phrasing items in a true-false format, and using pictorials. Picture-oriented attitude scales are especially appropriate for measuring the attitudes of young students.

YES	☐		
NO	☐	1.	Is a person with a disability usually sick?
NOT SURE	☐		
YES	☐		
NO	☐	2.	Can a person who is blind go to the store?
NOT SURE	☐		
YES	☐		
NO	☐	3.	If someone can't talk, do you think he's retarded?
NOT SURE	☐		
YES	☐		
NO	☐	4.	Were people with disabilities born that way?
NOT SURE	☐		
YES	☐		
NO	☐	5.	Do you feel sorry for someone who is disabled?
NOT SURE	☐		
YES	☐		
NO	☐	6.	Can blind people hear the same as other people?
NOT SURE	☐		
YES	☐		
NO	☐	7.	If a person is retarded, does it mean that he/she will never grow up?
NOT SURE	☐		
YES	☐		
NO	☐	8.	Are all deaf people alike?
NOT SURE	☐		
YES	☐		
NO	☐	9.	Can a person in a wheelchair be a teacher?
NOT SURE	☐		
YES	☐		
NO	☐	10.	Do all children have a right to go to your school?
NOT SURE	☐		

FIGURE 5.1   Sample probe on disabilities.

Source: E. Barnes, C. Berrigan, and D. Biklen, *What's the difference? Teaching positive attitudes toward people with disabilities* (Syracuse, NY: Human Policy Press, 1978), p. 5. Copyright 1978. Reprinted by permission of the publisher.

Knowledge of Individual Differences Probes

You also can use individual differences probes to assess your students' understanding of differences and factual knowledge about various groups ("What does it mean to have a learning disability?"); stereotypic views of others (True or false: " Homeless people are adults who don't work and choose to be homeless"); needs of other individuals ("What are three things that you would have difficulty doing in this classroom if you didn't speak English?"); ways to interact with others ("If you had a hearing impairment, how would you want others to interact with you?"); and devices and aids designed to help individuals ("What is a device that a student with one arm could use?"). A sample probe on disabilities is presented in Figure 5.1.

Student Drawings

Having students draw a picture of a scene depicting other individuals can be a valuable way of assessing their attitudes. To assess students' feelings accurately, you can also ask them to write a story explaining their picture. For example, examine the picture in Figure 5.2. How

FIGURE 5.2   Student drawing depicting an individual with a disability.

would you rate the attitude toward individuals with disabilities of the student who drew this picture? At first, the drawing may suggest that the student has a negative attitude. However, the accompanying story shows the student's attitude much more clearly. The student explained the picture by stating, "People with disabilities are almost always made fun of. This picture shows a person with a disability crying because of the way other people laugh at him. Put yourself in his position."

HOW CAN I TEACH ACCEPTANCE OF INDIVIDUAL DIFFERENCES RELATED TO DISABILITY?

Attitude Change and Information-Sharing Strategies

When students have negative attitudes toward individuals they view as different, you can foster positive attitudes by using a variety of *attitude change* and *information-sharing strategies.* A key factor in the success of these strategies is to establish an *equal-status relationship,* in which both parties view each other as equal in social, educational, or vocational status. To be successful, attitude change strategies should provide information, direct contact, and experiences that counter stereotyped views of others perceived as different.

Many different strategies to change attitudes, share information, and teach students about individual differences are described in this chapter. Figure 5.3 is a checklist for selecting a strategy that works in your own classroom situation. You also can get help from students, their families, and other educators in planning and implementing these strategies (Denti & Meyers, 1997).

Many of the strategies used to teach acceptance of individual differences related to disability can be adapted to teach students about individual differences related to culture, language, gender, and socioeconomic status as well.

Teacher Attitudes and Behaviors

REFLECTIVE

What are your attitudes and behaviors in regard to individual differences? Are there individual differences with which you feel comfortable? Uncomfortable? How do you reveal these attitudes to others? How did you develop these attitudes and behaviors?

Teachers like Mr. Monroig can begin to create a classroom environment that accepts diversity by examining their own attitudes and behaviors concerning individual differences and the inclusion of various types of learners (Davern, 1999; Huntze, 1994). Because students look up to and are influenced by their teachers, you can serve as a role model by demonstrating attitudes and behaviors that show you are comfortable with individual differences and respect *all of your students* (Giangreco et al., 1995). You also can show how to interact with students, provide opportunities for social interactions between students, and comment positively when students interact appropriately (Calloway, 1999). Finally, when referring to students, you can model appropriate language by avoiding language that sets students apart or describes them in terms of their abilities, disabilities, cultural backgrounds, sex, or interests (e.g., "our CP kids" or the use of nicknames for students with unusual names). It is important to act promptly and decisively when students act inappropriately and hurt others. You can also promote the status of *all students* by being aware of their interests, hobbies, and talents, sharing this information with others, and giving *all students* opportunities to act as leaders.

Several attitude change strategies exist. You can determine which strategy to use in your classroom by answering the following questions:

❖   Is the strategy appropriate for my students?
❖   What skills do I need to implement the strategy? Do I have these skills?
❖   What resources do I need to implement the strategy? Do I have these resources?
❖   Does the strategy teach critical information about the group and the acceptance of individual differences?
❖   Does the strategy present positive, nonstereotypic examples of the group?
❖   Does the strategy establish an equal-status relationship?
❖   Does the strategy offer students activities in which to learn about the group and individual differences?
❖   Does the strategy promote follow-up activities and additional opportunities for learning about the group and individual differences?

FIGURE 5.3   Attitude change strategy checklist.

REFLECTING ON PROFESSIONAL PRACTICES

Empowering Language

Ms. Ryan, a teacher education student, realized that her field placement in the FDR School gave her a lot of "food for thought." While she was learning about assessment, curriculum, teaching, and working with students and their families, several incidents forced her to reflect on the issues of teacher behavior and the language used in special education and their effects on students and professionals.

The first incident occurred during an informal conversation with a teacher while the students were working. The teacher nodded toward a student who was struggling with his work and said, "Can you believe he was supposed to be mainstreamed?" The second incident occurred later that same day. As the teacher prepared materials for a math assessment, the paraeducator approached her and asked, "They get to use calculators?" The teacher responded, "Well, they are special education students."

During the third incident, Ms. Ryan observed another teacher who approached her students' differences in a very different way. One student asked the teacher why another student received extra time to complete an assignment, saying, "That's not fair." The teacher responded, "Just like you, all the students in the class are learning new things in their own ways. In this class, we do not expect everyone to learn, look, sound, and act the same." Later, the teacher told the students, "In your

lives, you are going to meet a lot of people who are different from you, and it is these differences that make life special. Think about how boring it would be if we were all the same."

The final incident occurred when Ms. Ryan attended a planning team meeting that included a student and the student's family. The team discussed the student's needs, rather than the student's disability category, and strategies to enhance learning. Team members and the student noted that "he was good at some things and had difficulty with other things." The teachers listened carefully to the comments made by the student and the family and said that they believed that the student could succeed in their classroom. They told the student that "trying is one of the stepping stones to learning."

How did the behaviors and language of the teachers in the first two incidents differ from the behaviors and language of the teachers in the second two incidents? How were the students, teachers, and family members affected by the language associated with special education and individual differences? How can you use language and behaviors that show your acceptance of individual differences? How can you help students discuss their individual differences in empowering ways?

Source: Ryan (September 17, 1998; personal communication).

Disability Simulations

A very effective method that Mr. Monroig used to teach his students about individuals with disabilities was the use of *disability simulations*, in which students experience how it feels to have a disability (Horne, 1998). In addition to demonstrating the difficulties encountered by individuals with disabilities, simulations expose students to the adaptations that individuals with disabilities use. Simulations of varying disabilities and sample follow-up questions are presented in Figure 5.4.

When using simulations, you need to be aware of some limitations. Attitude changes related to simulations tend to be brief and may result in a feeling of sympathy. You also need to make sure that students don't trivialize the experience and think that having a disability is fun and games (e.g., wheeling around in a wheelchair). You can counter these limited reactions and make the simulations more effective by using several guidelines. You can select simulations that are as realistic as possible and tell the students that they must take the activities seriously and not quit until they are complete.

INFORMATIONAL

Additional simulation activities are available in Freedman-Harvey and Johnson (1998), Horne (1998), Hallenback and McMaster (1991), Raschke and Dedrick (1986), and Wesson and Mandell (1989).

VISUAL IMPAIRMENT SIMULATIONS

Activity

Have students wear blindfolds during part of the school day. Blindfold one student and assign another student as a helper to follow the blindfolded student around the room and building. Periodically, have the helper and the blindfolded student change roles. Structure the activity so that students must move around in the classroom, eat a meal, go to the bathroom, and move to other classes. Have the blindfolded student complete a form, with the helper providing verbal assistance only.

Follow-up Questions

1. What difficulties did you have during the activity? What difficulties did you observe as a helper?
2. What did you do that helped you perform the activities without seeing?
3. What did the helper do to help you perform the activities?
4. What changes could be made in school to assist students who can't see? At home?

HEARING IMPAIRMENT SIMULATIONS

Activity

Show a movie or video without the sound. Ask students questions that can be answered only after having heard the sound. Show the same film or video again with the sound and have students respond to the same questions.

Follow-up Questions

1. How did your answers differ?
2. What information did you use to answer the questions after the first viewing?

PHYSICAL DISABILITIES SIMULATIONS

Activity

Put a dowel rod in the joints of the students' elbows while their arms are positioned behind their backs. Ask students to try to comb their hair, tie their shoes, write a story, draw, and eat.

Follow-up Questions

1. Were you successful at combing your hair? Tying your shoes? Writing the story? Drawing? Eating?
2. What other activities would you have difficulty doing if you had limited use of your hands?
3. Are there any strategies or devices that you could use to perform the tasks?

Activity

Place students in wheelchairs and have them maneuver around the classroom and the school. Structure the activity so that students attempt to drink from a water fountain, write on the blackboard, make a phone call, go to the bathroom, and transfer themselves onto a toilet. Because of the potential architectural barriers in the school, have a same-sex peer assist and observe the student in the wheelchair.

Follow-up Questions

1. What difficulties did you encounter in maneuvering around the school?
2. What were the reactions of other students who saw you in the wheelchair? How did their reactions make you feel?
3. What are some barriers that would make it hard for a person who uses a wheelchair to move around on a street? In a store?
4. What modifications can make it easier for individuals who use wheelchairs to maneuver in schools? In streets, stores, or homes?

FIGURE 5.4 Sample disability simulations and follow-up questions.

Source: Hochman (1979).

SPEECH IMPAIRMENT SIMULATIONS

Activity

Assign students in pairs. Have one student try to communicate messages to the other by using physical gestures only, by talking without moving the tongue, and by using a communication board.

Follow-up Questions

1. What strategies did you use to communicate the message?
2. How did you understand your partner's message?
3. If you had difficulty talking, how would you want others to talk to you?

LEARNING DISABILITIES SIMULATIONS

Activity

Place a mirror and a sheet of paper on the students' desks so that students can see the reflection of the paper in the mirror. Have the students write a sentence and read a paragraph while looking in the mirror. Then have the students do the same tasks without looking in the mirror. Compare their ability to do the tasks under the two different conditions.

Follow-up Questions

1. What difficulties did you experience in writing and reading while looking in the mirror?
2. How did it feel to have difficulty writing and reading?
3. What other tasks would be hard if you saw this way all the time?

FIGURE 5.4 (continued)

During the simulations, you can assign an observer to watch and, if necessary, help students who are participating in the activities. Afterward, you can have students reflect on the simulations by conducting group discussions and by asking students to write about their experiences. A participant reaction form that can be used to help students reflect on their experiences is presented in Figure 5.5.

Successful Individuals with Disabilities

Many famous individuals have some type of disability. Lessons and assignments on the achievements of highly successful individuals with disabilities, and how they dealt with and compensated for their disability, can help present disabilities in a more positive light (Jairrels, Brazil, & Patton, 1999). You can have students write about a friend or relative who has a disability or complete a research report on the causes of different disabilities.

Guest Speakers

You can expose students directly to individuals with disabilities by inviting to class guest speakers who have disabilities (Calloway, 1999; Denti & Meyers, 1997). You can find potential guest speakers by contacting local community agencies, professional and advocacy organizations, and special education teachers. Meet with any potential speakers to determine how relevant and appropriate it would be to invite them.

Once a speaker has been selected, you can meet with this individual to discuss the goals of the presentation and possible topics to be covered. Speakers may want to address such topics as the problems they encounter now, as well as those they experienced when

REFLECTIVE

Simulate several disabilities for part or all of a day. How did the simulations make you feel? How did others treat you? What problems did you experience? What did you learn? How did you adapt to the various disabilities?

they were the students' age; school and childhood experiences; hobbies and interests; family; jobs; a typical day; future plans; causes of their disability; ways to prevent their disability (if possible); adaptations they need; ways of interacting with others; and adaptive devices they use. Speakers can be encouraged to speak in a language that your students can understand, and use short anecdotes and humorous stories that present their independent lives in a positive light.

To help speakers tailor their remarks to students, you can provide background information about the class (age level, grade level, exposure to and understanding of disabilities) and possible questions students may ask. Before the speaker comes to class, you can have students identify the questions they have about the disability to be discussed. Because some students may hesitate to ask questions, you can help overcome their reluctance by initially asking the speaker some of the questions the students previously identified.

PARTICIPANT REACTION FORM

Participant's Name_____

Activity _____   Date_____

I. Describe your reactions to this activity by completing the following:
   1. Describe your behaviors during the activity. What did you do?
   2. Describe your emotions during the activity. How did you feel after the activity?
   3. How were your reactions to this experience different than what you expected? Explain.

II. Rate your reactions to the activity on the scale provided.
   SD = strongly disagree   D = disagree   A = agree   SA = strongly agree

1. This activity made me feel incompetent.	SD	D	A	SA
2. This activity was easier to do than expected.	SD	D	A	SA
3. One of the worst things in the world would be to do this activity every day for the rest of my life.	SD	D	A	SA
4. This activity made me feel dumb.	SD	D	A	SA
5. This activity was fun to do.	SD	D	A	SA
6. This activity made me think a long time about this disability.	SD	D	A	SA
7. This activity made me feel helpless.	SD	D	A	SA

III. Rate your reactions to persons with this disability by completing the following.
   SD = strongly disagree   D = disagree   A = agree   SA = strongly agree

1. A person with this disability would have a hard time having a boyfriend or girlfriend.	SD	D	A	SA
2. A person with this disability could never have a professional occupation.	SD	D	A	SA
3. A person with this disability would have a very hard time being a parent.	SD	D	A	SA
4. A person with this disability would have a hard time liking him or herself.	SD	D	A	SA
5. A person with this disability needs a lot of assistance keeping house.	SD	D	A	SA
6. A person with this disability has few friends.	SD	D	A	SA
7. A person with this disability would probably never be able to vote in national elections.	SD	D	A	SA
8. A person with this disability cannot keep track of his or her own finances.	SD	D	A	SA
9. A person with this disability has few leisure activities he or she really enjoys.	SD	D	A	SA
10. A person with this disability would enjoy coming to visit me at my house.	SD	D	A	SA

FIGURE 5.5   Simulation participant reaction form.

Source: Simulations promote understanding of handicapping conditions by C. Wesson and C. Mandell, *Teaching Exceptional Children,* vol. 21, 1989, p. 34. Copyright 1989 by The Council for Exceptional Children. Reprinted by permission.

Students with disabilities and their family members can also share information. With the permission of the student, family members can talk about the characteristics of the disability and the child's needs. They can also use home videos, photographs, and items that depict their child's life and needs. Family members also can address the modifications and adaptive devices their child needs, as well as questions and concerns raised by the students. If a family member is not able to address the class, a professional who works with the student can serve as a guest speaker.

Films and Books

Many films and videos depict the lives of persons with individual differences (Kelly, 1997; Safran, 1998, 2000). Movies such as *Forrest Gump, Shine, Nell, Philadelphia, My Left Foot, Children of a Lesser God, Awakenings,* and *Rain Man* can be viewed and discussed. Videocassettes from professional organizations and television stations are available to introduce students to various disabilities and individual differences (Schwartz, 1995). For example, the Alexander Graham Bell Association for the Deaf provides a video that simulates different types of hearing losses.

Books about individuals with disabilities can promote positive attitudes and can teach students about individual differences and disabilities (Bryde, 1998; Prater, 1998). They also can be used to help your students with disabilities understand their own disabilities more clearly and relate to others with disabilities (Robinson, 1999). You can increase the effectiveness of these books with guided discussions and activities related to the story's plot, information about disabilities, and the similarities between the characters and your students (Favazza & Odom, 1997). Bryde (1998), Prater (1998, 2000), Winsor (1998), Dunnagan and Capan (1996), Bunch (1996), Zvirin (1994, 1996), Blaska and Lynch (1995), and Schroeder-Davis (1994) have

INFORMATIONAL

Safran (1998, 2000) offers a list of films about individuals with disabilities and guidelines for selecting and using them in classrooms.

SET YOUR SITES

A list of more than 2,000 films about individuals with disabilities is available at the website Films and Disabilities (www.caravan.demon.co.uk).

SET YOUR SITES

You can obtain information on children's books about individuals with disabilities by visiting the website www.kidsource.com/NICHCY/literature.html.

Teachers can use books to teach students about individual differences.

✓ REFLECTING ON YOUR PRACTICES

Selecting Children's Books About Individual Differences

You can examine the appropriateness of the books you use to teach students about individual differences by considering the following:

◆ Does the author have the background to accurately depict and present information about the group(s) discussed?

◆ Are the language, plot, and style of the book appropriate for your students and free of bias?

◆ Is the book factually correct, realistic, and presented in a culturally appropriate manner?

◆ Are individuals with differences depicted in a variety of situations and settings that represent their own cultural norms?

◆ Are individuals with differences portrayed in a positive, well-rounded, independent, complex, and nonstereotypic way?

◆ Does the book recognize and include the contributions of individuals from diverse groups?

◆ Does the book introduce students to the adaptations and devices that individuals with certain disabilities need?

◆ Does the book allow the students to develop an equal-status relationship with others and learn about the things they share with others?

◆ Does the book help students understand subtle stereotypes and present diversity within and across groups?

◆ In what proportion are individuals from different groups shown in the book's illustrations?

◆ Are the book's illustrations accurate, current, and nonstereotypical?

◆ Will the book and the illustrations stimulate questions and discussions about individuals with differences?

How would you rate your selection of children's books about individual differences? ( ) Excellent ( ) Good ( ) Needs Improvement ( ) Needs Much Improvement

What are some goals and steps you could adopt to improve your selection of children's books about individual differences?

Sources: Blaska and Lynch (1995), Kibler (1996), Mandlebaum, Thompson, and VandenBroek (1995), and Slapin, Seale, and Gonzales (1992).

INFORMATIONAL

Smead (1999) offers an annotated bibliography of 24 books presenting personal accounts of exceptionality.

compiled helpful lists of books about disabilities and giftedness that teachers can use with their students across a range of age and grade levels.

Older students can be introduced to individuals with disabilities via literature and first-person accounts of exceptionality (Smead, 1999). *The Handicapped in Literature: A Psychosocial Perspective* (Bowers, 1980) includes selections from H. G. Wells, Carson McCullers, Somerset Maugham, and Kurt Vonnegut; *The Exceptional Child Through Literature* (Landau, Epstein, & Stone, 1978) contains short stories by Joyce Carol Oates, John Steinbeck, and Alfred Kazin. Both include follow-up discussion questions that can be used to give students insights into the experiences and feelings of persons with disabilities. Landau et al. (1978) offer a bibliography of adult books concerning individuals with disabilities. Guidelines for using folktales to promote a greater understanding of individuals with disabilities also are available (Barnes, Berrigan, & Biklen, 1978).

Instructional Materials

Commercially developed materials to teach students about individual differences also are available (Denti & Meyers, 1997). These usually include a variety of learning activities, materials to implement the activities, multimedia materials, and a teacher's guide. For example, The Children's Museum of Boston has developed a series of seven units to teach students about individual differences and disabilities called *What If You Couldn't . . . ?* that can be rented or bought by contacting the museum at (800) 370-5487. The website for

Teachers can use a variety of instructional materials, including puppets, to teach children about disabilities and individual differences.

The Children's Museum of Boston is www.tcmboston.org. Other programs include the California Ability Awareness Program (916-228-2422), Include Us (http://IncludeUs.com, 888-462-5833), Lessons for Understanding (www.ici.coled.umn.edu/ici/pub/curricula.html, 612-624-4512), Friends Who Care (312-726-6200), and Count Me In (www.pacer.org/main/publist.html, 612-827-2966).

You also can promote acceptance by creating a classroom environment that supports the acceptance of individual differences. For example, you can introduce materials that stimulate discussions, such as photographs and posters of individuals with disabilities, and multiracial dolls and stuffed animals that depict individuals with disabilities.

Kids on the Block (www.kotb.com, 800-368-KIDS) offers awareness programs on educational differences and social/safety issues. For example, it offers puppet shows involving life-sized puppets representing students with disabilities in real-life situations. The vignettes encourage the audience to explore their feelings toward individuals with disabilities and to ask questions about persons with specific disabilities. In addition, Kids on the Block offers programs on medical conditions (AIDS, diabetes) and on such topics as aging, divorce, teen pregnancy, child abuse, substance abuse, and cultural differences.

Kids on the Block has developed two disability awareness programs including activities, stories, stickers, and posters to promote the acceptance and appreciation of individual differences: "Each and Every One" for primary grades and "Each and Every One" for intermediate grades. A series of books for children based on the Kids on the Block puppets and supplementary materials (chatabout cards, buttons, activity books, audiocassettes, and videocassettes) also are available.

Information About Adaptive Devices

Since many students with disabilities may use adaptive devices, teaching others about these devices can be beneficial. Wherever possible, it is best for the students with disabilities to

SET YOUR SITES

Info to Go at Gallaudet University (www.gallaudet.edu/~nicd, 202-651-5051) developed two series of materials to teach students in grades 3 and 4 and in grades 5 to 12 about deafness and hearing loss.

introduce and explain the aids and devices they use. Students can be shown the devices and allowed to touch and experiment with them. For example, a student with a hearing impairment could explain the parts and maintenance of the hearing aid and then have other students use a hearing aid for a brief period. If students do not feel comfortable showing and explaining the aids they use, a professional or family member can do so.

Collaborative Problem Solving

REFLECTIVE

Think about how to use collaborative problem solving in the following situation. In the social studies class, students are required to take notes. Some of the students have trouble doing this. What solutions do you think other students would suggest?

Collaborative problem solving can sensitize students about when and how to assist classmates by presenting scenarios on classroom and interpersonal situations that students are likely to encounter in the inclusive classroom (Salisbury et al., 1997). For example, a scenario of a student who plays alone during recess can be presented . Afterward, students can discuss it collaboratively and brainstorm possible solutions. You can promote the discussion by helping students identify the issues, providing additional information when necessary, and sharing their own beliefs about fairness. Once potential solutions are generated, the class can evaluate their completeness, fairness, feasibility, ability to solve the problem, and impact on peers, teachers, and the targeted student(s). Following this discussion, the class can select a solution, which is then implemented and evaluated.

HOW CAN I TEACH ACCEPTANCE OF INDIVIDUAL DIFFERENCES RELATED TO CULTURE, LANGUAGE, GENDER, AND SOCIOECONOMIC STATUS?

Learning activities can teach students to accept individual differences related to culture, language, gender, and socioeconomic status. These activities can be integrated into your curriculum to create a classroom that welcomes, acknowledges, and celebrates the value and experiences of *all students*.

Promote Acceptance of Cultural Diversity

Many students may view peers who come from other cultures and speak other languages as different, and may seldom interact with them because of their unique language, clothes, and customs. You can help students overcome these attitudes by teaching them about different cultures and the value of cultural diversity. With these activities, students gain a multicultural perspective that allows them to identify underlying and obvious similarities and differences among various groups. An environment that accepts other cultures can enhance the self-esteem and learning performance of *all students* by affirming their cultures, languages, and experiences. Additional guidelines on creating and using a multicultural curriculum in different content areas are presented in Chapter 8.

Derman-Sparks (1989) has developed an antibias curriculum on issues of color, language, gender, and disability. It includes a variety of activities to teach students to be sensitive to the needs of others, think critically, interact with others, and develop a positive self-identity based on one's own strengths rather than on the weaknesses of others. When teaching students about cultural diversity, you can consider the following guidelines:

SET YOUR SITES

The Freedom Forum Center (www.freedomforum.org, 615-321-9588) offers information and training to help schools promote religious tolerance.

INFORMATIONAL

Menkart (1999) offers guidelines on enhancing the effectiveness of heritage month celebrations.

◆ Examine cultural diversity with the belief that *all students* have a culture that is to be valued and affirmed.

- Teach initially about cultural diversity by noting the variety of students and adults in the classroom and then extending the discussion beyond the classroom.
- Collect information about your students' cultural backgrounds.
- Help students view the similarities among groups through their differences.
- Make cultural diversity activities an ongoing and integral part of the curriculum rather than a one-day "visit" to a culture during holidays or other special occasions.
- Relate experiences of cultural diversity to real life and give students hands-on experiences that address their interests.
- Teach students about the various types of individual behavior within all cultures, and emphasize the idea that families and individuals experience and live their culture in personal ways (Derman-Sparks, 1989; Martin, 1987).

Incorporate Cultural Diversity into the Classroom

You can incorporate acceptance of cultural diversity into your classroom in a variety of ways (see Figure 5.6). Use multicultural children's books and incorporate periodicals and magazines on multicultural issues into the curriculum (Jairrels et al., 1999; Taylor, 2000). For example, in literature discussion groups, students can read and discuss books such as Alma Flor Ada's *My Name Is Maria Isabel* (1993), which uses the theme of a student losing her name to show the importance of respecting the unique traits of all persons. Students can then develop character study journals in which they think about, write about, and maintain connections with the characters' feelings, and situations, as well as their similarities to and differences from the characters (Montgomery, 1999). In addition, you

INFORMATIONAL

Reviews and lists of children's literature about various cultures and religions across many grade levels are available (Book Links Advisory Board, 1994; Consortium of Latin American Studies Programs, 1998; Kaplan, 1994; Kea, 1998; Mandlebaum et al., 1995; Miller-Lachman & Taylor, 1995; Office of Diversity Concerns, 1999; Taylor, 2000). More information on multicultural children's literature can be obtained from the Council on Interracial Books for Children (212-757-5339).

SET YOUR SITES

Information about multicultural books and resources for students is available at such websites as the Internet School Library Media Center Multicultural Resources for Children (http://falcon.jmu.edu/~ramseyil/multipub.htm), Cynthia Leitich Smith Children's Literature Resources (www.cynthialeitichsmith.com/index1.htm), the Multicultural Book Review Homepage (www.isomedia.com/homes/jmele/homepage.html), and the Center for the Study of Books in Spanish for Children and Adolescents (http://coyote.csusm.edu/campus_centers/csb/index.htm).

- Share information about your own cultural background, and ask students and their family members to do likewise.
- Discuss the similarities and differences among cultures including music, foods, customs, holidays, and languages.
- Make artifacts from different cultures.
- Read ethnic stories to and with students.
- Listen to music from different cultures and learn ethnic songs. A variety of music examples, lesson plans, audiocassettes, videocassettes, and practical strategies for teaching music from a multicultural perspective are available from the Music Educators National Conference Publication Sales (www.menc.org, 800-828-0229).
- Decorate the room, bulletin boards, and hallways with artwork, symbols, and murals that reflect a multicultural perspective.
- Make a class calendar that recognizes the holidays and customs of all cultures, and celebrate holidays that are common to several cultures in a way that recognizes each culture's customs.
- Plan multicultural lunches in which students and their families work together to cook multiethnic dishes. Have students interview family members about their dishes and write about their findings, which can be posted next to each dish.
- Take field trips that introduce students to the lifestyles of persons from different cultures.
- Show movies and videos that highlight aspects of different cultures.
- Teach students ethnic games, and encourage them to use cross-cultural and cross-gender toys and other objects.
- Give students multicolored paints, paper, other art materials, and skin-tone crayons.
- Have students maintain an ethnic feelings book that summarizes their reactions to multicultural awareness activities and their experiences with their culture and other cultures.

FIGURE 5.6   Activities to promote acceptance of cultural diversity.

Sources: Derman-Sparks (1989), Nieto (1996), and Schniedewind and Davidson (1997).

Students can be resources for helping their peers learn about cultural diversity.

SET YOUR SITES

You can obtain print- and media-based materials and information on teaching about diversity, fairness, equity, and tolerance by contacting Teaching Tolerance (www.splcenter.org), the Anti-Defamation League (www.adl.org, 212-885-7970), Rethinking Schools (www.rethinkingschools.org, 800-669-4192), and the Equity Assistance Resource Center (www.nyu.edu/education/metro center/eac/catalog.html, 732-445-2071).

INFORMATIONAL

Tiedt and Tiedt (1995) describe many activities that teachers can use to help students learn about and value language diversity.

can examine textbooks and other materials for inclusion of all groups and the roles they play in the specific content area.

You also can use multicultural teaching and audiovisual materials and include the contributions of members of different groups in the content areas. For example, discussing the work of African American and Russian scientists or Hispanic and Irish poets in science and English classes, respectively, can teach students about the contributions of those ethnic groups. Students can also be assigned to read books about different cultures and biographies of women who have made significant contributions to society.

Teach About Language Diversity

Acceptance of language diversity can increase the self-esteem and school performance of students who are learning English and students who speak dialects of English. Acceptance also demonstrates a positive attitude toward students' language abilities and cultural backgrounds (Salend, 1997). Rather than viewing language diversity as a barrier to success in school, schools need to view it as an educational resource. This diversity offers teachers and students many opportunities to learn about the nature and power of language and to function successfully in the multicultural world in which they live (Adger, Wolfram, & Detwyler, 1993). Therefore, schools need to support, maintain, and strengthen students' linguistic varieties and promote a view of bilingualism as an asset (Gullingsrud, 1998; Moll, 1992).

Many strategies can be used to promote acceptance of language diversity. When teaching, you can use diverse cultural and language referents, teach and offer support in students' native languages, encourage and teach students to use bilingual dictionaries, allow students to ask and answer questions in their native languages, and use peers to tutor and help students in their native languages (Gonzalez, 1992). You can also establish social and work areas in the classroom and give students opportunities to work and interact with peers from diverse backgrounds (Hagiwara, 1998).

IDEAS FOR IMPLEMENTATION

Affirming Acceptance of Linguistic Diversity

Ms. White's school has had an influx of students who are learning English. Several of these students were ridiculed because of their accents and their difficulties in understanding and talking with others. Ms. White was asked to serve on a schoolwide committee to counter this teasing and help all students feel comfortable in their new school. At the first meeting, she suggested that community members who speak the students' native languages should be invited to join the committee.

The committee decided to start by creating a school environment that welcomed students and their families and reflected the different languages spoken in the community. They posted signs, bulletin board notices, and greetings in several languages throughout the school. They also displayed books and materials written in several languages in classrooms, in the school's office, and in the school library and posted students' work in several languages. Occasionally, the school played music in different languages over the loudspeaker and invited speakers and storytellers who spoke various languages to address different classes. The changes appeared to work. Several teachers noted that the new students seemed to feel more comfortable in school and that many of the English-speaking students were attempting to speak to them by using the new students' native language.

Here are some other strategies you can use to create a school environment that accepts diversity in language:

- Encourage students to use their native language in school, and teach some words from their language to others.
- Teach lessons about languages other than English. For example, you can teach lessons that compare the English alphabet with the alphabets of other languages.
- Stock the classroom with bilingual books.
- Ask students to explain customs, games, folktales, songs, or objects from their culture in their native language, and show videos and play music in various languages.
- Use various languages in school newsletters and other written communications.
- Have students write journal entries and poems, contribute pieces to school publications, sing songs, and perform plays in their native languages.
- Use simulation activities. For example, *BARNGA: A Simulation Game on Cultural Clashes* (800-370-2665) can help secondary school students learn about the difficulties and isolation that immigrants experience when they arrive in a new country.
- Learn to pronounce students' names correctly, and learn greetings and words in the students' languages.
- Give students opportunities to communicate with pen pals from other regions of the United States and other countries via the Internet.
- Tell students that being bilingual and bicultural can enhance their opportunities for success and employment.
- Give awards and recognition for excellence in speaking languages that may not be part of typical foreign language courses offered at the school.

Sources: Freeman and Freeman (1992), Gullingsrud (1998), Hagiwara (1998), and Nieto (1996).

Teach about Dialect Differences

You know, it's funny. I speak English and Black English. Outside of school I hear a lot of white kids trying to speak like I do. They listen to rap music and try to speak like they are black. But when I'm in school, the same students make faces when I sometimes use Black English in class. It's like they don't respect our language or are afraid of it. (Salend, 1997, p. 38)

African American English allows African Americans to connect with their cultural roots and to express solidarity with one another.

African American English   Since all English-speaking students speak a dialect, you also will work with students who speak various dialects of English, such as African American English, also referred to as *Black English* or *ebonics*. African American English allows African Americans to connect with their cultural roots and express power and solidarity with each other, as well as to continually evolve new cultural forms based on the language, among them music (such as rap), creative imagery, and slang (Lee, 1994). Simultaneously, it allows all Americans, especially youth, to participate in African American culture through the use of Black English patterns in current music, movies, and commercials (Wade-Lewis, December 2, 1991; personal communication).

While African American English has maintained a number of vocabulary items from African languages, it generally employs the vocabulary of English, with some phonology, morphology, syntax, nuance, tone, and gesture from African languages and other dialects of English (Alexander, 1985). Some phonological features of African American English include dropping the *t* when it is the final letter of a consonant cluster (*act* is pronounced *ak*), replacing the voiced *th* with *d (this* is pronounced *dis),* and substituting *i* for the *e (pen* is pronounced *pin).* Some syntactical features of African American English include using the verb *to be* to indicate ongoing action or a repeated occurrence and deleting *to be* when it is followed by a predicate, verb, adjective, or noun in the present tense ("The coffee be cold" indicates that the coffee is always cold, while "The coffee cold" means that the coffee is cold only today), employing *it* to indicate presence or to make statements, omitting *-ed* in the past tense, using double negatives in a single sentence, deleting plural markers when additional words in the sentence denote more than one ("He got three pencil" for "He has three pencils"), adding *s* to make plural forms of words ("peoples," "womans," "childrens"), denoting possession through position and context rather than using *'s* ("John car big" for "John's car is big"), and stressing subjects in a sentence by using subject/noun-pronoun redundancy ("My mother she be taking me to the hospital" for "My mother takes me to the hospital").

The grammatical and stylistic differences between African American English and standard English can be largely attributed to differences between African languages and English. Lexical features include words that have meanings only to speakers of the dialect, such as *bad* being the equivalent of *good* or *great* in standard English and *half-stepping*, meaning getting by without doing your best. Stylistic elements of African American English include subtlety, angled body movements, and intonation (Alexander, 1985). Rhetorical elements include exaggeration through the use of uncommon words and expressions and alliteration; mimicry of the speech and mannerisms of others; use of proverbs, puns, metaphors, and improvisation; displaying a sense of fearlessness; and use of innuendo and sound effects (Webb-Johnson, 1992).

Rather than making students who speak other dialects of English feel deficient and dysfunctional by interrupting and correcting them in midsentence, you can create a classroom that acknowledges and affirms the use of standard and other dialects of English as appropriate in various school and societal contexts (Day, 1998; Schorr, 1997). One effective approach for creating such a classroom is the *bridge system*, which encourages students to be bidialectical and to understand that different dialects are used in different situations. In this approach, you help students understand when to use standard English and when it is appropriate to use other dialects. For example, when you need to prompt students to use standard English, you can ask, "How can you say that in school language?" In addition, you can help students become bidialectal by showing respect for students' dialects and the cultures they reflect; acknowledging the oral traditions of some students' cultures; exposing students to and discussing with them other English dialects through literature, books, songs, poetry, and films; and discussing and role playing situations in which standard English and other dialects of English would be appropriate (Alexander, 1985; Thompson, 1990).

Employ Sociolinguistic Education

Sociolinguistic education can be integrated into all aspects of the curriculum. This fosters an understanding and appreciation of language diversity and counters negative reactions to language and dialect differences. Sociolinguistic education gives students information to identify, understand, and examine language variations and the relationship of language to power in schools and society (Adger, 1997).

Adger et al. (1993) have developed a curriculum that teaches students about language and dialect awareness and variation. This curriculum introduces students to language variations that challenge some of the negative stereotypes and attitudes associated with language and dialect differences. It also helps them to understand and experiment with patterns of language variation and to appreciate the cultural-historical perspective of language and dialect variations (Adger et al., 1993). Students learn how language works, and the roles and functions of language, by studying and comparing some of the different dialects of English, such as New England speech, Southern speech, Appalachian English, and African American English in terms of dialect differences, cultural

INFORMATIONAL

Day (1998) has developed a program to teach standard American English to African American English speakers.

and linguistic conventions, and historical developments. For example, students listen to and contrast the stories of *Cinderella,* told in a standard English dialect such as New England or Midwestern English, and *Ashley Lou and the Prince,* told in Appalachian English. For younger students, dialectic differences can be taught by reading and listening to stories, poems, and songs in different dialects.

Sociolinguistic education also can help students discover and understand the connections among different languages and dialects, as well as the differences among languages (Gonzalez, 1992; Tiedt & Tiedt, 1995). Students can study various aspects of languages and dialects and examine how words, sayings, riddles, and stories in different languages may share the same derivations. For example, students can experiment with Spanish words ending in *cia* (e.g., *distancia*) and English words ending in *ce* (e.g., *distance*) to begin to understand the commonalities of Spanish and English. Students and teachers can learn and use parallel sayings in English and other languages, and attempt to create their own sayings in many languages and dialects.

SET YOUR SITES

The Women's Educational Equity Act Equity Resource Center (www.edc.org/WomensEquity, 617-969-7100) offers information and resources to promote gender equity.

INFORMATIONAL

Odean (1997) provides an annotated bibliography of over 600 books about girls.

Teach Gender Equity

An effective program to teach students about cultural diversity should include activities that promote an understanding of gender equity. These activities can be integrated into all content areas to help female and male students expand their options in terms of behaviors, feelings, interests, career aspirations, and abilities. Gender equity activities also make *all students* aware of the negative effects of gender bias and of ways to combat sexism. For example, as part of your math class, you can have students graph the number of male and female athletes mentioned in their local newspaper (Rutledge, 1997). A variety of curriculum activities, media, books for children and adults, photographs, posters, toys, games, and professional organizations that you can use as resources for teaching students about gender equity and sexual harassment are available (Cohn, Hoffman, & Mozenter, 1994; Hodgin, Levin, & Matthews, 1997; Odean, 1997; Schniedewind & Davidson, 1997; Stein & Sjostrom, 1994).

Teach About Family Differences

In light of the different kinds of families that students live in, accepting cultural diversity also can include teaching about family differences (Sapon-Shevin, 1999). By teaching about family differences, you can acknowledge the different family arrangements of your students. You also can use the stories of students' families as the basis for interdisciplinary lessons (Nieto, 1996). Since students have a variety of family arrangements, it is important to be careful when assigning projects (e.g., family trees) or holding events (e.g., mother–daughter activities) that relate to or assume that students live in traditional nuclear families; instead, frame these assignments in a more inclusive manner. Other suggestions and resources for teaching about family differences were presented in Chapter 3.

Teach About Homelessness and the Migrant Lifestyle

SET YOUR SITES

Information about books on the migrant and immigrant experience is available from The Resource Center of the Americas (www.americas.org, 800-452-8382).

Frequent changes in schools can cause homeless and migrant students to be targets of ridicule by peers. To counteract this problem, you can teach students about the lifestyles of these students. This should be done carefully to avoid stigmatizing these students. The homeless and migrant lifestyles can be presented by guest speakers and through multi-

IDEAS FOR IMPLEMENTATION

Promoting Gender Equity

After taking a workshop on gender bias in the classroom, Ms. Stillwell tried to assess its extent in her classroom. She observed that her students appeared to segregate themselves when playing during recess and lunch. Boys sat and played with boys, and girls sat and played with girls. She also noted that she and her students frequently used male-based metaphors such as telling the class that "you guys can tackle that problem."

Ms. Stillwell decided to change her behavior and the behavior of her students. She used self-recording to keep track of her interactions with her male and female students. She also introduced several vignettes showing positive and negative interactions in schools between male and female students. Students acted out these vignettes and then discussed them in small mixed-sex groups. Each group then shared its reactions to the vignettes with the class. Ms. Stillwell continued to observe her own and her students' behaviors and noticed many improvements that made her feel better. However, she knew that she needed to continue to confront this issue and other issues in her classroom.

Here are some other strategies you can use to create an inclusive classroom that promotes gender equity:

◆ Help students recognize when they are responding in a sexist manner, and teach them how to challenge sex-role stereotyping in school and society.

◆ Model a commitment to gender equity by challenging students' stereotypic behavior and by using language that includes both genders.

◆ Teach students how their attitudes and behavior relating to sex roles are affected by television, movies, music, books, advertisements and the behavior of others.

◆ Avoid grouping students on the basis of gender, such as by forming separate lines, teams, seating arrangements, and academic learning groups and by comparing students by gender.

◆ Assign students of both sexes to class and school jobs on a rotating basis.

◆ Establish a classroom and school environment that encourages female and male students to play and work together. For example, decorate the classroom with pictures of males and females performing a variety of activities and use cooperative learning.

◆ Use nonsexist teaching materials that challenge stereotypical roles and, when possible, modify sexist teaching materials.

◆ Encourage male and female students to participate in a variety of physical education and extracurricular activities.

Sources: Sapon-Shevin (1999) and Schniedewind and Davidson (1997).

---

media and children's books. For example, Whittaker, Salend, and Gutierrez (1997), Kibler (1996), and Johanneson (1999) offer suggestions and resources for integrating into the curriculum reading and writing activities that reflect the experiences of migrant students and their families. Included are an annotated bibliography of monolingual and bilingual children's literature about the migrant experience. These resources and activities can be used to sensitize *all students* to the unique experiences of migrant students, as well as the importance of migrant workers to society.

Photographs and videocassettes depicting the migrant lifestyle or homelessness can give students direct, real-life experiences with issues related to these individuals. For example, the plight of migrant workers in the last 40 years can be examined and discussed through the use of such videos as *Harvest of Shame* (Murrow, 1960), *New Harvest, Old*

Shame (Corporation for Public Broadcasting, 1990), and *Legacy of Shame* (Columbia Broadcasting System, 1995), which depict the economic, social, health, living, and political conditions of migrant workers in the 1960s, 1980s, and 1990s, respectively. You also can show the value and importance of the work of migrants by having migrant students and their families discuss their experiences and the places where they have lived; by developing a map that traces the path of migrant families; by establishing a pen pal system whereby full-year students write to their migrant classmates who are traveling around the country; by visiting farms and talking with migrant workers; and by discussing the importance of migrant workers to our society.

Teach About AIDS

SET YOUR SITES

The American Foundation for AIDS Research (www.amfar.org, 212-806-1600) provides *Learning AIDS,* a comprehensive list and critique of over 2,000 videos, books, brochures, monographs, and teaching materials about AIDS.

Students often learn about conditions such as AIDS through television and other media. As a result, they often have misconceptions about AIDS and are afraid to be in classrooms with students who have AIDS. Several strategies can be used to overcome these negative attitudes and misconceptions. A trained professional or an individual with AIDS can be invited to speak about the social and medical aspects of the disease. Many curriculum materials and resources for teachers are available (Byrom & Katz, 1991; Colson & Colson, 1993; Lerro, 1994; Stuart et al., 1995). These often include print materials and videos that give specific information about AIDS. These resources help students understand the impact of their health habits and choices. They also help students develop the decision-making, assertive communication, and self-esteem-enhancing skills necessary to take control of their lives and resist peer pressure. Bryde (1998), Byrom and Katz (1991), and Sweeney, Clark, and Silva (1995) have compiled lists of resources and children's literature on HIV prevention and AIDS education.

Teach About Stereotyping

Many students gain negative perceptions of others through stereotypes. It is important to help students understand and challenge the process of stereotyping, in addition to learning about a group's experiences and history (Martin, 1987). You can counter the harmful effects of stereotyping by doing the following:

REFLECTIVE

Think about a situation in which you were stereotyped. What factors contributed to that stereotype? How did it make you feel? How did it affect the outcome of the situation? Think about a situation in which you stereotyped someone. What factors contributed to that stereotype? How did it make you feel? What would you do differently?

- ❖ Invite individuals who challenge stereotypes to speak to the class.
- ❖ Have students read books and view videos that challenge stereotypes and address discrimination.
- ❖ Display pictures and materials that challenge stereotypes.
- ❖ Discuss and critique how language, books, television shows, commercials, cartoons, jokes, toys, and common everyday items (such as lunch boxes) create and foster stereotypes.
- ❖ Compare items, images, and words and expressions that portray various groups.
- ❖ List and discuss stereotypes that students have about others, as well as the stereotypes that others have about them (Derman-Sparks, 1989; Martin, 1987).

Teach About Discrimination

INFORMATIONAL

Banks (1991a) and Tiedt and Tiedt (1995) identify many resources and activities for teaching students about discrimination.

Issues of cultural diversity are related to issues of power in schools and society. Therefore, it is important to confront discrimination and its harmful effects. Case studies and short stories on various cultures and instances of discrimination can be used to stimulate group discussions that introduce students to a variety of perspectives, experiences, and ideas. The purpose of such discussions is to help them reach conclusions, as well as question and affirm their own viewpoints.

Students can learn about these issues by experiencing them. For example, you can group students according to some arbitrary trait (e.g., hair color, eye color, type of clothing) and then treat the groups in different ways in terms of rules, assignments, compliments, grading procedures, privileges, homework, and class jobs. You can also show students what it means to be discriminated against by assigning several groups the same task while varying the resources each group is given to complete the task, so that the different performance of the groups is related to resources rather than ability. After these activities, you and your students can discuss their reactions and the effects of discrimination on individuals.

Teach How to Respond to Stereotyping and Discrimination

"I'm going to make my eyes straight and blue," 4-year-old Kim tells her teacher. "Why do you want to change your lovely eyes?" her teacher asks wonderingly. Kim: "It's prettier." Teacher: "Kim, I don't think straight eyes are prettier than yours are. Your mommy and daddy and grandpa don't think so either. We like you just the way you are, with your beautiful, dark brown eyes shaped just as they are. Why do you think straight and blue eyes are prettier?" Kim: "Sarah said I had ugly eyes, she likes Julie's better." Teacher: "Sarah is wrong to say you have ugly eyes. It's not true and it is unfair and hurtful to say so. In this classroom we respect how everyone looks. Let's go and talk with her about it." (Derman-Sparks, 1989, p. 34)

Once students learn about the negative effects of prejudice, they can be taught how to respond to stereotyping and discrimination. You can establish an inclusive classroom environment by modeling acceptance of all students and by establishing the rule that gender, race, ethnicity, language skills, ability, religion, physical appearance, sexual orientation, or socioeconomic status is not a reason for excluding or teasing someone. If someone breaks the rule, you should act immediately to support the student who has been discriminated against and to help the student describe his or her reaction to the student(s) who engaged in the exclusionary behavior. It is also important to help the excluding student(s) understand the harmful effects of prejudice (Derman-Sparks, 1989).

Role playing also can help students learn how to respond to discrimination and stereotyping. For example, you can present a bias-related incident and ask students to role play their responses. Afterward, the students can discuss their experiences and reactions.

Sometimes students express a desire to change their physical appearance. When this happens, tell students immediately that they are fine; assure them that others love them the way they are; explain to them that others who do not like them that way are wrong; point out that there are many people who have the same traits; and confront others who made negative statements that triggered the students' reactions (Derman-Sparks, 1989).

INFORMATIONAL

Aronson (1997) provides resources for teaching your students about individual differences in body size and type.

REFLECTIVE

Think about how you would respond to the following situations: Students are telling anti-Semitic jokes; using terms such as *Indian giver;* mimicking a student's accent; denying their racial, ethnic, or religious identities; or teasing a male student who likes to sew.

HOW CAN I FACILITATE FRIENDSHIPS?

Friendships in and outside of school are important for *all students* and are one of the benefits of inclusion programs. However, because some of your students may have few friends and limited peer support, you may need to use a variety of strategies to promote the development of friendships and peer support systems. When using these strategies, be careful that they don't inadvertently reinforce caregiving and parenting actions rather than friendship interactions (Kishi & Meyer, 1994).

Teach About Friendships

You can help promote friendships by integrating teaching about friendships into the curriculum (Froschl & Gropper, 1999; Wilson, 1999). This can include teaching the meaning and importance of friendship, the qualities of good friendship, and the problems that some students have in trying to make friends. For example, you can provide students with insights about friendships by talking about the importance of your friendships and the things you like to do with friends. Students can then explore their own friendships by developing a friendship chart that includes the names of several of their friends, the activities they do with their friends, the qualities they like in their friends, and how they met each friend; writing a friendship poem; or creating a wall with each block indicating a barrier to friendships (Froschl & Gropper, 1999; Schaffner & Buswell, 1992).

You also can use reading, writing, and content area teaching activities related to the theme of friendship (Searcy, 1996). Palincsar, Parecki, and McPhail (1995) developed a thematic unit on friendship. It includes interactive readings of children's books on friendship, writing personal accounts of how the stories changed their views about friendships; supported retelling of the stories; designing and implementing performances of the stories such as drama, art, and puppet shows; and maintaining a friendship journal with entries about students' friendships. Falvey and Rosenberg (1995) used a social studies lesson with secondary-level students that connected a diagram on the relationships among world leaders during the early 1900s with a similar diagram on the students' relationships with their friends.

INFORMATIONAL

DeGeorge (1998) compiled a list of children's books about friendship and described a model for using children's literature to teach friendship skills.

Mutual friendships in and outside of school are important for all students and are one of the benefits of inclusion.

Offer Social Skills Instruction

Teaching about friendships also should include teaching social skills. *All students* can learn how to initiate, respond to, and maintain positive, equal-status social interactions with their peers, and also how to deal with rejection and refusal (Clark & Smith, 1999; Wenz-Gross & Siperstein, 1997). For example, you can have students role play responses to various friendship-making situations (Froschl & Gropper, 1999). You can also use curricula that teach students friendship skills (Kamps, Ellis, Mancina, & Greene, 1995), such as the Play Time/Social Time Curriculum (Odom et al., 1993) to teach sharing toys and materials, listening and talking to friends, and complimenting, encouraging, and helping friends. More information on teaching social skills is presented in Chapters 6 and 7.

These activities can be supplemented by using different materials and children's literature to teach students about friendship. Inwald (1994) has developed a program called, *Cap It Off With a Smile: A Guide for Making and Keeping Friends,* which includes a children's book, an activity book, and an audiocassette of songs designed to teach children how to make and keep friends. *Making Friends* is a video series that gives students opportunities to learn and practice strategies for making friends (Making Friends, n.d.).

INFORMATIONAL
Rosenthal-Malek (1997) has developed a metacognitive strategy social skills training program to help students develop their friendship-making skills.

SET YOUR SITES
You can obtain information on a computer simulation program about making friends on the playground by visiting the Tom Snyder Productions website (www.teachtsp.com, 800-342-0236).

Foster Communication Among Students

Since students' sensory, speech, and cognitive abilities can affect their social interactions, you also may need to teach your students how to interact and communicate with classmates with disabilities (Helmstetter et al., 1994; Turnbull & Ruef, 1997). You can help students understand the communication needs of others by teaching and modeling ways of interacting with others. For example, you can show your students the videos *How to Talk to a Person Who Can't Hear* (available by calling 888-744-6843), *The Ten Commandments of Communicating with People with Disabilities* (available by calling 800-543-2119), and *A VideoGuide to (Dis)Ability Awareness* (available by calling 800-621-1136). *The Ten Commandments of Communicating with People with Disabilities* uses humorous situations to present guidelines for interacting with such individuals. *A VideoGuide to (Dis)Ability Awareness* uses a more traditional and straightforward approach. Guidelines for communicating with individuals with disabilities that can be shared with your students are presented in Figure 5.7.

Alternative communication systems that students with disabilities use, such as Braille and sign language, can be introduced in a variety of ways that also promote academic skills. You can teach students the manual alphabet and then have them practice their spelling by spelling the words manually. Similarly, rather than writing the numbers for a math problem on the chalkboard, you can present them using numerical hand signs. Basic signs can be introduced to students and used for assignments. Students who have learned Braille can be asked to read and write in Braille.

Use Circles of Friends

You also can use circles of friends to help students understand support systems and friendships (Forest & Lusthaus, 1989). To do this, give students a sheet with four concentric circles, each larger and farther away from the center of the sheet, which contains a drawing of a stick figure representing a student. First, ask students to fill in the first

REFLECTIVE
Make a circle of friends for yourself. How have your friends and support group assisted you during stressful times?

COMMUNICATING WITH INDIVIDUALS WITH DISABILITIES

◆ View the individual as a person, not as a disability.
◆ Refrain from "talking down" or speaking in a condescending way.
◆ Talk directly to the individual even if the individual uses an interpreter.
◆ Be yourself, relax, be considerate, and treat the individual with respect.
◆ Talk using language and about topics that are age appropriate.
◆ Don't apologize for using common expressions that may relate to the individual's disability such as "I've got to run" or "Have you seen Mary?"
◆ Greet the individual as you would others. If the individual cannot shake your hand, he or she will make you aware of that.
◆ Understand that the environment can affect communication. An overly noisy or dark room can make communication difficult for individuals with speech and sensory disabilities.
◆ Don't assume that the individual needs your assistance; ask.

COMMUNICATING WITH INDIVIDUALS WHO USE WHEELCHAIRS

◆ Respect the individual's space by refraining from hanging on to the wheelchair.
◆ Sit or kneel at the individual's eye level when the conversation is going to continue for a long period of time.
◆ Don't assume that the individual wants you to push the wheelchair.

COMMUNICATING WITH INDIVIDUALS WITH VISUAL DISABILITIES

◆ Introduce yourself and any companions when encountering the individual.
◆ Speak in a normal voice.
◆ Direct communications to the individual by using the individual's name.
◆ Tell the individual when you are leaving or ending the conversation.

COMMUNICATING WITH INDIVIDUALS WITH HEARING DISABILITIES

◆ Make sure you have the individual's attention before speaking.
◆ Speak clearly and in short sentences.
◆ Avoid raising your voice or exaggerating your mouth movements.
◆ Refrain from repeating yourself. If the individual doesn't understand, rephrase your message or write it out.
◆ Use facial expressions, physical gestures, and body movements.

COMMUNICATING WITH INDIVIDUALS WITH SPEECH/LANGUAGE DIFFICULTIES

◆ Focus your attention on the individual.
◆ Avoid correcting or speaking for the individual.
◆ Be encouraging and patient.
◆ Seek clarification when you don't understand by repeating what you did understand.

FIGURE 5.7 Guidelines for communication with individuals with disabilities.
Sources: Access Resources (n.d.) and Mid-Hudson Library System (1990).

circle (the one closest to the stick figure) by listing the people whom they love and who are closest to them. The second circle contains a list of the people they like, such as their best friends. The third circle contains a list of groups that they like and do things with, like members of their teams or community organizations. Finally, the fourth circle contains a list of individuals who are paid to be part of their lives, such as a doctor or teacher. Students' circles are then shared with their peers, and the meaning and importance of friendships are discussed, including strategies for helping students make friends and expand their circle of friends.

Create a Friendly Classroom Environment

You also can support the development of friendships by creating a friendly classroom environment that promotes social interactions among students. To do this, you can decorate the classroom with posters and bulletin boards on the theme of friendship and use learning centers where students work together.

You also can use friendship activities including games, songs, and art activities, as well as physical (e.g., shake hands or link arms with a friend) and verbal (e.g., give your friend a compliment) friendship prompts, to establish an environment that supports friendships (Brown & Odom, 1995). For example, teach students songs with the theme of friendship, including recorded songs such as *Friends* (Linhart & Klingman, 1976), *You've Got a Friend* (Taylor, 1971), *That's What Friends Are For* (Bayer Sager & Bacharach, 1985), and *With a Little Help from My Friends* (Lennon & McCartney, 1967), as well as nonrecorded songs that appear in music books such as *All I Need Is a Friend* (Worsley, 1995), *Best of Friends* (Fidel & Johnston, 1986), and *Best Friends* (Ravosa & Jones, 1981). Art activities can include creating friendship murals, bulletin boards, posters, and books with illustrations.

An environment that supports friendships also can be created by stocking the classroom with age-appropriate toys, materials, and games that students like to use with others. A variety of resources are available to assist you and students' families in identifying appropriate toys. The National Lekotek Center (www.lekotek.org, 800-573-4446) provides services to foster the play-related abilities of students with disabilities, including a Toy Resource Helpline (800-366-PLAY) and a toy lending program. It also disseminates *The Toy Guide for the Differently-Abled Kids,* developed by Toys'R'Us and the National Parent Network (www.npnd.org, 703-684-6763). Guides and catalogs such as the *Oppenheim Toy Portfolio* (www.toyportfolio.com, 800-kids-450) also are available to help you locate appropriate toys for your students.

You also can create a friendly school environment by using cooperative grouping so that students work and play together in groups (Calloway, 1999; Salisbury, Gallucci, Palombaro, & Peck, 1995). For example, during recess you can teach students simple, noncompetitive, and enjoyable games that don't require a lot of skill or language abilities. When using these games, consider how they can be adapted by modifying the rules, using adaptive devices, and employing personal assistance strategies such as playing as a team (Demchak, 1994). Technology-based collaborative activities such as using computer graphics to produce newsletters, fliers, invitations, banners, and illustrations for the classroom also can promote friendships (Male, 1994). Specific guidelines for using cooperative learning groups are presented in Chapter 9.

A friendly classroom environment can be fostered by activities that promote a sense of class cohesiveness. Such group activities promote friendships and acceptance by creating a class identity that recognizes the similarities among students and the unique contributions of each class member. For example, students can create a class book, mural, newsletter, or tree that includes and recognizes the work and participation of everyone in the class. Throughout the school year, students can use many different getting-acquainted activities such as playing name recognition games, developing a class directory, and interviewing each other (Searcy, 1996). Sapon-Shevin (1999), Schniedewind and Davidson (1997), Jones and Jones (1998), Chuoke and Eyman (1997), and Canfield and Wells (1976) outlined activities and games that teachers can use to introduce new students to the group and promote class cohesiveness, giving all students a common experience on which to build future friendships (see Figure 5.8).

SET YOUR SITES

The National Down Syndrome Society (www.ndss.org, 800-221-4602) provides free posters designed to promote friendships among students with and without disabilities.

SET YOUR SITES

Kapable Kids (www.kapablekids.com, 800-356-1564) adapts toys so that they can be used by students with disabilities. People of Every Stripe (www.teleport.com/~people, 503-282-0612) makes dolls that have prosthetic limbs, hearing aids, and eyeglasses.

SET YOUR SITES

Ideas and resources for cooperative games can be obtained from Worldwide Games 800-888-0987), Educators for Social Responsibility (www.quest.edu/slarticle4.htm, 800-370-2515), and the Flaghouse Corporation (www.Flaghouse.com, 800-793-7900).

INFORMATIONAL

Fad, Ross, and Boston (1995) offer guidelines for using cooperative groups to promote friendships and teach social skills.

Create a class history or class photo album that is updated periodically and includes a summary of the year's activities, as well as work produced by and information about each student.

Create special class days, such as T-Shirt Day, when all students wear their favorite T-shirts.

Create a class web page.

Publish a class newspaper/newsletter, to which each student contributes a piece or drawing during the school year.

Have students work in groups to complete a "Classmates Scavenger Hunt" by giving each group a list of feelings (e.g., "A classmate who makes others feel good"), interests (e.g., "A classmate who likes to draw"), and skills (e.g., "A classmate who is good at math") that is completed by placing the names of classmates who have those feelings, interests, or skills on a poster.

Make a class mural and have each student complete part of it.

Construct a class tree. Each branch of the tree can contain a picture of a student or a work produced by that student.

Compile a *Who's Who* book of the class, with each student having a page devoted to his or her interests, achievements, and so on.

Have a class applause in which the whole class acknowledges the accomplishments of classmates.

FIGURE 5.8   Activities to promote a sense of class cohesiveness.

Use Peer-Based Strategies

Peer Support Committees and Class Meetings

Peer support committees and class meetings can be used to address classroom social interaction problems, promote friendships, and ensure that *all students* are valued members of the class (Carpenter, Bloom, & Boat, 1999). The peer support committee identifies problems that students or the class as a whole are experiencing and creates strategies to address them, such as establishing buddy systems, peer helpers, and study partners. The committee also brainstorms strategies for promoting friendships in the classroom and involving students in all academic and social aspects of the school, including extracurricular activities (Stainback, Stainback, & Wilkinson, 1992). Typically, membership on the committee is rotated so that each member of the class has an opportunity to serve.

Some teachers also have a positive-comment box in the classroom. Class members who see another student performing a kind act that supports others record the action on a slip of paper that is placed in the comment box. At the end of the day, positive actions are shared with the class.

Peer Buddy and Partner Systems

INFORMATIONAL

Hughes et al. (1999) describe the steps in creating a high school peer buddy system.

Friendships also can be promoted through the use of peer buddy or partner systems (English, Goldstein, Shafer, & Kaczmarek, 1997; Hughes et al., 1999). Peers, particularly those who are valued and respected, can help their partners by introducing them to various academic and social features of the school. For example, peer buddies can help students learn the school's locker system, interact with classmates during lunch and recess, and encourage classmates to attend extracurricular activities. You can meet periodically with peer partners to examine their success in supporting each other and to rotate partners.

Deal with Name-Calling and Teasing

We're always stressing concern for others. The wrinkled-paper activity is a good one to use. . . . They start out with a piece of clean paper and each child says something mean to the paper and crumbles it. Then . . . we decide that we're going to say something nice to the paper; and when you say a nice thing about it, you smooth it out. Then when each child has had a chance to do that, you take a look at the paper. Each child sees that even though they said something nice and tried to smooth it out, the wrinkles are still in the paper. The hurt doesn't go away—just like the wrinkles don't leave. So we have that [paper] hanging in our room. And if someone says a put-down, we look at the wrinkled paper, remember what it was telling us. Think twice before you say something. (Jan, grade 2/3 teacher) (Salisbury et al., 1995, p. 134)

You also can promote friendships by dealing appropriately with name-calling and minimizing its negative effects (Albinger, 1995). Froschl and Gropper (1999), Levine and Wharton (1993), and Friends of Project 10 (1993) suggest that you respond to name-calling and teasing by:

- Establishing a rule about no name-calling and teasing;
- Making it clear to students that name-calling and teasing will not be tolerated;
- Responding immediately to incidents of name-calling and teasing with direct consequences;
- Following up incidents of name-calling and teasing with a discussion of differences and discrimination;
- Helping students recognize and explore the reasons why they are uncomfortable with individual differences; and
- Helping students to understand individual differences by giving them information.

INFORMATIONAL

Salend and Schobel (1981) developed a positive approach to name-calling, which involves using a series of activities that teach the importance, meaning, derivation, and function of names, as well as the negative effects of calling others names.

Encourage Participation in Extracurricular and Community-Based Activities

Many friendships begin outside of the classroom and school, so students should be encouraged to meet and make new friends through extracurricular and community-based activities. Because these activities provide opportunities to share mutually enjoyable activities, similarities among students are highlighted. You can work with other professionals, family members, students, and community groups to offer and adapt afterschool activities that allow various groups of students to participate and interact socially. More information on involving students in these activities is presented in Chapter 6.

INFORMATIONAL

Falvey, Coots, and Terry-Gage (1992) offer lists of extracurricular activities for preschool, elementary, and secondary students.

Involve Family Members

Family members can work with you to support budding friendships, develop friendship goals and plans, and problem-solve ways to facilitate friendships (Wiener & Sunohara, 1998). Family members can create opportunities for interactions outside of school (e.g., encourage their children to invite friends home or to attend a community event with the family), make their home an enjoyable place for children to gather, encourage and assist their children and others in attending extracurricular activities (e.g., learn about afterschool and community activities and provide transportation), and volunteer to lead or attend these activities. To help family members do these things, you can offer them resources and workshops, and can suggest games and activities that promote friendships among children (Searcy, 1996).

SUMMARY

This chapter offered many strategies for teaching students to accept individual differences and develop friendships. As you review the questions posed in this chapter, consider the following questions and remember the following points.

How Do Attitudes Toward Individual Differences Develop?

Many students have misconceptions about and stereotypic views of individual differences. Also, several factors appear to interact to influence attitudes toward individual differences, including cultural background, gender, age, socioeconomic status, childrearing practices, and exposure to the media.

How Can I Assess Attitudes Toward Individual Differences?

In addition to using observations and sociometric measures (see Chapter 12), you can assess attitudes toward individual differences by using attitude change assessment instruments, knowledge of individual differences probes, and student drawings.

How Can I Teach Acceptance of Individual Differences Related to Disability?

You can teach students about individual differences by modeling desired attitudes and behaviors and by using simulations. You can also study the lives of successful individuals with disabilities, invite guest speakers, and use films, children's books, and teaching materials about disabilities. Other methods include teaching about adaptive devices, and using collaborative problem solving.

How Can I Teach Acceptance of Individual Differences Related to Culture, Language, Gender, and Socioeconomic Status?

You can integrate into your curriculum and classroom learning activities and materials that promote acceptance of cultural and linguistic diversity and gender equity. These activities and materials can also be used to teach students about family differences, homelessness, the migrant lifestyle, AIDS, stereotyping, and discrimination.

How Can I Facilitate Friendships?

You can facilitate friendships among students by teaching about friendships, teaching social skills, using activities that develop social skills and encourage communication among students, using circles of friends, creating a friendly classroom environment, and using peer-based strategies. Other methods include dealing with name-calling and teasing, encouraging students to participate in extracurricular and community-based activities, and involving families.

What Would You Do in Today's Diverse Classroom?

Although your students are doing well academically, you are concerned about their social interaction patterns in your class. You observe your students' interactions inside and outside the class and notice the following:

❖ Linh asked Henry if he wanted to play soccer with her. Henry said, "No. Girls don't know how to play soccer, and you talk funny." As Henry went to play with some of the other boys, Linh walked away with tears in her eyes.

❖ Several students rolled their eyes when you assigned Delbert to their cooperative learning group. As students moved to their groups, you heard them make fun of Delbert because "he is slow" and wears "old and lame clothes."

1. What are some of the factors that might cause your students to have difficulty socializing with one another?

2. What are some other ways you could identify your students' attitudes toward Linh and Delbert?

3. What are some strategies you could use to encourage your students to accept Linh and Delbert and each other's individual differences?

4. What are some strategies you could use to help your students make friends with Linh and Delbert?

CHAPTER 6

CREATING SUCCESSFUL TRANSITIONS TO INCLUSIVE SETTINGS

Nick

Nick is about to be placed in Mr. Roberts's general education class. Nick's special education teacher, Ms. Thomas, contacts Mr. Roberts to plan a program to help Nick make a successful transition. She shares information about Nick with Mr. Roberts. They also discuss and compare the essential components that students need to succeed in their respective classrooms. Based on these similarities and differences, they identify skills and information that Nick will need to make a smooth adjustment to Mr. Roberts's class.

Although Nick will not enter Mr. Roberts's class for several weeks, Ms. Thomas and Mr. Roberts agree that they should begin the transition program immediately. Ms. Thomas introduces Nick to the textbooks and assignments he will encounter in Mr. Roberts's class. She starts to give Nick homework assignments and tests that parallel those given by Mr. Roberts.

Nick also visits Mr. Roberts's class, and Ms. Thomas makes a video of a typical teaching session. Ms. Thomas reviews the video with Nick to discuss classroom procedures and other critical elements of the classroom environment. In addition to introducing Nick to the routines and expectations of the general education classroom, Ms. Thomas uses the video to encourage Nick to discuss any questions and concerns he has about the new setting.

Ms. Thomas also uses the video to teach Nick appropriate note-taking skills. At first, Nick and Ms. Thomas watch the video together while Ms. Thomas shows how to take notes. To make sure Nick understands the different note-taking techniques and when to apply them, Ms. Thomas periodically stops the video and reviews with Nick why certain information is or is not recorded and why a specific format is used. As Nick's note-taking skills improve, Ms. Thomas and Nick visit Mr. Roberts's class and take notes. Afterward they compare their notes, emphasizing the critical factors that make for good note taking.

What other factors should you consider when planning a transitional program to prepare students such as Nick for success in a general education classroom? What other transitions do students make? How can you help them make these transitions? After reading this chapter, you should be able to answer these as well as the following questions:

◆ How can I help students make the transition to general education classrooms?
◆ How can I help students from specialized schools and preschool programs make the transition to inclusive settings?
◆ How can I help students from linguistically and culturally diverse backgrounds make the transition to inclusive settings?
◆ How can I help students make the transition from school to adulthood?
◆ How can I help students develop self-determination?

Beginnings and transitions are difficult. Placement in inclusive settings involves many beginnings and transitions for students. Moving from one setting to another, students must learn to adjust to different curriculum demands, teaching styles, behavioral expectations, classroom designs, and student socialization patterns (Helmstetter, et al., 1998; Logan & Malone, 1998). Students moving from a special day school to an integrated program within the community's public school system, or leaving school to search for work or to enter a postsecondary program, will encounter new expectations, rules, extracurricular activities, and personnel.

It is essential to work collaboratively with other professionals, family members, and students to prepare students for the many transitions they face. It is also crucial to teach students the skills that will help them succeed in inclusive settings (Monda-Amaya, Dieker, & Reed, 1998). This chapter offers a variety of strategies for helping students make the transition to inclusive settings. These strategies are appropriate for students with disabilities, but they also can be used to help *all students* function in inclusive settings and make transitions to new environments.

HOW CAN I HELP STUDENTS MAKE THE TRANSITION TO GENERAL EDUCATION CLASSROOMS?

Understand Students' Unique Abilities and Needs

Before students are placed in inclusive settings, their general education teachers can be given information about them. This information can include the students' needs and ability levels, as well as background information to help teachers develop a program that will

What language(s) does the student speak? What language(s) does the family speak?

How does the student communicate?

What are the student's academic strengths? Academic weaknesses?

What instructional approaches, arrangements, and materials have been effective with the student? Which have not been effective?

What adaptive devices and technology does the student require?

What instructional and testing modifications does the student require?

What type and amount of adult and peer support does the student need?

What factors and variables motivate the student?

What instructional activities are appropriate for use with the student?

What cultural factors should be considered in designing an educational program for the student? For involving the family in the educational program?

What social and behavioral skills does the student possess and need to develop?

What are the student's hobbies and interests?

Who are the student's friends?

In what school clubs or extracurricular activities does/could the student participate?

How does the student get along with her or his peers?

How does the student feel about her or his disability?

What school personnel and community agencies will be working with the student? What services will they provide?

To what extent will the student's parents be involved in the planning process?

What communication system will be used to communicate between professionals? With family members?

What are the student's medical and medication needs?

Has the student been prepared to enter the inclusive setting?

What are the student's educational, social, cultural, linguistic, medical, and physical strengths and needs?

What classroom management strategies and classroom design adaptations have been successful?

What alternative assessment strategies, procedures, and test modifications have been used with the student?

What school-based supportive and community-based services have been used with the student? What are the outcomes of these services?

What cultural and linguistic factors have been considered in designing an educational program for the student? For involving the family in the educational program?

FIGURE 6.1   Sample information sharing questions.

help students make the transition to inclusive settings (Lassman, Jolivette, & Wehby, 1999). Figure 6.1 presents questions that can guide the information-sharing process.

For students with sensory disabilities, their general education teachers can receive information on the nature of the sensory loss, as well as the amount of residual hearing or vision. For students with hearing impairments, teachers also can be informed of the students' communication abilities. For students who are learning English as a second language, teachers should be apprised of their language abilities and the best approaches for helping them learn English. Finally, for students with special physical and health needs, teachers need information about health and medical issues and concerns, assistive devices, social skill development, and teaching and physical design accommodations (Wadsworth & Knight, 1999).

Use Transenvironmental Programming

Anderson-Inman's (1986) four-step transenvironmental programming model can serve as a framework for developing a program to prepare students for success in inclusive settings. The four steps in the model are (1) environmental assessment, (2) intervention and preparation, (3) generalization to the new setting, and (4) evaluation in the new environment. *Environmental assessment* involves determining what the orientation program

INFORMATIONAL

O'Shea (1994) and McKenzie and Houk (1993) offer guidelines for helping students make the transition to the general education classroom.

TABLE 6.1   Sample Transenvironmental Programming Model

General Education Class	Special Education Class
Ms. G. uses textbooks, computers, and other instructional media.	Mr. K. can teach the students to use textbooks and other instructional media.
Students interact with each other during recess.	Mr. K. can teach the student to initiate and engage in play with others.
Ms. G. expects students to raise their hands before speaking.	Mr. K. can teach the student to follow the rules of the general education classroom.
Ms. G. gives an hour of homework three times per week.	Mr. K. can give the student an hour of homework three times per week.
Ms. G. presents information through lectures and expects students to take notes.	Mr. K. can teach the student listening and note-taking skills.

should include by identifying the key skills that promote success in inclusive settings. In the *intervention and preparation* phase, the skills identified in the environmental assessment are taught to students using a variety of strategies. The next two steps are to *promote* and *evaluate* use of the skills in inclusive settings. A sample transenvironmental programming model for a student is presented in Table 6.1.

Environmental Assessment

INFORMATIONAL

Welch (1994) offers guidelines for conducting an environmental assessment and an overview of commercially available environmental assessment instruments. Monda-Amaya et al. (1998), the Institute on Community Integration (n.d.), Fuchs et al. (1994), and George and Lewis (1991) have developed checklists, inventories, and interview protocols that can help you plan the transition to general education settings.

REFLECTIVE

Think about your transition from high school to college. What problems did you experience? How did peers help?

The content and goals of the transitional program are developed from an environmental assessment. This assessment involves analyzing the critical features of the new learning environment that affect student performance (see Figure 6.2) and interviewing teachers and students (Campbell, Campbell, & Brady, 1998; Monda-Amaya et al., 1998). For students with different languages and cultures, you also should consider the language used to teach, as well as the cultural factors that affect performance. In addition, you can assess other features of the general education program, such as routines in the cafeteria and at assemblies, movement between classes, and expectations in physical education, art, and music classes. After information on the inclusive settings is collected, you and your colleagues can meet to analyze the differences between the two settings, identify areas where teaching will be needed to help students succeed in the inclusive setting, and plan strategies to address these areas (Fuchs, Fernstrom, Scott, Fuchs, & Vandermeer, 1994). In planning the transitional program, you also may need to determine the order in which skills will be taught, as well as which skills will be taught before and after students have been placed in inclusive settings.

Some schools include a classmate on the placement team to help identify the content of the transitional program (Villa & Thousand, 1992). The student can provide input in such areas as books and materials needed, social interaction patterns, class routines, and student dress. Peers also can help to welcome and orient students to their new environment.

Intervention and Preparation

In the intervention and preparation phase of the transenvironmental model, a variety of teaching strategies are used to prepare students to succeed in the new learning environment. These strategies and procedures are described next.

Teacher: **Subject:**

Grade: **Date:**   **Teacher Completing the Observation:**

A. TEACHING MATERIALS AND SUPPORT PERSONNEL

1. What textbooks and teaching materials are used in the class? How difficult are these texts and teaching materials?
2. What supplementary materials are used in the class? How difficult are these materials? What are their unique features?
3. What types of media and technology are often used in the classroom?
4. What type(s) of support personnel are available in the classroom? How often are they available?
5. What teaching adaptations does the teacher employ?

B. PRESENTATION OF SUBJECT MATTER

1. How does the teacher present information to students (e.g., lecture, small groups, cooperative learning groups, learning centers)?
2. What is the language and vocabulary level used by the teacher?

C. LEARNER RESPONSE VARIABLES

1. How do students respond in the class (e.g., take notes, read aloud, participate in class, copy from the board)?
2. In what ways can a student request help in the classroom?
3. How are directions given to students? How many directions are given at one time?

D. STUDENT EVALUATION

1. How often and in what ways does the teacher evaluate student progress?
2. How are grades determined?
3. What types of tests are given?
4. What test modifications does the teacher use for students?
5. Does the teacher assign homework? (What type? How much? How often?)
6. Does the teacher assign special projects or extra-credit work? Please explain.

E. CLASSROOM MANAGEMENT

1. What is the teacher's management system?
2. What are the stated rules in the classroom?
3. What are the unstated rules in the classroom?
4. What are the consequences of following the rules? What are the consequences of not following the rules?
5. In what ways and how often does the teacher reinforce the students?
6. Does the teacher follow any special routines? What are they?

F. SOCIAL INTERACTIONS

1. How would you describe the social interactions inside and outside the classroom (e.g., individualistic, cooperative, competitive)?
2. What are the student norms in this class concerning dress, appearance, and interests?
3. What are the students' attitudes toward individual differences?
4. What is the language and vocabulary level of the students?
5. In what locations and ways do students interact in the classroom and the school?
6. What strategies does the teacher employ to promote friendships among students?
7. What personality variables does the teacher exhibit that seem to affect the class?

G. PHYSICAL DESIGN

1. What, if any, architectural barriers exist in the classroom?
2. How does the classroom's design affect the students' academic performance and social interactions?

FIGURE 6.2 Sample environmental assessment form.

Source: Adapted from Preparing secondary students for the mainstream by S. J. Salend and D. Viglianti, *Teaching Exceptional Children,* vol. 14, 1982, pp. 138–139. Copyright 1982 by The Council for Exceptional Children. Reprinted by permission.

Teachers can help students adapt to inclusive settings by teaching them about their surroundings.

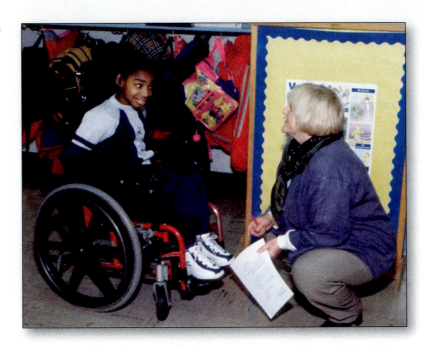

Teach Classroom Procedures and Successful Behaviors   As students move to inclusive classrooms, they need to be taught the procedures and routines of the new setting, as well as the skills that will help them succeed (Monda-Amaya et al., 1998). They can be introduced to several aspects of the new classroom setting such as the teacher's style, class rules, class jobs, and special events, as well as class routines such as lunch count, homework, attendance, and the like. The class schedule can be reviewed, and necessary materials and supplies for specific classes can be identified. You can explain procedures for storing materials; using learning centers, media, materials, and other equipment; working on seatwork activities and in small groups; getting help; handing in completed assignments; seeking permission to leave the room; and making transitions to activities and classes. You can also tour the classroom to show students the design of the room, the behaviors that they will need to succeed, and the location of teaching materials. Once new students move into inclusive classrooms, classmates can be peer helpers to assist them in learning about the class and school routines.

Use Preteaching   *Preteaching* can be used to prepare students for the academic, behavioral, and social expectations of the inclusive setting. In preteaching, the special educator uses the curriculum, teaching style, and instructional format of the teacher in the general education classroom. For example, you can use preteaching to introduce students to the general education curriculum, successful note-taking and homework completion strategies, and the teaching materials and formats (commercially produced teaching programs, media, software) used in inclusive settings.

Use Videos   As we saw in the chapter-opening vignette, videos of inclusive settings can help introduce students to the important factors that affect academic performance and interactions with other students and promote the use of already learned skills in the new setting (Salend, 1995). You can use videos of the new setting to help students identify and discuss key factors of the classroom, such as stated and unstated rules, teacher expectations, classroom routines, and the ways in which students ask for help. A video of students in social activities can provide information on student interaction patterns, peer norms, interests, and language levels.

You also can use videos to prepare students to function in the general education setting. Like Nick, your students can learn and practice note-taking skills by viewing videos of teacher-directed activities in inclusive settings. Students also can learn appropriate responses to many general education classroom situations. For example, they can view scenes from inclusive settings and discuss appropriate responses. Videos also can be used to create a tour of the new school and the new classroom that students can view before they enter the new setting. Finally, videos made by special educators or supportive service personnel showing good behavior management techniques and teaching adaptations, physical handling, and the use of assistive technology can be viewed by general educators (Phelps, 1995).

Teach Learning Strategies   An important part of a transitional program is teaching *learning strategies,* the "techniques, principles, or rules that will facilitate the acquisition, manipulation, integration, storage, and retrieval of information across situations and settings" (Alley & Deshler, 1979, p. 13). Learning strategy instruction teaches students how to learn, solve problems, and complete tasks independently (Sturomski, 1997). In determining if a specific learning strategy should be included in the transitional program, you can address the following questions:

◆ Is the strategy critical for success in the general education classroom?
◆ Is the strategy required in many settings?
◆ Does the strategy enable the student to solve problems independently? (Lebzelter & Nowacek, 1999).

Ellis, Deshler, Lenz, Schumaker, and Clark (1991) and Sturomski (1997) provide a model for teaching learning strategies that you can use to help students succeed in inclusive settings. The model includes the following steps:

◆ Select a strategy that is appropriate for the tasks or the setting and that will improve students' performance.
◆ Allow students to perform a task to determine what strategy they now use and how effectively they use it.
◆ Help students understand the problems caused by their current strategy, and get them interested in learning the new strategy.
◆ Explain and describe the new strategy, its application, and its advantages compared to those of the old strategy.
◆ Obtain a commitment from students to learn the new strategy.
◆ Describe and model the new strategy for students, including a description of each step as you demonstrate it.
◆ Teach students to rehearse the strategy verbally.
◆ Give students opportunities to practice the strategy with materials written at their level and then with materials used in the general education classroom.
◆ Develop an understanding of when to use the strategy.
◆ Offer feedback on the student's use of the strategy.
◆ Assess students' mastery of the strategy.
◆ Develop systems to help students remember the steps of the strategy, such as self-monitoring checklists.
◆ Promote generalization of the strategy across many different situations and settings.

REFLECTIVE

If you were going to make a video of your classroom and school, what features would you highlight?

INFORMATIONAL

Lebzelter and Nowacek (1999) offer a checklist that you can use to evaluate learning strategies and assess their usefulness for individual students.

INFORMATIONAL

Meltzer, Roditi, Houser, and Perlman (1998) offer strategies that teachers and students can use to assess students' use of learning strategies. Montague (1997) offers questions that teachers can use to assess students' acquisition, use, maintenance, and generalization of learning strategies.

REFLECTIVE

What learning strategies do you use? Are they successful? How did you learn them? What other learning strategies might be helpful to you?

INFORMATIONAL

Ellis and Lenz (1996) offer guidelines and Heaton and O'Shea (1995) offer a mnemonic strategy called STRATEGY that can help you develop mnemonic learning strategies.

REFLECTIVE

With which tasks and processes do your students have trouble? Can you develop a learning strategy to help them?

SET YOUR SITES

Additional information on learning strategies is available from the Center for Research on Learning at the University of Kansas (www.ku-crl.org, 785-864-4780).

In later chapters, we will discuss other learning strategies that students can be taught to promote their learning abilities and mastery of particular types of material.

Designing Learning Strategies   You also can design learning strategies for students (Lombardi, 1995). First, identify and sequence the key parts of the task or process. To make it easier for students to remember and use the strategy, try to limit the number of steps to seven. Each step should be briefly stated and should begin with a verb. Next, find a word relating to each part of the task or process that will trigger a memory of that part. The words are then used to create a mnemonic that will help students remember the steps, such as an acronym using the first letter of each word. As students develop skill in using learning strategies, they can be taught to develop their own learning strategies.

You also can help students use learning strategies by developing cognitive credit cards (Edmunds, 1999). These laminated cards provide cues that prompt students to use a learning strategy or guide them in thinking about how to process information.

Promote Students' Independent Work Skills   Although teachers may be able to help students frequently in smaller classes, general education classes may be large, limiting the assistance they can provide. Therefore, to succeed in inclusive settings, students must learn to work independently. You can use a gradual approach in teaching this transitional skill. At first, you can require students to work without teacher assistance for short periods of time; later, the interval can be increased.

Written Assignments   Students in inclusive classrooms are expected to work independently on many written assignments. Since the grades on these assignments are often based, in part, on their appearance, the *HOW* technique, outlined here, can provide students with a structure for producing acceptable papers.

H = HEADING

1. First and last names
2. Today's date
3. Subject/Period
4. Page number if needed

O = ORGANIZED

1. On the front side of the paper
2. Left margin
3. Right margin
4. At least one blank line at the top
5. At least one blank line at the bottom
6. Uniform spacing

W = WRITTEN NEATLY

1. Words and numbers on the line
2. Words and numbers written neatly
3. Neat erasing and crossing out (Archer & Gleason, 1996, p. 121)

Independent Assignments   Since students also have to complete many assignments on their own, a *job card* can help them learn to function independently (Cohen & de Bettencourt, 1988). Using the job card, students determine what materials they need

REFLECTING ON PROFESSIONAL PRACTICES

Teaching Students to Use Learning Strategies

Ms. Washington, a seventh-grade teacher, has noticed that several of her students are not prepared for class physically and mentally. She observes the students closely for several days to determine which skills and strategies they use successfully and which ones they seem to lack. She then meets with the students to talk about her concerns and how their current approaches are affecting their performance. Though initially reluctant, the students indicate that they aren't pleased with their classroom performance and would like to do better. She discusses a learning strategy called PREP and explains how it might help them. PREP involves four stages:

Prepare materials

- Get the notebook, study guide, pencil, and textbook ready for class.
- Mark difficult-to-understand parts of notes, the study guide, and textbook.

Review what you know

- Read notes, study guide, and textbook cues.
- Relate cues to what you already know about the topic.
- List at least three things you already know about the topic.

Establish a positive mind set

- Tell yourself to learn.
- Suppress put-downs.
- Make a positive statement.

Pinpoint goals

- Decide what you want to find out.
- Note participation goals. (Ellis, 1989, p. 36)

After reviewing the strategy and briefly explaining each step, Ms. Washington asks the students to decide if they are willing to make a commitment to learning this strategy. One student says "No" and Ms. Washington tells her that she does not have to learn it, but if she changes her mind, she can learn it at another time. The other students indicate that they are willing to try to learn the strategy. To increase their motivation and reinforce their commitment, Ms. Washington has the students set goals.

Ms. Washington begins by modeling and demonstrating the strategy by verbalizing and "thinking out loud" so that students can experience the thinking processes they will need when using the strategy. She models the proce-

dure several times, using a variety of materials from the class, and reviews how she uses the PREP acronym to remember the steps in the strategy. Students discuss how the PREP strategy compares with their current approaches to learning, as well as the overt and covert behaviors necessary to implement the strategy.

Next, Ms. Washington has the students attempt to learn the steps of the strategy. She divides them into teams and has each team rehearse and memorize the strategy and its proper sequence. To help some students learn the strategy, she gives them cue cards. As students memorize the steps, Ms. Washington gives them cue cards containing less information. When the students can give the steps in the correct sequence, Ms. Washington has them apply the strategy with materials from the classroom. Students work in cooperative learning groups to practice the strategy and receive feedback from their peers. Ms. Washington circulates around the room, observes students using the strategy, and provides feedback. She encourages the students to concentrate on becoming skilled in using the strategy and not to be concerned about the accuracy of the content. As students become adept in using the strategy, Ms. Washington gives them other materials so that they can apply the strategy in many different situations. When students are able to do this, Ms. Washington gives them a test to check their mastery of the material.

Once students master the strategy, Ms. Washington encourages them to use it in her class. She observes them to see if they are employing the strategy and keeps records of their academic performance. Periodically, Ms. Washington reviews the strategy procedures. She cues students to use the strategy through verbal reminders, cue cards, listing the strategy on the board, and reviewing its components. Because the strategy has greatly improved the students' performance, Ms. Washington is working with some of the other teachers to help students use it in their classrooms.

Why did Ms. Washington decide to teach her students to use learning strategies? What methods did she use to teach her students to use learning strategies? What did Ms. Washington do to involve her students in mastering learning strategies? What did she do to help her students use the learning strategies in her class and in their other classes? How would you teach your students to use learning strategies?

An important transitional skill for success in inclusive settings is the ability to work independently.

to do the assignment, the best ways to obtain the materials, where to complete the assignment, the amount of time needed to finish it, and the procedures for handing in their work and finishing assignments early. Archer (1988) also has proposed a model for training students to complete independent assignments:

Step 1: Plan it.
Read the directions and circle the words that tell you what to do.
Get out the material you need.
Tell yourself what to do.

Step 2: Complete it.
Do all items.
If you can't do an item, go ahead or ask for help.
Use HOW.

Step 3: Check it.
Did you do everything?
Did you get the right answers?
Did you proofread?

Step 4: Turn it in. (Archer, 1988, p. 56)

Develop Students' Organization Skills   You also can help students work independently by helping them develop their organizational skills. Several strategies that can help students become more organized will now be described.

Assignment Notebooks   In many general education classrooms, students take notes and record information in their notebooks according to the specifications of their teacher(s). Students can be taught to color code their notebooks by content area, listing assignments in the notebook including page numbers, dates when the assignments are due, and relevant information needed to complete the task. Spector, Decker, and Shaw (1991) suggest that you periodically check students' notebooks for neatness, organization,

Date	Date Due	Class/ Subject	Materials Needed	Assignment	Date Completed

FIGURE 6.3   Sample assignment log.

completeness, and currency, and that you remind students to use them for important assignments, projects, and tests. You also can have students use a homework buddy, a peer who can be contacted for missed assignments and further clarification. To help prevent the loss of notebooks, encourage students to use folders to carry assignments and other relevant materials and information. Finally, remind students to put their names in all textbooks and cover them (Williamson, 1997).

Assignment Logs   Shields and Heron (1989) suggest that students be taught to use an assignment log to keep track of assignments. The log consists of two pocket folders with built-in space to store assignment sheets that contain the name of the assignment, a description of it, the dates the assignment was given and is due, and a place for a family member's signature. When assignments are given, students complete the information on the assignment sheet and place the sheet in the pocket folder labeled "To Be Completed." When the assignment is completed, the assignment sheet is updated (signed by a family member) and put in the "Completed Work" pocket folder. A sample assignment log is presented in Figure 6.3.

Daily and Weekly Schedules   A transitional program also can help students learn how to keep track of the many activities that occur in inclusive settings. Students can become more productive by developing a schedule charting their daily activities, including the time of day and the activity that should and did occur during that time period. At the beginning, you can help students plan their schedules. Later on, as they develop skill in planning and following their schedules, they can plan their own schedules and record the obstacles they encounter in following them. In developing their schedules, students can be taught to do the following:

IDEAS FOR IMPLEMENTATION

Teaching Organizational Skills

Josh, a tenth grader, is having a tough time adjusting to high school. When he does an assignment, he usually receives a good grade. However, far too often, his notebook is messy and incomplete, and he forgets to do his assignments and to study for tests. In addition to his classes, Josh participates in extracurricular activities and occasionally works at a local restaurant.

His family and teachers, frustrated by his erratic performance, decide that a weekly schedule will help Josh organize his activities and complete his schoolwork. At first, each Monday, Josh meets with Ms. Gates, one of his teachers, to plan his schedule. They divide each day into hourly time slots, list class assignments and tests, and outline afterschool and home activities as well as job-related commitments. They then determine which activities have specific time commitments and record them in the schedule. Next, they list Josh's weekly assignments and due dates and estimate the amount of time needed to complete them. Josh and Ms. Gates then establish priorities and enter the items in the schedule. Finally, they review the schedule to ensure that all activities have been given sufficient time and that there is a balance among activities. Throughout the week, Ms. Gates checks Josh's progress in following the schedule. As Josh masters the steps in planning and implementing his schedule, Ms. Gates encourages him to develop his own schedule and monitor his own performance.

Here are some other strategies you can use to create an inclusive and supportive classroom that helps students develop their organizational skills:

◆ Teach students to maintain calendars on which they list their homework, exams, long-term assignments, and classroom and school activities, and encourage them to look at the calendar every day to determine daily activities and plan for long-term projects.

◆ Use class time to review schedules, notebooks, folders, and desks in order to reorganize them and throw out unnecessary materials.

◆ Give students space and materials in which to store items. For example, give them cartons to organize their desk materials or have them make simple desk organizers (see Williamson, 1997).

◆ Teach students to use sticky pads to record self-reminders.

◆ Mark a notebook page that is 20 pages from the last sheet to remind students to purchase a new notebook.

◆ Conduct a scavenger hunt using students' desks and lockers that causes students to clean these areas up.

◆ Train students to provide feedback to peers on organizing their materials and desks.

Sources: Archer and Gleason (1996), Gajria (1995), and Williamson (1997).

◆ Identify specific goals to be accomplished.

◆ Consider and allot time for all types of activities, including studying, social activities, relaxation, and personal responsibilities.

◆ Consider the times of the day at which they are most alert and least likely to be interrupted.

◆ Avoid studying material from one class for long periods of time.

◆ Divide study time into several short periods rather than one long period.

TIME MANAGEMENT CALENDAR, THE UNCALENDAR

WHAT NEEDS TO BE DONE THIS WEEK?

SCHOOL TASK	DUE	TIME TO DO IT
Book report	Friday	6 hrs.
Math Homework	Monday & Wednesday	2 hrs.
Social Studies	Tuesday & Thursday	2 hrs.

HOME

TASK	DUE	TIME
Clean Car	Sat	1 hr.

WORK

TASK	TIME
McDonalds	4-8 M-F

WEEKEND	DATE	MONDAY	DATE	TUESDAY	DATE	WEDNESDAY	DATE	THURSDAY	DATE	FRIDAY	DATE
SCHEDULE		**SCHEDULE**		**SCHEDULE**		**SCHEDULE**		**SCHEDULE**		**SCHEDULE**	
		7-8am bus ride (Homework) 8-3pm School 4-8pm Work 8:30-10:00 Homework									

Tasks:	Time:	Tasks:	Time:	Tasks:	Time:	Tasks:	Time:	Tasks:	Time:	Tasks:	Time:
Book Report	2 hr.	Math Book Report (w/Patty)	1 hr. 1 hr.	Soc St. Book Report	1 hr. 1 hr.	Math Book Report (w/Patty)	1 hr. 1 hr.	Soc St. Book Report	1 hr. 1 hr.	Clean Car	1 hr.

Comments:	Comments:	Comments:	Comments:	Comments:	Comments:
Need help outlining Book Report- See Patty		Have Patty proofread book report			

FIGURE 6.4 Sample weekly log.

Source: Teaching organizational skills to students with learning disabilities by J. M. Shields & T. E. Heron, *Teaching Exceptional Children,* vol. 21, 1989, p. 11. Copyright 1989 by The Council for Exceptional Children. Reprinted by permission.

◆ Be aware of their attention span when planning study periods.

◆ Arrange school tasks based on due dates, importance of tasks, and time demands.

◆ Group similar tasks together.

◆ Schedule time for relaxation.

◆ Reward studying by planning other activities (Mercer & Mercer, 1993; Pauk, 1984).

A sample schedule is presented in Figure 6.4.

Generalization

Once a transitional skill has been learned in one setting, you can take steps to promote *generalization,* the transfer of training to the inclusive setting. In planning for generalization, you must consider the student's abilities, as well as the nature of the general education classroom, including academic content, activities, and teaching style. Since

IDEAS FOR IMPLEMENTATION

Promoting Generalization

Diana, an 11th-grade student, is having difficulty in her science and social studies classes, which present information through textbooks. Her social studies, science, and resource room teachers meet to discuss Diana's performance and agree that she would benefit from learning SQ3R, a text comprehension strategy. Diana's resource room teacher introduces the strategy and helps her learn it in that setting. However, her other teachers notice that Diana often fails to apply the strategy in their classrooms. To help her do so, they give her the following self-monitoring checklist, which presents the skills Diana should demonstrate when using the strategy in social studies and science:

STEPS	YES	NO
1. Did I survey the chapter?		
a. Headings and titles		
b. First paragraph		
c. Visual aids		
d. Summary paragraphs		
2. Have I asked questions?		
3. Did I read the selection?		
4. Did I recite the main points?		
5. Did I produce a summary of the main points?		

Diana's use of the strategy increases, and her performance in science and social studies improves.

Here are some other strategies you can use to promote generalization:

- Discuss with students other settings in which they could use the strategies and skills.
- Work with students to identify similarities and differences among settings.
- Role play the use of the strategies and skills in other situations.
- Ask teachers to help and prompt students to use the strategies and skills.
- Help students understand the link between the strategies and skills and improved performance in the inclusive setting.
- Provide opportunities to practice the strategies and skills in inclusive settings.

transfer of training to other settings does not occur spontaneously, you must have a systematic plan to promote it.

You can promote generalization by training the students to perform under the conditions and expectations that they will encounter in the general education classroom. This can be done by introducing various factors of the general education classroom into the special education or bilingual education classroom and by giving students the opportunity to experience them. Similarly, a student who will be placed in the general education classroom can be taught to perform under the conditions that exist there. You also can use several strategies to prepare students for the demands of the general education classroom, including changing reinforcement, cues, materials, the ways students respond, and dimensions of the stimulus, settings, and teachers (Vaughn, Bos, & Lund, 1986). Descriptions and examples of these generalization techniques are presented in Figure 6.5.

CHANGE REINFORCEMENT

Description/Methods

Vary amount, power, and type of reinforcers.

- ❖ Fade amount of reinforcement.

- ❖ Decrease power of reinforcer from tangible reinforcers to verbal praise.
- ❖ Increase power of reinforcer when changing to mainstreamed setting.
- ❖ Use same reinforcers in different settings.

Examples

- ❖ Reduce frequency of reinforcement from completion of each assignment to completion of day's assignments.
- ❖ Limit use of stars/stickers and add more specific statements, e.g., "Hey, you did a really good job in your math book today."
- ❖ Give points in regular classroom although not needed in the resource room.
- ❖ Encourage all teachers working with student to use the same reinforcement program.

CHANGE CUES

Description/Methods

Vary instructions systematically.

- ❖ Use alternate/parallel directions.

- ❖ Change directions.

- ❖ Use photograph.
- ❖ Use picture to represent object.
- ❖ Use line drawing or symbol representation.
- ❖ Use varying print forms.

Examples

- ❖ Use variations of cue, e.g., "Find the . . ."; "Give me the . . ."; "Point to the . . ."
- ❖ Change length and vocabulary of directions to better represent the directions given in the regular classroom, e.g., "Open your book to page 42 and do the problems in set A."
- ❖ Move from real objects to miniature objects.
- ❖ Use actual photograph of object or situation.
- ❖ Move from object/photograph to picture of object or situation.
- ❖ Use drawings from workbooks to represent objects or situations.
- ❖ Vary lower and upper case letters; vary print by using manuscript, boldface, primary type.
- ❖ Move from manuscript to cursive.

CHANGE MATERIALS

Description/Methods

Vary materials within task.

- ❖ Change medium.

- ❖ Change media.

Examples

- ❖ Use unlined paper, lined paper; change size of lines; change color of paper.
- ❖ Use various writing instruments such as markers, pencil, pen, typewriter.
- ❖ Use materials such as films, microcomputers, filmstrips to present skills/concepts.
- ❖ Provide opportunity for student to phase into mainstream.

CHANGE RESPONSE SET

Description/Methods

Vary mode of responding.

- ❖ Change how student is to respond.

- ❖ Change time allowed for responding.

Examples

- ❖ Ask child to write answers rather than always responding orally.
- ❖ Teach student to respond to a variety of question types such as multiple choice, true/false, short answer.
- ❖ Decrease time allowed to complete math facts.

FIGURE 6.5 Generalization techniques.

Source: But they can do it in my room: Strategies for promoting generalization by S. Vaughn, C. S. Bos, and K. A. Lund, *Teaching Exceptional Children,* Vol. 18, 1986, pp. 177–178. Copyright 1986 by The Council for Exceptional Children. Reprinted with permission.

(continued)

CHANGE SOME DIMENSION(S) OF THE STIMULUS

Description/Methods

Vary the stimulus systematically.

◇ Use single stimulus and change size, color, shape.

◇ Add to number of distractors.

◇ Use concrete (real) object.
◇ Use toy or miniature representation.

Examples

◇ Teach colors by changing the size, shape, and shade of "orange" objects.
◇ Teach sight words by increasing number of words from which child is to choose.
◇ Introduce rhyming words by using real objects.
◇ Use miniature objects when real objects are impractical.

CHANGE SETTING(S)

Description/Methods

Vary instructional work space.

◇ Move from more structured to less structured work arrangements.

Examples

◇ Move one-to-one teaching to different areas within classroom.
◇ Provide opportunity for independent work.
◇ Move from one-to-one instruction to small-group format.
◇ Provide opportunity for student to interact in large group.

CHANGE TEACHERS

Description/Methods

Vary instructors.

◇ Assign child to work with different teacher.

Examples

◇ Select tasks so that child has opportunities to work with instructional aide, peer tutor, volunteer, regular classroom teacher, and parents.

FIGURE 6.5   (continued)

HOW CAN I HELP STUDENTS FROM SPECIALIZED SCHOOLS AND PRESCHOOL PROGRAMS MAKE THE TRANSITION TO INCLUSIVE SETTINGS?

Plan the Transitional Program

INFORMATIONAL

Hadden and Fowler (1997) and Drinkwater and Demchak (1995) offer guidelines and forms for designing programs that help students and families make the transition from preschool and early childhood programs to inclusive schools.

Students moving from special day schools and preschool programs also need transitional programs to prepare them to enter inclusive settings (Udell et al., 1998). In planning and using a transitional program for these students, you need to work with other educators and with students' families to develop a transition timeline, prepare students for the transition, collect data on students' performance, establish communication procedures, and evaluate the transition process. Such a transitional program can introduce students to the new school's personnel and describe their roles; to the school's physical design, including the location of the cafeteria, gymnasium, and auditorium; and to important rules, procedures, and extracurricular activities. You can orient students to the new setting by giving them a map of the school with key areas and suggested routes highlighted, assigning a reliable student to help the new students learn how to get around the school, and color coding the students' schedule (Gillet, 1986).

Adapt Transitional Models

George, Valore, Quinn, and Varisco (1997) and Goodman (1979) have developed models for integrating students from specialized schools into schools within their community. These models also can be adapted to plan transitions from preschool programs or from hospital and institutional settings to school. The models involve:

1. *Deciding on placement.* At first, teachers, determine which community school is appropriate based on location, attitudes of school personnel, availability of services, and needs of the students. They identify key personnel in the sending and receiving schools and programs, and they gather and share information about the students who will be moving from one setting to another.

2. *Approximating the new environment.* Teachers in the special school help students adjust to the new school by trying to duplicate the demands, conditions, and teaching methods of the new setting.

3. *Leveling of academic skills.* Students are prepared for the academic requirements of the new setting and start using the new school's textbooks, teaching materials, and assignments.

4. *Building skills in the new school.* Staff from the special school meet with teachers, administrators, and support staff from the new school to discuss strategies that have been used successfully with the students. Educational goals are developed and shared with teachers at the new school. The support needs of students and their teachers at the new school are identified, and appropriate strategies are instituted.

5. *Visiting the school.* Students visit and tour the new school to get a picture of the important aspects of the school and its physical design.

6. *Starting with small units of time.* At first, some students may attend the new school for a brief period to help them adjust gradually. As students become comfortable in the new school, the attendance period increases until the students spend the whole school day in the new setting.

7. *Accompanying and advocating for the student.* At first, a staff member from the sending school may accompany the students to the new school to serve as a resource for the students and the staff. At the same time, a staff member from the receiving school serves as an advocate to assist the students in the new setting.

8. *Promoting social acceptance and academic success.* Teachers in the new school promote the social acceptance of the new students by locating their work area near class leaders or assigning them an important class job. Teachers also teach peers about individual differences and friendships. In addition, they use appropriate teaching adaptations and monitor their effectiveness.

9. *Opening lines of communication.* Ongoing communication systems between personnel from the sending and receiving schools and between the receiving school and the home are established.

10. *Scheduling follow-up.* As part of the communication system, follow-up meetings are held to discuss the students' progress and to resolve conflicts.

INFORMATIONAL

Stuart and Goodsitt (1996), Doelling and Bryde (1995), and Phelps (1995) offer guidelines for helping students and their families make the transition from hospitals and rehabilitation centers to school and home.

How Can I Help Students from Linguistically and Culturally Diverse Backgrounds Make the Transition to Inclusive Settings?

INFORMATIONAL

Romero and Parrino (1994) developed the *Planned Alternation of Languages (PAL)* approach to help prepare second language learners to make the transition to general education classes.

Many of the transitional strategies previously discussed are appropriate for linguistically and culturally diverse students. However, a transitional program for these students can also include teaching cultural norms, language, and socialization skills, as well as the terminology related to each content area. A good transitional program for these students also will help them master the language skills necessary for academic learning, such as listening, reading, speaking, and writing. It will also teach students *pragmatics*, the functional and cultural aspects of language.

Teach Cultural Norms

A transitional program for students with various languages and cultures can teach them the cultural norms and communication skills that guide social and academic classroom life (Li, 1992). For example, some teachers may expect students to raise their hands to ask for help. However, some students, because of their cultural backgrounds, may hesitate to seek assistance in that way because they are taught not to draw attention to themselves. A transitional program should also help make students aware of the culture of the school, including routines, language, and customs. You can help students learn these different cultural behaviors by (1) acknowledging and understanding their cul-

A transitional program for students from linguistically and culturally diverse backgrounds should help students develop an awareness of routines, language, and customs.

tural perspective; (2) explaining to the students the new perspective and the environmental conditions associated with it; (3) using modeling, role playing, prompting, and scripting to teach new behaviors; and (4) understanding that it may take some time for these students to develop competence in the new culture. You also can help students make the transition to your class and school by assigning them class jobs, giving them peer helpers, and labeling objects in the classroom in their native language.

Orient Students to the School

Several activities can be used to orient students to their new school. When students first arrive, you can give them a list of common school vocabulary words and concepts. You also can pair these students with a peer who can serve as a host until they are acclimated. In addition, you can give students a tour of the school and photos labeled with the names of important locations and school personnel.

INFORMATIONAL

Bruns and Fowler (1999) offer guidelines for designing culturally sensitive transition plans.

Teach Basic Interpersonal Communication Skills

Since the language of social interactions in schools is English, many second language learners also need help in developing the *basic interpersonal communication skills (BICS)* to be successful in general education settings. BICS and other social skills can be taught using many strategies that give students valuable experiences. Some of these strategies are described here. These strategies also can be used to help students develop the social interaction skills that support friendships (see Chapter 5).

Modeling

Modeling allows students to view language and social interaction patterns. For example, students can observe peers in the inclusive classroom during a social interaction activity or view a video of such an activity (Buggey, 1999). You can then review these observations with students, emphasizing language, behaviors, and cues that promote social interactions—specifically, strategies and language for beginning and maintaining social interactions.

Role Playing

Students can develop BICS and social skills by role playing social interaction situations (Hartas & Donahue, 1997). Where possible, the role play should take place in the environment in which the behavior is to be used. After the role play, you can give students feedback on their performance.

Prompting

You can use prompting to help students learn relevant cues for using appropriate interpersonal skills. In prompting, students are taught to use the environment to learn new skills. For example, students and teachers can visit the playground, identify stimuli, and discuss how these stimuli can be used to promote socialization. Specifically, playground equipment, such as the slide, can serve as a prompt to elicit questions and statements such as "Do you want to play?", "This is fun!", and "Is it my turn?"

Scripting

Since much of the dialogue in social conversation is predictable and often redundant, you can show students the language and structure of social interactions via scripts that outline conversations that might occur in a specific setting. For example, a typical conversation at lunchtime can be scripted to include questions and responses relating to the day's events ("How are you doing today?"), menus ("Are you buying lunch today?"), and school or class events ("Are you going to the game after school?").

Teach Cognitive Academic Language Proficiency Skills

The strategies for teaching BICS also can be used to teach *cognitive academic language proficiency (CALP)* skills. CALP can be taught by giving students techniques for understanding the teaching terms used in inclusive settings. Students can be encouraged to list words and concepts used in the classroom discussions, textbooks, and assignments in a word file for retrieval as needed. For quick retrieval, the file can be organized alphabetically or by content area. As students master specific terms, those terms can be deleted or moved to an inactive section of the file. Students can also keep a record of key words and concepts by using the *divided page* method. Students divide a page into three columns. In column one, they list the term, phrase, or concept. The context in which it is used is given in column two, and the word is defined briefly in column three. Students can then keep a separate list for each new chapter or by subject area. These methods of listing difficult terms can be adapted for students who are learning English by recording information in their dominant language. For example, the primary language equivalent of words and phrases can be included in a word list or as separate sections of the divided page.

Cognitive Academic Language Learning Approach

Chamot and O'Malley (1989) have developed the *Cognitive Academic Language Learning Approach (CALLA)* to help students develop the cognitive academic language proficiency skills necessary for success in inclusive classrooms. CALLA was designed for students who speak primary languages other than English, but it can also be used to plan a transitional program for *all students.* CALLA has three components: content-based curriculum, academic language development, and learning strategy instruction.

Content-Based Curriculum   In the content-based curriculum component of CALLA, students are gradually introduced to the curriculum of the general education classroom in the bilingual education or ESL program using the materials used in the inclusive setting. It is recommended that students be introduced to the content areas in the following sequence: science, mathematics, social studies, and language arts.

Academic Language Development   In this component, students practice using English as the language of instruction while their teachers support them through the use of concrete objects, visual aids, and gestures. Possible activities include learning academic vocabulary in different content areas, understanding oral presentations accompanied by visuals, and participating in activities by using hands-on materials such as manipulatives and models.

METACOGNITIVE STRATEGIES

Advance organization   Previewing the main ideas and concepts of the material to be learned, often by skimming the text for the organizing principle.
Advance preparation   Rehearsing the language needed for an oral or written task.
Organizational planning   Planning the parts, sequence, and main ideas to be expressed orally or in writing.
Selective attention   Attending to or scanning key words, phrases, linguistic markers, sentences, or types of information.
Self-monitoring   Checking one's comprehension during listening or reading, or checking one's oral or written production while it is taking place.
Self-evaluation   Judging how well one has accomplished a learning task.
Self-management   Seeking or arranging the conditions that help one learn, such as finding opportunities for additional language or content input and practice.

COGNITIVE STRATEGIES

Resourcing   Using reference materials such as dictionaries, encyclopedias, or textbooks.
Grouping   Classifying words, terminology, numbers, or concepts according to their attributes.
Note taking   Writing down key words and concepts in abbreviated verbal, graphic, or numerical form.
Summarizing   Making a mental or written summary of information gained through listening or reading.
Deduction   Applying rules to understand or produce language or solve problems.
Imagery   Using visual images (either mental or actual) to understand and remember new information or to make a mental representation of a problem.
Auditory representation   Playing in the back of one's mind the sound of a word, phrase, or fact in order to assist comprehension and recall.
Elaboration   Relating new information to prior knowledge, relating different parts of new information to each other, or making meaningful personal associations with the new information.
Transfer   Using what is already known about language to assist comprehension or production.
Inferencing   Using information in the text to guess meanings of new items, predict outcomes, or complete missing parts.

SOCIAL AND AFFECTIVE STRATEGIES

Questioning for clarification   Eliciting from a teacher or peer additional explanation, rephrasing, examples, or verification.
Cooperation   Working together with peers to solve a problem, pool information, check a learning task, or get feedback on oral or written performance.
Self-talk   Reducing anxiety by using mental techniques that make one feel competent to do the learning task.

FIGURE 6.6   Learning strategies taught in the Cognitive Academic Language Learning Approach (CALLA).
Source: J. M. O'Malley and A. U. Chamot, *Learning strategies in second language acquisition* (New York: Cambridge University Press, 1990), pp. 198–199. Copyright 1990 by Cambridge University Press. Reprinted by permission of the publisher.

Learning Strategy Instruction   In the third component, students master techniques that make it easier to learn language and subject matter content. These learning strategies are presented in Figure 6.6.

Offer Newcomer Programs

To help immigrant students adjust, many school districts have developed *newcomer programs,* which offer students academic and support services to help them make the transition to and succeed in inclusive classrooms (Schnur, 1999). The services offered include (1) activities and classes to orient students to the school and society; (2) a special curriculum that promotes the learning of English, multicultural awareness, academic content, and students' native languages; (3) support services such as counseling, tutoring, family training, information, medical and referral services, career education, and transportation; and (4) individualized and innovative teaching by specially trained teachers. After spending up to 1 year in a newcomer program, students transfer to bilingual/ESL or general education classrooms within the school district.

HOW CAN I HELP STUDENTS MAKE THE TRANSITION FROM SCHOOL TO ADULTHOOD?

Develop an Individualized Transition Plan

As we mentioned earlier, the IDEA requires comprehensive planning teams to develop and implement Individualized Transition Plans (ITPs) that are part of the IEPs of students 14 years of age and older. These ITPs help students make the transition from school to adult life. The IDEA defines transition services as "a coordinated set of activities for a student, designed within an outcome-oriented process, which promotes movement from school to postschool activities, including postsecondary education, vocational training, integrated employment, continuing education, adult services, independent living or community participation. The coordinated set of activities must: (a) be based upon the individual student's needs; (b) take into account student's preferences and interests; and (c) include instruction, community experiences, the development of employment and other post-school adult living objectives, and if appropriate, the acquisition of daily living skills and functional vocational evaluation."

In designing ITPs, planning teams should use person-centered planning (Miner & Bates, 1997) and actively involve students in the process (Thoma, 1999) (see the guidelines for student involvement in the planning process in Chapter 2). The process should include the following:

◆ An assessment of students' career goals and interests, independence, hobbies, interpersonal relations, self-determination, decision-making skills, self-advocacy, and communication levels (Clark [1996] provides an overview of standardized and informal procedures that you can use to assess the transitional planning needs of students)

◆ An assessment of students' current and desired skill levels in making the transition to postsecondary education, employment, community participation, and/or residential living

◆ An assessment of the new environment to identify the physical, social, emotional, and cognitive skills necessary to perform effectively in the new setting

◆ A list of the related services and adaptive devices that can affect success in the new environment, as well as any potential barriers such as transportation problems

◆ A statement of the goals and objectives of the transitional program, including those related to student empowerment, self-determination, self-evaluation, and decision-making skills

◆ A list of teaching strategies, approaches, materials, adaptations, and experiences, as well as the supportive and community-based services necessary to achieve the stated goals of the transitional program

◆ A statement of each participating agency's role and responsibilities, including interagency collaborations

◆ A description of the communication systems that will be used to share information among professionals, among community agencies, and between school and family members

◆ A system for evaluating the success of the transition program on a regular basis (Dunn, 1996; Grigal, Test, Beattie, & Wood, 1997; Mental Retardation Institute, 1991)

INFORMATIONAL

Asselin, Todd-Allen, and deFur (1998) outline the roles and responsibilities of transition specialists to help students and their families make transitions.

INDIVIDUALIZED TRANSITION PLAN

Planning Meeting Date _____

Name of Student Alan _____   Date of Birth 16 years old at time of meeting _____

Planning Team Alan, Alan's mother, Mrs. Thomas (classroom teacher), Jeff R.
(job coach), Mr. Jones (school administrator) and John M. (paraprofessional)

Transition Options	Goal	School Representatives and Responsibilities	Parent/Family Responsibilities	Agencies Involved Responsibilities and Contact Person	Supportive IEP Goal(s)/Objective(s)
Vocational Placements		1. Teacher will increase from 2 hrs. weekly to 5 hrs. weekly the time Alan spends working at the nursery.	1. Alan's mother will begin to give Alan a regular, weekly allowance.	1. Job coach/teacher will arrange Alan's schedule next year to include more community-based vocational experiences.	—communication
Competitive	X				—identify job(s) he likes
Supportive	X				—behavior relaxation, identification of feelings
Sheltered	___	2. Job coach will expand the types of jobs Alan performs from maintenance tasks to more nursery trade related tasks.	2. Mother will begin to explore vocational options/interests by: a) checking with friends who own businesses to see if any have training opportunities for Alan; and b) spending time with Alan visiting different places and talking with Alan about the different jobs observed on these "exploration trips."	2. School administrator will initiate canvass of local businesses to explore potential vocational training sites for Alan including: a) local automotive parts refurbishing site b) local shipping company c) local supermarket chain d) local restaurant	—money management —skill mastery in designated tasks/jobs
Specify the above or other X					—rooming via uniform care and laundry, etc.
It is unclear whether Alan will be better able to perform in a competitive or supportive work environment 5 years from now, but both options are being explored.		3. Job coach will introduce two additional vocational experiences for Alan each of the next 3 years so that Alan can, in his last 2 years of school, choose a vocational area of preference and refine his skills in these.	3. Mother will assign Alan some household "jobs" so Alan has the opportunity to be responsible for chores.	3. Contact at local VESID office will visit school to provide overview training to staff re: job-related skills development.	—functional time telling —learning how to use staff lounge for break/meal times —social skills training (co-workers)
Identify current and past vocational experiences. Alan currently spends 2 hours each week working at a local nursery.				4. Job coach/teacher will perform functional assessment at each worksite to identify areas in which Alan needs support.	

FIGURE 6.7 Sample component of an ITP.

Source: J. O'Neill, C. Gothelf, S. Cohen, L. Lehman, & S. B. Woolf, *Supplement for transition coordinators: A curricular approach to support the transition to adulthood of adolescents with visual or dual sensory impairments and cognitive disabilities* (New York: Hunter College of the City University of New York and the Jewish Guild for the Blind, 1990; ERIC Documentation Reproduction Service No. EC 300 449–453).

A component of a sample transitional plan is presented in Figure 6.7. Transitional programming for students who are leaving school is designed to prepare them to participate actively in their communities and to become self-sufficient and independent. Therefore, transitional programming often addresses four areas: employment, living arrangements, leisure, and postsecondary education (Smith, Edelen-Smith, & Stodden, 1995).

SET YOUR SITES

You can obtain information and resources on transitions for individuals with disabilities by contacting the Institute on Community Integration (www.ici.coled.umn.edu/ici, 612-624-4512).

Prepare Students for Employment

An important outcome for many young people leaving high school is employment so that they can earn money, interact with others, and advance in their careers. The unemployment rate for non-college-bound young people and those with disabilities is still quite high, and these groups are less likely to aspire to high-status occupations (Rojewski, 1996). Most students with disabilities who find employment often work in part-time, unskilled positions that pay at or below the minimum wage and offer few opportunities for advancement. These low-wage positions limit the opportunities for self-sufficiency and a reasonable quality of life.

The employment outcomes of students with disabilities are also related to gender and ethnicity (Blackorby & Wagner, 1996; Doren & Benz, 1998). Although females with disabilities are less likely to find employment than males, they are more likely to live independently. White students with disabilities are more likely to find employment and receive higher wages than students of color and those who speak languages other than English.

Students with diverse languages and cultures and female students are often channeled into less challenging careers. You can begin to address these disparities by showing *all students* the importance of work inside and outside the home, the range of jobs that people perform, the preparation for these jobs, the fear-of-success syndrome, and sex-role and cultural stereotyping and their impact on career choices (Bartholomew & Schnorr, 1994).

Several models are available to address the difficulties that students with disabilities experience in finding a job. These models are outlined below.

Competitive Employment

Young people who are leaving school need help in making the transition to competitive and supported employment. *Competitive employment* involves working as a regular employee in an integrated setting with coworkers who are not disabled and being paid at least the minimum wage (Berkell & Gaylord-Ross, 1989). Individuals usually find competitive employment through a job training program, with the help of family and friends, or through a rehabilitation agency.

Supported Employment

While some individuals with disabilities may find competitive employment, many others benefit from supported employment (Wehman, West, & Kregel, 1999). *Supported employment* provides ongoing assistance as individuals learn how to obtain, perform, and hold a job; travel to and from work; interact with coworkers; work successfully in integrated community settings; and receive a salary that reflects the prevailing wage rate.

Job Coach

Because a key component of all supportive employment models is a *job coach* or a supported employment specialist, you may be asked to work collaboratively with these professionals, families, and employers. While the functions of the job coach depend on the supported employment model, this person may perform many different functions, including the following:

INFORMATIONAL

Hutchins and Renzaglia (1998) developed a family vocational interview that you can use to involve families in the transition planning process.

INFORMATIONAL

Patton, de la Garza, and Harmon (1997) developed assessment and learning activities to prepare students for success in competitive and supported employment settings.

◆ Assessing students' job skills and preferences for employment and placing them appropriately

◆ Training students in job-related, travel, and interpersonal skills and enlisting the aid of employers and coworkers to help them function successfully

◆ Monitoring the satisfaction of the student, employer, coworkers, and families

◆ Gradually eliminating the coaching services and providing periodic follow up services

Career Education Programs

A good career education program can help students make the transition to work (Morningstar, 1997). Career education should begin in elementary school and occur throughout schooling. It should include career awareness, orientation, exploration, preparation, and placement (Razeghi, 1998).

Elementary School Years   In elementary school, career education programs usually focus on *career awareness,* an understanding of the various occupations and jobs available, the importance of work, and an initial self-awareness of career interests. These programs also introduce students to daily living and social skills, attitudes, values, and concepts related to work through classroom jobs, homework, chores at home, money, and hobbies.

Middle School/Junior High Years   In middle school/junior high school, career education programs usually focus on *career orientation,* an identification of career interests through practical experience and exposure to a variety of occupations. Through field trips, speakers, special vocational classes, small job tryouts, and integrated curricula, students become familiar with work settings, attitudes, and job-related and interpersonal skills. They also develop an appreciation of the values associated with working.

High School Years   In high school, career education programs often focus on career exploration, preparation, and placement. *Career exploration* activities give students simulated and direct experiences with many occupations to help them determine their career goals and interests. For example, students can visit work settings and observe workers as they perform their jobs. Vocational guidance and counseling also help students obtain information about a variety of jobs. *Career preparation* helps students adjust to work by offering teaching, support, and work experiences through vocational education programs. A career preparation program includes training in specific job-related skills and the opportunity to use these skills in simulated or real work settings. *Career placement,* the placement of students in jobs or other postsecondary settings, often occurs at around the time of graduation from high school.

In high school, students may join *community-based learning programs* such as cooperative work education or work-study programs (Benz, Yovanoff, & Doren, 1997). In community-based learning programs, students are taught in their communities. They attend school and work part-time to blend their academic and vocational development. Through an agreement between schools and employers, students' educational and work experiences are coordinated. Students are encouraged to complete school while getting the training and experiences needed for future employment. Community-based learning programs give students financial aid and the opportunity to learn job-related skills and experiences.

SET YOUR SITES

The Job Accommodation Network (http://janweb.icdi.wvu.edu, 800-526-7234) offers information about job accommodations and help in hiring and training individuals with disabilities.

INFORMATIONAL

Beakley and Yoder (1998) offer guidelines for establishing community-based learning programs.

SET YOUR SITES

Help in establishing service learning programs is available from the National Service-Learning Clearinghouse (www.nicsl.coled. umn.edu, 800-808-7378), the National Helpers Network (www.nationalhelpers.org, 800-646-4623), and the Association for Supervision and Curriculum Development's Service Learning/Experiential Learning Network (SELNET) (www.ascd.org, 800-933-2723).

SET YOUR SITES

Information and resources to help students make the transition from school to work are available from the National School-to-Work Learning and Information Center (www.stw.ed.gov, 800-251-7236).

REFLECTIVE

How did you become interested in teaching? What career education programs helped you to make that decision? What job-related and interpersonal skills do you need to be an effective teacher? What career education experiences helped you develop those skills? How did your cultural background and gender affect your career choice?

Service Learning Programs

In *service learning* programs, students perform and reflect on their roles that benefit the community. These programs provide real-life experiences that teach students about the world of work and career choices and help them develop communication, social, problem-solving, and self-determination skills (Krystal, 1999; Yoder, Retish, & Wade, 1996). Service learning activities that connect the curriculum to important activities and actions in the community can motivate and teach students about themselves, others, and society (Burns, Storey, & Certo, 1999). For example, such programs can involve working in a homeless shelter or in a program for elderly persons or preschoolers.

Functional Curriculum and Career Education Models

An important part of transitional programming for students is a *functional curriculum.* In this curriculum, goals and methods tailored to individual students prepare them for a successful transition to adult living, including living, working, and socializing in their communities. When determining the individualized goals of a functional curriculum, teachers examine the importance of each goal to students' current and future needs. They also consider the relevance of each goal to the student's age and current level of performance.

Many functional curriculum and career education models are available. The *Life-Centered Career Education (LCCE)* model targets life-centered competencies involving daily living skills, personal-social skills, and occupational guidance and preparation to be integrated into the general education curriculum (Brolin, 1993). Clark and Kolstoe (1990) have developed the *School Based Career Education Model.* This model provides career education services and functional activities from preschool through adulthood, including values, attitudes, habits, human relationships, occupational information, and job and daily living skills. Cronin and Patton's (1993) *Domains of Adulthood* model gives teachers guidelines for providing students with experiences in employment/education, home and family, leisure pursuits, community involvement, physical/emotional health, and personal responsibility and relationships. Life skills and functional activities that can be integrated into the curriculum for elementary (Mannix, 1992) and secondary (Mannix, 1995) students also are available.

Foster Independent Living Arrangements

As students leave school, they also may need help in learning to live in community-based living arrangements. Clark and Kolstoe (1990, pp. 349–350) identified the most common such arrangements:

1. Independent living (alone or with a spouse, significant other, or roommates) in a house, mobile home, or apartment, with no supervision or support
2. Semi-independent living (alone or with someone else) in a house, mobile home, or apartment, with periodic supervision
3. Living at home with family members, with minimal or no supervision
4. Group home living with 6 to 10 other residents, with minimal but continuous supervision
5. Family care or foster home living, with close and continuous supervision

Other living arrangements include personal care facilities where staff offer help with daily living skills and provide comprehensive care.

To make a successful transition, students need training to overcome negative attitudes, environmental constraints (such as the availability of transportation, shopping, and leisure activities), and socioeconomic barriers. In addition, students can learn how to be self-sufficient and take care of their needs, maintain the property, and seek help from others when necessary.

Promote Students' Participation in Leisure Activities

Though often overlooked, leisure is an important quality-of-life issue and a key component for students who are leaving school. Through leisure and recreational activities, individuals can develop a satisfying social life. This increases their psychological and personal well-being, their development of self-determination, and their integration into inclusive settings (Dattilo & Hoge, 1999; Johnson, Bullock, & Ashton-Shaeffer, 1999). Unfortunately, studies of the leisure activities of individuals with disabilities reveal that they are less likely to belong to school or community groups and participate in recreational activities than their peers who are not disabled (Hoge & Dattilo, 1995).

Leisure Education

Because leisure is important for everyone, more and more leisure education services are being provided to students so that they can interact with others in community-based leisure activities throughout life. Leisure education teaches students to function independently during free-time activities at school, at home, and in the community; decide

SET YOUR SITES

Disability Resource Monthly (www.disabilityresources.org, 631-585-0290) is a newsletter that monitors, reviews, and reports on resources for independent living, and Independent Living USA maintains a website (www.ilusa.com) that addresses issues and resources related to independent living arrangements for individuals with disabilities.

All students should be encouraged to participate in leisure and afterschool activities.

which leisure activities they enjoy; participate in leisure and recreational activities with others; and engage in useful free-time activities.

Set Your Sites

Information and resources for adapting leisure and physical activities can be obtained from the National Consortium on Physical Education and Recreation for Individuals with Disabilities (http://ncperid.usf.edu, 770-423-6544), the American Alliance for Health, Physical Education, Recreation and Dance (www.aahperd.org, 800-213-7193), and FitnessLink (www.fitnesslink.com).

Recreational and Leisure Resources for Individuals with Disabilities

As an outgrowth of the disability rights movement, more recreational and leisure resources are now available for individuals with disabilities (Johnson et al., 1999). Publications such as *Laugh with Accent* (800-787-8444) and *Tales from the Cripped* (fax no. 716-244-6599) discuss disability issues humorously. Information about travel for individuals with disabilities can be obtained from *Access Travel USA: A Directory for People with Disabilities* (800-345-4789) and *New Horizons for the Air Traveler with a Disability* (301-322-4961). *Living Without Limits* is a syndicated radio program focused on lifestyle issues for individuals with disabilities that is available on the Internet (www.thriveonline.com./health/lwl.about.html). Resources to aid individuals with dis-

IDEAS FOR IMPLEMENTATION

Promoting Leisure Skills

On Mondays, Ms. Whatley asked her students to describe the things they did over the weekend. Since many students said they watched television or were bored and did nothing, Ms. Whatley decided to teach them about the leisure and recreation activities available in the community. She began by discussing her own leisure activities and how much she enjoyed playing soccer and going to concerts with her friends. She also gave the class materials about community leisure activities such as newspaper articles, fliers from parks and museums, newspaper and magazine reviews of movies, musics, and dance, and newspaper sports pages and had her students read them. As a follow-up activity, she invited members of leisure groups in the community to speak to students about their groups' activities. Three weeks later, Mondays seemed brighter to Ms. Whatley, as many of her students spoke about their participation in and enjoyment of leisure activities.

Here are some other strategies you can use to promote students' leisure skills:

◆ Allow and encourage students to select their own free-time activities.

◆ Encourage students to write and talk about their leisure activities and to participate in afterschool activities.

◆ Give students opportunities and teach them skills to try new activities and toys.

◆ Teach students how to initiate play with others and role play leisure situations.

◆ Take students on field trips to leisure facilities in the community.

◆ Teach students about social and recreational opportunities. For example, *I Belong Out There* (Program Development Associates, 1995) is a video with an accompanying booklet, including checklists and resources, that introduces individuals with disabilities to recreational opportunities and describes how to find them.

◆ Teach scoring for a variety of recreational games.

◆ Seek the help of others, such as a therapeutic recreation specialist, physical educator, community recreation personnel, and families.

abilities in driving (American Automobile Association, 1995; Plank, 1992), dressing (Schwarz, 1995), and enjoying and participating in the performing arts (Bailey, 1993) and yoga (Sumar, 1998) also are available.

Explore Postsecondary Opportunities

A growing number of students with disabilities are thinking of going to college (Dukes & Shaw, 1998). These students will benefit from a transitional program that helps them develop the skills necessary to succeed there, including understanding and informing others of their disability and the accommodations they will need. A transitional program also can address these students' attitudes and help them develop strategies for dealing with large classes, as well as reading, writing, testing, and course load demands (Synatschk, 1995).

Brandt and Berry (1991) and Grasso-Ryan and Price (1992) offer guidelines for preparing students with disabilities for postsecondary settings, including suggestions for planning and goal setting, promoting academic preparation, and developing social skills. Brinckerhoff (1996) offers a timetable for transition planning to succeed in college. Aune and Ness (1991) have developed *Tools for Transition* for teachers who are helping students make the transition to college. The eight units of Tools for Transition are (1) Understanding My Learning Style, (2) Using Study Strategies, (3) Planning Accommodations in School, (4) Self-Advocacy, (5) Exploring Careers, (6) Choosing a Type of Postsecondary School, (7) Choosing and Applying to a Postsecondary School, and (8) Interpersonal Skills. Brinckerhoff (1994) also developed a series of seminars to teach self-advocacy skills to college-bound students with disabilities.

HOW CAN I HELP STUDENTS DEVELOP SELF-DETERMINATION?

An important quality-of-life issue and an aspect of success in inclusive settings is the development of self-determination, "[the] personal attitudes and abilities that facilitate an individual's identification and pursuit of goals . . . reflected in personal attitudes of empowerment, active participation in decisionmaking, and self-directed action to achieve personally valued goals" (Powers et al., 1996, p. 292). Whether moving to a general education setting or to adulthood, self-determination skills can help students control their lives and adjust to the independence and choices associated with inclusive settings and adulthood (Thoma, 1999; Wehmeyer & Schwartz, 1997). Since self-determination involves lifelong experiences and opportunities, you can collaborate with other teachers and family members to include goals related to self-determination on students' IEPs and ITPs, and use the strategies described below to help students develop self-determination (Hasazi, Furney, & Destefano, 1999).

Offer Choices and Solicit Preferences

Allowing students to make choices and express their preferences can promote self-determination. Because the school day involves a series of choices, you can integrate

INFORMATIONAL

Heuttig and O'Connor (1999), Johnson et al., (1999), Reilly (1999), and Schleien, Ray, and Green (1997) provide a variety of leisure education materials, activities and resources, and Longmuir and Axelson (1996) offer resources, for using assistive technology for recreation.

SET YOUR SITES

Information to help you include individuals with disabilities in the arts is available from the National Arts and Disability Center (http://nadc.ucla.edu, 310-794-1141), and in recreation, parks, and tourism from the National Center on Accessibility (www.indiana.edu/%7Enca, 765-349-9240).

INFORMATIONAL

Hall, Kleinert, and Kearns (2000) offer information about postsecondary programs for students with moderate and severe disabilities.

INFORMATIONAL

Wehmeyer (1996) developed a student self-report strategy that you can use to measure your students' self-determination.

REFLECTIVE

Would you describe yourself as self-determined? If so, how did you develop self-determination? If not, what factors hindered you?

activities involving choices into both teaching and nonteaching parts of the daily schedule (Wall & Dattilo, 1995). If students have difficulty making choices, you can start by providing them with options. Cooperative learning arrangements, student-selected projects and rewards, self-management and metacognitive techniques, and learning strategies also allow students to guide their own learning.

Identifying and expressing preferences, needs, and strengths, and planning to meet these needs and desires, also promotes students' self-determination. A variety of strategies can be used to involve students in assessing their learning needs, learning styles, and preferences (see Chapter 12) and to help you assess the preferences and choices of students with severe disabilities (Hughes, Pitkin, & Lorden, 1998). As we saw in Chapter 2, students also can be empowered by attending and participating in meetings to develop their educational program and IEP.

INFORMATIONAL

Battle, Dickens-Wright, and Murphy (1998) offer guidelines to help students develop effective self-advocacy skills, and learning strategies. PROACT (Ellis, 1998) and ASSERT (Kling, 2000) are available for the same purpose.

SET YOUR SITES

LDOnline (www.ldonline.org) offers KidZone, which provides information, stories, and artwork that can help students with learning disabilities understand their conditions and develop their self-advocacy skills.

Develop Self-Advocacy Skills

By developing self-advocacy skills, students become actively involved in determining and meeting their educational and social-emotional needs and career goals (Battle, Dickens-Wright, & Murphy, 1999). An important aspect of self-advocacy is understanding and achieving one's needs and goals. You can work with others to help students understand their abilities, disabilities, needs, interests, and legal rights, as well as show them how to communicate this information to others and how to achieve their goals (Kling, 2000). Other self-advocacy skills that can be taught to students include making eye contact with others, asking for help when needed, expressing appreciation to others, supporting others, explaining their needs and accommodations to others, and presenting themselves positively (Gajria, 1995).

Promote Self-Esteem

Promoting self-esteem in students can improve their ability to advocate for themselves (Field, Hoffman, & Posch, 1997). Students with low self-esteem often make negative statements about themselves that hinder their performance, such as "I'm not good at this and I'll never complete it." You can promote self-esteem by helping students understand the harmful effects of low self-esteem, and by structuring academic and social situations so that students succeed (Gajria, 1995). Other methods include recognizing students' achievements and talents, teaching them to use self-management techniques, asking them to perform meaningful classroom and school-based jobs, and posting their work in the classroom and throughout the school (Nahmias, 1995). Additional suggestions for promoting students' self-esteem are presented in Chapter 7.

Provide Attribution Training

Students' self-determination and self-esteem can be fostered by *attribution training*, which involves teaching students to analyze the events and actions that lead to success and failure. Students who understand attribution recognize and acknowledge that their positive performance is due to effort ("I spent a lot of time studying for this test"), ability ("I'm good at social studies"), and other factors within themselves. Students who fail to understand attribution often attribute their poor performance to bad luck ("I got the

After reading each sentence, please place an 'X' on the line where you feel it should go.

My feelings about the task:

1. I thought this task was

very easy   kind of easy   just right   kind of hard   very hard

2. I gave this task

no effort   a little effort   good effort for awhile   a lot of effort   my best effort

3. On this task I think my answers were

all wrong   mostly wrong   half and half   mostly right   all right

On this task I was:

Successful because: Unsuccessful because:

1. The task was easy   1. The task was difficult

not important   kind of important   very important   not important   kind of important   very important

2. I tried   2. I did not try

not important   kind of important   very important   not important   kind of important   very important

3. I was lucky   3. I was not lucky

not important   kind of important   very important   not important   kind of important   very important

4. I am capable/good at this   4. I am not capable/good at this

not important   kind of important   very important   not important   kind of important   very important

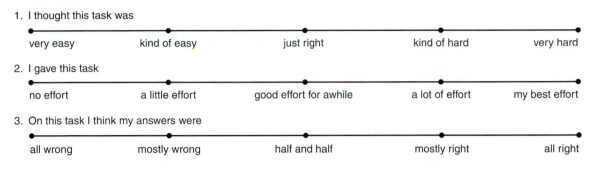

FIGURE 6.8 Sample attribution self-report.

Source: Self-task: Strategies for success in math by N. Corral & S. D. Antia, *Teaching Exceptional Children,* Vol. 29, 1997, pp. 42–45. Copyright 1997 by The Council for Exceptional Children. Reprinted with permission.

hardest test"), teacher error ("The teacher didn't teach that"), lack of ability ("I'm not good at math"), or other external factors. A sample self-report that you can use to assess your students' attributions is presented in Figure 6.8.

You can work with others to help students learn to use positive attributions by teaching them (1) to understand how attributions and effort affect performance, (2) to view failure as the first part of learning and a sign of the need to work harder, (3) to focus on improvement and to analyze past successes, and (4) to talk about mistakes and assume responsibility for successful outcomes (Oxer & Klevit, 1995). You also can encourage students to use positive attributions by modeling them, having students self-record them, responding to students' correct responses with effort feedback ("You're really working hard") or ability feedback ("You have the skill to do this"), and

INFORMATIONAL

Duchardt, Deshler, and Schumaker (1995) developed a learning strategy called BELIEF and accompanying graphic devices to help students identify and change their ineffective attributions.

by responding to students' incorrect responses with a strategy or informational feedback ("Try another way of doing this") (Corral & Antia, 1997; Yasutake, Bryan, & Dohrn, 1996).

Provide Access to Positive Role Models

Access to positive role models can promote self-determination in students. These role models can be found in affinity support groups, mentors, and communications that focus on the needs, interests, and experiences of students.

Affinity Support Groups

You can foster self-determination by promoting positive group and individual identities in students. This can be done by introducing students to affinity support groups of peers with common traits (Stainback, Stainback, East, & Sapon-Shevin, 1994). For example, you and your colleagues at school can establish an affinity support group of students with disabilities. Like other school groups made up of individuals with similar characteristics (e.g., sports teams, performing arts groups, academic clubs), this affinity support group can help students understand and value the skills and qualities they bring to school and learn to respect the individuality of others. The group can define their goals and activities: sharing experiences, expressing needs and interests, planning school activities, performing community service, and serving as an advocacy group to support each other.

Mentors

Mentors, self-determined, successful adults with disabilities who guide and assist younger individuals with disabilities, can be valuable in helping students make the transition to adulthood and develop self-determination (Field, 1996; Reiff, Gerber, & Ginsberg, 1996). Mentors and protégés are matched on the basis of shared interests, needs, goals, and personalities. Mentors serve as models of appropriate qualities and behaviors, teach and share knowledge, listen to the thoughts and feelings of protégés, offer advice, support, and encouragement, and promote protégés to others (Searcy et al., 1995). For example, by sharing their experiences and meeting regularly with protégés, mentors serve as role models for students attending colleges and universities, working in competitive employment situations, living independently, participating in community recreation activities, and having a family life. Mentors also can help protégés understand their talents and develop confidence in their abilities.

Same-race and same-language mentors, and personnel who understand the students' language and culture, also can help students from different cultural and language backgrounds make the many school- and society-based transitions they face (Campbell-Whatley, Algozzine, & Obiakor, 1997). Mentors from the community can help culturally and linguistically diverse students with various aspects of schooling, as well as helping them continue to value their cultural and linguistic identities. For example, same-language mentors can share their past and current experiences as second language learners. This allows them to relate to students and their experiences in learning a new language, and helps students to make school- and society-based transitions.

INFORMATIONAL

Stainback et al. (1994) offer suggestions for helping students form affinity support groups that are managed by the students themselves rather than by adults and that are inclusive rather than exclusive.

SET YOUR SITES

Information and resources to help you establish a mentoring program are available from the National Mentoring Partnership (www.mentoring.org, 202-729-4340).

INFORMATIONAL

Campbell-Whatley (1999) and Miller (1997) offer guidelines for developing mentoring programs for students.

REFLECTIVE

Have you mentored others? Have you been mentored by others? Were these arrangements formal or informal? What roles did the mentor perform? What outcomes and barriers were associated with these experiences? Was it easier to be a mentor or a protégé?

Mentors can help students make transitions to adulthood and can help them develop self-determination.

Provide Access to Communications

For persons with disabilities, self-determination and advocacy skills also can be promoted by access to communications that focus on their needs, interests, and experiences. For example, periodicals such as *The Disability Rag and ReSource* (502-459-5343), *Mainstream* (www.mainstream-mag.com, 619-234-3138), and *Kaleidoscope: International Magazine of Literature, Fine Arts, and Disability* (330-762-9755) publish articles, reviews, fiction, essays, and photographs on various issues affecting individuals with disabilities. Magazines that address disability-related issues are available on audiocassette, in Braille, and in other specialized formats from the National Library Service for the Blind and Physically Handicapped (www.lcweb.loc.gov/nls/nls.html, 202-707-5100). Individuals with disabilities also can develop solidarity and share their experiences by using the Internet and by joining a disabilities rights group. For example, *The Ability Online Support Network* (www.ablelink.org, 416-650-6207) offers a forum in which students with disabilities can interact with peers with and without disabilities, as well as with adult mentors.

Use Self-Determination Curricula

Curricula to help students develop the attitudes, knowledge, and skills to act with self-determination also are available. *Steps to Self-Determination* (Field & Hoffman, 1996) is an experience-based curriculum that teaches students many skills related to self-determination that can be used in inclusive settings. Serna and Lau-Smith (1995) developed the *Learning with PURPOSE* curriculum for students and the *PURPOSE-PLANNING* curriculum for families. These curricula can be used in inclusive settings to help students develop self-determination. Ludi and Martin's (1995) *Self-Determination: The Road to Personal Freedom* curriculum is designed for students from culturally and linguistically diverse backgrounds. It includes units on communication, self-understanding, rights, responsibilities, and self-advocacy. *Project Take Charge* (Powers et al., 1996) is a curriculum that offers strategies to promote adolescent independence and self-determination.

REFLECTING ON YOUR PRACTICES

Promoting Students' Self-determination

You can evaluate the extent to which you promote your students' self-determination by addressing the following questions:

◆ Do I integrate into the daily schedule activities that encourage students to make choices?

◆ Am I aware of students' preferences?

◆ Do I encourage IEP teams to consider students' self-determination skills?

◆ Have I made it easy for students to attend and participate in IEP meetings?

◆ Have I taught students to advocate for themselves?

◆ Do I create a learning environment that helps students feel good about themselves?

◆ Do I encourage students to analyze how their actions contribute to success and failure?

◆ Do I give students opportunities to have positive role models, and to participate in service learning and community-based programs?

◆ Do I give students access to resources that focus on their needs, interests, and experiences?

◆ Do I use curricula and teaching materials and activities to promote students' self-determination?

How would you rate the extent to which you promote self-determination in your students? ( ) Excellent ( ) Good ( ) Needs Improvement ( ) Needs Much Improvement

What are some goals and steps you could take to improve your students' self-determination?

SUMMARY

This chapter offered guidelines for planning and using transitional programs to prepare students for success in inclusive settings. As you review the questions posed in this chapter, remember the following points.

How Can I Help Students Make the Transition to General Education Classrooms?

You can help students make this transition by understanding their unique abilities and needs, using transenvironmental programming, identifying and teaching essential classroom procedures and behaviors, and helping students to use their skills in different settings. You can help students succeed by teaching them to use learning strategies that can improve their independent work and organizational skills.

How Can I Help Students from Specialized Schools and Preschool Programs Make the Transition to Inclusive Settings?

You can work with others to develop a transitional plan and adapt a variety of transitional models.

How Can I Help Students from Linguistically and Culturally Diverse Backgrounds Make the Transition to Inclusive Settings?

You can teach students the accepted cultural norms, orient them to the new school, help them develop basic communication and cognitive academic language proficiency skills, and offer newcomer programs.

What Would You Do in Today's Diverse Classroom?

It is the middle of the school year, and your principal tells you that you will be receiving two new students next week: Carolina and Henry.

❖ Carolina recently arrived in this country to be reunited with her family. Her records indicate that she attended school sporadically in her native country. She is now developing her English skills and has already learned some basic conversational skills. Carolina enjoys being with others, and they enjoy being with her.

❖ Henry has been in a self-contained class for students with learning disabilities for the past 3 years. During that time his learning and behavior improved, and the multidisciplinary team believes that he is ready to learn in a general education class. His special education teacher reports that he needs help organizing himself and working independently.

1. What additional information would you like to have about Carolina and Henry in order to plan transitional programs for them?

2. What goals would you have for their transitional programs?

3. What teaching and generalization strategies would you use to help Carolina and Henry succeed in your class?

4. How could you promote Carolina's and Henry's self-determination skills?

How Can I Help Students Make the Transition from School to Adulthood?

You can develop an ITP that addresses students' needs in the areas of employment, independent living arrangements, leisure, and postsecondary education.

How Can I Help Students Develop Self-Determination?

You can offer students choices, ask about their preferences, help them develop self-advocacy skills and self-esteem, provide attribution training and access to positive role models and communications, and use self-determination curricula.

CHAPTER 7

CREATING A CLASSROOM ENVIRONMENT TIIAT PROMOTES POSITIVE BEHAVIOR

Jaime

Just as Ms. McLeod is beginning to read to her students, Jaime approaches her with another book and asks her if she will read it. Ms. McLeod tells Jaime that she cannot read it now and asks him to please put it away. Jaime goes to the back of the group, sits down, and begins to play with the book. Ms. McLeod again asks him to put the book away. Jaime stands up, walks halfway to his desk, and returns to the group, still carrying the book. Again, Ms. McLeod asks him to put it away, and he finally complies.

The class begins to discuss the story, with Ms. McLeod asking the students various questions. Jaime touches another student's sneakers, and the student swats Jaime's hand away. Jaime then makes faces at Maria, who is sitting next to him. Maria laughs and starts sticking her tongue out at Jaime. Jaime raises his hand to respond to a question but cannot remember what he wants to say when Ms. McLeod calls on him, and starts making up a story and telling jokes. The class laughs, and Ms. McLeod tells Jaime to pay attention.

As Ms. McLeod begins to give directions for independent work, Jaime opens and closes his velcro sneakers. Ms. McLeod asks him to stop and get to work. He works on the assignment for 2 minutes and then "walks" on his knees to the wastepaper basket. The class laughs, and Ms. McLeod tells Jaime to return to his seat and get to work. When he reaches his desk, he begins to search for a missing crayon, naming each one as he puts it back in the box. His classmates laugh at these names, and Ms. McLeod reminds Jaime to work on the assignment. At the end of the period, Ms. McLeod collects the students' work. Although Jaime's responses were correct, he completed only 2 of the 10 questions.

What strategies could Ms. McLeod use to help Jaime improve his learning and behavior? After reading this chapter, you should be able to answer this as well as the following questions.

◇ What legal guidelines must I consider when designing disciplinary actions for students with disabilities?
◇ How can I conduct a functional behavioral assessment?
◇ How can I promote positive classroom behavior in students?
◇ How can I prevent students from harming others?
◇ How can I adapt the classroom design to accommodate students' learning, social and physical needs?

REFLECTIVE

What social and behavioral skills are important for success in your classroom?

For students to be successful in inclusive settings, their classroom behavior must be consistent with teachers' demands and academic expectations and must promote their learning and socialization with peers (Carpenter & McKee-Higgins, 1996). Appropriate academic and behavioral skills allow students to become part of the class, the school, and the community. Unfortunately, for reasons both inside and outside classroom, the behavior of some students like Jaime may interfere with their learning and socialization. Therefore, you may need to use different strategies and physical design changes to help your students to learn and socialize. A good classroom management system includes understanding students' learning and social needs, using an engaging and appropriate curriculum, and using innovative teaching practices and adaptations to instruction. It is also important to create a welcoming and comfortable learning environment, as well as to communicate with students, respect them, and care for them.

WHAT LEGAL GUIDELINES MUST I CONSIDER WHEN DESIGNING DISCIPLINARY ACTIONS FOR STUDENTS WITH DISABILITIES?

If students are classified as having a disability under either the IDEA or Section 504 of the Rehabilitation Act of 1973, you need to work collaboratively with placement teams to use certain rules and guidelines when disciplining them. In reviewing the legal status of disciplinary actions used with students with disabilities, Yell and Peterson (1995) identified three categories: permitted procedures, controlled procedures, and prohibited procedures.

◇ *Permitted disciplinary procedures* are inconspicuous strategies that are included in the school district's disciplinary policies, are typically used with *all students,* and do not change a student's placement or deny the student's right to an education. They should not have a strongly negative impact on the student's IEP goals. Such disciplinary procedures include verbal reprimands, warnings, restricting privileges, removing points as part of a token system, detention, or temporary delay of services or activities such as recess.

❖ *Controlled disciplinary procedures* are interventions that are allowable if they are appropriate and unabusive and do not interfere with the student's IEP goals. These strategies can also be used if they do not discriminate between students and do not represent a unilateral change in a student's placement. When using controlled discipline (e.g., short-term suspension), you should keep written records to document its appropriate use (Maloney, 1994).

❖ *Prohibited disciplinary procedures* are actions that result in a unilateral change in a student's placement and are therefore not permissible. They include expulsion or indefinite suspension.

Another important factor that you must consider when disciplining students with disabilities is *reasonableness,* which concerns rules that have a school-related rationale and rational procedures for helping students comply with the rules (Valente, 1994). In *Cole v. Greenfield-Central Community Schools* (1986), a federal court ruled that schools can use reasonable discipline with students with disabilities. The court identified four questions that help determine the reasonableness of a procedure: (1) Does the teacher have the authority to discipline students? (2) Is the rule that was violated related to an educational function? (3) Was the student who broke the rule the one who was disciplined? (4) Was the disciplinary procedure consistent with the seriousness of the rule violation? (Yell & Peterson, 1995).

The IDEA amendments of 1997 contain new provisions that you will have to consider when disciplining students with disabilities. Under these provisions, school personnel can discipline a student with disabilities in the same ways they discipline students without disabilities. However, students with disabilities cannot be suspended or placed in an interim alternative setting for more than 10 days unless the disciplinary action is related to carrying a weapon to school or knowingly possessing, using, or selling illegal drugs at school. In these cases, the IEP team can unilaterally place a student for up to 45 days in an interim alternative setting. The alternative setting must provide a general education, the special education services outlined in the student's IEP, and services to address the student's behavior.

In making the decision, the IEP team also must conduct a *manifestation determination,* an examination to determine if the student's disability made it difficult for the student to control the behavior and understand its impact and consequences. In doing so, the team considers many relevant data including evaluation and diagnostic test results, information provided by students and their families, observations of the students, the behavior to be disciplined, the appropriateness of the student's placement, and the extent to which the placement occurred as intended. If the team determines that the student's behavior was related to the disability, the team examines and modifies the student's IEP and behavioral intervention plan. If the team decides that the student's behavior was not related to the disability, the student can be disciplined in the same way as students without disabilities.

The IDEA amendments of 1997 also require the IEP team to conduct a functional behavioral assessment and use a behavioral intervention plan for students whose behavior results in suspension or removal to an interim alternative setting. For students whose behavior impedes their learning or the learning of others, the IEP team must consider positive behavioral interventions, strategies and supports focused on the student's behavior. This also may include a functional behavioral assessment and a behavioral intervention plan (Zurkowski, Kelly, & Griswold, 1998). (In the following sections, you will learn how to conduct a functional behavioral assessment and how to implement specific positive behavioral interventions.)

INFORMATIONAL

Yell (1997) reviews the law concerning teacher liability for student injury and misbehavior.

How Can I Conduct a Functional Behavioral Assessment?

A *functional behavioral assessment (FBA)* involves gathering information to measure specific student behaviors; determine why, where, and when a student uses these behaviors; and what social, affective, cultural, and/or environmental and contextual factors appear to predict and maintain the behaviors (Sugai, Horner, & Sprague, 1999; Tilly et al., 1998). An FBA helps you develop a plan to change a student's behavior by examining the reason for the behavior and identifying strategies that address the conditions (e.g., events, factors, individuals, activities, antecedents, and consequences) in which the behavior is most likely and least likely to occur (McConnell, Hilvitz, & Cox, 1998). Guidelines for conducting an FBA and examples relating to the chapter-opening vignette of Jaime and Ms. McLeod are presented below.

Identify the Problematic Behavior

First, the team identifies the behavior that will be examined by the FBA by considering the following questions: (1) What does the student do that causes a problem? (2) Does the student have the skill and the communication and physical abilities to perform the behavior? (3) How does the behavior affect the student's learning, socialization, and self-concept, as well as classmates and adults? For example, in the chapter-opening vignette, Jaime's poor on-task behavior seems to be undermining both his learning and the classroom environment.

The team also needs to examine the relationship, if any, between the behavior and the student's cultural and language background. Some students from diverse backgrounds may have different cultural perspectives from their teachers, and communication problems between students and teachers often are interpreted by teachers as behavioral problems. For example, a student may appear passive in class, which may be interpreted as evidence of immaturity and lack of interest. However, in the student's culture, the behavior may be considered a mark of respect for the teacher as an authority figure (Gutierrez, 1994).

Define the Behavior

Next, the behavior is defined in observable and measurable terms by listing its characteristics. For example, Jaime's on-task behavior can be defined as having his eyes on the teacher or an instructional object, making comments related to the task, being in his work area, and having his hands on the desk or on appropriate teaching materials.

Use an Observational Recording System to Record the Behavior

After the behavior has been defined, the team selects an appropriate observational recording method and uses it during times that are typical and representative. Examples of different recording systems are presented in Figure 7.1.

Event Recording

If the behavior to be observed has a definite beginning and end and occurs for brief time periods, event recording is a good choice. In *event recording,* the observer counts the

Date	Length of Sessions	Number of Events
9/11	30 minutes	卌
9/15	30 minutes	卌 卌 l
9/20	30 minutes	lll

(a) Event Recording of Call-outs

Date	Occurrence Number	Time		Total Duration
		Start	End	
5/8	1	9:20	9:25	5 minutes
	2	9:27	9:30	3 minutes
5/9	1	10:01	10:03	2 minutes
	2	10:05	10:06	1 minute
	3	10:10	10:14	4 minutes

(b) Duration Recording of Out-of-seat Behavior

15 Sec	15 Sec	15 Sec	15 Sec
+	−	−	+
+	+	−	−
+	−	−	−
−	+	+	+
+	+	−	+

(c) Interval Recording of On-task Behavior

(d) The observation of Jack took place on the school playground during a 15-minute recess period. The playground is made up of an open area for group games and an area with typical playground equipment of swings, a jungle gym, and two slides. During the first 5 minutes of observation, Jack played by himself on a swing with no interactions with his peers, who were also swinging or waiting for a turn. One of the waiting students asked Jack for a turn on the swing. Jack ignored the request, neither slowing down the swing, making eye contact, nor verbally responding to the student. The teacher's aide then intervened, asking Jack to finish his ride so others could have a turn. Jack responded by jumping off the swing in midflight and loudly cursing at the aide. The aide then removed Jack from the playground.

FIGURE 7.1   Examples of observational recording strategies.

number of behaviors that occurred during the observation period, as shown in Figure 7.1a. For example, event recording can be used to count the number of times Jaime was on task during a typical 30-minute teacher-directed activity. Data collected using event recording are displayed as either a frequency (number of times the behavior occurred) or a rate (number of times it occurred per length of observation).

You can use an inexpensive grocery, stitch, or golf counter for event recording. If a mechanical counter is not available, marks can be made on a pad, an index card, a chalkboard, or a piece of paper taped to the wrist. You also can use a transfer system in which

Observing students and recording their behavior can provide valuable information for a functional behavioral assessment.

you place small objects (e.g., poker chips, paper clips) in one pocket and transfer an object to another pocket each time the behavior occurs. The number of objects transferred to the second pocket gives an accurate measure of the behavior.

Duration and Latency Recording

If time is an important factor in the observed behavior, a good recording strategy would be either duration or latency recording. In *duration recording*, shown in Figure 7.1b, the observer records how long a behavior lasts. *Latency recording*, on the other hand, is used to determine the delay between receiving instructions and beginning a task. For example, duration recording can be used to find out how much time Jaime spends on task. Latency recording would be used to assess how long it took Jaime to begin an assignment after the directions were given. The findings of both recording systems can be presented as the total length of time or as an average. Duration recording data also can be summarized as the percentage of time the student engaged in the behavior by dividing the amount of time the behavior lasts by the length of the observation period and multiplying by 100.

Interval Recording or Time Sampling

With *interval recording and time sampling*, the observation period is divided into equal intervals, and the observer notes whether the behavior occurred during each interval; a plus ($+$) indicates occurrence and a minus ($-$) indicates nonoccurrence. A $+$ does not indicate how many times the behavior occurred in that interval, but only that it did occur. Therefore, this system shows the percentage of intervals in which the behavior occurred rather than how often it occurred.

The interval percentage is calculated by dividing the number of intervals in which the behavior occurred by the total number of intervals in the observation period and then multiplying by 100. For example, you might use interval recording to record Jaime's on-task behavior. After defining the behavior, you would divide the observation period into intervals and construct a corresponding interval score sheet, as shown in Figure 7.1c. You would then record whether or not Jaime was on task during each interval. The number of intervals in which the behavior occurred would be divided by the total number of intervals to determine the percentage of intervals in which he was on task.

Anecdotal Records

An anecdotal record, also known as *continuous recording*, is often useful in reporting the results of the observation. An *anecdotal record* is a narrative of the events that took place during the observation. Wright (1967) offers several suggestions for writing narrative anecdotal reports:

◆ Describe the activities, design, individuals, and their relationships to the setting in which the observation occurred.
◆ Report in observable terms all of the student's verbal and nonverbal behaviors, as well as the responses of others to these behaviors.
◆ Avoid interpretations.
◆ Indicate the sequence and duration of events.

A sample anecdotal record is presented in Figure 7.1d.

Obtain Additional Information About the Student and the Behavior

An important part of an FBA is determining the student's skills, strengths, weaknesses, interests, hobbies, preferences, self-concept, attitudes, health, culture, language, and experiences. Often this information is obtained by interviewing the student, teachers, family members, ancillary support personnel, and peers (Fox, Conroy, & Heckaman, 1998; Larson & Maag, 1998). For example, Ms. McLeod could ask Jaime to respond to the following questions: (1) What do I expect you to do during class time? (2) How did the activities and assignments make you feel? (3) Can you tell me why we couldn't read the book you wanted us to read? (4) What usually happens after you make faces at other students or touch them? and (5) Why did you walk to your desk on your hands and knees?

Perform an Antecedents-Behavior-Consequences (A-B-C) Analysis

While recording behavior, an A-B-C analysis also is used to identify the antecedents and consequences of the student's behavior. *Antecedents* and *consequences* are the events, stimuli, objects, actions, and activities that precede and trigger the behavior, and follow and maintain the behavior, respectively.

Analyze the Data and Develop Hypothesis Statements

First, the team identifies the antecedents and consequences of the behavior by addressing the following: (1) What happens before and after the behavior that makes it more or less likely that the behavior will occur? (2) Under what conditions (e.g., events, time, motivations, environmental factors, individuals, activities, instructional, behavioral, and procedural expectations, cultural perspectives, and other antecedents and consequences) is

REFLECTIVE

How would you define, in observable and measurable terms, and what recording strategies would you use to assess out-of-seat, inattentive, aggressive, tardy, noisy, and disruptive behavior?

INFORMATIONAL

Interviews and survey questions to identify the perspectives of teachers, students, and family members on student behavior are available (Kern, Dunlap, Clarke, & Childs, 1994; Lawry, Storey, & Danko, 1993; Lewis, Scott, & Sugai, 1994; O'Neill et al., 1997; Reid & Maag, 1998).

In analyzing the antecedents of student behavior, consider if the behavior is related to the following:

◆ Physiological factors such as medications, allergies, hunger/thirst, odors, or temperature levels
◆ Home factors or the student's cultural perspective
◆ Student's learning, motivation, communication, and physical abilities
◆ The physical design of the classroom, such as the seating arrangement, the student's proximity to the teacher and peers, classroom areas, transitions, scheduling changes, and noise levels
◆ The behavior of peers
◆ Certain days, the time of day, the length of the activity, the activities or events preceding or following the behavior or events outside the classroom
◆ The way the material is presented or the way the student responds
◆ The curriculum and the teaching activities, such as certain content areas and instructional activities, or the task's directions, difficulty and staff support
◆ Group size and/or composition or the presence and behavior of peers and adults

In analyzing the consequences of student behavior, consider the following:

◆ What are the behaviors and reactions of specific peers and/or adults?
◆ What is the effect of the behavior on the classroom atmosphere?
◆ How does the behavior affect progress on the activity or the assigned task?
◆ How does the behavior relate to and affect the student's cultural perspective?
◆ What encourages or discourages the behavior?

FIGURE 7.2   A-B-C analysis questions.

the behavior most likely and least likely to occur? For example, possible antecedents for Jaime's behavior include the location of the teacher and Jaime's work area; the type, duration, and difficulty of the activity; auditory and visual stimuli in the room; and the availability of other materials such as crayons and books. Possible consequences for Jaime's behavior include attention from the teacher and peers, avoiding an unpleasant activity, performing a pleasant activity, and releasing physical energy.

The A-B-C data are then analyzed and summarized to identify when, where, with whom, and under what conditions the behavior is most likely and least likely to occur (see Figure 7.2 for questions that can guide you in analyzing the behavior's antecedents and consequences). The A-B-C analysis data are also analyzed to try to determine why the student uses the behavior, also referred to as the *perceived function* of the behavior. The team can identify the perceived function of the behavior by considering the following: (1) What does the student appear to be communicating via the behavior? (2) How does the behavior benefit the student (e.g., getting attention or help from others, avoiding or escaping from an undesirable activity, access to a desired activity or peers, increased status and self-concept, sense of power and control, sensory stimulation or feedback, satisfaction)? (3) What is the purpose of the behavior in the student's culture? (4) How does the behavior relate to the student's language background?

Next, the interview and A-B-C analysis data are used to develop hypotheses about the student and the behavior, which are verified (Sasso, Peck, & Garrison-Harrell, 1998). *Specific hypotheses* relate to the purpose of the behavior and the conditions associated with it, including possible antecedents and consequences. For example, a specific hypothesis related to Jaime's behavior would be that when Jaime is given a teacher-directed or independent academic activity, Jaime will use many off-tasks behaviors to gain attention from peers and the teacher and to avoid a difficult activity.

Consider Sociocultural Factors

When analyzing the A-B-C information to determine hypotheses, the team should consider the impact of cultural perspectives and language background on the student's behavior and communication. To do this, behavior and communication must be examined in a social/cultural context. For example, three cultural factors that may affect students' behavior in school are outlined below: time, respect for elders, and individual versus group performance. However, although this framework for comparing students may be useful in understanding certain cognitive styles and associated behaviors, you should be careful in generalizing a specific behavior to any cultural group. Thus, rather than considering these behaviors as characteristic of the group as a whole, you should view them as attitudes or behaviors that an individual may consider in learning and interacting with others (Anderson & Fenichel, 1989).

Time

Different cultural groups have different concepts of time. The Euro-American culture views timeliness as essential and as a key characteristic in judging competence. Students are expected to be on time and to complete assignments on time. Other cultures may also view time as important, but as secondary to relationships and performance (Cloud & Landurand, n.d.). For some students, helping a friend with a problem may be considered more important than completing an assignment by the deadline. Students who have different concepts of time may also have difficulties on timed tests or assignments.

Respect for Elders

Cultures, and therefore individuals, have different ways to show respect for elders and authority figures such as teachers. In many cultures, teachers and other school personnel are viewed as prestigious and valued individuals who are worthy of respect. Respect may be demonstrated in many different ways, such as not making eye contact with adults, not speaking to adults unless spoken to first, not asking questions, and using formal titles (Ramirez, 1989). Mainstream culture in the United States does not always show respect for elders and teachers in these ways. Therefore, the behaviors mentioned above may be interpreted as communication or behavior problems rather than as cultural marks of respect.

Individual versus Group Performance

The Euro-American culture is founded on such notions as rugged individualism. By contrast, many other cultures view group cooperation as more important. For students from these cultures, responsibility to society is seen as an essential aspect of competence, and their classroom performance is shaped by their commitment to the group and the community rather than to individual success. As a result, for some African American, Native American, and Hispanic American students who are brought up to believe in a group solidarity orientation, their behavior may be designed to avoid being viewed as "acting white" or "acting Anglo" (Fordham & Ogbu, 1986; Ramirez, 1989).

Humility is important in cultures that value group solidarity. By contrast, cultures that emphasize individuality award status based on individual achievement. Students from cultures that view achievement as contributing to the success of the group may perform better on tasks perceived as benefiting a group (LaFramboise & Graff-Low, 1989). They may avoid situations that bring attention to themselves, such as reading out loud,

INFORMATIONAL

Cartledge, Kea, and Ida (2000) and Craig et al. (2000) offer reviews of culturally based student behaviors that may be misinterpreted by teachers.

answering questions, gaining the teacher's praise, disclosing themselves, revealing problems, or demonstrating expertise.

Develop a Behavioral Intervention Plan

REFLECTIVE

African American and Hispanic males and poor students receive harsher discipline for all types of behavioral offenses than their white peers and are more often suspended and physically punished (Evans & Richardson, 1995). Why do you think this is the case?

Based on its information and hypotheses, the team collaboratively develops a behavioral intervention plan focusing on the student's behavior, characteristics, and needs (Scheuermann, & Webber, 1999). The plan should identify specific measurable goals and the individuals and services responsible for helping the student achieve these goals. It also should outline the positive, culturally appropriate, teaching and behavioral supports and strategies that change the antecedent events and consequences by addressing the following issues: (1) What antecedents and consequences can I change to increase/decrease the behavior? (2) What strategies, curricular adaptations, and physical design modifications can I use to increase/decrease the behavior? (3) Which of these changes are most likely to be effective, acceptable, easy to use, culturally sensitive, least intrusive, and beneficial to others and the learning environment? For example, Ms. McLeod can try to change Jaime's behavior by moving his seat closer to her, adjusting the activity to Jaime's teaching and motivational level, limiting the distractions in the room, and praising Jaime and others. Strategies for increasing appropriate behavior and decreasing inappropriate behavior and modifying the physical environment that Ms. McLeod can use are discussed later in this chapter.

SET YOUR SITES

For more information and resources in conducting an FBA and creating behavioral intervention plans, contact the Center for Effective Collaboration and Practice (www.air-dc.org/cecp/cecp.html, 888-457-1551).

Evaluate the Plan

The team continues to collect data to examine how effectively the plan is influencing the student's behavior, learning, and socialization. Students from various cultural and language backgrounds also may respond differently to their teachers' behavior management strategies, so the team also needs to be aware of how the plan influences' students' cultural perspectives (Ewing & Duhaney, 1996). Based on these data and feedback from others, the team revises the plan, changes the interventions, and collects additional data if necessary.

REFLECTIVE

Perform an FBA on one of your behaviors, such as studying or eating. How could you use the results to change your behavior?

HOW CAN I PROMOTE POSITIVE CLASSROOM BEHAVIOR IN STUDENTS?

Many supports and strategies to promote good classroom behavior exist. They include affective education techniques, antecedents-based interventions, consequences-based interventions, self-management techniques, group-oriented management systems, and behavior reduction techniques. These methods are described below.

SET YOUR SITES

Information and resources from other teachers on behavior management strategies are available at the website www.quasar.ualberta.ca/ddc/incl/intro.htm#top.

Affective Education Techniques

Affective education strategies and programs help students understand their feelings, attitudes, and values. These strategies and programs involve students in resolving conflicts. They also try to promote students' emotional, behavioral, and social development by increasing their self-esteem and their ability to express emotions effectively (Abrams, 1992). Students who feel good about themselves and know how to express their feelings tend not to have behavior problems.

> ## VIDEO INSIGHT
> **Survival Lessons: School-based Mental Health Programs**
> In this ABC News video segment, we visit Francis Scott Key Elementary and Middle School and Eastern High School, where full-time school-based mental health programs have been set up to identify and help troubled children.
>
> With your classmates or in your teaching journal, reflect on these questions:
>
> 1. How does the implementation of school-based mental-health programs reflect the four principles of inclusion (diversity, individual needs, reflective practice, and collaboration)?
> 2. If your school did not have a school-based mental health program and you noticed a student in your inclusive classroom exhibiting the signs of mental health problems, what would you do?
> 3. How are other students in the inclusive classroom affected when their peers are troubled and don't receive guidance or positive messages from adults?

Develop Students' Self-Esteem

You can establish a good learning environment by helping students develop their self-esteem. This is done by building and maintaining rapport with students. Rapport can be established by talking to students about topics that interest them, sharing your own interests, giving emotional support, letting them perform activities in which they excel, greeting students by name, participating in after-school activities with them, recognizing special events in students' lives such as birthdays, displaying kindness, spending informal time with students, and complimenting them (Johns & Carr, 1995; Oxer & Klevit, 1995).

In addition to defusing difficult classroom situations, humor can help you and your students develop a good relationship and a positive classroom atmosphere. When using humor, make sure that it is not directed toward students and is free of racial, ethnic, religious, sexual, and gender bias and sarcasm.

Use Values Clarification

Values clarification views classroom misbehavior as a result of confused values (Raths, Harmin, & Simon, 1978). Values clarification activities that are part of the curriculum allow students to examine their attitudes, interests, and feelings and learn how these values affect their behavior. For example, after students express their attitudes or opinions or use a specific behavior, you might ask them, "How did that affect you and others?", "Why is that important to you?", and "Did you consider any alternatives?" You can also use values clarification by creating a nonjudgmental, open, and trusting environment. Such an atmosphere encourages students to share their values, feelings, and beliefs and respect those of others (Abrams, 1992).

INFORMATIONAL

Strategies and activities for using values clarification in the classroom are available (Hawley & Hawley, 1975; Howe & Howe, 1975; Simon, Howe, & Kirschenbaum, 1972).

Use Life Space Interviewing

Life Space Interviewing involves talking empathetically with students who are having problems in school (Raymond, 1994). This may take the form of Emotional First Aid, Clinical Exploitation of Life Events, or both. Emotional First Aid provides temporary

IDEAS FOR IMPLEMENTATION

Promoting Students' Self-Esteem

Ms. Vang noticed that several of her students often made derogatory comments about themselves and seemed reluctant to volunteer and participate in classroom activities. Concerned about their attitude, Ms. Vang decided to develop some activities to help her students feel better about themselves and her classroom. To make students aware of their strengths, she posted their work on bulletin boards and acknowledged their contributions by having the class applaud them. She also set up a rotating system so that all students could act as classroom leaders and perform jobs.

Here are some other strategies you can use to create an inclusive and supportive classroom that promotes students' self-esteem:

◆ Build students' confidence by praising them, focusing on improvement, showing faith in their abilities, and acknowledging the difficulty of tasks.

◆ Give students learning activities that they can succeed at and enjoy.

◆ Relate mistakes to effort and learning and remind students of past success.

◆ Encourage students to help each other and give students choices.

◆ Recognize and show appreciation for students' interests, hobbies, and cultural and language backgrounds.

◆ Make teaching personal by relating it to students' experiences.

◆ Use facial expressions and eye contact to show interest, concern, and warmth. For example, smile at students and laugh with them at appropriate times.

Sources: Oxer and Klevit (1995) and Tiedt and Tiedt (1995).

INFORMATIONAL

Fecser and Long (1997) and Wood and Long (1990) offer guidelines on using Life Space Interviewing.

emotional support by helping students deal with frustration, anger, panic, and hostility. Clinical Exploitation of Life Events helps students examine an incident by conducting a reality check, focusing on the students' behavior, and helping students feel less guilty. It also helps students understand and develop self-control.

Dialogue with Students

INFORMATIONAL

McCarty and Chalmers (1997) offer a list of children's books dealing with anger.

You can use dialoguing to help students understand their behavior and work out alternatives to inappropriate behaviors. This process involves (1) meeting with students to discover their view of the problem; (2) helping students identify the real problems; (3) phrasing the problems in the students' words; (4) helping them to solve the problems; and (5) discussing their solutions (Research Press, 1992).

Use Teacher Effectiveness Training

Teacher Effectiveness Training (Gordon, 1974) uses several strategies to help students and teachers communicate. One strategy is *active listening,* which involves the following:

◆ *Using door openers.* Teachers encourage students to express their feelings and ideas ("It looks like you're feeling sad about something. Would you like to talk about it?").

◆ *Using reflective comments.* Teachers reflect back the feelings and experiences shared by students ("When the other students said bad things about your friend, it made you sad.").

⬧ *Acknowledging comments.* Teachers show understanding of students' comments and encourage students to continue to share their feelings ("Yes, I see. What else would you like to tell me?").

⬧ *Avoiding roadblocks to communication.* Teachers encourage communication and avoid threatening, advising, lecturing, labeling, analyzing, consoling, and criticizing students, moralizing to students, and changing the focus of the discussion.

⬧ *Resolving problems using a no-lose approach.* Teachers and students focus on the problem, and seek and agree to solutions that are acceptable to all parties.

Gordon (1974) also suggests that teachers respond to students' behaviors, both appropriate and inappropriate, with *I-statements,* which express teachers' feelings about students' behavior. I-statements usually include the following: (1) a review of the student's behavior ("When you . . ."); (2) a mention of how the behavior made the teacher feel ("It made me feel . . ."); and (3) a comment on the reasons why the teacher felt that way ("Because . . .").

Conduct Class Meetings

Students, as a group, also can share their opinions and brainstorm solutions to class behavior problems, concerns about schoolwork, and general topics that concern students during *class meetings* (Jones & Jones, 1998). Class meetings are designed to help students understand the perspectives of others, so they are especially effective for resolving conflicts between students based on cultural differences (Meier, 1992). You can promote discussion by presenting open-ended topics using *defining* questions ("What does it mean to interrupt the class?"), *personalizing* questions ("How do you feel when someone interrupts the class?"), and *creative thinking* questions ("How can we stop others from interrupting the class?"). In class discussions, all students have a right to share their opinions without being criticized by others, and only positive, constructive suggestions should be presented.

Classroom problems and tensions between students can be identified and handled by placing a box in the classroom where students and adults submit compliments and descriptions of problems and situations that made them feel upset, sad, annoyed, or angry (Bloom et al., 1999). Compliments and concerns can be shared with the class, and all students can brainstorm possible solutions to concerns.

Use Peer Mediation

Classroom and school-related conflicts, particularly those based on age and cultural differences, can be handled by *peer mediation,* "an approach to resolve conflicts in which disputants, or people who disagree, have the chance to sit face to face and talk uninterrupted so each side of the dispute is heard. After the problem is defined, solutions are created and then evaluated" (Schrumpf, Crawford, & Usadel, 1991, p. 41). Students trained to serve as peer mediators use communication, problem solving, and critical thinking to solve conflicts (Johnson & Johnson, 1996). Peer mediation involves the following steps:

Step 1. Start the session. Peer mediators introduce themselves and the peer mediation process, welcome the disputants, and establish the ground rules. All students involved commit to the ground rules, which include the following:

Class meetings allow students to share their opinions about and brain-storm solutions to classroom problems.

mediators remain neutral, all comments are confidential, do not interrupt others, and both parties agree to solve the problem.

Step 2. Gather information. Peer mediators collect information by asking disputants to discuss the conflict from their perspective (e.g., "Please tell me what happened"). Afterward, peer mediators summarize their statements, ask for additional information (e.g., "Would you like to add any additional comments or information?"), asks questions to clarify the situation, and acknowledge the concerns of all parties.

Step 3. Focus on common interests. Peer mediators help disputants find common interests by asking each person the following questions: "What do you really want?" "How do you think the other person feels?" "What do you have in common with each other?" "What happens if no agreement is reached?" Peer mediators share the comments of both parties and emphasize the things they have in common.

Step 4. Create options. Peer mediators use brainstorming and questioning to help disputants generate options for solving the conflict by asking, "What can be done to solve the problem?"

Step 5. Evaluate the options and choose a solution. Peer mediators ask the disputants to evaluate the options and choose those they feel might work. If the disputants agree on a solution, peer mediators help them analyze it and summarize the main points of the agreement.

Step 6. Write the agreement and end the session. Peer mediators write out the agreement, share it with the disputants, ask the disputants to acknowledge their agreement, encourage them to shake hands, and thank the disputants for their participation.

INFORMATIONAL

A good peer mediation and conflict resolution program is the *Teaching Students to be Peacemakers Program* (Johnson & Johnson, 1996).

SET YOUR SITES

You can get help in establishing a peer mediation program from the Conflict Resolution/Peer Mediation Research Project (www.coe.ufl.edu/ CRPM/CRPMhome.html) and the website www.columbia.edu/ ~dd185/peermed.html.

Use Cooperative Discipline

Cooperative discipline is a collaborative approach to help students improve their class-room behavior and interactions with others, develop self-esteem, and become effective learners (Oxer & Klevit, 1995). Students, families, and professionals work as a team to create and use a variety of strategies (Payne & Brown, 1994). Students learn to use self-management techniques and serve as peer tutors, peer mediators, and counselors. Family members communicate and meet with professionals and students. The purpose of these meetings is to discuss concerns and improvements and to work out solutions to be used in school and at home. Teachers use positive reinforcement, dialoguing, classroom meetings, and group-oriented systems, as well as strategies to improve students' learning and self-esteem. Administrators promote the program by supporting students, families, and professionals and by conducting classroom observations.

Antecedent-Based Interventions

Antecedent-based interventions are changes in classroom events and stimuli that pre-cede behavior. They also include curricular and teaching accommodations (see Chapters 8 to 11) and classroom design changes (discussed later in this chapter). Antecedent-based interventions will now be discussed.

Be Aware of Nonverbal Communication

Nonverbal communication includes physical distance and personal space, eye contact and facial expressions, and gestures and body movements (Marable & Raimondi, 1995). When nonverbal communication is not understood, the result can be miscommunication and conflicts between students and teachers (Banbury & Hebert, 1992). Therefore, your nonverbal messages should be consistent with students' behavioral expectations, pro-mote positive interactions, and communicate attitudes.

   Nonverbal behaviors also should be consistent with students' cultural backgrounds. For example, individuals from some cultures may feel comfortable standing close to persons they are talking to, while those from other cultures may view this closeness as a sign of aggressiveness. Physical gestures may also have different meanings in different cultures. For example, to some Southeast Asian groups, crossing the fingers to indicate good luck is viewed as obscene. Hand gestures are considered rude, as they are used with animals or to challenge others to a fight (National Coalition of Advocates for Students, 1991).

   You should be sensitive to the nonverbal behaviors of your students and respond to them with congruent nonverbal and verbal messages. Examples of such nonverbal and verbal messages that you can use to promote positive classroom behaviors are presented in Table 7.1.

REFLECTIVE

Observe several individuals with whom you deal regularly. How do they interact nonverbally with others? Are their nonverbal and verbal behaviors congruent? When these behaviors are incongruent, on which type of behavior do you rely?

Use Teacher Proximity and Movement

Your proximity and movement can promote good behavior (Marable & Raimondi, 1995). This can be done by (1) standing near students who have behavior problems; (2) placing students' desks near you; (3) talking briefly with students while walking around the room; (4) delivering praise, reprimands, and consequences while standing close to students; and (5) monitoring your movement patterns to ensure that *all students* receive attention

TABLE 7.1   Congruency of Verbal and Nonverbal Messages

	Approving/ Accepting	Disapproving/ Critical	Assertive/ Confident	Passive/ Indifferent
Verbal message	"I like what you are doing."	"I don't like what you are doing."	"I mean what I say."	"I don't care."
Physical distance	Sit or stand in close proximity to other person.	Distance self from other person; encroach uninvited into other's personal space.	Physically elevate self; move slowly into personal space of other person.	Distance self from other person.
Facial expressions	Engage in frequent eye contact; open eyes wide; raise brows; smile.	Engage in too much or too little eye contact; open eyes wide in fixed, frozen expression; squint or glare; turn corners of eyebrows down; purse or tightly close lips; frown; tighten jaw muscle.	Engage in prolonged, neutral eye contact; lift eyebrows; drop head and raise eyebrow.	Avert gaze; stare blankly; cast eyes down or let them wander; let eyes droop.
Body movements	Nod affirmatively; "open" posture; uncross arms/legs; place arms at side; show palms; lean forward; lean head and trunk to one side; orient body toward other person; grasp or pat shoulder or arm; place hand to chest.	Shake head slowly; "close" posture; fold arms across chest; lean away from person; hold head/trunk straight; square shoulders; thrust chin out; use gestures of negation, e.g., finger shaking, hand held up like a stop signal.	Place hands on hips; lean forward; touch shoulder; tap on desk; drop hand on desk; join fingers at tips and make a steeple.	Lean away from other person; place head in palm of hand; fold hands behind back or upward in front; drum fingers on table; tap with feet; swing crossed leg or foot; sit with leg over chair.

Source: *Do you see what I mean?* by M. M. Banbury and C. R. Hebert, *Teaching Exceptional Children,* vol. 24, no. 2, p. 36. Copyright 1992 by The Council for Exceptional Children. Reprinted by permission.

and interact with you (Gunter, Shores, Jack, Rasmussen, & Flowers, 1995). When using proximity, you should be aware of its effects on students. For example, Ewing and Duhaney (1996) noted that African American students may view it as lack of trust in students.

Use Cues

Cues can be used to promote good classroom behavior. For example, color cues can indicate acceptable noise levels in the classroom. Red can signal that the noise is too high, yellow that moderate noise is appropriate, and green that there are no restrictions on the noise level.

INFORMATIONAL

Chalmers, Olson, and Zurkowski (1999) offer guidelines for using music to foster positive classroom behavior.

Verbal and nonverbal cues such as physical gestures can be used to prompt group or individual responses. These cues also can establish routines, promote efficiency, or signal to students that their behavior is unacceptable and should be changed. When working with students from different cultural and language backgrounds, you should use culturally appropriate cues.

Consider Scheduling Alternatives

Good scheduling (see Figure 7.3) also can improve student behavior. A regular schedule with ongoing classroom routines helps students understand the day's events. Since many

CONSIDER STUDENT CHARACTERISTICS AND NEEDS

◆ Examine the objectives, activities, and priorities in students' IEPs.
◆ Adapt the schedule and the length of activities based on students' ages and attention spans.
◆ Involve students in planning the schedule for negotiable events such as free-time activities.
◆ Begin the school day with a lesson or activity that is motivating and interesting to students.
◆ Plan activities so that less popular activities are followed by activities that students enjoy.
◆ Teach difficult material and concepts when students are most alert.
◆ Alternate movement and discussion activities with passive and quiet activities, and alternate small-group and large-group activities.
◆ Work with individual students during activities that require limited supervision.
◆ Give students breaks that allow them to move around and interact socially.
◆ Give students several alternatives when they complete an assigned activity early.

HELP STUDENTS LEARN THE SCHEDULE

◆ Post the schedule in a prominent location using an appropriate format for the students' ages.
◆ Review the schedule periodically with students.
◆ Record the schedule on loop tapes that automatically rewind and then repeat the same message.
◆ Avoid frequently changing the schedule.
◆ Share the schedule with families and other professionals.

FIGURE 7.3   Classroom scheduling guidelines.
Sources: Meier (1992), Murdick and Petch-Hogan (1996), Murray (1991), and Ruef, Higgins, Glaeser, and Patnode (1998).

students with disabilities also receive instruction and services from support personnel, you may need to coordinate their schedules with other professionals. Also, since these students will miss work and assignments while outside the room, you need to establish procedures for making up these assignments.

Many school districts are moving toward block scheduling, which involves expanding teaching periods to 80–120 minutes in middle and high schools and 40–50 minutes in elementary schools (Santos & Rettig, 1999). Block scheduling allows teachers to be more creative, cover content in greater depth, integrate content across the curriculum, and use more student-centered learning and assessment activities (DiRocco, 1999). In some school districts, block scheduling makes it easier to include students with disabilities in general education classrooms. Teachers have more flexibility in planning schedules, decreasing disruptions and transitions, and limiting the number of classes these students take at one time. This reduces the amount of information these students must remember and the homework they have to complete.

INFORMATIONAL

Santos and Rettig (1999) offer guidelines for meeting the needs of students with disabilities in schools that use block scheduling.

REFLECTIVE

What is your opinion of block scheduling? How would it affect your teaching and your students' learning?

Help Students Make Transitions

Transitions from one period to the next, and from one activity to the next within a class period, are a significant part of the school day. These transitions can lead to disruptive behaviors that interfere with student learning. You can minimize problems with transitions by allowing students to practice making transitions and by making adaptations in the classroom routine (Buck, 1999). You can use verbal, musical, or physical cues to signal students that it is time to get ready for a new activity and that they have 5 minutes left to complete their work (Gibson & Govendo, 1999). In addition, you can use pictorial cue cards that prompt students to (1) listen to directions, (2) put their materials away, and (3) get ready for the next activity. You also can reward groups or individual students for making an orderly and smooth transition, pair students together to help each other finish an activity, and review several motivating aspects of the next activity.

Having clear expectations and giving students specific directions on moving to the next activity can help them make the transition. For example, rather than telling students to "Get ready for physical education class," you can say, "Finish working on your assignment, put all your materials neatly in your desk or bookbag, check to see that you have your sneakers and gym uniform, and line up quietly." When students come from a less structured social activity like recess to a setting that requires quiet and attention, a transitional activity is important. For example, following recess, have students write in a journal one thing that was discussed in social studies class the previous day. This can help prepare them for the day's lesson and smooth the transition.

Establish, Teach, and Enforce Rules

To create an effective, efficient, and pleasant learning environment, it is important to establish, teach, and enforce classroom rules. It is desirable for students to be involved in developing the rules, and students are more likely to follow rules that they help create. Therefore, you can work with students to develop no more than eight rules that address cooperative and productive learning behaviors, guide classroom interactions, and are acceptable both to them and to you (Rademacher, Callahan, & Pederson-Seelye, 1998). You can ask students what rules they think the class needs, present classroom problems and ask students to brainstorm solutions and rules to address these problems, or have students create a classroom constitution or mission statement (Bloom et al., 1999; Fleming, 1996). Students also can help determine the consequences for following rules and the violations for breaking them. This process should have some flexibility based on students' individual differences and circumstances.

You can follow several guidelines to make the rules meaningful to students (Hardman & Smith, 1999). Phrase rules so that they are concise, stated in the students' language, easily understood, and usable in many situations and settings. Each rule should begin with an action verb. It should include a behavioral expectation that is defined in observable terms and the benefits of following the rule. When exceptions to rules exist, identify the exceptions and discuss them in advance. Similarly, when allowances need to be made for students, particularly those with disabilities in order to accommodate their unique needs and behaviors, the rationales for these allowances can be discussed and explained to the class.

Whenever possible, state rules in positive terms. For example, a rule for in-seat behavior can be stated as "Work at your desk" rather than "Don't get out of your seat." Rules also can be stated in terms of students' responsibilities such as "Show respect for yourself by doing your best." Rules also may be needed and phrased to help students respect *all students*. For example, you may want to introduce rules related to teasing and name-calling such as "Be polite, show respect for others, and treat others fairly."

It also is important that you help students learn the rules. You can do this by describing and demonstrating the observable behaviors that make up the rules, giving examples of rule violations and behaviors related to the rules, and role playing rule-following and rule-violating behaviors. You can also discuss the rationale for the rules, the contexts in which rules apply, and the benefits of each rule. At the beginning, you can review the rules frequently with the class, asking students periodically to recite them or practice one of them. It also is important to praise students for following the rules

REFLECTING ON YOUR PRACTICES

Examining Rules

You can examine your classroom rules by considering the following:

◆ Are your rules necessary to prevent harm to others or their property?

◆ Do your rules promote the personal comfort of others?

◆ Do your rules promote learning?

◆ Do your rules encourage students to make friends?

◆ Do your rules address respectful behavior directed at peers, the teacher, the teacher's aide, or others in school?

◆ Are your rules logical and reasonable?

◆ How do your rules affect the class?

◆ Are your rules consistent with the school's rules and procedures?

◆ How do you involve your students in creating rules?

◆ Are your rules consistent with students' ages, maturity levels, cultural backgrounds, and learning and physical and behavioral needs?

◆ Do you have enough rules?

◆ Are your rules stated in positive terms and in language students can understand?

◆ Are your rules stated in observable terms?

◆ Are your consequences for following and not following the rules appropriate and fair?

◆ Are your rules easily enforceable?

How would you rate your rules? ( ) Excellent ( ) Good ( ) Needs Improvement ( ) Needs Much Improvement

What steps could you adopt to improve your classroom rules?

---

and to offer positive and corrective feedback to students who initially fail to comply so that they can succeed in the future. For example, when a student breaks a rule, you can state the rule, request compliance, and offer options for complying with it (Colvin, Ainge, & Nelson, 1997).

Posting the rules on a neat, colorful sign in an easy-to-see location in the room also can help students remember them. Some students with disabilities and younger students may have difficulty reading, so pictures representing the rules are often helpful. You also can personalize this method by taking and posting photographs of students acting out the rules, labeling the photos, and using them as prompts for appropriate behavior (Lazarus, 1998). Additionally, you can help students understand the rules and commit to following them by enforcing the rules immediately and consistently and by reminding students of the rules when a class member complies with them.

Teach Social Skills

With social skills teaching, students like Jaime can discover how to learn and socialize with others. You can help students develop their social skills by clearly explaining the behavior, its importance, and when it should be used. You also can demonstrate, explain, role play, and practice using the behavior, as well as ask students to use it in natural settings. Finally, you can provide feedback and promote use of the behavior in various settings. Elksnin and Elksnin (1998) provide a list of programs to teach social skills to students. Guidelines for evaluating the effectiveness, cost, target group and setting, ease of use, instructional approach, and depth of content of these programs, as well as generalization and maintenance, also are available (Carter & Sugai, 1989; Sabornie & Beard, 1990).

INFORMATIONAL

Allsopp, Santos, and Linn (2000) offer strategies for teaching social skills.

Consequence-Based Interventions

Consequence-based interventions are changes in the classroom events and stimuli that follow a behavior. Several consequence-based interventions will now be described.

Use Positive Reinforcement

A widely used, highly effective method for motivating students to obey rules is *positive reinforcement.* With this method, a stimulus is given after a behavior occurs. The stimulus increases the rate of the behavior or makes it more likely that the behavior will occur again. Stimuli that increase the probability of a repeated behavior are called *positive reinforcers.* For example, you can use verbal and physical (e.g., smiling, signaling OK, thumbs up) praise as a positive reinforcer to increase a variety of classroom behaviors.

When using positive reinforcement, you need to consider several things. First, it is critical to be consistent and make sure that reinforcers desired by students are delivered after the behavior occurs, especially when the behavior is being learned. As the student becomes successful, gradually deliver the reinforcement less often and less quickly and raise the standards that students must meet to receive reinforcement.

One type of positive reinforcement used by many classroom teachers is the *Premack Principle* (Premack, 1959). According to this principle, students can do something they like if they complete a less popular task first. For example, a student who works on an assignment for a while can earn an opportunity to work on the computer.

Classroom Lottery   A positive reinforcement system that can promote good behavior is the *classroom lottery,* in which you write students' names on "lottery" tickets and place the tickets in a jar in full view of the class. At the end of the class or at various times during the day, you or a designated student draws names from the jar, and those selected receive reinforcement. The lottery system can be modified by having the class earn a group reward when the number of tickets accumulated exceeds a preestablished number.

Select Appropriate Reinforcers

A key component of positive reinforcement is the reinforcers or rewards that students receive. You can use a variety of culturally relevant edible, tangible, activity, social, and group reinforcers. However, you should be careful in using reinforcers because they can have negative effects on student motivation and performance (Okolo, Bard, & Gardner, 1995). You can solve this problem by using reinforcers only when necessary, embedding rewards in the activity, making the rewards more subtle, using rewards for improved performance, combining rewards with praise, fading out the use of rewards, and encouraging students to reinforce themselves via self-statements (Fulk & Montgomery-Grymes, 1994). Other guidelines for motivating students are presented in Chapter 9.

Many food reinforcers have little nutritional value and can cause health problems, so you should work with family members and health professionals to evaluate them with respect to students' health needs and allergic reactions. Activity reinforcers, which allow students to perform an enjoyable task or activity, are highly motivating alternatives. One flexible activity reinforcer is free time. It can be varied to allow students to work alone, with a peer, or with adults. Students also can use free time to go to the library, play a favorite game, sit where they choose in the room, make an arts project, or perform a supervised activity in the gymnasium.

Class jobs also can motivate students. At first, you may assign class jobs—handing out and collecting papers, cleaning the classroom, making class announcements, taking attendance, running errands, and so on. When students perform these jobs well, they can be given jobs that require more responsibility, such as working in the main office, helping the janitorial staff, running media hardware, tutoring peers and younger students, and helping teachers grade papers.

A potent reinforcer that many teachers use is praise and teacher attention. Effective use of praise can promote self-esteem in students, strengthen the bond between you and your students, reinforce appropriate behavior, and create a positive environment in the classroom. Guidelines for using praise are presented in Chapter 9.

Administer Reinforcement Surveys

Many behavior management systems fail because the reinforcers are not appropriate and effective. One way to solve this problem is to ask for students' preferences via a reinforcement survey. Many reinforcement surveys exist. You can also develop your own surveys tailored to the characteristics of your students and classrooms.

Raschke (1981) identified three formats for reinforcement surveys: open-ended, multiple-choice, and rank order. The *open-ended* format asks students to identify reinforcers by completing statements about their preferences ("If I could choose the game we will play the next time we go to recess, it would be . . ."). The *multiple-choice* format allows students to select one or more choices from a list of potential reinforcers ("If I had 15 minutes of free time in class, I'd like to (1) work on the computer, (2) play a game with a friend, or (3) listen to music on the headphones"). For the *rank order* format, students grade their preferences from strong to weak using a number system.

You can consider several factors when developing reinforcement surveys. Items can be phrased using student language rather than professional jargon (*reward* rather than *reinforcer*) and can reflect a range of reinforcement. In addition, the effectiveness ("Do students like the reinforcers and engage in the activities?"), availability ("Will I be able to give the reinforcer at the appropriate times?"), practicality ("Is the reinforcer consistent with the class and school rules?"), cultural relevance ("Is the reinforcer consistent with the student's cultural background?"), and cost ("Will the reinforcer prove too expensive to maintain?") of reinforcers on the survey can be examined. Finally, since students may have reading and/or writing difficulties, you may need to read items for students as well as record their responses.

INFORMATIONAL

Raschke (1981) provides examples of many types of reinforcement surveys, and Mason and Egel (1995) offer guidelines for using reinforcement surveys with students with developmental disabilities.

Use Contracting

You and your students may work together to develop a *contract*, a written agreement that outlines the behaviors and results of a specific behavior management system (Lassman et al., 1999). Contracts should give immediate and frequent reinforcement. They should be structured for success by calling at first for small changes in behavior. Both parties must consider the contract fair, and it must be stated in language that the students can read and understand.

This is a contract between _____ and
                                    Student's or class's name
_____ . The contract starts on _____ and ends
    Teacher's name
on _____ . We will renegotiate it on _____ .
    During _____
                    Environmental conditions (times, classes, activities)
I (we) agree to _____.
                            Behavior student(s) will demonstrate
If I (we) do, I (we) will _____.
                                Reinforcer to be delivered
The teacher will help by _____.
I (we) will help by _____.

                                        _____
                                                Teacher's Signature

                                        _____
                                        Student or Class Representative's Signature

                                        _____
                                                Date

FIGURE 7.4   Sample contract outline.

A contract should include the following elements:

◆ A statement of the behavior(s) the student is to increase/decrease in observable terms
◆ A statement of the environment in which the contract will be used
◆ A list of the types and amounts of reinforcers and who will provide them
◆ A schedule for the delivery of reinforcers
◆ A list of the things the teacher and student(s) can do to increase the success of the system
◆ A time frame for the contract, including a date for renegotiation
◆ Signatures of the student(s) and teacher

Figure 7.4 presents an outline of a sample contract.

Self-Management Interventions

INFORMATIONAL

Johnson and Johnson (1999), King-Sears and Bonfil (2000) and McConnell (1999) developed guidelines for teaching students to use self-management strategies.

Self-management intervention strategies, also called *cognitive behavioral interventions,* actively involve students in monitoring and changing their behaviors. Several of these strategies that have been used in many different inclusive settings are described here (King-Sears, 1999; McDougall, 1998). You may want to use combinations of these strategies. Students can be taught to use them by introducing the target behavior(s) and the self-management strategies and giving students opportunities to practice and master them (Daniels, 1998).

Self-Monitoring   In *self-monitoring,* also called *self-recording,* students measure their behaviors by using a data-collection system (Callahan & Rademacher, 1999). For

Students can use self-management strategies to monitor and change their behavior.

example, students can be taught to increase their on-task behavior during a lecture class by placing a + in a box when they pay attention for several minutes and a − if they do not. Sample self-recording systems are presented in Figure 7.5.

You can increase your students' ability to record their own behavior by using a *countoon,* a recording sheet with a picture of the behavior and space for students to record each occurrence. A countoon for in-seat behavior, for example, would include a drawing of a student sitting in a chair with a box under the chair for recording.

Self-Evaluation   In *self-evaluation* or *self-assessment,* students are taught to evaluate their in-class behavior according to some standard or scale. For example, students can rate their on-task and disruptive behavior using a 0 to 5 point (unacceptable to excellent) rating scale. Students then earn points, which they exchange for reinforcers, based on both their behavior and the accuracy of their rating.

Self-Reinforcement   In *self-reinforcement,* students are taught to evaluate their behavior and then deliver self-selected rewards if appropriate. For example, after showing the correct behavior, students reinforce themselves by working for 15 minutes on the computer.

INFORMATIONAL

Alber and Heward (1997) provide guidelines for teaching students to recruit positive teacher attention.

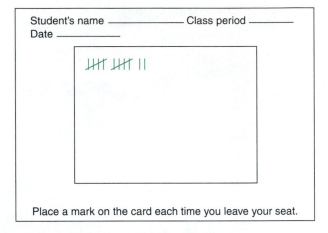

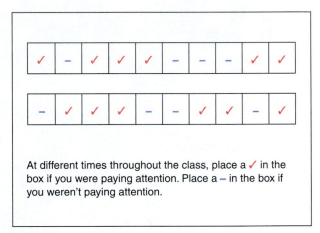

FIGURE 7.5   Examples of self-recording systems.

Source: Adapted from M. Broden, R. V. Hall, and B. Mitts, *Journal of Applied Behavior Analysis,* vol. 4 (1971), pp. 193, 496. Copyright 1971 by the Society for the Experimental Analysis of Behavior, Inc.

Self-Managed Free-Token Response-Cost   One system that has been used successfully by students with disabilities in inclusive settings is a *student-managed free-token response-cost* system. In this system, you give the student an index card with a certain number of symbols. The symbols represent the number of inappropriate behaviors the student may exhibit before losing the agreed-on reinforcement. After each inappropriate behavior, the student crosses out one of the symbols on the index card. If any symbols remain at the end of the class time, the student receives the agreed-on reinforcement.

Self-Instruction   *Self-instruction* teaches students to regulate their behaviors by verbalizing to themselves the questions and responses necessary to (1) identify problems ("What am I being asked to do?"), (2) generate potential solutions ("What are the ways to do it?"), (3) evaluate solutions ("What is the best way?"), (4) use appropriate solutions ("Did I do it?"), and (5) determine if the solutions were effective ("Did it work?"). To help them do this, you can use *cueing cards,* index cards with pictures of the self-teaching

REFLECTING ON PROFESSIONAL PRACTICES

Using Self-Management Strategies

Kris is having difficulty completing assignments because she is frequently off task—leaving her seat, talking to classmates, playing with objects, and looking around the room. Kris's teacher, Mr. Bevier, is concerned about this behavior and decides that Kris could benefit from a strategy that increases her awareness of it. Mr. Bevier meets with Kris. They discuss her behavior and the use of a self-management strategy, which Kris agrees to try. Before starting, they meet again to discuss the system and the behavior. At first, they talk about the importance of Kris paying attention. Mr. Bevier explains that on-task behavior means eyes on the materials and/or on the teacher. Next, he demonstrates specific, observable examples of on-task and off-task behaviors, emphasizing the features of each. Afterward, he asks Kris to show examples and nonexamples of on-task behavior.

Mr. Bevier and Kris then discuss the self-management system and its benefit. Next, Mr. Bevier demonstrates the system for Kris and thinks out loud as he uses it, which prompts a discussion about the actual conditions in which the system will be used. Before using the system in class, they role play it. Mr. Bevier assesses Kris's use of the system and gives her feedback.

Mr. Bevier and Kris meet again, but this time he asks her to complete a reinforcement survey. The survey includes the following completion items:

The things I like to do at school are
I am proudest in this class when I
When I have free time in class, I like to
The best reward the teacher could give me is
Something that I would work hard for is

Mr. Bevier is surprised by Kris's responses. Rather than wanting tangible items such as stickers, Kris states that she would prefer a class job and extra time to spend with the teacher or her friends. Mr. Bevier and Kris agree that if she succeeds in changing her behavior, she may choose a reward from among a class job, free time with a friend or Mr. Bevier, and the opportunity to work with a friend.

Next, they try the system in class. It involves placing on Kris's desk a 4- by 6-inch index card that contains 10 drawings of eyes. When Kris fails to engage in on-task behavior, she crosses out one of the eyes. If any eyes remain at the end of the class period, Kris can choose one of the activities they discussed. With this system, Kris is able to increase her on-task behavior, and Mr. Bevier notices that Kris is doing more assignments and completing them more accurately.

Why did Mr. Bevier use a self-management system with Kris? What did he do to promote the success of the system? What steps did Mr. Bevier use to teach Kris to use the system? How could you use self-management strategies in your class? What benefits would they have for you and your students?

---

steps for following directions ("stop, look, listen" and "think") that are placed on the students' desks to guide them (Swaggart, 1998).

Self-Managing Peer Interactions A self-management system that students can use to deal with the inappropriate behavior of their peers is 3-Steps (Schmid, 1998). When students are being bothered by peers, they use 3-Steps by (1) telling peers "Stop! I don't like that," (2) ignoring or walking away from peers if they do not stop, and (3) informing the teacher that they told them to stop, tried to ignore them, and are now seeking the teacher's help.

REFLECTIVE

Choose a behavior you would like to increase or decrease. Select one of the self-management strategies and keep track of your progress. Were you successful? If so, why? If not, why?

Group-Oriented Management Systems

Group influence can be used to promote good behavior and decrease misbehavior by using *group-oriented systems.* Group-oriented management systems have several advantages over traditional methods: they foster cohesiveness and cooperation among members; they teach responsibility to the group and enlist the class in solving classroom problems; they allow you to manage behavior effectively and efficiently; they are adaptable to a variety of behaviors and classrooms; and they give students a positive, practical, and acceptable method of dealing effectively with the problems of peers.

When using group-oriented management systems, there are several possible problems. Because the success of these systems depends on the behavior of the whole group or class, a single disruptive individual can prevent the class from achieving its goals. If this happens, the offender can be removed and dealt with individually. Group-oriented management systems also can result in peer pressure and scapegoating, so you must carefully observe the impact of these systems on your students. You can attempt to minimize problems by establishing criterion levels that *all students and groups* can achieve. You can choose target behaviors that benefit *all students,* allowing those who do not want to participate in a group to opt out. You also can use heterogeneous groups and limit the competition between groups so that groups compete against a criterion level rather than against other groups (Maag & Webber, 1995).

Use Interdependent Group Systems

When several students in a class have a behavior problem, a good strategy is an *interdependent* group system. The system is applied to the entire group, and its success depends on the behavior of the group. Popular reinforcers for groups of students are free time, a class trip, a party for the class, time to play a group game, or a special privilege.

Group Free-Token Response-Cost System   One effective interdependent group system is a *group response-cost* system with free tokens (Salend & Allen, 1985). The group is given a certain number of tokens, which are placed in full view of the students and in easy reach of the teacher (such as paper strips on an easel or marks on the chalkboard). A token is removed each time a class member misbehaves. If any tokens remain at the end of the time period, the agreed-on reinforcement is given to the whole group. As the group becomes successful, the number of tokens given can gradually be decreased. Adaptations of this system include allowing students to be responsible for removing the tokens (Salend & Lamb, 1986) and making each token worth a set amount. An illustration of the group response-cost system is presented in Figure 7.6a.

Good Behavior Game   The *Good Behavior Game* is an interdependent group system whereby the class is divided into two or more groups. Each group's inappropriate behaviors are recorded by a slash on the blackboard (see Figure 7.6b). If the total number of slashes is less than the number specified by the teacher, the groups earn special privileges.

You can modify the Good Behavior Game to account for different types and frequencies of misbehaviors. The system can be tailored to the students by having different groups work on different target behaviors and with different criterion levels. To minimize the competition between groups, each group can earn the reinforcement if the number of misbehaviors is less than the group's own frequency level. For example, one group may work on decreasing calling out and have a criterion level of 25, and another group may work on reducing cursing and have a criterion level of 8. Rather than competing, each group earns reinforcement if its number of slashes is less than its own criterion level. You also can modify the Good Behavior Game by giving groups merit cards for positive behaviors of the group or of individual members. These merit cards are then used to remove slashes that the group has previously earned (Tankersley, 1995).

A. Illustration of group response-cost system. The class is given free tokens (chalkboard 1), which are removed when a disruptive behavior occurs (chalkboard 2). If any tokens remain at the end of the class, the group receives reinforcement (chalkboard 3).

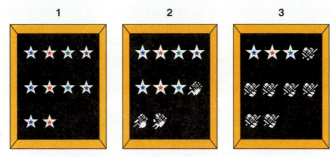

B. The Good Behavior Game

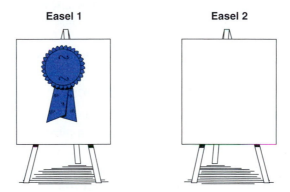

C. Illustration of a group timeout ribbon system. When the timeout ribbon is in place (easel 1), the group earns tokens. However, when the timeout ribbon is removed (easel 2), no tokens are delivered to the group.

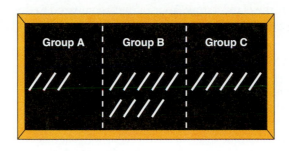

FIGURE 7.6 Illustrations of group-oriented management strategies.

Source: Group oriented behavioral contingencies by S. J. Salend, *Teaching Exceptional Children,* vol. 20, 1987, pp. 54 (a and b) and 55 (c). Copyright 1987 by The Council for Exceptional Children. Reprinted with permission.

Group Evaluation   You also can use a variety of group-evaluation systems to promote good classroom behavior. Two examples are the group average group-evaluation system (Salend, Whittaker, Raab, & Giek, 1991) and the consensus-based interdependent group-evaluation system (Salend, Whittaker, & Reeder, 1993). In the *group average system,* you give an evaluation form to each student in the group and ask each student to rate the group's behavior. You then determine a group rating by computing an average of the students' ratings. You also rate the group's behavior using the same form, and the group rating is compared to your rating. The group earns points, which are exchanged for reinforcers, based on its behavior and accuracy in rating its behavior.

The *consensus-based system* consists of (1) dividing the class into teams and giving each team an evaluation form; (2) having each team use a consensus method for determining the team's ratings of the class's behavior; (3) having the teacher rate the class's behavior using the same evaluation form; (4) comparing each team's ratings to the teacher's rating; and (5) giving reinforcement to each team based on the behavior of the class and the team's accuracy in rating that behavior.

Group evaluation also can be adapted so that one student's evaluation of the behavior of the whole group determines the reinforcement for the whole class (Salend, Reeder, Katz, & Russell, 1992). In this system, you and your students rate the class's behavior using the same evaluation form. You then randomly select a student whose rating represents the class's rating. Your rating is compared to this student's rating, and the group receives reinforcement based on the class's behavior and the student's agreement with your rating.

Group Timeout Ribbon   The *group timeout ribbon* method uses a ribbon, leather string, piece of rope, or piece of colored paper placed where all students can see it and close to the teacher. While the class behaves appropriately, the ribbon remains in its location and the class earns tokens that can be exchanged for reinforcers. As the class succeeds, the time interval for receiving a token can be increased.

If a student misbehaves, the ribbon is removed for 1 to 5 minutes; during that time, the group loses the opportunity to earn tokens. After the group behaves appropriately for a specified brief period of time, the ribbon is returned and the group can earn tokens again. However, if a student misbehaves while the ribbon is removed, the timeout period is extended. As the class learns the system, students can remove the ribbon and give themselves tokens. An example of a group timeout ribbon system is presented in Figure 7.6c.

Use Dependent Group Systems

In a *dependent* group system, a student's behavior problem is reinforced by his or her peers. In this system, the contingency is applied to the whole class, depending on the behavior of one member.

Use Independent Group Systems

In an *independent* group system, individual students are reinforced based on their own performance or behavior. Thus, reinforcement is available to each student, depending on that student's behavior.

Token Economy Systems   One independent group system that works well in both general and special education classes is a *token economy* system (Anderson & Katsiyannis, 1997; Lyon & Lagarde, 1997). Students earn tokens for showing appropriate behavior and can redeem these tokens for social, activity, tangible, and edible reinforcers. The steps of token economy systems are as follows:

> *Step 1. Collaborate with students and their families to determine the rules and behaviors that students must use to receive tokens.*
> *Step 2. Choose tokens that are safe, attractive, durable, inexpensive, easy to handle and dispense, and controllable by the teacher.* In selecting tokens, consider the

Some teachers find that token economy systems are effective.

age and cognitive abilities of students and the number of tokens needed per student.

Step 3. Identify the reinforcers that students want and determine how many tokens each item is worth. You can establish a store where students may go to buy items with their tokens and allow students to work in the store on a rotating basis. Keep a record of what items students buy and stock the store with those items. Consider using an auction system in which students bid for available items.

Step 4. Collect other materials needed for the token economy system, such as a container for students to store their tokens and a chart to keep a tally of students' tokens. You also can establish a bank where students can store their tokens, earn interest when saving them for a period of time, and invest in stocks, commodity futures, certificates of deposit, and Treasury bills (Adair & Schneider, 1993; Cook, 1999).

Step 5. Arrange the room for effective and efficient use of the system. For example, desks can be arranged so that you have easy access to all students when dispensing tokens.

Step 6. Introduce and explain the token system to students.

Step 7. Use the token system. At first, give large numbers of tokens to students by catching students behaving appropriately, and allow students to exchange their tokens for reinforcers on a regular basis to show that the tokens have real value. Pair the delivery of tokens with praise and tell the students exactly which appropriate behavior(s) was exhibited. Use a timer to remind you to dispense tokens.

Step 8. Determine how to handle incorrect behavior. You can use a timeout card, which is placed on students' desks for a brief period to indicate that no tokens can be earned. When students behave appropriately for a brief, specified time period, the timeout card is removed and students can earn tokens. Avoid taking away tokens when students do not have enough tokens.

Step 9. Revise the system to correct any problems. For example, if a student is suspected of stealing tokens from others, give the student tokens that are unique in shape or color.

Step 10. Begin to phase out the token system. You can do this by increasing the number of appropriate responses necessary to earn a token, increasing the number of tokens needed for a specific reinforcer, giving tokens on an intermittent schedule, using fewer verbal prompts, giving students fewer chances to exchange tokens for reinforcers, and using a graduated reinforcement system that moves toward the use of naturally occurring reinforcers.

Behavior Reduction Interventions

Teachers also are concerned about misbehavior and its impact on the learning environment and other students. There are many ways of decreasing misbehavior. When selecting a procedure, consider the following questions: Is the strategy aversive? Does it produce bad side effects? Is it effective? Does it allow me to teach another behavior to replace the undesirable one? (Alberto & Troutman, 1995).

Another issue to consider is the *Least Restrictive Alternative* principle, also referred to as the *Least Intrusive Alternative.* Use this principle as a guide in selecting methods that reduce the problem behavior without limiting a student's freedom more than necessary and without being physically or psychologically unappealing (McDonnell, 1993). Several methods for decreasing misbehavior, ranging from most to least intrusive, are presented below.

Use Redirection and Corrective Teaching

Redirection involves making comments or using behaviors designed to interrupt the misbehavior and prompt students to use appropriate behavior and work on the activity at hand (Colvin et al., 1997). Typically, this involves removing the individuals, objects, or stimuli that appear to be causing the misbehavior. Other redirection strategies include introducing a new stimulus to recapture the student's attention, signaling the student verbally and nonverbally to stop a behavior, offering to help the student with a task, engaging the student in conversation, reminding the student to focus on the assignment, changing the activity or some aspect of it, giving the student a choice between good behavior and a minor punishment such as a loss of recess, modeling calm and controlled behavior, and using humor (Garey & Wambold, 1994).

Corrective teaching is used to redirect and prompt students to behave well. Each time students misbehave, use corrective teaching by (1) approaching students individually with a positive or empathetic comment, (2) briefly describing the misbehavior, (3) briefly describing the desired behavior, (4) explaining why the desired behavior is important, (5) having students practice and role play or repeat the steps in the desired behavior, and (6) delivering feedback, praise, or points (West et al., 1995).

Employ Interspersed Requests

Interspersed requests, also known as *pretask requests* and *behavioral momentum,* can be used to decrease students' avoidance and challenging behaviors and to help students make transitions, learn difficult material, and avoid a series of escalating misbehaviors (Maag, 2000; Sprague & Horner, 1990). Interspersed requests motivate students to do a difficult or unpleasant task by first asking them to perform several easier tasks that they can complete successfully in a short period of time. You do this by asking students to do two to five easy tasks before giving them a task that they might resist or refuse to perform.

Use Positive Reductive Procedures/ Differential Reinforcement Techniques

In using *positive reductive procedures*, also called *differential reinforcement techniques*, you reinforce and increase a positive behavior that cannot coexist with the misbehavior that you want to decrease; this reduces the incidence of misbehavior (Drasgow, 1998). For example, to have a student stop swearing, you could reinforce the student for *not* swearing.

REFLECTIVE

What are some behaviors that may serve as positive, incompatible alternatives to misbehaviors such as calling out, being off task, being out of one's seat, and swearing?

Use Planned Ignoring

In *planned ignoring*, also called *extinction*, the positive reinforcers of a behavior are withheld or ended. When this happens, the behavior decreases. For example, you may be inadvertently maintaining a student's habit of calling out by reminding the student to raise his or her hand and by responding to the student's comments. Rather than giving the student attention through these reminders, you could decrease the behavior by ignoring the student's calling out.

Planned ignoring takes time to be effective and often initially increases the rate and/or intensity of misbehavior. Therefore, you should use it only for behaviors that can be changed gradually and when you can identify and withhold all reinforcers that are maintaining these behaviors. You can speed up the effectiveness of planned ignoring by combining it with reinforcement of appropriate alternative behaviors. Planned ignoring should not be used for behaviors maintained by reinforcers that cannot be withdrawn, such as peer attention. Finally, planned ignoring may increase aggressive behavior.

Consider Verbal Reprimands

Occasionally, you may need to use verbal reprimands to deal with misbehavior (Fiore, Becker, & Nero, 1993; Kehle, Clark, & Jenson, 1996). You can make these reprimands more effective by using them infrequently, by making them brief, firm, and matter-of-fact, and by delivering them immediately after the misbehavior occurs and in close contact to the student. Reprimands should be specific statements that direct students to engage in an appropriate alternative behavior ("Stop now, and do your work.") rather than questions ("Why aren't you doing your work?"). You also should combine reprimands with nonverbal behaviors such as eye contact, and avoid the use of sarcasm and judgmental language ("You're a bad boy/girl"), which can harm students' self-esteem and cause negative comments from peers.

Rather than use a public verbal reprimand, you can speak to students privately about behavior problems. In these meetings, you can briefly and succinctly tell them what you think, ask probing questions such as "Are you having problems with the assignment?", and discuss a plan for acting appropriately (Johns & Carr, 1995).

HOW CAN I PREVENT STUDENTS FROM HARMING OTHERS?

Students Who Are Bullies

You may need to deal with bullying or peer harassment, which may take the form of extorting lunch money, taunting, name-calling, spreading false rumors, and using verbal and physical threats (McNamara, 1996). You also can work with students and their families and professionals to create a safe, caring school environment that does not tolerate bullying and harassment and that fosters and acknowledges acceptance of individual differences and the development of friendships (Froschl & Gropper, 1999; see Chapter 5). In addition to confronting and disciplining bullies quickly and firmly, and creating rules and policies that address peer harassment, you can help bullies develop empathy for others and engage in acts that benefit and show respect for others. For example, students who have used bullying can be asked to apologize and do something nice for their victims, clean up part of the school, reflect on how harassment makes their victims feel, or keep a journal of their acts of kindness (Garrity, Jens, Porter, Sager, & Short-Camilli, 1997). You also can create a classroom environment that does not tolerate bullying by having students make "No Bullying Zone" posters, identifying and recording instances of bullying, and discussing alternatives. Victims of bullying need to learn how to respond in an assertive way that does not make the situation worse. They must also understand when and how to get help from adults. Students who are neither bullies nor victims need to learn how to actively support victims and how to counteract bullies and their harassing acts.

Students with Aggressive and Violent Behaviors

As we have seen in our nation's schools, all segments of society and all parts of the country are encountering violence (Rudo, Powell, & Dunlap, 1998; Webber, 1997). Although the number of crimes committed by juveniles has declined in the last 20 years, the rate and level of school-based violent acts has increased (Grant, Van Acker, Guerra, Duplechain, & Coen, 1998). The age of students who commit violent acts and crimes has decreased (Tobin & Sugai, 1999).

Students experience violence in several forms: carrying guns and weapons to school, fighting in school, and being threatened or injured with a weapon at school. You can minimize the likelihood of a crisis by designing a learning environment that involves students in a meaningful, relevant, and multicultural curriculum, deals effectively with student problems and misbehavior, and promotes friendships, trust, understanding, and respect for others.

By being aware of the warning signs, you may be able to prevent violence from occurring. While the signs vary, some of the common indicators of an escalating situation are verbal abuse (e.g., cursing and threats), shouting, body tenseness, and threatening physical gestures.

If you encounter a violent incident, you should attempt to follow the school policies for dealing with such situations. These policies often include assessing the situation, evacuating the classroom as soon as possible, getting help, and trying to defuse the situation. Some strategies that you use to defuse a crisis include the following:

◆ Remain calm and controlled.
◆ Allow the student to vent anger and feelings verbally.

◆ Ignore irrelevant comments and have the student focus on the relevant issues.

◆ Listen to the student without interrupting or denying the student's feelings.

◆ Use the student's name, and speak in a clear, moderate voice and in a slow, empathetic manner.

◆ Establish limits that clearly and concisely inform the student of the choices and consequences.

◆ Maintain a positive body posture, with the hands open and in view and eye contact without staring.

◆ Consider the culture and experiential background of the student.

◆ Remain close to the student while respecting the student's personal space.

◆ Persuade the student to leave the room.

◆ Ask the student to carefully lay down any weapon carried.

After the incident, you may need to continue to calm the student down, give support, send for medical assistance (if necessary), notify administrators and/or the police, file a report, counsel students, contact family members, and seek counseling.

INFORMATIONAL

Murdick, Gartin, and Yalowitz (1995) and Berry (1995) offer teachers precrisis, crisis, and post-crisis guidelines for dealing with violent behaviors.

SET YOUR SITES

More information and resources on how to respond to a crisis in school are available from the UCLA Center for Mental Health in Schools (www.smhp.psych.ucla.edu/specres.htm).

HOW CAN I ADAPT THE CLASSROOM DESIGN TO ACCOMMODATE STUDENTS' LEARNING, SOCIAL, AND PHYSICAL NEEDS?

The design of the classroom environment can complement your teaching style and help students learn, behave well, and develop social skills. In planning your classroom's design, consider the following: objects and areas in the room that cannot be altered easily (doors, windows, lights, outlets, cabinets, shelves, chalkboards, and bulletin boards), unique classroom problems and student needs, class size, amount and type of furniture, traffic patterns, ventilation, glare and temperature, and your teaching style and educational philosophy (Murdick & Petch-Hogan, 1996; Wadsworth & Knight, 1999).

You can affirm students and the value of education by creating a cheerful and inviting classroom that is clean, well lit, odor free, colorful, and respectful of your students' unique identities and needs. Your classroom can also be designed to ensure student safety if you check to make sure that electrical wires are anchored and covered, dangerous materials and equipment are locked in cabinets, sharp edges and broken furniture are removed, and walls, floors, and equipment are in good condition (Rikhye, Gothelf, & Appell, 1989).

INFORMATIONAL

Everston, Emmer, Clements, Sanford, and Worsham (1989) suggest that teachers assess classroom effectiveness by simulating their movements during a typical day, and by pretending to be a student and examining visibility, movement patterns, and accessibility of materials from the student's perspective.

Seating Arrangements

Generally, students are seated in areas that allow them to see clearly all presentations and displays. These locations also allow you to see and reach your students. When small-group teacher-directed instruction is used, students can be seated in a semicircle facing you. In a larger-group teacher-directed activity, it may be better for *all students* to face you sitting in a row, circular, or horseshoe arrangement. When students work in groups, they can arrange their desks so that they face each other, allowing them to share information efficiently and quietly. You also can encourage students to personalize their work area by placing photos, posters, slogans, and small plants on their desktops (Voltz & Damiano-Lantz, 1993).

Each student's desk should be of the right size and should be placed so as to include the student in all classroom activities and maintain good posture and body alignment (Rikhye et al., 1989). The space around students' desks should be large enough to give you easy access to students in order to monitor performance and distribute papers. Students also need a place to store their materials. When students' desks are not large enough, tote trays can be used to store their supplies (Everston et al., 1989).

Teacher's Desk

The location of your desk allows you to monitor behavior and progress and to move quickly if a problem occurs. For monitoring students, your desk can be placed in an area that provides a view of the whole classroom. Any obstacles that prevent you from scanning different parts of the room can be removed. When you are working with students in other parts of the room, you can sit facing the other students in the class.

Teaching Materials

Storing, organizing, categorizing, and labeling materials can make the classroom a more orderly, efficient place and promote student independence and individualized teaching. Cohen and de Bettencourt (1988) offer teachers a system for categorizing their materials:

1. Create a file box of all classroom materials, with each card including the material's name, objectives, level of difficulty, and possible modifications.
2. Develop a code, and label each material by the type of activity. For example, a * could indicate a software program, and a # could indicate a role play.
3. Assign each material a level of difficulty.
4. Color code and place materials in separate locations by content area.

Bulletin Boards and Walls

Bulletin boards can help you create a pleasant, attractive environment that promotes learning and class pride. *Decorative* bulletin boards make the room attractive and interesting and often relate to a theme. *Motivational* bulletin boards encourage students by showing progress and publicly displaying their work. *Instructional* bulletin boards, or *teaching walls,* often include an acquisition wall, which introduces new concepts and material, and a maintenance wall, which reviews previously learned concepts (Cummins & Lombardi, 1989). *Manipulative* bulletin boards use materials that students can manipulate to learn new skills.

Displays should be planned so that they are at the students' eye level. Whenever possible, involve students in decorating areas of the room. Mobiles, posters, pictures, and other forms of student artwork (e.g., a class collage that includes a contribution from each student) can make the walls and ceiling of the classroom colorful and attractive.

You also can include a space for displaying student assignments, as well as pictures, posters, and art forms that reflect the students' families, homes, neighborhoods, and other cultural groups that may not be represented in the classroom. Posting the daily as-

Posting student's work can make the classroom more attractive and can motivate students.

signment schedule and examples of products on part of the bulletin board or wall can help students remember to perform all assigned tasks. Wall displays can include a clock and calendar large enough to be seen from all parts of the classroom and a list of class rules (Everston et al., 1989).

Learning Centers and Specialized Areas

Learning centers provide variety in the classroom and help you individualize instruction. They also can help students develop independent skills and learn to work collaboratively.

You also may want to establish special areas of the room for specific functions. For example, a couch or rocking chair can be placed in a quiet part of the room to give students a place to relax when the classroom pace is hectic, to think about what they have just learned, to be alone, or to gain control of their behavior. A room location where groups of students can read together or meet with a peer can promote socialization. High-traffic areas should be free from congestion, separated from each other, easily accessible, and spacious.

Classroom Design Adaptations

Many students, especially those with disabilities, need specific classroom design modifications in order to perform as well as possible. Guidelines for physical adaptations of general education classrooms are outlined here. (Also see Chapter 2 for further discussion of the educational needs of these students.)

IDEAS FOR IMPLEMENTATION

Using Learning Centers

Ms. Carty's classroom has four centers, and groups of students rotate among them every 30 minutes. As the students work at the different centers, Ms. Carty circulates around the room to monitor the groups and offer help and directions.

At the telling-time station, students work in small groups on activities that involve telling time. At the reading center, six students are making puppets and writing dialogue for a puppet show they are going to present to the whole class on a story they have been reading. At the measurement center, students are learning about centimeters and inches by measuring the length of each other's arms, legs, fingers, and bodies. Students then record their findings, compare their measurements, and write word problems based on their measurements. At the art center, students are creating murals that show the different characteristics of the students in their group. When students complete their murals, Ms. Carty plans to place them on a bulletin board in the hallway outside the room.

Here are some other strategies you can use to create learning centers:

◆ Teach students how to use the centers independently and how to work in small groups. Explain the appropriate times for using the centers and the number of students that each center can accommodate.

◆ Use a variety of centers that allow students to explore new skills and practice those they have learned. *Skill centers* let students practice skills such as math facts, spelling words, alphabetizing, and defining

vocabulary. *Discovery/enrichment centers* use many different learning activities (science experiments, math applications) that require students to increase their knowledge. A *listening center* offers instruction or recreation through listening. Arts and crafts, music, creative writing, and poetry are often the focus of activities in a *creativity center*.

◆ Include activities at each center geared to a range of student academic levels, interests, and needs.

◆ Develop and organize materials in the center so that students can work on them independently and can easily locate, select, and return them.

◆ Consider the equipment and furniture needs of students with physical and sensory disabilities when creating learning centers.

◆ Make self-correction an integral part of centers. For example, you can include a checkout center, where students can check their assignments or have their work checked by others (Kemp et al., 1995). Typically, checkout centers include answer keys, audiocassettes of correct answers, and reference materials to help students check and revise their work and that of others.

◆ Observe how students work and socialize in learning centers, evaluate their products, and change materials and activities as they master new skills.

Sources: Maxim (1995) and Pike, Compain, and Mumper (1994).

Students from Diverse Cultural and Language Backgrounds

You can arrange the classroom environment to help second language learners learn English by making language part of all classroom routines. For instance, you can label work areas and objects in the classroom. You also can give students access to materials and learning activities, set up social and work areas, listening areas, and meeting areas, and allow students to sit and work with peer models (Ostrosky & Kaiser, 1991).

Students with Hearing Impairments

Classroom design adaptations should help students with hearing impairments gain information from teachers and interact with peers. To make it easier to use lip reading and residual hearing, the desks of students with hearing impairments can be placed in a central location, about two rows from the front, where students can see the teacher's and other students' lips. Hearing and lip reading also can be fostered by having the students sit in swivel chairs on casters. This makes it easy for them to move and to follow conversations. If students with hearing impairments cannot see the speaker's lips, they can be allowed to change their seats. During lectures or other teacher-directed activities, these students can be seated near the teacher and to one side of the room, where they have a direct line of sight to the lips of peers and teachers. A semicircular seating arrangement can promote lip reading during small-group instruction.

Lighting and noise levels should also be considered in setting up work areas for students with hearing impairments. Glaring light can hinder lip reading; therefore, the source of information should not be located in a poorly lighted area or one where the light is behind the speaker. Structural noises such as those of heating and cooling units, furniture movements, and external airborne noises, such as cars or construction outside the school, can be reduced by using carpets and acoustic tiles on the floor, drapes on windows, and sound-absorbent room dividers. Also, classes containing students with hearing impairments can be placed in rooms in quiet locations and away from noise centers such as gymnasiums, cafeterias, and busy hallways and corridors. The acoustical environment and the noise level in the classroom also can be improved by placing cork protectors on the edges of desks to reduce the sounds of desks closing, tips on the ends of the legs of chairs and desks, and absorbent materials on the walls (Mangiardi, 1993).

Students with hearing impairments may benefit from sitting next to an alert and competent peer who can help them follow along during verbal conversations by indicating changes in the speaker. A peer also can be assigned to give these students information conveyed on the intercom system. Peers also can be responsible for helping students with hearing impairments react to fire drills (flashing lights for fire alarms also can be located throughout the school). However, as students with hearing impairments adjust to the general education classroom, the help they receive from peers should be phased out if possible.

Students with Visual Impairments

Several classroom design adaptations can help students with visual impairments function successfully in inclusive settings. You can encourage them to use their residual vision by providing a glare-free and well-lighted work area. You also can reduce problems associated with glare by using a gray-green chalkboard, placing translucent shades on windows, installing furniture and equipment with matte finishes, and positioning desks so that the light comes over the shoulder of the student's nondominant hand. During teacher-directed activities, the student should not have to look directly into the light to see the teacher. To reduce the fatigue associated with bending over, desks should have adjustable tops.

The work area for students with visual impairments should offer an unobstructed, direct trail to the major parts of the room. When these students first come to your classroom, they can be taught how to move around the room and from their desk to the major classroom locations. These students can be taught to navigate the classroom by using *trace trailing,* directing them to the routes between their desks and major classroom landmarks by having them touch the surfaces of objects on the path. Visual descriptions of the room and routes can supplement trace trailing and help students develop a mental picture of the room. When the room is rearranged, provide time so that these students can learn to adjust to the new arrangement. Students with visual disabilities also may benefit from tactile symbols and signs in Braille placed in important locations in the classroom.

These students' work areas should be in a quiet place, away from potentially harmful objects such as hot radiators, half-open doors, and paper cutters. Pathways throughout the room should be free of objects, and all students should be reminded not to leave things in pathways. To help all students compensate for their visual impairment by increased attention to verbal information, they should be seated where they can hear others well. Masking tape markers on the floor can help students with visual impairments keep their desks properly aligned. Since students with visual impairments may need prosthetic devices and optical aids, you also should consider providing them with a sufficient, convenient, safe space to store this equipment. For example, a music stand or drafting table can be placed next to the students' work areas to reduce the problems of using large-print books.

SET YOUR SITES

For more information on creating an accessible classroom, contact The Center for Universal Design (www.design.ncsu.edu/cud, 800-647-6777) and visit the website www.MakingLife.Easier.com.

Students with Health and Physical Disabilities

Students with physical disabilities who use wheelchairs or prostheses will need aisles and doorways at least 32 inches wide so that they can maneuver easily and safely in the classroom. If possible, arrange desks and classroom furniture with aisles that can accommodate crutches, canes, and turning space for wheelchairs. Some students may also need space to recline during the school day. Students with orthopedic impairments also will benefit from lowered shelves, hooks, storage areas, telephones, fire alarms, water fountains, and door knobs, as well as handrails in the bathroom and at the chalkboard. Ramps and access to electrical outlets and water to operate and rinse their equipment are also important (Knight & Wadsworth, 1993; Wadsworth & Knight, 1999).

For students who use wheelchairs, the type of floor coverings in the classroom is important. Floors should have a nonslip surface; deep pile, shag, or sculptured rugs can limit mobility. Floors should be covered with tightly looped, commercial-grade carpet smooth enough to allow wheelchairs to move easily and strong enough to withstand frequent use. To keep the rug from fraying or rippling, tape it down from wall to wall without placing padding underneath it.

Although students with physical disabilities should have the same type of furniture as their peers, the height of the work area can be adjusted to accommodate wheelchairs or prostheses. Therefore, you may want to request that your classroom include desks with adjustable-height work stations. Some students may need stand-up desks; others may use a desk top or lap board placed on their wheelchairs. These desks can have a cork surface to hold students' work with push pins. Some students also may use special chairs with abductors or adductors.

Furniture that is rounded, with padding on the edges and with no protrusions, is appropriate for many students with physical disabilities. Work areas should be at least 28 inches high to allow students who use wheelchairs to get close to them. Because the reach of students who use wheelchairs is restricted, work tables should not be wider than 42 inches. For comfortable seating, chairs can be curvilinear, have seat heights at least 16 inches above the ground, and be strong enough to support students who wish to pull up

IDEAS FOR IMPLEMENTATION

Transferring Students Who Use Wheelchairs

When Ms. Wade felt a twinge in her back as she helped transfer Mickey from his wheelchair to his seat, she knew she had to talk with Mr. Roman, the occupational therapist. When she caught up with Mr. Roman, he smiled and said, "Welcome to the club. Luckily, there are some things that you can do so that you won't hurt your back. Before you move Mickey, loosen up so that your muscles are ready to be exerted, tell Mickey what is going to happen, and encourage him to help you in the transfer. Then, lift him with your legs, not your back, and keep your back straight. Try to maintain a smooth, steady movement and a wide base of support by placing one foot in front of the other and getting as close as possible to Mickey. As you move, take short steps and avoid becoming twisted when changing directions." The next time Ms. Wade saw Mr. Roman, she thanked him and said, "It's a piece of cake."

Here are some other strategies you can use when transferring students who use wheelchairs:

◆ Wear comfortable footwear that minimizes the likelihood of slipping on the floor.
◆ Encourage students who are able to bear some weight by standing to wear slip-resistant footwear and sturdy belts.
◆ Use walls or sturdy objects to assist in maintaining balance.
◆ Consult with a physical or occupational therapist.

Source: Parette and Hourcade (1986).

on and out of the chairs. Work areas for students with physical disabilities can include space for computers or other adaptive devices that they may need.

Since students with physical disabilities will have to work at the chalkboard, at least one chalkboard in the classroom can be lowered to 24 inches from the floor. To help students work at the chalkboard, attach a sturdy vertical bar as a handrail.

Teachers must understand the importance of body positioning and know how to move and transfer students who use wheelchairs. To prevent pressure sores and help students maintain proper positioning, their position should be changed every 20 to 30 minutes. Posting photographs and descriptions of suggested positions for students with physical disabilities can remind you and others to use the right positioning and transferring techniques (Rikhye et al., 1989). Equipment such as side-lying frames, walkers, crawling assists, floor sitters, chair inserts, straps, standing aids, and beanbag chairs also can help students maintain or change positions.

Several classroom adaptations can help students whose movements are limited. Buddies can be assigned to bring assignments and materials to the students' desks. You can allow these students to leave class early to get to their next class and avoid the rush in the hallway. Securing papers by taping them to the students' desks, and using clipboards or metal cookie sheets and magnets, can help with writing assignments. Similarly, connecting writing utensils to strings taped to students' desks can help students retrieve them when dropped. Desks with textured surfaces or with a barrier around the edge also can help prevent papers, books, and writing utensils from falling. Rikhye et al. (1989) note that built-up utensils, velcro fasteners, cut-out cups, switches, and nonslip placemats can be used for students with physical disabilities.

INFORMATIONAL

Kolar (1996) offers suggestions to help teachers to meet the seating and positioning needs of students with physical disabilities and to select wheeled mobility aids.

INFORMATIONAL

Parette and Hourcade (1986) offer guidelines for moving students forward, backward, and sideways in their wheelchairs and transferring students to toilets and the classroom floor.

Students with Behavior and Attention Disorders

Since it is easier for you to control students, monitor performance, and deliver cues and nonverbal feedback when students are sitting nearby, you may want to locate the work areas of students with behavior and attention disorders near you. Placing these students near good peer models can also help them learn the right classroom behaviors. To make peer models more effective, you can praise them. This reinforces and promotes good behaviors in *all students*.

You also can give students personalized spaces in the classroom and examine the movement patterns in the classroom when determining the work areas for students with behavior and attention disorders. Avoid putting the desks of these students in parts of the room that have a lot of activity, such as near learning centers, media, pencil sharpeners, windows, open doors, and visually loaded areas of the room (Bender & Mathes, 1995). You also can decrease visual distractions by placing a cloth over them when they are not important for learning (Evans, Tickle, Toppel, & Nichols, 1997).

Some teachers use a study carrel for students with attention problems. However, study carrels should not be used often because they may isolate or stigmatize these students. You can reduce the potential problems of study carrels by discussing how individuals learn and function best in different ways, allowing all students to use the study carrel, referring to it in a positive way, and using it for several purposes, such as a relaxation area and a computer or media center.

SUMMARY

This chapter offered guidelines for helping students learn in inclusive classrooms by promoting good classroom behavior and modifying the classroom design for various types of students. As you review the chapter, consider the following questions and remember the following points.

What Legal Guidelines Must I Consider When Designing Disciplinary Actions for Students with Disabilities?

The legal factors to keep in mind when designing disciplinary actions for students with disabilities include using reasonable procedures, determining whether the student's behavior is related to the student's disability, conducting an FBA and designing a behavioral intervention plan for students who misbehave.

How Can I Conduct a Functional Behavioral Assessment?

An FBA involves identifying and defining the problem behavior, recording the behavior using an observational recording system, obtaining more information about the student and the behavior, performing an A-B-C analysis, analyzing the data and developing hypothesis statements, considering sociocultural factors, and developing and evaluating a behavioral intervention plan.

How Can I Promote Positive Classroom Behavior in Students?

You can use affective education techniques, antecedents-based interventions, consequences-based interventions, self-management techniques, group-oriented management systems, and behavior reduction techniques.

What Would You Do in Today's Diverse Classroom?

It is 2 months into the semester and one of your students, Victor, is misbehaving. During teaching activities, he often calls out answers without your permission, talks to other students, sings, and makes inappropriate noises. When this happens, you reprimand Victor and remind him to raise his hand. He rarely completes his assignments, and several of your students have complained that he bothers them.

1. How would you assess Victor's behavior and the environmental events that seem to be associated with it?

2. What environmental factors might be antecedents and consequences of Victor's behavior?

3. What should be the goals of Victor's behavioral intervention plan?

4. What strategies, curricular adaptations, and physical design changes could be included in Victor's behavioral intervention plan?

5. How would you evaluate the effectiveness of Victor's behavioral intervention plan?

It is August, and your principal has given you the list for your inclusion class. Your class of 23 students will include 1 student with a hearing disability, 1 student with a visual disability, 3 students with learning disabilities, 1 student with a behavior disorder, and 2 students who are learning English. Sketch a classroom plan including seating arrangements, the teacher's and students' desks, teaching materials, bulletin boards and walls, specialized areas, and learning centers.

1. What factors did you consider in designing your classroom?

2. How does the design relate to your educational philosophy and teaching style?

3. How has it been adapted for students with disabilities and students from diverse cultural and language backgrounds?

How Can I Prevent Students from Harming Others?

You can work with students and their families and professionals to create a safe, caring school environment that does not tolerate bullying, harassment, and violence of any kind. This collaboration should also foster and acknowledge acceptance of individual differences and the development of friendships. You should be aware of the warning signs of violence and of the steps to take when violence occurs.

How Can I Adapt the Classroom Design to Accommodate Students' Learning, Social, and Physical Needs?

You can consider such factors as seating arrangements; positioning the teacher's desk; organizing teaching materials; designing bulletin boards, walls, specialized areas, and learning centers; and using classroom design adaptations.

PART III

Differentiating Instruction for All Students

P art III of the book, which includes Chapters 8, 9, 10 and 11, is designed to help you vary your teaching to promote the learning of *all students* by accommodating their individual needs in inclusive classrooms. Chapter 8 introduces the concept of differentiating instruction for *all students,* as well as how to use instructional technology and assistive devices for this purpose. Chapter 9 provides strategies for fostering learning when using large- and small-group instruction for *all students*, including how to use the principles of effective teaching and cooperative learning. Chapter 10 offers guidelines for teaching and differentiating instruction so that you can help *all students* learn to read, write, and spell. Chapter 11 presents ways to adapt content area instruction to help *all students* learn by providing guidelines for differentiating mathematics, science, and social studies instruction.

CHAPTER
8

DIFFERENTIATING INSTRUCTION FOR DIVERSE LEARNERS

Tom

Tom, a student with severe disabilities, has been fully included in all classroom activities in Ms. Taravella's class. Ms. Taravella's students have been reading books and sharing them with their classmates through a variety of activities. Tom has been reading a book on a CD-ROM, which allows him to read and listen to the book being read. When he encounters a word that he doesn't know, Tom clicks on a button and the word is read for him.

After completing their reading, students choose a strategy for sharing their books from a list of activities that vary in both difficulty and learning style. The activities include writing a letter or summary about the book, creating a CD-ROM of the story, and making a poster or drawing related to the book. To make sure that students select activities appropriate to their learning levels, Ms. Taravella focuses their choices. She also keeps a record of students' choices and encourages them to try new activities. While Tom's peers work on activities like composing their own ending to their books, writing and videorecording a short play, or making a diorama about the book, Tom and the teacher's aide work together to draw pictures of scenes from the book. These pictures are scanned and transferred to a slide show using presentation software that is narrated by Tom and other students.

What other modifications could Ms. Taravella use to differentiate instruction for Tom and her other students? After reading this chapter, you should be able to answer this as well as the following questions:

◆ How can I differentiate instruction for students?
◆ How can I differentiate instruction for students who have difficulty reading and gaining information from print materials?
◆ How can I differentiate instruction for students from diverse cultural and language backgrounds?
◆ How can I use instructional technology and assistive devices to differentiate instruction for students?

Tom and Ms. Taravella's other students were successful learners because Ms. Taravella used a variety of teaching and curricular adaptations to differentiate instruction for her students. In this process, educators use instructional arrangements, strategies, resources, materials, curricular approaches, and teaching and assistive technology to accommodate the individual learning needs, strengths, preferences, and styles of their students, as well as their experiential, cultural, and language backgrounds (Scott, Vitale, & Masten, 1998). This chapter describes proven adaptations for differentiating instruction to address the many unique learning needs of students. While these adaptations can be used to help various types of students learn, they also can be used to differentiate instruction for *all students.* For example, while Ms. Taravella used multilevel teaching to differentiate instruction for Tom, she also used it to ensure the learning of *all* of her students.

How Can I Differentiate Instruction for Students?

Tailor Teaching Strategies to the Needs of Students and the Learning Environment

The types of teaching strategies students will need can be determined and specified by the planning team. The strategies chosen will depend on several factors, including the students' needs and the learning environment. Cohen and Lynch (1991) and Arllen, Gable, and Hendrickson (1996) offer excellent models for selecting teaching modifications for students. These models have seven steps.

Step 1: Clarification of elements under the teacher's control. The planning team identifies the variables under the teacher's control. These include the physical and social environment of the classroom, the organization and objectives of the lesson, and the choice of teaching activities, materials, and media. Other variables examined include the availability of support personnel, management strategies, and evaluation techniques. In examining the learning environment, you can consider the following issues:

◆ What are the themes, goals, and objectives of the lesson/activity?
◆ What teaching materials and arrangements will be used in the lesson/activity?
◆ When, where, and how long will this lesson/activity occur?
◆ Will students be able to participate in this lesson/activity in the same ways as their classmates?

◈ What supports and/or accommodations are needed to help students participate fully?

◈ How can the curriculum be supplemented or changed to address the different learning needs of students?

◈ How can the lesson/activity be adapted to students' learning styles, language, culture, experiences, behavioral needs, interests, talents, strengths, difficulties, and IEPs?

◈ How can the lesson/activity be adapted in terms of the type and amount of work, teaching materials used, grouping patterns, assistance needed, pace and time, and the products produced?

◈ Can the student participate in the activity but work on other skills or work with others on an activity that has different goals?

◈ How can the lesson/activity be adapted to motivate and engage students?

◈ What materials will be needed to engage students in the lesson/activity?

◈ How can the classroom environment be changed to engage students in the lesson/activity (Dyck et al., 1997; Jorgensen, 1995)?

Step 2: Development of a modification menu. The planning team lists potential modifications that can be used with the student.

Step 3: Decision on whether a problem exists. If a problem exists, the planning team meets with teachers to determine its extent.

Step 4: Development of a problem statement. The planning team agrees on and states the problem in a clear and understandable way.

Step 5: Selection and grouping of modifications. The planning team reviews the modification menu delineated in step 2 and selects various alternatives that address the problem(s) stated in step 4.

Step 6: Ranking of modification options. The planning team ranks each alternative suggested in step 5 according to potential impact, prior effectiveness, teacher's ability, and number of outside resources and time requirements for the modification.

Step 7: Modification implementation. The planning team selects a teaching modification based on the rankings computed in step 6, which is then used and evaluated.

INFORMATIONAL

Knowlton (1998) offers a model for designing personalized curricular supports for students with developmental disabilities.

VIDEO INSIGHT

Common Miracles: The New American Revolution in Learning

In this ABC News video segment, we learn about recent changes in the American educational system based on new understandings about teaching, learning, and what school systems can do to help *all students* learn.

With your classmates or in your teaching journal, reflect on these questions:

1. Recall that the four principles of inclusion are: diversity, individual needs, reflective practice, and collaboration. How is each of these principles exemplified in the different teaching strategies shown in the video segment?

2. In the video, Howard Gardner says the question teachers should be asking is not "How smart are you?" but "How are you smart?" How can you differentiate instruction for students with diverse learning needs in your inclusive classroom so that you tap into their unique strengths, abilities and intelligences?

INFORMATIONAL

Guidelines for identifying students' learning styles and designing teaching strategies and environments accordingly are available (Carbo, 1994; Dunn, 1996; Johnston, 1998).

SET YOUR SITES

Information and resources on learning styles are available from the Center for the Study of Learning and Teaching Styles (www. learningstyles.net).

INFORMATIONAL

Dunn, Griggs, Olson, Beasley, and Gorman (1995) and Kavale, Hirshoren, and Forness (1998) debate the research and merits of teaching based on learning styles.

REFLECTIVE

How do you prefer to learn and teach? How do you adapt when the teaching strategy and environment are different from the way you prefer to learn? Should teachers match teaching to students' learning styles all of the time? Should students be taught to adapt their learning styles to the various teaching styles they will encounter in schools?

Consider Students' Learning Styles

When choosing methods to differentiate instruction, you should consider students' learning styles (Hodgin & Wooliscroft, 1997; Nickelsburg, 1995). Note the situations and conditions that appear to influence individual students, and adjust learning and assessment activities to accommodate students' learning styles (Garrick Duhaney & Whittington-Couse, 1998; Kubina & Cooper, 2000). You can use different types of reinforcement and feedback to increase students' motivation and acknowledge their performance. You also can structure the classroom so that noise levels, students' nearness to others, distractions, movement, and desk arrangements are acceptable to students. Whenever possible, you can adjust the lighting, temperature, ventilation, and students' work locations. For example, you can let students choose whether to work at their desks, on the floor, or in some other place (e.g., a soft lounge chair). Finally, when planning the length and nature of learning activities and daily and weekly schedules, you can think about the various learning style needs of students such as attention span, ability to move while learning, time of day, and grouping considerations such as learning alone or in groups and with or without adults present.

Learning and teaching styles also are classified as either *field independent* or *field sensitive*. Field-independent students appear to work best on individual tasks such as independent projects and relate formally to teachers; field-sensitive students prefer to work in groups and establish personal relationships with others, including teachers. Field-independent teachers foster learning through competition and independent assignments; field-sensitive teachers use personal and conversational teaching techniques.

Another important consideration is *locus of control,* an individual's belief about the relationship between effort and achievement. Individuals who believe that their actions cause them to succeed or fail are said to have an *internal* locus of control. By contrast, those who believe that circumstances outside of their control affect their performance are said to have an *external* locus of control. Hoover and Collier (1989) noted that because of acculturation, many students from diverse cultural and language backgrounds may behave in ways that indicate an external locus of control. They suggest that you can help these students by training them to see mistakes as temporary and as correctable through hard work.

Learning styles can be affected in other ways by cultural factors. For example, some cultures emphasize learning through verbal rather than visual descriptions; other cultures emphasize physical modeling over pictorials. Students' socioeconomic status can also influence their learning and cognitive styles (Garcia & Ortiz, 1988).

Consider Students' Sensory Abilities

Students with sensory disabilities have unique needs. For students with visual disabilities, you must present information orally; for students with hearing disabilities, you should use visual forms. At all times, you should encourage independence. Because the sensory functioning of students with sensory disabilities varies tremendously, you need to consider their unique needs and abilities when modifying your teaching methods.

Differentiating Instruction for Students with Visual Disabilities

You can use many different strategies to differentiate instruction for students with visual disabilities (Torres & Corn, 1990). However, understand that as students grow older, they may be reluctant to use special materials in the presence of their peers.

First, you can help them follow along in class by giving important directions verbally or recording them, phrasing questions and comments so that they include students' names, and using peers to read directions and materials, describe events in the classroom, and take notes. You also can help these students learn by giving them opportunities to learn by doing, such as touching objects and materials and using manipulatives, and by providing them with large-print books, photo-enlarged handouts and tests, Braille reference books and dictionaries, adaptive computer software, and audiocassettes.

When developing materials for students to use or when writing at the chalkboard, you can use larger letters and numerals, tactile illustrations, raised-line drawings, and graphics that avoid clutter and emphasize contrast. Use computers to produce large, clear typewritten materials. Avoid the use of purple dittos and multicolored chalk, as they are often difficult to see. Tracing over the letters, numerals, and pictorials with a black felt-tip marker or black ballpoint pen makes it easier to see dittos, and placing a piece of yellow acetate over a page of print enhances the contrast and darkens the print. Students with visual impairments may suffer from visual fatigue during activities that require continuous use of visual skills. In these situations, it may be helpful to give students additional time to complete assignments and tests or to reduce the number and length of activities that call for visual concentration.

You also can make it easier for students to learn by giving them a copy of notes, verbalizing notes as they are being written on the board, sharing notes with students' other teachers, and allowing students to take notes using a laptop computer. In addition, you can give students desk copies of important visual materials such as charts or maps; explain in greater detail information presented visually; and refer to information on the board by name.

Student learning can also be promoted by using several strategies to help students locate learning materials and move around the classroom and the school. You can use *o'-clock* directions to describe the location of an object on a flat surface (e.g., "Your book is at three o'clock and your pencil is at nine o'clock"). If an object is nearby and in danger of being knocked over, guide the student's hand to the object or hand the student the object by gently touching his or her hand with the object. When giving directions to specific places in the classroom or school, use nonvisual statements and remember that directions for going left and right should be in relation to the student's body rather than yours. At first, it may be helpful to assign students a buddy to help them move through the school. When students become skilled in traveling around the school, ask them to perform errands and class jobs. It also is important to identify yourself by name or voice when walking up to students with visual impairments. Finally, don't leave a room without telling these students that you are leaving.

Differentiating Instruction for Students with Hearing Disabilities

Many strategies are available for differentiating instruction for students with hearing impairments (Mangiardi, 1993): using good communication techniques, which include standing still and facing the person when speaking; speaking clearly, at a moderate pace, using short sentences; speaking in a normal voice; maintaining a proper speaking distance; keeping the mouth area clear; using facial and body gestures; speaking in an area where the light is on your lips and face; and providing transitions to indicate a change in the subject. Try to limit movement and unnecessary gestures, and present all spelling and vocabulary words in sentences (context), as many words presented in isolation look alike to lip readers. In addition, you can use visual signals to gain the student's attention, and use media such as an overhead projector to present material so that the student can view the material and your lips simultaneously. If necessary, rephrase, repeat, summarize, or simplify your comments and questions, as well as those of other students, to make them more understandable, and ask questions to check understanding of orally presented directions and content. When using media, shine a light on the speaker's face when the room is darkened for films or slides, and give the student the script of a video, or a record to help the student follow along.

You also can use visually oriented techniques to help students learn. Offer demonstrations and provide examples. Supplement information presented orally with real objects, manipulatives, and concrete visual aids (e.g., maps, globes). Write daily assignments, the schedule, important directions and information, technical terms, and new vocabulary on the board, and give students test directions, assignments, vocabulary lists, models, feedback, and lecture outlines in writing. Teach the student to look up difficult-to-pronounce words in the dictionary.

Peers also can be helpful in teaching students with hearing impairments. For example, they can share their notes, using carbon paper, and point to speakers during a group discussion. A peer also can ensure that the student is following along in the correct place when the class is working on an assignment, indicate that someone is talking over the intercom, and then share the intercom message.

Using Educational Interpreters Effectively An *educational interpreter*, a professional who helps to transfer information between individuals who do not communicate in the same way, can assist you in differentiating instruction for students with hearing impairments. Depending on the student's preference, many different educational interpreting methods exist. A signed system interpreter translates spoken language directed to a student with a hearing impairment into a signed system such as Conceptually Accurate Signed English (CASE). An oral interpreter helps the student understand verbal messages by silently mouthing the complete message or a paraphrase of it. In both of these methods, voice interpretation is used if the student needs help in converting his or her responses into the mode preferred by those who are communicating with the student.

INFORMATIONAL

Guidelines for using educational interpreters in schools and classrooms are available (New York State Education Department, n.d.; Salend & Longo, 1994).

An educational interpreter can improve the student's academic performance in the general education classroom by translating directions, content, and assignments presented orally by teachers, as well as the comments of peers. The interpreter can also share the student's responses and questions with teachers and peers (Jones, Clark, & Soltz, 1997). Early in the school year, you and the interpreter can meet to agree on the responsibilities of both persons. Generally, the teacher has primary responsibility and the interpreter aids communication (Salend & Longo, 1994). To help teachers and interpreters communicate, planning meetings can be scheduled on a regular basis.

Since interpreters may not know the content and teaching strategies used in the classroom, it is helpful to orient them to the curriculum and to give them copies of textbooks and other relevant materials. A knowledge of class routines, projects, and long-term assignments can assist interpreters in helping students understand assignments. With a difficult unit, including technical vocabulary and other content that may be hard to explain by alternative means, you and the interpreter can meet to discuss key terms. For example, when teaching a unit about the geological history of the earth, you could give the interpreter a list of key terms and copies of lesson plans so that the interpreter can plan in advance how to translate and explain such terms as *Paleozoic era, Oligocene epoch*, and *Jurassic period.*

Students with hearing impairments may need the service of an educational interpreter.

To maximize the effectiveness of the interpreter in your classroom, you can

◇ be sensitive to the time delays caused by interpreting.

◇ talk to the students, not to the interpreter.

◇ avoid directing comments to the interpreter during class time. Signals can be used to indicate the need for discussion after class.

◇ encourage the interpreter to seek help when communication problems arise during class that affect the translation process.

◇ avoid involving the interpreter in disciplining the student for misbehavior unless this misbehavior is directed at the interpreter. When the interpreter is involved in disciplinary actions, help students understand the roles and perspectives of the persons involved.

◇ place the interpreter in a position that makes interpretation easy.

Maintaining Hearing Aids   A hearing aid that does not work properly can hinder your attempts to differentiate instruction for students with hearing impairments. You may need to help these students monitor and maintain the working condition of their hearing aids. Periodically, you can examine a student's hearing aid by using an inexpensive plastic stethoscope, which allows you to hear what the student hears and to detect malfunctions and their causes. A whistling sound may indicate that the earmold doesn't fit, the battery or the receiver is malfunctioning, or the volume control is too loud. No sound often suggests that the cord or the battery is not working. If a faint sound is heard, the problem may be caused by a worn-down or incorrect battery, a broken cord, or an incorrect setting for the volume or tone control. When the sound varies from on to off, the battery and cord connections may be loose or corroded. If the battery and cord are connected properly, the fluctuating signal may be caused by a broken receiver. Finally, a sound that is distorted or too loud can be caused by a weak battery, improper battery or cord connections, an incorrect tone control setting, a damaged earphone, or a wax-clogged earmold or earphone.

You can help maintain the hearing aid in working condition by keeping it out of excessively hot or cold locations and by making sure that it does not get wet. When you suspect that a hearing aid is not working properly and the problem cannot be corrected, you should immediately contact the student's family and the speech and language therapist for assistance.

Consider Treatment Acceptability

When selecting strategies to differentiate instruction, another important factor to consider is *treatment acceptability,* the extent to which you view a specific teaching strategy as easy to use, effective, appropriate for the setting, fair, and reasonable (Gajria & Salend, 1996). Reasonableness can be assessed by examining the strategy in terms of how much extra time and what resources are needed to use it, whether it will require important changes in your teaching style, whether it is consistent with your philosophy, whether it is intrusive, how it will affect others, and how much it will cost. In general, you are more likely to use a strategy that is practical, easy to use, immediately effective, and not disruptive to your classroom routine and teaching style (Margolis & McGettigan, 1988).

An important aspect of treatment acceptability is the impact of the strategy on specific students and their peers. You are more likely to use strategies you perceive as fair and benefiting *all students.* Other factors related to students include age appropriateness, risks such as student embarrassment or isolation, intrusiveness into the student's personal space, and student cooperation (Epps, Prescott, & Horner, 1990). For example, giving a student a math assignment while the other students are working on social studies can isolate the student. Make sure that the strategy does not adversely affect either the students or their classmates.

When adapting your teaching methods, you also need to consider students' reactions to and perceptions of these changes. In general, students prefer teachers who adapt their teaching methods and believe that *all students* benefit from these accommodations. Some students, however, particularly those with disabilities, are concerned that modifications in tests, textbooks, and homework may isolate them from their general education peers (Vaugh, Schumm, & Kouzekanani, 1993).

Use Individualized Adaptations

Individualized adaptations are modifications in the ways information is presented or the ways students respond. Frequently, teaching modifications are used to help some students who are learning the same material as their classmates. Individualized adaptations include using adapted materials, adaptive equipment, and technology; using peer and adult assistance; delivering verbal cues and physical prompts; changing the skill sequence; and adjusting classroom rules (Ayres, Belle, Greene, O'Connor, & Meyer, n.d.). Some individualized adaptations that you may consider include altering the pace of instruction, designing alternative projects to allow students to demonstrate mastery, focusing on fewer objectives, and adapting or modifying students' requirements and assessments.

Use Multilevel Teaching

All lessons and curricular areas can be individualized by using *multilevel teaching* (Murray, 1991). In this system, students are given lessons in the same curricular areas as their peers but at varying levels of difficulty (Giangreco et al., 1995). Multilevel teaching also involves using flexible learning objectives that are adapted to the needs of students. For example, a student with a severe disability might practice writing numbers by copying the same problems that other students are using to practice addition of decimals. Collicott (1991) described a four-step process for designing multilevel lessons:

> *Step 1: Identify the underlying concepts.* Identify and examine the objectives and materials of the lesson, and determine the content and skill level differences.
>
> *Step 2: Consider the various possible teaching methods.* Consider the different learning styles, and the cognitive and participation levels of students, as well as the different modes that can be used to present the lesson.
>
> *Step 3: Consider the ways in which students practice and perform.* Consider the different ways students can practice and show mastery of skills and concepts. In addition, teach students to accept different modes for demonstrating skill mastery and understanding of concepts.
>
> *Step 4: Consider methods of evaluation.* Consider a variety of ways to assess students' mastery.

REFLECTIVE

Think about a lesson you recently taught. How did/could you use multilevel teaching to adapt the lesson to the needs of a student with a severe disability? A student with a mild disability? A student who is gifted and talented? A second language learner?

Use Curriculum Overlapping

Curriculum overlapping involves teaching a diverse group of students individualized skills from different curricular areas (Ayres et al., n.d.). In this method, teaching of a practical, functional, specific skill related to the student's academic program is embedded in learning activities across the curriculum. For example, when the class is working on social studies and science lessons, a student can be working on following multi-task directions within those content areas.

Use Tiered Assignments

Tiered assignments allow you to tailor assignments to meet the needs of individual students (Tomlinson, 1995b). In this method, you identify concepts that need to be learned and allow students to respond in alternative ways that differ in complexity and learning style. For example, after reading a book, students can display their learning by writing a book report or review, designing a book jacket, writing a play, drawing a picture, composing a poem, or making a video.

Use Universally Designed Teaching Materials

You also can individualize lessons and activities by using teaching materials that are *universally designed.* These materials have been developed for use with students who have a wide range of ability levels. This allows you to tailor them based on students' learning styles and cognitive, physical, sensory, cultural, and language needs (United States Office of Special Programs, 1999). Universally designed materials offer options that allow learners to receive and respond to information in a variety of formats. For example, *Wiggleworks* is a universally designed technology-based instructional material developed by

Scholastic (www.scholastic.com). It uses many different teaching formats that allow a wide range of students to read stories and record their responses. Therefore, when reading, students can have the text highlighted, enlarged, or read aloud by the computer. Similarly, students can record their responses by typing text, drawing, speaking, or entering words from a list into their text.

How Can I Differentiate Instruction for Students Who Have Difficulty Reading and Gaining Information from Print Materials?

You probably present a lot of content to your students using print materials. However, since many students have difficulty reading and gaining information from print materials, you may need to use alternative teacher- and student-directed strategies instead. These methods are described in the following sections.

Use Teacher-Directed Text Comprehension Strategies

Previewing

Informational

Andrews, Winograd, and DeVille (1996) offer prereading activities for use with students who have hearing impairments and students who are second language learners.

Before assigning a reading selection, you can use prereading activities to preview new vocabulary and word pronunciation, motivate students, and activate their prior knowledge. Scanning the selection and discussing the meaning of boldfaced or italicized terms is helpful. New vocabulary words can be placed in a word file of index cards by chapter, with each new term placed on a separate card with its definition and the page number on which it appears (Wood & Wooley, 1986).

Previews, structured overviews, and prereading organizers can help students understand the purpose of the reading selection, activate their prior knowledge, direct their attention to the relevant information in the selection, and help them identify what they know about the selection's topic (Gartland, 1994). For example, you can give students a list of important vocabulary with definitions or an outline of the selection's main points and discuss them before reading or have students complete an outline as they read the selection. As students read the assignment, emphasize key points by underlining and highlighting them; by repeating, discussing and summarizing them; and by questioning students about graphs, pictures, and diagrams.

You also can use marginal glosses to help students identify and understand essential information presented in print (Stewart & Cross, 1991). Like the marginal notes in this book, marginal glosses are written on textbook pages that include statements, questions, notes, and activities that help students understand and interact with the material.

Activating students' prior knowledge before reading the selection also can help them understand the new material. This can be done by using brainstorming, by discussing and predicting components of the story, by building semantic webs, and by using a *K-W-L* strategy: *K* (students identify what they KNOW about the reading selection and the topic), *W* (students create questions or statements related to what they WANT to learn from reading about the topic), and *L* (students discuss what they have LEARNED from reading about the topic) (Schirmer, 1997).

You can improve students' comprehension skills by asking them to do a writing activity related to the assignment before they read the selection. Learning logs, study guides, written summaries, and questions related to readings can be used to help students understand the material by allowing them to organize their thoughts.

Questioning

A popular strategy for guiding text comprehension—having students respond to questions about the text before, during, and after reading—can focus their attention on the purpose of the assignment (Pedrotty Bryant, Ugel, Thompson, & Hamff, 1999). Manzo and Manzo (1990) identified five types of questions that you can use:

1. *Predictable questions* about the facts presented in the selection (who, what, where, when, why, and how)
2. *Mind-opening questions* related to the written and oral language components of the selection
3. *Introspective questions*, which cause students to reflect on the material
4. *Ponderable questions*, which present dilemmas or situations that have no right or wrong answer
5. *Elaborative knowledge questions*, which ask students to incorporate their prior knowledge into information presented in the selection

You can help students answer chapter questions correctly by modifying the type and timing of the questions. At first, you can present questions that deal with factual information. Then you can move to those that require inference and more complex skills. Rather than using open-ended questions, you can rephrase them, using simpler language or a multiple-choice format. You can help students gain information from books by using *prequestions* posed before the selection is read and *postquestions* posed afterward. Postquestions are particularly effective in promoting recall by establishing the need for review. Be careful in using prequestions; they can cause students to focus too much on information related to the answers while ignoring other content.

You can help students develop text comprehension skills by asking them to generate their own questions and summarize a selection's content in their own words. Students can be taught to create their own questions through a procedure called *REQUEST*, which involves reading silently, asking questions about the text, responding to the questions, repeating the procedure with other parts of the selection, making predictions about what will happen, reading silently, and discussing their predictions (Manzo, 1969).

Reciprocal Teaching

Text comprehension skills also can be improved by *reciprocal teaching*, which involves a dialogue between you and your students (Carter, 1997; Palincsar & Klenk, 1991). Here you ask students to read a selection silently, summarize it, discuss and clarify problem areas and unclear vocabulary, use questions to check understanding, and give students the opportunity to predict future content. After you model these strategies, students take the role of the teacher while you provide help through prompting ("What type of question would a teacher ask in this situation?"), instructing ("A summary is a short statement that

INFORMATIONAL

Palincsar and Klenk (1991) give guidelines to prepare teachers and students to use reciprocal teaching.

Story maps can facilitate students' reading comprehension.

includes only essential information"), modifying the activity ("If you can't predict what's going to happen, summarize the information again"), praising students ("That was a good prediction"), and offering corrective feedback ("What information could help you make your prediction?").

Story-Mapping

INFORMATIONAL

Boyle and Weishaar (1997) have developed TRAVEL, a learning strategy to help students create cognitive organizers to help them understand text.

Some students may benefit from *story-mapping,* in which you help them identify the structure and the major elements of a story by using a visual representation of the major elements (Gardill & Jitendra, 1999). Give students story maps that contain spaces for them to list the setting (characters, time, and place), the problem, the goal, the action, the outcome, and the characters' reactions. As students read information on the components of the story map, ask them to discuss the information and write the correct response on their story map. As students learn to do this, they can complete the story map independently.

POSSE

POSSE is a series of strategies for use before, during, and after reading text to promote text comprehension (Englert & Marriage, 1991). Before reading the text, students predict what ideas are in the story and organize their thoughts through the use of semantic webs. During reading, students search for and summarize the main ideas. After reading, they evaluate the selection and their comprehension by comparing their predictions with the actual outcomes, clarifying vocabulary and referents, and predicting what the author will present next. The teacher supports students in these activities by using POSSE strategy sheets, self-statement cue cards, student–teacher dialogues and think-alouds, mapping, questioning, and reciprocal teaching.

Teach Student-Directed Text Comprehension Strategies

In addition to using teacher-directed strategies, you can teach students to use a variety of student-directed comprehension strategies, which are described in the following sections.

Finding the Main Idea

Students can learn to identify the main idea of a paragraph, which is usually embedded in the topic sentence. This sentence is usually the first sentence of the paragraph. Students also can be taught to identify main points by looking for repetition of the same word or words throughout the paragraph (Crank & Keimig, 1988) and by using an instructional program (Jitendra, Cole, Hoppes, & Wilson, 1998).

Surveying

Students can be taught to survey reading assignment through use of *SQ3R*, a technique that consists of the following steps:

Survey. Surveying allows students to look for clues to the content of the chapter. In surveying, students can do the following: (1) examine the title of the chapter and try to anticipate what information will be presented; (2) read the first paragraph to try to determine the objectives of the chapter; (3) review the headings and subheadings to identify main points; (4) analyze visual aids to find relevant supporting information and related details; and (5) read the final paragraph to summarize the main points.

Question. Questioning helps students identify important content by formulating questions based on restating headings and subheadings and their own reactions to the material.

Read. Reading enables students to examine sections more closely and to answer the questions raised in the questioning phase.

Recite. Reciting helps students recall the information for further use. In this step, students can be encouraged to study the information they have just covered.

Review. Reviewing also helps students remember the content. This can be done by having them prepare an oral or written summary of the main topics.

INFORMATIONAL

Bradstad and Stumpf (1987) provide excellent guidelines for training students to learn each step involved in using SQ3R.

Multipass   A modified version of SQ3R is *multipass*, in which students review the content of a reading selection three times (Schumaker et al., 1982). In the first pass, or *survey*, students become familiar with the structure and organization of the selection by examining the chapter title, introductory and summary paragraphs, headings, visual displays, and organization of the chapter. The survey pass concludes with students paraphrasing the content of the selection.

The second review, the *size-up* pass, helps students identify the main points of the chapter. Students read the chapter questions; those that can be answered after the survey pass are checked off. They then survey the material to answer those questions that do not have check marks by paying attention to cues, phrasing cued information as a question, skimming paragraphs to determine the answers, and paraphrasing the answers and all the material they can remember.

In the final or *sort-out* pass, students read the selection again and answer the accompanying questions. Again, students check off each completed question and move on until all questions are answered.

Other similar techniques, such as SOS (Schumaker, Deshler, Alley, & Warner, 1983), OK5R (Pauk, 1984), PQST (Pauk, 1984), PARTS (Ellis, 1996), and SCROL (Grant, 1993), also can be selected based on the ability levels of students.

Self-Questioning

Students can be taught to use several self-questioning procedures to improve their text comprehension skills (Lebzelter & Nowacek, 1999). In one self-questioning technique, students determine the reasons for studying the passage, identify the passage's main ideas by underlining them, generate a question associated with each main idea and write it in the margin, find the answer to the question and write it in the margin, and review all the questions and answers (Wong & Jones, 1982). Another self-questioning strategy, *ASK IT,* involves teaching students to develop and use symbols for who, what, where, when, why, which, and how questions, as well as to write questions, answer them, and talk about their answers (Schumaker, Deshler, Nolan, & Alley, 1994).

Paraphrasing

Paraphrasing requires students to read text, ask questions about it to determine the main idea and other relevant information, and paraphrase the answers to these questions (Lebzelter & Nowacek, 1999). Paraphrased statements should consist of a complete sentence; be correct and logical; and provide new and useful information (Schumaker, Denton, & Deshler, 1984).

Outlining

Outlining chapters allow students to identify, sequence, and group main and secondary points so that they can better understand what they have read. Students can learn to use a separate outline for each topic, identify essential parts of a topic using Roman numerals, present subtopics by subdividing each main heading using capital letters, and group information within a subdivision in a sequence using numbers.

Summarizing

INFORMATIONAL

Thistlethwaite (1991) provides a six-phase model for teaching students to use summarization, and Chan (1991) offers a list of questions that students can use in creating summaries.

Another approach to teaching text comprehension skills is *summarization* (Swanson & De la Paz, 1998). Gajria (1988) identified five basic rules students can employ in summarizing text: (1) identify and group main points; (2) eliminate information that is repeated or unnecessary; (3) find the topic sentence; (4) devise topic sentences for paragraphs that have none; and (5) delete phrases and sentences that fail to present new or relevant information.

Paragraph Restatements and Paragraph Shrinking

INFORMATIONAL

Jenkins, Heliotis, Stein, and Haynes (1987) provide guidelines for teaching students to use paragraph restatements.

Paragraph restatements help students actively process reading material by encouraging them to create original sentences that summarize the main points of the selection. The sentences should include the fewest possible words. They can be written in the textbook, recorded as notes on a separate sheet, or constructed mentally. In *paragraph shrinking,* students read a paragraph orally and then state its main idea in 10 words or less by identifying the most important information about who or what the paragraph is about (Fuchs, Fuchs, & Kazdan, 1999).

Critical Thinking Maps

Teaching students to use *critical thinking maps* can help them interpret and comprehend textbook information (Bock & Barger, 1998; Idol, 1987a). Students complete the map during or after reading the selection by listing the following: (1) the main point(s) of the selection; (2) the important facts, actions, examples, events, or steps that lead to and support the main point(s); (3) their interpretations, opinions, and prior knowledge of the content of the chapter, as well as any additional viewpoints of the author and their conclusions about the information presented; and (4) the relationship between the information presented and events and issues in society and their lives.

Visual Imagery

Visual imagery requires students to read a section of a book, create an image for every sentence read, contrast each new image with the prior one, and evaluate the images to make sure that they are complete. You can teach students to use visual imagery by asking them to create visual images for concrete objects, having them visualize familiar objects and settings, asking them to create images while listening to high-imagery stories, and having them devise images as they read.

Verbal Rehearsal

In verbal rehearsal, students pause after reading several sentences to themselves and verbalize to themselves the selection's content. At the beginning, you can cue students to use verbal rehearsal by placing red dots at various points in the selection.

Enhance the Readability of Materials

Students with reading and learning difficulties must often use commercially produced and teacher-developed print materials whose readability levels are too high for them. You can increase students' understanding of reading matter by modifying the material, making the text less complex, using the principles of typographic design, and using audiocassettes, videocassettes, and electronic literacy activities.

Highlight Essential Information

You can make print materials more readable by highlighting critical information. This will help students identify main points and locate essential information. Cues linking questions with the location of the answers in the selection can help students learn how to find the answers. For example, you can color code study questions and their answers in the text. Pairing questions with the numbers of pages containing the answers, simplifying vocabulary by paraphrasing questions, defining important and difficult terms, breaking multiple-part questions into separate questions, or recording questions on cassettes and including the pages where the answers occur are other helpful methods. (Chalmers, 1991; Wood & Wooley, 1986).

Use the Principles of Typographic Design

Since the visual look of text also affects its readability, you can use the principles of typographic and visual design to produce materials that promote speed, clarity, and understanding (Hoener, Salend, & Kay, 1997). Because computers are now becoming more

REFLECTIVE

Try the various text comprehension strategies using material in this textbook or in a textbook for the grade and subject matter you would like to teach. Which strategies were easiest? Which ones were most effective?

IDEAS FOR IMPLEMENTATION

Adjusting the Complexity of Text Language

Ms. Mantel's class had several students whose reading abilities varied widely. Sometimes, they were able to read the material and understand it. At other times, they struggled. Ms. Mantel noticed that her students' reading abilities appeared to be related to the linguistic complexity of the text. She began to simplify the choice and arrangements of words and sentences in the selections that caused her students the most trouble. First, she examined the length of sentences and shortened them. She broke long sentences into two or three shorter sentences. Second, she highlighted main ideas, concepts, and words. Third, she helped her students understand the order of the concepts presented by using signal words such as *first, second,* and *third.* Fourth, because her students had difficulty understanding the relationship between concepts, she used words that show relationships, such as *because, after,* and *since.*

Here are some other strategies you can use to reduce the linguistic complexity of text to help students understand it:

◇ Eliminate unnecessary words and sections that may distract students.

◇ Use coordinate and subordinate conjunctions to establish cohesive ties between concepts.

◇ Use clear pronoun references and word substitution to clarify relationships.

◇ Rephrase paragraphs so that they begin with a topic sentence followed by supporting details.

◇ Present a series of events or actions in chronological order, and cluster information that is related.

◇ Embed the definition of new words in paragraphs, and avoid using different words that have identical meanings.

◇ Insert text and examples to clarify main points.

◇ Present text in the present tense and avoid use of the passive voice.

◇ Create visual aids that present content.

Sources: Beech (1983), Mercer and Mercer (1993), Reynolds and Salend (1990), and Wood and Wooley (1986).

available in classrooms, various dimensions of typographic design can help you design and produce printed materials that are very readable and legible. These dimensions are outlined below.

Type size: 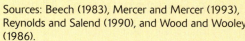 and type that is too large requires excessive eye movements to follow the text and can cause the reader to pause more often while reading a line.

You can make material more readable by using typefaces with simple designs, as well as those familiar to students. In terms of type size, 12- to 14-point type is easier to read than smaller or larger print at typical reading distances. However, larger type may be more appropriate for young students who are beginning to read and for students who have visual difficulties.

Case   Lowercase letters provide cues that help readers perceive and remember differences in letters and word shapes. For this reason, text should be printed in lowercase and capital letters where grammatically appropriate. ALL-CAPITAL PRINTING CAN

Teachers can use the principles of typographic design to produce highly readable and legible materials for use with students.

SLOW DOWN THE READING PROCESS and is appropriate for use with short, non-continuous text that needs to be HIGHLIGHTED, such as headings and subheadings, or for an essential word in a sentence or paragraph.

Style   Style refers to variants such as *italics* and **boldface.** *The use of italics or boldface variants slows reading of continuous text* and should be used only to **emphasize** and *highlight* small amounts of text embedded in sentences and paragraphs or to make headings stand out. Italics and boldface are preferable to underlining to highlight important material; underlining can distract the reader and make it harder to discriminate letters. For example, underlining can cause students to perceive y as v or u and g as a.

Proportional and Monospaced Type   `Monospaced type uses the same horizontal space for all letters,` while proportionally spaced type varies the horizontal space of letters, depending on their form. Proportionally spaced type makes reading easier by providing additional perceptual cues for letter recognition and enhancing the flow of the text.

Line Length   Line length refers to the number of characters and spaces in a line. Material that is printed in long lines may cause fatigue by making it difficult to find the next line to read, while text that is printed in short lines
demands that students' eyes
change lines frequently.

You can use several strategies to design materials that have appropriate line length. One method is to count characters and spaces and to maintain a line length and character count of between 60 and 80. Another method is to structure the material by using line lengths of six to eight words. This method adjusts the line length to the linguistic complexity of the material and therefore the reading skill of students.

Spacing   When designing print materials, it is useful to view space as a hierarchy that proceeds from smallest to largest as follows: (1) space between letters, (2) space between words, (3) space between lines, (4) space between paragraphs, (5) space between columns, (6) space between sections, and (7) space from the text area to the edge of the page. Failure to follow these spatial relationships can confuse and frustrate readers. For example, if the space between letters exceeds the space between words, the words appear to "fall apart," and if the space between words is greater than the space between lines, the lines break up and the eye may be tempted to move down rather than across. Therefore, you should examine the impact of all spaces on a page and make adjustments when necessary.

Justification   Justification refers to the alignment of the edges of text. Left-justified or aligned text is the best choice for readability at all reading levels, as it makes it easier for the reader to track the text. Right-justified text results in uneven word and letter spacing of text and can cause students with reading difficulties to experience distracting modulations in the flow of text.

Centered text slows the reading process and is best used
for special purposes like titles or lists.

Right-aligned text disturbs the flow of reading because the
eye does not know
where to go to begin reading the next

line.

Background   Since students' ability to read also can be affected by the color contrast between the text and the background, material should consist of black or blue text on a white background.

Use Electronic Literacy

Some students may benefit from electronic literacy, which involves the use of digitally presented, interactive teaching activities to support and improve understanding (Horney & Anderson-Inman, 1999; Topping & McKenna, 1999). Electronically presented reading activities such as electronic books differentiate instruction for students through help menus that connect them to

- translation resources that offer help through the use of digitized pronunciations and definitions of words or video clips of sign language translations;
- teaching resources and/or strategy prompts embedded in the selection to allow students to review material, understand context cues, look ahead to preview material, respond to questions, ask questions about the material, engage in games and simulations, pay attention to underlined or highlighted information, receive corrective feedback, and construct mental pictures;
- illustrative resources that offer students access to examples, comparisons, and visuals of concepts through the use of graphics, animation, and sound;
- informational or supplementary resources that provide additional information and enrichment via access to multimedia presentations, electronic encyclopedias, dictionaries, and databases;
- summarizing resources that offer students graphics, outlines, and overviews of the structure, content, and major features of the text;

REFLECTING ON YOUR PRACTICES

Examining the Readability and Legibility of Your Materials

You can examine the readability and legibility of the materials you develop for students by considering the following questions:

◆ Are the materials too wordy?

◆ Are key terms and concepts highlighted?

◆ Do you use words that students can read and understand?

◆ Are definitions and examples of new and difficult words and concepts embedded in the text?

◆ Are the lengths of sentences and paragraphs appropriate?

◆ Do sentences contain no more than one complex idea?

◆ Do you avoid using double negatives, abbreviations, contractions, acronyms, quotations, and parentheses?

◆ Do paragraphs begin with a topic sentence and present information and events logically and in chronological order?

◆ Do you number or letter directions, lists, and steps?

◆ Are transitions to and connections between concepts clearly established?

◆ Are the visual aids necessary, are they placed in the right locations, and do they explain, highlight, or summarize the material?

◆ Are there too many visuals and unnecessary stimuli or text?

◆ Are the materials grammatically correct and presented in a tense and voice that students can understand?

◆ Do you use type sizes and typefaces that are simple and familiar to students?

◆ Do you present text in lowercase and capital letters when grammatically appropriate?

◆ Do you use brief, highlighted headings?

◆ Do you use boldface and italics sparingly and only to highlight headings or small amounts of text within sentences or paragraphs?

◆ Do you use proportionally spaced type and appropriate line lengths?

◆ Do you use left-justified margins and wider margins at the bottom of the page?

◆ Is the overall spacing consistent, and does it provide a logical structure for the reader to follow?

◆ Is the length of the material appropriate, and are pages numbered?

◆ Is there appropriate contrast between lettering color and background color?

How would you rate the readability and legibility of your materials? ( ) Excellent ( ) Good ( ) Needs Improvement ( ) Needs Much Improvement

What steps could you adopt to improve the readability and legibility of your materials?

Sources: Boone et al., (1999) and Hoener et al. (1997).

◆ collaborative resources that allow students to work together; and

◆ notational resources that allow students to take notes, construct post-its, summarize main points, and highlight text electronically as they read (Horney & Anderson-Inman, 1999; McKenna, Reinking, Labbo, & Kieffer, 1999)

Provide Audiocassettes and Videocassettes

You can foster text comprehension by giving students audiocassettes of the text that are commercially produced or made by volunteers. For example, groups of students can be asked to prepare an audiocassette of textbook material. For repeated use by many students, cassettes can be stored in the library and checked out when needed.

When cassettes of written materials are prepared, the clarity of the cassette can be enhanced by recording in a quiet location, keeping the microphone in a fixed position approximately 6 inches from the speaker's mouth, and adjusting the volume so that clicks are minimized (Mercer & Mercer, 1993). Audiocassettes also can be made more effective through the use of variable speech-control recorders that allow users to control the playback speed (Raskind & Higgins, 1998).

In preparing cassettes for students, it is often helpful for the speaker to read in a clear, coherent voice at a rate of 120 to 175 words per minute, with pauses appropriate to punctuation. It also is important to limit the amount of information presented, emphasize vocabulary words, and explain graphic information. Before making the cassette, you can read the selection and determine which text should be read verbatim, paraphrased, or deleted. Each cassette can begin with a statement of the title of the selection, the authors' names, the chapters or sections recorded, and the directions for using the tape. The beginning of the cassette can include study questions or an advance organizer to orient the listener to the important points of the selection (Mercer & Mercer, 1993). You can encourage students to rehearse or apply the content presented by including study questions on the cassette or giving students a corresponding study guide. For example, a reminder such as "Stop here and list three changes in the United States that were a result of the Industrial Revolution" can guide students. At strategic points throughout the cassette, you also can give students a summary of the information.

Videocassettes of content that is related to or parallels the material presented in textbooks and other print materials also can orient students to content in these materials. Videocassettes also provide direct visual experience with the material that can improve students' understanding and memory of the content to be mastered.

SET YOUR SITES

You can obtain recordings of textbooks for students with disabilities from the National Library Service for the Blind and Physically Handicapped (www.lcweb.loc.gov/nls, 202-707-5100), the American Printing House for the Blind (www.aph.org, 502-895-2405), or Recordings for the Blind and Dyslexic (www.rfbd.org, 800-221-4792). Contact these organizations as early as possible so that the recordings are available when needed.

HOW CAN I DIFFERENTIATE INSTRUCTION FOR STUDENTS FROM DIVERSE CULTURAL AND LANGUAGE BACKGROUNDS?

In addition to using cooperative learning and the other strategies presented in this book, you can consider the following guidelines when modifying your teaching for students from diverse cultural and language backgrounds. Again, these guidelines can be used to enhance instruction for *all students*.

Use a Multicultural Curriculum

One means of making learning relevant for all students is by using a *multicultural curriculum*, which acknowledges the voices, histories, experiences, and contributions of all ethnic and cultural groups. The goal of a multicultural curriculum is to help *all students* do the following: (1) understand, view, and appreciate events from various cultural perspectives; (2) understand and function in their own and other cultures; (3) take personal actions to promote racial and ethnic harmony and to counter racism and discrimination; (4) understand various cultural and ethnic alternatives; (5) develop their academic skills; and (6) improve their ability to make reflective personal and public decisions and actions that contribute to changing society and culture (Banks, 1991a; Grant & Sleeter, 1994). Multicultural education is often seen as focusing on the needs of students of color and students who speak languages other than English. However, a true multicultural curriculum should teach information about all groups and should be directed at all students

A multicultural curriculum should teach information about all groups and should be directed at all students.

(Nieto, 1996). Besides including all students, the multicultural curriculum should address all content areas (Miller-Lachmann & Taylor, 1995). For example, a science lesson on plants can include a discussion of plants in other countries and in various regions of the United States. The Native American counting technique that uses knots in a rope can be taught as part of a math lesson.

Banks and Banks (1993) identified four hierarchical methods for incorporating multicultural information into the curriculum. In the *contributions* approach, various ethnic heroes, highlights, holidays, and cultural events are added to the curriculum. In the *additive* approach, content, concepts, themes, and issues related to various cultures are added to the curriculum. In both of these approaches, no substantive changes are made in the organization or goals of the curriculum. As a result, while students are introduced to the contributions of various cultural groups, they are often given little information about various cultural groups, and fail to understand the social and political realities behind the experiences of these groups (Miller-Lachmann & Taylor, 1995).

The *transformation* approach to multicultural curriculum reform tries to modify the curriculum by encouraging students to examine and explore content, concepts, themes, issues, problems, and concerns from various cultural perspectives. In this approach, students learn to think critically and reflect on the viewpoints of different cultural, gender, and social class groups. For example, a lesson on the impact of the North American Free Trade Agreement (NAFTA) can compare its impact from the perspectives of groups in all countries of North America.

The *social action* approach, though similar to the transformation approach, encourages and teaches students to identify social problems and take action to solve them. Students are given opportunities to challenge and change practices that they consider unfair. For example, as part of a mathematics lesson, a class might analyze data on the number of girls in advanced mathematics and science classes. They can then propose and evaluate actions to address the problems that discourage girls from taking these classes.

REFLECTIVE

How has your cultural background influenced your perspectives? How are your cultural perspectives similar to and different from those of others? How would multicultural education influence your cultural perspectives?

Parallel Lessons

You can make your curriculum multicultural by using *parallel lessons,* which allow students to learn about individuals and content from both the mainstream culture and other cultures. For example, a lesson on Abraham Lincoln could be paired with a lesson on Benito Juarez, a comparable historical figure in his country (Gonzalez, 1992).

Constructive Controversy

INFORMATIONAL

Leigh and Lamorey (1996) offer guidelines for incorporating contemporary issues into the curriculum.

Multiple perspectives on various issues in the curriculum can be examined using *constructive controversy,* a cooperative learning technique (Mendez, 1991). With this method, students are placed in groups of four. Each group consists of two dyads, each of which examines a different perspective on a controversial topic. First, the dyads obtain information and prepare arguments to support their perspectives. Each dyad then presents its case, while the other dyad listens and asks questions to seek clarification. Afterward, each dyad challenges the other's case and questions the facts and logical arguments presented. The dyads then switch roles and prepare a case for the opposite side of the issue. Next, working together, the group agrees on the arguments that are valid on both sides of the issue and prepares a report or presentation. If the group cannot achieve a consensus, a minority report or a report outlining the agreements and disagreements is prepared.

Use Multicultural Teaching Materials

INFORMATIONAL

Santos et al. (2000) offer guidelines for selecting culturally and linguistically appropriate early childhood materials.

A multicultural curriculum should contain teaching materials that reflect a wide range of experiences and aspirations (Santos, Fowler, Corso, & Bruns, 2000). Therefore, materials such as textbooks, children's books, books containing rhymes, songs, and stories, media, poetry, toys, puppets, instruments, manipulatives, and art supplies that reflect cultural, ethnic, linguistic, and gender diversity should be used frequently and should be fully integrated into the curriculum. Other activities and materials for promoting an acceptance and appreciation of cultural diversity are presented in Chapter 5. Guidelines for evaluating multicultural teaching materials are presented in Figure 8.1

SET YOUR SITES

The National Seeking Educational Equity and Diversity Project on Inclusive Curriculum (SEED Project) (www.wellesley.edu/WCW/projects/seed.html, 781-283-2520) offers help in developing inclusive, gender-fair, and multicultural curriculums.

SET YOUR SITES

Teaching for Change (www.teachingforchange.org, 800-763-9131) maintains a website that provides information about multicultural books, videos, and CD-ROMs.

Use Culturally Relevant Teaching Strategies

Teaching strategies should reflect the students' experiences, cultural perspectives, and developmental ages (Franklin, James, & Watson, 1996). Your teaching strategies should be aligned with your students' cultural backgrounds and preferred learning styles. For example, because many Native American students are socialized by and learn traditions through observation, imitation, and listening, they may perform better when teachers use observational and experiential learning (Swisher, 1997). You can use observational learning by allowing students to work on experiential activities, use manipulatives, and view concrete examples and models of new and difficult-to-learn skills.

Franklin (1992) examined the research on effective strategies for teaching students from diverse cultural and language backgrounds, and identified several strategies that appear to be successful with African American students and other groups of students:

> *Emphasizing verbal interactions.* Use activities that encourage students to respond verbally to the material in creative ways such as group discussions, role plays, storytelling, group recitations, choral and responsive reading, and rap.
> *Teaching students to use self-talk.* Encourage and teach students to learn new material by verbalizing it to themselves.

To what extent do the materials include the various social and cultural groups in U.S. society?

How are various groups portrayed in the materials?

Are the viewpoints, attitudes, reactions, experiences, and feelings of various cultural groups accurately presented?

Do the materials present a varied group of credible individuals to whom students can relate in terms of lifestyle, values, speech and language, and actions?

Are individuals from diverse backgrounds depicted in a wide range of social and professional activities?

Do the materials show a variety of situations, conflicts, issues, and problems as experienced by different groups?

Are a wide range of perspectives on situations and issues offered?

Does the material incorporate the history, heritage, experiences, language, and traditions of various groups?

Are the experiences of and issues important to various groups presented in a realistic manner that allows students to recognize and understand their complexities?

Are culturally diverse examples, situations, experiences, and anecdotes included throughout the materials?

Are the materials factually correct?

Are the experiences, contributions, and content of various groups fully integrated into the materials and the curriculum?

Are graphics accurate, inclusive, and ethnically sensitive?

Do the materials avoid stereotypes and generalizations about groups?

Are members of various groups presented as having a range of physical features (e.g., hair texture, skin color, facial features)?

Is the language of the materials inclusive, and does it reflect various groups?

Do the materials include learning activities that help students develop a multicultural perspective?

FIGURE 8.1   Guidelines for evaluating multicultural teaching materials.

Sources: Banks (1991a), Garcia and Malkin (1993), Miller-Lachmann and Taylor (1995), Santos et al. (2000), and Taylor (2000).

Facilitating divergent thinking. Encourage students to explore and devise unique solutions to issues and problems through activities such as brainstorming, group discussions, debates, and responding to open-ended questions.

Using small-group instruction and cooperative learning. Allow students to work in small groups, and use cooperative learning arrangements including peer tutoring and cross-age tutoring.

Employing verve in the classroom. Introduce *verve,* a high level of energy, exuberance, and action, into the classroom by displaying enthusiasm for teaching and learning, using choral responding, moving around the classroom, varying your voice quality, snapping your fingers, using facial expressions, and encouraging students to use their bodies to act out and demonstrate content.

Focusing on real-world tasks. Introduce content, language, and learning by relating them to students' home, school, and community life, and to their cultures and experiences.

Promoting teacher–student interactions. Use teaching methods based on exchanges between students and teachers. Ask frequent questions, affirm students' responses, give feedback, offer demonstrations and explanations, and rephrase, review, and summarize material.

Use Reciprocal Interaction Teaching Approaches

Teaching models using task analysis, structured drills, teacher-directed instruction, and independent seatwork may not be effective with many students, including second language learners, because they fail to provide a language context for students (Ortiz & Yates, 1989). Therefore, you can supplement teaching activities that emphasize the development of skills with *reciprocal interaction teaching approaches (RITA)* that foster empowerment, reflection, analysis, and learning through verbal and written dialogues between students and teachers and among students (Echevarria & McDonough, 1995). In using reciprocal interaction, you use students' prior knowledge and experiences to add a context that promotes comprehension and incorporates language development and use in all activities and content areas. The curriculum and teaching focus on meaningful, authentic activities related to students' lives, and they target higher-level critical thinking skills rather than basic skills.

When implementing RITA, you also use student-centered teaching and dialogues, student–student interactions, problem-solving situations, tasks that promote internal motivation, and guided questioning to help students control their learning (Wiig, Freedman, & Secord, 1992). Higher-level thinking is promoted through teacher modeling and thinking aloud, presenting new information as collaborative problems to be solved or provocative ideas and experiences, posing open-ended questions, asking students to justify their responses and explain their reasoning, helping students explore alternative perspectives, encouraging students to evaluate and monitor their thinking and that of others, and viewing students' miscues as opportunities to discuss new information (Englert, Tarrant, & Mariage, 1992). The elements of lessons based on RITA are presented in Figure 8.2.

You also can employ *scaffolding*, breaking down comments students don't understand or a task students have difficulty performing into smaller components that promote understanding or mastery. Scaffolding methods include relating the task to students' prior knowledge, using visual and language cues, modeling effective strategies, and highlighting the key parts of the task (Beaumont, 1992). As students gain skill or mastery, scaffolding supports are gradually removed so that students function independently to understand, apply, and integrate their new learning.

1. *Thematic focus.* The teacher selects a theme or idea to serve as a starting point to focus the discussion and has a general plan for how the theme will unfold, including how to "chunk" the text to permit optimal exploration of the theme.
2. *Activation and use of background and relevant schemata.* The teacher either "hooks into" or provides students with pertinent background knowledge and relevant schemata necessary for understanding a text. Background knowledge and schemata are then woven into the discussion that follows.
3. *Direct teaching.* When necessary, the teacher provides direct teaching of a skill or concept.
4. *Promotion of more complex language and expression.* The teacher elicits more extended student contributions by using a variety of elicitation techniques, for example, invitation to expand ("Tell me more about _____"), questions ("What do you mean by _____"), restatements ("In other words, _____"), and pauses.
5. *Elicitation of bases for statements or positions.* The teacher promotes students' use of text, pictures, and reasoning to support an argument or position. Without overwhelming students, the teacher probes for the bases of students' statements: "How do you know?" "What makes you think that?" "Show us where it says _____ ."
6. *Few "known-answer" questions.* Much of the discussion centers on questions and answers for which there might be more than one correct answer.
7. *Responsivity to student contributions.* While having an initial plan and maintaining the focus and coherence of the discussion, the teacher is also responsive to students' statements and the opportunities they provide.
8. *Connected discourse.* The discussion is characterized by multiple, interactive, connected turns, and succeeding utterances that build upon and extend previous ones.
9. *A challenging, but nonthreatening, atmosphere.* The teacher creates a "zone of proximal development" where a challenging atmosphere is balanced by a positive affective climate. The teacher is more collaborator than evaluator and creates an atmosphere that challenges students and allows them to negotiate and construct the meaning of the text.
10. *General participation, including self-selected turns.* The teacher encourages general participation among students. The teacher does not hold exclusive rights to determine who talks, and students are encouraged to volunteer or otherwise influence the selection of speaking turns.

FIGURE 8.2 Elements of reciprocal interactive teaching lessons.

Source: Interactive reading instruction: A comparison of proximal and distal effects by J. Echevarria, *Teaching Exceptional Children,* vol. 61, 1995, p. 538. Copyright 1995 by The Council for Exceptional Children. Reprinted with permission.

When using RITA, you also can promote teacher–student interactions through the use of confirmation checks ("Are you saying. . .?"), comprehension checks ("Do you understand what I just said?" "Tell me in your own words what I'm saying"), clarification requests ("Can you explain that again?" "In a different way?"), repetitions, and expansions. Conversational interactions also can be fostered by you and your students asking who, where, why, when, and what questions.

Use Effective ESL Approaches

Instruction for second language learners can be differentiated by using effective ESL approaches such as total physical response, sheltered English, natural language approaches, and new vocabulary and concept instructional techniques.

Total Physical Response

Total physical response (TPR) improves students' vocabulary through modeling, repeated practice, and movement (Asher, 1977). In TPR, you model the message by emphasizing physical gestures and objects. (You state the message, model, and physically emphasize movements related to the concept of, say, sharpening a pencil.) Next, the class as a group responds to your directions. (You ask the students to sharpen their pencils and the students, as a group, make the appropriate motion.) Finally, individual students respond to verbal commands given by you and their peers. (Individual students are asked by you and their peers to sharpen a pencil.) As students develop skills, the complexity of the language skills taught increases. Adaptations of TPR include having students write statements and comply with written statements (Freeman & Freeman, 1992).

Sheltered English

Sheltered English or *content-based instruction*, uses cues, gestures, media, manipulatives, drama, and visual stimuli and aids to teach new vocabulary and concepts. When using a sheltered English approach, present lessons that cover grade-level content and teach students the terminology needed to understand the concepts in specific content areas. Create a context, present information orally and visually, use hands-on activities and media, and help students learn by restating, paraphrasing, simplifying, and expanding the material. It is also important to connect the curriculum to students' culture, experiences, and language and to promote interactions among students.

Lessons using a sheltered English approach typically are organized in the following sequence:

1. Identify, define, and teach terminology that is essential to understanding the lesson and related to the curriculum. Key terms are posted as a visual reference for students and are added to students' word banks.
2. Select and explain the main concepts to students.
3. Help students learn and understand the main concepts by presenting content using visual aids, objects, physical gestures, facial expressions, and manipulatives. Where possible, allow students to experience the concepts.
4. Make instruction meaningful by giving students opportunities to relate the concepts to their experiences.
5. Check students' understanding, encourage them to seek clarification, and offer feedback.
6. Encourage students to work and interact with their peers (Echevarria, 1995).

IDEAS FOR IMPLEMENTATION

Differentiating Instruction for Second Language Learners

Ms. Phalen's class included several second language learners. The class was learning about the cycle of the butterfly. First, Ms. Phalen read and discussed a book on this topic with her students. They talked about such terms as *caterpillar, cocoon,* and *butterfly.* Then Ms. Phalen had the students reenact the cycle of the butterfly. She told them to roll themselves into a little ball. Then she asked them to pretend that they were caterpillars. They acted like caterpillars, and then became a cocoon and broke out of the cocoon as butterflies. With their arms outstretched like butterflies, the students then "flew" around the room. After this activity, Ms. Phalen had her students work in small groups to draw pictures of the cycle of the butterfly.

Here are some other strategies you can use to differentiate instruction for second language learners:

- Establish a relaxed learning environment that encourages students to take risks and attempt to use both languages, and emphasize communication rather than language form. For example, correct students indirectly by restating their incorrect comments in correct form (If the student says "My notebook home," you say, "I see, your notebook is at home.")
- Begin new lessons with reviews of relevant previously learned concepts, and show the relationships between previously learned concepts and new material.
- Relate material and examples to students' experiences, use cultural referents, and use real-world language and meaningful, functional activities.
- Be consistent in your use of language, and use repetition to help students acquire the rhythm, pitch, volume, and tone of their new language.

- Use gestures, facial expressions, voice changes, pantomimes, demonstrations, rephrasing, visuals, props, manipulatives, and other cues to provide a context that conveys the meaning of new terms and concepts.
- Introduce new material in context, discussing changes in the context while it is occurring. Talk about what has occurred in context so that ambiguities are reduced.
- Develop students' language competence by using questioning, art forms, drama, simulations, role plays, storytelling, music, and games.
- Supplement oral instruction and descriptions with visual materials such as charts, maps, graphs, pictures, and graphic organizers.
- Make it easier for students to understand and respond by articulating clearly; pausing often; limiting the use of idiomatic expressions, slang, and pronouns; highlighting key words through increased volume and slight exaggeration; using rephrasing, simple vocabulary, and shorter sentences; and giving students enough wait time.
- Allow students to express their knowledge, understanding, and intended meaning nonverbally. For example, rather than asking a student to define a word or concept, ask the student to draw a picture depicting it.
- Encourage and show students how to use bilingual dictionaries and pictionaries.
- Offer regular summaries of important content, and check students' understanding frequently.

Sources: Brice and Roseberry-McKibbin (1999), Freeman and Freeman (1989), Fueyo (1997), Gersten (1999), and Maldonado-Colon (1995).

Natural Language Techniques

You also can help students develop language by using natural language techniques: expansion, expatiation, parallel talk, and self-talk (Lowenthal, 1995). *Expansion* allows you to present a language model by expanding on students' incomplete sentences or thoughts. *Expatiation* occurs when you add new information to the comments of students. *Parallel talk* involves describing an event that students are seeing or doing. *Self-talk* consists of talking about your actions, experiences, or feelings.

New Vocabulary and Concept Teaching Techniques

Effective teaching for second language learners requires you to help them learn new vocabulary and concepts. To aid these students, focus on a few essential vocabulary key words and concepts. In addition, teach vocabulary in context rather than in isolation, and teach related words and concepts together. When introducing new vocabulary and concepts, you can consider the following sequence:

Step 1: Analyze the concept to be taught and highlight its key features, including the concept's structure and characteristics. Determine if the context is important for understanding the concept.

Step 2: Introduce and label the concept in a variety of situations. If possible, present the concept by using clear, consistent language, concrete materials, and manipulatives.

Step 3: Show and discuss examples and nonexamples of the concept, moving from easy to difficult. Present and use the concept in many naturally occurring situations, and elaborate on the characteristics that define the concept and distinguish it from others.

Step 4: Contrast the concept with other related concepts.

Step 5: Allow students to practice using the concept in functional activities related to their interests and learning levels (Prater, 1993).

REFLECTIVE

Watch a television show or film in a second language. What factors helped you understand the content?

Encourage Students to Respond

You may need to encourage second language learners and students with speech and language difficulties to respond verbally. You can promote student responding by using open-ended questions, by allowing students to use gestures until they develop language competence, and by praising and expanding on students' contributions and seeking more information when necessary (McNeill & Fowler, 1996). Give students enough time to interact and discuss material before responding, and encourage students to share their opinions, ask questions, and expand on the comments of others. You also can stimulate the use of language by providing experiences that encourage discussion, such as introducing new objects into the classroom; changing the classroom environment; allowing students to work and play together; sending students on errands; creating situations in which students need to ask for help; asking students to recount events or talk about doing something while doing it; and using visuals that display pictorial absurdities (Westby, 1992).

How Can I Use Instructional Technology and Assistive Devices to Differentiate Instruction for Students?

Instructional Technology

INFORMATIONAL

While instructional technology can enhance student learning, several concerns also have been raised (Stoll, 1995).

SET YOUR SITES

Teacherzone.com (www. teacherzone.com) offers information and resources about instructional technology and accounts of how schools use it.

Recent technological developments now allow you to use instructional technology and interactive multimedia to create motivating and contextualized learning environments for students. Interactive multimedia link text, sound, animation, video, and graphics to present information to students in a nonlinear, instantaneous fashion that promotes critical thinking skills and social interactions (Wissick, 1996). These technologies can be integrated across the curriculum to differentiate instruction and allow students to be more actively involved in directing their learning. You can also use technology to modify the ways in which material is presented and responded to, promote reading and note taking, improve communication, promote cultural diversity, motivate students to learn, and use adaptive devices for individuals with physical and sensory disabilities. Several related multimedia teaching technologies are described in the following section.

Computers

You can supplement and individualize teaching by using computers and computer-assisted instruction. Computers can individualize instruction by directing students to items related to their skill levels and allowing students to work at their own pace. However, the effectiveness of computer-based instruction depends on the software program used. Many programs are open to criticism; you should carefully evaluate the ones you use. A form for evaluating software programs is presented in Figure 8.3.

Hypertext/Hypermedia

Hypertext or *hypermedia* is a computerized teaching system that provides alternative nonsequential and nonlinear formats for mastering content, including additional text, specialized graphics, digital video clips, animated presentations, and computer-produced speech and sound effects (Boone, Higgins, Falba, & Langley, 1993). Hypermedia systems offer experiential or direct learning opportunities and are especially helpful for second language learners (Bermudez & Palumbo, 1994). Most traditional print materials present content in a linear fashion. Hypermedia, by contrast, allows students to view and link information via television monitors, videodiscs, and videocassettes controlled by a computer into a unified lesson based on students' needs and interests. Hypermedia provides a media-rich environment that allows students to control their learning and the order and format in which they access information. In hypertext, information such as words, letters, numbers, sentences, paragraphs, and pictures presented on one screen is linked to supplemental, related content on other screens that students access based on their needs and interests. Hypermedia also can be used to create and share portfolios of students' work (Edyburn, 1994) (see Chapter 12).

LEARNER/TEACHER NEEDS

	YES	NO
1. Does the program reach the target population for which it was designed?	☐	☐
2. Will the program motivate the students to learn?	☐	☐
3. Is the content relevant to the instructional needs of the students?	☐	☐
4. Will the material be effective with individual learning styles?	☐	☐
5. Does the format appeal to the students?	☐	☐
6. Is the material relevant to daily living experiences?	☐	☐

INSTRUCTIONAL INTEGRITY

	YES	NO
1. Does the program state behavioral/instructional objectives?	☐	☐
2. Is the teaching/learning mode identified (drill and practice, diagnosis, tutorial, simulation, inquiry, game, problem solving)?	☐	☐
3. Is the program organized and presented in a sequential manner and in appropriate developmental steps?	☐	☐
4. Is the material presented at a concrete level and in a variety of ways?	☐	☐
5. Is the content presented clearly?	☐	☐
6. Does the program use a multisensory approach?	☐	☐
7. Is the use of graphics, sound, and color appropriate?	☐	☐
8. Does the program provide meaningful interaction for the students?	☐	☐
9. Does the program provide for user self-pacing?	☐	☐
10. Does the material require the purchase of accompanying printed material, or is it self-sufficient?	☐	☐
11. Does the material prescribe to a number of sources or just the publisher's own materials?	☐	☐
12. Does the material provide direct instruction?	☐	☐
13. Does the material provide immediate feedback?	☐	☐
14. Does the material provide a variety of built-in reinforcements?	☐	☐
15. Does the program offer supplementary materials or suggested activities for reinforcement?	☐	☐
16. Does the content use past learning or experiential background?	☐	☐
17. Is the material presented on a meaningful and appropriate language level?	☐	☐

	YES	NO
18. Is the required reading presented at the students' level of functioning?	☐	☐
19. Does the program provide "flexible" branching so that the content and reading levels meet the needs of individual student levels?	☐	☐
20. Does the program allow the student adequate time to complete learning segments?	☐	☐
21. Is the program designed to alert the teacher to a student who is experiencing difficulty with the content?	☐	☐
22. Does the material meet race, sex, and cultural distributions of the student population?	☐	☐

TECHNICAL ADEQUACY AND UTILITY

	YES	NO
1. Are the teacher's instructions well organized, useful, and easy to understand?	☐	☐
2. Does the material require extensive preparation or training on the teacher's part?	☐	☐
3. Is the material of high quality?	☐	☐
4. Is the material reusable?	☐	☐
5. Is the material durable for repeated and prolonged use?	☐	☐
6. Is the size of the print clear and well spaced?	☐	☐
7. Does the speed of presentation match individual learning styles?	☐	☐
8. Does the student need typing skills to use the program?	☐	☐
9. Is it "kid-proof?"	☐	☐
10. Can a student use the program without supervision?	☐	☐
11. Is a printout of student performance available, if desired?	☐	☐
12. Is the initial cost of this nonconsumable material reasonable?	☐	☐
13. Is the program packaged so that it can be easily and safely stored?	☐	☐
14. Can the program be used in a regular classroom, resource room, media center, agency, or institution?	☐	☐
15. Does the publisher provide a policy for replacement of parts?	☐	☐
16. Does the publisher provide for preview and/or demonstration of the program?	☐	☐
17. Has the publisher provided the program so that it is available for use on at least two different models of microcomputer hardware?	☐	☐

FIGURE 8.3 Computer software evaluation form.

Source: From Microcomputers: Powerful learning tools with proper programming by A. Hannaford and E. Sloane, *Teaching Exceptional Children,* vol. 14, 1981, p. 56. Copyright 1981 by The Council for Exceptional Children. Reprinted with permission.

Videocassette Recorders

Videocassette recorders (VCRs) can help you present information. High-resolution color video cameras can display images of three-dimensional objects, photographs, slides, and documents, and allow students to record activities that can be included in the learning products they produce in school. The taping, stopping, and starting capabilities of VCRs allow demonstrations, experiments, and other classroom activities to be taped and then played back to highlight or repeat key parts or information. Videocassettes can facilitate modeling and prompting and can be used in simulation activities or group discussions. Videocassette recordings of sessions also help students learn to use new teaching strategies and adaptations and allow you to evaluate new teaching formats. For example, a videocassette of a successful cooperative learning group can be viewed and discussed to focus students' attention on the behaviors and roles that help groups work collaboratively. Students can also show mastery of content in video-based projects such as writing, producing, and recording a news program, play, or video; role playing a reading selection; simulating an activity; or explaining how to solve a problem or perform an experiment. These video-based projects also can be included in students' portfolios, and video technology can be used to record other assignments to create a video portfolio (see Chapter 12).

Videocassettes of shows, movies, or documentaries can be used as teaching tools. In particular, videocassettes can be used to give students experiences with various aspects of society and cultural diversity. For example, a video of excerpts from a television show on the homeless can stimulate a discussion on the plight of the homeless.

Videodiscs

You can present content via *videodiscs* containing frames of realistic computer graphic displays, videocassette segments, slides, motion pictures, audio information, and sound effects. With remote control, you can quickly access high-quality visual and auditory information randomly or continuously, and you can halt the presentation to highlight critical information or to ask students questions. Thus, videodisc teaching allows students to hear explanations; and view colorful, animated, and expressive visual displays and demonstrations, computer graphics, and sound effects that accurately depict concepts and material in a gradual and systematic way (Boone, Higgins, & Williams, 1997).

Digital Cameras

Digital cameras give you and your students access to technology in order to create video-based projects. Users can immediately see the recorded image, store it in memory, delete it, or download it directly to computers so that it can be edited, enlarged, e-mailed, embedded in web pages, added to student products or learning materials, or printed (Lazarus, 1998).

CD-ROM Based Materials

CD-ROM-based teaching materials have many multimedia features that can help you differentiate your instruction. For example, CD-ROM books can be presented through the use of music, speech, and dynamic illustrations to motivate students and promote concept and vocabulary development across content areas, as well as reading and listening comprehension (Blanck, 1994). These CD-ROM materials can present text and illustrations using different voices and languages for the various characters. Individual words and

INFORMATIONAL

Blubaugh (1999) offers guidelines that increase the effectiveness of videos and television programs used in classrooms.

SET YOUR SITES

Video Placement Worldwide (www.vpw.com, 813-823-9595) offers free, sponsored videos and educational materials via the World Wide Web, and the website www.libraryvideo.com (800-843-3620) maintains a database of over 10,000 videos on a wide range of subjects.

INFORMATIONAL

Boone et al. (1997) offer guidelines for integrating videodiscs into teaching activities.

SET YOUR SITES

For information and resources on the use of digital cameras, visit the Digital Camera Resource website (www.dcresource.com).

text can be repeated, defined, presented in sign language, or translated into another language by highlighting the text to be pronounced or pressing a button (Andrews & Jordan, 1998). CD-ROM technology also allows you and your students to adjust the pace of the oral reading, magnify the text, vary the colors of the illustrations, and compare their reading to the oral reading on the CD-ROM. CD-ROM equipment that allows you and your students to develop materials and products also is available. For example, students can use CD-ROM technology to develop, publish, and animate their stories.

CD-ROM technology is also being used to make teaching and reference materials more accessible and understandable to students. Because this technology integrates graphics, spoken text, video segments, animation, and sound effects, information presented in encyclopedias and dictionaries can become more meaningful and motivating to students.

Captioned Television and Liquid Crystal Display Computer Projection Panels

Captioned television and liquid crystal display (LCD) computer projection panels are other valuable teaching methods, particularly for students with hearing disabilities and second language learners. The dialogue that accompanies closed-caption television shows and films can be presented visually on the screen via a device that receives closed-caption signals connected to the television. Captioned television was developed for students with hearing disabilities, but it can be used with a wide variety of students, including those with reading difficulties and those who speak different languages; it provides an auditory and a visual context for learning new vocabulary and information (Gartland, 1994). For example, set-top television translators can convert closed captions from one language into another (Brier, 1998). Students with visual disabilities may benefit from descriptive video, a specialized sound track system that enhances television viewing by describing events, characters' actions and body language, and scenes during pauses in the dialogue.

LCD computer projection panels promote information sharing by interfacing a computer with an overhead projector so that students can view more easily the information displayed on the monitor. With LCD panels, you can display images from multimedia sources with more colors and sharper resolution. You can also teach content in ways that are interesting, multidimensional, motivating, and tailored to students' needs.

Virtual Reality

Virtual reality systems allow students to experience what it feels like to see, touch, smell, and move through artificial, three-dimensional, interactive environments with the use of head-mounted goggles, headsets, or specially designed gloves and body suits that present computer-generated images. For example, virtual reality systems allow students to experience Newton's law of gravity firsthand or teach them how to use power wheelchairs.

Internet

The Internet provides you and your students with access to the information superhighway, as well as many exploratory and discovery-based learning and communication

SET YOUR SITES

You can obtain information about captioned videos, films, and educational materials by contacting the website www.cfv.org.

SET YOUR SITES

To control students' access to inappropriate material available on the Internet, you may need to use software and Internet management systems such as www.safekids.com, www.safeteens.com, www.netnanny.com, www.cyberpatrol.com, www.safesurf.com, or www.surfmonkey.com.

SET YOUR SITES

To help you and your students evaluate the credibility of websites, visit http://lii.org (click on Internet Info, Evaluation) www.library.cornell.edu//okuref/webeval.html.

INFORMATIONAL

Teicher (1999) presents activities, resources, and websites that can help you teach students about Internet safety and responsibility.

experiences. It allows students to control the curriculum more effectively, and it offers them options related to what and how they learn. When using the Internet with students, you need to teach them how to sort through and assess the reliability of large amounts of often contradictory information. You also need to establish and teach students rules and etiquette for using the Internet, including accessing the right material, refraining from giving out personal information and pictures, interacting with others, using copyrighted material, understanding confidentiality and plagiarism, recognizing and dealing with advertising, avoiding mischief and viruses, and misusing Internet accounts (Bakken & Aloia, 1998; Teicher, 1999).

The Internet allows students to learn and communicate with others. Bulletin board folders, e-mail, and chat groups offer students opportunities to talk to, share information and experiences with, and learn from others (LeLoup & Ponterio, 1998). Internet bulletin boards allow students to locate and meet others with whom they may want to interact. E-mail gives them the chance to send private messages to and receive them from other individuals, as well as to develop social and academic skills (Trollinger & Slavkin, 1999). Chat groups or computer conferences offer students a forum to talk with others. Through the Internet, students and classes can have computer pals from other schools in the district, geographic region, country, and world with whom they communicate and learn (Burtch, 1999). These interactions give students direct opportunities to learn about and with others, to experience different ways of life, and to learn and use a second language.

The Internet provides you and your students with access to an enormous electronic library of resources, pictorials, and databases containing information about virtually every subject and content area and in every language. Internet connections allow you and your students to examine and browse through these electronic documents. Students can visit and access information from museums via the Internet, and use streaming audio and video technology to watch or hear live or prerecorded broadcasts of events occurring throughout the world.

Software programs that help individuals with disabilities use the Internet are available. For example, pwWebSpeak and Home Page Reader, which are available in several languages, allow individuals with visual, dexterity-based, and reading disabilities to browse and navigate the Internet by presenting computer text and graphics that are read aloud or by displaying text in large type.

You also can use the Internet to create districtwide, schoolwide, and classroom web pages, also referred to as *home pages*. Creating a web page for your class is a good way to involve students in learning about the Internet and communicating with other students, families, and individuals throughout the world. For example, your class can work as a group to plan, design, and create a classroom web page including pictorials, graphics, animation, and text relating to important aspects of your class. You also can post students' work on their web page, and students can receive and respond to inquiries from others about their web page.

Assistive Devices

Computer technology has been used to develop many assistive devices to promote the learning, independence and communication abilities of students with various disabilities. These devices, described below, are an integral part of students' IEPs.

Devices for Students with Physical Disabilities

For students who have difficulty speaking intelligibly, assistive communication devices are invaluable. Low-technology devices, such as communication boards, are nonelectric and tend to be made by clinicians or are homemade. High-technology devices require the use of an electrical power source.

High-technology assistive communication systems based on computer hardware and software and output devices transform word input into speech. Students can input a phrase or press a key that activates the computer's speech capabilities. Specific vocabulary sets can be programmed based on students' educational and communicative needs, as well as the setting in which they need to communicate. As the technology evolves, these devices are being improved and made more portable through the use of auditory scanning, dynamic computer screen displays, and digitized speech that sounds more natural (Blackstone, 1996).

Students with physical disabilities also may have problems inputting information into the computer in traditional ways (such as pressing more than one key at a time). To meet their needs, alternative methods have been developed (see Figure 8.4). These students also may benefit from modifications to the standard keyboard such as alternative keyboards, keyguards, stickers to signify keys, key locks, and word prediction programs. They also may need to use such built-in systems as sticky keys, mousekeys, repeatkeys, slowkeys, bouncekeys, and serial keys (Vanderheiden, 1996).

Assistive devices also help individuals with disabilities to organize and take notes in class. Some students are using laptop computers with word processing programs and lightweight, voice-activated microcassette recorders for note-taking. Personal digital assistants (PDAs) allow students to take notes that include illustrations. PDAs

INFORMATIONAL

Peters-Walters (1998) offers guidelines for designing websites for use by individuals with disabilities.

REFLECTIVE

Students from culturally and linguistically diverse backgrounds, lower socioeconomic groups, and single-parent families have less access to computers and the Internet than other groups. (Sanger, 1999). Will this disparity create a greater gap between students? What implications would this disparity have for your use of technology to teach?

REFLECTIVE

What teaching technologies did you use as a student? As a teacher? What were the positive and negative effects of these technologies on your learning and your students' learning?

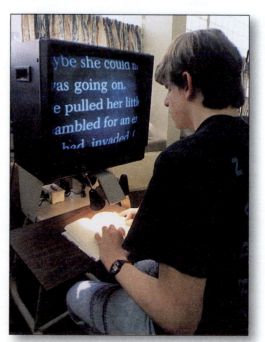

Assistive technology and adaptive devices are helping students succeed in inclusive settings.

1. *Voice recognition:* The computer recognizes the user's speech and converts it into action.
2. *Key guard:* A device that modifies the traditional keyboard to change the size and spacing of the keys. It may include a key lock that automatically toggles specialty keys.
3. *Keyboard alteration programs:* Programs that modify the keyboard in terms of key accept time and key repeating.
4. *Graphics tablet:* A small slate that may be covered by templates of words, pictures, numerals, and letters that are input when touched by a special stylus.
5. *Adapted switches:* Switches controlled by pressure or body movements. They can be activated by foot, head, cheek, chin, and eye movements.
6. *Scanning systems:* An array of letters, phrases, and numerals displayed on the screen at a rate that is adjusted to the student's need. The student selects the message from the scanner by using the keyboard or a switch.
7. *Touch screens/light pens:* Devices that allow the student to activate the computer by touching or writing on the screen.
8. *Joystick:* A stick that is moved in different directions, controlling the movement of the cursor.
9. *Mouthstick:* A tool that is placed in the mouth and used to press buttons and activate switches.
10. *Headband:* A headband-like device that is worn by the student to control the computer through head or eye movements.
11. *Sip and puff systems:* A long command tube attached to a computer or wheelchair on which the student sucks.
12. *Skateboard:* A block of wood on rollers attached to the student's arm that is moved in different directions to control cursor movements.
13. *Mouse:* A mouselike object that is moved in different directions to control the computer. Adaptations of the mouse can be controlled by using the numeric pad of the keyboard (keyboard mouse) or by a headsetlike device, such as a headband, that conveys directions to the computer via head movements.
14. *Eye gaze:* Use of eye gazes and scanning to select stimuli that appear on the computer screen.

FIGURE 8.4 Alternative methods of inputting information into computers.

INFORMATIONAL

Cook and Cavalier (1999) offer guidelines and a training sequence for using robotics with students.

SET YOUR SITES

Information and resources about robotics are available from the Robotics Internet Resources Page (www-robotics.cs.umass.edu/robotics. html) and the Robotics Institute (www.frc.ri.cmu.edu/robotics-faq, 978-670-4270).

provide access to information and resources available through other technologies such as the Internet. PDAs and paging systems also can help students recall and access information and remember the correct sequence of tasks and routines, as well as organize schedules, information, and events. Software programs are being developed and refined that provide wireless connections to the Internet, fax machines, and cellular telephone connections, as well as read, edit, and transmit electronic handwriting via e-mail.

Computer technology has also helped increase the range of movements and thus the independence of individuals with physical disabilities (Cook & Cavalier, 1999). Robotic devices and computerized systems in the home can be programmed to turn on the oven, shut off lights, lock doors, and adjust the sound of the television so that these individuals can live on their own. Infrared remote control systems also allow individuals to control and operate devices and appliances.

Devices for Students with Visual and Reading Disabilities

Several adaptive devices have been developed to help use print materials. Various lightweight, inexpensive text scanners and character-recognition software such as the

Kurzweil 3000 recognize letters, group letters into words, pronounce words, and provide the correct pronunciation of words in a sentence in several languages. Printed materials are scanned and stored in memory. Students can then view the printed page, hear the text being read aloud, look up the meaning of unfamiliar words, highlight important content, and insert bookmarks. When selecting a scanning-based reading adaptive device, you should consider the ability of the scanner to scan accurately and the availability of an automatic document/page feeder.

Computer-based screen-reading programs allow computers to read text letter by letter, read it by phonetic markers, or convert words, sentences, and paragraphs into fluent speech. These programs, which can be read in different voices and languages, also allow users to search for or highlight words, sentences, and paragraphs that can be read aloud.

Technological adaptations also are being developed to help students with visual and reading disabilities use computers. Voice-activated programs assist students in using computer-based technology. Digitized books help students use printed materials including textbooks. Electronic dictionaries with digitized speech help students define unfamiliar words. Screen magnification programs enlarge computer-generated text and graphics to an appropriate size and adjust the colors on the screen to offer users the best contrast. Font enlargement features also allow users to adjust the size of the fonts in which text is presented, limiting the number of words per line and the number of lines per page.

A variety of optical aids including hand-held magnifiers, magnifiers mounted on a base, and magnifiers attached to eyeglass frames or incorporated in the lenses magnify printed materials for individuals with visual disabilities. The *Low Vision Enhancement System (LVES)* is a head-mounted display and camera system that uses video magnification and contrast enhancement technology to enhance vision. Another optical aid, the *Apollo Laser Electronic Aid*, uses a closed-circuit television system that enlarges visual stimuli aimed through its lens. It helps students obtain information presented on the chalkboard by enlarging white lettering on a black background, and it helps them read books by enlarging black lettering on a white background.

Communication systems for individuals with visual disabilities also exist. *Tele-Braille* helps deaf and blind individuals communicate by converting a message typed on a Braille keyboard into print on a video monitor, which is read by a sighted person. The sighted person then types a response, which is converted into a Braille display. *VersaBraille*, which produces a Braille readout of information presented on a computer screen, also allows individuals with visual impairments to communicate with others. *Braille and Speak* is a handheld note-taker that allows students to record notes in class in Braille and then reads the notes back using a speech synthesizer. Computers with large-print, Braille, and voice output capabilities also allow students with visual disabilities to communicate. These students also may benefit from the use of Braille printers, refreshable Braille displays, and Braille note-takers (Blackstone, 1996).

Electronic travel aids can increase the independent movement of students with visual disabilities. The *Mowat Sensor* is a handheld electronic device that uses vibrations to alert students to barriers in their path and to indicate the distance to obstacles. The *Laser Cane* emits three laser beams that provide a sound signaling objects, dropoffs, or low-hanging obstacles in the user's path.

SET YOUR SITES

You can obtain information on voice activated software by contacting Dragon Systems (www.dragonsys.com, 800-437-2466) or IBM (www-4.ibm.com/software/speech, 800-825-5263).

SET YOUR SITES

Trio Publications publishes the *Illustrated Directory of Disability Products,* a catalog of high- and low-tech products that promote the independence of individuals with disabilities.

Devices for Students with Hearing Disabilities

Technology is making a profound improvement in assistive devices for individuals with hearing disabilities. New types of hearing aids based on digital technology contain powerful computer chips that filter out background noises, deliver more realistic sound, and tailor the sound to the individual's needs and acoustic setting. Systems that convert verbal statements to print allow individuals with and without hearing disabilities to communicate. The *teletypewriter* translates speech into a visual display on a screen that can be read by individuals with hearing disabilities. Telecommunication Devices for the Deaf (TDD or TTY) allow these individuals to communicate by telephone. The individual with a hearing impairment types a message that is sent to a Relay Center, which then converts the call orally and relays it to the individual who does not have a hearing loss.

Some students with hearing disabilities may benefit from assistive communication devices that use infrared (IR), frequency modulation (FM), or inductive coupling (McFadyen, 1996). In these systems, the speaker wears a microphone/transmitter and students wear sound receivers. Verbal messages from the speaker are transmitted to the students' receivers.

With computer software and adaptive devices, students with hearing disabilities can read printed material presented on computers. In such systems, the text and graphics appear on the video monitor accompanied by a video of a signer who signs the text. For students who have some hearing, a digitized voice can read the text as the signer signs it.

Devices for Students from Diverse Language Backgrounds

SET YOUR SITES

The Consortium for Speech Translation Advanced Research (www.c-star.org,) has created a synthesized speech system that translates spoken words from one language into another language.

REFLECTIVE

What technological aids have you used to enhance your skills as a learner? To make your life easier? What have been the positive and negative impacts of using these devices?

Students who are learning English also may benefit from technology that provides meaningful, active, sensory-based activities (Soska, 1994). This technology allows students to hear the pronunciation of words and sentences in their new language and then to record their own attempts to speak the new language. The *Language Master* is an electronic dictionary, thesaurus, and grammar and spell checker that pronounces words, gives definitions and synonyms, corrects the spelling of phonetic words, and offers educational games involving over 83,000 words. The Language Master allows you and your students to play, record, and erase oral material on stimulus cards and write on the stimulus cards to provide visual cues.

Bilingual word processing programs provide bilingual online assistance with dictionaries, thesauruses, and spell and grammar checkers. Interactive videodiscs and CD-ROM programs offer many opportunities for students to develop their vocabulary, word recognition, and reading and listening comprehension skills.

SUMMARY

This chapter offered guidelines for differentiating instruction to address the diverse learning needs of students. As you review the questions posed in this chapter, remember the following points:

How Can I Differentiate Instruction for Students?

You can tailor teaching strategies to the needs of students and the learning environment. It is also important to consider students' learning styles, sensory abilities, and the acceptability

REFLECTING ON PROFESSIONAL PRACTICES

Using Instructional Technology and Assistive Devices

Mr. Nealon, a social studies teacher, and Ms. Camac, the school's technology specialist, were excited about developing and teaching a unit on the Vietnam War using instructional technology. They started to develop the unit by searching the Internet for content, online lesson plans, and teaching resources about the war. They also participated in a chat room related to teaching and technology, which also provided suggestions for the unit. Then they identified and reviewed interesting and relevant websites and resources and created their unit. They also visited the websites, which provided help in designing various web-based activities.

Since their students' experience with the Internet varied, Mr. Nealon and Ms. Camac began by teaching students about the Internet and how to use it. They provided an overview of how to access and navigate the Internet and paired experienced users with novices to perform a World Wide Web scavenger hunt that required them to conduct searches for various topics. They brainstormed with students and framed rules for use of the Internet by having students respond to such questions as "What would you do if you were asked for personal information or your password?", "What would you do if someone wanted to meet you or sell you something?" and "What would you do if you received or encountered offensive material?" They also told students not to believe everything they read or heard via the Internet. They gave students guidelines for examining and verifying sites and information, which included identifying the individuals who created the site, the dates on which it was created and updated, the location and organizational affiliation of the site, and the content of the site.

Once they were convinced that students could use the technology appropriately, Mr. Nealon and Ms. Camac assigned students to work in groups. Each group selected a variety of learning activities from a menu that included

◆ viewing a videodisc that portrayed actual battles and presented interviews with soldiers;
◆ taking a three-dimensional panoramic tour of the Vietnam Memorial through pictures that Ms. Camac had taken last summer with a digital camera and downloaded to a computer;
◆ watching videos of news reports from the 1960s and 1970s and documentaries about the Vietnam War and antiwar activities throughout the United States and the world;
◆ exchanging e-mail messages with military experts and leaders of the antiwar movement;
◆ using virtual reality to attend rallies for and against the war;
◆ examining primary source documents online;
◆ hearing eyewitness accounts of the war from the viewpoint of soldiers, protestors, and Vietnamese citizens;
◆ making an online visit to an exhibition on the Vietnam War at the Smithsonian Museum; and
◆ establishing a keypal relationship with Vietnamese and U.S. students and their families.

While the groups worked, Mr. Nealon and Ms. Camac helped them. When computers froze because students tried to download too much information, they helped students reboot them. They also aided students who had difficulty reading information from websites by using Internet screen reading programs and reformatting the text and images so that they were easier for students to read.

Mr. Nealon and Ms. Camac also allowed each group to choose its own final product. Group projects included writing and making a video of a play about the Vietnam War, preparing a presentation about the war using presentation software, conducting an online survey of the community's knowledge of the Vietnam War, and creating a memorial to Vietnam Veterans and the Peace Movement. All students helped to develop their group's project. Steven, a student with a severe disability, used his assistive communication system to speak lines in his group's play, and Marta, a second language learner, helped her group translate their community survey into Spanish.

Mr. Nealon and Ms. Camac shared the groups' projects by posting them on the class's web page. They were pleased when they received e-mail messages from other teachers and their students' families about the students' products and requests to use activities from their unit.

What strategies did Mr. Nealon and Ms. Camac use to differentiate instruction for their students? What process and resources did they use to create and implement their technology-based unit? How do you think their students and their families felt about this unit? What difficulties might you encounter in using instructional technology activities in your classroom? How could you attempt to solve these difficulties?

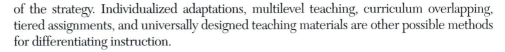

What Would You Do in Today's Diverse Classroom?

Your class includes the following students:

◆ Alexis is an inconsistent reader. Her reading difficulties are greatest when she is asked to read handouts and tests. She also has trouble understanding text. Alexis likes to work with others, and works hard to please her teachers and her family.

◆ Raymond, a student with cerebral palsy, has difficulty walking and limited use of his hands. While he can speak, it is very hard to understand him. Because of his communication difficulties, it is hard to assess his cognitive abilities. However, the professionals who work with him report that he has normal intelligence.

◆ Carla, a student with a moderate hearing impairment, has difficulty following orally presented information and directions. She relies heavily on gestures and visual stimuli. Usually she can understand face-to-face communications. Her speech, which is impaired, is intelligible to others. However, she needs to be prodded to speak in class.

◆ Malik is an African American student who is in the gifted and talented program. Despite his intellectual abilities, his performance is erratic. Occasionally, he appears to be bored in class and rushes through his work so that he can work with others or use one of the learning centers.

1. How would you determine the appropriate strategies to differentiate instruction for Alexis, Raymond, Carla, and Malik?

2. What strategies would you use to differentiate instruction for these students?

3. How could you use instructional technology and assistive devices to differentiate instruction for Alexis, Raymond, Carla, and Malik?

4. What difficulties might you encounter in differentiating instruction for these students?

of the strategy. Individualized adaptations, multilevel teaching, curriculum overlapping, tiered assignments, and universally designed teaching materials are other possible methods for differentiating instruction.

How Can I Differentiate Instruction for Students Who Have Difficulty Reading and Gaining Information from Print Materials?

You can use a variety of teacher- and student-directed strategies. In addition, you can make materials more readable by modifying them, reducing their linguistic complexity, using the principles of typographic design, and using audiocassettes, videocassettes, and electronic literacy activities.

How Can I Differentiate Instruction for Students from Diverse Cultural and Language Backgrounds?

You can use a multicultural curriculum, multicultural instructional materials, culturally relevant teaching strategies, reciprocal interaction, and effective ESL techniques. You can also encourage students to respond.

How Can I Use Instructional Technology and Assistive Devices to Differentiate Instruction for Students?

Recent developments in instructional technology allow you to create differentiated, interactive, motivating, and contextualized learning environments for students by using computers, hypertext/hypermedia, videocassette recorders, videodiscs, digital cameras, CD-ROMs, caption television and liquid crystal display projection panels, presentation software, virtual reality, and the Internet. You also can use assistive devices to help students communicate with others, use computers, be organized, take notes, increase their range of movements and mobility, read text, hear sounds, and learn a second language.

CHAPTER
9

DIFFERENTIATING LARGE- AND SMALL- GROUP INSTRUCTION FOR DIVERSE LEARNERS

Mr. Armstrong

Mr. Armstrong begins his lesson by reminding students that "we have been learning about nouns and verbs" and asking them to tell him something they did over the weekend. Students reply, "I went camping with my family," "I went to the movies," and "I played with my friends." Mr. Armstrong repeats each sentence and asks students to identify the nouns and verbs in the sentence, pausing for several seconds before randomly picking a student to respond.

Mr. Armstrong tells the students, "Today, we are going to learn about adjectives." He then defines an adjective and models finding the adjectives in a series of sentences. Then, using sentences he has written on the blackboard, he asks students to identify the nouns, verbs, and adjectives. Sometimes he asks a peer if he or she agrees with a student's response.

Next, he asks students to open their books to a page containing a series of sentences. He has students read a sentence and think about which words in the sentence are nouns, verbs, and adjectives. Then he picks a word from the sentence and has students indicate whether it is a noun, verb, or adjective by arranging their fingers in the shape of an N (noun), V (verb), or A (adjective). Occasionally, he asks students to justify their responses ("Why do you think that word is an adjective?").

Mr. Armstrong concludes the lesson by giving students independent assignments that involve identifying the nouns, verbs, and adjectives in sentences. He differentiates the assignment for students by having some students work on five sentences while others work on three sentences. As students work on the assignment, he circulates around the room, praising them, providing feedback, and assisting them. For homework, he asks students to interview family members concerning what they did today. They must then write five sentences concerning their families' activities containing nouns, verbs, and adjectives, and identify them by placing an N over the nouns, a V over the verbs, and an A over the adjectives.

What other adaptations could Mr. Armstrong use to differentiate instruction for his students? After reading this chapter, you should be able to answer this as well as the following questions.

◈ How can I adapt large-group instruction for students?
◈ How can I use effective instruction?
◈ How can I successfully use cooperative learning arrangements with students?

L ike Mr. Armstrong, you teach in many different ways. You use oral presentations, effective instruction, and cooperative learning to help students learn. However, if *all of your students* are to benefit from these varied arrangements, you must adapt these arrangements to the unique needs of your students and your curriculum. This chapter offers strategies that you can use to differentiate large- and small-group instruction for *all students*.

HOW CAN I ADAPT LARGE-GROUP INSTRUCTION FOR STUDENTS?

The following section offers information on strategies you can use to foster student learning when you are teaching large groups of students.

Have Students Work Collaboratively

The amount of information students gain from teacher-directed presentations can be increased by using a variety of learning arrangements in which students work collaboratively, such as collaborative discussion teams, Send a Problem, Numbered Heads Together, Think-Pair-Share, and Bookends.

Collaborative Discussion Teams

Collaborative discussion teams can be used throughout the presentation. After a certain amount of time, usually 10 to 15 minutes, teams can respond to discussion questions, react to material presented, or predict what will happen or be discussed next. Teams can then be called on to share their responses. At the end of the presentations, teams can summarize the main points and check each other's comprehension.

Send a Problem

In the Send a Problem technique, groups make up questions that are answered by other groups. This is done by developing a list of questions related to material being presented in class, recording the answers to each question, and passing the questions from group to group (Goor & Schwenn, 1993).

Numbered Heads Together

Numbered Heads Together can be used to help students review and check their understanding of orally presented information (Kagan, 1990). You can use this method by doing the following:

1. Assign students to mixed ability groups of three or four.
2. Assign a number (1, 2, 3, or 4) to each student in each group.
3. Break up the oral presentation by periodically asking the class a question and telling each group to "put your heads together and make sure that everyone in your group knows the answer."
4. Tell the groups to end their discussion, call a number, ask all students with that number to raise their hands, select one of the students with that number to answer, and ask the other students with that number to agree with or expand on the answer.

Think-Pair-Share

Think-Pair-Share is another cooperative learning strategy that helps students master content presented orally. The process is as follows:

1. Pair students randomly.
2. Give students a question, problem, or situation.
3. Ask individual students to think about the question.
4. Have students discuss their responses with their partners.
5. Select several pairs to share their thoughts and responses with the class (Mallette, Pomerantz, & Sacca, 1991).

Bookends

Bookends is a cooperative learning strategy in which students meet in small groups before an oral presentation to share their existing knowledge about the topic to be presented. The groups also generate questions on the topic, and these questions are discussed during or after the oral presentation.

Use Presentation Software/Overhead Projector

You can supplement your large-group teaching by using presentation software or an overhead projector. These technologies help students by providing visual support and computer-generated text and graphics. They also allow you to present content and highlight main points and key vocabulary while maintaining eye contact with students. With these technologies, you can also model and provide students with high-quality notes. Presentation software or transparencies can be made more effective by using color, simple and realistic visuals, photographs rather than line drawings, consistent backgrounds, easy-to-read color combinations, and the principles of graphic design (see Chapter 8) (Thoms, 1999).

REFLECTING ON YOUR PRACTICES

Delivering Oral Presentations to Students

You can examine your success in giving oral presentations to students by addressing the following questions:

◇ Are the objectives, purpose, and relevance of the oral presentation stated at the beginning?

◇ Are prerequisite information and key terms reviewed and explained so that students understand them?

◇ Has the relationship between the new material and old material been established?

◇ Are the pace and sequence of the presentation appropriate?

◇ Is student interest maintained by using changes in voice level, stories to make a point, jokes, and humorous anecdotes?

◇ Are ordinal numbers and time cues (*first, second, finally*) used to organize information for students?

◇ Are important concepts and critical points emphasized by varying voice quality and by using cues (e.g., "It is important that you remember")—speaking them with emphasis, writing them on the blackboard, and repeating them?

◇ Are examples, illustrations, charts, diagrams, advance organizers, and maps used to make the material more concrete and to supplement oral material?

◇ Are individuals, places, or things referred to by nouns rather than pronouns, and by using specific numerals instead of ambiguous ones (using *two* instead of a *couple*)?

◇ Are vague terms ("these kinds of things," "somewhere") and phrases ("to make a long story short," "as you all know") avoided?

◇ Are questions asked that require students to think about the information presented and that assess understanding and recall?

◇ Do you pause periodically to have students discuss and review new content and their notes, jot down questions, and rehearse important points?

◇ Do students have opportunities to ask questions during and after the class?

◇ Do students have time at the end of class to review, discuss, summarize, and organize the main points and their notes?

How would you rate your oral presentations?
( ) Excellent ( ) Good ( ) Needs Improvement
( ) Needs Much Improvement
What steps could you adopt to improve your oral presentations?

Encourage Students to Ask Questions

To benefit from oral instruction and to understand assignments and directions, students can ask questions. However, many students may be reluctant to do so. To help these students overcome their fear of asking questions, you can praise them for asking questions, give them time to write down and ask questions during class, give students the correct answer and ask them to state the corresponding question, and teach students when and how to ask questions.

Help Students Take Notes

The amount of information gained from the teacher's oral presentations also depends on the students' ability to take notes. A variety of strategies for improving students' note-taking skills are presented below.

Outlines

You can give students a framework for note taking by using a listening guide (Shields & Heron, 1989) or a skeleton/slot/frame outline (Lazarus, 1996). A *listening guide* is a list

Civil War

A. The sides
   1. The Union:

   2. The Confederacy:

   3. The Border States:
     a.   c.
     b.   d.

B. Advantages of each side
   1. The Union:
     a.   c.
     b.   d.
   2. The Confederacy:
     a.   c.
     b.   d.

C. The strategy of each side:
   1. The Union:
     a.
     b.
     c.
   2. The Confederacy:
     a.
     b.
     c.

D. Key individuals to know
   1. Abraham Lincoln
   2. Jefferson Davis
   3. Stonewall Jackson
   4. Robert E. Lee
   5. Ulysses S. Grant
   6. Clara Barton

FIGURE 9.1 Sample listening guide for Civil War unit lecture.
Source: Developed by Peter Goss, social studies teacher, New Paltz Central Schools, New Paltz, New York.

of important terms and concepts that parallels the order in which they will be presented in class. Students add to this list by writing supplemental information and supportive details. A *skeleton/slot/frame outline* presents a sequential overview of the key terms and main points as an outline made up of incomplete statements with visual cues such as spaces, letters, and labels that can help students determine the amount and type of information to be recorded (Figure 9.1). Students listen to the lecture or read the textbook chapter and fill in the blanks to complete the outline, which then serves as the students' notes. You can encourage students to use outlines by periodically pairing students to check each other's outlines and sometimes collecting them.

If giving students outlines is not feasible, you can encourage note taking by listing the major points on the chalkboard. You also can structure students' notes at the beginning of class by listing questions on the blackboard relating to the day's work and then discussing answers to them at the end of class.

INFORMATIONAL

Lazarus (1996) offers guidelines for developing and using skeleton guided notes.

Highlighting Main Points

To help students determine important points to include in their notes, you can emphasize these points by pausing for attention, using introductory phrases, and changing inflection. You also can highlight main points by writing them on the board and reviewing them before you erase them.

Another method that can help students identify important points is *oral quizzing*, in which the teacher allots time at the end of the class to respond to students' questions and to ask questions based on the material presented. End-of-class time can also be devoted to summarizing and reviewing main points and discussing what points should be in the students' notes (Weishaar & Boyle, 1997). Pairing students to check each other's notes after class also ensures that students' notes are in the desired format and include relevant

Teachers can use a variety of strategies to help students take notes.

content. In addition, you can check the accuracy, completeness, usability, and style of student notes by regularly collecting and reviewing them.

Peer Note Takers and Audiocassette Recorders

For students who have difficulty taking notes, peer note takers can be used. This can be done by giving the peer carbon paper or by using a photocopying machine.

When selecting peer note takers, you should consider their mastery of the content, sensitivity to students who need help with note taking, and ability to work independently. Students also can record class sessions on an audiocassette. The cassette can be replayed after class using a variable speech-control tape recorder that allows students to listen to notes at their own pace. Whether students are using peer note takers or audiocassettes, they can be required to take notes during class. This allows them to practice their note-taking skills and keep alert in class. It also helps prevent resentment from other students who may feel that students with peer note takers have to do less work.

Teach Note-Taking Skills and Strategies

You can help students learn to use a variety of note-taking skills and strategies. Students can improve their note-taking skills by using several behaviors before, during, and after the class. These behaviors and note-taking skills are presented in Figure 9.2.

Since the note-taking strategy selected depends on the content, students also can be taught to match their strategy to the material. A *chart* is used when the speaker is contrasting information. When information is ordered by the date of occurrence, students can use a *timeline*, which involves making a horizontal line across the page and recording the events and dates in sequence. If the material is presented in steps, then

REFLECTIVE

What strategies do your instructors use to promote your note taking in class?

REFLECTIVE

What skills and strategies do you use to pay attention and take notes in class? Are they successful? How do they compare with the strategies presented in this book?

INFORMATIONAL

Strategies that can help students take notes include CALL UP and "A" NOTES (Czarnecki, Rosko, & Fine, 1998) and LINKS and AWARE (Suritsky & Hughes, 1996).

BEFORE THE CLASS

◈ Try to anticipate what the teacher will cover by reading the assigned material and reviewing notes from previous classes.

◈ Bring writing utensils, notebooks, and an audiocassette recorder if necessary.

◈ Come to class mentally and physically prepared.

◈ Select a seat near the speaker, and take a good listening posture.

◈ List the name of the class, page number, and date on each page to ensure continuity.

◈ Organize notebook pages into two columns, one on the left for checking understanding and the other on the right for recording notes.

DURING THE CLASS

◈ Pay attention, and avoid being distracted by outside stimuli.

◈ Listen to and watch for verbal and nonverbal cues from the speaker and the audience.

◈ Write legibly, and record notes in your own words.

◈ Jot down only critical points and essential details.

◈ Write complete statements rather than unconnected words or phrases.

◈ Record the teacher's examples to clarify information.

◈ Listen for key phrases that indicate important information and transitions from one point to another.

◈ Highlight important ideas through highlighting, underlining, extra spacing, and boxing.

◈ Skip a line to indicate transitions between material.

◈ Draw diagrams and sketches to help you understand key points and concepts.

◈ Use symbols. For example, a ? can indicate missed information, and an = can indicate a relationship between two concepts.

NEAR THE END OF CLASS

◈ Add any missing words, incomplete thoughts, related details, or original ideas.

◈ Summarize the main points using a *noteshrink* technique, which involves surveying the notes, identifying and highlighting main points, and listing these points in the quiz column.

AFTER THE CLASS

◈ Review and edit notes.

◈ Identify important points and information that needs further clarification, and then seek additional explanations from teachers and/or peers.

◈ Ask the teacher or a peer to provide missed information.

◈ Indicate an overlap between the textbook and the teacher's comments.

◈ Record the length of time spent on a topic.

FIGURE 9.2   Recommended student note-taking skills.
Sources: Learning Resource Center (n.d.) and Suritsky and Hughes (1996).

stepwise, or numerical, note taking is best. Examples of these three systems are presented in Figure 9.3.

Foster Students' Listening Skills

Since listening is critical in order to learn from teacher directed presentations, you can foster students' listening skills. Periodically, you can ask questions about critical content and have students try to predict what will be discussed next. To increase listening, you can also provide visual aids, vary the pace of the oral presentation to emphasize critical points, move around the room, place the student near the speaker, and minimize unimportant and distracting noises and activities. Additional strategies to help students learn to listen are presented next.

INFORMATIONAL

Anderson-Inman, Knox-Quinn, and Horney (1996) offer guidelines for using computer-based study strategies to take notes in class and from textbooks.

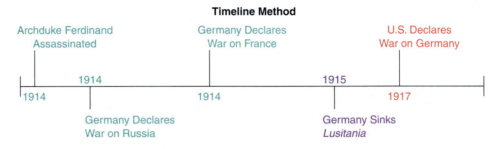

Chart Method

	Hamilton	*Jefferson*
Cabinet Position	Secretary of the Treasury	Secretary of State
Political Party	Federalist	Republican
Constitutional	Supported England	Supported France

Timeline Method

Archduke Ferdinand Assassinated		Germany Declares War on France		U.S. Declares War on Germany
	1914		1915	
1914		1914		1917
	Germany Declares War on Russia		Germany Sinks *Lusitania*	

Stepwise Method

The three principles underlying Roosevelt's "Good Neighbor" Policy:
1. Noninterference in affairs of independent countries
2. Concern for economic policies of Latin American countries
3. Establishment of inter-American cooperation

FIGURE 9.3 Three methods of note taking.

Motivating Students to Listen

To motivate students to listen, use gestures, eye contact, facial expressions, pauses, and voice changes. Keeping students actively involved in learning is also important. You also can help students listen by teaching them to ask questions of their peers, expanding on and using their responses, using activities that require students to use objects or work in small groups, relating lesson content to their lives and interests using attractive materials, and varying the schedule so that students are not passive for long periods of time.

Paraphrasing

Paraphrasing requires students to convert the information they have learned into their own words. Paraphrasing skills can be taught by asking students to paraphrase directions, assignment instructions, or peer comments.

Using Cues

Both nonverbal and verbal cues can help students listen. *Nonverbal* cues, such as eye contact and gestures, as well as awareness of the reactions of their peers, can increase a student's listening skills. For example, if a student observes others in the class looking intently at the teacher, it can indicate the need to listen carefully. Gloeckler and Simpson (1988) believe that students' listening skills can be improved by using a cue card that lists the guidelines for listening.

Students can be taught how to respond to *verbal* cues such as pacing, inflection, and loudness. They can also learn the words and statements that teachers use to highlight and organize key points. A videocassette recorder can be used to teach these skills. It allows students to experience different speaking styles, and can be stopped and replayed to demonstrate key points.

Screening

An efficient listener knows how to distinguish between important and less important information. Successful listeners listen for ideas as well as facts; judge the speaker's comments rather than the speaker's style; are flexible; and concentrate, pay attention, and avoid distractions (Communication Briefings, 1989a).

Listening Materials

Many materials that help teach listening skills have been developed for elementary and secondary students. These materials teach a variety of listening skills, including identifying and paying attention to auditory stimuli; using memory strategies such as visualization, rehearsal, and grouping; following directions; determining the sequence, main ideas, and details of the information; identifying supporting information; and making inferences and predicting outcomes.

Gain and Maintain Students' Attention

An important aspect of listening to and following directions is paying attention. However, many students have difficulty focusing their attention. You may have to use several attention-getting strategies, such as (1) directing them to listen carefully ("Listen carefully to what I say"); (2) giving clear, emphatic instructions ("Put your finger on the top of the page"); (3) pausing before speaking to make sure that all students are paying attention; and (4) limiting distractions. You also can use cues, such as a verbal statement or physical gesture (raising a hand, blinking the lights, ringing a bell), to alert students to the need to pay attention.

Once you have gained students' attention, you can use several methods to maintain it. First, you can present material rapidly and have students respond often. For example, you can select students randomly to respond, remind students that they may be called on next, ask students to add information to or explain an answer given by a peer, and use repetition by asking students to answer the same questions several times. You also can group students with peers who can stay attentive, maintain eye contact with all students, create suspense, change activities frequently, and vary the ways of presenting material and asking students to respond.

Give Clear and Detailed Directions

Students will perform better during large-group instruction if you use certain techniques for giving clear and detailed directions. When explaining assignments, make certain that all students are attentive, pausing when they are not. Start by describing the assignment and the reasons for working on it. Give directions visually and review them orally, using terms that the students understand. When giving directions orally, you can simplify the vocabulary, cut down on unnecessary words and irrelevant information, and use consistent terms from assignment to assignment. Students can copy the directions in their notebooks. For students

Teachers may need to modify the ways they give directions to students.

who have difficulty copying from the blackboard or writing, a teacher-prepared handout can be given, using the writing style (manuscript or cursive) to which these students are accustomed. Directions for completing assignments can also be recorded on an audiocassette.

In presenting directions that have several steps, you can number and list the steps in order. For example, an assignment using dictionary skills can be presented by listing the steps:

1. Use the dictionary guide words.
2. Check the pronunciation of each word.
3. Write the definition.

Students will also understand directions more clearly if you provide a model of the assignment, describe the qualities you will use in evaluating it, encourage students to ask questions about the assignment, and have students paraphrase and explain the directions to the rest of the class (Rademacher, 2000). You may also question students to see how well they understand the instructions ("What steps are you required to follow in doing this assignment?" "Can you anticipate any problems in doing this assignment?"), the materials they need to complete the assignment (What materials do you need?), the ways they can get help ("If you have a problem, who should you ask for help?"), and the things they can do if they finish the assignment ("What can you do if you finish early?"). Finally, to ensure understanding, students can complete several problems from the assignment under your supervision before beginning to work independently.

For students who continue to have problems in following directions, you can break directions into shorter, more meaningful statements. When possible, give no more than two instructions at a time. These students can work on one part of the assignment at a time and can check with an adult before advancing to the next part. Long assignments can be divided into several shorter ones, with students completing one part before working on the next.

You can help students with reading and language problems understand written directions via a *rebus* system, in which pictures represent important words in the directions

(Cohen & de Bettencourt, 1988). Recurring words and their corresponding rebus can be placed in a location in the room where all students can see them. Second language learners also may benefit from using a bilingual dictionary/pictionary or keeping a list in English and their native language of words teachers commonly use when giving directions.

Another way to help students follow directions is to allow time for students to receive teacher assistance. A signup sheet posted in the classroom can be used to schedule teacher–student meetings. The times when adults are available to provide help can be listed, and students can sign their names next to the desired time.

Motivate Students

Motivation is an important aspect of learning, listening, and following directions. Because of their past history of struggle or failure, some students with special needs may lack the motivation necessary to be successful learners. Successful techniques for motivating students include those that give students a sense of control and choice regarding their learning; personalizing instruction with respect to students' skills, interests, experiences, career goals, and cultural and language backgrounds; keeping students engaged and interested in learning activities; and acknowledging students' effort, improvement, and performance.

INFORMATIONAL

Rademacher, Cowart, Sparks, and Chism (1997) have developed the Quality Assignment Planning Worksheet and the Assignment Idea Chart to help you plan and use lessons that motivate your students.

Student-Directed Learning

Students who become involved and participate in instruction gain a sense of ownership in education, which increases their motivation and learning. To promote student-directed learning, link instruction to students' real-world experiences and interests, use a thematic approach, understand and adapt instruction to students' cultural and language backgrounds and learning styles, use a problem-solving approach to learning, and allow students to help choose learning goals and activities (Voltz & Damiano-Lantz, 1993). To encourage students to participate, create an environment in which students and teachers ask questions, express opinions, and are urged to elaborate on their responses as well as those of others. In addition, use open-ended learning activities and independent projects that allow students to identify activities, learning products, and areas of interest to be studied (Hertzog, 1998a; Tomlinson, 1995b).

INFORMATIONAL

Hertzog (1998a) offers guidelines for using open-ended learning activities.

INFORMATIONAL

Margolis (1999) has developed the *Student Motivation: A Problem Solving Questionnaire* to help use, analyze, and promote student motivation.

How Can I Use Effective Instruction?

Elements of Effective Instruction

What are the elements of effective lessons? These elements, which can be used for both large- and small-group instruction (Stein, Carnine, & Dixon, 1998), are discussed here. When using these techniques with second language learners, teachers should provide contextual cues and should integrate tasks into a meaningful whole (Ortiz & Yates, 1989).

These elements are effective in helping students to master basic skills. However, you will also need to use other teaching frameworks and formats to promote learning and the development of higher-order thinking and problem-solving abilities. Therefore, you should also use alternative methods such as reciprocal interaction teaching approaches,

IDEAS FOR IMPLEMENTATION

Motivating Students

Ms. Wilhem notices that her students are not as enthusiastic as they were earlier in the school year. Some students are not completing their assignments, and fewer students are participating in class. The number of yawns and notes passed in class seems to be increasing.

To reverse this cycle, Ms. Wilhem decides to change the major assignment for her upcoming unit on spreadsheets. Noticing that her students spend a lot of time talking about getting jobs and buying a car and clothes, she decides to have them research a career and develop a spreadsheet that outlines their expenditures during the first year of employment. She also asks them to write a narrative answering the following questions: Why did you choose this career? What education or training do you need? What is the anticipated demand for this career? What is the beginning salary?

She asks students to share their spreadsheets and narratives with the class. All of the students complete the assignment and seem to enjoy sharing their findings. Here are some other strategies you can use to motivate students:

◇ Survey students at the beginning of a unit to determine what they already know about it and what questions they have.

◇ Give students choices in terms of content and process, including what, when, and

how they learn. For example, you can ask students to identify innovative ways to demonstrate mastery, such as role plays, skits, and art projects.

◇ Use activities, materials, and examples that are interesting, creative, challenging, and relevant to students' academic abilities, cultural perspectives, and lifestyles.

◇ Personalize instruction by using the students' names, interests, and experiences, as well as incorporating popular characters, items, and trends in classroom examples and assignments.

◇ Display enthusiasm for learning and for the material being presented.

◇ Use suspense, fantasy, curiosity, games, technology, simulations, experiments, color, uncertainty, novelty, activities, and sensory experiences that arouse students' curiosity.

◇ Vary the teaching format, grouping arrangements, and student products, and incorporate self-correction and self-reinforcement into learning activities.

Sources: Fulk and Montgomery-Grymes (1994) and Okolo et al. (1995).

cooperative learning, hands-on learning activities, technology-based instruction, and individualized learning activities discussed in other sections of this book.

Element 1: Establish the Lesson's Purpose by Explaining Its Goals and Objectives

You can begin the lesson by identifying its purpose and emphasizing how the lesson's objectives relate to students' lives. This helps to focus their attention on the new information. When students know the lesson's purpose, they will understand your goals and the importance of the content.

You also can start the lesson with an *anticipatory set,* a statement or an activity that introduces the material and motivates students to learn it by relating the goals of the lesson to their interests, strengths, and future life events (Hunter, 1981). The anticipatory set is often an enjoyable activity that establishes the relevance of the new material and clarifies its relationship to previously learned material. For example, in the chapter-opening vignette, Mr. Armstrong used an anticipatory set that asked students to talk about something they did over the weekend.

Element 2: Review Prerequisite Skills

After clarifying the lesson's purpose, it is important for you to review previously learned relevant skills. For example, in learning to tell time, it might help students if you review such skills as identifying the big and small hands of the clock and identifying the numerals 1 through 12. You can review prerequisite skills by correcting and discussing homework, asking students to define key terms, having them apply concepts, or assigning an activity requiring mastery of prior relevant material.

Element 3: Use Task Analysis and Introduce Content in Separate Steps Followed by Practice

Next, specific points are presented to students in small, sequential steps. Task analysis can help you identify the steps used to master a skill and individualize the lesson according to the various skill levels of students. *Task analysis* is a systematic process of stating and sequencing the parts of a task to determine what subtasks must be performed in order to master the task. A sample task analysis is presented in Figure 9.4.

REFLECTIVE

How would you task analyze a motor skill such as brushing your teeth? How would you task analyze a cognitive skill such as measuring a line using a ruler?

Each skill completes the statement *The student will*

1. verbally identify the clock and its function.
2. verbally identify the numbers on the clock.
3. discriminate the little hand as the hour hand and the big hand as the minute hand.
4. state the number of minutes in an hour and number of seconds in a minute.
5. state the time when the time is set
    a. on the hour.
    b. on the half hour.
    c. on the quarter hour.
    d. in 10-minute intervals.
    e. in 5-minute intervals
    f. in 1-minute intervals.
6. position the hands of the clock when given a specific time
    a. on the hour.
    b. on the half hour.
    c. on the quarter hour.
    d. in 10-minute intervals.
    e. in 5-minute intervals.
    f. in 1-minute intervals.
7. write the time when the time is set
    a. on the hour.
    b. on the half hour.
    c. on the quarter hour.
    d. in 10-minute intervals.
    e. in 5-minute intervals.
    f. in 1-minute intervals.

FIGURE 9.4 Task analysis of telling time.

Element 4: Give Clear Directions, Explanations, and Relevant Examples

Give students detailed explanations and examples of content using clear, explicit statements. Avoid using confusing wording ("you know," "a lot," "these things") and try to use terms that students understand. While the rate of presentation will depend on the students' skills and the complexity of the material, you should try to maintain a swift pace. However, to ensure understanding, you can repeat key points, terms, and concepts, and adjust the pace of the lesson to allow for reteaching and repetition.

Model-Lead-Test   When introducing a new concept or strategy, you can model it for students, identifying and emphasizing the key features. One effective modeling procedure is the *model-lead-test* strategy. It involves modelling and orally presenting the material, helping students understand it through prompts and practice, and testing student mastery. When modelling new content, you can make the demonstration very clear and exaggerate the salient features. It also is a good idea to offer specific examples as well as nonexamples to help make abstract information more concrete.

Element 5: Provide Time for Active and Guided Practice

Practice activities allow *all students* to respond so that you can ensure that they have mastered the skill. It is often best to structure time for practice after you introduce small amounts of difficult or new material. Since success during practice helps students learn, you should strive for a practice success rate of at least 75 to 80 percent and prepare practice activities that require students to respond to both easier and harder items (Rosenshine, 1986). Good practice activities include responding to the teacher's questions, summarizing major points, and using peer tutoring.

Academic Learning Games   *Academic learning games* can motivate students to practice skills and concepts learned in lessons. These games should be challenging and motivating, structured to involve *all students*, and match the content to be taught (Newby, Stepich, Lehman, & Russell, 1996). Academic games may take several forms. When space is limited, a gameboard is feasible; if space is available, a movement-oriented game is appropriate.

In academic games, the academic component is controlled by the teacher, who can vary the level of the skill, the presentation, and the response modes to match the needs and levels of many different students. Thus, students of varying abilities can interact within the same teaching format, yet use skills that differ in complexity. For example, some students can focus on addition of fractions with a common denominator, while other students can solve problems requiring the division of fractions.

Games can stress cooperation rather than competition. One cooperative strategy requires players to strive for a common goal. In this technique, winning occurs when the whole group achieves the goal. Devising game pawns as puzzle pieces also fosters cooperation in an academic game. For example, each player's pawn can be part of a puzzle that is completed when each player reaches a specified goal. Competition with oneself can be built into common-goal games by setting individualized time limits or by increasing the difficulty of the content. The time limits and content levels can be based on a previously established standard or a prior level of performance.

You can help players cooperate by phrasing questions so that they require the input of more than one player to be answered correctly. For example, the academic question

INFORMATIONAL

Blum and Yocom (1996) offer guidelines for designing academic learning games to use in inclusive settings.

Academic games should promote the involvement of all participants.

"What do you get when you add the number of players on a baseball team to the number of eggs in a dozen, then multiply that number by the number of players on a basketball team, and then divide that number by the number of students in this class?" can be answered by having players collaborate.

Rules too can be designed to optimize cooperation. A rule that requires players to change teams or movers periodically during the game can promote cooperation. A rule that periodically requires one player to move toward the goal, depending on the academic performance of another player, also fosters a coalition of game players. Another cooperative rule allows a player who has reached the goal to aid the other players by helping to answer questions put to them.

REFLECTIVE

Identify a game you or your students like to play. How can you apply the principles presented here to make this game cooperative?

Element 6: Promote Active Responding and Check for Understanding

Rather than asking students if they have questions, you can promote active responding and check for understanding after presenting each new point. When checking for understanding, you can have all students respond actively and identify main points or state agreement or disagreement with the comments and responses of their peers.

Questioning   You can promote active student responding and check for understanding by asking questions. Questions can be stated clearly, at the language and ability levels of various students, and distributed fairly so that *all students* must respond openly. Thus, rather than targeting a question to a specific student ("Jack, who was the president during the Civil War?"), you can phrase questions using comments such as "Everyone listen and then tell me" or "I want you all to think before you answer." Also, you can randomly select students to respond, give them at least 5 to 10 seconds to formulate their answers, and then ask other students to respond to these answers. Questions also can be directed to students so that they expand on their first answers or those of others. If students fail to respond to the question, you can ask them if they know the answer, ask them about related knowledge, direct the question to another student, or provide the correct answer. When questioning students, avoid promoting inattention by repeating questions, answering questions for them, or supplementing incomplete answers.

Questions can be adjusted to the difficulty of the content and the skill levels of the students (Flanagan, 1998). To check understanding of simple facts or basic rules, you can use product questions that ask students to give the answer or to restate information and procedures, such as "What is the '*i* before *e*' rule?" To check students' ability to use complex skills, you can ask questions that require them to apply basic rules or generalizations. For example, asking students to spell *receive* involves a more complex skill than merely asking them to repeat the rule. You also can use process questions that ask students to discuss how they arrived at an answer.

Questioning techniques can be adapted for students who are second language learners. You can encourage these students to answer questions by providing visual supports and clues such as pictures, gestures, and words; initially asking students questions that require only one- or two-word answers; rephrasing questions when necessary; asking complex questions that can be answered in many different ways; probing responses such as "I don't know"; and repeating and elaborating on students' answers.

Active Student Responding   To encourage active student responding and the review of content that needs to be overlearned, you can use *choral responding,* in which students answer simultaneously on a cue from the teacher, such as "Everyone whisper the answer when I say *three,"* or have students tell their classmates the answer, or have students write down their answer and then check each student's response.

INFORMATIONAL

Heward et al. (1996) offer guidelines for developing and using preprinted and write-on response cards.

Response cards also help students respond. Heward et al. (1996) define *response cards* as "cards, signs, or items that are simultaneously held up by students in the class to display their responses to questions or problems presented by the teacher" (p. 5). Preprinted response cards are given to students so that they can select the cards that give their responses. These cards are appropriate for content that has a limited number of answers, such as true/false questions or questions that require agreement or disagreement. Write-on response cards allow students to record their answers on blank cards or boards and then erase them. These cards are typically used when teachers want students to recall information.

Group responses that allow each member of the group to respond with a physical gesture also are desirable. For example, students can respond to a question with a "yes" or "no" answer by placing their thumbs up or down, respectively. It can be motivating for students to plan with teachers different ways to answer using physical gestures.

Element 7: Give Prompt, Specific Feedback

Students' responses should be followed by frequent, prompt, clear, and constructive feedback from you or other students and adults in the classroom (McDonnell, 1998). The type of feedback can be related to the nature of the response. Therefore, in determining what type of feedback to use, you can categorize students' responses as *correct and confident, correct but unsure, partly correct,* or *incorrect.* If the answer is correct and confident, you can confirm it with praise and ask additional questions at the same or a more difficult level. If the answer is not correct and confident, another type of feedback can be used.

Process Feedback   Students who are unsure of their correct responses may need *process feedback*, in which you praise students and reinforce their answer by restating why it was correct. Besides responding to correct answers, it is important to provide feedback to students whose answers are partly correct. You can confirm the part of the answer that is correct and then restate or simplify the question to address the incorrect part.

You also can respond to students' errors with techniques such as corrective and instructive feedback, prompting, and cuing. If these strategies are not effective, you can call on other students to provide the answer and recheck understanding of the question later in the session.

Corrective Feedback   *Corrective feedback* shows students how to work more effectively. When using corrective feedback, you identify errors and show students how to correct them. Corrective feedback is more effective in promoting learning than *general feedback*, in which responses are identified simply as correct or incorrect; *right-only feedback,* in which only correct responses are identified; or *wrong-only feedback,* in which only incorrect responses are identified.

When students fail to respond, or give an incomplete or incorrect answer, you can use corrective feedback by restating the question, rephrasing it, or changing it to activate the students' knowledge of the content. If the students' responses are incorrect and extensive teaching will not help them find the correct answer, you can clarify the directions, recheck mastery of prerequisite skills, teach a lower-level skill from the task analysis, provide additional practice, and modify your teaching style. When the students' incorrect answers are caused by lack of effort, attention, or preparation, you can emphasize the need to improve in these areas.

Instructive Feedback   *Instructive feedback* promotes learning by giving students extra information and teaching on the task or content. After students answer, you offer instructive feedback by giving verbal or visual information that expands on the target skills being taught (e.g., defining a sight word or giving a word's antonym), parallels the skills being taught (e.g., linking a numeral with its corresponding number word), or offers new information (e.g., describing the color of something) (Werts, Wolery, Gast, & Holcombe, 1996).

Prompting   You can help correct students' errors by using a variety of visual, auditory, or tactile prompts. Prompts can be categorized from most to least intrusive, including *manual prompts,* in which the student is physically guided through the task; *modeling prompts*, in which the student observes someone else perform the task; *oral prompts* that describe how to perform the task; and *visual prompts* that show the student the correct process or answer in a graphic presentation (Schloss, 1986). Prompts can be used sequentially, depending on the skills of the students and the complexity of the task.

Praising   Praise coupled with comments about strengths and weaknesses can provide valuable feedback to students and improve their work. You can increase your use of praise by recording the number of times you praise students. Displaying a cue in an area of the room that you frequently see (e.g., a smiling face on the back wall of the classroom) and finding a student to praise each time you make eye contact with the cue will increase your use of praise.

Praise also can be delivered nonverbally, such as with a smile, the OK sign, or the thumbs-up sign. Since some studies have shown that frequent praise can reduce students' independence, self-confidence, and creativity (Brophy, 1981), you should distribute praise evenly and examine its effect on students. Rather than just praising on-task behavior and task correctness, use praise to encourage independence, determination, and creativity.

You can follow several guidelines to make your praise more effective. Your praise statements should describe the specific behavior that is being praised (rather than saying "This is a good paper," say, "You really did a good job of using topic sentences to begin your paragraphs in this paper") and should be tailored to the age, skill level, and cultural background of the students. It also is important to use praise to acknowledge effort as well as specific outcomes, and to individualize praise so that the students' achievements are evaluated in comparison to their own performance rather than the performance of others. You can increase the credibility of the praise by using diverse and spontaneous statements.

Student-Directed Feedback   Students also can be a valuable source of feedback. They can be encouraged and taught to use self-monitoring and self-correction techniques to record and analyze their own progress. They can chart their mastery of a specific skill by graphing their percentage or number correct every day. Students can also be given answer keys to correct their own work, or they can exchange papers with peers and offer feedback to peers on their work. For example, you can establish a checkout area where students can get written or taped answer keys to correct their own work or have their work checked by peers or teacher aides.

Element 8: *Offer Time for Independent Activities*

You can end successful lessons by giving students independent activities that allow them to demonstrate mastery of the material. Make sure that the activities fit the students' instructional levels and needs. You can motivate students to complete independent activities by modeling strategies for completing assignments; communicating expectations in terms of accuracy, time, format, and appearance; and monitoring student performance and offering prompt feedback (Englert et al., 1992). If completed assignments do not meet your expectations, students can be required to redo them until the product meets your standards.

You can modify independent assignments by providing help or access to peer tutors. Students can ask for help by placing a help sign or card on their desks, raising their hands, or signing a list (Everston et al., 1989). At first, you can provide help by asking questions and making statements that help students assume responsibility for figuring out answers, such as "What things can help you figure out the answer?" and "Have you asked three of your classmates for help before asking me?" (Gibson & Govendo, 1999).

Although it is appropriate to modify the tasks, do not have students work in a different content area from the rest of the class since this might isolate them. Also, when possible, students should complete assignments and work with materials similar to those that other students are using.

Boyer (1998) developed a time-saving system of teacher-created graphic templates, forms, and cues that are stamped on student assignments to individualize and modify them. These templates allow all students to work on the same assignments by using visual prompts that adjust the workload of students, inform students how to complete assignments, adapt the ways in which students respond to items, and vary the time students have to complete the assignment. Sample stamps are presented in Figure 9.5.

IDEAS FOR IMPLEMENTATION

Adapting Independent Assignments

Ms. Maphas's class included a wide range of students. Some students completed independent assignments quickly; others took more time. Concerned about student frustration and the need to avoid isolating students, Ms. Maphas decided to modify her independent assignments. First, rather than having students work on one long assignment, she decided to give several shorter assignments that covered the same content. She also prepared different versions of assignments that modified their content to meet students' skill levels by decreasing the number of items students had to answer, by interspersing items on previously mastered content with items on new material, and by placing the most important items to be completed at the beginning of the assignment. She also built in opportunities for students to receive feedback by asking students to correct their own work or to seek feedback after completing a specific number of items tailored to the students' skill levels.

Here are some other strategies you can use to help students complete independent assignments:

◇ Give clear and concise directions in a list of steps.
◇ Provide cues to highlight key parts of directions, details of items, and changes in item types.
◇ Offer examples of correct response formats.
◇ Divide assignments into sections by folding, drawing lines, cutting off parts of the page, boxing, and blocking out with an index card or a heavy crayon.
◇ Provide enough space for students to record their answers, and limit the amount of distracting visual stimuli.
◇ Scan assignments onto a computer and allow students to complete the assignment using a computer.
◇ Limit the types of questions.

Sources: Chalmers (1991), Fulk and Montgomery-Grymes (1994), Gillet (1986), Reichel (1997), and Shank and Hooser (1999).

Effective teachers provide students with opportunities to work independently and request teacher assistance.

Stamps for Adjusting Workload

Complete the following:
_____ All
_____ All Odd
_____ All Even
_____ Every Third
_____ First Five
_____ First Ten

This stamp is effective when an assignment has several of the same type of questions/problems (e.g. math worksheet). The teacher can select all or a portion of the items for the student to complete.

Select
——— ● items
——— ▲ items
——— ★ items
to complete

Teacher codes questions by importance, type, or level using the symbols and then writes down how many of each type the student should complete. The student then self-selects from the questions on the page. This provides the student control in work completion – the teacher sets clear expectations while the student is still allowed some choice in work completion.

Complete all circled items.

Allows the teacher to select specific items to be completed by the student.

Stamps for Setting Clear Expectations for Written Assignments

Remember:
_____ . ? !
_____ complete sentences
_____ capital letters

Prompts students to pay attention to certain aspects of writing as they complete a writing assignment.

To be graded for:
_____ content/organization
_____ sentence structure
_____ capitalization/punctuation
_____ spelling
_____ form
_____ neatness
_____ all of the above

Teacher checks off what the student is to focus attention on when completing the written assignment. One or more things can be checked off.

FIGURE 9.5 Sample stamps to differentiate student assignments.
Source: M. M. Boyer, *Using stamps to differentiate student assignments* (Phoenix, AZ: Author, 1995). Reprinted by permission.

Stamps to Differentiate the Student Response Required

Assignment can be completed
—— orally with the teacher
—— with an adult
—— as we discussed

Allows the teacher to alter the method of student response. Excellent for students who have difficulty organizing thoughts and ideas in writing or those with handwriting/graphomotor deficits. Teacher can specify that the student complete the assignment a certain way (e.g. dictated to a parent, using a tape recorder, in note form, etc.).

Do the ★ items orally with the teacher.

Allows the teacher to alter the method of student response on selected items. Useful on quizzes or tests with students who need more time to complete written work. For example, essay questions could be completed orally with the teacher during class testing time rather than making arrangements for additional time to complete the item(s) in writing.

Complete:
—— independently
—— with a learning buddy
—— in a cooperative group
of ——————

This stamp allows the teacher to adjust how students work within the classroom — alone or in some type of cooperative group.

Stamps for Providing Additional Time to Complete Assignments

Do you need additional time to complete this assignment?

YES   **NO**

If yes, see the teacher to make arrangements.

Allows the student to inform the teacher of the need for additional time in a private and unobtrusive way. Arrangements for additional time can then be made. Excellent for quizzes and tests and other tasks where time is often limited.

Incomplete — Complete by

——————————

FIGURE 9.5 (continued)

INFORMATIONAL

Olympia, Andrews, Valum, and Jenson (1993) developed a program to give teachers guidelines for using cooperative homework teams.

SET YOUR SITES

Students can obtain online homework assistance by visiting the websites www.homeworkcentral.com, www.jahl.org, www.schoolwork.org, and www.searchopolis.com.

Element 9: Summarize Main Points and Evaluate Mastery

At the end of the lesson, summarize the main points and evaluate students' understanding and mastery of the content. You can assess students' mastery of content in a 1- to 5-minute probe or by asking them to complete a learning log indicating what they learned, how they learned it, what they are confused about, and what additional information they would like to learn (Flanagan, 1998). Since maintenance of skills is critical for building a foundation for learning new skills, weekly and monthly maintenance probes also are desirable. The results of these assessments can be recorded, shared with students, and used to make teaching decisions. Additional guidelines for evaluating student mastery and progress are presented in Chapter 12.

Homework   Homework can be very useful in evaluating student mastery of content. You can use homework to individualize instruction, promote learning through practice and application, allow students to complete work not finished in school, teach independent study skills and work habits, and communicate to families the skills and materials that are being covered in school.

HOW CAN I SUCCESSFULLY USE COOPERATIVE LEARNING ARRANGEMENTS WITH STUDENTS?

Rather than structuring learning so that students work individually, competitively, or in large groups, you can have students work together in cooperative learning arrangements. In *cooperative learning arrangements,* students work in small groups with their peers to achieve a shared academic goal rather than competing against or working separately from their classmates. You structure the learning environment so that each class member contributes to the group's goal. When learning is structured cooperatively, students are accountable not only for their own achievement but also for those of other group members, as the group's evaluation is based on the group's product. Cooperative learning is especially worthwhile for heterogeneous student populations. It promotes friendships and encourages mutual respect and learning among students of various academic abilities and different language, racial, and ethnic backgrounds (Marr, 1997).

Cooperative learning activities have three important components: positive interdependence, individual accountability, and face-to-face interactions. *Positive interdependence* is established when students understand that they must work together to achieve their goal. You can promote positive interdependence by using cooperative learning activities with mutual goals, role interdependence and specialization, resource sharing, and group rewards. *Individual accountability* is understanding that each group member is responsible for contributing to the group and learning the material. This is often established by giving individualized tests or probes, adding group members' scores together, assigning specific parts of an assignment to different group members, randomly selecting group members to respond for the group, asking all members of the group to present part of the project, asking students to keep a journal of their contributions to the group, or tailoring roles to the ability levels of students (Whittaker, 1996). Building individual accountability into cooperative learning groups helps to reduce the *free-rider effect,* in which some members fail to contribute and allow others to do the majority of the work (Slavin, 1990). *Face-to-face interactions* occur when students encourage and help each other learn the material.

IDEAS FOR IMPLEMENTATION

Helping Students Complete Homework

Ms. Rios felt strongly about the value of homework and assigned it 4 days a week. She checked her students' assignments daily and noticed that Matt often failed to complete his homework. When questioned about his homework, Matt said, "The problems were too hard," "I did not know what to do," or simply "I can't do this."

Recognizing Matt's difficulties, Ms. Rios approached Matt's friend, Jamal, who completed his homework, to see if he would be willing to work with Matt as a homework buddy. Jamal agreed and Ms. Rios spoke to Matt, who also was interested in working with Jamal. Both Matt and Jamal were responsible for making sure that their partner had recorded the assignment in his assignment notebooks. Before starting their homework, Matt and Jamal spoke over the phone or worked at each other's home to make sure that they both understood the material presented in class and the homework assignment. As they worked on their homework assignments, they monitored each other's work, offered feedback, and discussed any difficulties.

Here are some other strategies you can use to help students complete homework:

◆ Adjust the amount and type of homework by shortening assignments, extending time lines, using other evaluation strategies, and modifying the types of assignments and the responses required.

◆ Coordinate homework assignments—particularly for secondary-level students who may have different teachers in each content area.

◆ Establish, teach, and follow regular routines for assigning, collecting, evaluating, and returning homework.

◆ Give clear, explicit directions and monitor students' understanding of their assignments and the guidelines for completing them.

◆ Encourage students who have difficulty with homework to record assignments in their notebooks, to use homework planners, and to use a daily or weekly teacher-prepared homework assignment sheet or checklist. Encourage students to check with a classmate about homework assignments.

◆ Give students opportunities to begin their homework in class.

◆ Motivate students to complete their homework by making homework creative and enjoyable, connecting assignments to real-life situations, evaluating it frequently and immediately, and displaying exemplary homework assignments. For example, homework assignments can include games or interviews with family members about events being studied in class.

◆ Give homework grades that become part of the report card grade.

◆ Make families an important part of the homework process by asking them to sign homework, contacting them about the purpose of homework and the amount and type of homework given, and offering suggestions on how to help their children complete their homework. For example, you can offer families information on how to give feedback, use positive reinforcement, schedule time to do homework, establish a proper, distraction-free environment, deal with frustration, and avoid completing homework for the child.

◆ Understand that families may have to deal with more pressing home issues than homework.

◆ Offer multilingual homework hotlines via the telephone, television, fax, or e-mail.

Sources: Bryan and Sullivan-Burstein (1997), Gajria and Salend, (1995), Jayanthi, Bursuck, Epstein, and Polloway (1997), and Stormont-Spurgin (1997).

Students benefit academically and socially from working in cooperative learning groups.

Since social and group processing skills also are necessary to cooperative learning and help the group work smoothly, these skills can be taught and evaluated as part of cooperative learning. Another important element of cooperative learning is the ongoing monitoring of the groups. This can be done by circulating around the room to observe and assist groups (Nesbit & Rogers, 1997).

Guidelines for using cooperative learning arrangements are discussed below.

Select an Appropriate Cooperative Learning Format

Cooperative learning begins by selecting an appropriate format. The format you choose will depend on the needs and characteristics of your students, as well as their experiences in working cooperatively. Generally, it is wise to start by having students work in pairs before they work in groups (Muth, 1997).

The cooperative learning format selected also will depend on the content, objectives, and mastery levels of the assignment. According to Maheady, Harper, and Mallette (1991), peer tutoring, Classwide Peer Tutoring (CWPT), Student Teams-Achievement Divisions, and Team-Assisted Instruction are best for teaching basic skills and factual knowledge in content areas; Jigsaw is appropriate for text mastery; and Learning Together is the desired format for teaching higher-level cognitive material and having students learn how to work together and reach a consensus on controversial material.

Peer Tutoring

In *peer tutoring,* one student tutors and assists another in learning a new skill. Peer tutoring increases student learning and fosters positive attitudes toward school (Longwill & Kleinert, 1998). It also promotes a greater sense of responsibility and an improved self-concept, as well as increased academic skills in tutors. When using peer tutoring, you can do the following:

◆ Establish specific goals for the sessions.
◆ Plan particular learning activities and select appropriate materials to meet the identified goals.
◆ Select tutors who have mastered the content to be taught.
◆ Train students to be successful tutors, including how to establish rapport, present the material and tasks, record tutees' responses, use prompts, and offer feedback.
◆ Train tutees so that they understand the peer tutoring process and are willing to work with a tutor.
◆ Match tutors and tutees.
◆ Schedule sessions for no longer than 30 minutes and no more than three times per week.
◆ Monitor and evaluate the tutoring process periodically and provide feedback to both members of the dyad.
◆ Allay families' potential concerns by explaining to them the role and value of peer tutoring.

Plan tutoring sessions so that students with special needs are not always the ones being tutored. For example, if a student performs well in math, this student could teach math to a student who tutored to him or her in learning capitalization rules. Students who are not proficient at teaching academic skills can teach nonacademic skills related to their hobbies or interests.

INFORMATIONAL

Longwill and Kleinert (1998) offer guidelines for setting up a high school peer tutoring program.

Classwide Peer Tutoring

Classwide Peer Tutoring (CWPT) is effective in teaching reading, spelling, vocabulary, math, and social studies to a wide range of students educated in a variety of settings (Allsopp, 1997; Arreaga-Mayer, 1998). Randomly divide the class into two groups and set up tutoring dyads within both groups. During the first 10 to 15 minutes of the period, one student tutors the other. The members of each dyad then reverse their roles and continue for another equal time period.

You should train students to tutor using a set procedure that involves the following:

1. Tutors present material that requires a response from tutees ("Spell the word," "Answer the question").
2. Tutees say and write their responses. A correct response earns two points. An incorrect response prompts tutors to offer the correct response, ask tutees to write this response three times, and award a point to tutees for correcting their errors.
3. You circulate around the classroom to give bonus points for appropriate tutee and tutor behavior.

After this procedure is repeated throughout the week, students take individual tests and receive points for each correct response. All points earned by the groups are totaled at the end of the week, and the group with the most points is acknowledged through badges, stickers, certificates, public posting of names, or additional free time (Maheady et al., 1991). You can make this system less competitive by giving all groups a chance to earn rewards and acknowledgment if they achieve their goals or exceed a previously established point total. The Peabody Classwide Peer Tutoring system offers variations of these steps to teach reading and math (Mathes, Grek, Howard, Babyak, & Allen, 1999; Phillips, Hamlett, Fuchs, & Fuchs, 1993).

Student Teams-Achievement Divisions

Another cooperative learning arrangement is *Student Teams-Achievement Divisions (STAD).* Kagan (1992) outlines the steps:

1. Content is presented by the teacher.
2. Teams are formed, work on study sheets, and prepare for quizzes on the content.
3. Students take quizzes individually; their improvement above an individually assigned "base score" earns points for their respective teams (base scores are averages of the students' two latest quizzes).
4. Teachers recognize team and individual improvement by distributing a newsletter on the teams' performance or giving teams special activities.

A variation of STAD is *Teams-Games-Tournaments (TGT),* in which triads work together and compete with other teams in weekly tournaments (Slavin, 1990).

Jigsaw

The *Jigsaw* format divides students into groups, with each student assigned a task that is essential in reaching the group's goal (Aronson, Blaney, Stephan, Sikes, & Snapp, 1978). Every member makes a contribution that is integrated with the work of others to produce the group's product. When teams work on the same task, expert groups can be formed by having a member of each group meet with peers from other groups who have been assigned the same subtask. The expert group members work together to complete their assignment and then share the results with their original jigsaw groups.

You can structure the students' assignment so that each group member can succeed. For example, one general education classroom teacher taught a lesson about Dr. Martin Luther King, Jr., by giving each student one segment of Dr. King's life to learn about and teach to others in their group. Students who were assigned the same aspect of Dr. King's life met in expert groups to complete their part; then the original group answered questions on all segments of Dr. King's life.

Learning Together

A cooperative learning format that places more responsibility on group members is Johnson and Johnson's (1986) *Learning Together Approach.* In this format, students are assigned to teams, and each team is given an assignment. Teams decide whether to divide the task into its components or approach the task as a whole group. All group members are involved in the team's decisions by offering their knowledge and skills and by seeking help and clarification from others. Every group produces one product, which represents the combined contributions of all group members. You then grade this product, with each student in the group receiving the group grade. For example, you could use Learning Together to teach students about mammals by dividing the class into groups and having each group develop part of a bulletin board display with information and artwork about a particular mammal. The students in each group then would contribute to the group's display by reporting information, doing artwork, or dictating material about mammals.

Team-Assisted Instruction

Team-Assisted Instruction (TAI) is a cooperative learning system in which heterogeneous groups of students work to master individualized assignments (Slavin, Madden, & Leavey, 1984). While other cooperative learning formats are group paced, TAI combines cooperative learning with individualized instruction. In TAI, individual group members work on their own assignments and help other group members with their assignments. Group members are then rewarded if their team's performance meets or exceeds a preestablished criterion.

Establish Guidelines for Working Cooperatively

You and your students can establish guidelines for working cooperatively. Johnson (1988) outlines several guidelines that foster cooperation:

Each group will produce one product.
Each group member will help other group members understand the material.
Each group member will seek help from her or his peers.
Each group member will stay in his or her group.
No group member will change her or his ideas unless logically persuaded to do so.
Each group member will indicate acceptance of the group's product by signing her or his name.

Maheady et al. (1991) identified three problems that may occur in cooperative learning arrangements: increased noise, complaints about partners, and cheating. They suggest that noise can be minimized by developing and posting rules, developing signals that make students aware of their noise levels, assigning a student to monitor the group's noise level, providing rewards for groups that follow the rules, and teaching students to use their quiet voices. Complaints can be dealt with by discussing them with the group and by reinforcing students who work collaboratively, and cheating can be lessened by random checks of each group's work.

The issue of equitable contributions of each member to the group can be addressed via a Group Project Work Log, a process log or journal of the group's activities, including a description of each student's contribution and effort (Goor & Schwenn, 1993). Individual group members can also keep a journal of their participation and contributions. You can remind students that the standard classroom behaviors will be used during cooperative learning lessons.

Form Heterogeneous Cooperative Groups

Assign students to cooperative, heterogeneous groups by considering their sex, race, ethnicity, language ability, disability, and academic and social skill levels. You also can consider characteristics such as motivation, personality, and communication skills. For example, students who sit quietly and do not participate could be assigned to a highly supportive team. Whittaker (1991) identified a variety of strategies for dealing with students with reading and/or learning problems, behavior and emotional disorders, short attention spans, and auditory and visual difficulties.

Another factor to consider in forming groups is the students' ability to work together. You can get this information through observation and/or by administering a sociogram (see Chapter 12). While groups can be changed for each cooperative lesson, keeping the

SET YOUR SITES

Your students' cooperative learning groups can work with students from all over the world by contacting the Global Schoolhouse (www.gsn.org).

INFORMATIONAL

Dishon and O'Leary (1991) offer guidelines for assigning students to heterogeneous cooperative groups.

students in the same group for several weeks provides the continuity that is helpful in developing cooperative skills. How long a group remains together can depend on the students' ages, the nature of the task, and the group's interpersonal skills. At the beginning, you can use small groups of two or three students, increasing them to five when students become accustomed to cooperative learning. When forming new groups, start with activities that help students get acquainted.

Arrange the Classroom for Cooperative Learning

To structure your classrooms for cooperative work, arrange the students' desks or tables in clusters, place individual desks in pairs for peer tutoring, or block off a carpeted corner of the room. For larger groups, desks can be placed in circles rather than rows, which prevent eye contact and communication. Bookshelves, screens, movable chalkboards, and easels can divide the classroom into separate areas. Since the time needed to complete cooperative projects may vary, you can give groups a safe area to store in-progress projects and other materials.

Another way to promote cooperative work is to post cooperative group reminders. For example, you can post a chart with strategies for respecting the individuality of each group member. These strategies include referring to each group member by name, speaking quietly, and encouraging all members to participate (Ammer, 1998).

Develop Students' Cooperative Skills

Cooperative learning depends on the quality of the interactions of group members. Because many students have little experience with this arrangement, you may have to devote some time to helping students learn to work together effectively (Goodwin, 1999). Interpersonal skills that students must develop to work well together include getting to know and trust peers, communicating directly and clearly, listening actively, supporting, encouraging, and complementing others, accepting differences, managing resources, balancing personal and group goals, building consensus, and resolving conflicts (Prater, Bruhl, & Serna, 1998; Siperstein & Leffert, 1999).

INFORMATIONAL

Goodwin (1992), Kagan (1992), and Goor and Schwenn (1993) offer team-building activities to help students get to know each other and develop cooperative skills, and Vernon, Schumaker, and Deshler (1995) have developed the Cooperative Strategies Series to teach students cooperative and teamwork skills.

Johnson and Johnson (1990) suggest that you use a *T-chart* to help students develop cooperative skills. This involves (1) drawing a horizontal line and writing the cooperative skill on the line; (2) drawing a vertical line from the middle of the horizontal line; (3) listing students' responses to the question "What would the skill look like?" on one side of the vertical line; and (4) listing students' responses to the question "What would the skill sound like?" on the other side of the vertical line.

You also can use the *round robin,* the *round table,* and the *paraphrase passport* to promote team-building and communication skills. Round robin gives each student a chance to participate and to share comments and reactions with others. Whereas round robin involves oral sharing, round table involves passing a pencil and paper around so that each student can contribute to the group's response. The paraphrase passport requires students to paraphrase the statements of their teammate who has just spoken and then share their own ideas and perspectives.

Communication and consensus skills can be fostered by such strategies as *Talking Chips* and *Spend-a-Buck* (Karnes, Collins, Maheady, Harper, & Mallette, 1997). Talking Chips helps students participate equally by giving each of them a set number of talking chips, which are placed in the middle of the work area each time a student speaks. Once students use up all their chips, they cannot speak until all group members have used all their chips. Spend-a-Buck helps groups reach a consensus by giving each group member four quarters, which are then spent on the group's options.

You can also help students learn to work cooperatively by giving them opportunities to practice specific skills. For example, because put-downs of group members can hinder cooperation, you can help the class practice how to respond appropriately to these statements. First, students should brainstorm all constructive ways to respond to put-downs directed at themselves or other group members. Students can be given time to practice responding to put-downs. To follow up, you can lead the students in a discussion of the most effective responses to put-downs, possibly listing them on a chart for further reference.

Another method of teaching cooperative learning skills is *role delineation,* in which each member of the group is given a specific role. For example, to produce a written product, a team might need a reader, a discussion leader to promote brainstorming and decision making, a secretary to record all contributions, and a writer to edit the product. Other students might be assigned the roles of keeping the group on task, keeping track of time, explaining word meanings, managing materials, monitoring the group's noise level, operating media, encouraging all group members to participate and help others, providing positive comments, and presenting the group's product to the class. Periodically, students can complete evaluation sheets that ask them to react to the roles and contributions of group members, as well as suggest what the group could do to improve.

Monitoring groups and providing feedback can build cooperative skills. Therefore, it is important for you to observe groups, model cooperative skills, intervene when necessary, and provide feedback on group processing skills. After students complete a cooperative lesson, they can be encouraged to reflect on their experience by responding to such questions as "What did members do to help your group accomplish its goal?", "What did members do that hindered your group in achieving its goal?", and "What will your group do differently next time?"

Students also can comment on how well the group is working collaboratively by writing and keeping a journal. Finally, students can give feedback on their own collaborative skills by completing a form such as the one presented in Figure 9.6.

Evaluate Cooperative Learning

You can evaluate groups based on their mastery of subject matter, as well as on their ability to work together. To promote peer support and group accountability, students are evaluated as a group, and each student's learning contributes to the group's evaluation. A popular method for evaluating cooperative learning is the *group project/group grade* format. The group submits for evaluation one final product (a report, an oral presentation) that represents all members' contributions. You then evaluate the product and give each group member the same grade.

In another evaluation format, *contract grading,* groups contract for a grade based on the amount of work they agree to do according to a set of criteria. Thus, group members who have different skill levels can perform different parts of the task according to their ability. For example, a cooperative lesson might contain five activities, some more difficult than others, with each activity worth 10 points. The contract between you and the groups might then specify the criteria the groups must meet to achieve an A (50 points), a B (40 points), or a C (30 points). Additional guidelines for using contract grading are discussed in Chapter 12.

Group Evaluation Form

1. I learned something from my group members.

2. I asked questions when I did not understand something.

3. I used praise.

4. I felt good about working with my group members.

5. Someone said something nice about what I was doing to help my group.

6. We worked well together.

7. Everyone did something to help the group.

8. We were able to make decisions as a group.

9. When we did not agree on something, we worked it out by ourselves.

10. My group members needed my help to get the project done.

FIGURE 9.6 Cooperative skills evaluation form.

Source: Developed by Selina Watts-Delisfort, special education teacher, Newburgh Central Schools, Newburgh, New York.

REFLECTING ON PROFESSIONAL PRACTICES

Using Cooperative Learning

After reading about and attending several inservice sessions on cooperative learning, Ms. Johnson decides to try it with her students. She divides the students into groups and gives each group an assignment to work on together. She then circulates throughout the room and observes the groups. In one group, Luis, a second language learner, sits quietly and does not participate in his group's project. Luis does not speak throughout the activity, and no one speaks to him. In another group, students rely on Maria to do the assignment while they talk about an upcoming school event. In still another group, students fight over who will draw a picture that will be part of the group's project.

Frustrated but not about to give up, Ms. Johnson realizes that she needs to help her students learn to work collaboratively. She decides to start by having pairs of students study for a quiz together and receive their average grade score. Next, she has students work together in peer tutoring dyads; she arranges it so that all students serve as both tutors and tutees.

She also teaches her students how to develop specific collaborative skills. For example, she has them discuss the need to encourage all group members to participate. They then brainstorm, role play, and practice ways to encourage others to contribute to the group. Another lesson focuses on the need for and use of quiet voices.

After several lessons on collaborative skills, Ms. Johnson asks students to perform a science experiment and write a report while working in cooperative learning groups. She tells them that they will be working cooperatively and asks, "How will I know if you're cooperating? What will I see and hear if you're working cooperatively?" The students' responses are listed on the blackboard and discussed.

To ensure the participation of all students, Ms. Johnson assigns shy or quiet students like Luis to groups with supportive peers. To make sure that all students contribute to and understand the group's project, she tells the class that she will randomly select group members to explain parts of the group's report. To help groups work efficiently, she assigns one student in each group to be the group's recorder and another student to make sure that each member of the group participates.

As the groups work on their projects, Ms. Johnson monitors their progress and observes their use of collaborative skills. When students demonstrate such skills, she acknowledges them. Periodically, she praises a group to the whole class and asks groups to model various collaborative skills. She also asks each group to keep a record of the skills they use. At the end of the class session, she and the students discuss and reflect on their collaborative skills.

Why do you think Ms. Johnson wanted her students to use cooperative learning? What problems did she encounter? How did she attempt to solve these problems? What other problems might teachers encounter in using cooperative learning? How can teachers address these problems? What have been your experiences in using cooperative learning as a teacher? As a student?

One evaluation system that gives students strong incentives to help others learn the material is the *group average.* Individual grades on a quiz or part of a project are averaged into a group grade. Each group member receives the average grade. For example, each group member could be given an individualized test tailored to his or her abilities in math. Thus, one student might be tested on addition, another on subtraction, and another on multiplication. During the week, group members help each other master their assignments and prepare for their tests. At first, some students may resist the concept of group grades. You can minimize this resistance by assuring students that group members will be assigned only work that they can complete. Inform students that if all group members do their best and help others, they will all receive high grades. You can modify the group average by using improvement scores. In this system, students are assigned

You can obtain information and resources about cooperative learning by visiting the website Cooperative Learning: Response to Diversity (www.cde.ca.gov/iasa/cooplrng.html, 916-657-3837).

a base score, depending on their prior performance, and earn points for their teams by improving on their base score.

In addition to evaluating the group for mastery of content, you can evaluate each student in terms of effort and ability to work together by giving each team member a percentage grade representing his or her effort and ability to work with others. Since team members will have a clearer idea of the contribution of each group member, the group can determine the effort and teamwork grade for each member. However, since students may feel uncomfortable rating their peers, you should be careful about requiring an effort grade. Kagan (1992) has developed several forms that you can use to obtain evaluations from teammates.

SUMMARY

This chapter offered guidelines for differentiating large- and small-group instruction to meet the unique learning needs of students. As you review the questions posed in this chapter, remember the following points.

How Can I Adapt Large-Group Instruction for Students?

You can have students work collaboratively, use presentation software or an overhead, encourage students to ask questions, help students take notes, teach note-taking skills and strategies, foster students' listening skills, gain and maintain students' attention, and motivate students.

How Can I Use Effective Instruction?

To teach effectively, you should establish the lesson's purpose; review prerequisite skills; give clear directions, explanations, and relevant examples; provide time for active and guided practice; promote active responding and check for comprehension; give prompt and specific feedback; offer time for independent activities; and summarize main points and evaluate mastery.

How Can I Successfully Use Cooperative Learning Arrangements with Students?

You can select an appropriate cooperative learning format, establish guidelines for working collaboratively, form heterogeneous cooperative groups, arrange the classroom for cooperative learning, develop students' cooperative skills, and evaluate cooperative learning.

What Would You Do in Today's Diverse Classroom?

As a teacher in an inclusion classroom, you encounter the following situations:

◆ Although your students claim that they are studying, they are doing poorly on tests. You ask them how they study for tests. They tell you that they study notes from class. You examine their notes and notice that they are often incomplete and focused on material that you do not consider relevant.

◆ You have been using cooperative learning, and several families have started to complain. They feel that their children did the work for the group and received a poor grade because others did not do their share.

◆ Several of your students are not completing their homework. When you ask for an explanation, students say, "You give too much homework; I have other responsibilities," "I forget what the assignment was," and "It's too noisy at home." Since you consider homework as part of their grades, these students are in danger of failing.

1. What problem(s) are you encountering in each situation?

2. What would you do to address each situation?

3. What resources and support would you need in using strategies to address each situation?

CHAPTER
10

DIFFERENTIATING READING, WRITING, AND SPELLING INSTRUCTION

Ms. Pike

Ms. Pike's students slowly begin to arrive at school. When they enter her class, they start working on either independent reading or journal writing. After about 20 minutes, all her students have arrived, and the class discusses such topics as important school, community, or current events or a review of a new movie or book.

Following the class meeting, Ms. Pike shares a book with students. She is reading the African folktale Why Mosquitoes Buzz in People's Ears, *which is part of a theme on understanding people from diverse cultures. Before reading the story, Ms. Pike discusses the African reverence for nature and the use of animals in folktales to represent human traits. Also, as part of the theme, students are reading and writing about female and male scientists and mathematicians from diverse ethnic backgrounds and examining historical events from the perspectives of different groups.*

As a follow-up activity to her lesson on folktales, Ms. Pike asks her students to work in groups to write and illustrate a short folktale using animals as the characters in the story, to be read to or performed for the class in a week. Before assigning students to groups, Ms. Pike conducts a lesson and discussion on folktales. While the students work, Ms. Pike circulates around the room to observe and meet with individual students and groups. One group conference focuses on why that group selected a camel to be their main character; another conference deals with creating a story line.

The group activity is followed by individualized reading. Students independently read books about individuals from various cultures that they have selected from a list prepared and previewed by Ms. Pike and the class. Students who select the same book to read are grouped together, and meet with Ms. Pike to discuss the book and work on group projects. Occasionally, Ms. Pike teaches a mini-lesson to help students learn a sound–symbol correspondence, blending, and a specific reading or writing strategy.

The students and Ms. Pike also read these books during the afternoon sustained silent reading period. After working in their literature groups, students react to what they have read by making entries in their reading journals. Ms. Pike periodically collects and reads the journals and responds to students' entries via written comments or individual conferences.

What strategies is Ms. Pike using to promote the literacy skills of her students? After reading this chapter, you should be able to answer this as well as the following questions.

◇ How can I help students learn to read?
◇ How can I help students learn to write?
◇ How can I help students learn to spell?

I n addition to differentiating instruction for diverse learners and teaching that involves the use of large and small groups, teachers like Ms. Pike also need to help students develop literacy skills. This chapter offers guidelines for differentiating instruction so that you can help your students learn to read, write, and spell.

How Can I Help Students Learn to Read?

Motivate Students to Read

Informational

Sanacore (1999) offers guidelines for reading aloud to students.

Since students develop their reading proficiency by reading regularly, it is important to motivate *all students* to read (Holloway, 1999). You can do this by promoting a positive attitude toward reading by modeling the enjoyment of reading and demonstrating that reading can be fun; using reading materials that are interesting to students and related to their lives; reading aloud to students; giving students a range of reading choices; creating a relaxed learning and reading environment; playing recordings of students' favorite stories; giving students a variety of ways to express their reactions to material they have read; and acknowledging students' attempts to read, as well as their progress (Arthur & Burch, 1993; Carbo, 1997; Sanacore, 1999). Like Ms. Pike did in the chapter-opening vignette, you can motivate students to read by selecting reading selections that relate to students' experiences and cultures.

Use a Balanced Approach

Most reading programs are based on a particular teaching philosophy, and therefore they differ in their instructional approach. In planning reading instruction for your students, select approaches that are appropriate to your students' individual learning needs and characteristics. In addition, examine the impact of these approaches on your students' rate of learning and emotional responsiveness. Some students may benefit from one specific reading approach. Most students, however, perform best if you use a balanced approach that combines elements of the various approaches described in the following sections.

Phonetic Approaches

Phonetic reading approaches teach students to recognize and understand the phonological features of language and of individual words. These approaches also teach students strategies for decoding or "sounding out" new and unknown words. Therefore, phonics instruction is geared to teaching students the relationship between letters, and it focuses on helping students learn to blend and segment sounds within words. Teachers using a phonetic approach to reading start with relatively easy words and progress to more difficult words as students develop *phonemic awareness,* the understanding that words are made up of different sounds (Kameenui, 1996).

Phonetic approaches are categorized as synthetic or analytic. The *synthetic* approach develops phonetic skills by teaching students the specific symbol–grapheme (e.g., *g*) to sound–phoneme (e.g., *guh*) correspondence rules. Once students learn the sound and symbol rules, they are taught to synthesize the sounds into words through blending. To use this approach, you would:

1. Introduce letters and their names to students.
2. Teach students the sounds associated with each letter.
3. Give students opportunities to develop automaticity in grapheme–phoneme relationships.
4. Teach students how to blend sounds into words.
5. Offer activities that allow students to apply their skills to unknown words.

In the *analytic* approach to phonetics instruction, grapheme–phoneme correspondence is learned by teaching students to analyze words. These word analysis skills help

INFORMATIONAL

Chard and Dickson (1999), Edelen-Smith (1997), Mathes et al. (1999), and Smith (1998) present assessment techniques, training programs, and teaching strategies to assess and promote the phonemic awareness of students.

Phonics instruction teaches students the relationship between letters and sound.

students understand that letters within words sound alike and are written the same way. When using the analytic approach, do the following:

1. Give students a list of words that have a common phonic element.
2. Question students about the similarities and differences in the look and sound of the words.
3. Help students determine the common phonetic patterns in the words.
4. Have students state the rule concerning the phonetic pattern.

Another analytic method uses a *linguistic* approach to teach reading. Students learn to read and spell words within word families that have the same phonetic patterns. Through repeated presentations of these word families, students learn the rules of sound–symbol correspondence. For example, the *at* family would be introduced together, using such words as *bat, cat, fat, hat, rat,* and *sat.*

Phonetic approaches may present some problems for students with disabilities. Students taught using these phonetic approaches tend not to guess words that do not follow phonetic rules; read more regular words than irregular words; and tend to pronounce words based on graphic and phonetic cues rather than semantic and syntactic cues. Students may have difficulty in identifying words that do not follow phonetic patterns and in isolating and blending sounds, so you may need to supplement phonetics instruction with other approaches.

Whole Word Approaches

Whole word approaches help students make the link between whole words and their oral counterparts. In the whole word approach, meaning also is emphasized. New words are taught within sentences and passages or in isolation. Students taught through whole word methods tend to attempt to read unfamiliar words, use context cues rather than graphic cues, and substitute familiar words for new words. You can modify whole word approaches by decreasing the number of words to be learned, using flash cards that contain the word and a pictorial of the word, offering spaced practice sessions, providing opportunities for overlearning, and delivering more frequent reinforcement (Harris & Sipay, 1985).

Basal Readers   Whole word approaches often employ basal readers. These readers are designed to teach students to recognize, read, and define the common words that appear in the basal series. More complex words are introduced gradually as students progress through the series. Basal readers cover a wide range of reading levels, usually from readiness kindergarten materials to eighth grade, allowing students to work at different levels in the general education classroom. Each level may have several books that correspond to specific skills within the skill sequence on which the series is based. The skill sequence usually follows a continuum of reading readiness, word identification, vocabulary, comprehension, and study skills. As students develop their skills, phonics and word analysis skills are taught to increase word recognition skills.

In the basal series, vocabulary and new skills are introduced in a gradual, logical sequence. You can guide groups of students through a story using *directed reading,* which includes three components: preparation, reading, and discussion (Harris & Sipay, 1985). During the preparation stage, you stimulate students' interest and present new words and concepts from the selection. Next, the students read the selection silently after discussing the story's title and the accompanying pictures. Then the group discusses the story. Afterward, each member takes a turn reading the story aloud. Students then practice skills and words introduced in the story through some type of follow-up activity.

INFORMATIONAL

Chard and Osborn (1999) offer guidelines and activities for using a phonetic approach to teach letter–sound correspondence, regular and irregular words, story reading, and word analysis.

INFORMATIONAL

Lebzelter and Nowacek (1999) describe two learning strategies, DISSECT and WIST (Word Identification Strategy Training), that you can teach students to help them decode words.

INFORMATIONAL

Bryant, Ugel, Thompson, and Hamff (1999) offer activities for teaching word identification, vocabulary, and comprehension.

Language Experience Approach

A *language experience* approach is based on the belief that what students think about, they can talk about; what students can say, they can write or have someone write for them; and what students can write, they can read. Language experience approaches are highly individualized; they use the students' interests, hobbies, and experiences as the basis for creating reading materials that are highly motivating and foster creativity.

To implement a language experience approach, provide students with guided and varied experiences and encourage them to share their thoughts, ideas, and feelings through artwork, speaking, and writing. Initially, students share their reactions and experiences by dictating stories to you; these stories form the core of the reading program. You guide the formation of the story, helping students make revisions and teaching them about grammar, punctuation, spelling, syntax, and vocabulary. As students develop a sufficient number of words that they can recognize, easy books are introduced. They also are encouraged to write and then read their own stories, poems, and plays.

Whole Language Approach

One philosophy for promoting literacy that may be particularly appropriate for *all students,* including those from culturally and linguistically diverse backgrounds, is *whole language* (Lopez-Reyna, 1996). A whole language approach uses students' natural language and experiences in and out of school to immerse *all students* in a supportive, stimulating, natural learning environment that promotes their literacy. In a whole language approach, reading, writing, listening, speaking, and thinking are integrated into each lesson and activity, and learning is viewed as proceeding from the whole to the part rather than the reverse. Rather than teaching students specific skills, whole language programs teach strategies that help them control their learning and the books and stories they read.

In a whole language approach, the emphasis is on reading for meaning rather than learning decoding skills in isolation (Dudley-Marling & Fine, 1997). Students are motivated to read and improve their reading by reading authentic, relevant, and functional materials that make sense to them and relate to their experiences. Students are encouraged to take risks, and errors are viewed as attempts to learn and make sense of the world. Rather than using basal readers or skill development programs, whole language reading materials are high-quality fiction and nonfiction books and resources that the students need or want to read. Thus, the whole language classroom is stocked with books that vary in difficulty and content, such as novels, short stories, dictionaries, and encyclopedias.

The whole language curriculum is developmental, and is often organized around themes and units that increase language and reading skills. Teachers and students develop and structure curricula to offer teaching experiences related to real problems and ideas. At first, students read meaningful, predictable whole texts. Next, they use the familiar words in these texts to learn new words and phrases. While learning to read, students also learn to write. They are encouraged to write about their experiences by composing letters, maintaining journals, making lists, labeling objects in the classroom, and keeping records.

In the whole language approach, you do several things to promote students' literacy. This includes motivating students, structuring the environment, evaluating progress, supplying and exposing students to relevant and meaningful materials and experiences, serving as a model for students, involving them in learning, and working with students to create a community of learners. When using a whole language approach, you do not teach

Teachers can promote students' reading skills by helping them select interesting and appropriate reading materials.

phonetic, spelling, and writing skills directly. Instead, you teach these skills in the context of numerous authentic reading and writing activities. Thus, rather than teaching students phonics and writing skills in a strict sequence, you encourage students to examine and discover the textual features of words and the grammatical features of written text as they read and write every day.

The role of phonics and the teaching of spelling, punctuation, and grammar using a whole language approach have been debated, and some educators have raised concerns about the efficacy of this approach. These critics argue that a whole language approach fails to provide students, particularly those who are having trouble reading, with systematic teaching focused on learning the phonetic and writing skills necessary to be successful readers and writers. They also note that students with reading difficulties need more intensive phonics teaching to promote phonemic awareness before reading for meaning can proceed. In response to this criticism, some teachers using a whole language approach are incorporating phonics instruction into their curriculum to help students understand the text they read (Drecktrah & Chiang, 1997; Morgan, 1995; Steinberg, 1998).

Components of Whole Language Programs   Butler (n.d.) described the components of a balanced whole language program. These components are discussed here.

Reading Aloud to Students.   Read quality literature from a variety of genres to introduce students to the enjoyment and excitement of reading. Reading to students also allows you to model good oral reading, promote vocabulary development and good reading habits, and offer background knowledge in such areas as story structure and content. When reading to students, you can introduce the selection by discussing the title and cover of the book and by asking students to make predictions about the book. You also can introduce the author and illustrator and talk with students about other books they have read by the author or on a similar topic or theme.

As you read to students, you can promote their interest and understanding by using animated expressions, displaying illustrations so that *all students* can see and react to them, relating the book to students' experiences, discussing the book in a lively, inviting, and thought-provoking manner, and offering students a variety of learning activities (i.e., writing, drama, art) to respond to and express their feelings about the selection (Hoffman, Roser, & Battle, 1993).

Shared Book Reading.   You and your students sit close together and share in reading a variety of materials. You read a new or familiar story; students react to it through arts and crafts, drama, reading, or writing; and students then reread the story on their own. Big books with large print and pictures are particularly appropriate for shared book reading, as they allow you to display the words the students are reading.

Sustained Silent Reading.   During sustained silent reading, also referred to as *Drop Everything and Read (DEAR) time,* you, your students, and other members of the class read self-selected materials for an extended period of time. Typically, the rules for sustained silent reading are: (1) read silently, (2) do not interrupt others, and (3) do not change books.

INFORMATIONAL

Alber (1996) offers guidelines for creating interest, holding students accountable, and preventing disruptions during sustained silent reading.

Guided Reading.   Work with students in small groups to explore books and ideas. In addition, demonstrate reading strategies and help students learn how to use them. For example, you may demonstrate and discuss with students successful strategies for selecting a book, using context clues, or reading with a purpose.

An important component of guided reading is the *group reading conference,* a time when groups discuss books or selections that they have been reading independently. Structure the conference by asking open-ended questions that require students to think, express an opinion, and relate the selection to their own experiences. For example, you can use *literature circles* or *literature discussion groups,* small groups of students who work collaboratively to share their reactions to and discuss various aspects of books that all group members have decided to read (Goforth, 1998).

INFORMATIONAL

Keefe (1995a) offers guidelines for using literature circles to create a community of readers in the classroom.

Literature Response Journals.   *Literature response journals* can be used as a follow-up to sustained silent reading periods or literature discussion groups. In these journals, students describe their reactions to and thoughts about the material they have been reading, as well as any questions they have. Students also are encouraged to write about their opinions and emotional responses to the book, relate the book to their own experiences, and make predictions about the book and its characters. You can read students' journals and offer comments that encourage students to redirect, expand, and refocus their reactions and questions.

One type of literature response journal is the character study journal, in which students make entries related to an interesting character (Galda, Cullinan, & Strickland, 1997). While reading the selection, students react to and write about their character, including the character's dilemmas, feelings, and responses.

Individualized Reading.   Students learn to control their literacy by reading selections addressing their individual needs and teaching levels. They keep records of books read and their responses to these books and receive assistance from their teachers.

Language Experience.   Promote students' literacy by using students' language generated during both planned experiences organized by you and spontaneous experiences that happen during the day. Students' responses to these experiences are recorded and presented to them in a written format.

Children's Writing.   Students learn the writing process and write in a variety of genres. Because of the importance of writing, it is discussed in greater detail later in this chapter.

Modeled Writing.   You model writing, providing students with the opportunity to observe composing and other elements of the writing process.

Opportunities for Sharing.   Students share their products with others through such activities as the writers' circle, the author's chair, or literature response groups, which are discussed later in this chapter.

INFORMATIONAL

Pike et al. (1994) offer guidelines and examples of thematic units that integrate reading, writing, and content area learning, as well as suggestions for organizing the classroom to promote the use of a whole language approach.

Integrating Reading and Writing Throughout the Curriculum.   Give students opportunities to read and write across the curriculum. You also can use *thematic units*, which integrate reading, writing, speaking, and listening to help students master content area material. When using thematic units, you typically structure and connect a series of reading, writing, and content area learning activities based on a particular theme (Englert, Mariage, Garmon, & Tarrant, 1998). Lessons involving reading, writing, speaking, and listening related to the selected theme are then taught across the various content areas.

Whole Language Curricular Adaptations   When using a whole language approach, you also can use a variety of teaching strategies and curricular adaptations. Some of these are discussed here.

Environmental Print.   Environmental print—that is, materials that are found in students' natural environments—can help students who are learning English read and give meaning to printed symbols. Environmental print can be used to promote literacy through role plays, journals, and copying. You also can establish learning centers that allow students to read magazines and newspapers written at different levels of difficulty, as well as signs, labels, posters, calendars, advertisements, menus, and wall charts.

**SET YOUR SITES**

The Story Arts website (www.storyarts.org) offers folktales and stories that can be used in the classroom, as well as resources and strategies that help teachers and students to use storytelling.

Storytelling.   Storytelling can help students construct meaning from text, promote listening comprehension and vocabulary skills, and motivate students to read. While *all students* benefit from storytelling, it is a particularly good teaching technique for students whose cultures have an oral tradition and for those who are learning a second language (Maldonado-Colon, 1991).

INFORMATIONAL

Bligh (1996) and Perry (1997) offer guidelines for using picture books and provide a bibliography of recommended picture books.

Picture Books.   You can motivate students to read and write through the use of *picture books,* short books that use pictures and illustrations to enhance the reader's understanding of the meaning and content of the story (Bligh, 1996). Picture books also can help students learn a wide range of reading strategies, such as prediction and using context and syntactical cues (Bligh, 1996).

Frames.   Frames outline important components of stories and provide cues to help students understand and write in a variety of genres. One effective frame is the *circle story,* which is developed by plotting a story's important components in a clockwise sequence on a circle diagram.

Story Grammars.   Story grammars are outlines of the ways stories are organized. They often involve identifying and articulating a reading selection's main characters, story lines, conflicts, and ending (Dimino, Taylor, & Gersten, 1995). Story grammars

✓ REFLECTING ON YOUR PRACTICES

Using a Whole Language Approach

You can examine your use of a whole language approach by considering the following questions:

◈ Do you maintain a classroom environment that is print rich through the use of charts, mobiles, logos, signs, flash cards, and posters, as well as the labeling of objects and areas in the classroom?

◈ How do you create opportunities for students to interact verbally with their peers, talk about their ideas and reactions, and participate actively in lessons?

◈ How often and in what ways do you give students access to high-quality literature?

◈ What techniques do you use to give students choices concerning the books they read, the topics they write about, and the projects they complete?

◈ Are reading and writing activities focused on students' experiences, interests, and background knowledge?

◈ Do you model reading and writing by demonstrating and sharing your ongoing efforts in these areas?

◈ Are centers for reading, writing, speaking, listening, and content area learning available to students?

◈ Do you display work on bulletin boards, blackboards, doors, and walls that has been written and read by students?

◈ How do you create a comfortable physical environment for learning?

◈ Do you maintain a classroom library of books and materials related to students' interests and cultural backgrounds?

◈ Is your classroom stocked with books that contain repetitive language, an interesting story line, pictures related to the text, and a predictable structure?

◈ Do students maintain personal and dialogue journals and logs of books read, and do they make and read invitations, cards, and recipes?

How would you rate your use of a whole language approach? ( ) Excellent ( ) Good ( ) Needs Improvement ( ) Needs Much Improvement

What steps could you adopt to improve your use of a whole language approach?

Sources: Franklin (1992), Goodman (1986), Hollingsworth and Reutzel (1988), Pike et al. (1994), and Ruiz, Rueda, Figueroa, and Boothroyd (1995).

---

motivate students to read and allow students to expand on their experiences by generating stories.

Choral Reading.   Choral reading involves you and your students reading poems, predictable books, stories, and student-authored materials together (Englert et al., 1998). It can promote students' fluency, vocabulary development, diction, self-confidence, and motivation to read, and can help establish the relationship between oral and written language.

Drama.   Through drama, students can act out and retell stories through miming, gestures, role playing, and the use of props.

Recursive Encounters.   Students practice language and reading through repetition of themes, including recursive experiences, so that they are repeatedly exposed to poems, songs, riddles, discussions, and stories. For example, repeated reading of a book or a selection can increase students' fluency and aid them in learning the rhythm, volume, tone, and language patterns of their second language.

Use Remedial Reading Programs and Strategies

Because many students, particularly those with disabilities, have difficulty reading, you may need to supplement your reading instruction with some of the remedial reading programs and strategies described below.

Cooperative Integrated Reading and Composition

INFORMATIONAL

Calderon, Hertz-Lazarowitz, and Tinajero (1991) adapted the CIRC model for use in multiethnic and bilingual classrooms.

Cooperative Integrated Reading and Composition (CIRC) is a program designed to teach reading and writing skills that uses basal readers, direct instruction, integrated reading and writing, and cooperative learning (Slavin, Madden, & Stevens, 1990). Initially, you assign students to dyads within reading groups. These dyads are then placed in teams made up of dyads from two other reading groups. You teach with dyads, groups, and individuals directly, and meet daily to lead reading groups while students complete assigned activities by working in dyads or with the whole team. The teaching sequence usually includes the following elements:

Teacher-directed, basal-related tasks. Introduce and discuss a story from the students' regular basal readers. Structured activities are used to set the purpose of the reading, introduce new vocabulary, review vocabulary from prior lessons, and encourage students to discuss the story.

Partner reading. Students work in their dyads, read the story silently, and then read it aloud, alternating readers. When one student is reading, the other student is listening and offering feedback when errors are made.

Story structure and story-related writing. Halfway through the story, students are asked to respond to various story-structure tasks and comprehension questions, such as identifying main characters, describing the setting and the problem, and making predictions about the story. After reading the story, students work as a team to respond to comprehension questions and produce a written product on a topic relating to it.

Words out loud. Students work in dyads or with the whole team to learn to read and define a list of new or difficult words from the story.

Word meaning. Students look up the definitions of vocabulary words from the story, record paraphrased definitions in their notebooks, and write sentences that illustrate the meaning of the words.

Story retelling. After reading and discussing the story in their groups, students retell the main points of the story, which are checked by their partners, who have a list of essential story elements.

Spelling. Students test each other on a list of spelling words until all words are spelled correctly.

Partner checking. Partners sign an assignment sheet to indicate that their peer has completed the task(s) successfully.

Tests. Students take tests to assess their mastery of the reading material.

Direct instruction in reading comprehension. One day each week, you teach students directly on specific reading comprehension skills such as identifying the main idea, predicting, and summarizing.

Integrated language arts and writing. Offer students direct instruction on writing strategies and specific language arts objectives, including the use of a process approach to teach writing.

Independent home reading. Students select a trade book and read it every night for at least 20 minutes. Family members verify students' home reading by initialing a form that is sent to teachers.

Team rewards. Teams are rewarded at the end of the week based on the whole team's performance on quizzes, compositions, and other related activities (Slavin et al., 1990).

Reading Recovery

Reading Recovery is an individualized teaching program designed to help students develop their reading and phonics skills through the use of meaningful reading activities (Clay, 1985; Dudley-Marling & Murphy, 1997). In addition to participating in reading activities in their classrooms, students in Reading Recovery programs receive 30 minutes of individualized instruction each day from a specially trained teacher who teaches letters and sounds within the context of reading text (Stahl, 1998). Students use a variety of activities to learn to read words that occur often, read aloud from familiar and new books, write responses to the material they have just read, and learn a variety of word identification and text comprehension strategies. Teachers monitor their progress, offer feedback, teach specific skills, and use appropriate teaching strategies.

Multisensory Strategies

Multisensory strategies teach letters and words using combinations of visual, auditory, kinesthetic, and tactile modalities. Several multisensory strategies are available, including writing the word in chalk, spelling the word after saying it, tracing three-dimensional letters with students' eyes shut, and tracing letters on the students' backs.

Fernald Method   A multisensory, whole word, language experience strategy that was developed for students with learning problems is the *Fernald method,* which involves four steps: tracing, writing without tracing, recognition in print, and word analysis (Fernald, 1943; Stahl, 1998).

Orton-Gillingham-Stillman Strategy   The *Orton-Gillingham-Stillman strategy* uses a multisensory synthetic phonics approach to teaching reading (Rooney, 1995; Stahl, 1998). At first, students are taught letter–sound symbol correspondence by viewing the letters, hearing the sounds they make, linking the letters to their sounds, and writing the letters. Once 10 letters (*a, b, f, h, i, j, k, m, p, t*) are mastered, blending of the sounds is taught. Blending is followed by story writing, syllabification, dictionary skills, and instruction in spelling rules.

SET YOUR SITES

You can obtain additional information about the Orton-Gillingham-Stillman strategy from the International Dyslexia Association (www.interdys.org, 410-296-0232).

Use Programmed Reading Materials

A highly structured approach to the teaching of reading involves *programmed materials,* which present information in small, discrete steps that follow a planned sequence of skills. Each skill within the sequence is presented so that students can review, practice, overlearn, and apply the skill while receiving feedback. Errors are corrected before students can proceed to the next skill. You follow the presentation sequence by adhering to the directions outlined in the manual.

Use Cuing Strategies

Cuing can help students read difficult or unfamiliar words. Cues can be divided into two types: teacher cues and student cues. *Teacher cues* are used by the teacher to help a student make the correct response and include language, visual, and physical cues. *Student cues* are used by students to determine the correct response and include configuration and context cues.

Language Cues

Language cues use the students' language skills as the basis for triggering the correct response. For example, if a student had difficulty decoding the word *store,* a vocabulary cue such as "You buy things at a . . ." might elicit the correct response. Other language-oriented cues include rhyming ("it rhymes with *door*"), word associations ("Choo! Choo!" to cue the word *train*), analogies ("Light is to day as dark is to night"), and antonyms ("It's the opposite of *hot*" for *cold*).

Visual Cues

Visual cues can help students focus on certain aspects of words. For instance, attention to medial vowels can be fostered visually by color cues (make the medial vowel a different color than the other letters), size cues (enlarge the medial vowel while keeping the other letters constant, such as *cAt*), or graphic cues (accentuate the medial vowel by underlining or circling it, such as *c<u>a</u>t*). Visual cues are valuable in correcting reversals. For example, difficulty discriminating *b* and *d* can be reduced by cuing one of the letters graphically.

Picture cuing, in which pictures depicting words are drawn above words that are difficult to read, is especially helpful in reading nouns and prepositions. For example, if a student typically reads the word *saw* as *was,* a drawing of a saw above the word *saw* would help the student make this distinction. Finally, visual cues, such as pointing to an object in the classroom or showing a numeral, can be used to prompt the reading of words that correspond, respectively, to objects in the classroom and number words.

Physical Cues

Physical cues are most effective in communicating words or concepts with perceptually salient features. These words can be cued by miming the distinct qualities or actions associated with them. In addition to miming, you can use finger spelling as a cue to elicit a correct response.

Configuration Cues

Configuration cues relate to the outline of the word and can be useful when there are noticeable differences in the shape and length of words. Students use configuration cues when they note the length of the words and the size and graphic characteristics of the letters. While research on the effectiveness of configuration cues is inconclusive, it appears that they are most effective when used with context and other cuing strategies.

Context Cues

The context in which the word is presented can provide useful cues for determining the pronunciation of unknown words. Potential context cues that students can use include syntactic, semantic, and picture features of the text. Context cues are best suited for words that occur near the middle or the end of the sentence.

REFLECTIVE

How could you use cues to help students who have difficulty reading the following words? *laugh, bee, floor, eat, yellow, jump, seven, quiet, why, small.*

Thompson and Taymans (1994) developed the FIGURE learning strategy to teach students how to use context cues. The steps in this strategy are:

*F*inish the sentence without the word.
*I*nspect the picture.
*G*lance at the beginning of the word.
*U*se your brain to think of a word that makes sense.
*R*eread the sentence with the word.
*E*mploy another word if you need to (p. 21).

Syntactic Cues   Syntactic cues deal with the grammatical structure of the sentence containing the word. The syntactic structure of English dictates that only certain words can fit into a particular part of a sentence or statement. Thus, students can be taught to use parts of sentences to figure out difficult words.

Semantic Cues   Semantic cues, available by examining the meanings of the text, can help students improve their word identification skills. Semantic cues can be taught by having students closely examine the sentence containing the unknown word, as well as the entire reading selection in which the word appears. These cues are particularly appropriate when students are learning to read abstract words.

Pictorial Cues   Many reading passages contain illustrations to promote comprehension and motivation. These pictorial cues also can help students recognize new words by helping them establish the context of the story. To maximize the effects of illustrations on word recognition, the students' attention can be directed to the word and the illustration.

Involve Families

The active involvement of families also can help students learn to read (Saint-Laurent, Giasson, & Couture, 1997). Family members can serve as role models by reading a variety of materials, showing their children that reading is useful, fun, interesting, and informative. Family members also can promote reading development by giving their children access to interesting and appropriate books; using rhyming, word games, and poetry to help students hear the sounds within words; reading with their children and asking them to respond to who, what, where, when, and why questions; and having children retell stories.

HOW CAN I HELP STUDENTS LEARN TO WRITE?

Make Writing Meaningful and an Integral Part of the Curriculum

One content area directly related to reading that occurs throughout the school curriculum is written language. However, rather than assume that students are improving their writing skills by writing during reading and content area assignments, the teaching of written expression should be an ongoing part of the students' instructional program.

INFORMATIONAL

Salembier and Cheng (1997) have developed SCUBA-DIVE, a learning strategy that helps students use six different cues to decode unfamiliar words.

REFLECTIVE

What cuing strategies do you use when you encounter a word you don't know? When working with students?

SET YOUR SITES

You can obtain information, research, and resources about the teaching of reading from the International Reading Association (www.reading.org, 302-731-1600).

Family members can promote literacy by showing that reading is fun, interesting, and informative.

SET YOUR SITES

The National Council of Teachers of English (www.ncte.org, 800-369-6283) offers information and resources that can assist you in teaching reading and writing.

Instruction in writing should be meaningful and should allow students to write for social, creative, recreational, and occupational purposes, as well as to express opinions and share information. Students also should be allowed to perform meaningful writing tasks that have an authentic audience, are of interest to them, and serve a real purpose. Other ways to make writing meaningful include allowing students to select the topics they will write about, teaching students to set goals for their writing, having them share their work with others, allowing them to work on the same product for a long period of time, and integrating writing into other teaching and social activities (Graham, 1992).

Use Journals

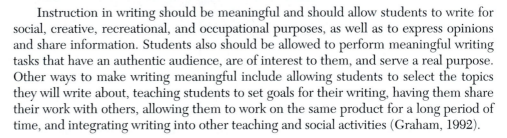

INFORMATIONAL

Kluwin (1996) describes how to use dialogue journals to encourage students working in dyads to write to each other.

Journals in which students write about their personal reactions to events and their experiences are a good way to make writing meaningful (Rose, 1999). For example, students can maintain a *personal journal* or a *dialogue journal.* In the personal journal, students write about their own lives, including such topics as family members, friends, feelings, hobbies, and personal events. The dialogue journal, in which you and your students write confidential responses to each other, can motivate students to write while promoting a good relationship between you and your students. As students become comfortable with writing in their journals, you can probe the meaning of their statements and seek more in-depth responses by using probing questions, making comments, sharing observations, responding to students' questions, and asking for more detail. Students also can be asked to maintain *simulated journals* in which they take and write about the perspective of another person (Pike et al., 1994), or a *buddy journal* in which they maintain a written conversation with one of their classmates (Bromley, 1998).

Students also can be encouraged to write by linking writing to their culture and experiences. All students can be given opportunities to write poems, essays, and short stories that express their ideas and cultural experiences. As they write about their cultural backgrounds, students also learn about and understand the cultural experiences of their classmates.

Use a Process-Oriented Approach to Writing Instruction

Although there is considerable overlap in the stages of writing, many researchers advocate a process-oriented approach in teaching writing (Calkins, 1994; Graves, 1994). Research indicates that when this approach is combined with strategy instruction and computer-supported writing, students with disabilities improve their writing (Graves, 1995; Hunt-Berg, Rankin, & Beukelman, 1994).

A process-oriented approach to writing, integral to whole language instruction, is viewed as consisting of four holistic subprocesses: planning/prewriting, drafting, revising and editing, and publishing. These subprocesses lead to writing activities that have a real purpose and a real audience. The subprocesses and writing strategies, together with computer-supported writing applications, are presented in the following sections.

Planning/Prewriting

During the planning or prewriting phase, students determine the purpose of the writing task, generate and group ideas, identify the audience, and plan how to present the content to the reader. Prewriting activities to help students plan their writing are discussed here.

Idea Generation   Allowing students to work on topics they themselves have chosen can foster idea generation because students will probably choose topics familiar to them. When students select their own topics and make decisions about content, they develop a sense of ownership toward writing. Multimedia, computer software, simulations, trips, interviews, pictorial representations, music, sensory explorations, creative imagery, speakers, demonstrations, interviews, brainstorming, and researching can be used to help students select topics.

Because writing is linked to reading, students can obtain ideas for writing from reading. Reading and discussing passages before writing can help students select topics and add details to their writing. Younger students can write stories by changing the characters or action in a story they have just listened to or read. Predictable books can stimulate such story writing since they often follow repetitive story lines. Students also can be given books containing pictures that tell a story and asked to write the text that tells the story.

Story Starters/Enders   Some students may benefit from the use of *story starters* or *story enders,* in which they are given the first or last paragraph of a story, or the initial or ending sentence of a paragraph, and asked to complete the story or paragraph. Music, pictures, and videos also can prompt students to write by serving as starters. Similarly, you can use story frames in which students complete blank frames by writing in information related to the frame. In addition, you can use paragraph organization worksheets and paragraph draft outlines to help students plan and organize their writing.

Outlines and Semantic Maps   Ideas generated by students can be organized by helping students to develop an *outline,* which includes the main topics and supporting ideas grouped together, as well as the order in which the ideas will be presented. Students also can be taught to organize their writing by developing a *semantic map,* a diagram or map of the key ideas and words that make up the topic. Mapping allows students to identify main points and to plan the interrelationship between them. In introducing semantic maps, you can ask questions that help students understand their own decision-making processes and learn from others. Software programs such as

INFORMATIONAL

Ellis (1997) outlines the steps in POWER, a learning strategy that can be used to prompt students to use a writing process approach.

INFORMATIONAL

Graham (1992) describes a strategy to help students establish writing goals by teaching them to use a planning strategy called *PLANS.*

Inspiration, Semantic Mapper, and Semnet can help students develop outlines and semantic maps (Raskind & Higgins, 1998). A sample writing semantic map is presented in Figure 10.1.

Drafting

In the drafting phase, writers transform their ideas and plans into sentences and paragraphs. They attempt to establish a relationship and an order between sentences and paragraphs and make appropriate word choices. While it should not be emphasized in the drafting stage, some attention to the rules of grammar, punctuation, and spelling may be appropriate. In a writing process approach, these skills are taught using the students' own writing through individualized or group lessons. During this step, you encourage students to plan their draft and provide time to revise it.

You can help students prepare the draft in several ways. These include asking questions to help students explore alternatives, offering suggestions, encouraging students, and focusing attention on the writing task. You also can give students self-evaluation questions and encourage them to use the self-evaluation guidelines throughout the writing process. Sample self-evaluation questions for writing stories are presented in Figure 10.2.

FIGURE 10.1   A sample writing semantic map.

Does each paragraph start with a topic sentence?
Does each paragraph include relevant supporting information?
Are the paragraphs organized appropriately?
Are the main characters introduced and described?
Is the location of the story presented and described?
Is the time of the story introduced?
Does the story include a starting event?
Does the story include the main characters' reactions to the starting event?
Does the story present actions to resolve conflicts?
Does the story have an ending?
Does the ending include the outcome's effects on the main characters?

FIGURE 10.2   Sample writing self-evaluation questions.

Editing and Revising

In this phase, students edit their drafts by making revisions, additions, and deletions to ensure that their products achieve their writing goals. You can introduce students to revision by reviewing a sample paper as a group. The class can identify the positive aspects of the paper, as well as the problems a reader would have in reading it. The discussion should focus on the content, organization, and word choices rather than on mechanical errors. The class can then complete the revision by correcting the problems identified in the paper as a group. For example, you and your students can help classmates generate a list of synonyms to replace nondescriptive words (such as *nice, great, fine,* and *good*) that have been used repeatedly. The Find (Search) and Replace functions of many word processing programs can then be used to locate the nondescriptive word and replace it with the new word.

Students also can be taught to correct their own papers and to do content, organizational, and mechanical editing by maintain an editing log (see Figure 10.3). The editing log includes the date, the error, the correction, and the rule being applied.

INFORMATIONAL

Strategies such as *DEFENDS, TOWER, PENS, SEARCH,* and *WRITER* can be used to monitor the quality of students' writing (Ellis & Covert, 1996; Mercer & Mercer, 1993).

Proofreading   Proofreading is an important part of the editing and revising processes. Students can be taught to review their written products to check for misspelled words, sentence fragments, and errors in punctuation, capitalization, and grammar. You can help students proofread their work by giving them a proofreading checklist.

One strategy that trains students to use these proofreading skills in a systematic way is *COPS* (Schumaker, Nolan, & Deshler, 1985). In this procedure, students learn to proofread their papers by asking:

C = Have I capitalized letters that need to be capitalized?
O = What is the overall appearance of my paper?
P = Have I used proper punctuation?
S = Are the words I used spelled correctly?

Name _____

Date	Error and Correction	Rule
1/25/2000	*Error:* The student suddenly jumped out of his seat, however, the teacher ignored him. *Correction:* The student suddenly jumped out of his seat; however, the teacher ignored him. or The student suddenly jumped out of his seat. However, the teacher ignored him.	This is called a comma splice or run-on sentence. It can be corrected by replacing the first comma with a semicolon or with a period and a capital letter to start a new sentence.
1/25/2000	*Error:* The boys father met them at school. *Correction:* The boys' father met them at school.	The father "belongs" to the boys, so *boys* should be possessive. The apostrophe comes after the *s* because the word *boys* is plural.

FIGURE 10.3 Sample editing log.
Source: Prepared by Catharine Whittaker.

Editing Symbols

Mark	Explanation	Example
⬯	Circle words that are spelled incorrectly.	My freind and I went to the zoo last Sunday.
/	Change a capital letter to a small leter.	Mary and Jim watched Television for one hour.
≡	Change a small letter to a capital letter.	bob loves the way I play horn.
∧	Add letters, words, or sentences.	My friend lives in the brick house next door. ∧
⊙	Add a period.	My dog, Frisky, and I are private detectives⊙
ℓ	Take out letters, words, or punctuation.	Last summer Bob went and flew an airplane in Alaska.
∧	Add a comma.	Bob visited Alaska, Ohio, and Florida.

FIGURE 10.4 Editing symbols.

Source: Motivate reluctant learning disabled writers by J. Whitt, P. V. Paul, and C. J. Reynolds, *Teaching Exceptional Children*, vol. 20, 1988, p. 38. Copyright 1988 by The Council for Exceptional Children. Reprinted with permission.

Students can improve their proofreading skills by using proofreader's marks. You can train students to use these marks by teaching them the system and modeling its use when giving feedback on written assignments. Additionally, you can give students a handout of editing symbols paired with examples of their use, as shown in Figure 10.4.

Models   You can foster the editing process by giving students writing sample models that show the correct format, writing style, and organization of content. The value of the model can be increased by reviewing it with students and marking it with comments highlighting the qualities that help to make it an excellent product. For example, you can emphasize the topic sentence by circling it and writing "This is a good topic sentence. It introduces the reader to the content in the paragraph." Similarly, the inclusion of specific sections in the written product can be noted to ensure that the student's paper includes all the necessary sections.

In addition to providing students with a model, teachers can promote writing by providing a checklist of items they will use in evaluating the paper. The checklist can then guide students in evaluating their papers before handing them in.

Collaborative Writing Groups   Collaborative writing groups can be an excellent way of helping students, as well as promoting a positive environment for writing and improving the writing skills of students from various language and cultural backgrounds. Stu-

Collaborative writing groups can foster students' writing.

dents can work in collaboration by reading their products to the group or to individual group members; editing the products of group members; brainstorming ideas for writing; developing outlines as a group; and producing a group product such as a class newsletter.

Fleming (1988) proposed three models for using collaboration in the writing process: the chunk model, the blended model, and the raisin bread model. In the *chunk* model, each group member contributes a specific part of the written product. *Blended* writing requires the group to reach a consensus in composing and discussing each sentence in a writing assignment. The *raisin bread* model allows one group member to transform the contributions of individual group members into a larger group draft.

Collaborative groups can be particularly helpful in revising written assignments. One collaborative strategy is the *author's chair* (Graves & Hansen, 1983). In this technique, once their product has been completed, students read it aloud to their peers, who discuss its positive features and ask questions about strategy, meaning, and writing style.

MacArthur et al. (1991) developed a peer-revising strategy to help students working in dyads provide feedback to each other. The strategy requires students to do the following:

Listen to each other's papers and read along.
Tell what your partner's paper is about and what you liked best.
Reread your partner's paper and make notes:
    Is everything clear?
    Can any details be added?
Discuss your suggestions with your partner.
Revise your own paper and correct errors.
Exchange papers and check for errors in sentences, capitalization, punctuation, and spelling. (Graham, 1992, p. 141)

Students can work together in groups to offer feedback on content, sequence, and vocabulary and to edit drafts (Hallenbeck, 1996). You can establish guidelines for peer writing groups, including focusing on feedback that emphasizes the positive aspects of the product; being specific; directing feedback at the work rather than the author; phrasing negative reactions as questions; giving reactions orally or in writing; and offering writers time to respond to the reactions of their peers (Levy, 1999).

Editing groups allow editing to be done by the group rather than by individual students. In editing groups, each member reads his or her product aloud while peer editors follow along on a photocopy. Peer editors record their reactions and comments on their photocopy and then present and discuss the written product as a group. Editing groups can be modified so that each group focuses on a specific aspect of the written product.

In addition to training peers to give valuable and specific feedback, you can guide students in learning how to accept feedback. You can help students receive feedback from others by establishing rules for accepting reactions from others, including the following:

> Listen carefully to all comments from others.
> Ask for feedback from as many people as possible.
> Do not dispute or dismiss feedback from others.
> Seek further clarification or examples when you don't understand another person's reaction.
> Check your understanding of another person's reaction by paraphrasing the statements in your own words.

Writers' Workshop   Another collaborative writing strategy designed to create a community of writers is the Writers' Workshop, where students write every day and receive feedback from peers and teachers on topics they select (Milem & Garcia, 1996). The Writers' Workshop is divided into four parts: status of the class, mini-lessons, workshop proper, and sharing. In the status component, you work with individual students to identify the project(s) on which they are working, the help they will need, and the progress they are making. Mini-lessons, approximately 5 minutes long, offer students direct instruction on specific skills such as process skills (e.g., idea generation), grammar and spelling skills, writing skills (e.g., paragraph development), and classroom routines. The majority of the Writers' Workshop consists of the workshop proper, during which you and your students actively write. In addition to writing, you circulate around the room to monitor student progress, help students hear their own voices and solve minor problems, and confer with individual students. In the final component, students share their work with others, receive feedback, and publish their work.

INFORMATIONAL

Isaacson and Gleason (1998) offer a variety of strategies to assess students' written language, and McAlister, Nelson, and Bahr (1999) offer strategies for assessing students' understanding of and attitudes toward a writing process approach.

Publishing

Publishing students' written products presents an excellent opportunity for sharing their work with others and for receiving feedback. For example, students can publish their work in books that they design. Technology also can be a valuable resource in the fourth stage of the writing process: publishing. For instance, students also can "publish" their work via the Internet.

Provide Feedback

Feedback should facilitate, not frustrate, the writing process. A teacher conference is an excellent means of providing feedback and encouraging students to reflect on their writing. By meeting individually with students you serve as both reader and coach, helping students learn to examine their writing in terms of ideas and content, organization, voice, word choice, fluency, and use of conventions. For example, in a writing conference with students, you can ask them: "Why did you select this topic?," "Is the introduction inviting?," "What changes did you make when editing your piece?," and "What was easy and difficult for you when writing this piece?"

REFLECTING ON PROFESSIONAL PRACTICES

Using a Process Approach to Teaching Writing

Ms. Rogers notices that many of her students are having difficulty with writing assignments. A review of their written products reveals that they are extremely short and disorganized, lack important elements, and include irrelevant information. To correct these problems, Ms. Rogers decides to try a different approach to teaching students to write.

Ms. Rogers begins by writing a description of herself, reading it to her students and asking them to guess who is being described. After the students guess correctly, Ms. Rogers explains how she wrote it. She draws a semantic map on the board and demonstrates how she used it to list the important characteristics she wanted to mention in her description. She then gives the students a semantic map outline and asks them to complete it using the characteristics that best describe themselves.

The next day, Ms. Rogers asks the students to use their semantic maps to write a five-sentence draft that describes themselves. After the drafts are completed, Ms. Rogers collects them, selects students to read them to the class, and has the class guess who wrote each piece. Ms. Rogers concludes the day's writing lesson by telling students that tomorrow they will work on revising their descriptions.

Ms. Rogers begins the next day's lesson by explaining the purpose of revising a draft. Using her description of herself, Ms. Rogers asks students to identify things they liked about it. After this is done, she asks them to identify ways in which the description could be improved. Following this discussion, Ms. Rogers reviews several guidelines for giving and accepting feedback.

She then selects a student's draft and role plays giving feedback with the student.

Ms. Rogers then places students in dyads, gives each group member a checklist to guide the feedback process, and asks members to read each other's papers and share their reactions. While students work collaboratively, Ms. Rogers monitors their progress and assists them in developing collaborative skills. During the last 15 minutes of the period, Ms. Rogers and the whole class discuss how it feels to give and receive feedback.

The next day's writing period is devoted to revising students' drafts based on the feedback they have received. Ms. Rogers works on her draft, and circulates around the room to monitor student progress and to confer with individual students. After students revise their writing, they type their product on the computer and share their printout with their dyad partner. They then make final revisions, and a copy of each student's description is printed out and compiled into a class book called *Who's Who*, which is shared with students' families, other teachers, and the principal and is posted on the class's web page.

Why did Ms. Rogers decide to use a process approach to teach writing? What procedures and strategies did she use to implement a writing process approach? What are the advantages of using a process approach to teach writing? What are the potential problems with this approach? What resources would you need to implement a process approach to teach writing?

Initially, you can focus on the positive aspects of the students' writing, and acknowledge and encourage them to write by praising them, sharing their stories with others by reading them in class, and posting their writing in the room or elsewhere in the school. Because identifying all errors can frustrate students, corrective feedback should focus on no more than two writing problems at a time. You can pinpoint errors that interfere with the writer's ability to make the product understandable to the reader rather than emphasize grammar, punctuation, spelling, and usage errors. Instruction to correct grammatical and spelling errors can focus on skills that are within the student's repertoire and occur within the context of the student's writing.

Teach Students to Use Learning Strategies

You can help students improve their writing by teaching them to use learning strategies. For example, Graham and Harris (cited in Graham, Harris, & Sawyer, 1987) have developed a learning strategy for teaching students to write a narrative story. This self-instructional strategy has five steps:

REFLECTIVE

How did you learn to write? When you write a paper for class or a letter to a friend, what processes do you use? How does the use of a computer and a word processing program affect your writing?

SET YOUR SITES

The National Writing Project (www.nwp.berkeley.edu, 510-642-0963) maintains a website that offers teacher-centered activities to improve the teaching and learning of writing.

1. Look at the picture (stimulus item).
2. Let your mind be free.
3. Write down the story part reminder (W-W-W; What = 2; How = 2).
4. Write down story parts for each part reminder.
5. Write your story; use good parts and make sense. (Graham et al., 1987, p. 7)

Similarly, the mnemonic *W-W-W; What = 2; How = 2* helps students remember the following:

1. Who is the main character? Who else is in the story?
2. When does the story take place?
3. Where does the story take place?
4. What does the main character want to do?
5. What happens when he or she tries to do it?
6. How does the story end?
7. How does the main character feel? (Graham et al., 1987, p. 7)

INFORMATIONAL

Other learning strategies that can be taught to students include TREE (Sexton, Harris, & Graham, 1998), PLAN and WRITE (De La Paz, 1999), STOP and DARE (De La Paz & Graham, 1997), and STOP and LIST (Troia, Graham, & Harris, 1999).

Use Computer-Supported Writing Applications

Students can improve their writing skills and the writing products they produce by using computer-supported writing applications (MacArthur, 1999). Several of these applications are described below.

Word Processing

Word processing allows students to store, copy, cut and paste, insert, format, print text, and choose font types and sizes electronically. Word processing has several advantages. It allows students to focus on the writing process; minimizes spelling errors; facilitates publication; eliminates handwriting problems so that all students produce a neat, clean copy; provides students with a novel experience that motivates them to write; makes text revision easy by allowing students to move text around and insert words; eliminates the tedious process of copying; and allows students to insert graphics that illustrate and support written text (Bangert-Drowns, 1993). Word processing programs also offer students access to electronic thesauruses and dictionaries that can guide them in making appropriate and varied word choices.

Talking word processors that "read" the text on the computer screen and enlarged print systems can enhance the writing capabilities of students with visual and reading disabilities (MacArthur, 1996). Talking word processors allow students to detect syntax errors, receive feedback on spelling as they enter words, and hear their text read. Word processors that have voice output systems can provide immediate auditory and visual feedback to users concerning keystrokes and various commands as they type, as well as orally reviewing individual letters and words, sentences, paragraphs, highlighted text, and whole documents after the text has been typed. These applications can be combined with text windowing, the simultaneous visual highlighting of text as it is read to help students focus on, monitor, and proofread their writing. Because most talking word processors pronounce words based on phonetic spellings, some word processing programs include pronunciation editing, which allows students to adjust the speech of the program so that words that are not phonetically based are pronounced correctly. A variety of special monitors and print enlargement programs also are available for students who can benefit from word processing through the use of enlarged print.

Talk-type or voice-activated word processing programs based on computerized speech recognition can help students improve their writing and overcome their spelling

Students can improve their writing skills through the use of computer-supported writing applications, such as word processing.

difficulties (Higgins & Raskind, 1995). In these programs, the individual talks into a headphone-mounted microphone, pausing briefly after each word. The individual's comments then appear as electronic text on a video monitor and may be revised via word processing (Wetzel, 1996). Researchers are developing voice recognition systems that are not speaker dependent, require little pretraining to use, process a large vocabulary accurately, screen background noises, and recognize continuous speech.

Students with disabilities may experience difficulties using word processing such as having difficulty remembering functions that require multiple key presses or syntax codes, using inefficient cursor movements, using deletion procedures inappropriately, and experiencing problems in saving and loading files and using the return key to organize text on the monitor. Therefore, some students may need to use word processing programs that have safeguards to prevent the loss of documents, offer easy-to-read manuals and directions for use, and contain pictures and cues as prompts. Students also may benefit from word processing programs that use simple keystrokes to delete and insert text and move the cursor; offer prompting and verification to help students save documents and load features; include easy-to-use menus; and use language that students can understand.

To benefit from word processing, students may need instruction in keyboarding skills and the word processing program. Such training should teach students to enter and save text; return to the menu; print copies; load disks; clear memory; center, justify, add, delete, and move text; skip lines; and move the cursor. Keyboarding skills also can be taught to students through the use of typing teaching programs that accept only correct responses, provide numerous practice activities, introduce skills gradually, contain graphics for finger positions, and offer frequent feedback (Majsterek, 1990). Prompt cards that display the keys and their functions help students to remember key functions and patterns of multiple-key pressing. Typing teaching programs that analyze students' typing patterns, including strengths and weaknesses, and plan customized programs tailored to students' unique learning styles also are available.

IDEAS FOR IMPLEMENTATION

Teaching Handwriting

Although Ms. Stepanovich had her students write using computers, she also wanted them to develop the legibility and fluency of their handwriting so that they could express themselves in writing. During handwriting activities, she noticed that several students had poor writing posture that interfered with the size, slant, proportion, alignment, and spacing of letters. Therefore, Ms. Stepanovich used modeling to teach her students proper posture and paper positioning. She asked students to watch her as she wrote at her desk and told them, "Look at me when I write. I sit upright, with my back against the back seat of my chair and both of my feet on the floor. As I write, I lean my shoulders and upper back forward in a straight line, place my elbows extended slightly at the edge of my desk, and use my forearms as a pivot for my movements. I hold my pen lightly between the index finger and the middle finger, with the thumb to the side and the index finger on top. My thumb is bent to hold the pen high in the hand and the utensil rests near the knuckle of the index finger, and my pinky and ring fingers touch the paper."

Ms. Stepanovich also created and posted charts that showed students how to position their paper when writing. For manuscript writing, a chart demonstrated how to hold the paper perpendicular to the front of the body, with the left side placed so that it is aligned with the center of the body. For cursive writing, the charts showed right-handers slanting the paper counterclockwise and left-handers slanting it clockwise. As students wrote, Ms. Stepanovich guided them physically, encouraged them to look at the charts, and gave them feedback on their posture and their ability to hold the pen correctly.

Here are some other strategies you can use to improve your students' handwriting:

- Focus initial instruction on helping students develop the prerequisite fine motor, visual motor, and visual discrimination skills needed for handwriting by using activities such as cutting, tracing, coloring, fingerpainting, discriminating, and copying shapes.
- Teach the meaning of the directional concepts that guide letter formation instruction such as *up, down, top, center, bottom, around, left, right, across, middle,* and *diagonal.*
- Use a combination of procedures that include modeling, self-instruction, copying, cueing, and teaching the basic strokes.
- Help students hold the writing utensil by using tape, foam rubber bands, a triangle or grips that can be purchased to slip over the writing utensil, or specialized writing utensils such as large-diameter pencils, crayons, holders, and writing frames.
- Adapt writing paper by emphasizing the base lines and marking the starting and end points with green and red dots, respectively.
- Use paper with colored, solid, and dashed lines to help students learn correct letter heights and paper with perpendicular lines to teach proper spacing.
- Offer left-handed students left-handed models, group them together, teach them to write letters vertically or with a slight backward slant, have them write on the left side of the blackboard, and provide them with left-handed desks.
- Place a chart presenting lowercase and uppercase letters, the numerals 1 through 10, and their corresponding stroke directions in a location in the room that *all students* can see.

Sources: Aber, Bachman, Campbell, and O'Malley (1994) and Kurtz (1994).

Spell Checkers

Word processing programs come with a spell checker, which can help students with spelling difficulties and aid them in revising their writing (MacArthur, 1999). Spell checkers review written text and identify spelling errors and other words that do not match the program's dictionary. Students then correct the spelling errors by typing in the correct spelling or by choosing from a list of alternatives presented by the spell checker. Students can add words to the spell checker's dictionary to tailor it to their unique spelling needs. Those with reading disabilities may benefit from programs that use talking spell checkers to read word choices to them, while other students may prefer a program that offers a definition of each word presented as an alternative. Spell checkers that present word choices in short lists also may assist students with reading and spelling difficulties.

However, spell checkers have several limitations (MacArthur, Graham, Haynes, & DeLaPaz, 1996). They often cannot identify words that are spelled correctly but used in the wrong context, such as homonyms. Spell checks often identify correctly spelled words as errors if these words are not available in their dictionaries, such as proper nouns, uncommon words, and specialized vocabulary. Spell checkers also may not be able to provide the correct spelling of every word that has been misspelled. In particular, they cannot suggest the correct spelling of words when the student's version does not resemble the correct spelling. Ashton (1999) developed The CHECK procedure, a mnemonic learning strategy designed to help students use spell checkers. The steps in this procedure are:

Check: Check the beginning sound of the word.
            What other letter(s) could make that beginning sound?
Hunt: Hunt for the correct consonants.
            Have you included all the consonants in the rest of the word?
Examine: Examine the vowels.
            What other vowel(s) could make the same sound(s)?
Changes: Changes in suggested word lists may give hints.
            What words are being suggested? Is that one you're looking for?
Keep: Keep repeating Steps 1 through 4.
            Need help? Try dictionaries and asking others for assistance.
            (Ashton, 1999, p. 24)

Some programs also offer spelling assistance (Hunt-Berg et al., 1994). As students type text, the spelling assistance program immediately indicates that a spelling error has occurred and then asks if the student would like to correct the word at that time or spell check the entire document when it is completed. Other spelling assistance programs offer students a list of word choices based on the first few letters typed. Students can then select and enter the desired word from the list into the document.

Macros, which record keystrokes in a file so that they can be used repeatedly, also can be used to assist students with spelling and writing by reducing the number of keystrokes. Macros can be set up to aid students in spelling words and text, writing out abbreviations, producing repetitive strings of words, and formatting paragraphs and pages (Behrmann, 1994). Students also can create abbreviation expanders for frequently used words and text to minimize keystrokes (Raskind & Higgins, 1998).

INFORMATIONAL

McNaughton, Hughes, and Ofiesh (1997) developed INSPECT, a learning strategy to teach students to use a spell checker.

Word Cueing and Prediction

Word cueing and prediction programs offer students choices of words and phrases as they compose text and are helpful for students who have difficulty recalling words (MacArthur, 1998). As students type text, a changing list of predicted words and phrases appears on the screen. Students can then decide to select the predicted words and insert them into their written products or to continue typing. The word and phrase banks that are integral parts of these programs can be customized for students based on their needs and the topic and content of their written product.

Whereas word cueing programs offer choices based on the first letters typed by students, word prediction programs offer word and phrase options based on context, word frequency (i.e., how frequently the word is used in English), word recency (i.e., how recently the word has been used by the writer), grammatical correctness, and commonly associated words and phrases. Thesaurus programs also can improve students' writing by increasing the variety of words used in writing and limiting word repetition.

Text Organization, Grammar, and Punctuation Assistance

Programs that help students organize the text and check text for syntax, punctuation, capitalization, usage, and style can be useful (Sturm, Rankin, Beukelman, & Schutz-Muehling, 1997). Some word processing programs have interactive prompting capabilities that help students write effectively. These programs provide prompts and guidelines that appear on the screen to guide development of the student's product. You can tailor these and create your own prompts to adapt to the different types of writing assignments and needs of students. Some programs offer students assistance in generating ideas to write about, selecting a writing style, and conforming to the writing style selected. Graphics-based programs allow students to create pictorials and then compose the corresponding text (Bahr, Nelson, & Van Meter, 1996).

Grammar checkers identify grammatical and punctuation errors and present alternatives to address them. Students then examine the alternatives and select the option that they believe best corrects the error. Many of these programs guide students in selecting an appropriate alternative by offering prompts, as well as reviews and explanations of the different selections and their corresponding grammatical applications. Some programs also help students produce grammatically correct written products by automatically capitalizing proper nouns and the first words of sentences.

INFORMATIONAL

Sturm et al. (1997) offer guidelines for selecting appropriate software for computer-assisted writing.

INFORMATIONAL

Smith, Boone, and Higgins (1998) offer guidelines for using the Internet as part of the writing process.

HOW CAN I HELP STUDENTS LEARN TO SPELL?

Use a Combination of Approaches

A skill area that can affect both writing and reading is spelling. Reading is a decoding process; spelling is an encoding process. Consequently, many students who experience difficulties in reading also are likely to have problems with spelling. These students may benefit from a spelling program that combines several of the approaches presented in the following sections (Greene, 1995).

Rule-Governed Approaches

Rule-governed models promote spelling skills by teaching students to use morphemic and phonemic analysis and basic spelling rules (Oldrieve, 1997). In using rule-governed approaches, you help students learn spelling rules and patterns by asking them to analyze words that follow the same grapheme–phoneme correspondence, to discuss similarities and differences in words, to identify the rules that apply, to practice the use of the rule with unfamiliar words, and to learn exceptions to the rule.

One rule-governed model for teaching spelling is the *linguistic* approach, in which spelling instruction focuses on the rules of spelling and patterns related to whole words. Once the students learn a series of words with similar spelling, opportunities to generalize the rule to other words in the family arise. For example, students are taught the *oat* family using the words *boat* and *coat.* Later, they apply the pattern to words from that family such as *goat, moat,* and *float.*

One linguistic approach that teaches spelling by having students compare and contrast words that conform to related spelling patterns is *Directed Spelling Thinking Activity (DSTA)*

(Graham, Harris, & Loynachan, 1996). DSTA involves selecting two or more different but related spelling patterns (e.g., short vowel [CVC] and long vowel [CVCe] word patterns) and choosing words that illustrate the word patterns selected, as well as one or two words that do not fit the patterns. After students write the selected words, you display their spellings and ask them to describe how to spell the words. You also present models of the correct spelling of the words, acknowledging students' attempts to spell them, highlighting the parts of the words that caused difficulty, reviewing each of the words, and having students sort them into their respective spelling patterns. You then ask students to identify other words that fit the word pattern categories and request explicit statements concerning the orthographic patterns associated with the respective word categories. Then you provide reading and writing activities that offer students opportunities to apply the orthographic patterns discussed.

While the linguistic approach is based on learning spelling patterns within whole words, the *phonetic* approach is based on learning to apply phoneme–grapheme correspondence within parts of words. Thus, a phonetic approach to spelling involves teaching students the sound–symbol correspondence for individual letters and combinations of letters (such as digraphs and diphthongs). Students then apply these rules by breaking words into syllables, pronouncing each syllable, and writing the letter(s) that correspond to each sound. While phonetic approaches to teaching spelling have been successful, words that represent irregularities in the English language, including multiple-letter sounds, word pronunciations, and unstressed syllables, are deterrents to phonetic spelling.

Cognitive Approaches

Cognitive approaches to spelling are based on the view that spelling is a developmental process and that students go through predictable phases as they learn orthographic skills and learn to spell. Wong (1986) proposes a *cognitive* approach to teaching spelling that uses a spelling grid and a seven-step questioning procedure. The five-column spelling grid is designed to teach structural analysis of words. Its use begins with the teacher writing a spelling word, pronouncing it, and discussing its meaning. Next, students complete the spelling grid by reading the word in column one; recording the number of syllables in the word in column two; dividing the word into syllables in column three; breaking the word into its root and suffix and writing the suffix in column four; and writing the modification of the spelling of the root word in column five. The self-questioning strategy entails students asking themselves the following questions:

1. Do I know the word?
2. How many syllables do I hear in this word? (Write down the number.)
3. I'll spell the word.
4. Do I have the right number of syllables down?
5. If yes, is there any part of the word I'm not sure of the spelling? I'll underline that part and try spelling the word again.
6. Now, does it look right to me? If it does, I'll leave it alone. If it still doesn't look right, I'll underline the part of the spelling I'm not sure of and try again. (If the word I spelled does not have the right number of syllables, let me hear the word in my head again and find the missing syllable. Then I'll go back to steps 5 and 6.)
7. When I finish spelling, I tell myself I'm a good worker. I've tried hard at spelling. (Wong, 1986, p. 172)

Whole Word Approaches

Whole word approaches help students focus on the whole word through a variety of multisensory activities. Whole word approaches include test-study-test procedures, corrected-test methods, and word study techniques.

Test-Study-Test Procedures   Perhaps the most frequently used method of spelling instruction is the *test-study-test* method. In this method, students take a pretest on a fixed list of words, study the words they misspell, and take a posttest to assess mastery. You also can use a study-test procedure in which students study all the week's spelling words and then take a test. When posttesting students with these procedures, it is recommended that teachers intersperse known and unknown words in the test.

You can adapt test-study-test procedures by decreasing the number of spelling words given to students from five to three to increase their spelling performance. Thus, rather than have students try to master a large list of words each week, you can break down the list so that students study and are tested on three words each day. You also can use a flow word list rather than a fixed list. Flow lists can help you individualize spelling by allowing students who master spelling words to delete those words from the list and replace them with new words. Whether using a fixed or flow list of spelling words, you can give students time to work at their own rate and can require them to demonstrate mastery over a period of time.

Corrected-Test Methods   The *corrected-test* method allows you to guide students in correcting their spelling errors by spelling words orally while students correct them; spelling words and accentuating each letter as students simultaneously point to each letter in the word; spelling words while students write the correct letter above the crossed-out, incorrect letter; writing the correct spelling on students' papers near the incorrectly spelled word, which students then correct; and copying students' errors, modeling the correct spelling, and observing students as they write the word correctly.

Word Study Techniques   *Word study* techniques include a wide range of activities designed to help students remember spelling words. Harris, Graham, and Freeman (1988) found that a student-controlled five-step word study procedure was effective in helping students learn new spelling words. The multistep word study procedure included verbalizing the word; writing and saying the word; comparing the written word to a model; tracing and saying the word; writing the word from memory and checking it; and repeating prior steps as necessary. You also can use word study methods that encourage students to close their eyes and visualize the spelling word, or verbalize the word while writing it, or finger spelling or writing words in the air.

Radabaugh and Yukish (1982) suggest that you match the word study strategies to the learning styles of your students. For visual learners, they recommend that students:

1. View the word while you read the word to them.
2. Study the word, read it, spell it, and read it again.
3. Attempt to spell the word orally three times without the model.
4. Write the word and check its spelling.

For auditory learners, they recommend that students:

1. Listen to you read, spell, and read the word.
2. Read the word and then attempt to spell it.
3. Listen to you spell the word and then repeat it after you.
4. Spell the word without assistance.

Adapt Spelling Instruction

Many students, including those with disabilities, may exhibit problems in spelling. You can adapt spelling instruction for them in the following ways.

REFLECTIVE

What approaches were used by your teachers to teach you spelling? What were the strengths of these approaches? What were their weaknesses?

INFORMATIONAL

Richards and Gipe (1993) offer a variety of spelling activities that you can use to integrate spelling into your language arts programs.

Explain the Importance of Spelling

Explaining the importance and relevance of spelling can motivate students to improve their spelling skills (Fulk & Stormont-Spurgin, 1995). You can emphasize the relevance of spelling by helping students see the connection between spelling, reading, and writing.

Teach Dictionary Skills

Spelling problems can be minimized by encouraging students to use the dictionary to confirm the spelling of unknown or irregular words, spelling demons, confusing rules, and difficult word combinations. Therefore, students need to learn dictionary skills, including alphabetizing, locating words, using guide words, and understanding syllabification and pronunciation. Students in primary grades can use a picture dictionary until they learn the skills needed to use a regular dictionary. You can have students make personal dictionaries or word books that include pages for each letter of the alphabet, with weekly entries of spelling words in sentences and their definitions on the appropriate page (Richards & Gipe, 1993; Issacson & Gleason, 1997). As students write, they consult their personal dictionaries to help them with word choice and spelling. Personal dictionaries also can be developed for math, science, and social studies words (Scheuermann, Jacobs, McCall, & Knies, 1994).

Teach Students to Proofread and to Correct Spelling Errors

Spelling errors can be reduced by having students proofread their work (McNaughton, Hughes & Clark, 1997). You can train students to proofread for spelling errors by giving them a list of words and having them identify and correct the misspellings; assigning them to find the spelling errors in the assignments of their peers; listing the number of errors in a student's assignment and having students locate and correct the errors; and marking words that may be incorrectly spelled and having students check them. Posting an alphabetical list of words frequently misspelled in a central location in the room, encouraging students to maintain a list of words they frequently misspell in their notebooks, and assigning peers to serve as a "human dictionary" or "super speller" to assist their classmates can help students learn to identify and deal with spelling demons (Fagen, Graves, & Tessier-Switlick, 1984).

Students also can be encouraged and taught to correct their own spelling errors. Fulk and Stormont-Spurgin (1995) suggest that students correct their spelling by (1) comparing their spelling of words to a correct spelling model; (2) noting incorrect letter(s) by crossing them out, boxing, or circling them; (3) writing the correct letters above the incorrect letters; and (4) writing the correct spelling on a line next to the incorrect spelling. Error identification and correction also can be fostered by teaching students to use a spell checker.

Use Spelling Games

Games can motivate students and give them the opportunity to practice spelling skills in a nonthreatening environment. Teacher-made games include spelling bingo, hangman, spelling baseball, and spelling lotto. Commercially produced games include Scrabble, Spello, and Boggle.

Use Computer Programs

Computer programs have been successful in improving students' spelling (Fulk & Stormont-Spurgin, 1995). These programs offer students opportunities to practice their spelling skills within individualized teaching formats and instructional learning games.

For example, *Simon Spells* is a software program that teaches students to spell 1,000 frequently read or written words (Ochoa, Vasquez, & Gerber, 1999).

Teach Students to Use Cues

Students can use meaning and sound-alike cues, mnemonic devices, and configuration clues to figure out the correct spellings (Cunningham, 1998). For example, some students may benefit from drawing blocks around the outline of the word to remember its configuration. Students can be encouraged to select cues that make sense to them and relate to their experiences and culture.

You also can use classroom posters to provide students with spelling cues. For example, you can post spelling strategy charts to give students a range of spelling techniques, alphabet wall charts to assist students who reverse letters, wall calendars that offer correct spellings for the months and days of the week, and vocabulary wall charts that present the correct spelling of content area vocabulary words (Beckman, 1999).

Have Students Record Their Progress and Correct Their Own Spelling Errors

Self-recording motivates students by giving them a visual representation of their progress. For example, students can keep a cumulative chart or graph of words spelled correctly, maintain weekly graphs that measure performance on pretests and posttests, or self-correct and track their spelling performance on writing tasks. Students also can correct their own work and then set spelling goals for themselves based on their prior performance and chart their success in achieving their goals (Goddard & Heron, 1998).

Provide Time to Review Words Previously Learned

Students with disabilities may experience difficulty remembering words previously mastered. Therefore, you can provide time to review and study previously learned words and use spelling words in other situations.

Model Appropriate Spelling Techniques

You can improve the spelling skills of students by giving them oral and written models to imitate. When writing on the blackboard, you can periodically emphasize the spelling of words, and occasionally spell words or have peers spell them for the class. You also can model a positive attitude toward spelling by teaching spelling with enthusiasm and encouraging positive attributions regarding the use of spelling strategies (Fulk, 1997).

Teach Students to Use the Spell Checker

As we discussed earlier in this chapter, you can help students with spelling by teaching them to use spell checkers. Students who do not have access to word processing programs may benefit from handheld electronic spell checkers. For example, students can be given a written product and asked to underline misspelled words and write their correct spellings after using their handheld spell checkers.

Choose Relevant Spelling Words

You can motivate students and improve their spelling by focusing initially on a core of frequently used words, as well as on words that are part of the student's listening and spelling vocabulary. Graham (1992) suggests that students' spelling words be selected by both students and teachers and be those that frequently appear in students' writing products.

Teach Useful Prefixes, Suffixes, and Root Words

Teaching students useful prefixes, suffixes, and root words can help them to spell and define new multisyllabic words (Cunningham, 1998).

Analyze Students' Spelling Errors

You can observe students while they spell and note the types of errors they make through error analysis. For example, many second language learners may engage in *cross-linguistically developed* spelling, spelling words incorrectly by using elements from their first and second languages. Appropriate spelling instruction can be based on the students' error patterns.

SUMMARY

This chapter presented guidelines and strategies for differentiating reading, writing, and spelling instruction. As you review the questions posed in this chapter, remember the following points.

How Can I Help Students Learn to Read?

You can motivate them to read; use a balanced approach, remedial reading strategies, programmed reading materials, and cuing strategies; and involve families.

How Can I Help Students Learn to Write?

You can make writing a meaningful, integral part of the curriculum, use a process-oriented approach to writing instruction, teach students to use learning strategies, and employ computer-supported applications.

How Can I Help Students Learn to Spell?

You can help students learn to spell by employing a combination of approaches and by adapting spelling instruction.

 ## What Would You Do in Today's Diverse Classroom?

Richard is having difficulty with reading, writing, and spelling. He reads haltingly and stiffly and often has to read words several times as he attempts to sound them out. His writing, which is very limited, is disorganized, contains repetitive words and irrelevant information, and is very difficult to follow. Because of his poor handwriting, even Richard has difficulty deciphering his writing. He also struggles with spelling and can spell only a few sight words. When he encounters a word he cannot spell, he attempts to spell it phonetically.

1. What would you do to help Richard learn to read?
2. What would you do to help Richard learn to write?
3. What would you do to help Richard learn to spell?
4. What resources and support from others would be useful in helping Richard learn to read, write, and spell?

CHAPTER
11

DIFFERENTIATING MATHEMATICS, SCIENCE, AND SOCIAL STUDIES INSTRUCTION

Ms. Hofbart

Ms. Hofbart and her students are beginning to study geometry, including perimeter and area. She begins by reading the book The Dot and the Line *(Juster, 1963) to her students to help them develop an appreciation of geometry as a means of describing the physical world. She then asks her students to identify shapes in the classroom, draw these shapes, and write journal entries describing them. For homework, students are asked to find pictures of two-dimensional figures in newspapers and magazines, and write about and orally describe these shapes. Ms. Hofbart uses students' homework in class by having them exchange their geometric shapes so that they can describe the figures their classmates have collected.*

The students experiment with shapes by performing geoboard activities. Using tanagrams, they also sort shapes, investigate the properties of shapes, discuss the similarities and differences among the shapes, and create new shapes.

Ms. Hofbart uses computer graphics to create an overhead transparency of various shapes in the classroom, and uses the transparency and colored pens to introduce the concepts of area and perimeter. Students are then given different shapes and asked to shade the parts of the shapes that relate to perimeter and area.

Ms. Hofbart also has students work in cooperative learning groups to experiment with, brainstorm about, and solve problems. In their groups, students research and write about the cultural origins and meanings of geometric shapes. One group reports about the Egyptian pyramids, including information about the area and perimeter of these structures, while another group uses the Internet to gather and present information about Mayan ruins and geometric shapes. As a culminating activity, Ms.

Hofbart asks each group to design a school yard playground. Groups begin by collecting data about the various dimensions of the playground and students' favorite pieces of playground equipment. They then create and draw their playground, considering such questions as these: Is the space provided large enough for all the equipment? How much room should be left between pieces of equipment? Should there be open space for group games? Are there alternative ways of organizing the space to accommodate the equipment? Groups share their designs with the whole class.

At the end of the unit, Ms. Hofbart works with her students to create portfolios that demonstrate students' knowledge of geometric shapes, perimeter, and area. The portfolio items they select include drawings of various geometric shapes, geoboard activities, journal entries describing the shapes in the classroom, diagrams and measurements of local areas of interest, worksheets of completed examples, tests, quizzes, and the cooperative learning group project on designing a school yard playground.

What additional strategies can Ms. Hofbart use to promote the mathematics skills of her students? After reading this chapter, you should be able to answer this as well as the following questions.

◆ How can I differentiate mathematics instruction?
◆ How can I differentiate science and social studies instruction?

Many strategies for differentiating classroom instruction to enhance learning, motivation, and social development can be used across academic disciplines (see Chapters 8 and 9). However, like Ms. Hofbart, you may find that you must make adaptations to a specific content area to promote learning for students. This chapter offers guidelines for differentiating mathematics, science, and social studies instruction.

How Can I Differentiate Mathematics Instruction?

Use a Problem-Solving Approach

The National Council of Teachers of Mathematics (NCTM) established guidelines that promote five general mathematical goals for *all students*: (1) learning to value mathematics; (2) developing confidence in one's mathematical ability; (3) becoming mathematical problem solvers; (4) learning to communicate mathematically; and (5) learning to reason mathematically. To achieve these goals, the NCTM endorsed a problem-solving approach to the teaching and assessment of mathematics that gives *all students* opportunities to work and interact with others in using mathematics to solve meaningful problems and evaluating their own mathematical performance.

Many students with disabilities experience problems in learning mathematics (Cawley, Parmar, Yan, & Miller, 1998; Xin & Jitendra, 1999). However, these students can im-

Problem solving can be aided by using manipulatives and other teaching aids.

prove their computational and mathematics reasoning skills when they are taught using a problem-solving curriculum that involves them in experiencing, thinking about, and solving meaningful mathematical problems (Bottge, 1999; Woodward & Baxter, 1997). In addition to improving the mathematical understanding of students with disabilities, a problem-solving approach fosters mathematical fluency, promotes a positive attitude toward mathematics, and prepares students for the world of work and independent living (Bley & Thornton, 1995).

Because of learning, language, and behavioral difficulties, some students may initially have difficulty with a problem-solving approach. You can help these students benefit from and succeed with this approach by planning and organizing instruction according to the following principles, many of which also can be used to structure your teaching of science and social studies.

SET YOUR SITES

Math Forum (www.forum. swarthmore.edu) and Mega Mathematics (www.cs.uidaho.edu/~ casey931/mega-math) offer links to mathematics lessons and activities.

Present Mathematics Appropriately

Organize Instruction to Follow a Developmental Sequence

You can follow an instructional sequence that involves first introducing new concepts by using three-dimensional objects such as concrete aids and manipulatives; then using semiconcrete aids, such as demonstrations or illustrations on overheads, in computers, and in textbooks to develop proficiency; and finally, promoting speed and accuracy by using abstract strategies such as mathematical symbols and oral and written language (Allsopp, 1999). Following this developmental approach, Miller and Mercer (1993) suggest that you use a graduated word problem sequence in which students first work on word problems without irrelevant information, then progress to word problems with irrelevant information, and finally create their own word problems.

Introduce Concepts and Present Problems Through Everyday Situations

INFORMATIONAL

Patton, Cronin, Bassett, and Koppel (1997) offer guidelines and resources for focusing mathematics teaching on the real-life demands of adulthood.

INFORMATIONAL

Midkiff and Cramer (1993) and Hopkins (1993) provide lists of children's books that relate language arts instruction and students' experiences to mathematics.

INFORMATIONAL

De la Cruz, Cage, and Lian (2000) offer examples of multicultural games to teach mathematics.

INFORMATIONAL

Mitchell, Baab, Campbell-LaVoie, and Prion (1992) have developed the Mathematics of the Environment Curriculum that teaches math by having students apply it to environmental issues in different countries using actual information about population, food, energy, and cultural factors.

You can promote learning, motivate students, and help them learn to value mathematics by connecting mathematics to situations and problems that are familiar and meaningful to them (Mittag & Van Reusen, 1999; Thornton, Langrall, & Jones, 1997). You can present math problems related to real-life situations, and discuss the relevance of learning a new skill and the situations in which the skill can be applied. For example, students can investigate problems by gathering data from shopping, sports statistics, or checkbook recordings. These data can then be used to determine if enough money is available for purchases, if a sports figure is having a successful season, or if a bank account has been credited with the appropriate interest.

By linking mathematical problems to other subject areas such as reading, you can make mathematical connections to the practical, civic, professional, recreational, and cultural aspects of students' lives. For example, *Math Curse* (Scieszka, 1995) uses humor to explain that students encounter math all the time, and *Counting on Frank* (Clement, 1991) can be used as part of a problem-solving approach demonstrating the importance of counting and ratios.

You also can connect mathematics to students' cultural backgrounds. Materials that explore the different cultural origins of mathematics, discuss mathematical solutions and practices developed and used in all parts of the world, present the achievements of mathematicians from various language and cultural backgrounds, and offer various culturally diverse, practical applications of mathematics can be used to relate students' experiences to mathematics. Connections to students' lives and cultures also can be established by using rhythms, songs, raps, and chants that teach mathematics, as well as by employing strategies that were used to teach mathematics in students' native countries (Scott & Raborn, 1996). You also can frame word problems using familiar community and multicultural and nonsexist references so that students conduct problem-solving activities focused on problems in the community.

Teach the Language of Mathematics

Like other content areas, math has its own terminology. Learning the language of mathematics can promote mathematical literacy and proficiency, communication, and reasoning and give students a framework for solving problems (Gurganus & Del Mastro, 1998). In particular, students who are second language learners can learn math more easily by using methods that foster their understanding of English language mathematics vocabulary, such as using concrete activities and developing a picture file or bilingual glossary of frequently used math terms (Scott & Raborn, 1996).

Bley and Thornton (1995) propose that you and your students develop and maintain a math dictionary that contains definitions, visual explanations, examples, and graphics of mathematical terminology. For example, the dictionary can contain definitions and examples of such math terms as *sums, differences, quotients, proper fractions, mixed numbers,* and *reciprocals.* Students having difficulty with the term *denominator,* for example, can locate its definition and view examples ("The denominator is the bottom part of a fraction that indicates the number of parts. In this fraction, the 6 is the denominator."). In addition, students can write in their notebooks definitions for mathematical terms using their own words. They also can create a mathematical operations chart that lists various mathematical symbols, terms, and the words that imply different mathematical operations and terms.

Use Teaching Aids

Teach Students to Use Manipulatives and Concrete Teaching Aids

Manipulatives and concrete teaching aids can promote students' understanding of abstract and symbolic concepts by introducing these concepts in a nonthreatening way that makes the connection between mathematics and students' lives (Lambert, 1996; Rose, 1999). They also offer students opportunities to explore concepts before learning standard math terms and notation (Trafton & Claus, 1994). Manipulatives are particularly valuable in helping students with language difficulties learn math concepts (Garnett, 1989).

Marzola (1987) offered a list of commercially produced manipulatives that can be used to teach a variety of concepts including place value, computations, money, time, measurement, fractions, decimals, percent, and geometry. For example, the *Stern Structural Arithmetic Program* (Stern, 1965) employs blocks to teach K-3 arithmetic concepts, and colored Cuisenairre rods of varying lengths have been developed to demonstrate many principles of mathematics.

INFORMATIONAL

Brosnan (1997) describes a variety of geoboard activities that you can use to teach mathematics.

When using manipulatives and concrete teaching aids to teach math concepts, the following guidelines are helpful. At first, introduce them by modeling their use and explaining the concepts illustrated. Next, allow students to experiment with the materials and describe their actions. You can structure students' use of the materials by asking questions that guide their experimentation. To promote generalization, give students opportunities to use a variety of manipulatives. When using manipulatives with students who have behavioral difficulties, you may need to remind them of the classroom rules and reinforce them for complying with the procedures for using and handling the materials.

Use Visuals to Illustrate Concepts, Problems, Solutions, and Interrelationships

Oral math instruction can be supplemented by the use of visuals. Drawings and diagrams of new concepts and interrelationships can help students discuss and visualize mathematical ideas, concepts, and solutions (Woodward, Baxter, & Robinson, 1999). Students gain a visual, concrete framework for understanding the foundations of the process, as well as the steps necessary to solve problems (Allsopp, 1999). Because material used to present mathematics is usually difficult to read, misunderstandings related to reading mathematical language can be minimized by using drawings and diagrams that depict difficult content.

When offering depictions of math concepts and problem-solving techniques, you can discuss patterns and relationships, highlight essential information, and focus students' attention by using colored chalk, marking pens, or computer graphics. For example, when introducing students to the definitions of and differences among equilateral, isosceles, and scalene triangles, you can record the definitions and present examples of each type of triangle and then highlight key words in the definition and shade key sides.

You also can encourage students to visualize solutions to math problems, draw pictures, illustrate and translate findings, and record notes to help them solve problems. For example, if the class is asked to determine the number of different outfits Raul could create after receiving four new shirts, three new ties, and two new pairs of pants, students could solve the problem by drawing pictures of Raul's clothing and connecting the different pictorials with arrows to answer the question.

Students also can learn to solve problems by using graphs. They can be taught how and when to create different types of graphs (e.g., circle, bar, line, histogram) to help them visualize and present solutions to problems.

Use Instructional Technology and Teach Students to Use It

Instructional technology can enhance and support mathematics instruction by offering you and your students visual and auditory stimuli and interactive simulations that can make mathematics come alive for students and help them collect real data and explore solutions to problems (Babbitt & Miller, 1996; Woodward, 1999). These stimuli, including software programs, spreadsheets, databases, computer simulations, and graphics programs and graphing calculators, also can help students solve math problems (Drier, Dawson, & Garofalo, 1999). The Internet and CD-ROM programs allow students to access real data that can be used in solving meaningful problems.

Instructional technology can help you structure lessons so that students with different learning abilities can work together to solve problems. For example, the video-based *The Adventures of Jasper Woodbury* and *Bart's Pet Project* present stories and math problems visually. These problems can be used with students who have different reading abilities (Bottge & Hasselbring, 1999; Goldman & Hasselbring, 1997). The video series *The Wonderful Problems of Fizz and Martina* stimulates students to talk about mathematical solutions and work collaboratively to help the characters solve problems that require mathematical solutions (Dockterman, 1995).

Encourage and Teach Students to Use Calculators

Calculators can help students develop their mathematical literacy and solve problems by giving them the ability to learn, retrieve, and check computation facts, thus promoting their independence and increasing their speed in solving problems (Woodward, 1999). For these reasons, the NCTM has called for teachers to provide students with calculators. Horton, Lovitt, and White (1992) found that when students with disabilities used calculators, their performance was equivalent to that of their general education peers.

You can begin to teach students to use calculators by employing software or an overhead projector transparency to display the calculator keyboard. Each key can then be located, its function described, and examples of its use presented. Next, students can practice locating keys and performing simple calculations. While students are using their calculators, you can periodically remind them that they still need to review and estimate their answers.

Some students who have difficulty computing with calculators, such as those who reverse numbers, may benefit from a talking calculator, which states the numerals entered and computed (Raskind & Higgins, 1998). The *Speech Plus Calculator* developed by Telesensory Systems has a 24-word vocabulary that can help students perform addition, subtraction, multiplication, division, square root, and percentage calculations by stating the function or name of each key as it is pressed. Calculators that provide a printout or display of all numerals and operations entered ($9 - 6 = 3$) may be helpful for students with motor, memory, or attention difficulties because they offer products that can be checked for memory and accuracy (Bley & Thornton, 1995). Some students may need to use calculators with large-print numbers.

Use a Variety of Instructional Approaches

Use Peer-Mediated Instruction

With peer-mediated instruction such as cooperative learning arrangements (see Chapter 9), students work in groups to communicate about and experiment with solutions to mathematical problems (Muth, 1997; Thornton et al., 1007). Peer-mediated instruction allows students to work in groups to ask questions, share ideas, clarify thoughts, experiment, brainstorm, and present solutions with their classmates. Students can understand many perspectives and solutions to mathematical problems and appreciate that math problems can be approached and solved in a variety of ways.

Use Mathematics Programs and Curriculums to Guide and Support Instruction

SET YOUR SITES

Tools for Understanding has a website (www.ups.edu/community/tofu) that offers a curriculum, resources, and lesson plans for teaching common math topics to help secondary students achieve math literacy.

You can use use several problem-solving mathematics programs and curriculums to guide and support instruction (Checkley, 1996; Goldsmith & Mark, 1999). *MiC* is a middle school math curriculum designed to teach numbers, algebra, geometry, and probability and statistics by using real-world problems, interdisciplinary instruction, teacher questioning, and experimentation. *Core-Plus* also uses problem solving to help students understand important mathematical concepts. The problems posed in Core-Plus are designed to promote and accommodate cultural and linguistic diversity. *Number, Data and Space* tries to promote students' mathematical thinking and literacy by using meaningful mathematical problems. The *Interactive Mathematics Program* uses a problem-based approach to teach algebra, geometry, and trigonometry (Alper, Fendel, Fraser, & Resek, 1996). *Everyday Mathematics* uses student-centered problem-solving activities and teaching related to real-life situations and to science, geography, and other content areas (Woodward & Baxter, 1997).

Students who are learning a second language may benefit from *Finding Out/Descubrimiento* (De Avila, 1988) and the *Second Language Approach to Mathematics Skills* (Cuevas, 1984), which promote math literacy through the use of hands-on, relevant activities that reduce abstractions. Other math curriculum materials designed for second language learners are *Children's Math Worlds, Mathematics in Context, EQUALS,* and *Visual Mathematics* (Secada & De La Cruz, 1996).

Offer Students Specialized Instruction in Solving Word Problems

While many students have difficulty solving mathematics word problems, students with learning difficulties may experience particular difficulties. Therefore, these students will need specialized instruction in approaching and solving word problems (Xin & Jitendra, 1999).

Such factors as syntactic complexity, vocabulary level, context, amount of irrelevant information, sequence, and number of ideas presented can make it difficult to solve word problems. You can improve your students' abilities by simplifying the syntax, using vocabulary students understand, deleting irrelevant information, limiting the number of ideas presented, and rearranging the information and presenting it in the order students can follow in solving the problem.

The problem-solving skills of students, particularly those who are learning English, can be enhanced by incorporating writing tasks into mathematics instruction (Davison & Pearce, 1992). Students can keep a math journal that contains reactions to and notes on mathematics activities and teaching, as well as explanations, clarifications, and

IDEAS FOR IMPLEMENTATION

Developing Students' Word Problem-Solving Skills

Although Ms. Ventnor's students were making progress in developing their computation skills, she was concerned about the difficulties they were having with word problems. To help them, she decided to focus on developing their problem-solving skills. She started by presenting word problems through the use of pictorials, highlighting important words in problems, and having students write or state math problems without computing the answers. She also began to personalize problems by using students' names and relating problems to their interests, cultures, experiences, and classroom or current events. When presenting these problems, she asked students to paraphrase the problems in their own words, and had them work in groups to act out word problems, create drawings of the problems, and compose problems to be solved by their classmates. As her students began to develop their problem-solving skills, she asked them to solve problems and minimized the complexity of the calculations by using easier and smaller numbers.

Here are some other strategies you can use to develop your students' word problem-solving skills:

◇ Teach students how to differentiate between relevant and irrelevant information by presenting problems that have too little or too much information.

◇ Teach students the unique features of the various problem types.

◇ Write number cues above specific parts of word problems to show the steps students can follow to solve the problems.

◇ Encourage students to estimate answers and brainstorm solutions to word problems.

◇ Teach students to look for patterns in problems, use charts and graphs to organize data, and relate solutions to previous problems.

◇ Give students diagrams and teach them to draw diagrams to identify the important features of word problems.

◇ Give students problems that have more than one answer and problems that can be solved in several ways.

◇ Encourage and recognize multiple solution strategies to solve problems.

Sources: Jitendra, Hoff, and Beck (1999), Leon (1991), and Parmar, Cawley, and Frazita (1996).

---

applications of math problems (Scott & Raborn, 1996). Students also can write their story problems; write letters to others outlining a mathematical solution, rule, or concept; and develop a math project that requires them to collect data, compute results, develop graphs and other pictorials, and share conclusions.

Students also can be taught to identify the critical elements of word problems, eliminate irrelevant details, and sequence information in the order in which it will be needed. These skills can be developed by teaching students to underline the question and circle the given parts of the problem, by providing practice items in which students restate the specifics of the problem in their own words, and by having students act out the problem.

Teach Students to Use Self-Management Techniques and Learning Strategies

Self-management techniques and learning strategies can be taught to help students solve problems involving a variety of mathematical procedures (Miller, Strawser, & Mercer, 1996).

Techniques such as self-monitoring checklists prompt students to remember the steps necessary to complete a task. In devising self-monitoring checklists, you can do the following:

◆ Identify the skills necessary to complete the task.
◆ List the skills in order.
◆ Create a mnemonic that will help students remember the steps in the process.
◆ Develop a self-monitoring checklist that appears on the students' instructional worksheets.
◆ Model the use of the self-monitoring checklist and the mnemonic strategy for students while describing each step.
◆ Gradually eliminate the use of the checklist (Frank & Brown, 1992).

Self-management also can be effective in helping students learn the math facts and computation skills needed to solve problems that require multistep math operations (Maccini & Hughes, 1997; McDougall & Brady, 1998). For example, self-instruction teaches students to perform computations by describing to themselves the steps and questions necessary to identify and perform the calculations.

Several learning strategies have been developed to help students solve mathematical problems (Babbit & Miller, 1996; Montague, 1997). In general, the steps in these strategies include the following:

Step 1: Read the problem. First, students read the problem to determine the question and to find unknown words and clue words. Clue words are those words that indicate the correct operation to be used. For example, the words *all together, both, together, in all, and, plus,* and *sum* suggest that the problem involves addition; words like *left, lost, spend,* and *remain* indicate that the correct operation is subtraction. When students encounter unknown words, they can ask you to pronounce and define them.

Step 2: Reread the problem. Read the problem a second time to identify and paraphrase relevant information, which can be highlighted by underlining, while deleting irrelevant information and facts. Focus on determining what mathematical process and unit can be used to express the answer.

Step 3: Visualize and draw the problem. Students visualize the problem and draw a representation of the information given.

Step 4: Make a plan and write the problem. Students hypothesize and write the steps in solving the problem in order with the appropriate sign.

Step 5: Estimate the answer. Before solving the problem, students estimate the answer. The estimate provides a framework for determining the reasonableness of their response.

Step 6: Solve the problem. Students solve the problem, as outlined in step 4, by calculating each step in the process, giving attention to the correctness of the calculations and the unit used to express the answer.

Step 7: Check the answer. Students check their work and compare their answer to their estimate. They examine each step in terms of necessity, order, operation selected, and correctness of calculations.

Give Students Models, Cues, and Prompts

Students with learning difficulties may understand the processes used to solve problems involving several operations executed in a particular sequence, but they may need

INFORMATIONAL

Choate (1990) and Karrison and Carroll (1991) offer guidelines for teaching the steps necessary for solving word problems, including studying the problem, devising checklists, identifying clues and key words, and illustrating problems.

INFORMATIONAL

Successful self-instructional techniques for teaching computation skills include equal additions (Sugai & Smith, 1986), count-bys (Lloyd, Saltzman, & Kauffman, 1981), touch math (Miller, Miller, Wheeler, & Selinger, 1989), count-ons, zero facts, doubles, and turn-around (Jones, Thornton, & Toohey, 1985).

INFORMATIONAL

Miller et al. (1996) offer examples of acronym mnemonics that can be used to help students solve word problems.

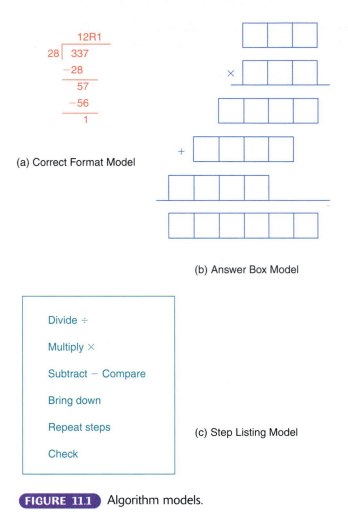

(a) Correct Format Model

(b) Answer Box Model

Divide ÷

Multiply ×

Subtract − Compare

Bring down

Repeat steps

Check

(c) Step Listing Model

FIGURE 11.1   Algorithm models.

models, cues, and prompts to guide them in performing these operations. Problem-solving assignments can be coded so that they include a model for calculating the answer. The model can vary, depending on the skill level and needs of the students. Sample models are presented in Figure 11.1. Flip charts can offer students a model of the correct format and order in approaching a task (Bley & Thornton, 1995). Each page of the flip chart represents a step students must perform to complete the task. A sample flip chart for division of fractions is presented in Figure 11.2.

Charts also can be placed in the room to help students. These charts can present math terms, facts, and symbols (*subtract = take away = −*), as well as the steps to follow for a specific type of problem, such as the steps in dividing fractions. For example, a fraction strip chart presenting strips divided into halves, thirds, fourths, and so on can be posted to help students learn the concepts associated with fractions.

Cues also can be used with students who have difficulty remembering the order in which to solve computation items. Arrows can be drawn to indicate the direction in which students should proceed. Cues such as green and red dots, go and stop signs, and answer boxes tell students when to proceed or stop when working on a specific item.

Attention to signs (+, −, ×) can be emphasized by color coding, boldfacing, and underlining. It can also be fostered by listing the sign and its operation at the top of each

---

Chart 1: Identify the divisor

$$\frac{a}{b} \div \frac{c}{d}$$

Chart 2: Invert the divisor

$$\frac{c}{d} \quad \text{becomes} \quad \frac{d}{c}$$

Chart 3: Multiply fractions and reduce to the lowest terms

$$\frac{a}{b} \times \frac{d}{c} = \frac{ad}{bc}$$

FIGURE 11.2 Flip chart for dividing fractions.

worksheet (+ = add: 6 + 3 = 9) and teaching students to trace the sign before beginning the computation.

Another type of cue, *boxing*, or placing boxes around items, can focus students' attention on specific problems within a group. When boxing items, you should leave enough space within the box to do the calculations needed to solve the item. As students' skills increase, they can be encouraged to assume responsibility for boxing items.

Boxing also can aid students who have problems placing their answer in the correct column. A color-coded, smaller box or broken line can be drawn to delineate columns so that students place their answers appropriately. Problems with aligning answers also can be minimized by having students use centimeter graph paper, on which only one digit can be written in each box, or by turning lined paper so that the lines run vertically. Alignment problems also can be reduced by teaching students to estimate the answer and check its reasonableness. An answer that deviates significantly from the estimate may indicate an alignment problem, and students can check their work accordingly.

You can use visual and verbal prompts to help students solve problems (Phillips et al., 1993). For example, students can be given a visual that prompts them to read the problem, underline the important information, cross out useless information, ask what type of problem it is, and ask what operations should be used.

Help Students Develop Their Math Facts and Computation Skills

You can promote the success of a problem-solving approach to mathematics by offering instruction that helps students develop their math facts and computation skills (Lock, 1996). A *demonstration plus model* strategy has been successful in helping students with learning problems develop computational skills (Rivera & Deutsch-Smith, 1988). The strategy involves these steps:

Step 1: You demonstrate the procedures for solving a specific type of computation problem while presenting the key words for each step.

Step 2: Students view your example and perform the steps in the computation while giving the key words for each step.

Step 3: Students complete additional problems, referring to your example if necessary.

Vary the Instructional Sequence

Some students who are having difficulty learning math facts and computation skills may benefit from modifications in their sequence. For example, while the traditional teaching sequence for addition computation skills is based on the numeric value of the sum, Thornton and Toohey (1985) suggest that teachers use a teaching sequence that progresses from count-ons (e.g., +1, +2, +3) to zero facts (3 + 0, 7 + 0) to doubles (3 + 3, 8 + 8) to 10 sums (4 + 6, 3 + 7).

Varying the teaching sequence to cluster math facts can make it easier to remember them. Rather than teaching math facts in isolation, you can present related math facts together (Thornton, Tucker, Dossey, & Bazik, 1983). For example, students can learn the cluster of multiplying by 2 together. As students demonstrate mastery, they can practice mixed groups of math facts (Garnett, 1989).

Promote Mastery and Automaticity

An important goal of math instruction in basic facts is to have students respond quickly and accurately. You can offer students a variety of activities that promote mastery and automaticity, such as using student- or peer-directed flash cards and having students listen to math facts on a Language Master or an audiocassette. Independent assignments and homework also can be used to help students develop automaticity. Rather than giving students a large number of items, Parmar and Cawley (1991) suggest that you give them assignments with two sample computation items, discuss the key features of the items, and ask students to create and answer new items that resemble the sample items.

Use Remedial Programs

Several programs are available to help students develop their math skills and to supplement math instruction. These programs include Project Math (Cawley, Fitzmaurice, Sedlak, & Althaus, 1976), Computational Arithmetic Program (Smith & Lovitt, 1982), Milliken Wordmath (Coffland & Baldwin, 1985), Corrective Mathematics Program (Engelmann & Carnine, 1982), Distar Arithmetic (Engelmann & Carnine, 1975, 1976), Enright S.O.L.V.E.: Action Problem Solving (Enright, 1987), Developing Key Concepts for Solving Word Problems (Panchyshyn & Monroe, 1986), Problem Solving Experiences in Mathematics (Charles, 1984), and the Strategic Math Series (SMS) (Mercer & Miller, 1992).

Match Instruction to Students' Error Types

The instructional strategy selected often will depend on the types of errors that students make. Taylor (1992) offers the following suggestions:

◆ When a step in an algorithm is omitted, consider teaching students a self-monitoring strategy to check that all steps have been completed.

◆ When a placement error is made, give students opportunities to practice the rule and provide feedback.

◆ When the error involves problems with regrouping, use manipulatives, concrete materials, and pictorial displays.

◆ When a step in the process is substituted for, use role playing in which the students review the steps in the process by acting out the role of the teacher.

Chiang and Ratajczak (1990) noted that when errors indicate conceptual misunderstandings, you can break down the task into smaller and simpler units, make sure that students have mastered prerequisite skills, offer them prompts and cues, and teach them to use self-instruction and self-monitoring techniques.

Provide Feedback and Use Assessment to Guide Future Teaching

Offer Prompt Feedback

Prompt feedback is an important part of effective mathematics instruction. Allsopp (1999) suggests that you use corrective feedback to tell students that their response is correct or incorrect, identify which part is correct or incorrect, and offer students a strategy to obtain the correct response.

Involve Students in the Assessment Process

The NCTM calls for involving students in the assessment process to help them gain insight into their knowledge of math and the ways in which they think about math. Therefore, you can consider using student-centered strategies that involve students in setting goals, choosing appropriate assessment techniques, and identifying helpful teaching strategies and materials such as portfolio assessment, learning logs, think-alouds, and student interviews. (These student-centered assessment strategies are discussed in Chapter 12.) Student-centered assessment also includes public demonstrations that focus on the process and products of learning. These demonstrations are a means of assessing students' understanding and identifying the approaches they use to solve real-world problems (Rivera, 1996).

As part of the self-assessment process, students can be taught to estimate and check their answers. They can learn to locate and correct their errors. You can provide an error analysis and correction sheet that asks students to list the problem, the steps in solving the problem, the correct answer(s), the errors made, and the reason for the errors. Students also can be taught to evaluate their mastery of concepts by graphing their performance on computer programs, worksheets, and follow-up probes. A checking center equipped with answer keys, teacher's guides, supplementary materials, peer tutors, and recordings of potential solutions can promote self-checking and minimize the demands on your time.

Assess Mastery and Progress Over Time

Maintaining skills is important for students with disabilities, so you can periodically conduct reviews and probes to assess their mastery and retention of previously learned skills. You can give students feedback on their performance and encourage them to record their own progress over time.

How Can I Differentiate Science and Social Studies Instruction?

In addition to the strategies for differentiating instruction presented in this section, many of the suggestions for teaching mathematics outlined in the previous section also apply to teaching science and social studies.

Choose and Use Appropriate Instructional Materials

While the specific content in each area is different, science and social studies share several teaching methods. Both areas are often taught using content-oriented approaches that rely on oral presentations and textbooks. Because some students, including students with disabilities, may sometimes have difficulty learning information from oral presentations and textbooks, science and social studies teaching should be differentiated by using appropriate instructional materials.

Choose Textbooks Carefully

Much of the content in science and social studies, particularly at the middle and secondary levels, is presented in textbooks that are often difficult for students, particularly those with learning difficulties, to use (Bryant et al., 1999; Wood, 1995). It is important to determine the readability level of the textbook and to use the teacher- and student-directed text comprehension strategies we reviewed in Chapter 8. In addition, textbooks for students should be chosen carefully in terms of structure, coherence, content, and audience appropriateness.

Textbooks also should relate to students' background knowledge. Unfortunately, many textbooks and instructional materials do not include the accomplishments or perspectives of individuals from diverse cultural and language backgrounds. Many of them ignore other cultures and female students, use stereotyping, offer only one interpretation of issues, avoid important issues, and present information about certain groups in isola-

Choosing appropriate textbooks is a crucial part of content area instruction.

REFLECTING ON YOUR PRACTICES

Selecting Textbooks

In selecting the textbooks you use, consider the following questions:

◇ Is the content appropriate and up-to-date?

◇ Is the language clear and appropriate for students?

◇ Are there informative headings and subheadings?

◇ Does the textbook provide signals to highlight main points and key vocabulary (marginal notations, graphic aids, pointer words and phrases)?

◇ Is information presented in an organized fashion (using preview or introductory statements, topic sentences, summary statements, lists, enumeration words)?

◇ Does the textbook offer transitions that help the reader adjust to changes in topics?

◇ Does the textbook come with support materials to help students learn, such as study guides, graphic organizers, concept maps, illustrations, pictorials, supplemental learning activities, a table of contents, an index, a glossary, appendices, and computer programs?

◇ Are the pictorial and graphic aids easy to read and interpret?

◇ Do the illustrations provide a visual framework for understanding the material and supplementing the text?

◇ Are illustrations referred to and explained?

◇ Are chronological sequences or events presented in order of occurrence?

◇ Is the content balanced, as well as sufficiently broad and deep?

◇ Does the textbook clearly establish and highlight the relationships among important facts, concepts, and roles?

◇ Does the textbook include information about and the perspectives of individuals from diverse cultural backgrounds, as well as their contributions?

◇ Does the textbook include strategies to check for student understanding, such as interspersed and review questions and activities that help students identify, understand, apply, and assess their mastery of critical information?

◇ Is the textbook interesting looking, and does it make good use of space and colors?

How would you rate your selection of textbooks?
( ) Excellent ( ) Good ( ) Needs Improvement
( ) Needs Much Improvement
    What steps could you take to improve your selection of textbooks?

Sources: Armbruster and Anderson (1988), Ellis (1996), Harniss, Hollenbeck, Crawford, and Carnine (1994), and Lovitt and Horton (1994).

---

tion. Because of the bias in many textbooks, many teachers rely on hands-on, activity-based teaching approaches instead.

Consider Electronic Textbooks

Technological advances are resulting in the development of handheld electronic textbooks that have several advantages over traditional textbooks (Bronner, 1998). Electronic textbooks have built-in dictionaries. They allow students to conduct word searches and download information from the Internet and other electronic sources. They also help students to understand the material by allowing them to access on-line resources such as graphics, pictures, audio, and video.

Teach Students How to Use Textbooks and Instructional Materials

Students can be taught how to use and obtain information from the textbooks and instructional materials used in the general education classroom. You can examine the vocabulary and concept development that students will need to use the book and teach students how to identify and define these terms. For example, you and your students can review chapters from the book, selecting key terms and concepts that they can define by using the book's glossary or another resource, such as a dictionary or an encyclopedia. When students become adept at this task, they can be encouraged to perform the steps alone.

Because information is usually presented in a similar way from chapter to chapter in textbooks and instructional materials, reviewing the organization of the materials is also helpful. This involves reviewing and explaining the functions of and interrelationships among the material's components (table of contents, text, glossary, index, appendices) and the elements of the book's chapters (titles, objectives, abstract, headings, summary, study guides, follow-up questions, references, alternative learning activities).

You also can help students learn to use text headings to enhance their reading and learning from textbooks by teaching them to use learning strategies such as *SCROL* (Grant, 1993). The SCROL strategy involves the following:

Survey: Students read the headings and subheadings and ask themselves, "What do I know about this topic?" and "What information is going to be presented?"

Connect: Students ask, "How do the headings and subheadings relate to each other?" and list key words that provide connections.

Read: Students read the headings and outline the major ideas and supporting details without looking back at the text.

Outline: Students record the headings and outline the major ideas and supporting details without looking back at the text.

Look back: Students look back at the heading and subheadings, and check and correct their outlines.

When teaching about textbooks and instructional materials, it may be helpful to teach students the strategies used by the author(s) to present content. Students can learn to identify five patterns that are typically used by authors: enumeration, time order, compare-contrast, cause-effect, and problem solution. These strategies are often repeated throughout the book, so students can be taught to analyze a book by examining the numbering (*1, 2, 3*), lettering (*a, b, c*), or word (*first, second, third*) system used to show the relative importance of information, as well as the order of ideas; the typographic signs (*boldfacing, underlining, color cueing, boxing*) used to highlight critical information; and the word signals that indicate the equal importance of information (*furthermore, likewise*), elaboration (*moreover*), rebuttal and clarification (*nevertheless, however, but*), summarization (*therefore, consequently*), and termination (*finally, in conclusion*).

You also can help students by showing them how to gain information from visual displays. Prompt them to examine illustrations and to preview the graphics to get a general idea of their purpose. You can teach them to read the title, captions, and headings to determine relevant information about the graphic; identify the units of measurement; and discuss, relate, and generalize graphic information to the text.

Many textbooks and instructional materials often come with supplemental materials such as student activity worksheets and overviews. Therefore, students can receive some training in completing the activity worksheets and interpreting information presented in graphic displays. For example, you can help students learn to complete end-of-chapter questions by training them to do the following:

◆ Read each question to determine what is being asked.
◆ Identify words in the question that can guide the reader to the correct answer.

INFORMATIONAL

Harmon, Katims, and Whittington (1999) developed the Person-Event-Place (PEP) strategy to help students learn to use social studies textbooks.

REFLECTIVE

How is this book organized to present information? What strategies are used to highlight information? What aspects of the book help promote your learning?

INFORMATIONAL

Ellis (1996) developed SNIPS, and Barry, cited in Ellis and Lenz (1987), developed the *Reading Visual Aids Strategy (RVAS)* to help students gain information from visual aids and graphic presentations.

- ◈ Determine the requirement of the question and the format of the answer.
- ◈ Convert appropriate parts of the question into part of the answer.
- ◈ Identify the paragraphs of the chapter that relate to the question.
- ◈ Locate the answer to the question by reading the chapter.
- ◈ Write the answer to the question.
- ◈ Check the answer for accuracy and form.

Learning to look for highlighted information that is usually italicized or boldfaced also can help students identify main points that often contain answers to study questions.

Note Taking from Textbooks   Good note-taking skills are invaluable in learning from textbooks. A useful method to teach students involves setting up a margin, about 2 inches from the left side of the paper, where students can jot down questions based on the information presented in the chapter, on chapter subheadings, and on discussion/ study questions. Students also can use this column to list vocabulary words and their definitions. They can use the rest of the page to record answers to the questions and other critical information from the chapter.

If the school allows it, highlighting information in a textbook can help students identify parts of a chapter that are critical for class discussions and can assist them in studying for exams (Pauk, 1984). When marking in a textbook, <u>students can be taught to use double lines to delineate text that denotes main ideas</u> and <u>single lines to identify supporting ideas</u>. [When several continuous lines present essential content, students can use a vertical bracket in the margin rather than underlining.]

Symbols in margins and in the text are also helpful. Asterisks in the margins can be used to identify and rate important content, and question marks in the margins can prompt students to seek clarification for material that they do not agree with or do not understand. Finally, students can be taught to circle key words and to box words that indicate enumeration and transition.

Use Study Guides

You can prepare *study guides* to help students identify the critical information in assignments and provide activities to help students master it (Boyle & Yeager, 1997). Study guides contain a series of statements, questions, and/or activities that help students identify and learn critical information from textbooks and oral presentations. They can be used to teach content-specific vocabulary, structure content-specific readings, practice and review previously learned material, and introduce new material.

While study guides vary, they often include the reading assignment, objectives, rationale, text references, a chapter summary, an outline, study questions, activities, definitions of key terms, and student evaluation probes. Study guides also can take the form of a *framed outline,* an ordered list of the chapter's main points with key words blanked out. The students fill in the blanks while reading the selection or listening to a lecture in class. You also can use hypertext to develop computerized study guides for students (Lovitt & Horton, 1994).

Wood (1995) identified five types of study guides that can be used to assist students in reading informational text: the point of view reading guide, interactive reading guide, learning-from-text guide, textbook activity guide, and reading road map. Samples of a point of view reading guide, an interactive reading guide, and a reading road map are presented in Figure 11.3.

The point of view reading guide uses an interview format to prompt students to see events and material from multiple viewpoints (see Figure 11.3A). This guide requires students to assume the roles and perspectives of the individuals depicted in the text. For

---

✶ **REFLECTIVE**

Look back at the notes you have taken for this book. What note-taking strategies did you use? How well do you use them? Which strategies do you find to be most efficient?

example, when reading about the abolition of slavery, students can be asked to provide text and reader-based information by responding to the question "As an abolitionist, how did you feel about slavery?"

The interactive reading guide is designed so that students can work collaboratively to complete it (see Figure 11.3B). This reading guide asks students "to predict, develop associations, write, chart, outline, or re-tell information in their own words to a partner or a group" (Wood, 1995, p. 138). Once groups or pairs complete the guide, they discuss their responses with the whole class.

The learning-from-text guide is structured so that students progress from answering questions about the textbook that proceed from a literal level ("What is erosion?") to an inferential level ("How does erosion affect people?") to a generalization or evaluative level ("If you were on a committee to minimize the effects of erosion in your community, what things would you want the committee to do?").

The textbook activity guide provides students with a study guide that prompts them to use self-monitoring and metacognitive strategies as they read the textbook. For

INFORMATIONAL

Higgins, Boone, and Lovitt (1996) describe the use and effectiveness of hypermedia-developed study guides.

A: Point of view reading guide

Chapter 11: The War of 1812

You are about to be interviewed as if you were a person living in the United States in the early 1800s. Describe your reactions to each of the events discussed next.

Planting the Seeds of War (p. 285)

  1. As a merchant in a coastal town, tell why your business is doing poorly.

The War Debate (p. 285–7)

  2. Explain why you decided to become a war hawk. Who was your leader?

  3. Tell why many of your fellow townspeople lowered their flags at half mast. What else did they do?

  4. What was the reaction of Great Britain to you and your people at that time?

  5. In your opinion, is America ready to fight? Explain why you feel this way.

Perry's Victory (p. 287)

  6. In what ways were your predictions either correct or incorrect about Americans' readiness to fight this war?

  7. Tell about your experiences under Captain Perry's command.

Death of Tecumseh (p. 288)

  8. Mr. Harrison, describe what really happened near the Thames River in Canada.

  9. What was Richard Johnson's role in that battle?

10. Now, what are your future plans?

Death of the Creek Confederacy (p. 288)

11. Explain how your people, the Cherokees, actually helped the United States.

12. Tell about your leader.

British Invasion (p. 288–90)

13. As a British soldier, what happened when you got to Washington, D.C.?

14. You headed to Fort McHenry after D.C.; what was the outcome?

15. General Jackson, it's your turn. Tell about your army and how you defeated the British in New Orleans.

The Treaty of Ghent (p. 290)

16. We will end our interview with some final observations from the merchant questioned earlier. We will give you some names and people. Tell how they fare now that the war is over: the British, the Indians, the United States, Harrison, Jackson.

FIGURE 11.3   Sample study guides.

Interaction codes:

- ⭕ = Individual
- ⊙⊙ = Pairs
- ⊗⊗ = Group
- ◯ = Whole class

Chapter 12: "Japan—An Island Country"

⊗⊗ 1. In your group, write down everything you can think of relative to the topics listed below on Japan. Your group's associations will then be shared with the class.

```
        location ———— Japan ———— major cities
            land  ╱  ╱    │  ╲ ╲  industry
          seasons          │       products
                          food
```

⭕
⊙⊙ 2. Read page 156 and jot down 5 things about the topography of Japan. Share this information with your partner.

◯ 3. Read to remember all you can about the "Seasons of Japan." The associations of the class will then be written on the board for discussion.

⊙⊙ 4. a. Take turns "whisper reading" the three sections under "Feeding the People of Japan." After each section, retell, with the aid of your partner, the information in your own words.

   b. What have you learned about the following?
      terraces, paddies, thresh, other crops, fisheries

⊗⊗ 5. Put two pencils together and allow each person in the group to try eating with chopsticks. Discuss your experiences with the group.

⊙⊙ 6. With your partner, use your prior knowledge to predict if the following statements are true or false *before* reading the section on "Industrialized Japan." Return to these statements *after* reading to see if you've changed your view. In all cases, be sure to explain your answers. You do not have to agree with your partner.

   a. Japan does not produce its own raw materials but instead gets them from other countries.
   b. Japan is one of the top 10 shipbuilding countries.
   c. Japan makes more cars than the U.S.
   d. Silk used to be produced by silkworms but now it is a manmade fiber.
   e. Silkworms eat mulberry leaves.
   f. The thread from a single cocoon is 600 feet long.

⭕ 7. After reading, write down 3 new things you learned about the following topics.
⊗⊗ Compare these responses with those of your group.

         Other industries of Japan
         Old and new ways of living

⭕ 8. Read the section on "Cities of Japan." Each group member is to choose a city;
⊗⊗ show its location on the map in the textbook, and report on some facts about it.

⭕ 9. Return to the major topics introduced in the first activity. Skim over your chapter
◯ reading guide responses with these topics in mind. Next, be ready to contribute, along with the class, anything you have learned about these topics.

FIGURE 11.3 (continued)

C: Reading road map

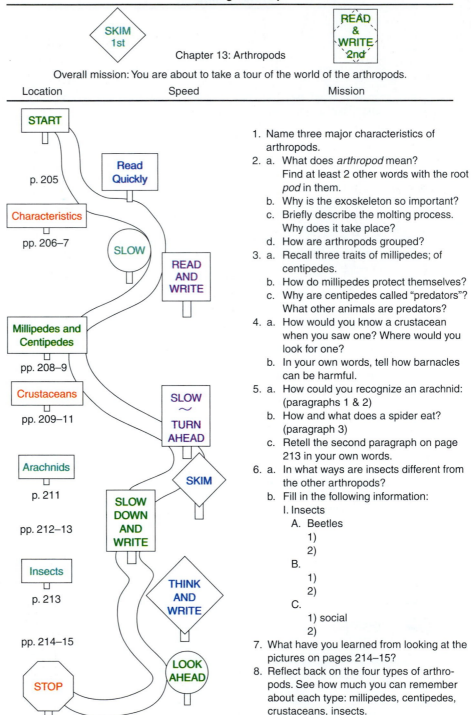

Chapter 13: Arthropods

Overall mission: You are about to take a tour of the world of the arthropods.

Location	Speed	Mission

1. Name three major characteristics of arthropods.
2. a. What does *arthropod* mean?
      Find at least 2 other words with the root *pod* in them.
   b. Why is the exoskeleton so important?
   c. Briefly describe the molting process. Why does it take place?
   d. How are arthropods grouped?
3. a. Recall three traits of millipedes; of centipedes.
   b. How do millipedes protect themselves?
   c. Why are centipedes called "predators"? What other animals are predators?
4. a. How would you know a crustacean when you saw one? Where would you look for one?
   b. In your own words, tell how barnacles can be harmful.
5. a. How could you recognize an arachnid: (paragraphs 1 & 2)
   b. How and what does a spider eat? (paragraph 3)
   c. Retell the second paragraph on page 213 in your own words.
6. a. In what ways are insects different from the other arthropods?
   b. Fill in the following information:
      I. Insects
         A. Beetles
            1)
            2)
         B.
            1)
            2)
         C.
            1) social
            2)
7. What have you learned from looking at the pictures on pages 214–15?
8. Reflect back on the four types of arthropods. See how much you can remember about each type: millipedes, centipedes, crustaceans, insects.

FIGURE 11.3 (continued)

example, as students read textbooks, they are guided to assess their understanding of the material by responding to self-monitoring statements such as "I understand this information," "I don't think I understand this information," and "I don't understand this information and need help." Metacognitive strategy codes also direct students to use various metacognitive strategies to enhance their understanding of the textbook material. For example, metacognitive strategy codes can prompt students to relate new information to their prior knowledge, predict information, paraphrase information in their own words, survey material, create a chart, map, or outline, and use self-questioning.

The reading road map gives students a time frame for adjusting their reading rate based on the importance of the textbook material (see Figure 11.3C). A reading road map "includes missions (interspersed questions and activities), road signs (indicating the speed or rate of reading), and location signs (headings and page or paragraph numbers)" (Wood, 1995, p. 141).

In developing and using study guides, consider the following:

◆ Create separate study guides for each chapter, unit of content, or class presentation.
◆ Identify the key words, main points, and important concepts to be highlighted.
◆ Adjust the readability of the study guide, highlight critical vocabulary and points, and give students cues to indicate the pages and paragraphs where answers and relevant information to complete the study guides are located.
◆ Be creative and use pictures, drawings, and activities that engage students' attention and provide motivation.
◆ Devise interspersed questions, brief sentences, and multimodality activities focusing on the critical components of the material so that they are consistent with the order of the information presented in the textbook or in class.
◆ Give students enough space to write their answers on the study guide.
◆ Distribute the study guides, explain their purpose, and model how to use and complete them.
◆ Have students complete the study guides individually or in groups.
◆ Discuss and review the answers and offer students feedback on their performance.

Use Adapted Textbooks and a Parallel Alternative Curriculum

Many students with disabilities may have difficulty reading on-grade science and social studies textbooks. For these students, it may be appropriate to use *adapted textbooks*, which present the same content as the on-grade textbook but at a lower readability level. You can find appropriate adapted textbooks corresponding to on-grade textbooks by contacting representatives from book companies.

In addition to adapted textbooks, *Parallel Alternative Curriculum (PAC)* materials have been developed for students with learning difficulties. These materials supplement the textbook by providing students with alternative ways to master critical information (Mercer & Mercer, 1993).

SET YOUR SITES

Information on teaching science to students with disabilities can be obtained from the Educational Resource Information Center Clearinghouse for Science, Math, and Environmental Education (www.ericse.org, 800-276-0462).

Use Content Enhancements

Content enhancements are strategies that help students identify, organize, understand, and remember important content. They help students understand abstract information and see the relationship between different pieces or types of information (Bulgren & Lenz, 1996). A variety of content enhancements are presented next.

INFORMATIONAL

Boudah, Lenz, Bulgren, Schumaker, and Deshler (2000) offer guidelines for using a unit organizer, an interactive content enhancement technique.

Advance and Post Organizers

Advance and *post organizers* are written or oral statements, activities, and/or illustrations that offer students a framework for determining and understanding the essential information in a learning activity (Munk, Bruckert, Call, Stoehrmann, & Radandt, 1998). Advance organizers are used at the beginning of a lesson to orient students to the content to be presented. Post organizers are used at the end of the lesson to help students review and remember the content that has been presented. For example, when assigning a reading selection in a science textbook, you can focus students' reading via an advance organizer such as "Read pages 65 to 68 on mirrors and find out how a mirror works. Pay careful attention to such terms as *plane mirror, virtual image, parabolic mirror, principal axis, principal focus,* and *focal length.*" Similarly, a class-developed outline that summarizes the main points of a presentation on the geography of California could serve as a post organizer. In addition to social studies and science, advance and post organizers can be used to teach in all content areas. Several types of advance and post organizers are described below.

Graphic Organizers   One advance or post organizer is a *graphic organizer,* also called a *structured overview,* which identifies and presents key terms before students encounter them in class and textbooks. A graphic organizer is a visual-spatial illustration of the key terms that comprise concepts and their interrelationships. It presents information through the use of webs, matrices, timelines, process chains, cycles, and networks. Graphic organizers help students identify and organize important information so that they can make comparisons, clarify relationships, develop inferences, and draw conclusions (Griffin & Tulbert, 1995).

    Crank and Bulgren (1993) identified three types of graphic organizers: central and hierarchical, directional, and comparative. *Central* and *hierarchical* graphic organizers are structured around one central topic (i.e., an idea or a concept) and are typically used to depict concepts and the elements that describe them. In a central graphic organizer, important information related to the central topic is depicted visually as radiating outward from the central topic. In a hierarchical graphic organizer, supporting information is presented in order of importance, with items being supraordinate to other items. *Directional* graphic organizers present information in a sequence and are often used to depict cause-effect information or content that can be presented in a timeline or flowchart. Directional organizers are often used to present processes and procedures. *Comparative* graphic organizers are used to compare two or more concepts and typically include information presented in a matrix or chart.

    You can develop graphic organizers by doing the following:

INFORMATIONAL

Crank and Bulgren (1993) and Ellis (1994, 1997, 1998) offer illustrations for hierarchical, cause-effect, compare-contrast, and sequential process graphic organizers.

◆ Preview and analyze the curriculum area or textbook to identify key information, concepts, and terms.
◆ Construct an outline of the main information. Arrange the information, concepts, and terms students are to learn based on their interrelationships.
◆ Select a graphic organizer format that coincides with the organization of the information to be learned.
◆ Delete information you want students to contribute.
◆ Include additional terms that are important for students to know.
◆ Add graphics to motivate students and promote mastery of the information.
◆ Assess the graphic organizer for completeness and organization.
◆ Prepare three versions of the graphic organizer: a completed version, a semicompleted version, and a blank version. Use the blank version with students who write quickly. Use the semicompleted version with students who have some

Graphic organizers help students make comparisons, clarify relationships, formulate inferences, and draw conclusions.

difficulty copying and organizing information. Use the completed version with students who have significant difficulties copying and organizing information.

◆ Introduce the graphic organizer to the students.

◆ Include additional information relevant to the overview (Dye, 2000; Lovitt & Horton, 1994).

As students become accustomed to using graphic organizers, they can be encouraged to develop their own. Scanlon, Deshler, and Schumaker (1996) developed a learning strategy called ORDER to help students develop their own graphic organizers.

Semantic Webs   *Semantic webs*, also called *semantic maps*, like graphic organizers, provide a visual depiction of important points, as well as the relationships between these points, and can be developed by students (Rose, 1999). Semantic webs can be used to introduce, review, and clarify new and previously learned material. A semantic web includes a key word or phrase that relates to the main point of the content, which serves as the focal point of the web; web strands, which are subordinate ideas related to the key word; strand supports, which include details and information related to each web strand; and strand ties, which establish the interrelationships between different strands. Semantic webs may take other shapes as well (see Figure 11.4).

Anticipation Guides   The *anticipation guide* is an advance organizer that introduces students to new content by having them respond to several oral or written statements or questions concerning the material. For example, an anticipation guide might include a series of true/false statements that the students answer and discuss before reading a chapter in the textbook (see Figure 11.5). The steps in constructing anticipation guides are as follows:

1. Analyze the text and determine the main points.
2. Convert main points into short, declarative, concrete statements that students can understand.

INFORMATIONAL

Boyle and Yeager (1997) describe TRAVEL, a learning strategy that helps students generate their own semantic webs.

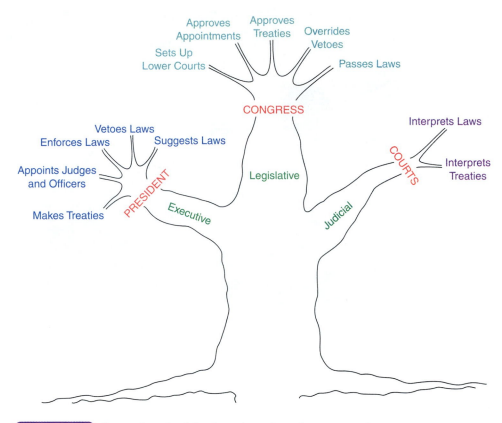

FIGURE 11.4   Semantic web of the three branches of government.

3. Present statements to students in a way that leads to anticipation and prediction.
4. Have students discuss their predictions and responses to the statements.
5. Discuss the students' reading of the text selection, and then compare and evaluate their responses with the information presented in the text.

Concept-Teaching Routines   Many science and social studies concepts can be taught using a *concept teaching routine.* This involves presenting new concepts in the form of a concept diagram containing the relevant characteristics of the concept. The

REFLECTIVE

Develop a graphic organizer, concept teaching routine, anticipation guide, or semantic web for the content presented in this chapter.

> Working as a group, read the statements and place a *T* next to those that are true and an *F* next to those that are false. Be prepared to explain the reasons for rating a statement as true or false.
>
> ◇ Ninety-five percent of the energy needs of the United States are provided by fossil fuels.
> ◇ Spacecraft and many homes use solar energy.
> ◇ Hydroelectric power has no negative effects on the environment.
> ◇ Fossil fuels produce more energy per gram than nonfossil fuels.
> ◇ Before the radiation decays, radioactive wastes must be stored for a thousand years.

FIGURE 11.5   Anticipation guide on energy resources.

Concept Name:	democracy		

Definitions: A democracy is a form of government in which the people hold the ruling power, citizens are equal, the individual is valued, and compromise is necessary.

Characteristics Present in the Concept:

Always	Sometimes	Never
form of government	direct representation	king rules
people hold power	indirect representation	dictator rules
individual is valued		
citizens equal		
compromise necessary		

Example:

Germany today

Athens
(about 500 B.C.)

Nonexample:

Germany under Hitler

Macedonia
(under Alexander)

FIGURE 11.6   Sample concept teaching routine.

Source: J. Bulgren, J. B. Schumaker, and D. Deshler, Effectiveness of a concept teaching routine in enhancing the performance of LD students in secondary-level mainstream classes. *Learning Disability Quarterly,* vol. 11, 1988. Copyright 1988. Reprinted by permission.

concept diagram can also be used to help students review for tests. A sample concept diagram is presented in Figure 11.6.

Use a Variety of Instructional Approaches and Practices

You can differentiate social studies and science instruction by using a variety of approaches and practices such as the ones described below.

Use Activities-Oriented Approaches

Instead of a content-oriented approach to teaching science and social studies, you can use an activities-oriented approach. This approach uses discovery and inquiry to help students develop their own knowledge and understanding of science and social studies based on their experiences. When using an activities-oriented approach, offer students a variety of active educational experiences that provide engagement, exploration, development, and extension (Guillaume, Yopp, & Yopp, 1996; Gurganus, Janas, & Schmitt, 1995). The learning cycle begins with the *engagement phase,* in which real-life activities,

SET YOUR SITES

You can obtain information, resources, and standards for teaching science from the National Science Teachers Association (www.nsta.org, 703-243-7100).

REFLECTING ON PROFESSIONAL PRACTICES

Using Semantic Webs

Mr. Tejada collects and grades students' notebooks at the end of each unit of instruction. He notices that his students are handing in notebooks that lack many pieces of information from classes and textbook readings that he feels are important. As a result, many students are having difficulty in class and are doing poorly on tests.

To help his students identify and retain information, Mr. Tejada decides to use semantic webs to help them review and organize material relating to the unit they are studying on the federal government. After asking students to read about the roles of the three branches of government, Mr. Tejada writes the key words *Executive, Legislative,* and *Judicial* on the board. He asks students what these words mean and then asks them to brainstorm related ideas and concepts. As students present their ideas, Mr. Tejada asks the class to determine whether the ideas are new and relevant and should be listed on the board or whether they are not relevant or overlap with the ideas already on the board. He then asks the students to work in groups to examine the relationships between the con-

cepts listed on the board and group the related concepts together under the key words. After reviewing their groupings, Mr. Tejada and his students create a tree-like semantic web that contains the branches of the government and the duties performed by the president, Congress, and the courts (see Figure 11.4). The students then review the web, add new material based on texts and classroom discussions, and copy it in their notebooks. To further reinforce the concept of checks and balances, Mr. Tejada draws a picture of a seesaw balanced by an equal number of checkmarks on both sides.

Before the unit ends, Mr. Tejada collects students' notebooks and is pleased to see that they have copied the webs and pictorials. He also is pleased when his students' knowledge of the material has improved.

Why did Mr. Tejada decide to use semantic webs? How do content enhancements like semantic webs benefit students? What steps and strategies did Mr. Tejada follow in using semantic webs? What other strategies could he use to help his students learn the material?

problems, and questions are used to motivate students to learn about the topic and to assess their prior knowledge. Students explore the content and phenomena by manipulating materials and start to address the questions presented in the engagement phase. For example, as part of a unit on simple machines, you can ask students to identify simple machines that they use and have them take apart broken household appliances. During the *exploration phase,* students formulate new ideas and questions to be developed in the later phases. For example, you can have students explore how the household appliances work, identify their components, and develop hypotheses about how to fix them. In the *development phase,* students add to their understanding by gathering more information and drawing conclusions about the concepts, the phenomena, and the questions previously generated. Using our example, students can access the Internet to learn more about the appliances and to draw conclusions about how they work. The final stage, *extension,* gives students opportunities to apply their learning to new and different situations as well as to their own experiences. In our example, students can hypothesize how other machines and household appliances that they use work.

An effective activities-oriented approach provides students with hands-on and multisensory experiences and materials. Hands-on learning offers students concrete experiences that establish a foundation for learning abstract concepts. Hands-on and multisensory activities also allow students to explore and discover content. In addition, these activities reduce the language and literacy demands that may interfere with the learning of students with disabilities and students who are learning a second language (Lee & Fradd, 1995). For example, students can learn about electricity by building electric circuits and can become familiar with the geography of a region by making a topographical map out of papier-mâché.

IDEAS FOR IMPLEMENTATION

Ensuring Safety in Laboratory Settings

Ms. Castro's chemistry class included several students with sensory and physical disabilities. She was concerned about their ability to use and learn from the frequent laboratory experiments that students performed. Her principal and several of her colleagues suggested that she purchase specialized equipment such as spoons with sliding covers, glassware with raised letters and numbers, lightweight fire extinguishers, and devices with visual and auditory on/off indicators and warnings. They also recommended that she label important areas, material, and substances in the room and assign students to work with lab partners.

Here are some other strategies you can use to ensure safety in the laboratory:

◇ Post, discuss, and distribute to students the rules, safety considerations, and evacuation procedures before beginning an experiment.

◇ Make sure that students wear safety equipment such as splashproof goggles and rubber gloves and aprons.

◇ Use print and sandpaper labeling for hazardous materials, and make sure that combustible gas supplies contain odorants.

◇ Provide adapted laboratory stations for students who need them. An adapted station may include a work surface 30 inches from the floor, accessible and modified equipment controls, appropriate space for clearance, and wider than usual aisles.

◇ Equip the laboratory with adjustable-height storage units, pull-out or drop-leaf shelves and countertops, single-action lever controls and blade-type handles, and flexible connections to water, electrical, and gas lines.

Source: Kucera (1993).

Organize Instruction Around Big Ideas and Interdisciplinary Themes

Activities-oriented approaches focus on depth of understanding rather than broad coverage of science and social studies. Kameenui and Carnine (1998) suggest that you organize science and social studies around *big ideas:* critical topics, concepts, issues, problems, experiences, or principles that assist students in organizing, interrelating, and applying information so that meaningful links can be established between the content and students' lives. Organizing instruction through big ideas also gives students a framework for learning "smaller ideas" such as facts related to the broader concepts and big ideas being studied (Ellis, 1997).

Student learning can also be promoted by linking instruction to important broad, common, and interdisciplinary themes that can accommodate the diverse learning abilities of students (Barab & Landa, 1997). Interdisciplinary themes can link the various science and social studies disciplines, as well as relate them to other subject areas. For example, an integrated programming unit on the Incas of Peru could include a social studies investigation of the geographical area affected by the Incas, Incan cultural traditions, and Incan religious beliefs. In science class, students could study the scientific, medical, and agricultural methods of the Incas. In math, they could learn about the Incan system of record keeping based on cords and knots. For art, students could learn about cultural symbols associated with the Incas and produce art forms that reflect these traditional symbols. Throughout this unit, students can read and write about the Incas.

INFORMATIONAL

Roberts and Kellough (1996) and Maxim (1995) offer guidelines and examples for developing and using thematic instruction.

When selecting common and interdisciplinary themes around which to organize instruction, you should consider several factors, including whether the themes (1) are feasible in terms of motivation, relevance to the curriculum and students' lives, length of time, and the availability of materials and resources; (2) provide enough opportunities to teach basic- and higher-level content, information, and skills; (3) capture students' imagination; (4) address a range of learning styles, abilities, and teaching approaches; and (5) relate to meaningful and worthwhile contextualized content (Barab & Landa, 1997; Savage & Armstrong, 1996). Once themes are selected, you formulate objectives and develop, select, and organize the content and teaching resources. You then implement a variety of theme-connected direct and hands-on learning activities that integrate science, social studies, language arts, music, art, and other content areas. Finally, you devise appropriate assessment procedures to be used throughout the unit (Roberts & Kellough, 1996). Interdisciplinary thematic units usually end with students completing an activity that allows them to summarize and present their learning.

Relate Instruction to Students' Lives and General Societal Problems

SET YOUR SITES

The Association for Supervision and Curriculum Development's Problem-based Learning Network (PBL NET) (www.ascd.org, 630-907-5956) offers information, resources, and an electronic forum on problem-based learning.

Relating science to practical, civic, professional, recreational, and cultural events and problems that are familiar and relevant to students can promote learning, increase motivation, and help students learn to value science and social studies. In using problem-based learning, you present students with information, issues, and problems related to real-life situations and discuss with students the relevance of these problems to their lives, as well as the situations in which this content can be applied (Krynock & Robb, 1999). For example, students can investigate important social problems such as the water supply, the weather, pollution, nutrition, and solar energy.

Science can also be connected to students' cultural backgrounds (Raborn & Daniel, 1999). Learning activities and instructional materials that explore the different cultural and historical origins of science, discuss scientific solutions and practices developed and used in all parts of the world, highlight the achievements of scientists and historians from

Relating science to practical problems that are relevant to students can promote learning and motivation.

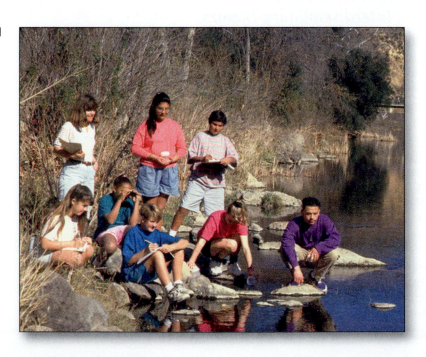

various cultural and language backgrounds, and present a range of culturally diverse practical applications of science can be used to help students understand the multicultural aspects of science. Connections to students' lives and cultures also can be established by having students perform activities that address community problems; use artifacts, buildings, geographical sites, museums, and other resources in the students' community; and interview community members to illustrate and reinforce concepts, issues, phenomena, and events (Lee & Fradd, 1998; Taylor, Gutierrez, Whittaker, & Salend, 1995).

Instruction also can foster the development of *social responsibility*, an interest in and concern for the well-being of others and the environment. Social responsibility encourages the development of social consciousness, which helps students explore their hopes for the future and the impact of their actions on others. A curriculum to teach students social responsibility can help them develop an understanding of our social and ecological interdependence, a sense of what it means to be part of a community, a sense of history, and basic social skills including communication, conflict management, and perspective taking (Berman, 1990). Social responsibility can be taught throughout the curriculum by examining real-word issues. For example, mathematics classes can explore the impact of math (such as statistics) on the political process; science classes can address the relationship between science, technology, and the world; and social studies classes can examine racism in society.

Use Effective Questioning Techniques

Another way to foster and direct student learning is by using effective questioning strategies that promote critical thinking and reflection. Maxim (1995) identified three types of questions teachers typically ask: literal, inferential, and critical. *Literal questions* focus on content derived from class presentations and instructional materials. *Inferential questions* require students to provide answers that are not explicitly stated in the presentation and instructional materials. *Critical questions* ask students to provide personal judgments and reactions to the content.

Use Specially Designed Programs and Curriculums

Specially designed programs and curriculums are available and can be integrated into existing science and social studies instructional programs. Educators have developed activity-based science programs for students with visual disabilities called *Science Activities for the Visually Impaired (SAVI)* and programs for students with physical disabilities called *Science Enrichment Learning for Learners with Physical Handicaps (SELPH)*. These programs use a laboratory approach to teaching science that stresses observations, manipulation of materials, and the development of scientific language. *Project MAVIS (Materials Adaptations for Visually Impaired Students)* has adapted social studies materials for students with visual and physical disabilities, but these materials also can be used with other students. The *Full Option Science System (FOSS)* (Encyclopedia Britannica Co., 1992) is based on SAVI and SELPH and offers a hands-on, laboratory-based K-6 curriculum structured around four themes: Scientific Reasoning, Physical Science, Earth Science, and Life Science. The FOSS also uses discovery learning, cooperative learning groups, interdisciplinary activities, and activities to teach scientific language and the use of scientific equipment and tools.

Other laboratory-based curriculum models and materials include *Science for All Children (SAC)* (Cawley, Miller, Sentman, & Bennet, 1993) and *Applications in Biology/Chemistry (ABC)* (Prescott, Rinard, Cockerill, & Baker, 1996). *SAC* is a curriculum model for students in grades 1 through 6 that is organized around four interrelated themes and thinking processes: Systems, Change, Structure, and Relationship. It has

SET YOUR SITES

You can obtain information and resources to integrate social responsibility into your curriculum from Educators for Social Responsibility (www.esrnational.org).

REFLECTIVE

Select a content area and create literal, inferential, and critical questions. Share and critique your questions with a partner.

SET YOUR SITES

Information on FOSS, SAVI, and SELPH can be obtained from the Center for Multisensory Learning (www.lhs.berkeley.edu/foss/CML.html, 510-642-8941).

SET YOUR SITES

You can obtain information about Great Explorations in Math and Science (GEMS), an activities-oriented curriculum, and other activities from the Lawrence Hall of Science (www.lhs.berkeley.edu/GEMS, 510-642-7771).

been designed as a multiple-option curriculum that allows you to adapt the activities to the cognitive, cultural, language, and social-personal needs of your students. The *ABC* curriculum seeks to promote the science literacy skills of secondary students in the middle 50 percent range by linking science concepts to personal and societal contexts and the world of work. Through the use of real-world activities, job profiles, cooperative learning, learning style adaptations, laboratory exercises, and hands-on activities, the ABC curriculum provides you with a framework for teaching science in context.

Science curricula and programs designed to address the needs of students from culturally and linguistically diverse backgrounds also are available. De Avila (1988) has developed a collaborative learning, hands-on, problem-solving math and science program for second language learners that includes materials in English and Spanish and pictorial directions called *Finding Out/Descubrimiento.* Educational Equity Concepts (n.d.) has developed *Beginning Science Equitably,* an early childhood science program offering developmentally appropriate activities that help *all students* develop the visual-spatial, problem-solving, and decision-making skills that promote positive attitudes toward and future success in science. The program includes a hands-on curriculum that introduces a variety of science concepts using the scientific method and a series of science activities that families perform to help their children learn about science. Additional information about this program can be obtained by contacting Educational Equity Concepts at (212)-725-1803.

INFORMATIONAL

Bulgren et al. (1997) have developed a recall enhancement routine that can help you plan and use mnemonic strategies to improve your students' memory.

Improve Students' Memory

Because content-oriented approaches to teaching science and social studies require students to retain large amounts of information and many new terms, training in develop-

IDEAS FOR IMPLEMENTATION

Promoting Students' Memory

Mr. Contreras was very surprised by the difficulty many students had in memorizing information and decided to use a variety of strategies to help his students remember it. During science instruction, he taught students to use a first-letter mnemonic strategy to memorize the colors of the spectrum. By using the first letter of each word in the list, students created a word, name, or sentence that helped them remember and retrieve information. One group of students learned about the mnemonic "Roy G Biv," a name composed of the first letter of each color of the light spectrum. Another time, when students were having trouble memorizing the names of the states in the United States, he taught them to categorize states according to geographic location and then memorize each geographic cluster.

Here are some other strategies you can use to improve students' memory:

- ◇ Have students work with partners to rehearse critical information and check each other's memory of the material.
- ◇ Give students opportunities to review small amounts of material frequently rather than trying to memorize large amounts of information at once.
- ◇ Encourage students to use mnemonics by teaching them to use such learning strategies as the FIRST-Letter Mnemonic Strategy and LISTS (Nagel, Schumaker, & Deshler, 1986) and the Paired Associates Strategy (Bulgren, Schumaker, & Deshler [in Bulgren, Hock, Schumaker, & Deshler, 1995]).
- ◇ Teach students to use mental visualization, in which they create a mental picture of the content. For example, to remember the definition of *stalactite,* they can visualize a stalactite mentally.

ing memory skills can help students succeed in inclusive settings. A variety of methods can be used to help students remember content, including pictures, acronyms, and rhymes (Bulgren, Deshler, & Schumaker, 1997). For example, your students can learn the acronymn HOMES to prompt their memory of the Great Lakes.

Key Word Method   An effective strategy for helping students remember science and social studies vocabulary is the *key word* method (Mastropieri & Scruggs, 1998). This mnemonic device associates the new vocabulary word with a word that sounds similar to an easy-to-remember illustration. Mastropieri (1988) outlines the steps in the key word method:

1. *Recoding.* The new vocabulary word is recoded into a key word that sounds similar and is familiar to the student. The key word should be one that students can easily picture. For example, the key word for the word *Sauro* might be a *saw*.
2. *Relating.* An *interactive illustration*—a mental picture or drawing of the key word interacting with the definition of the vocabulary word—is created. A sentence describing the interaction also is developed. For example, the definition of *Sauro* and the key word *saw* can be depicted using the sentence "A lizard is sawing."
3. *Retrieving.* On hearing the new vocabulary word, students retrieve its definition by thinking of the key word, creating the interactive illustration and/or its corresponding sentence, and stating the definition.

Use Instructional Technology and Multimedia

As we discussed in Chapter 8, instructional technology and multimedia can enhance science and social studies instruction and play a key role in activities-based approaches. Instructional technology, virtual reality, and multimedia can be used to introduce, review, and apply science and social studies concepts. Using these devices, students can experience events, places, and phenomena such as scientific experiments, geographic locations around the world, or historical events. For example, multimedia applications allow students to perform complicated scientific experiments such as those involving chemical reactions on the computer. In addition to providing an opportunity to obtain and observe unique aspects of the content, these instructional delivery systems can motivate students and stimulate their curiosity.

Through the Internet and telecommunications, students can learn science and social studies by being linked to data and educational resources, problem-solving experiences, and interactions with students and professionals around the world. For example, the National Geographic Society and the Technical Education Research Center sponsor the Kids Network (www.nrel.gov, 303-275-3044), an international telecommunications-based curriculum that teaches science and geography to elementary and middle school students. Units in the curriculum focus on real-life, socially significant problems such as the water supply, weather, pollution, nutrition, and solar energy. Students work in small groups to develop questions, conduct experiments, collect and analyze data related to their questions, and share their findings. Students can receive assistance from the Kids Network staff such as computer graphs and maps. They can also exchange and share information and their findings with students throughout the world.

Take Students on Field Trips

Field trips also can make learning more meaningful and real for students. In particular, visits to historical and science museums, as well as ecological and historical sites, allow

INFORMATIONAL

Greene (1994) describes a variety of mnemonic strategies to help students improve their spelling, word recognition, reading comprehension, mathematics, and study skills.

INFORMATIONAL

Several learning strategies have been developed to help students learn to use the key word method, including LINCS and IT FITS (Hughes, 1996; Lebzelter & Nowacek, 1999).

INFORMATIONAL

Coleman (1997) provides a list of companies that produce software simulations of science experiments.

INFORMATIONAL

Savage and Armstrong (1996) and Trowbridge and Bybee (1996) offer descriptions and examples of how instructional technology and multimedia can be used to teach science and social studies.

SET YOUR SITES

Project ASSIST (All Students in Supported Inquiry-Based Science with Technology) (www.edc.org/FSC/ASSIST, 617-969-7100) offers resources and support to help you in using technology to teach science.

SET YOUR SITES

You can obtain information, resources, and standards for teaching social studies from the National Council for the Social Studies (www.ncss.org, 202-966-7840), the Center for Civic Education (www.civiced.org, 202-861-8800), the National Council on Economic Education (www.nationalcouncil.org, 800-338-1192), the National Council for Geographic Education (www.ncge.org, 724-357-6290), the National Center for History in the Schools (www.sscnet.ucla.edu/nchs, 310-825-4702), and the ERIC Clearinghouse for Social Studies/Social Science Education (www.indiana.edu/~ssdc/eric-chess.html, 800-266-3815).

INFORMATIONAL

Ebenezer and Lau (1999) offer guidelines for using the Internet to teach science and appropriate websites.

students to experience what they hear and read about. Many museums and sites offer students hands-on experiences that promote learning and provide information. To help you and your students benefit from field trips, many museums and sites provide teacher training programs, model curricula and teaching strategies, special tours, exhibits, and materials for school groups, as well as traveling exhibits that prepare students for and build upon experiences at the museum.

Before taking your class on a trip, you may want to make a previsit to familiarize yourself with various aspects of the facility (e.g., exhibits and activities, admission costs, accessibility of the facility, rules on photography, availability of restrooms, lunchrooms, and coatrooms) and meet with the facility's staff concerning the size and unique needs of your class and the availability and scope of guided tours. The value of field trips also can be enhanced

IDEAS FOR IMPLEMENTATION

Promoting Math and Science Education for All Students

The teachers in the Madison School were shocked and disappointed at the small number of female students who had enrolled in their afterschool science and math program. Unsure of the reasons for the low turnout, the teachers spoke to several of their female students, who said that they didn't sign up for the program because "science is for nerds and boys," "my friends will think I'm weird," and "I'm not good at science and math." Struck by these comments, the teachers decided to revamp their math and science teaching so that it appealed to *all students*. First, they started to use textbooks, instructional materials, and activities that presented females in nonstereotypic science and math roles. They also developed and taught an interdisciplinary unit about scientists and mathematicians who are female, from culturally and linguistically diverse backgrounds, or have disabilities. They invited several local scientists and mathematicians from these diverse groups to speak about their jobs and training. As a culminating activity, students worked in cooperative learning groups to study why females, individuals from diverse backgrounds, and people with disabilities are underrepresented in science and mathematics.

Here are some other strategies you can use to promote math and science education for all students:

◆ Model and encourage *all students* to have a positive attitude toward math and science and take intellectual risks.

◆ Establish a learning environment that fosters high expectations for *all students*

and allows them to be active, inquiring participants.

◆ Provide students with a historical and multicultural understanding of math and science.

◆ Present problems and situations so that *all students* are depicted in active, nonstereotypic ways, and avoid using statements, materials, and pictorials that suggest that certain groups of students are not skilled in math and science.

◆ Emphasize the problem-solving aspects of math and science rather than speed and competition.

◆ Teach math and science using real-life situations, cooperative learning groups, projects, and games. For example, as part of a unit on pollution, students can work in cooperative learning groups to study water, air, and noise pollution in their own communities.

◆ Communicate and demonstrate to students, their families, and other teachers the importance of seeking advanced training and pursuing careers in math and science.

◆ Contact scientists and mathematicians in your community to serve as mentors for your students.

◆ Assign class and school jobs to *all students* that require them to solve problems and use their math and science skills.

Sources: Kellermaier (1996) and Rop (1998).

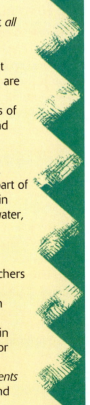

by giving students a variety of pretrip learning experiences that prepare them for the information and experiences they will be exposed to on the field trip; explaining to students how they should behave on the trip; giving them notepads on which to take notes and make sketches; asking for and answering questions on the ride to the site; and discussing positive and negative aspects of the trip with students on the ride back to school (Roberts & Kellough, 1996). In addition to preparing students for the field trip, you can prepare chaperones by giving them information about the facility and outlining their responsibilities.

You can enhance the educational benefit of field trips by videotaping them. These videos can be viewed and discussed in class and serve as a basis for lessons to help students understand important information presented on the trip. Students also can show the video and discuss it with other classes or students who were not able to take the field trip.

Students also can make "field trips" to various museums and scientific and historical sites via the Internet (Bridges & DeVaull, 1999). For example, the American Museum of Natural History's National Center for Science Literacy, Education and Technology offers a website (www.amnh.org) with a variety of on-line activities that make scientists and exhibitions available to schools and families.

Address the Needs of Diverse Learners

Female students, students from various cultural and language backgrounds, and students with disabilities are often underrepresented in advanced math and science classes and in careers in these fields (Rop, 1998). This underrepresentation is often attributed to math/science anxiety, as well as to societal expectations and norms that make it acceptable for these students to ignore or question their abilities in science and math. There also is evidence that teachers treat male and female students differently, encouraging males to achieve in math and science and discouraging females. Therefore, you need to be aware of your behavior, and of societal pressures, so that you can change any such tendencies and create a classroom that encourages math and science competence in *all students*.

SET YOUR SITES

The Association for Supervision and Curriculum Development (www.ascd.org) maintains a list of virtual field-trip sites that you can request via e-mail (amachi@ascd.org) or phone (703-549-9110).

SET YOUR SITES

The National Science Foundation has the Program for Persons with Disabilities (www.ehr.nsf.gov/EHR/HRD, 703-306-1636), which offers resources and funds programs to support the science and math education of individuals with disabilities.

SET YOUR SITES

On-line resources are available to help your students with mathematics and science (www.ed.gov/pubs/emath) and to help you create an equitable environment to teach these subjects (www.equity.enc.org).

It is important for all students to have role models who have been successful in math and science.

SUMMARY

This chapter presented guidelines and strategies for differentiating mathematics, science, and social studies instruction. As you review the questions posed in this chapter, remember the following points.

How Can I Differentiate Mathematics Instruction?

Use a problem-solving approach that involves students in learning mathematics by experiencing and thinking about meaningful problems related to their lives. In addition, present mathematics appropriately, use teaching aids and a variety of instructional approaches, help students develop their math facts and computation skills, and provide feedback and use assessment to guide future teaching.

How Can I Differentiate Science and Social Studies Instruction?

Choose textbooks carefully, consider using electronic textbooks, teach students how to use textbooks and instructional materials, and use study guides, adapted textbooks, a parallel alternative curriculum, and content enhancements. In addition, you can promote students' memory, use activities-oriented approaches, organize instruction around big ideas and interdisciplinary themes, and relate instruction to students' lives and social problems. You also can use effective questioning techniques, instructional technology and multimedia, and specially designed programs and curriculums, take students on field trips, and address the needs of diverse learners.

 ## What Would You Do in Today's Diverse Classroom?

Felicia, one of your students, is having difficulty in mathematics, science, and social studies. She has learned about half of her basic mathematics facts and is struggling to understand word problems and more abstract concepts. An examination of her science and social studies notebooks indicates that she is not identifying important information from textbooks and lessons.

1. What would you do to help Felicia learn mathematics, science, and social studies?
2. What resources and support from others would be useful in helping Felicia learn mathematics, science, and social studies?

Using a textbook in a subject area and a grade level you would like to teach, create a point of view reading guide, an interactive reading guide, a learning-from-text guide, a textbook activity guide, and a reading road map.

1. Which study guide(s) are easiest for you to develop? Why?
2. Which one(s) would your students like best? Why?
3. Which one(s) would be most effective? Why?

PART IV

Evaluating Individual and Programmatic Progress

Y ou have learned about the fundamentals of inclusion, the need to create a school and classroom environment that supports learning for *all students,* and strategies for differentiating instruction to accommodate *all of your students.* With these components in place, it is essential for you to learn how to evaluate the effectiveness of your inclusion program. This evaluation can help you assess the impact of your program on *all* of your students, family members, and teachers, including yourself. It also can aid you in documenting the strengths of your inclusion program and pinpointing areas in need of revision.

Part IV, which consists of Chapter 12, provides a framework and specific strategies and resources for evaluating inclusion programs. Specifically, it presents guidelines for determining if your inclusion program is resulting in positive educational, social, behavioral, and self-concept outcomes for *all of your students.* It also provides techniques for examining students, family members' and educators' perceptions of and experiences with inclusion that can help you assess your students' progress and evaluate various programmatic components of your inclusion program.

CHAPTER
12

Evaluating Student Progress and the Effectiveness of Your Inclusion Program

Ms. Charles and Ms. Mackey

Ms. Charles, a general education teacher, and Ms. Mackey, a special education teacher, were asked by their principal to work together as a cooperative teaching team to start an inclusion class. Their class included 24 students, 7 of whom had been identified as having a disability. Ms. Charles and Ms. Mackey had worked together before to mainstream students, and they were both excited about working in an inclusive classroom. At first, they had some difficulty determining their responsibilities and blending their skills. As they worked together, they began to notice and respect each other's skills, perspectives, experiences, and areas of expertise. From their point of view, things were going well.

However, soon they were faced with the question of whether the inclusion program was benefitting their students. It first came up at a meeting with the students' families. Some families of students without disabilities expressed concerns about whether the needs of the students with disabilities would interfere with their children's education. A few of the families of students with disabilities also were worried about their children being ridiculed by others and about losing individualized services. Their principal also approached them with a request from the school board to provide data justifying the money being spent on the program. Even many of their colleagues were asking if the students were really successful in the inclusion program.

While Ms. Charles and Ms. Mackey felt that their inclusion program was benefitting their students, they knew they had to begin to document the program's outcomes. In addition to looking for strategies and resources in professional journals, they began to ask others how the academic, social, and behavioral progress of students educated in inclusion programs could be evaluated as an ongoing process.

How can Ms. Charles and Ms. Mackey evaluate the effectiveness of their inclusion program? After reading this chapter, you should be able to answer this as well as the following questions.

◇ How can I evaluate the academic performance of students?
◇ How can I evaluate the social and behavioral performance of students?
◇ How can I measure perceptions of my inclusion program?
◇ How can I improve the effectiveness of my inclusion program?

L ike Ms. Charles and Ms. Mackey, it is important for you to evaluate the effectiveness of your inclusion program by examining its impact on *all* of your students, on yourself and other teachers, and on students' families. An evaluation can assess the impact of your inclusion program on your students' academic, social, and behavioral performance. It can also allay the concern that the academic and behavioral needs of students with disabilities will require excessive school resources and teacher attention and therefore jeopardize the education of students without disabilities. Information on the perceptions of students, teachers, and family members regarding your inclusion program is also helpful in examining the overall effectiveness of your inclusion program. This information validates successful inclusive educational policies that should be continued, as well as pinpointing procedures that need to be revised.

HOW CAN I EVALUATE THE ACADEMIC PERFORMANCE OF STUDENTS?

An important goal of inclusion programs is to enhance the academic performance of *all students.* A variety of strategies for examining your program's impact on your students are presented below.

Standardized Testing

As we saw in Chapters 1 and 2, important aspects of the IDEA amendments of 1997 and educational reform efforts relate to the participation of *all students*, including those with disabilities, in statewide testing programs that measure higher educational standards. Student performance on these standardized statewide tests also can be used to examine the impact of your inclusion program on your students' academic performance. This is done by comparing the scores of students educated in inclusion classes with the scores of their counterparts who are not taught in inclusion classes (Waldron & McLeskey, 1998a). These test scores also can be used to contrast the performance of students with disabilities taught in inclusion classes with the performance of their classmates without disabilities (Gronna, Jenkins, and Chin-Chance, 1998a).

INFORMATIONAL

Lachat (1997) provides guidelines for examining the appropriateness of large-scale tests for students from various cultural and language backgrounds.

SET YOUR SITES

Information and resources on the inclusion of students with disabilities in statewide and districtwide assessments are available from the National Center on Educational Outcomes (www.coled.umn.edu/NCEO, 612-626-1530).

Types of Standardized Tests

Some states have developed performance assessments (Kearns, Kleinert, Clayton, Burdge, & Williams, 1998). However, most statewide and districtwide tests are either norm-referenced or criterion-referenced (Gronna et al., 1998a).

Norm-Referenced Testing   *Norm-referenced tests* provide measures of performance that allow teachers to compare a student's score to the scores of others. Norms are determined and are then used to compare students in terms of such variables as age and grade level. For example, norm-referenced testing may reveal that your inclusion program has improved a student's performance so that he or she is now reading at a third-grade level and doing mathematics at a fifth-grade level.

Criterion-Referenced Testing   In contrast to norm-referenced testing, *criterion-referenced testing* compares a student's performance to a specific level of skill mastery. That is, rather than giving the grade level at which students are functioning, criterion-referenced testing demonstrates specific skills mastered and not mastered by the student. For example, the test may show that a student in your inclusion program can now add and subtract decimals and fractions but still needs to learn how to multiply or divide them.

Testing Accommodations for Diverse Learners

Many diverse learners, including students with disabilities, will need accommodations in order to take part in statewide testing, as well as when they take tests in your classroom. *Testing accommodations*, also referred to as *alternative testing techniques*, are adaptations in testing administration and procedures that allow students to perform at their optimal level and demonstrate their knowledge and abilities.

The testing accommodations needed, which should appear in students' IEPs or Section 504 accommodation plans, are related to the instructional modifications used to help them learn content. They also depend on the purpose of the test, the nature of the items, and the regulations that guide the test's administration. For example, it would not be appropriate to provide a reader for students taking tests designed to assess their reading ability. However, a reader would be an appropriate testing accommodation for a math test that requires considerable reading. In addition, the accommodations, if used with general education students, should have little effect on their test performance (Tindal, Heath, Hollenbeck, Almond, & Harniss, 1998). After the testing accommodations are used, their effectiveness, usefulness, and fairness should be assessed (Elliott, Kratochwill, & Schulte, 1998).

Accommodations typically relate to presentation and response mode formats, and to scheduling and setting alternatives (Erickson, Ysseldyke, Thurlow, & Elliott, 1998). Another accommodation is to train students before they take the test (Elliott et al., 1998). A discussion of various alternative testing techniques follows.

Presentation of Items and Directions   Alternative testing techniques may include adaptations in the way test questions and directions are presented to students. You can help your students to understand test items and directions by simplifying the language used, formatting the test so that there is only one complete sentence per line, providing models and visuals, listing directions in the order in which they should be followed, and using cues to help students perform well (Elliott et al., 1998; Rein, 1995). For example, to indicate a change in directions among types of items, you can provide a sample of each type of problem set off in a box with each change in directions. Similarly, cues such as color coding, underlining, enlarging, or highlighting key words or phrases can

SET YOUR SITES

The National Center for Research on Evaluation, Standards, and Student Testing (CRESST) (www.cresst96.cse.ucla.edu, 310 206-1532) and the ERIC Clearinghouse on Assessment and Evaluation (www.ericae.net, 800-464-3742) maintain websites that offer information and resources on student assessment.

REFLECTIVE

What is your view of the inclusion of students with disabilities in statewide assessments? How will it affect them, you, and your school district?

SET YOUR SITES

FairTest, the National Center for Fair and Open Testing, an advocacy organization examining the misuses and problems associated with standardized testing and other forms of assessment and promoting fair and equitable assessment of students, maintains a website (www.fairtest.org, 617-864-4810).

INFORMATIONAL

Elliott et al. (1998) developed the Assessment Accommodation Checklist, and Fuchs, Karns, Eaton, and Hamlett (1999) developed the Dynamic Assessment of Test Accommodations (DATA) to help teachers select testing accommodations for students with a wide range of disabilities.

Alternative testing techniques may include adaptations in the manner in which test questions and directions are presented to students.

alert your students to the specifics of each item. Cues, such as arrows, can be placed at the bottom of the test pages to indicate those pages that are a continuous part of a section of the test; stop signs can be placed to indicate ending pages.

Some students will require the help of school personnel when taking tests. A proctor can read and/or simplify the test directions and questions for these students (Tindal et al., 1998). Proctors should be careful not to give students cues and additional information that may affect their performance. School personnel also can help students during the test by turning pages for them, helping them maintain their place in a standard exam booklet, delivering on-task and focusing prompts, and motivating students to sustain their effort (Elliott et al., 1998). Students with hearing disabilities may benefit from a trained teacher who can sign and interpret oral directions and translate their answers.

Some students may need specialized adaptations and equipment to gain information about test directions and items. Students with visual impairments may benefit from visual magnification aids, readers, verbal descriptions of pictorials, tactile materials, photo-enlarged examinations and answer sheets, and Braille or large-print versions of tests (Erin & Koenig, 1997). Students with hearing impairments may need to use devices that amplify sound. Audiocassettes of tests, and markers or masks to focus the students' attention and help them maintain their place during reading, can help students with reading disabilities.

Responses to Items   You also may need to make changes in the way students respond to test items or determine their answers. Some students who have problems with writing and speaking may need to indicate their responses by providing oral responses or pointing, respectively. Some students may benefit from fewer items per page or line, extra space between items, and a larger answer block (Thurlow, Ysseldyke, & Silverstein, 1995). Students who have difficulty transferring their responses to a separate answer sheet can be allowed to mark their responses on the test protocol or to fold test pages and position the answer sheet so that only one page appears (Erickson et al., 1998). To minimize difficulty transferring responses, school personnel can monitor students during testing to make sure that they record answers in the correct space, follow the correct sequence, and check to see that the question numbers correspond to the numbers on the answer sheet (Hughes, 1996).

Students who have difficulty with writing can be helped in several ways. Use of multiple-choice items instead of sentence completion and essay questions can minimize the amount of writing necessary to complete the test. When grammar, punctuation, and spelling are not essential aspects of the response, students can record their answers on an audiocassette or take an oral test. If the mechanics of written language are important in evaluating the response, students can dictate their complete response, including spelling, punctuation, paragraphing, and grammar, to a scribe (Kearns et al. 1998). Students can then review their response in written form and direct their recorder to the correct grammar, punctuation, and word choices. Devices such as word processors, Braille writers, speech synthesizers, pointers, electronic dictionaries, audiocassettes, and communication boards can help students who have difficulty answering orally or in writing to respond.

Because of their unique conditions, some students with disabilities may need to use aids to respond to test items. Computational aids such as calculators, software programs, and mathematics tables can be useful for students who have the ability to complete items but lack the memory skills to remember facts or word definitions.

Scheduling and Setting Alternatives

> It was my first high school final. I studied more than I ever had and thought I had a good chance of getting an A or B. I . . . took my regular seat at the large table by the window. During the teacher's directions, I forced myself to listen. I was doing good. Then I noticed this squirrel outside in the tree. . . . I watched the squirrel for 20 minutes. My teacher walked over and asked when I was going to start my exam. I looked away from the squirrel, but then I noticed this girl snapping her gum. . . . It was driving me crazy. I couldn't think. . . . She finally spit her gum out, but by that time it was too late. I didn't have enough time to finish now that I didn't even start the exam. . . . I felt sick to my stomach. I knew my mom would be mad. (Yehle & Wambold, 1998, p. 8)

You may need to adjust the scheduling of tests, as well as the location in which the tests are given. Some students with disabilities may not work as fast as their peers because of (1) difficulties processing information and staying on task, (2) the extra time required to use specialized testing techniques (such as dictating answers), (3) physical needs that cause them to tire easily, and (4) the declining effectiveness of their medications over time. Therefore, when planning testing for these students, you can consider scheduling alternatives such as giving them more time to complete tests; giving shorter versions of tests; allowing students to take breaks as needed; changing the time of day when the test is given; dividing the testing session into several shorter periods during the day; and allowing students to complete the test over a period of several days (Erickson et al., 1998).

Students who have difficulty remaining on task and are anxious about taking tests may perform better if they take the test in a small group or individually in a quiet place free of distractions. Students with physical disabilities may require adaptive furniture or devices, and students with sensory impairments may need specific environmental arrangements, such as specialized lighting or acoustics.

REFLECTIVE

Do alternative testing techniques give students with disabilities an advantage over other students? Would these techniques violate the integrity of your tests?

Test Adaptations for Second Language Learners   Since language proficiency can affect students' test performance, you may need to modify tests for second language learners and those who speak vernacular dialects of English. Consider the following adaptations:

◆ Provide context clues, and present items and directions using graphics and pictures.
◆ Teach students the language of academic testing, and give them bilingual dictionaries or glossaries for content area tests.

◇ Provide students with review sheets, lists of vocabulary, and important terms before giving tests.

◇ Use items that are easy to understand and low in language level.

◇ Allow students to demonstrate mastery of test material in alternative ways, such as with projects developed by cooperative learning groups or through the use of manipulatives or drama.

◇ Use a translator to administer the test, and allow students to respond in their native language or dialect.

Some teachers have tried to minimize the bias in English-language tests by translating them into the student's dominant language. However, translations do not remove the cultural bias in tests that are related to content, item, picture, and task selection. Some concepts in English, referred to as *empty concepts* (e.g., certain time and color concepts), may not exist in other cultures and languages. In addition, because words may have different levels of difficulty across languages and dialects, test translations may change the psychometric properties of the original test. Additionally, translation does not account for experiences and words that have different or multiple meanings in different cultures. Thus, despite the translation, the constructs underlying the test items still reflect the dominant culture and may not be appropriate for students from other cultures.

Training Prior to Testing   An appropriate alternative testing procedure for many students may be training prior to testing to improve their test-taking skills (Elliott et al., 1998). Instruction in test-taking skills can reduce some of the anxiety about testing that students experience and can help them feel comfortable with the test format (Berendt & Koski, 1999). Therefore, prior to testing, you can allow your students to practice taking tests, and give them time to work in groups to take and prepare for tests. These small groups can review notes and chapters, predict possible questions, and quiz members on specific facts, terms, and concepts.

You also can teach your students to develop their test-taking skills. Recommended test-taking skills that can be taught to students are presented in Figure 12.1.

Alternatives to Standardized Testing

Most students with disabilities should be able to participate in statewide tests with appropriate testing accommodations. However, students who are not working on general education goals or standards may not need to take part in these assessments (Erickson et al., 1998; Gronna, Jenkins, & Chin-Chance, 1998b). In these cases, you and your colleagues may want to use some of the assessment alternatives presented below. Because these methods are classroom-based techniques that align assessment with your curriculum and instruction, you also can use them to assess the progress of *all of your students,* provide a more complete picture of your students' performance, and examine the effectiveness of your inclusion program (Winn & Otis-Wilborn, 1999; Ysseldyke & Olsen, 1999).

Curriculum-Based Measurement

Curriculum-based measurement (CBM) provides individualized, direct, and repeated measures of students' proficiency and progress in the curriculum. Because CBM is an ongoing, dynamic process involving content derived directly from students' instructional programs, it provides continuous measurements of your students' progress (Jones, Southern, & Brigham, 1998). For instance, Ms. Charles and Ms. Mackey, the teachers we met at the beginning of this chapter, can examine their students' progress in reading

---

INFORMATIONAL

Fradd and Wilen (1990) provide guidelines for using interpreters and translators to assess the test performance of second language learners.

INFORMATIONAL

Hughes, Deshler, Ruhl, and Schumaker (1993) improved students' test performance by teaching them to use *PIRATES: Prepare* to succeed; *Inspect the instructions; Read,* remember, reduce; *Answer* or abandon; *Turn back; Estimate; Survey.* Hughes (1996) developed *ANSWER,* an essay test-taking learning strategy: *Analyze* the situation; *Notice* requirements; *Set* up an outline; *Work* in details; *Engineer* your answer; and *Review* your answer.

REFLECTIVE

What studying and test-taking strategies do you use? Are they successful? How did you learn these strategies?

SET YOUR SITES

The following websites can assist you in creating forms to use with informal assessment techniques: www.junior.apk.net/~jbarta/tutor/forms/index.html, www.freedback.com, and www.response-o-matic.com.

INFORMATIONAL

Idol, Nevin, and Paolucci-Whitcomb (1999) and Paulsen (1997) offer guidelines and models for using CBM to assess student performance in inclusive classrooms.

PRIOR TO TESTING

◆ Review the content to be studied over a spaced period of time rather than cramming.
◆ Determine the specific objectives of each study session.
◆ Study the most difficult content areas first.
◆ Make sure that the study area is conducive to studying.
◆ Gather all the materials necessary for studying, including notebooks, textbooks, paper, writing utensils, reference books, and calculators.
◆ Review prior tests in terms of format, length, response types, and the completeness of the responses required.
◆ Develop and use study guides, review sheets, vocabulary lists, and outlines of the material to be covered on the test.
◆ Sleep and eat well before the test.
◆ Develop a positive attitude about the test and your effort.

DURING TESTING

◆ Remain calm.
◆ Preview the test to determine the number and nature of test items before beginning the test.
◆ Be aware of the time left to complete the test.
◆ Develop an order and a timeline for working on the test based on the total time allotted to the test, the point values of sections (work on those sections worth the most points in descending order), and the difficulty of the items.
◆ Make three passes through the test. In the first pass, read all questions and respond to the ones you know how to answer, noting those that are somewhat difficult or very difficult. During the second pass, respond to those questions skipped in the first pass that have been identified as somewhat difficult. Answer all unanswered questions during the third pass.
◆ Read the directions to all parts of the test to determine what type of response is required, the aids allowed, the sequence to be followed in completing the test, the point values of items and sections of the test, and the time and space limits.
◆ Underline important parts of test items and directions.
◆ Seek clarification about the specifics of test items and directions.
◆ Identify and analyze critical words, look for word clues, and rephrase questions in language you can understand.
◆ Jot down on the test paper essential facts and formulas that you will use throughout the test.
◆ Check responses to make sure that they are correct, complete, neat, and marked appropriately.
◆ Stay with your first choice when you are unsure of an answer.
◆ Answer all questions. However, when you lose additional points for incorrect responses, answer only those questions that have a high probability of being correct.

WHEN WORKING ON MULTIPLE-CHOICE ITEMS

◆ Read the question and think of the answer before reading and carefully analyzing all the choices.
◆ Examine each response alternative, select the one that is most complete and inclusive, and eliminate choices that are obviously false or incorrect, that are not related to the content covered in class, or that are absurd or deal with nonsense or irrelevant material.
◆ Be aware that the choices *all of the above, none of the above,* and numbers that represent the middle range are often correct, as are alternatives that are unusually long or short.
◆ Be aware that when alternative answers are contradictory, one of them is likely to be correct, and that when two options provide similar information, neither of them should be considered.
◆ Use clues such as subject–verb agreement, verb tense, and modifiers such as *a* or *an* and other information from the stem of the item to determine the correct response.

WHEN WORKING ON MATCHING ITEMS

◆ Survey both lists to get an idea of the choices, to note if each column has an equal number of items, and to determine if an alternative can be used more than once.
◆ Read the initial item in the left-hand column first and then read each choice in the right-hand column before answering.
◆ Work on the easiest items first and skip items that are difficult.
◆ Record the correct answer if you know it immediately, and highlight choices in the right-hand column that have been used.
◆ Avoid guessing until all other items have been answered, as an incorrect match can multiply the number of errors.

FIGURE 12.1 Recommended student test-taking skills. (continued)

Sources: Hoy (1995), Hudson (1996), Hughes (1996), Langan (1982), Millman and Pauk (1969), Pauk (1984), and Putnam (1992).

WHEN WORKING ON TRUE-FALSE ITEMS

❖ Determine the type of true-false items on the test before beginning.

❖ Examine the questions for *specific determiners,* which are words that modify or limit a statement (e.g., *rarely, usually*). In general, false statements often include a qualifier that suggests that the statement is extreme or true 100 percent of the time (e.g., *no, never, every, always, all*).

❖ Words that moderate a statement (e.g., *sometimes, most, many, generally, usually*) often indicate that a statement is true. If true-false statements lack a specific determiner, the question should be marked *True* only if it is always true.

❖ Read all parts of the statement, and mark the statement *False* if any part of it is not true or correct.

❖ Highlight the negative words or prefixes in true-false statements and identify the meaning of the item while deleting the negatives.

WHEN WORKING ON SENTENCE COMPLETION ITEMS

❖ Answer sentence completion items by converting them into questions.

❖ Use the grammatical structure of the item to help you formulate the answer. If the stem ends in *a* or *an,* the correct answer probably starts with a consonant or a vowel, respectively. The verb form also indicates whether the answer is singular or plural.

❖ Use the number and length of the blanks provided as a clue. Often, two blanks with no words between them indicate that a two-word response, such as an individual's name, is the answer. Two blanks separated by words should be approached as two separate statements. A long blank tends to suggest that the correct answer is a phrase or a sentence.

WHEN WORKING ON ESSAY QUESTIONS

❖ Read the questions and record relevant points to be mentioned or addressed next to each question.

❖ Highlight key words related to directions and important information to be addressed.

❖ Work on the easiest questions first, rereading each question and adding new information or deleting irrelevant statements.

❖ Outline the response before writing, and then use the outline as a guide for composing the answer.

❖ Consider the following when writing the response: rephrase the question as the first sentence of the answer; present the answer in a logical order, with transitions from one paragraph to another; give specifics when necessary; use examples to support statements; and summarize the main points at the end of the essay.

❖ Proofread responses for clarity, organization, legibility, spelling, and grammar.

❖ Write down the outline and key points rather than leaving the question blank.

FIGURE 12.1   (continued)

by using CBM to record and graph measures of their students' performance on the selections they read every day in class.

CBM has several advantages over other methods of assessment, including linking testing, teaching, and evaluation, as well as making it easier to develop and evaluate IEPs (Fuchs & Fuchs, 1998; Jones, Southern, & Brigham, 1998). CBM provides information on the demands of instructional tasks. This allows you to determine the content and pace of an instructional program and to communicate information about your students' performance to their families and to other professionals (Paulsen, 1997).

Idol, Nevin, and Paolucci-Whitcomb (1999), Jones et al. (1998), and King-Sears, Burgess, and Lawson (1999) offer the following guidelines for conducting a CBM:

1. *Identify the content area(s) to be assessed.* CBM begins by examining and determining the content areas to be assessed.

2. *Define the school-related tasks that will constitute the assessment and the sample duration.* For example, you can measure reading by having students read aloud from their readers for a sample duration of 1 minute, and measure writing by the number of words written during a sample duration of 5 minutes.

3. *Determine if performance or progress measurement will be used.* Performance measurement involves changes on a specific task that remains constant throughout the CBM. Progress measurement evaluates student progress on sequentially ordered levels/objectives within the curriculum.

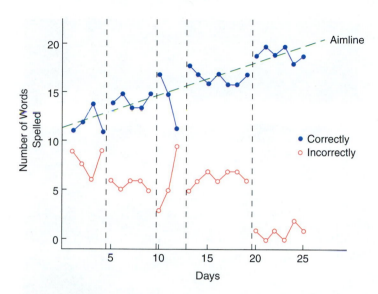

FIGURE 12.2 Graph of CBM of spelling.

4. *Prepare and organize the necessary materials.* Select material from the curriculum related to the assessment tasks in advance.

5. *Administer the CBM.*

6. *Decide how frequently the CBM will be administered.* Depending on your time, the students' skill, and the nature of the task, decide how frequently to administer the CBM.

7. *Record and graph students' performance over time.* A sample graph is presented in Figure 12.2. The vertical axis measures the student's performance on the school-related task (such as the number of words read or the number of words spelled). The horizontal axis indicates the day on which the CBM is given. Data points on the graph should provide a measure of the correct and incorrect responses. The diagonal broken line starting at the left and ending on the right side of the graph is called the *aimline;* it provides a reference point for judging students' progress and making decisions about their instructional program. The vertical broken lines indicate changes in the program. Gable, Arllen, Evans, and Whinnery (1997) offer additional guidelines for graphing student performance and interpreting these data.

8. *Analyze the results to determine students' progress in terms of skills mastered and not mastered.* You can use the data to identify the students who have mastered the skills and are ready for new instructional objectives; those who are progressing but need additional teaching to demonstrate mastery of skills; and those who have not progressed and need modifications in their instructional program. King-Sears et al. (1999) suggest that if students fail to make progress in three consecutive sessions, you need to teach a less difficult form of the task or an easier skill or change your teaching procedures.

9. *Examine and compare the efficacy of different instructional strategies.* You can examine the data to assess and compare the efficacy of different teaching methods and make decisions about students' educational programs (Allinder, 1996; Fuchs & Fuchs, 1998).

Authentic/Performance Assessment

You also can use *authentic/performance assessment* to measure the impact of your instructional programs on your students' academic performance (Poteet, Choate, & Stewart,

INFORMATIONAL

Wiggins (1997) and Herman, Aschbacher, and Winters (1992) provide questions that can guide you in selecting appropriate performance/authentic assessment tasks.

In authentic/performance assessment, students apply the knowledge and skills they have learned to contextualized problems and real-life settings.

REFLECTIVE
What performance/authentic assessment tasks might be appropriate for measuring your understanding of the material presented in this course and book?

INFORMATIONAL
States like Kentucky have established an alternate portfolio assessment system to involve students with moderate and severe cognitive disabilities in the statewide testing system (Kearns, Kleinert, & Kennedy, 1999).

INFORMATIONAL
Gelfer and Perkins (1998) and O'Malley and Valdez Pierce (1996) provide guidelines for developing portfolios with young children, and with students from various cultural and language backgrounds, respectively.

1996; Siegel-Causey & Allinder, 1998). In this type of assessment, students work on meaningful, complex, and relevant learning activities that are incorporated into the assessment process. The results of these activities are authentic products that reveal their ability to apply the knowledge and skills they have learned to contextualized problems and real-life settings. Teachers using authentic/performance assessment have students demonstrate their skills, problem-solving abilities, knowledge, and understanding by creating and making things, developing projects, solving problems, producing written products, responding to simulations, giving presentations and performances, conducting investigations, and designing and performing experiments (O'Malley & Valdez Pierce, 1996). For example, in an authentic assessment related to a unit on the plant life cycle, your students could create a children's book explaining this topic to others.

Portfolio Assessment

Authentic/performance assessment is closely related to *portfolio assessment,* which is used to assess student progress in inclusive classrooms (Banerji & Dailey, 1995; Jochum, Curran, & Reetz, 1998). Portfolio assessment involves teachers, students, and family members working together to create a continuous and purposeful collection of various authentic student products across a range of content areas throughout the school year that show the process and products associated with student learning (Danielson & Abrutyn, 1997). Portfolios are student-centered and archival in nature. They contain samples over time that are periodically reviewed by teachers, families, and students to reflect on and document progress, effort, attitudes, achievement, development, and the strategies students use to learn (Duffy, Jones, & Thomas, 1999). While portfolio assessment is appropriate for *all students,* it is particularly meaningful for students from various cultural and language backgrounds, whose progress may not be accurately measured by traditional testing strategies (O'Malley & Valdez Pierce 1996; Rueda & Garcia, 1997).

Here are some guidelines for using portfolio assessment that you may want to consider:

1. *Identify the goals of the portfolio.* Typically, the goals of students' portfolios are individualized, broadly stated, related directly to the curriculum, and cover an extended period of time. For students with disabilities, portfolio goals also can be linked to their IEPs, and portfolio goals for second language learners might relate to increasing their proficiency in English.

2. *Determine the type of portfolio.* Jochum et al. (1998) and Swicegood (1994) identified four types of portfolios: showcase, reflective, cumulative, and goal based. A *showcase portfolio* presents the student's best work and is often used to help students enter a specialized program or school or to apply for employment. A *reflective portfolio* helps teachers, students, and family members reflect on students' learning, including attitudes, strategies, and knowledge. A *cumulative portfolio* shows changes in the products and process associated with students' learning throughout the school year. A *goal-based portfolio* has preset goals and items are selected to fit those goals, such as goals from a student's IEP. Another type of portfolio is a *process portfolio,* which documents the steps and processes a student has used to complete a piece of work (Katz & Johnson-Kuby, 1996).

3. *Select a variety of real classroom products that address the goals of the portfolio.* Students and teachers jointly select a range of authentic classroom products related to the goals of the portfolio. Some schools also involve families and students' classmates in the selection process, and use video and audio recordings to document students' accomplishments. For example, you can use video and audio recordings to examine and document a student's progress on such learning activities as describing illustrations in a "big book," giving oral presentations, participating in meaningful conversations, retelling stories, or solving math problems.

A variety of strategies can be used to involve your students in selecting items. Some teachers schedule a selection day on which students choose items for their portfolios; others encourage students to select items that are in progress or completed. Carpenter, Ray, and Bloom (1995) offer several options for selecting items and involving students in the process, including items selected by students with and without a menu determined by teachers or outside sources such as the school board, items selected by teachers, and items selected by students and teachers together. You can help students select portfolio items by offering models, allowing students to learn from each other by sharing their portfolios, and creating and sharing evaluation criteria with students (Wesson & King, 1996).

4. *Establish procedures for collecting, storing, organizing, and noting the significance of students' products.* Portfolio items are usually stored in individualized folders such as file folders, binders, and boxes with dividers organized in a variety of ways: according to students' IEPs, academic or content area subjects, student interests, thematic units, or chronologically (e.g., early/intermediate/later works) (Reetz, 1995). You can ask your students to personalize their portfolios by covering them with photographs, pictures, and logos (Keefe, 1995b).

Technology and multimedia can be used to store items and organize electronic or digital portfolios (Niguidula, 1997; Stiggins, 1997). For example, videocassettes can be used to record students' performances and portfolio items, scanners to enter students' work on a computer diskette or laser disk, and CD writers and photo CD technology to record pictures and add sound and text. Software programs offer ways to scan student-produced projects and artwork; enter sound and video clips of student presentations; organize portfolios by subject, theme, or project; and link students' work to national and districtwide standards, rubrics, and individualized lesson plans (Bahr & Bahr, 1997; Edyburn, 1994). A sample hypermedia-based electronic portfolio is presented in Figure 12.3.

INFORMATIONAL

Jochum et al. (1998) outline the roles of students, family members, general and special educators, and ancillary support personnel in the portfolio process.

SET YOUR SITES

The Coalition of Essential Schools (www.ces.aisr.brown.edu, 401-863-3384) has developed a CD-ROM on digital portfolios.

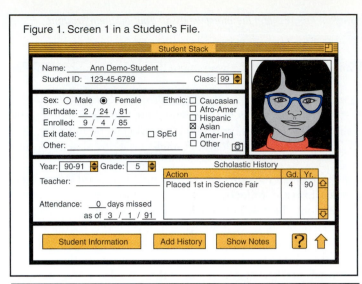

Figure 1. Screen 1 in a Student's File.

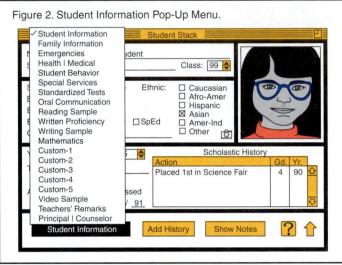

Figure 2. Student Information Pop-Up Menu.

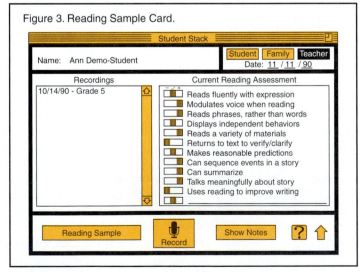

Figure 3. Reading Sample Card.

FIGURE 12.3 Sample hypermedia-based electronic portfolio.

Source: D. L. Edyburn, An equation to consider: The portfolio assessment knowledge base + technology = The Grady Profile. *LD Forum,* vol. 19, 1994, pp. 36, 37. Copyright 1994 by *LD Forum.* Reprinted with permission.

Date: 12/18/2000

Teacher Comments: This piece demonstrates James's ability to engage in the writing process and use story elements. James was given a choice of several themes and selected a theme relating to Thanksgiving. James completed the piece using a checklist that guided him in creating and organizing the elements of the story. When James first discussed the piece with me, I encouraged him to elaborate on his story.

Student Comments: I have been working on a story about Thanksgiving. I feel good about this item because I made up the story. In working on this story, I used a checklist that Ms. Feld gave me. The checklist asked me: What is the title of the story?, Who are the characters?, Where does the story take place?, What happens in the story?, and How does the story end?

FIGURE 12.4 Sample caption statement.

5. *Record the significance of items included in students' portfolios and help students reflect on them.* When selecting products for a portfolio, teachers and students write *caption statements,* brief descriptions that identify the document, provide the context in which it was produced, and reflect on why it was selected. For students who have difficulty writing caption statements, peer or adult scribes or audio and video recordings can be used to engage them in the self-reflection process (Jochum et al., 1998). A sample caption statement is presented in Figure 12.4.

Reetz (1995) and Countryman and Schroeder (1996) identified the following prompts, which can be used to help students compose caption statements:

Improvements
This piece shows my improvement in _____ . I used to _____ but now I _____ .

Pride
I am proud of this work because _____ . In this piece, notice how I _____ .

Special Efforts
This piece shows something that is hard for me. As you can see, I have worked hard to _____ .

IEP Objectives
This work shows my progress on _____ . I have learned to _____ . I will continue to _____ .

Content Areas
In (content area) I have been working on _____ . My goal is to _____ .

Thematic Units
I have been working on a unit relating to the theme of _____ . As part of this unit, I selected the following pieces: _____ . These pieces show that I _____ .

Projects
I have been working on a project about _____ . I learned _____ . The project shows I can _____ .

Difficulties
This piece shows the trouble I have with _____ .

Strategy Use
This piece shows that I used the following method: _____ . The steps I used were _____ and _____ .

You can help your students reflect on their portfolios by asking them to discuss why they selected a particular piece. Questions also can relate to learning outcomes (e.g., "What did you learn from working on this project?"), improvement (e.g., "If you could redo this, how would you improve it?" or "How is this piece different from your other pieces?"), process (e.g., "What process did you go through to complete this assignment?"), and strategy use (e.g., "What strategies did you use to work on this piece?" "Were they effective?"), as well as other aspects of student learning. You also can promote reflection by asking students to compare a recently completed item with an earlier work, by having students reflect on each other's work, by asking them to write letters for their portfolios explaining why a specific item was chosen, or by writing a portfolio introduction that compares items, identifies patterns, and interprets the meaning of the whole portfolio (Danielson & Abrutyn, 1997; Pike et al., 1994).

Many portfolios also include statements that summarize and reflect on the information presented in the portfolio and provide a framework for making decisions about students' educational programs (Keefe, 1995b). For example, you can ask your students to write summary statements about their writing portfolios by responding to the following questions: How have your attitudes toward writing changed?; What patterns have you noticed in your writing products?; Which writing project did you find most difficult? Why?; Which writing product do you consider your best? Why?; In which writing project did you learn the most about yourself as a writer? What did you learn?; and What changes have you noticed in your writing strategies over time?

6. *Review and evaluate portfolios and share them with others.* Portfolios should be reviewed and evaluated periodically by teachers, students, family members, and administrators throughout the school year during conferences (Countryman and Schroeder, 1996; Wesson & King, 1996). Students can share their portfolios with others by identifying the goals and purpose of their portfolios, explaining how their portfolios are organized and individualized to reflect their needs, providing an overview of the contents and special items in their portfolios, reviewing the criteria for evaluating their portfolios and individual items, and outlining what the portfolios show about their school performance and what they would like others to learn about them from their portfolios (Herbert & Schultz, 1996; Maxim, 1995). Others can then examine and evaluate students' portfolios using mutually agreed-on criteria that address the goals of the portfolio and examine the students' progress. The following questions can guide that process: (a) What does the portfolio reveal about the student's IEP and academic, behavioral, language, and social-emotional performance and skills?; (b) What are the student's strengths and instructional needs?; (c) What does the portfolio indicate about the student's learning style, attitudes, motivation, interests, cultural background, and use of learning strategies?; (d) Do items in the portfolio relate to each other? If so, what patterns do they reveal?; and (e) How can the information presented in the portfolio be used to plan the student's educational program? (Swicegood, 1994). Near the end of the conference, participants can be asked to write or dictate a note or letter to the portfolio stating what they feel is the most meaningful information in the portfolio, as well as what the portfolio indicates about the student's progress and educational program (Keefe, 1995b).

Rubrics

Authentic/performance assessment and portfolio assessment include the use of *rubrics*, statements specifying the criteria associated with different levels of proficiency for evaluating student performance (McTighe, 1997). Teachers using rubrics describe the various dimensions of assessment tasks, the different levels of performance, and the criteria describing each level, and then rate student performance on assessments and activities. Rubrics can

INFORMATIONAL

Countryman and Schroeder (1996) and Hebert and Schultz (1996) offer suggestions for helping students share their portfolios at conferences with their teachers and families, and Graham and Fahey (1999) describe how a collaborative assessment conference is used to engage teachers in a discussion of students' work.

REFLECTIVE

You applied for a job in a local school district by sending a resumé and a letter of interest. The superintendent's office asks you to come in for an interview and bring a portfolio showing your experiences and training. What items would you include in the portfolio? How would you organize and present them?

INFORMATIONAL

Finson and Ormsbee (1998) discuss and give examples of the use of rubrics in inclusive classrooms.

REFLECTING ON PROFESSIONAL PRACTICES

Using Student Portfolios

James moved into the school district in November and was placed in Ms. Feld's class. To prepare an educational program for James, Ms. Feld examined his performance on several norm-referenced tests administered while he attended his prior school. The test results indicated that James's reading and writing skills were significantly below grade level. However, they provided little information about his strengths and the teaching strategies that could be used to help him. Therefore, Ms. Feld decided to work with James to develop a reading and writing portfolio.

Throughout the school year, James and Ms. Feld selected a variety of items for his portfolio, including an audiocassette of James reading, a collection of pieces that he wrote based on a single theme using a process approach to writing, written summaries of books he read, a children's book that he wrote, and a self-recording graph of James's daily reading. The items were stored in an accordion file folder by date and subject area. James decorated the cover of his portfolio, and included a picture of his family and drawings of his favorite activities. When James and Ms. Feld selected an item for the portfolio, they discussed what it revealed about James's progress in reading and writing. After discussing the item's significance, each of them wrote a caption statement that was attached to the item.

During several family–teacher conferences throughout the school year, Ms. Feld and James shared his portfolio with his family. Before these meetings, James and Ms. Feld examined the whole portfolio and summarized what it demonstrated about James's progress in reading and writing. James began the conference by presenting his portfolio. First, he mentioned the goals and purpose of the portfolio and how it was organized. He then spoke about the content and special items in the portfolio, discussing why items were selected and what they showed about his learning. Ms. Feld spoke about James's progress by citing various portfolio items. James's family gave their reactions to his portfolio and asked questions about it. James, his family, and Ms. Feld discussed how his reading and writing had changed, the patterns that were evident in his reading and writing, the strategies he was using in these areas, and the changes in his attitude and motivation. They also talked about the skills and learning strategies that needed to be developed, as well as goals and plans for future work to address his instructional needs. At the end of the meetings, Ms. Feld, James, and James's family wrote notes summarizing their reactions to the portfolio, which then were included in the portfolio.

James's family was proud of him, and pleased to see real and understandable signs that James was learning. James's notes indicated that he was feeling good about himself and that he liked having some control over his learning. Ms. Feld felt much better knowing that her instructional program was helping James make progress in reading and writing.

Why did Ms. Feld decide to work with James to develop a portfolio? What roles did James perform in the portfolio process? What roles did James's family perform? How did Ms. Feld involve James and his family in the portfolio process? What was the impact of the portfolio on James, his family, and Ms. Feld? How could you use portfolios with your students?

help you clarify and communicate your expectations. They also make grading and feedback more objective and consistent, which in turn helps students understand the qualities associated with assignments and aids them in monitoring their own work (Goodrich, 1997; Schirmer, Bailey, & Fitzgerald, 1999). A writing rubric developed by Ms. Cheryl Ebert, an English teacher at the Johnson City (New York) High School, is presented in Figure 12.5.

SET YOUR SITES

The Center on Learning, Assessment, and School Structure (CLASS) maintains a website (www.classnj.org, 609-730-1199) that offers help in creating rubrics.

Technology-Based Testing

Advances in technology and multimedia allow you to assess students' responses to authentic situations and give students opportunities to use and develop their critical thinking, social, and metacognitive skills (Bahr & Bahr, 1997; Lawrence, 1994). For example, students can be given video clips of academic and social situations and asked to respond to them in a variety of ways.

Technology-based testing also allows you to modify the presentation and response modes of items to tailor exams to the skill levels of your students. For example, an exam

Criteria Quality	Focus on and Organization of Task	Narrative	Descriptive	Style and Diction	Grammar, Usage, and Mechanics
Excellent 90+ (A)	• Topic is approached in a unique and imaginative way. • Attitude and point of view remain the same for entire paper. • Paragraphs and sentences are organized and make sense.	• Opening situation is clearly established. • Characters are effectively introduced and developed. • Description is original and vivid. • Conflict is clearly developed. • Conflict is logically and completely solved.	• Very descriptive words or phrases are used. • Details are chosen to create a very clear picture or image for the reader throughout the writing.	• Uses well-chosen and appropriate words all of the time. • Expresses ideas in an imaginative and creative way. • Effective paragraphing. • Varies sentence structure.	• Can correctly use certain parts of speech, ending punctuation, and indentation at all times. • Correctly uses comma and quotations at all times. • Uses proper tense throughout. • Few or no spelling errors. • Capitalization correct throughout.
Quality 80+ (B)	• Topic is understood. • Attitude and point of view are clear, but not used throughout the paper. • Paragraphs are not always organized, but sentences are organized in a pattern.	• Opening situation is established. • Characters are adequately introduced and developed. • Includes some description. • A conflict is developed. • Conflict is solved.	• Descriptive words or phrases are used. • Details are chosen to create a good picture or image for the reader throughout the writing.	• Generally chooses appropriate words. • Expresses ideas clearly. • Some sentence structures are repetitious. • Some errors in sentences. • Correct paragraphing.	• Can correctly use certain parts of speech, ending punctuation, and indentation in most cases. • Correctly uses commas and quotations most of the time. • Uses proper tense throughout. • Minor spelling errors. • Capitalization appropriate.
Acceptable 70+ (C)	• Topic is understood, but ideas are not developed enough. • Attitude and point of view change throughout the writing. • Paragraphs are not always organized, and sentence order does not make sense.	• Opening situation is not appropriate or established. • Characters are not well developed. • Conflict is not established or does not make sense. • Conflict is not completely solved.	• Few descriptive words or phrases are used. • There are not enough details to keep the picture or image in the reader's mind.	• Sometimes chooses inappropriate words. • Meaning is clear, but word choice is not varied. • Some sentences are choppy. • Fragments/run-ons. • Errors in paragraphing.	• Word usage is limited. • Errors or omissions in the use of commas or quotations. • Errors in verb tense, but meaning is clear. • Several spelling errors, but meaning is clear.
Below Expectations	• Topic is not understood. • Attitude, point of view are unclear. • Paragraphs are not organized, nor do the sentences make sense.	• Lacking major elements of narrative structure.	• Almost no descriptive words or phrases are used. • Details, if any, do not create a picture for the reader.	• Chooses incorrect or inappropriate words. • Meaning is unclear or confusing, point is not made. • Many fragments and/or run-ons. • Incorrect or no paragraphing.	• Little or no knowledge of use of parts of speech or ending punctuation. • Commas, quotes, capitalization, punctuation errors throughout the paper. • Spelling errors interfere with understanding. • Constant shifting of verb tenses.

Name:
Narrative/Descriptive Writing Scoring Guide
Course Outcome: Students will be able to internalize a writing process which includes planning, composing, revising, and self-evaluating.

Assignment:
Date:

Notes:

FIGURE 12.5 Sample writing rubric.

Source: Developed by Cheryl Ebert, English teacher, Johnson City High School, Johnson City Central School District, Johnson City, NY

Advances in technology and multimedia are providing new ways to assess student learning.

administered via the computer can be structured so that the difficulty of each question depends on how the student performed on the prior question. If the student answers a question correctly, the computer can branch to a more difficult item; if he or she answers a question incorrectly, the computer can branch to an easier item. Technology-based assessment can also meet the needs of your linguistically diverse students by giving tests and interacting with students in their preferred language.

It is important to be aware of concerns about computer-based testing (FairTest, cited in Thurlow et al., 1995). These concerns include limiting test takers because it may take longer to read text presented on computer screens; making it more difficult to identify errors in material presented this way; preventing test takers from using such test-taking techniques as underlining or highlighting key words, eliminating choices, and scanning materials; failing to remove the cultural bias associated with testing; and placing students who do not have experience with technology at a disadvantage.

Dynamic Assessment

Dynamic assessment involves examining how students react to and benefit from instruction by using a test-train-retest model (Jitendra & Kameenui, 1993). While your students work on a task, you observe and offer help and feedback to improve their performance and skills. As students master skills, you offer less help and feedback and try to improve students' problem-solving abilities. One example of dynamic assessment is Feuerstein's (1979) *Learning Potential Assessment Model,* in which teachers offer students prompts and clues to promote skill acquisition as needed.

Observations

Although observational techniques are typically used to record students' social behaviors, you also can use them to document students' academic performance and academic-related behaviors (Meltzer et al., 1998). You can maintain recorded anecdotal records of students performing various content area activities, as well as observing students' products and/or the processes or strategies they use (Banerji & Dailey, 1995). Some teachers structure their observations by using teacher-made rating scales and checklists such as the one in Figure 12.6.

Student: _____

Teacher: _____

Date(s): _____

Directions: Use the following system to record student behavior:

   N = Student does not engage in the behavior.

   B = Student is beginning to engage in the behavior.

   D = Student is developing the behavior.

   P = Student has proficiency in the behavior.

Support your notations with comments.

Narratives	Behavior	Date(s)	Comments
Names characters			
Describes the setting			
Identifies time/place			
Identifies problems			
Identifies solutions			
Predicts story outcomes			
Identifies mood			
Describes author's view			
States theme of story			

FIGURE 12.6   Observation checklist of students' understanding of narrative text.

Source: Authentic assessment strategies by K. Pike and S. J. Salend, *Teaching Exceptional Children*, vol. 28, 1995, p. 16. Copyright 1995 by The Council for Exceptional Children. Reprinted by permission.

Observational techniques can be used to collect data on the amount of time planned for teaching, time actually spent teaching, and time spent by students on teaching activities in class, as well as the rates and sources of interruptions to planned teaching activities (Hollowood et al., 1994). These data also can be used to help determine if the presence of students with disabilities in general education classrooms reduces the teacher's attention and instructional time devoted to their classmates without disabilities.

Teacher-Made Tests

INFORMATIONAL

Test development software programs to help you in creating your own tests are available (Bahr & Bahr, 1997).

Traditional teacher-made tests are often used to evaluate students' performance in general education classrooms. Several factors you can consider when developing tests are presented below. When designing tests, you must be careful not to compromise the integrity of the test, course, or curriculum.

Test Content   The items on your tests should be directly related to the objectives of your instructional program. The tests should reflect not only *what* but also *how* content has been taught. Content taught via analysis, synthesis, or problem-solving techniques is best tested through essay questions, whereas factual and rote memory material may be tested by objective items. Additionally, the language and terminology used in both test directions and items should be consistent with those used in class.

The percentage of test questions related to specific content areas should reflect the amount of time your class spent on these topics. For example, on a test following a unit in which 30 percent of class time was spent on the U.S. Constitution, 30 percent of the test items should focus on material related to the Constitution. Shorter and more frequent tests of specific content rather than fewer, longer, and more comprehensive tests can help your students who have difficulty remembering large amounts of information.

Test Format   Even though many of your students can master the content necessary to perform well on a test, they may have difficulty with the test's format. Tests that cause confusion and distraction because of poor appearance or spatial design can defeat students before they begin. Therefore, items should be clearly and darkly printed on a solid, nondistracting background. Ideally, tests should be typed. If they must be written, the writing should be in the style (manuscript or cursive) familiar to the student.

Confusion can be minimized by proper spacing and sequencing of items (Rein, 1995). Items and the directions for completing them should appear on the same page so that students do not have to turn back and forth. Presenting items in a fixed, predictable, symmetrical sequence that emphasizes the transition from one item to another can help ensure that your students do not skip lines or fail to complete test items. Allowing students to write on the test itself rather than transferring answers to a separate page can reduce confusion for students with organizational difficulties. Providing enough space for responses allows students to complete an answer without continuing on another page and can structure the length of responses.

The needs of your students should also be considered in phrasing and structuring objective and essay-type questions. Guidelines you can use in writing test items are discussed here.

Multiple-Choice Items   Students' performance on multiple-choice items can be improved by composing well-written, grammatically correct items using language free of double negatives that students can read and understand (Maxim, 1995; Savage & Armstrong, 1996). The stem should provide a context for answering the item, contain only one major point and only relevant information, and be longer than the answer alternatives. The choices should be feasible and of the same length, should be presented vertically, and should not contain categorical words such as *always, all, only,* or *never.* Multiple-choice items can be tailored to the needs of students by reducing the number of choices and by eliminating more difficult choices, such as having to select *all of the above* or *none of the above.* Finally, allowing students to circle the answer they choose can alleviate problems in recording answers. An example of an adapted multiple choice item is as follows:

Directions: (Circle) the lettered choice that answers the question.

In which court case did the Supreme Court decide that *segregating students by race was unconstitutional?* (Note: Italicize text to highlight the information.)

(a) *Plessy* v. *Ferguson*
(b) *Baker* v. *Carr*
(c) *Newkirk* v. *Phalen School District*
(d) *Brown* v. *Board of Education of Topeka*

Matching Items   When writing matching items, you should consider several variables that can affect students' performance. Each matching section of the test should contain a maximum of 10 items. When more than 10 items are needed, group the additional items by content area in a separate matching section. There should be 25 percent more items in one column than in the other and only one correct response for each pair (Savage & Armstrong, 1996). Because students usually approach matching items by reading an item in the left-hand column and then reading all the available choices in the right-hand column, you can help your students save time and work in a coordinated fashion by listing the longer items in the left-hand column. For example, a matching item designed to assess mastery of vocabulary would have the definitions in the left-hand column and the vocabulary words in the right-hand column.

Place clear, unambiguous directions and both columns on the same page. This prevents the frustration some students encounter when matching questions are presented on more than one page. To avoid the disorganization that can occur when students respond by drawing lines connecting their choices from both columns, direct students to record the letter or number of their selection in the blank provided. You also can improve student performance on this type of test question by giving choices that are clear and concise, embedding an example in the matching question, labeling both columns, and organizing columns in a sensible and logical fashion (such as placing items in one column in numerical order and those in the other column in alphabetical order). An adapted matching item is as follows:

Directions: Write the letter from column 2 in the blank next to the best answer in column 1. The first one is done for you as an example.

Column 1		Column 2
__E__ 1.	A small, raised part of the land, lower than a mountain.	A. Peninsula
____ 2.	Land surrounded by water on three sides.	B. Plateau
____ 3.	An area of high, flat land.	C. Reservoir
____ 4.	A lake where a large water supply is stored.	D. Valley
____ 5.	Low land between mountains or hills.	E. Hill
____ 6.	Low and wet land.	F. Swamp

True-False Items   Many of your students may have difficulty responding to the true-false part of a test. In particular, they may have problems responding to items that require them to correct all false choices. To eliminate problems, phrase questions clearly and briefly, highlighting critical parts of the statements. Eliminate items that assess trivial information or values or that mislead students. Avoid stating items negatively. Focus each item on only one point, avoid items that ask students to change false statements into true statements, and limit the number of true-false questions per test (Maxim, 1995). Students who fail to discriminate the *T* and the *F*, or who write *T*'s that look like *F*'s and vice versa, should be allowed to record their response by circling either *True* or *False*. An adapted true-false question is as follows:

Directions: Read each statement. If the statement is *true*, circle (True). If the statement is *false*, circle (False).

True   False   1. The bee that lays eggs in the colony is the *queen*.

Sentence Completion Items   Sentence completion items can be especially difficult for students who have memory deficits. You can reduce the memory requirements of these items by making sure that they assess critical information and by providing several response choices or a word bank that includes a list of choices from which students select to complete the statement. For example, the sentence completion question *The outer layer of the atmosphere is called the* _____ can be modified by listing the choices of *stratosphere, exosphere,* and *ionosphere* under the blank. Where possible, the words in word banks can be categorized and placed together in the list. Because statements to be completed that come directly from print materials such as textbooks can be too vague when taken out of context, you should clearly phrase sentence completion items so that students can understand them. Additionally, word blanks should be placed near the end of items, be of the same length, kept to a minimum in each sentence, and require a one-word response or a short phrase (Newby et al., 1996). You also can modify the scoring of these items by accepting synonyms as correct responses and by not penalizing students for misspelling correct answers.

Essay Questions   Essay questions present unique problems for many students because of the numerous skills needed to answer them. You can adapt essay questions by making sure that they are focused, appropriate, and understandable in terms of readability and level of difficulty. Key words that guide students in analyzing and writing the essay can be highlighted and defined or students can be allowed to use a word list or dictionary.

You also can help your students interpret essay questions correctly and guide their essays in several ways. You can provide check sheets or outlines listing the components that can help them organize their response. Rather than using a single open-ended essay question, you can direct the organization and ensure the completeness of the response by using subquestions that divide the open-ended question into smaller sequential questions that can elicit all the parts of an accurate, well structured, detailed answer. Similarly, important concepts that students should include in their essays can be listed, highlighted, and located in a prominent place so that students will read them before writing their essays. For example, an essay question on the food groups can be adapted as follows:

Directions: When writing this essay, some terms you want to discuss include *minerals, vitamins, protein, carbohydrates, fats, calories, sugars,* and *grains.*

1. How are the basic food groups different? In writing your answer, discuss the following:

     What are the basic food groups?
     What are examples of the foods that make up the basic food groups?
     What nutrients does each food group provide?
     How many servings from each group should one have?

Readability of Items   Another factor to consider when developing a test is the readability of its items. Abstract sentences can be made more readable by simplifying the language and adding examples that illustrate the statements. For example, the essay terms requiring students to compare and contrast two concepts can be simplified by asking students to identify how the concepts are alike and different. In reading test items, misunderstandings can be avoided by using fewer pronouns to refer to important points, objects, or events. Additional information on making text and teacher-produced materials such as tests more readable and legible is presented in Chapter 8.

Scoring   The scoring of your tests can be modified to address the unique needs of students. This can be done by omitting certain questions, offering extra credit opportunities, giving bonus points for specific questions, allowing students to earn back

REFLECTING ON YOUR PRACTICES

Evaluating Teacher-Made Tests

You can evaluate your teacher-made tests by addressing the following:

Content

◇ Do items measure important information related to the objectives taught?

◇ Does the test require students to apply skills that they have not been specifically taught?

◇ Are the types of questions consistent with the strategies used to help students learn the content?

◇ Are the language and terms used in test directions and items consistent with those used in class?

◇ Does the percentage of items devoted to specific content areas reflect the amount of class time spent on those areas?

◇ Is the scope of the material being tested too broad? Too narrow?

Format and Readability

◇ Is the readability of the test appropriate?

◇ Are directions and items presented in language students can understand?

◇ Are cues provided to indicate a change in directions? To alert students to the specifics of each item?

◇ Is the length of the test reasonable?

◇ Is there a reasonable number of items per page?

◇ Do items on a page have proper spacing, and are they ordered correctly?

◇ Do students have to transfer their responses to a separate answer sheet?

◇ Do students have enough space to record their responses?

◇ Is the test legible, neat, and free of distracting features?

Multiple-Choice Items

◇ Does the stem provide a context for answering the item, and is it longer than the answer alternatives?

◇ Does the stem relate to only one point and include only relevant information?

◇ Are all the choices grammatically correct, free of double negatives, feasible, and of the same length?

◇ Is the correct choice clearly the best answer?

Matching Items

◇ Does the matching section include no more than 10 items?

◇ Are there 25 percent more choices in one column than in the other?

◇ Is an example embedded?

◇ Is there only one correct response for each pair?

◇ Are the directions and the columns presented on the same page?

◇ Are columns labeled and organized in a sensible, logical manner?

◇ Do students respond by writing the letter or number in a blank rather than drawing lines from column to column?

◇ Are the longer item statements listed in the left-hand column and the shorter statements in the right-hand column?

True-False Questions

◇ Are questions phrased clearly, without double negatives?

◇ Do items relate to relevant information?

◇ Are items focused on only one point?

◇ Do students respond by circling their choice of *True* or *False* rather than writing out their response?

◇ Are items unequivocally true or false?

Sentence Completion Items

◇ Do items relate to meaningful information?

◇ Are items understandable to students and have only one answer?

◇ Do items provide students with a sufficient context for answering?

◇ Are word blanks placed at the end of the item, of the same length, and kept to a minimum?

◇ Are response choices or word blanks provided?

Essay Questions

◇ Is the readability of the question appropriate?

◇ Are key words highlighted?

◇ Are open-ended questions divided into smaller sequential questions?

◇ Are students provided with a list of important concepts that should be discussed in the essay?

How would you rate your teacher-made tests? ( ) Excellent ( ) Good ( ) Needs Improvement ( ) Needs Much Improvement

What are some goals and steps you could adopt to improve your teacher-made tests?

points by correcting incorrect answers using their notes and textbooks, and giving partial credit for showing correct work (Hobbs, 1995). When grammar, spelling, and punctuation are not the elements being tested, you can consider not penalizing students for these errors or giving students separate grades for content and mechanics. For example, if an essay response on a social studies test is correct but contains many misspelled words, you could give separate grades for content and spelling. On essay tests, students initially can be given credit for an outline, web, diagram, or chart in place of a lengthy response.

In addition to grading the test, you can offer students corrective feedback on their test performance. When the test is returned, review it carefully with the class. You and your students should analyze tests to determine what types of errors were made and how often they occurred. If patterns of errors are noted, preparation for upcoming tests should address these trends. Error trends also can provide information for adapting tests to meet students' skills and preparing students for tests. For example, if students' tests showed problems with true-false items, you could use other types of items or review with the student strategies for handling true-false items.

Cooperative Group Testing   In *cooperative group testing,* students work collaboratively on open-ended tasks that have nonroutine solutions (Pomplun, 1996). You can then evaluate each group's product and cooperative behavior. Students also can be asked to respond individually to questions about their group's project. For example, in science, students can work in groups to develop a hypothesis related to recycling and then design, describe, and implement their study and report their conclusions. Each group member can brainstorm ways to test the hypothesis and record the group's decisions, activities, and findings.

Some teachers use a *two-tiered testing system* (Gajria, Giek, Hemrick, & Salend, 1992). In this system, students working in collaborative groups take a test, and each student receives the group grade. After the group test, students work individually on a

In cooperative group testing, students work collaboratively on open-ended tasks that have nonroutine solutions.

second test that covers similar material. Students can be given two separate grades, their two grades can be averaged together into one grade, or they can be allowed to select the higher grade.

Student Involvement   Your tests can be made fairer by involving students in the testing process. Curwin and Mendler (1988) suggest that you incorporate students' suggestions in writing and scoring tests. Ask them to submit possible test questions, have them test each other, and allow them to score each other's exams. Students also can be allowed to choose the type of test they take (Gajria et al., 1992). For example, you can create three versions of a test: multiple-choice, essay, and sentence completion. Your students can then select the test that best fits their response style and study habits. Similarly, you can structure your tests to give students some choice in responding to items (Rein, 1995). For example, a test can consist of 20 items with varying formats, and students can be directed to respond to any 15 of them.

Gathering Additional Information About the Academic Progress of Diverse Learners

In addition to using various types of standardized and nonstandardized assessments, you can gather additional information about your students' academic progress by using a variety of techniques described in the following sections.

Error Analysis

You can increase the amount of information obtained from formal and informal assessment procedures by using *error analysis.* This method is used to examine students' responses in order to identify areas of difficulty and patterns in the ways students approach a task. Error analysis usually focuses on identifying errors related to inappropriate use of rules and concepts, rather than careless random errors or those caused by lack of training.

Think-Aloud Techniques

The ways students approach a task can also be determined by *think-aloud techniques,* in which students state the processes they are using and describe their thoughts while working on a task. You can encourage students to think aloud by modeling the procedure and talking as you work through tasks and situations. You can also prompt students to think aloud by asking probing questions such as "What are you doing now?", "What are you thinking about?", and "How did you come up with that answer?" (Andrews & Mason, 1991).

Student Journals/Learning Logs

Student learning in inclusive settings also can be assessed through the use of *journals* or *learning logs.* Periodically, you can ask students to write comments in their journals on what they learned, how they learned it, what they do not understand, why they are confused, and what help they would like to receive. Students who have difficulty writing can maintain an audio log by recording their responses on audiocassette. You and the students can then examine the logs to identify instructional goals and modifications.

Students also can make journal entries on specific information covered in classes, attitudes toward a content area, how material covered in class relates to their lives, and additional questions that need to be studied. For example, after learning about decimals, students can be asked to respond to the following questions: (1) What are decimals, and why do we use them?; (2) What part of learning about decimals do you find easy? Hard?; and (3) Write a story to go with the problem $9.5 + 3.3 = 12.8$.

Self-Evaluation Questionnaires/Interviews

Self-evaluation questionnaires or *interviews* can provide information on students' perceptions of their educational needs, progress in learning new material, and strategies for completing a task. For example, according to Pike et al. (1994), a questionnaire or interview might focus on asking students to respond to the following questions: "What are some things you do well when you read?", "What are some areas in reading that cause you difficulty?", "In what ways is your reading improving?", and "What areas of your reading would you like to improve?"

Reporting Information About the Academic Progress of Diverse Learners

IEPs

Students' academic performance in inclusive settings also can be determined by examining their IEPs. For example, you can assess their progress by examining their success in attaining the goals outlined in their IEPs. If specific goals have not been achieved, the evaluation can attempt to explain why, and whether these goals are still appropriate.

Report Card Grades

Report card grades, which are reported periodically, are another indicator of student progress in inclusive classrooms. Because students with disabilities may receive the services of several teachers, the roles of these professionals in grading should be determined and conflicts should be resolved (Christiansen & Vogel, 1998). In addition, when grading students in inclusive classes, the issues of equity and fairness must be considered (Bradley & Calvin, 1998).

INFORMATIONAL

Christiansen and Vogel (1998) offer a decision-making model that teachers working collaboratively in inclusive classrooms can use to determine appropriate grading systems for student with disabilities.

Alternate Grading Systems   When grading students in inclusive classrooms, a variety of alternative grading systems can be considered (see Figure 12.7). The grading system chosen for each student should be included in the student's IEP (Hendrickson & Gable, 1997). In addition, Bradley and Calvin (1998) suggest that points and percentages rather than letter grades be used to grade different types of classroom products. They also believe it is important to minimize competition among students, avoid posting grades and scores, and give students opportunities to grade themselves and each other. In addition, they encourage you to weight a variety of activities to determine students' grades. For example, rather than giving grades based solely on test scores, points can be divided so that 40 percent of the grade is related to projects, 30 percent to test performance, 10 percent to class participation, 10 percent to homework, and 10 percent to effort. It is also important to examine the effectiveness of grading alternatives and their impact on all students. Finally, be prepared to offer a rationale for their use if students question you about their appropriateness.

REFLECTIVE

Do grading alternatives and accommodations compromise standards and reduce course integrity? Should grades be assigned only by the general education classroom teacher or through collaboration with others?

❖ *IEP grading:* Students' IEP goals and performance criteria serve as the foundation for grading. Teachers assign grades that acknowledge students' progress in meeting goals established at a certain skill level.

❖ *Contract grading:* Teachers and students determine the amount and quality of the work students must complete to receive a specific grade. In framing the contract, both teachers and students agree on the content the students hope to learn; activities, strategies, and resources that will help them acquire the skills; products students will produce to demonstrate mastery; strategies for evaluating their products; timelines for assignments, including penalties for lateness; and procedures for assigning a grade.

❖ *Pass/fail systems:* Minimum course competencies are specified and students who demonstrate mastery receive a P grade, while those who fail to meet the minimum standards are given an F grade. Some schools have modified traditional pass/fail grading system to include such distinctions as honors (HonorP), high pass (HP), pass (P), and low pass (LP).

❖ *Mastery level/criterion systems:* Students and teachers meet to divide the material into a hierarchy of skills and activities based on individual needs and abilities, as measured by a pretest. After completing learning activities, the students take a posttest or perform an activity to demonstrate mastery of the content. When students demonstrate mastery, they receive credit for that accomplishment and repeat the process with the next skill to be mastered.

❖ *Checklists and rating scales:* Teachers develop checklists and rating scales that describe the competencies associated with their courses and evaluate each student according to mastery of these competencies. Some school districts have revised their grading systems by creating rating scales for different grade levels. Students are rated on each skill using a scale that includes "not yet evident," "beginning," "developing," and "independent."

❖ *Multiple grading:* Teachers grade students in the areas of ability, effort, and achievement. The ability grade is based on the students' expected improvements in the content areas. The effort grade is a measure of the time and energy the students devoted to learning the content. The achievement grade assesses the students' mastery of the material in relation to others. Students' report cards can then include the three grades for each content area, or grades can be computed by averaging the three areas.

❖ *Level grading:* Teachers individualize the grading system by using a numeric subscript to indicate the level of difficulty on which the students' grades are based. For example, a grade of B6 indicates that a student is working in the B range at the sixth-grade level. Subscript systems can also be used to indicate whether students are working at grade level, above grade level, or below grade level.

❖ *Shared grading:* Teachers who are team teaching collaborate to assign grades based on both teachers' observations of students' performance. Before making their evaluations, teachers establish guidelines for determining and weighting valid criteria and measuring performance.

❖ *Descriptive grading:* Teachers write descriptive comments and give examples of students' performance that give students, families, and other teachers information on the students' skills, learning styles, effort, attitudes, and growth over time. Descriptive grading also can include copies of students' work and comments about strategies to improve students' performance.

FIGURE 12.7 Alternative grading systems.
Sources: Bradley and Calvin (1998), Cohen (1983), Hendrickson and Gable (1997), Kinnison, Hayes, and Acord (1981), Rojewski, Pollard, and Meers (1992), and Vasa (1981).

How Can I Evaluate the Social and Behavioral Performance of Students?

One premise of inclusion programs is that such programs will have a positive impact on students' social and behavioral development. For students with disabilities, desired social and behavioral outcomes include making friends, increasing their social and behavioral skills, and improving their self-concepts. For students without disabilities, social and behavioral outcomes include becoming more accepting and understanding of individual differences, more aware of and sensitive to the needs of others, and more willing to make friends with students with disabilities.

Observational Techniques

Through direct observations of interactions between students, you can gain insights into students' interaction patterns, as well as their social and behavioral competence (Gelzheiser, McLane, Meyers, & Pruzek, 1998). Data collected via observation can be supplemented by observations and interviews with family members, other teachers, and students. Still other information sources are documents revealing the number and types of discipline referrals, behavioral incidents, interruptions caused, and referrals to special education.

You can examine the interaction patterns of your students by observing them during various learning and social activities. This information can then be analyzed by considering the following questions:

◇ How often are students with and without disabilities interacting with each other?
◇ How long do these interactions last?
◇ What is the nature of these interactions (e.g., spontaneous, assistive, reciprocal, instructional, disciplinary, attention-seeking, playful)?
◇ Who is beginning and ending the interactions?
◇ How many students without disabilities are interacting with their peers with disabilities?
◇ What events, activities, individuals, objects, and other stimuli seem to promote interactions?
◇ What events, activities, individuals, objects, and other stimuli seem to limit interactions?
◇ What roles, if any, do race, gender, sexual orientation, and socioeconomic factors play in the interactions among students?
◇ Do the students with and without disabilities have the skills needed to interact with their peers?
◇ What are the outcomes of these interactions?

Observations of students' behavioral and social skills also can be recorded on checklists and rating scales (Taylor, 1997; Witt, Elliott, Daly, Gresham, & Kramer, 1998). These scales provide a list of behavioral and social skills that guide your observations of your students. To ensure that the results are accurate and representative of student behavior, you may want to ask several different individuals to rate your students in various settings. A sample rating scale based on the social and behavioral skills that teachers believe are important for success in inclusive classrooms is presented in Figure 12.8.

INFORMATIONAL

The *Educational Assessment of Social Interaction* (*EASI*) (Hunt, Alwell, Farron-Davis, & Goetz, 1996), the *Interactive Partnership Scale* (*IPS*) (Hunt et al., 1996), the *Social Inter-action Checklist* (*SIC*) (Kennedy et al., 1997), the *Social Contact Assessment Form* (Kennedy et al., 1997), and the *School-Based Social Network Form* (Kennedy et al., 1997) can help you record and categorize your observations of student interactions.

Sociometric Techniques

Data on the social relationships students prefer can be collected by using sociometric techniques (Sale & Carey, 1995). A peer-nomination sociogram involves asking students to respond confidentially to a series of questions that reveal classmates with whom they would like to perform a social or classroom activity. Because it is important to obtain information on both popular and unpopular students in the class, sociograms should include both acceptance (i.e., "Which 5 students from this class would you most like to invite to your birthday party?") and rejection ("Which 5 students from this class would you least like to sit next to during lunch?") questions. In addition to providing data on the acceptance or rejection of students, sociograms can help you identify students who need to improve their socialization skills.

Several structured sociometric rating procedures have been developed for teachers. They provide specific questions to ask students and standardized procedures to follow when administering the rating scale. For example, *How I Feel Toward Others* (Agard, Veldman, Kaufman, & Semmel, 1978) is a fixed-choice sociometric rating scale on which each class member rates every other class member as "likes very much" (friend), "all right" (feels neutral toward), "don't like" (does not want as a friend), or "don't know." Other structured sociometric rating scales include the *Perception of Social Closeness Scale* (Horne, 1981), the *Peer Acceptance Scale* (Bruininks, Rynders, & Gross, 1974) and the *Ohio Social Acceptance Scale* (Lorber, 1973). You can supplement data collected via sociograms by using the *Friendship Quality Scale* (Berndt & Perry, 1986), a structured interview that examines various dimensions of student friendships.

Self-Concept Measures

Many strategies have been developed to assess students' self-concepts. You can measure the academic self-concepts of your students and their perceptions of how they learn by asking them to complete such instruments as the *Student Self-Report System* (Meltzer & Roditi, 1994), the *Student Rating Scale* (Meltzer & Roditi, 1994), and the *Perception of Ability Scale for Students* (*PASS*) (Boersma & Chapman, 1992). Other instruments used to measure aspects of the self-concept of students in inclusion programs include the *Self-Perception Profile* (Renick & Harter, 1989), the *Loneliness and Social Dissatisfaction Scale* (Asher, Hymel, & Renshaw, 1985), and the *Social Alienation Scale* (Seidel & Vaughn, 1991).

Please rate each skill using the following scale:

Always	Usually	Sometimes	Rarely	Never
(1)	(2)	(3)	(4)	(5)

Behavioral and Social Skill	Always (1)	Usually (2)	Sometimes (3)	Rarely (4)	Never (5)
1. Follows directions	1	2	3	4	5
2. Asks for help when it's appropriate	1	2	3	4	5
3. Begins an assignment after teacher gives assignment to class	1	2	3	4	5
4. Obeys class rules	1	2	3	4	5
5. Doesn't speak when others are talking	1	2	3	4	5
6. Works well with others	1	2	3	4	5
7. Interacts cooperatively with others	1	2	3	4	5
8. Shares with others	1	2	3	4	5
9. Attends class regularly	1	2	3	4	5
10. Seeks teacher's permission before speaking	1	2	3	4	5
11. Works independently on assignments	1	2	3	4	5
12. Seeks teacher's permission before leaving seat	1	2	3	4	5
13. Brings necessary materials to class	1	2	3	4	5
14. Participates in class	1	2	3	4	5
15. Makes friends	1	2	3	4	5
16. Has a sense of humor	1	2	3	4	5

FIGURE 12.8   Inclusive setting behavioral and social skills rating scale.

HOW CAN I MEASURE PERCEPTIONS OF MY INCLUSION PROGRAM?

As we saw in Chapter 1, students, teachers, and family members have varied perceptions of inclusion that are often related to the effectiveness of the inclusion program. Therefore, any evaluation of your inclusion program must include an examination of the perceptions and experiences of students, teachers, and family members. This information can help you analyze the effectiveness of your inclusion program, validate successful inclusive educational policies that should be continued, and pinpoint procedures that need to be revised.

Students' Perceptions

Your students' perceptions are crucial in evaluating your inclusion program. Interviews and questionnaires can be used to collect information from students on the academic and social benefits of the program, as well as their insights and experiences. When using interviews and questionnaires, items and directions should be clearly stated and phrased using students' language rather than professional jargon. When professional terms like *inclusion* must be used, these terms should be defined so that your students can understand them.

You also need to consider whether or not it is appropriate to use phrases such as *students with and without disabilities* and to tailor specific items for both types of students. Because interviews and questionnaires may take a long time to complete, you may choose to administer them over several days. Interviews are particularly appropriate for younger students and those who have difficulty reading and writing (Best & Kahn, 1998). A list of potential interview questions is presented in Figure 12.9.

INFORMATIONAL

Bogdan and Biklen (1992) offer guidelines for interviewing students.

All students can benefit from inclusive teaching practices.

Others sometimes call your class an inclusion classroom. This means that students who learn, act, look, and speak in different ways are learning together in the same class. It also means that other teachers work with students in this classroom rather than taking them to another classroom.

I am going to ask you some questions about your class.

1. Do you think that all types of students learning in the same class is a good idea? Why or why not?
2. What things do you like about being in this class?
3. What things don't you like about being in this class?
4. What have you learned from being in this class?
5. In what areas are you doing well? Having difficulty?
6. Are you completing all your schoolwork and homework? If so, what things are helping you to complete your work? If not, what things are keeping you from completing your work?
7. What are your teachers doing to help you in your class?
8. How do you get along with other students in this class? How has being in this class affected your friendships and popularity?
9. In what afterschool activities do you participate? If none, why?
10. How do you think your classmates feel about being in this class?
11. What do you think your classmates learned from being in this class?
12. What changes have you observed in your classmates since being in this class?
13. What parts of being in this class have been hard for you? For your classmates? For your teacher(s)? Why?
14. What would you tell other students about being in this class?
15. What ways can you think of to make this class work better?

FIGURE 12.9   Sample student interview.

VIDEO INSIGHT

Evaluating the Effectiveness of Inclusion: A Video Case Study of Memorial High School

View these video segments online by visiting our companion web-site, located at http://www.prenhall.com/salend. *Once you enter the site, select the Video Case Study module on the navigation bar. There you will be able to down-load and view the video clips as well as respond to reflective questions. You can print out your answers or submit them via e-mail to a professor or study partner.*

In these video segments, we take a virtual field trip to Memorial High School, which has recently implemented an inclusion program. Watch interviews with Angie, Elizabeth, Blaine, David, and Efren—a mix of students with and without disabilities—as they discuss the principles of inclusion, and share their opinions of how well the inclusion program works at Memorial High School. After listening to their comments, use the guidelines presented in this chapter to provide your own assessment of the effectiveness of Memorial's inclusion program.

Questionnaires also allow you to investigate your students' feelings about and reactions to various aspects of inclusion programs. It is best to use a closed-form questionnaire that is easy for them to complete. This type of questionnaire has a yes-no or true-false format or asks students to mark a number or a statement that best indicates their response. For students who have reading and/or writing difficulties, you may need to read items for them as well as record their responses. A sample questionnaire is presented in Figure 12.10.

Please circle the word that best describes your feelings about your class:

	Yes	Maybe	No
1. I like being in a class with different types of students.	Yes	Maybe	No
2. I learned a lot, and so did others.	Yes	Maybe	No
3. I am more likely to help other students.	Yes	Maybe	No
4. I saw other students making fun of their classmates.	Yes	Maybe	No
5. I have improved at teaching others.	Yes	Maybe	No
6. I am more understanding of the behaviors and feelings of others.	Yes	Maybe	No
7. I was made fun of by my classmates.	Yes	Maybe	No
8. I feel better about myself.	Yes	Maybe	No
9. I feel that I belong in this class.	Yes	Maybe	No
10. I improved my schoolwork and grades.	Yes	Maybe	No
11. I am better at making friends.	Yes	Maybe	No
12. I improved at learning from others.	Yes	Maybe	No
13. I am less likely to make fun of others.	Yes	Maybe	No
14. I felt the same as the other students in my class.	Yes	Maybe	No
15. I received help from my teacher(s) when I needed it.	Yes	Maybe	No
16. I did most of my schoolwork without help.	Yes	Maybe	No
17. I liked having several teachers in the classroom.	Yes	Maybe	No
18. I liked working with other students.	Yes	Maybe	No
19. I enjoyed being in this classroom.	Yes	Maybe	No
20. I would like to be in a class like this next year.	Yes	Maybe	No

FIGURE 12.10   Sample student inclusion survey.
Note: See Companion Website for additional survey questions.

Teachers' Perceptions

Teachers are vital to the success of inclusion programs. Therefore, in evaluating inclusion programs, their perceptions of and experiences with inclusion are very important. This information can help school districts assess the impact of their inclusion programs on students, evaluate various aspects of these programs, and design and implement effective inclusion programs.

Questionnaires

Questionnaires and interviews can be used to elicit teachers' feelings about and reactions to inclusion programs, including their beliefs and concerns, as well as their feelings about the impact of the programs. Questionnaires and interviews also can address teachers' satisfaction with (1) their roles in implementing inclusion programs; (2) the quality of the resources they have received to implement inclusion; (3) their experiences in collaborating and communicating with others; (4) their skills and training to implement inclusion successfully; and (5) the policies and practices concerning inclusion of the school and the district.

Questionnaires have several advantages that make them particularly suitable for use with teachers. They are easily and quickly completed, and they maintain the confidentiality of the respondents. To make it easy to complete surveys, they should be presented using a yes-no or true-false format, or as a Likert-type scale that asks individuals to select a number or statement that best indicates their response. A sample questionnaire designed to assess teachers' perceptions of and experiences with inclusive education is presented in Figure 12.11.

Please indicate your feelings about and experiences with inclusion using the following scale:

Strongly Disagree (SD)	Disagree (D)	Neutral (N)	Agree (A)	Strongly Agree (SA)
1	2	3	4	5

	SD	D	N	A	SA
1. I feel that inclusion is a good idea.	1	2	3	4	5
2. I feel that I have the time and the training to implement inclusion successfully.	1	2	3	4	5
3. I feel that inclusion helps students develop friendships.	1	2	3	4	5
4. I feel that inclusion is working well in my class.	1	2	3	4	5
5. I feel that I receive the necessary support and assistance to implement inclusion successfully.	1	2	3	4	5
6. I feel that it is difficult to modify instruction and my teaching style to meet the needs of students with disabilities.	1	2	3	4	5
7. I feel that inclusion helps students academically.	1	2	3	4	5
8. I feel that having other adults in the classroom is an asset.	1	2	3	4	5
9. I feel that the demands of the curriculum make it difficult to implement inclusion.	1	2	3	4	5
10. I feel that I have been sufficiently involved in the inclusion process in my school.	1	2	3	4	5
11. I feel that I perform a subordinate role as a result of inclusion.	1	2	3	4	5
12. I feel that I do not have enough time to communicate and collaborate with others.	1	2	3	4	5
13. My students' academic performance has been negatively affected.	1	2	3	4	5
14. My students have become more accepting of individual differences.	1	2	3	4	5
15. My students feel better about themselves.	1	2	3	4	5
16. My students have picked up undesirable behaviors from their classmates.	1	2	3	4	5
17. My students have received less teacher attention.	1	2	3	4	5
18. My students have been teased by their classmates.	1	2	3	4	5
19. My students have grown socially and emotionally.	1	2	3	4	5
20. My students feel that they belong in my class.	1	2	3	4	5
21. My students feel positive about my class.	1	2	3	4	5
22. My students show pride in their work.	1	2	3	4	5

FIGURE 12.11   Sample teacher's inclusion survey.

Note: See Companion Website for additional survey questions.

Interviews

Interviews give teachers the opportunity to provide rich and descriptive examples, insights, and suggestions that can be valuable in evaluating inclusive educational programs (Panyan, Hillman, & Liggett, 1997). In addition to individual interviews, focus group interviews can be used (Stanovich, 1999). Potential interview questions that can be used to examine teachers' experiences in inclusion programs are presented in Figure 12.12.

Interviews with teachers also can provide valuable information that can pinpoint students' strengths and existing or potential problems in their academic, behavioral, and social-emotional performance by addressing the following questions:

1. How is inclusion working in your class? Your school? What is working well? What is not working well?
2. What factors have contributed to the success of inclusion in your class? At your school?
3. What factors have prevented inclusion from working in your class? At your school?
4. What are your biggest concerns about and frustrations with inclusion?
5. What things do you enjoy most about inclusion?
6. Do you have difficulty meeting the needs of students with certain types of disabilities? If so, what types of disabilities do these students have and what problems are you experiencing?
7. Do you feel that you have the support, resources, and time to implement inclusion effectively? If not, what support, resources, and scheduling arrangements would be helpful to you?
8. Do you feel that you have the skills and training to implement inclusion effectively? If not, what skills would you like to develop and what training would you like to receive?
9. Which individuals (give titles, not names) have been most helpful in assisting you to implement inclusion? How have these individuals assisted you? What additional assistance would you like to receive?
10. How has inclusion affected your students with disabilities? Please describe any benefits and/or negative consequences you have observed in these students.
11. What accommodations have been provided to meet the cultural and linguistic needs of your students? How effective have these accommodations been?
12. Have your students participated in the statewide testing program? If yes, what were the results? What, if any, alternative testing techniques were employed? Where they effective? If no, why not and what alternative assessment strategies have been employed?
13. How has inclusion affected your students without disabilities? Please describe any benefits and/or negative consequences you have observed for these students.
14. How has inclusion affected you as a professional and a person? Please describe any benefits and/or any negative consequences for you.
15. In what ways has your role changed as a result of your school's effort to implement inclusion? What do you enjoy about your new roles? What concerns do you have about your new roles?
16. How did it feel to collaborate with another professional? What was most difficult? Most enjoyable? Most surprising?
17. How did the collaboration process change throughout the school year?
18. What did you learn from collaborating with another professional?
19. What suggestions would you have for other professionals who are planning to work collaboratively?
20. If another professional asked you for advice about inclusion, what advice would you give?
21. What things has your school district done to facilitate inclusion in your school? To hinder inclusion in your school?
22. What schoolwide and districtwide inclusion practices would you like to see retained? What practices would you like to see revised?
23. What additional information would you like to have about inclusion?

FIGURE 12.12 Sample interview questions to examine the experiences of educators working in inclusive classrooms.

Sources: Banerji and Dailey (1995), Bennett et al. (1997), Downing et al. (1997), Giangreco et al. (1993), Janney, Snell, Beers, and Raynes (1995), Phillips et al. (1995), and York and Tundidor (1995).

◆ How is the student performing academically, socially, and behaviorally in your class?
◆ To what extent has the student achieved the goals listed in the IEP? If the goals have not been achieved, what is an explanation?
◆ Does the student complete classwork, homework, and other assigned projects?
◆ What methods, materials, instructional adaptations, and alternative testing techniques have been successful? Unsuccessful?
◆ What accommodations have been provided to meet the student's cultural and language needs? How effective have these accommodations been?
◆ How does the student get along with classmates?
◆ In what extracurricular activities does the student participate?
◆ Is the student receiving the necessary supportive services?
◆ How is the communication system with other personnel and the student's family working?

Teachers also can provide feedback on students' performance by completing a weekly or monthly rating scale such as the one presented in Figure 12.13.

DATE DISTRIBUTED:_____
DATE COMPLETED: _____
DATE RETURNED: _____
CLASS: _____
How are you feeling about _____'s:
                          (student's name)

	Please Rate	Comments
1. Goals	Not Clear----------------------Very Clear 1 2 3 4	
2. Participation in class	Passive------------------------------Active 1 2 3 4	
3. Behavior	Unmanageable----------- Manageable 1 2 3 4	
4. Progress	Unnoticeable------------------Noticeable 1 2 3 4	
5. Impact on classroom atmosphere	Negative------------------------- Positive 1 2 3 4	
6. Peer connections	Isolated------------------------Connected 1 2 3 4	
7. Request for my time/ attention	Too Demanding-Reasonable Amount 1 2 3 4	

Please list three positive comments and three concerns that you may have for _____ .
                                                                              (class)

POSITIVES	CONCERNS	Please list any initial thought you may have that address your concerns.
1.	1.	
2.	2.	
3.	3.	

FIGURE 12.13   Sample student progress rating form.

Source: Measuring perceptions about inclusion by M. Prom. *Teaching Exceptional Children,* vol. 31, 1999, pp. 38–42. Copyright 1999 by The Council for Exceptional Children. Reprinted by permission.

Journals

The needs, experiences, and feelings of teachers concerning inclusive education also can be examined through the use of journals (Phillips et al., 1995; Salend et al., 1997). In their journals, teachers can record their thoughts, observations, achievements, frustrations, conflicts, and reactions to their experiences, including their interactions with each other, students, family members, and other professionals. The journals can then be analyzed to identify and understand emerging patterns and recurring themes with respect to the concerns, needs, successes, perspectives, and experiences of educators.

Family Members' Perceptions

Family members are particularly affected by the impact of inclusion programs on their children. Therefore, they too can provide feedback on the academic, social, and behavioral development of their children. They can also assess the effectiveness of the school district's inclusion practices and policies, as well as identify and make recommendations about policies and practices that need revision (Giangreco, Edelman, Cloninger, & Dennis, 1993; Ryndak et al., 1995). Families can be especially informative about the social and emotional adjustment of their children, as well as their children's reactions to the inclusive setting and relationships with classroom peers. For example, family members may notice that their child is reluctant to go to school and has little contact with classmates outside of school. Similarly, family members can inform teachers that their child is spending too much time on homework and thus is having difficulty with the academic requirements of the inclusive class.

Interviews and Questionnaires

Schools should not assume that families are satisfied with the inclusion program. Their experiences with and perceptions of the program should be assessed as part of the evaluation of the program (Palmer et al., 1998). Interviews with or surveys of family members can focus on the following issues: (1) their beliefs and concerns about inclusion; (2) the experiences and perceptions of their children regarding the inclusion programs; and (3) the impact of the inclusion program on their children, other students, themselves, other families, and teachers (Davern, 1999). Interviews and surveys also can address their satisfaction with the quality of the educational program, their communication with school personnel, and the inclusion practices of the school and the district. A sample interview and a questionnaire on the perceptions and experiences of families concerning inclusion programs are provided in Figures 12.14 and 12.15, respectively.

1. Do you think that placing students with disabilities in general education classrooms with their peers who do not have disabilities is a good idea? Why or why not?
2. What things do you like about your child being in an inclusion classroom?
3. What concerns do (did) you have about your child being in an inclusion classroom? Do you still have these concerns?
4. How does your child feel about being in an inclusion classroom? What things does your child like about being in an inclusion classroom? What concerns, if any, does your child have about being in an inclusion classroom? How could these concerns be addressed?
5. How do you feel about the educational program your child is receiving in his or her inclusion classroom?
6. How do you feel about the special education and supportive services your child is receiving in his or her inclusion classroom?
7. How has being in an inclusion classroom affected your child academically, socially, and behaviorally? Please describe any benefits and/or negative consequences you have observed in your child. What factors led to these changes?
8. How has your child's placement in an inclusion classroom affected other students? His or her teachers? Other families? Other professionals who work with your child? Please describe any benefits and/or any negative consequences for these individuals.
9. How has your child's placement in an inclusion classroom affected you? Please describe any benefits and/or any negative consequences for you.
10. Have your goals for your child's future changed as a result of your child's being placed in an inclusion classroom? If yes, in what ways?
11. What roles have you performed in the inclusion process? Are you satisfied with your roles in the inclusion process? If so, what roles have been particularly important and satisfying? If not, why not, and what roles would you like to perform?
12. What things seem to make inclusion work well at your child's school? What things seem to prevent inclusion from working well at your child's school? In what ways can inclusion be improved in your child's class and school?
13. What schoolwide and districtwide inclusion practices would you like to see retained? What practices would you like to see revised?
14. What do you think of the access to, timeliness, and coordination of the services your child is receiving?
15. How is the communication system between you and the school working?
16. What additional information would you like to have about inclusion and your child's class?

FIGURE 12.14   Sample family interview questions concerning inclusive education programs.
Sources: Gibb et al. (1997), Green and Shinn (1995), Peck et al. (1992), Ryndak et al. (1995), and York and Tundidor (1995).

Please indicate your feelings about and experiences with inclusion using the following scale:

Strongly Disagree (SD)	Disagree (D)	Neutral (N)	Agree (A)	Strongly Agree (SA)
1	2	3	4	5

	SD	D	N	A	SA
1. I feel satisfied with the educational and supportive services my child is receiving.	1	2	3	4	5
2. I feel satisfied with the school's communication with families.	1	2	3	4	5
3. I feel that being in an inclusion class has been positive for my child.	1	2	3	4	5
4. I feel that inclusion helps children academically and socially.	1	2	3	4	5
5. I feel that families are adequately involved in the inclusion process.	1	2	3	4	5
6. I feel that the school district did a good job of explaining the inclusion program to me.	1	2	3	4	5
7. My child learned a lot.	1	2	3	4	5
8. My child talks positively about school.	1	2	3	4	5
9. My child feels proud of his/her classwork.					
10. My child has learned to feel comfortable interacting with other students.	1	2	3	4	5
11. My child has grown socially and emotionally.	1	2	3	4	5
12. My child's education has been negatively affected.	1	2	3	4	5
13. My child has received fewer services.	1	2	3	4	5
14. My child has made more friends.	1	2	3	4	5
15. My child has become more confident and outgoing.	1	2	3	4	5
16. My child has become more accepting of individual differences.	1	2	3	4	5
17. My child has picked up undesirable behavior from classmates.	1	2	3	4	5
18. My child has been teased by classmates.	1	2	3	4	5
19. My child has teased classmates.	1	2	3	4	5
20. My child would like to be in an inclusion class next year.	1	2	3	4	5

FIGURE 12.15 Sample family inclusion survey.
Note: See Companion Website for additional survey questions.

HOW CAN I IMPROVE THE EFFECTIVENESS OF MY INCLUSION PROGRAM?

After you have collected data on students' progress and on students', teachers', and family members' perceptions of your inclusion program, members of the school or school district's comprehensive planning team or inclusive educational program planning committee can analyze them. The data can be used to examine the impact of the program on student performance and to improve the program's effectiveness.

Examine the Impact on Student Performance

First, the committee can examine the impact of your inclusion program on the academic, social, and behavioral performance of your students by reviewing the results of standardized tests and the findings of alternative assessments. For example, your students' academic progress can be assessed by examining their statewide test results, as well as their progress in mastering their IEP goals. This information can be supplemented by an examination of other indicators of student progress and program effectiveness. Such indicators include data on graduation rates, participation in statewide tests, attendance patterns, participation in extracurricular activities, behavioral referrals, course failures, and accrual of credits (Sinclair et al., 1998; Thurlow, Ysseldyke, & Reid, 1997). For secondary students, data on the types of diploma students are receiving, as well as their success in attending college, finding a job, living independently, and being socially integrated into their communities can be measures of the ability of the inclusion program to help students make the transition from school to adulthood (SRI International, 1993).

Determine Program Strengths, Concerns, and Possible Solutions

The data on the perceptions of students, teachers, and family members regarding your inclusion program also can be analyzed to determine the strengths of the program and validate aspects of the program that appear to be working well. In addition, these data can be used to identify components of the program that need revision, as well as determining potential solutions. Possible concerns associated with inclusion programs and potential solutions to address these concerns are presented in Table 12.1 (pages 450–451).

SUMMARY

This chapter offered a variety of strategies for evaluating the progress of students and the effectiveness of inclusion programs. As you review the questions posed in this chapter, remember the following points.

How Can I Evaluate the Academic Performance of Students?

You can use standardized tests, testing accommodations, curriculum-based measurement, authentic/performance assessment, portfolio assessment, rubrics, technology-based testing, dynamic assessment, observation, and teacher-made tests. You also can gather additional information about students' academic progress by using error analysis, think-aloud techniques, student journals/learning logs, and self-evaluation questionnaires/interviews. Students' academic progress can be assessed by examining their IEPs and report card grades.

How Can I Evaluate the Social and Behavioral Performance of Students?

You can evaluate the impact of your inclusion program on your students' social and behavioral performance by using observational techniques, sociometric techniques, and self-concept measures.

TABLE 12.1 Possible Concerns About Inclusion and Potential Solutions

Possible Concerns	Potential Solutions
Students are not benefitting academically, socially, and behaviorally	• Collect and examine data on the impact of the program on students (see Chapter 12) • Meet with families (see Chapter 4) • Revise students' IEPs (see Chapter 2) • Use strategies to promote the academic development of students, such as teaching students to use learning strategies, adapting large- and small-group instruction, modifying instructional materials and techniques, employing technology, and using culturally relevant instructional strategies (see Chapters 2, 3, 5, and 8–11) • Use strategies to promote acceptance of individual differences and friendships (see Chapter 5) • Use strategies to modify classroom behavior (see Chapter 7) • Modify the classroom environment to promote students' academic, social, and behavioral development (see Chapter 7)
Students with disabilities are having a difficult time adjusting to inclusive classrooms	• Help students with disabilities make the transition to inclusive settings (see Chapter 6) • Learn about the needs of students with disabilities (see Chapter 2)
Students with disabilities are not participating in statewide and districtwide assessments	• Identify and use appropriate testing accommodations (see Chapter 12) • Differentiate instruction to promote the learning of all students (see Chapters 8–11)
Students from various cultural and language backgrounds are having difficulties in inclusive settings and are disproportionately represented	• Learn more about the unique needs of students from various cultural and language backgrounds (see Chapter 3) and about disproportionate representation (see Chapter 1) • Promote interactions among students (see Chapters 5 and 9) • Use culturally relevant instructional strategies and instructional materials, cooperative learning, and a diversified curriculum (see Chapters 8–11) • Communicate and collaborate with families and community organizations (see Chapter 4)
Teachers express negative attitudes about working in inclusion programs	• Give teachers information and research about inclusion programs (see Chapter 1) • Identify the sources of teachers' negative attitudes and plan activities to address these concerns (see Chapters 1, 4, and 12) • Provide opportunities to talk with teachers, family members, and students who have experience with successful inclusion programs (see Chapter 4) • Involve teachers in planning and evaluating all aspects of inclusion programs (see Chapters 1, 4, and 12)
Family and community members have negative attitudes about inclusion programs	• Give family and community members information and research about inclusion programs (see Chapter 1) • Identify the sources of these negative attitudes and plan activities to address these concerns (see Chapters 1, 4, and 12) • Invite family members, other professionals, and community members to visit inclusion programs (see Chapter 4) • Offer family and community members data on the impact of the inclusion program (see Chapter 12) • Involve family and community members in planning and evaluating all aspects of the inclusion program (see Chapters 1, 4, and 12)
General education teachers report that they are not receiving enough support from others	• Examine existing arrangements for providing teaching support (see Chapter 4) • Provide general education teachers with greater support from special educators, paraeducators, and ancillary support personnel (see Chapter 4)

(continued)

TABLE 12.1   (continued)

Possible Concerns	Potential Solutions
Teachers report difficulty meeting the requirements of the general education curriculum	• Give teachers appropriate curriculum materials, technology, and equipment (see Chapters 8–11) • Explore ways to diversify and modify the curriculum (see Chapters 2, 3, and 7–11)
Teachers indicate that the large class size reduces the success of the program and their ability to meet the needs of students	• Make sure that the class size is appropriate (see Chapters 1 and 4) • Encourage teachers to differentiate instruction, and use cooperative learning arrangements and peer-mediated instructional and behavior management techniques (see Chapters 7–11)
Teachers express concerns about educating students with certain types of disabilities in inclusive settings	• Identify teachers' specific concerns (see Chapters 1 and 12) • Provide teachers with training and information to understand and address the educational, social, medical, physical, cognitive, and behavioral needs of students (see Chapters 2 and 3) • Make sure that teachers and students are receiving the necessary assistance (see all chapters)
Teachers report that they do not have the expertise and training to implement inclusion effectively	• Conduct a needs assessment to identify teachers' training needs (see Chapter 12) • Offer systematic, ongoing, coordinated, and well-planned staff development activities (see Chapter 4) • Encourage teachers to visit model programs and attend professional conferences (see Chapter 4) • Provide teachers with access to professional journals and other resources addressing current trends, models, research and strategies (see all chapters)
Teachers report that there is not enough time for collaboration and communication among staff members	• Use flexible scheduling to give teachers the time to collaborate and communicate (see Chapter 4) • Maintain appropriate caseloads for teachers (see Chapters 1 and 4) • Schedule regular meetings (see Chapter 4)
Cooperative teaching teams report that they are having problems resolving problems involving teaching style, personality, and philosophical differences	• Examine the mechanism and variables used for matching teachers in cooperative teaching teams (see Chapter 4) • Offer training to help teachers work collaboratively (see Chapter 4) • Provide mechanisms for resolving disagreements among teachers working in teaching teams (see Chapter 4) • Establish mechanisms for ensuring equal-status, cooperative teaching relationships among teachers, and for sharing accountability for educational outcomes for all students (see Chapter 4) • Provide time for teachers to collaborate and coordinate instructional activities and supportive services (see Chapter 4)

How Can I Measure Perceptions of My Inclusion Program?

You can measure students', teachers', and family members' perceptions of your inclusion program by using questionnaires, interviews, and journals.

How Can I Improve the Effectiveness of My Inclusion Program?

You can work with others to analyze data on the impact of your program on student performance, to validate program strengths, to identify program components that need revision, and to determine strategies for improving the program.

What Would You Do in Today's Diverse Classroom?

Your inclusion classroom includes some of the students we met earlier in this book:

❖ Mary enjoys social studies, science, and socializing with her friends during lunch. She has difficulty communicating orally and in writing, and difficulty remembering content and applying it to new situations (see Chapter 1).

❖ Marty knows a lot about a variety of different topics and likes to share his knowledge with others. However, he struggles to complete his assignments and has difficulties with reading and math. Marty likes to interact with others but sometimes gets carried away, which bothers some of his friends (see Chapter 2).

❖ Carol has had a difficult time adjusting to the culture and language of the United States. She appears to be shy and withdrawn and has had some difficulties completing her assignments. Her difficulties in school appear to be having a negative effect on her self-esteem (see Chapter 3).

❖ Jaime exhibits a variety of behaviors that interfere with his learning. He has difficulty paying attention and completing assignments because he shifts from one activity to another (see Chapter 7).

❖ Tom's abilities and skills are significantly below those of his peers. He speaks in one-, two- or three-word sentences and often has difficulty understanding others. It takes him a while to learn things and generalize his new learning to new situations (see Chapter 8).

1. What would be the goals of your inclusion program for these students?

2. How would you evaluate the effectiveness of your inclusion program based on the academic, behavioral, and social performance of these students?

3. Would you include these students in your school's statewide and districtwide testing programs? If yes, what testing accommodations might they need? If no, what alternative techniques would you use to assess their progress?

4. What roles would the perceptions of students, other teachers, and family members play in your evaluation of your inclusion program? How would you gather information from these groups about the program?

5. How would you assess your perceptions of your inclusion program?

6. What difficulties might arise in educating these students in your inclusion program? How could you address these difficulties to improve the effectiveness of the program?

As a member of your grade level team, you are asked to prepare questions for a unit your team has been teaching. Using a unit you have developed or a textbook you use in your class, develop one essay, two multiple-choice, one matching, two true-false, two sentence completion items for inclusion in your team's test. How would you adapt the content and format of the test items for different types of students? What alternative testing procedures would you use for students with disabilities? For students from various cultural and language backgrounds?

REFERENCES

Aber, M. E., Bachman, B., Campbell, P., & O'Malley, G. (1994). Improving instruction in elementary schools. *Teaching Exceptional Children, 26*(3), 42–50.

Abrams, B. J. (1992). Values clarification for students with emotional disabilities. *Teaching Exceptional Children, 24*(3), 28–33.

Abrams, B. J., & Segal, A. (1998). How to prevent aggressive behavior. *Teaching Exceptional Children, 30*(4), 10–15.

Ada, A. F. (1993). *My name is Maria Isabel.* New York: Atheneum.

Adair, J. G., & Schneider, J. L. (1993). Banking on learning: An incentive system for adolescents in the resource room. *Teaching Exceptional Children, 25*(2), 30–34.

Adger, C. T. (1997). *Issues and implications of English dialects for teaching English as a second language.* Alexandria, VA: Teachers of English to Speakers of Other Languages, Inc.

Adger, C. T., Wolfram, W., & Detwyler, J. (1993). Language differences: A new approach for special educators. *Teaching Exceptional Children, 26*(1), 44–47.

Agard, J. A., Veldman, D. J., Kaufman, M. J., & Semmel, M. I. (1978). *How I feel toward others: An instrument of the PRIME instrument battery.* Baltimore: University Park Press.

Agostino v. Felton, 117 S. Ct. 1997 (1997).

Alber, S. R. (1996). Sustained silent reading: Practical suggestions for successful implementation. *Reading and Writing Quarterly: Overcoming Learning Difficulties, 12*(4), 403–406.

Alber, S. R., & Heward, H. L. (1997). Recruit it or lose it. Training students to recruit positive teacher attention. *Intervention in School and Clinic, 32*(5), 275–282.

Alberto, P. A., & Troutman, A. C. (1995). *Applied behavior analysis for teachers* (5th ed.). Upper Saddle River, NJ: Merrill/Prentice Hall.

Albinger, P. (1995). Stories from the resource room: Piano lessons, imaginary illness, and broken-down cars. *Journal of Learning Disabilities, 28*(10), 615–621.

Alexander, C. F. (1985). Black English dialect and the classroom teacher. In C. K. Brooks (Ed.), *Tapping potential: English and language arts for the black learner* (pp. 20–29). Urbana, IL: National Council of Teachers of English.

Alley, G., & Deshler, D. (1979). *Teaching the learning disabled adolescent: Strategies and methods.* Denver: Love.

Allinder, R. M. (1996). When some is not better than none: Effects of differential implementation of curriculum-based measurement. *Exceptional Children, 62*(6), 525–535.

Allington, R. L., & Broikou, K. A. (1988). Development of shared knowledge: A new role for classroom and specialist teachers. *The Reading Teacher, 41,* 806–811.

Allington, R. L., & Shake, M. C. (1986). Remedial reading: Achieving curricular congruence in classroom and clinic. *The Reading Teacher, 39,* 648–654.

Allsopp, D. H. (1997). Using classwide peer tutoring to teach beginning algebra problem-solving skills in heterogeneous classrooms. *Remedial and Special Education, 18*(6), 367–379.

Allsopp, D. H. (1999). Using modeling, manipulatives, and mnemonics with eighth grade math students. *Teaching Exceptional Children, 32*(2), 46–54.

Allsopp, D. H., Santos, K. E., & Linn, R. (2000). Collaborating to teach prosocial skills. *Intervention in School and Clinic, 35*(3), 141–146.

Alper, L., Fendel, D., Fraser, S., & Resek, D. (1996). Problem-based mathematics—Not just for the college-bound. *Educational Leadership, 53*(8), 18–21.

Alper, S., Schloss, P. J., & Schloss, C. N. (1994). *Families of students with disabilities: Consultation and advocacy.* Boston: Allyn & Bacon.

Alper, S., Schloss, P. J., & Schloss, C. N. (1996). Families of children with disabilities in elementary and middle school: Advocacy models and strategies. *Exceptional Children, 62*(3), 261–270.

Alvarez, L. (1995, October 1). Interpreting new worlds for parents. *The New York Times,* 29, 34.

American Association of University Women. (1992). *The AAUW report: How schools shortchange girls.* Washington, DC: Author.

American Association of University Women. (1998). *Gender gaps: Where schools still fail our children.* Washington, DC: Author.

American Automobile Association. (1995). *Disabled driver's mobility guide* (7th ed.). Heathrow, FL: Author.

American Federation of Teachers. (1993). *Draft AFT position on inclusion.* Washington, DC: Author.

American Psychiatric Association. (1994). *Diagnostic and statistical manual of mental disorders* (4th ed.). Washington, DC: Author.

Ammer, J. J. (1998). Peer evaluation model for enhancing writing performance of students with learning disabilities. *Reading and Writing Quarterly: Overcoming Learning Difficulties, 14*(3), 263–282.

Anderegg, M. L., & Vergason, G. A. (1992). Preparing teachers for their legal responsibilities in facing school-age suicide. *Teacher Education and Special Education, 15*(4), 295–299.

Anderegg, M. L., Vergason, G. A., & Smith, M. C. (1992). A visual representation of the grief cycle for use by teachers with families of children with disabilities. *Remedial and Special Education, 13*(2), 17–23.

Anderson, C., & Katsiyannis, A. (1997). By what token economy? A classroom learning tool for inclusive settings. *Teaching Exceptional Children, 29*(4), 65–67.

Anderson, J. D. (1997). Supporting the invisible minority. *Educational Leadership, 54*(7), 65–68.

Anderson, P. P., & Fenichel, E. S. (1989). *Serving culturally diverse families of infants and toddlers with disabilities.* Washington, DC: National Center for Clinical Infant Programs.

Anderson-Inman, L. (1986). Bridging the gap: Student-centered strategies for promoting the transfer of learning. *Exceptional Children, 52,* 562–572.

Anderson-Inman, L., Knox-Quinn, C., & Horney, M. A. (1996). Computer-based study strategies for students with learning disabilities: Individual differences associated with adoption level. *Journal of Learning Disabilities, 29*(5), 461–484.

Andrews, J. F., & Jordan, D. L. (1998). Multimedia stories for deaf children. *Teaching Exceptional Children, 30*(5), 28–33.

Andrews, J. F., & Mason, J. M. (1991). Strategy usage among deaf and hearing readers. *Exceptional Children, 57,* 536–545.

Andrews, J. F., Winograd, P., & DeVille, G. (1996). Using sign language summaries during prereading lessons. *Teaching Exceptional Children, 28*(3), 30–35.

Antonak, R. F., & Livneh, H. (1988). *The measurement of attitudes toward people with disabilities: Methods, psychometrics and scales.* Springfield, IL: Charles C. Thomas.

Archer, A. (1988). Strategies for responding to information. *Teaching Exceptional Children, 20,* 55–57.

Archer, A., & Gleason, M. (1996). Advanced skills for school success. *Intervention in School and Clinic, 32*(3), 119–123.

Arllen, N. L., Gable, R. A., & Hendrickson, J. M. (1996). Accommodating students with special needs in general education classrooms. *Preventing School Failure, 41*(1), 7–13.

Armbruster, B. B., & Anderson, T. H. (1988). On selecting "considerate" content area textbooks. *Remedial and Special Education, 9*(1), 47–52.

Aronson, D. (1997). No laughing matter. *Teaching Tolerance, 6*(2), 20–23.

Aronson, E., Blaney, N., Stephan, C., Sikes, J., & Snapp, M. (1978). *The jigsaw classroom.* Beverly Hills, CA: Sage.

Arreaga-Mayer, C. (1998). Increasing active student responding and improving academic performance through classwide peer tutoring. *Intervention in School and Clinic, 34*(2), 89–94, 117.

Arthur, B. M., & Burch, A. D. (1993). Motivation for reading is an affective concern. *Intervention in School and Clinic, 28*(5), 280–287.

Artiles, A. J., & Zamora-Duran, G. (1997). *Reducing disproportionate representation of culturally and linguistically diverse students in special and gifted education.* Reston, VA: Council for Exceptional Children.

Asher, J. J. (1977). *Learning author language through actions: The complete teacher's guide.* Los Gatos, CA: Sky Oaks.

Ashton, T. M. (1999). Spell checking: Making writing meaningful in the inclusive classroom. *Teaching Exceptional Children, 32*(2), 24–27.

Askov, E., & Greff, K. (1975). Handwriting: Copying versus tracing as the most effective type of practice. *Journal of Educational Research, 69,* 96–98.

Asselin, S. B., Todd-Allen, M., & deFur, S. (1998). Transition coordinators: Define yourselves. *Teaching Exceptional Children, 30*(3), 11–15.

Aune, E. P., & Ness, J. E. (1991). *Tools for transition: Preparing students with learning disabilities for postsecondary education.* Circle Pines, MN: American Guidance Service.

Ayres, B., Belle, C., Greene, K., O'Connor, J., & Meyer, L. H. (n.d.). *Examples of curricular adaptations for students with severe disabilities in the elementary classroom—Study Group Report Series No. 3.* Syracuse, NY: Division of Special Education, Syracuse University.

Babbitt, B. C., & Miller, S. P. (1996). Using hypermedia to improve the mathematics problem-solving skills of students with learning disabilities. *Journal of Learning Disabilities, 29*(4), 391–401, 412.

Baca, L. M. (1998). Bilingual special education: A judicial perspective. In L. M. Baca & H. T. Cervantes (Eds.), *The*

bilingual special education interface (3rd ed., pp. 76–97). Upper Saddle River, NJ: Merrill/Prentice Hall.

Baca, L. M., & Cervantes, H. T. (1998). *The bilingual special education interface* (3rd ed). Upper Saddle River, NJ: Merrill/Prentice Hall.

Baca, L. M., & de Valenzuela, J. S. (1998). Development of the bilingual special education interface. In L. M. Baca & H. T. Cervantes (Eds.), *The bilingual special education interface* (3rd ed., pp. 98–118). Upper Saddle River, NJ: Merrill/Prentice Hall.

Bahr, C. M., Nelson, N. W., & Van Meter, A. M. (1996). The effects of text-based and graphic-based software tools on planning and organizing stories. *Journal of Learning Disabilities, 29*(4), 355–370.

Bahr, M. W., & Bahr, C. M. (1997). Educational assessment in the next millennium: Contributions of technology. *Preventing School Failure, 41*(2), 90–94.

Bailey, D. (1993). *Wings to fly: Bridging theatre arts to students with special needs.* Bethesda, MD: Woodbine House.

Bailey, D. B., Skinner, D., Rodriguez, P., Gut, D., & Correa, V. (1999). Awareness, use and satisfaction with services for Latino parents of young children with disabilities. *Exceptional Children, 65*(3), 367–381.

Bailey, D. B., & Winton, P. (1987). Stability and change in parents' expectations about mainstreaming. *Topics in Early Childhood Special Education, 7,* 73–88.

Baker, J. M., & Zigmond, N. (1995). The meaning and practice of inclusion for students with learning disabilities: Themes and implications from five cases. *Journal of Special Education, 29*(2), 163–180.

Bakken, J. P., & Aloia, G. F. (1998). Evaluating the World Wide Web. *Teaching Exceptional Children, 30*(5), 48–52.

Baldwin, B. A. (1989). The cornucopia kids. *US Air Magazine, 11*(10), 30–34.

Banbury, M. M., & Hebert, C. R. (1992). Do you see what I mean? Body language in classroom interactions. *Teaching Exceptional Children, 24*(2), 32–38.

Banerji, M., & Dailey, R. A. (1995). A study of the effects of an inclusion model on students with specific learning disabilities. *Journal of Learning Disabilities, 28*(8), 511–522.

Bangert-Drowns, R. L. (1993). The word processor as an instructional tool: A meta-analysis of word processing in writing instruction. *Review of Educational Research, 63*(1), 69–93.

Banks, J. A. (1991a). A curriculum for empowerment, action, and change. In C. E. Sleeter (Ed.), *Empowerment through multicultural education* (pp. 125–141). Albany: State University of New York Press.

Banks, J. A. (1991b). *Teaching strategies for ethnic studies* (5th ed.). Boston: Allyn & Bacon.

Banks, J. A., & Banks, C. A. (1993). *Multicultural education: Issues and perspectives* (2nd ed.). Boston: Allyn & Bacon.

Barab, S., & Landa, A. (1997). Designing effective interdisciplinary anchors. *Educational Leadership, 54*(6), 52–55.

Barnes, E., Berrigan, C., & Biklen, D. (1978). *What's the difference? Teaching positive attitudes toward people with disabilities.* Syracuse, NY: Human Policy.

Bartholomew, C. G., & Schnorr, D. L. (1994). Gender equity: Suggestions for broadening the career options of female students. *The School Counselor, 41*(4), 245–255.

Bass, E., & Kaufman, K. (1996). *Free your mind: The book for gay, lesbian, and bisexual youth—and their allies.* New York: Harper Perennial.

Battle, D. A., Dickens-Wright, L. L., & Murphy, S. C. (1998). How to empower adolescents: Guidelines for effective self-advocacy. *Teaching Exceptional Children, 30*(3), 28–34.

Bauwens, J., & Hourcade, J. J. (1995). *Cooperative teaching: Rebuilding the school house.* Austin, TX: PRO-ED.

Bauwens, J., & Hourcade, J. J. (1997). Cooperative teaching: Pictures of possibilities. *Intervention in School and Clinic, 33*(2), 81–85, 89.

Bayer Sager, C., & Bacharach, B. (1985). *That's what friends are for.* Los Angeles: Warner-Tamerlane.

Beakley, B. A., & Yoder, S. L. (1998). Middle schoolers learn community skills. *Teaching Exceptional Children, 30*(3), 16–21.

Bear, G. G., Clever, A., & Proctor, W. A. (1991). Self-perceptions of nonhandicapped children and children with learning disabilities in integrated classes. *Journal of Special Education, 24*, 410–426.

Beaumont, C. (1992). Language intervention strategies for Hispanic LLD students. In H. W. Langdon & L. L. Cheng (Eds.), *Hispanic children and adults with communication disorders* (pp. 272–342). Gaithersburg, MD: Aspen.

Beckman, P. (1999). Strategies for independent learning in reading and spelling. *Teaching Exceptional Children, 32*(2), 93.

Bedard, E. (1995). Collaboration in educational planning: A parent's perspective. *LD Forum, 20*(3), 23–25.

Beech, M. C. (1983). Simplifying text for mainstreamed students. *Journal of Learning Disabilities, 16*, 400–402.

Behrmann, M. M. (1994). Assistive technology for students with mild disabilities. *Intervention in School and Clinic, 30*(2), 70–83.

Belcher, R. N., & Fletcher-Carter, R. (1999). Growing gifted students in the desert: Using alternative, community-based assessment and an enriched curriculum. *Teaching Exceptional Children, 32*(1), 17–24.

Bell, M. L., & Smith, B. R. (1996). Grandparents as primary caregivers. *Teaching Exceptional Children, 28*(2), 18–19.

Bender, W. N., & Mathes, M. Y. (1995). Students with ADHD in the inclusive classroom: A hierarchical approach to strategy selection. *Intervention in School and Clinic, 30*(4), 226–234.

Bender, W. N., & McLaughlin, P. J. (1997). Weapons violence in schools: Strategies for teachers confronting violence and hostage situations. *Intervention in School and Clinic, 32*(4), 211–216.

Bennett, L. (1997, Fall). Breaking the silence. *Teaching Tolerance,* 24–29.

Bennett, T., DeLuca, D., & Bruns, D. (1997). Putting inclusion into practice: Perspectives of teachers and parents. *Exceptional Children, 64*, 115–131.

Bennett, T., Rowe, V., & DeLuca, D. (1996). *Getting to know Abby. Focus on Autism and Other Developmental Delays, 11*, 183–188.

Benz, M. R., Yovanoff, P., & Doren, B. (1997). School-to-work components that predict postschool success for students with and without disabilities. *Exceptional Children, 63*(2), 151–165.

Berkell, D. E., & Gaylord-Ross, R. (1989). The concept of transition: Historical and current developments. In D. E. Berkell & J. M. Brown (Eds.), *Transition from school to work for persons with disabilities* (pp. 1–21). White Plains, NY: Longman.

Berman, S. (1990). Educating for social responsibility. *Educational Leadership, 48*(3), 75–80.

Bermudez, A. B., & Palumbo, D. B. (1994). Bridging the gap between literacy and technology: Hypermedia as a learning tool for limited English proficient students. *The Journal of Educational Issues of Language Minority Students, 14*, 165–184.

Berendt, P. R., & Koski, B. (1999). No shortcuts to success. *Educational Leadership, 56*(6), 45–47.

Berndt, T. J., & Perry, T. B. (1986). Children's perceptions of friendships as supportive relationships. *Developmental Psychology, 22*, 640–648.

Berry, R. L. (1995). Dealing with an aggressive student. *Teaching for Excellence, 8*(9), 1–2.

Best, J. W., & Kahn, J. V. (1998). *Research in education* (8th ed.). Boston: Allyn & Bacon.

Best, S. J., Bigge, J. L., & Sirvis, B. P. (1994). Physical and health impairments. In N. G. Haring, L. McCormick, & T. G. Haring (Eds.), *Exceptional children and youth* (6th ed., pp. 300–341). Upper Saddle River, NJ: Merrill/Prentice Hall.

Biklen, D., Corrigan, C., & Quick, D. (1989). Beyond obligation: Students' relations with each other in integrated classes. In D. Lipsky & A. Gartner (Eds.), *Beyond separate education: Quality education for all* (pp. 207–221). Baltimore: Paul H. Brookes.

Billings, H. K. (1963). An exploratory study of the attitudes of non-crippled children toward crippled children in three selected elementary schools. *Journal of Experimental Education, 31*, 381–387.

Blackorby, J., & Wagner, M. (1996). Longitudinal postschool outcomes of youth with disabilities: Findings from the National Longitudinal Transition Study. *Exceptional Children, 62*(5), 399–413.

Blackstone, S. W. (1996). Selecting, using, and evaluating communication devices. In J. C. Galvin & M. J. Scherer (Eds.), *Evaluating, selecting, and using appropriate assistive technology* (pp. 97–124). Gaithersburg, MD: Aspen.

Blanck, P. D. (1994). *Communications technology for everyone: Implications for the classroom and beyond.* Washington, DC: The Annenberg Washington Program in Policy Studies of Northwestern University.

Blaska, J. K., & Lynch, E. C. (1995, April). *Teaching about disabilities through children's literature.* Presentation at the annual meeting of the Council for Exceptional Children, Indianapolis, IN.

Blazer, B. (1999). Developing 504 classroom accommodation plans: A collaborative, systematic parent–student–teacher approach. *Teaching Exceptional Children, 32*(2), 28–33.

Bley, N. S., & Thornton, C. A. (1995). *Teaching mathematics to students with learning disabilities* (3rd ed.). Austin, TX: PRO-ED.

Bligh, T. (1996). Choosing and using picture books for mini-lessons with middle school students. *Reading and Writing Quarterly: Overcoming Learning Difficulties, 12*(4), 333–349.

Bloom, L. A., Perlmutter, J., & Burrell, L. (1999). The general educator: Applying constructivism to inclusive classrooms. *Intervention in School and Clinic, 34*(3), 132–136.

Blubaugh, D. (1999). Bringing cable into the classroom. *Educational Leadership, 56*(5), 61–65.

Blum, H. T., & Yocom, D. J. (1996). Using instructional games to foster student learning. *Teaching Exceptional Children, 29*(2), 60–63.

Board of Education of the Hendrick Hudson Central School District v. *Rowley,* 102 S. Ct. 3034 (1982).

Bock, M. A., & Barger, R. (1998). The popcorn book: A diagnostic teaching unit. *Intervention in School and Clinic, 33*(5), 290–303.

Boersma, F. J., & Chapman, J. W. (1992). *The Perception of Ability Scale for Students.* Los Angeles: Western Psychological Services.

Bogdan, R. C., & Biklen, S. K. (1992). *Qualitative research for education.* Boston: Allyn & Bacon.

Book Links Advisory Board. (1994). Today's children of color. *Book Links, 3*(3), 25–31.

Boone, R., Higgins, K., Falba, C., & Langley, W. (1993). Cooperative text: Reading and writing in a hypermedia environment. *LD Forum, 19*(1), 28–37.

Boone, R., Higgins, K., & Williams, D. (1997). Computer-based multimedia and videodiscs: Uses in supporting content-area instruction for students with learning disabilities. *Intervention in School and Clinic, 32*(5), 302–311.

Boone, R., Wolfe, P. S., & Schaufler, J. H. (1999). Written communication in special education: Meeting the needs of culturally and linguistically diverse families. *Multiple Voices, 3*(1), 25–36.

Bottge, B. A. (1999). Effects of contextualized math instruction on problem solving of average and below-average achieving students. *The Journal of Special Education, 33*(2), 81–92.

Bottge, B. A., & Hasselbring, T. S. (1999). Teaching mathematics to adolescents with disabilities in a multimedia environment. *Intervention in School and Clinic, 35*(2), 113–116.

Boudah, D. J., Lenz, B. K., Bulgren, J. A., Schumaker, J. B., & Deshler, D. D. (2000). Don't water down: Enhance content learning through the unit organizer routine. *Teaching Exceptional Children, 32*(3), 48–56.

Bowers, E. M. (1980). *The handicapped in literature: A psychosocial perspective.* Denver: Love.

Boyle, J. R., & Weishaar, M. (1997). The effects of expert-generated versus student-generated cognitive organizers on the reading comprehension of students with learning disabilities. *Learning Disabilities Research and Practice, 12*(4), 228–235.

Boyle, J. R., & Yeager, N. (1997). Blueprints for learning: Using frameworks for understanding. *Teaching Exceptional Children, 29*(4), 26–31.

Bradley, D. F., & Calvin, M. B. (1998). Grading modified assignments: Equity or compromise? *Teaching Exceptional Children, 31*(2), 24–29.

Bradsher, K. (1995a, April 17). Gap in wealth in U.S. called widest in west. *The New York Times,* A1, D4.

Bradsher, K. (1995b, August 14). Low ranking for poor American children. *The New York Times,* A9.

Bradstad, B. J., & Stumpf, S. M. (1987). *A guide book for teaching study skills and motivation* (2nd ed.). Boston: Allyn & Bacon.

Brandt, M. D., & Berry, J. O. (1991). Transitioning college bound students with LD. *Intervention in School and Clinic, 26,* 297–301.

Brantlinger, E. (1995). Social class in school: Students' perspectives. *Research Bulletin, 14,* 1–4.

Brice, A., & Roseberry-McKibbin, C. (1999). Turning frustration into success for English language learners. *Educational Leadership, 56*(7), 53–55.

Bridges, D. L., & DeVault, F. L. (1999). Now that we have it, what do we do with it? Using the Web in the classroom. *Intervention in School and Clinic, 34*(3), 181–187.

Brier, S. E. (1998, July 23). News watch. *The New York Times,* G3.

Brinckerhoff, L. C. (1994). Developing effective self-advocacy skills in college-bound students with learning disabilities. *Intervention in School and Clinic, 29*(4), 229–237.

Brinckerhoff, L. C. (1996). Making the transition to higher education: Opportunities for student empowerment. *Journal of Learning Disabilities, 29*(2), 118–136.

Brody, J. E. (1996, April 3). Enlisting a silent majority to fight school bullying. *The New York Times,* B9.

Brolin, D. E. (1993). *Life-centered career education: A competency-based approach.* Reston, VA: Council for Exceptional Children.

Bromley, K. D. (1998). *Language arts: Exploring connections.* Needham Heights, MA: Allyn & Bacon.

Bronheim, S. (n.d.). *An educator's guide to Tourette syndrome.* Bayside, NY: Tourette Syndrome Association.

Bronner, E. (1998, December 1). For more textbooks, a shift from printed page to screen. *The New York Times,* A1, A27.

Brooks-Gunn, J., & Duncan, G. J. (1997, Summer/Fall). The effects of poverty on children. *The Future of Children,* 55–71.

Brophy, J. E. (1981). Teacher praise: A functional analysis. *Review of Educational Research, 5,* 301–318.

Brosnan, P. A. (1997). Visual mathematics. *Teaching Exceptional Children, 29*(3), 18–22.

Brown v. *Board of Education of Topeka,* 347 U.S. 483 (1954).

Brown, L. W. (1997). Seizure disorders. In M. L. Batshaw (Ed.), *Children with disabilities* (4th ed., pp. 553–595). Baltimore: Paul H. Brookes.

Brown, W. H., & Odom, S. L. (1995). Naturalistic peer interventions for promoting preschool children's social interactions. *Preventing School Failure, 39*(4), 38–43.

Brownell, M. T., Yeager, E., Rennells, M. S., & Riley, T. (1997). Teachers working together: What teacher educators and researchers should know. *Teacher Education and Special Education, 20*(4), 340–359.

Bruininks, R. H., Rynders, J. E., & Gross, J. C. (1974). Social acceptance of mildly retarded pupils in resource rooms and regular classes. *American Journal of Mental Deficiency, 78,* 377–383.

Bruns, D. A., & Fowler, S. A. (1999). Culturally sensitive transition plans for young children and their families. *Teaching Exceptional Children, 31*(5), 26–30.

Bryan, T. (1997). Assessing the personal and social status of students with learning disabilities. *Learning Disabilities Research and Practice, 12*(1), 63–76.

Bryan, T., & Sullivan-Burstein, K. (1997). Homework how-to's. *Teaching Exceptional Children, 29*(6), 32–37.

Bryant, B. R. (1998). Assistive technology: An introduction. *Journal of Learning Disabilities, 31*(1), 2–3.

Bryant, B. R., & Seay, P. C. (1998). The Technology-Related Assistance to Individuals with Disabilities Act: Relevance to individuals with learning disabilities and their advocates. *Journal of Learning Disabilities, 31*(1), 4–15.

Bryant, D. P., & Bryant, B. R. (1998). Using assistive technology adaptations to include students with learning disabilities in cooperative learning activities. *Journal of Learning Disabilities, 31*(1), 41–54.

Bryant, D. P., Bryant, B. R., & Raskind, M. H. (1998). Using assistive technology to enhance the skills of students with learning disabilities. *Intervention in School and Clinic, 34*(1), 53–58.

Bryant, D. P., Ugel, N., Thompson, S., & Hamff, A. (1999). Instructional strategies for content-area reading instruction. *Intervention in School and Clinic, 34*(5), 293–302.

Bryde, S. (1998, April). *Using children's literature to teach about disabilities and other issues.* Presentation at the annual meeting of the Council for Exceptional Children, Minneapolis.

Buck, G. H. (1999). Smoothing the rough edges of classroom transitions. *Intervention in School and Clinic, 34*(4), 224–227, 235.

Buggey, T. (1999). Look! I'm on TV!: Using videotaped self-modeling to change behavior. *Teaching Exceptional Children, 31*(4), 27–30.

Bulgren, J. A., Deshler, D. D., & Schumaker, J. B. (1997). Use of a recall enhancement routine and strategies in inclusive secondary classes. *Learning Disabilities Research and Practice, 12*(4), 198–208.

Bulgren, J. A., Hock, M. F., Schumaker, J. B., & Deshler, D. D. (1995). The effects of instruction in a paired associates strategy on the information mastery performance of students and learning disabilities. *Learning Disabilities Research and Practice, 10*(1), 22–37.

Bulgren, J. A., & Lenz, B. K. (1996). Strategic instruction in the content areas. In D. D. Deshler, E. S. Ellis, & B. K. Lenz (Eds.), *Teaching adolescents with learning disabilities: Strategies and methods* (2nd ed., pp. 409–473). Denver: Love.

Bunch, G. (1996). *Kids, disabilities, and regular classrooms: An annotated bibliography of selected children's literature on disability.* Toronto: Inclusion Press.

Burcham, B. G., & DeMers, S. T. (1995). Comprehensive assessment of children and youth with ADHD. *Intervention in School and Clinic, 30*(4), 211–220.

Burnette, J. M. (1996). Including students with disabilities in general education classrooms: From policy to practice, *The ERIC Review, 4*(3), 2–11.

Burns, M., Storey, K., & Certo, N. J. (1999). Effect of service learning on attitudes towards students with severe disabilities. *Education and Training in Mental Retardation and Developmental Disabilities, 34*(1), 58–65.

Burtch, J. A. (1999). Technology is for everyone. *Educational Leadership, 56*(5), 33–34.

Butler, A. (n.d.). *The elements of the whole language program.* Crystal Lake, IL: Rigby.

Byrom, E., & Katz, G. (1991). *HIV prevention and AIDS education: Resources for special educators.* Reston, VA: Council for Exceptional Children.

Caffrey, J. A. (1997). *First star I see.* Fairport, NY: Verbal Image Press.

Calderon, M. E., Hertz-Lazarowitz, R., & Tinajero, J. V. (1991). Adapting CIRC to multiethnic and bilingual classrooms. *Cooperative Learning, 12*(1), 17–20.

Calkins, L. M. (1994). *The art of teaching writing.* Portsmouth, NH: Heinemann.

Callahan, K., & Rademacher, J. A. (1999). Using self-management strategies to increase the on-task behavior of a student with autism. *Journal of Positive Behavioral Interventions, 1*(2), 117–122.

Calloway, C. (1999). Promote friendship in the inclusive classroom. *Intervention in School and Clinic, 34*(3), 176–177.

Campbell, L. (1997). How teachers interpret MI theory. *Educational Leadership, 55*(1), 14–19.

Campbell, P. C., Campbell, R. C., & Brady, M. P. (1998). Team environmental assessment mapping system: A method for selecting curriculum goals for students with disabilities. *Education and Training in Mental Retardation and Developmental Disabilities, 33*(3), 264–272.

Campbell-Whatley, G. D. (1999, April). *Developing a mentoring program for students with disabilities.* Presentation at the annual meeting of the Council for Exceptional Children, Charlotte, NC.

Campbell-Whatley, G. D., Algozinne, B., & Obiakor, F. (1997). Using mentoring to improve academic programming for African American male youths with mild disabilities. *The School Counselor, 44,* 362–367.

Canfield, J., & Wells, H. C. (1976). *100 ways to enhance self-concept in the classroom.* Upper Saddle River, NJ: Prentice Hall.

Cantrell, R. P., & Cantrell, M. L. (1995). Recapturing a generation: The future of secondary programs for students with disabilities. *Preventing School Failure, 39*(3), 25–28.

Capper, C. A., & Pickett, R. S. (1994). The relationship between school structure and culture and student views of diversity and inclusive education. *The Special Education Leadership Review, 2*(1), 102–122.

Carbo, M. (1994). *Reading style inventory.* Syosset, NY: National Reading Styles Institute.

Carbo, M. (1997). Reading styles times twenty. *Educational Leadership, 54*(6), 38–42.

Carpenter, C. D., Bloom, L. A., & Boat, M. B. (1999). Guidelines for special educators: Achieving socially valid outcomes. *Intervention in School and Clinic, 34*(3), 143–149.

Carpenter, C. D., Ray, M. S., & Bloom, L. A. (1995). Portfolio assessment: Opportunities and challenges. *Intervention in School and Clinic, 31*(1), 34–41.

Carpenter, S. L., & McKee-Higgins, E. (1996). Behavior management in inclusive classrooms. *Remedial and Special Education, 17*(4), 195–203.

Carter, C. J. (1997). Why reciprocal teaching? *Educational Leadership, 54*(6), 64–68.

Carter, J., & Sugai, G. (1989). Social skills curriculum analysis. *Teaching Exceptional Children, 21,* 36–39.

Cartledge, G., Kea, C. D., & Ida, D. J. (2000). Anticipating differences—Celebrating strengths: Providing culturally competent services for students with serious emotional disturbance. *Teaching Exceptional Children, 32*(3), 30–37.

Cates, D. L., Markell, M. A., & Bettenhausen, S. (1995). At risk for abuse: A teacher's guide for recognizing and reporting child abuse. *Preventing School Failure, 39*(3), 6–9.

Cawley, J. F., Fitzmaurice, A. M., Sedlak, R., & Althaus, V. (1976). *Project math.* Tulsa, OK: Educational Progress.

Cawley, J. F., Miller, J., Sentman, R., & Bennett, S. (1993). *Science for all children.* Buffalo: State University Press of New York at Buffalo.

Cawley, J. F., Parmar, R. S., Yan, W., & Miller, J. H. (1998). Arithmetic computation performance of students with learning disabilities: Implications for curriculum. *Learning Disabilities Research and Practice, 13*(2), 68–74.

Cedar Rapids Community School District v. *Garret F.* 96-1793 S. Ct. (1999).

Center for Special Education Finance. (1995). *Supported education in Oregon: Resource implications of inclusion.* Palo Alto, CA: American Institutes of Research.

Chalmers, L. (1991). Classroom modifications for the mainstreamed student with mild handicaps. *Intervention in School and Clinic, 27*(1), 40–42, 51.

Chalmers, L., Olson, M. R., & Zurkowski, J. K. (1999). Music as a classroom tool. *Intervention in School and Clinic, 35*(1), 43–45, 52.

Chamot, A. U., & O'Malley, J. M. (1989). The cognitive academic language learning approach. In P. Rigg & V. G. Allen (Eds.), *When they don't all speak English: Integrating the ESL student into the regular classroom* (pp. 108–125). Urbana, IL: National Council of Teachers of English.

Chan, L. K. S. (1991). Promoting strategy generalization through self-instructional training in students with reading disabilities. *Journal of Learning Disabilities, 24,* 427–433.

Chard, D. J., & Dickson, S. V. (1999). Phonological awareness: Instructional and assessment guidelines. *Intervention in School and Clinic, 34*(5), 261–270.

Chard, D. J., & Osborn, J. (1999). Word recognition instruction: Paving the road to successful reading. *Intervention in School and Clinic, 34*(5), 271–277.

Charles, R. I. (1984). *Problem solving experiences in mathematics.* Menlo Park, CA: Addison-Wesley.

Chase Thomas, C., Correa, V. I., & Morsink, C. V. (1995). *Interactive teaming: Consultation and collaboration in special education programs* (2nd ed.). Upper Saddle River, NJ: Merrill/Prentice Hall.

Checkley, K. (1996, Summer). The teachers' picks: Standards-based curriculums boost interest, achievement in math. *Curriculum Update,* 4–5.

Chiang, B., & Ratajczak, L. (1990). Analyzing computational errors for instruction. *LD Forum, 15*(2), 21–22.

Chiong, J. A. (1998). *Racial categorization of multiracial children in schools.* Westport, CT: Bergin & Garvey.

Chira, S. (1995, March 19). Struggling to find stability when divorce is a pattern. *The New York Times,* 1, 42.

Choate, J. S. (1990). Study the problem. *Teaching Exceptional Children, 22*(4), 44–46.

Christiansen, J., & Vogel, J. R. (1998). A decision making model for grading students with disabilities. *Teaching Exceptional Children, 31*(2), 30–35.

Chuoke, M., & Eyman, B. (1997). Play fair—And not just at recess. *Educational Leadership, 54*(8), 53–55.

Clark, D. M., & Smith, S. W. (1999). Facilitating friendships: Including students with autism in the early elementary classroom. *Intervention in School and Clinic, 34*(4), 248–250.

Clark, E. (1996). Children and adolescents with traumatic brain injury: Reintegration challenges in educational settings. *Journal of Learning Disabilities, 29*(5), 549–560.

Clark, G. M., & Kolstoe, O. (1990). *Career development and transition education for adolescents with disabilities.* Boston: Allyn & Bacon.

Clay, M. M. (1985). *The early detection of reading difficulties* (3rd. ed.). Auckland, NZ: Heinemann.

Clement, R. (1991). *Counting on Frank.* Milwaukee: Gareth Stevens Children's Books.

Cloud, N., & Landurand, P. M. (n.d.). *Multisystem: Training program for special educators.* New York: Teachers College Press.

Clyde K. and Sheila K. v. Puyallup School District, 35 F.3d 1396, 9th Circuit, 1994.

Coates, R. D. (1989). The regular education initiative and opinions of regular classroom teachers. *Journal of Learning Disabilities, 22,* 532–536.

Coffland, J. A., & Baldwin, R. S. (1985). *Wordmath.* St. Louis: Milliken.

Cohen, L. M. (1994). Meeting the needs of gifted and talented minority language students. *Teaching Exceptional Children, 26*(1), 70–71.

Cohen, S. B. (1983). Assigning report card grades to the mainstreamed child. *Teaching Exceptional Children, 15,* 86–89.

Cohen, S. B., & de Bettencourt, L. V. (1988). Teaching children to be independent learners: A step by step strategy. In E. L. Meyen, G. A. Vergason, & R. J. Whelan (Eds.), *Effective instructional strategies for exceptional children* (pp. 319–334). Denver: Love.

Cohen, S. B., & Lynch, D. K. (1991). An instructional modification process. *Teaching Exceptional Children, 23*(4), 12–18.

Cohn, C., Hoffman, J., & Mozenter, A. (1994). *In real life: Sexual harassment in schools, training series and video.* Wayne, PA: PeopleTECH.

Cole v. Greenfield-Central Community Schools, 657 F.Supp. 56 (S.D. Ind. 1986).

Cole, C. M., & McLeskey, J. (1997). Secondary inclusion programs for students with mild disabilities. *Focus on Exceptional Children, 29*(6), 1–15.

Coleman, F. M. (1997). Software simulation enhances science experiments. *The Journal, 25*(2), 56–58.

Collet-Klingenberg, L. L. (1998). The reality of best practices in transition: A case study. *Exceptional Children, 65*(1), 67–78.

Collicott, J. (1991). Implementing multi-level teaching: Strategies for classroom teachers. In G. L. Porter & D. Richler (Eds.), *Changing Canadian schools: Perspectives on disability and inclusion* (pp. 191–218). Toronto: Roeher Institute.

Collier, C. (1996, January). *Cross cultural assessment: New tools and strategies.* Presentation at the nineteenth annual statewide conference for teachers of linguistically and culturally diverse students, Chicago.

Collier, V. (1995). Acquiring a second language for school. *Directions in Language and Education, 1*(4), 1–12.

Colson, S. E., & Colson, J. K. (1993). HIV/AIDS education for students with special needs. *Intervention in School and Clinic, 28*(5), 262–274.

Columbia Broadcasting System. (1995). *Legacy of shame.* New York: Author.

Colvin, G., Ainge, D., & Nelson, R. (1997). How to defuse confrontations. *Teaching Exceptional Children, 29*(6), 47–51.

Communication Briefings. (1989a). *Listening tips.* Pitman, NJ: Author.

Communication Briefings. (1989b). *Teamwork tips.* Pitman, NJ: Author.

Conaty, R. (1993). I learn differently. In National Center for Learning Disabilities (Ed.), *Their world* (pp. 17–19). New York: National Center for Learning Disabilities.

Conoley, J. C., & Sheridan, S. (1996). Pediatric traumatic brain injury: Challenges and interventions for families. *Journal of Learning Disabilities, 29*(6), 662–669.

Consortium of Latin American Studies Programs. (1998). *Americas award for children's and young adult literature.* Milwaukee: The Center for Latin America at the University of Wisconsin-Milwaukee.

Conture, E. G., & Fraser, J. (1990). *Stuttering and your child: Questions and answers.* Memphis, TN: Speech Foundation of America.

Cook, A. M., & Cavalier, A. R. (1999). Young children using assistive robotics for discovery and control. *Teaching Exceptional Children, 31*(5), 72–78.

Cook, B. G., Semmel, M. I., & Gerber, M. M. (1999). Attitudes of principals and special education teachers toward the inclusion of students with mild disabilities: Critical differences of opinion. *Remedial and Special Education, 20*(4), 199–207, 243.

Cook, D. (1999). Behavior bucks: A unique motivational program. *Intervention in School and Clinic, 34*(5), 307–308, 316.

Coots, J. J., Bishop, K. D., & Grenot-Scheyer, M. (1998). Supporting elementary age students with significant disabilities in general education classrooms: Personal perspectives on inclusion. *Education and Training in Mental Retardation and Developmental Disabilities, 33*(4), 317–330.

Corporation for Public Broadcasting. (1990). *New harvest, old shame.* Alexandria, VA: Author.

Corral, N., & Antia, S. D. (1997). Self-task: Strategies for success in math. *Teaching Exceptional Children, 29*(4), 42–45.

Countryman, L. L., & Schroeder, M. (1996). When students lead parent–teacher conferences. *Educational Leadership, 53*(7), 64–68.

Craig, S., Hull, K., Haggart, A. G., & Perez-Selles, M. (2000). Promoting cultural competence through teacher assistance teams. *Teaching Exceptional Children, 32*(3), 6–12.

Cramer, S., Erzkus, A., Mayweather, K., Pope, K., Roeder, J., & Tone, T. (1997). Connecting with siblings. *Teaching Exceptional Children, 30*(1), 46–51.

Crank, J. N., & Bulgren, J. A. (1993). Visual depictions as information organizers for enhancing achievement of students with learning disabilities. *Learning Disabilities Research and Practice, 8*(3), 140–147.

Crank, J. N., & Keimig, J. (1988, March). *Learning strategies assessment for secondary students.* Paper presented at the meeting of the Council for Exceptional Children, Washington, DC.

Cronin, M. E., & Patton, J. R. (1993). *Life skills instruction for all students with special needs: A practical guide for integrating real-life content into the curriculum.* Austin, TX: PRO-ED.

Cronin, M. E., Slade, D. L., Bechtel, C., & Anderson, P. (1992). Home–school partnerships: A cooperative approach to intervention. *Intervention in School and Clinic, 27*(5), 286–292.

Cuevas, G. J. (1984). Mathematics learning in English as a second language. *Journal for Research in Mathematics Education, 15,* 35–144.

Cummins, G. J., & Lonbardi, T. P. (1989). Bulletin board learning center makes spelling fun. *Teaching Exceptional Children, 21,* 33–35.

Cummins, J. (1981). Four misconceptions about the language proficiency in bilingual children. *Journal of the National Association of Bilingual Education, 5*(3), 31–45.

Cummins, J. (1984). *Bilingualism and special education: Issues in assessment and pedagogy.* San Diego, CA: College-Hill.

Cunningham, C. M., Callahan, C. M., Plucker, J. A., Roberson, S. C., & Rapkin, A. (1998). Identifying Hispanic students of outstanding talent: Psychometric integrity of a peer nomination form. *Exceptional Children, 64*(2), 197–209.

Cunningham, P. M. (1998). The multisyllabic word dilemma: Helping students build meaning, spell, and read "big" words. *Reading and Writing Quarterly: Overcoming Learning Difficulties, 14*(2), 189–218.

Curwin, R. L., & Mendler, A. N. (1988). *Discipline with dignity.* Alexandria, VA: Association for Supervision and Curriculum Development.

Czarnecki, E., Rosko, D., & Fine, E. (1998). How to call up notetaking skills. *Teaching Exceptional Children, 30*(6), 14–19.

D'Alonzo, B. J., Giordano, G., & Vanleeuwen, D. M. (1997). Perceptions by teachers about the benefits and liabilities of inclusion. *Preventing School Failure, 42*(1), 4–11.

D'Amato, R. C., & Rothlisberg, B. A. (1996). How education should respond to students with traumatic brain injury. *Journal of Learning Disabilities, 29*(6), 670–683.

Damico, J. S. (1991). Descriptive assessment of communicative ability in Limited English Proficient students. In E. Hamayan & J. S. Damico (Eds.), *Limiting bias in the assessment of bilingual students* (pp. 157–218). Austin, TX: PRO-ED.

Daniel R. R. v. State Board of Education, 874 F.2d 1036, 5th Circuit, 1989.

Daniels, V. I. (1998). How to manage disruptive behavior in inclusive classrooms. *Teaching Exceptional Children, 30*(4), 26–31.

Danielson, C., & Abrutyn, L. (1997). *An introduction to using portfolios in the classroom.* Alexandria, VA: Association for Supervision and Curriculum Development.

Dattilo, J., & Hoge, G. (1999). Effects of leisure education program on youth with mental retardation. *Education and Training in Mental Retardation and Developmental Disabilities, 34*(1), 20–34.

Davern, L. (1999). Parents' perspectives on personnel attitudes and characteristics in inclusive school settings: Implications for teacher preparation programs. *Teacher Education and Special Education, 22*(3), 165–182.

Davern, L., Ford, A., Marusa, J., & Schnorr, R. (1993). *How are we doing?: A review process for evaluating teams which are working in inclusive settings.* Syracuse, NY: Inclusive Education Project.

Davis, S. (1997). *Child labor in agriculture.* Charleston, WV: ERIC Clearinghouse on Rural Education and Small Schools. (ERIC Document Reproduction Service No. ED 405 159).

Davison, D. M., & Pearce, D. L. (1992). The influence of writing activities on mathematic learning of American Indian students. *The Journal of Educational Issues of Language Minority Students, 10,* 147–157.

Day, J. (1998, November). *A program to teach standard American English to African-American English speakers.* Presentation at the Council for Exceptional Children/Division of Diverse Exceptional Learners Symposium on Culturally and Linguistically Diverse Exceptional Learners, Washington, D.C.

De Avila, E. A. (1988). *Finding out/Descubrimiento.* Northvale, NJ: Santillana.

Deck, M., Scarborough, J. L., Sferrazza, M. S., & Estill, D. M. (1999). Serving students with disabilities: Perspectives of three school counselors. *Intervention in School and Clinic, 34*(3), 150–155.

DeGeorge, K. L. (1998). Friendship and stories: Using children's literature to teach friendship skills to children with learning disabilities. *Intervention in School and Clinic, 33*(3), 157–162.

De la Cruz, R. E., Cage, C. E., & Lian, M. J. (2000). Learning math and social skills through ancient multicultural games. *Teaching Exceptional Children, 32*(3), 38–42.

De La Paz, S. (1999). Self-regulated strategy instruction in regular education settings: Improving outcomes for students with and without learning disabilities. *Learning Disabilities Research and Practice, 14*(2), 92–106.

De La Paz, S., & Graham, S. (1997). Strategy instruction in planning: Effects on the writing performance and behavior of students with learning disabilities. *Exceptional Children, 63*(2), 167–181.

Demchak, M. (1994). Helping individuals with severe disabilities find leisure activities. *Teaching Exceptional Children, 27*(1), 48–53.

Dennis, R. E., & Giangreco, M. F. (1996). Creating conversation: Reflections on cultural sensitivity in family interviewing. *Exceptional Children, 63*(1), 103–116.

Deno, E. (1970). Special education as developmental capital. *Exceptional Children, 37,* 229–237.

Denti, L. G., & Meyers, S. B. (1997). Successful ability awareness programs. The key is in the planning. *Teaching Exceptional Children, 29*(4), 52–54.

Derman-Sparks, L. (1989). *Anti-bias curriculum.* Washington, DC: National Association for the Education of Young Children.

D'Errico, R. (1998, November 21). Grandparents defer dreams in order to serve loved ones. *The Times Herald-Record*, 4.

Diana v. California State Board of Education, No. C-70–37, RFP, (N.D. Cal., 1970).

Dimino, J. A., Taylor, R. M., & Gersten, R. M. (1995). Synthesis of the research on story grammar as a means to increase comprehension. *Reading and Writing Quarterly: Overcoming Learning Difficulties, 11*(1), 53–72.

DiRocco, M. D. (1999). How an alternating-day schedule empowers teachers. *Educational Leadership, 56*(4), 82–84.

Dishon, D., & O'Leary, P. W. (1991). Tips for heterogeneous group selection. *Cooperative Learning, 12*(1), 42–43.

Dockterman, D. A. (1995). Interactive learning: It's pushing the right buttons. *Educational Leadership, 53*(2), 58–59.

Doelling, J. E., & Bryde, S. (1995). School reentry and educational planning for the individual with traumatic brain injury. *Intervention in School and Clinic, 31*(2), 101–107.

Doelling, J. E., Bryde, S., & Parette, H. P. (1997). What are multidisciplinary and ecobehavioral approaches and how can they make a difference for students with traumatic brain injuries? *Teaching Exceptional Children, 30*(1), 56–60.

Donley, C. R., & Williams, G. (1997). Parents exhibit children's progress at a poster session. *Teaching Exceptional Children, 29*(4), 46–51.

Doren, B., & Benz, M. R. (1998). Employment inequality revisited: Predictors of better employment outcomes for young women with disabilities in transition. *The Journal of Special Education, 31*(4), 425–442.

Downing, J. E., Eichinger, J., & Williams, L. J. (1997). Inclusive education for students with severe disabilities. Comparative views of principals and educators at different levels of implementation. *Remedial and Special Education, 18*, 133–142, 165.

Doyle, M. B. (1997). *The paraprofessional's guide to the inclusive classroom*. Baltimore: Brookes.

Drecktrah, M. E., & Chiang, B. (1997). Instructional strategies used by general educators and teachers of students with learning disabilities. *Remedial and Special Education, 18*(3), 174–181.

Drier, H. S., Dawson, K. M., & Garofalo, J. (1999). Not your typical math class. *Educational Leadership, 56*(5), 21–25.

Drinkwater, S., & Demchak, M. (1995). The preschool checklist: Integration of children with severe disabilities. *Teaching Exceptional Children, 28*(1), 4–8.

Duchardt, B. A., Deshler, D. D., & Schumaker, J. B. (1995). A strategic intervention for enabling students with learning disabilities to identify and change their ineffective beliefs. *Learning Disability Quarterly, 18*(3), 186–201.

Dudley-Marling, C., & Fine, E. (1997). Politics of whole language. *Reading and Writing Quarterly: Overcoming Learning Difficulties, 13*, 247–260.

Dudley-Marling, C., & Murphy, S. (1997). A political critique of remedial reading programs: The example of reading recovery. *The Reading Teacher, 50*(6), 460–468.

Duffy, M. L., Jones, J., & Thomas, S. W. (1999). Using portfolios to foster independent thinking. *Intervention in School and Clinic, 35*(1), 34–37.

Dugger, C. W. (1998, March 21). Among young of immigrants, outlook rises. *The New York Times*, A1, A11.

Dukes, L. L., & Shaw, S. F. (1998). Not just children anymore: Personnel preparation regarding postsecondary education for adults with disabilities. *Teacher Education and Special Education, 21*(3), 205–213.

Dunn, C. (1996). A status report on transition planning for individuals with learning disabilities. *Journal of Learning Disabilities, 29*(1), 31–39.

Dunn, L. M. (1968). Special education for the mildly retarded—is much of it justifiable? *Exceptional Children, 35*, 5–22.

Dunn, R. (1996). *How to implement and supervise a learning styles program*. Alexandria, VA: Association for Supervision and Curriculum Development.

Dunn, R., Griggs, S. A., Olson, J., Beasley, M., & Gorman, B. S. (1995). A meta-analytic validation of the Dunn and Dunn model of learning style preferences. *The Journal of Educational Research, 88*, 353–362.

Dunnagan, K., & Capan, M. A. (1996). Exclusive books for inclusive readers. *Reading and Writing Quarterly: Overcoming Learning Difficulties, 12*(3), 309–323.

DuPaul, G. J., & Eckert, T. L. (1998). Academic interventions for students with attention-deficit/hyperactivity disorder: A review of the literature. *Reading and Writing Quarterly: Overcoming Learning Difficulties, 14*(1), 59–82.

Dyck, N., Sundbye, N., & Pemberton, J. (1997). A recipe for efficient co-teaching. *Teaching Exceptional Children, 30*(2), 42–45.

Dye, G. A. (2000). Graphic organizers to the rescue: Helping students link and remember information. *Teaching Exceptional Children, 32*(3), 72–76.

Easterbrookes, S. (1999). Improving practices for students with hearing impairments. *Exceptional Children, 65*(4), 537–554.

Ebenezer, J. V., & Lau, E. (1999). *Science on the Internet: A resource for K–12 teachers*. Upper Saddle River, NJ: Prentice Hall.

Echevarria, J. (1995). Sheltered instruction for students with learning disabilities who have limited English proficiency. *Intervention in School and Clinic, 30*(5), 302–305.

Echevarria, J., & McDonough, R. (1995). An alternative reading approach: Instructional conversations in a bilingual special education setting. *Learning Disabilities Research and Practice, 10*(2), 108–119.

Edelen-Smith, P. J. (1997). How now brown cow: Phoneme awareness activities for collaborative classrooms. *Intervention in School and Clinic, 33*(2), 103–111.

Edmunds, A. L. (1999). Cognitive credit cards: Acquiring learning strategies. *Teaching Exceptional Children, 31*(4), 68–73.

Educational Equity Concepts. (n.d.). *Beginning science equitably*. New York: Author.

Edwards, A. T. (1997). Let's stop ignoring our gay and lesbian youth. *Educational Leadership, 54*(7), 68–70.

Edyburn, D. L. (1994). An equation to consider: The portfolio assessment knowledge base + technology = The Grady Profile. *LD Forum, 19*(4), 35–37.

Elksnin, L. K., & Elksnin, N. (1998). Teaching social skills to students with learning and behavior problems. *Intervention in School and Clinic, 33*(3), 131–140.

Elliott, S. N., Kratochwill, T. R., & Schulte, T. R. (1998). The assessment accommodation checklist. *Teaching Exceptional Children, 31*(2), 10–14.

Ellis, E. S. (1989). A metacognitive intervention for increasing class participation. *Learning Disabilities Focus, 5*(1), 36–46.

Ellis, E. S. (1994). Integrating writing strategy instruction with content-area instruction: Part 1—Orienting students to organizational strategies. *Intervention in School and Clinic, 29*(3), 169–179.

Ellis, E. S. (1996). Reading strategy instruction. In D. D. Deshler, E. S. Ellis, & B. K. Lenz (Eds.), *Teaching adolescents with learning disabilities: Strategies and methods* (2nd ed., pp. 61–125). Denver: Love.

Ellis, E. S. (1997). Watering up the curriculum for adolescents with learning disabilities. *Remedial and Special Education, 18*(6), 326–346.

Ellis, E. S. (1998). Watering up the curriculum for adolescents with learning disabilities—Part 2. *Remedial and Special Education, 19*(2), 91–105.

Ellis, E. S., & Covert, G. (1996). Writing strategy instruction. In D. D. Deshler, E. S. Ellis, & B. K. Lenz (Eds.), *Teaching adolescents with learning disabilities: Strategies and methods* (2nd ed., pp. 127–207). Denver: Love.

Ellis, E. S., Deshler, D. D., Lenz, B. K., Schumaker, J. S., & Clark, F. L. (1991). An instructional model for teaching learning strategies. *Focus on Exceptional Children, 23*(6), 1–24.

Ellis, E. S., & Lenz, B. K. (1987). A component analysis of effective learning strategies for LD students. *Learning Disabilities Focus, 2,* 94–107.

Ellis, E. S., & Lenz, B. K. (1996). Perspectives on instruction in learning strategies. In D. D. Deshler, E. S. Ellis, & B. K. Lenz (Eds.), *Teaching adolescents with learning disabilities: Strategies and methods* (2nd ed., pp. 9–60). Denver: Love.

Embry, D. D. (1997). Does your school have a peaceful environment? Using an adult to create a climate for change and resiliency. *Intervention in School and Clinic, 32*(4), 217–222.

Encyclopedia Britannica Co. (1992). *Full option science system.* Chicago: Author.

Engleman, M. D., Griffin, H. C., Griffin, L. W., & Maddox, J. I. (1999). A teacher's guide to communicating with students with deaf-blindness. *Teaching Exceptional Children, 31*(5), 64–70.

Englemann, S., & Carnine, D. W. (1975). *Distar arithmetic level 1.* Chicago: Science Research Associates.

Englemann, S., & Carnine, D. W. (1976). *Distar arithmetic level 2.* Chicago: Science Research Associates.

Englemann, S., & Carnine, D. W. (1982). *Corrective mathematics program.* Chicago: Science Research Associates.

Englert, C. S., & Mariage, T. V. (1991). Making students partners in the comprehension process: Send for the reading POSSE. *Learning Disability Quarterly, 14,* 123–138.

Englert, C. S., Mariage, T. V., Garmon, M. A., & Tarrant, K. L. (1998). Accelerating reading progress in early literacy project classrooms. Three exploratory studies. *Remedial and Special Education, 19*(3), 142–159, 180.

Englert, C. S., Tarrant, K. L., & Mariage, T. V. (1992). Defining and redefining instructional practice in special education: Perspectives on good teaching. *Teacher Education and Special Education, 15*(2), 62–86.

English, K., Goldstein, H., Kaczmarek, L., & Shafer, K. (1996). "Buddy skills" for preschoolers. *Teaching Exceptional Children, 28*(3), 62–66.

English, K., Goldstein, H., Shafer, K., & Kaczmarek, L. (1997). Promoting interactions among preschoolers with and without disabilities: Effects of a buddy skills-training program. *Exceptional Children, 63*(2), 229–243.

Epps, S., Prescott, A. L., & Horner, R. H. (1990). Social acceptability of menstrual-care training methods for young women with developmental disabilities. *Education and Training in Mental Retardation, 25*(1), 33–44.

Erickson, R., Ysseldyke, J., Thurlow, M., & Elliott, J. (1998). Inclusive assessments and accountability systems: Tools of the trade in educational reform. *Teaching Exceptional Children, 31*(2), 4–9.

Erin, J. N., & Koenig, A. J. (1997). The student with a visual disability and a learning disability. *Journal of Learning Disabilities, 30*(3), 309–320.

Erwin, E. J., & Soodak, L. C. (1995). I never knew I could stand up to the system: Families' perspectives on pursuing inclusive education. *The Journal of the Association for Persons with Severe Handicaps, 20*(2), 136–146.

Etscheidt, S. K., & Bartlett, L. (1999). The IDEA amendments: A four-step approach for determining supplementary aids and services. *Exceptional Children, 65*(2), 163–174.

Evans, D. E., & Richardson, R. C. (1995). Corporal punishment: What teachers should know. *Teaching Exceptional Children, 27*(2), 33–36.

Evans, I. M., Salisbury, C. L., Palombaro, M. M., Berryman, J., & Hollowood, T. M. (1992). Acceptance of elementary-aged children with severe disabilities in an inclusive school. *Journal of the Association for Persons with Severe Handicaps, 17,* 205–212.

Evans, S., Tickle, B., Toppel, C., & Nichols, A. (1997). Here's help for young children exposed to drugs. *Teaching Exceptional Children, 29*(3), 60–62.

Everston, C. M., Emmer, E. T., Clements, B. S., Sanford, J. P., & Worsham, M. E. (1989). *Classroom management for elementary teachers* (2nd ed.). Upper Saddle River, NJ: Prentice Hall.

Ewing, N. J., & Duhaney, L. G. (1996, April). *Effective behavior management and counseling practices for culturally diverse students.* Presentation at the annual meeting of the Council for Exceptional Children, Orlando, FL.

Fad, K. S., Ross, M., & Boston, J. (1995). We're better together: Using cooperative learning to teach social skills to young children. *Teaching Exceptional Children, 27*(4), 28–34.

Fagen, S. A., Graves, D. L., & Tessier-Switlick, D. (1984). *Promoting successful mainstreaming: Reasonable classroom accommodations for learning disabled students.* Rockville, MD: Montgomery County Public Schools.

Falvey, M. A., Coots, J., & Terry-Gage, S. (1992). Extracurricular activities. In S. Stainback & W. Stainback (Eds.), *Curriculum considerations in inclusive classrooms: Facilitating learning for all students* (pp. 229–237). Baltimore: Paul H. Brookes.

Falvey, M. A., & Rosenberg, R. L. (1995). Developing and fostering friendships. In M. A. Falvey (Ed.), *Inclusive and heterogeneous schooling: Assessment, curriculum, and instruction* (pp. 267–284). Baltimore: Paul H. Brookes.

Favazza, P. C., & Odom, S. L. (1997). Promoting positive attitudes of kindergarten-age children toward people with disabilities. *Exceptional Children, 63*(3), 405–418.

Fecser, F. A., & Long, N. J. (1997). Life space crisis interventions. *Beyond Behavior, 8*(1), 10–15.

Fernald, G. (1943). *Remedial techniques in basic school subjects.* New York: McGraw-Hill.

Feuerstein, R. (1979). *The dynamic assessment of retarded performers: The Learning Potential Assessment Device. Theory, instruments and techniques.* Baltimore: University Park Press.

Fidel, S., & Johnston, R. (1986). Best of friends. In *The new illustrated Disney songbook* (pp. 205–207). New York: Harry N. Abrams.

Field, S. (1996). Self-determination instructional strategies for youth with learning disabilities. *Journal of Learning Disabilities, 29*(1), 40–52.

Field, S., & Hoffman, A. (1996). *Steps to self-determination.* Austin, TX: PRO-ED.

Field, S., Hoffman, A., & Posch, M. (1997). Self-determination during adolescence: A developmental perspective. *Remedial and Special Education, 18*(5), 285–293.

Finson, K. D., & Ormsbee, C. K. (1998). Rubrics and their use in inclusive settings. *Intervention in School and Clinic, 34*(2), 79–88.

Fiore, T. A., Becker, E. A., & Nero, R. C. (1993). Educational interventions for students with attention deficit disorders. *Exceptional Children, 60*(2), 163–173.

Fisher, D., Pumpian, I., & Sax, C. (1998). Parent and caregiver impressions of different educational models. *Remedial and Special Education, 19,* 173–180.

Flanagan, B. (1998, April). *Strategies for improving student comprehension of textbook content.* Presentation at the meeting of the Council for Exceptional Children, Minneapolis.

Fleming, D. (1996). Preamble to a more perfect classroom. *Educational Leadership, 54*(1), 73–76.

Fleming, M. B. (1988). Getting out of the writing vacuum. In J. Golub (Ed.), *Focus on collaborative learning* (pp. 77–84). Urbana, IL: National Council of Teachers of English.

Flor Ada, A. (1993). *My name is Maria Isabel.* New York: Atheneum.

Ford, B. A., Obiakor, F. E., & Patton, J. M. (1995). *Effective education of African-American exceptional learners: New perspectives.* Austin, TX: PRO-ED.

Ford, D. Y. (1998). The underrepresentation of minority students in gifted education: Problems and promises in recruitment and retention. *The Journal of Special Education, 32,* 4–14.

Fordham, S., & Ogbu, J. (1986). Black students' school success: Coping with the burden of "acting white." *The Urban Review, 18,* 176–206.

Forest, M., & Lusthaus, E. (1989). Promoting educational equality for all students: Circles and maps. In S. Stainback, W. Stainback, & M. Forest (Eds.), *Educating all students in the mainstream of regular education* (pp. 43–57). Baltimore: Paul H. Brookes.

Forest, M., & Lusthaus, E. (1990). Everyone belongs with MAPS action planning system. *Teaching Exceptional Children, 22*(2), 32–35.

Forness, S. R., Keogh, B. K., Macmillan, D. L., Kavale, K. A., & Gresham, F. M. (1998). What is so special about IQ? *Remedial and Special Education, 19*(6), 315–322.

Fossey, R., Hosie, T., Soniat, K., & Zirkel, P. (1995). Section 504 and "front line" educators: An expanded obligation to serve children with disabilities. *Preventing School Failure, 39*(2), 10–14.

Fox, J., Conroy, M., & Heckaman, K. (1998). Research issues in functional assessment of the challenging behaviors of students with emotional and behavioral disorders. *Behavioral Disorders, 24*(1), 26–33.

Fradd, S. H. (1993). *Creating the team to assist culturally and linguistically diverse students.* Tucson, AZ: Communication Skill Builders.

Fradd, S. H., & Weismantel, M. J. (1989). *Meeting the needs of culturally and linguistically different students: A handbook for educators.* Austin, TX: PRO-ED.

Fradd, S. H., & Wilen, D. K. (1990). *Using interpreters and translators to meet the needs of handicapped language minority students and their families.* Washington, DC: National Clearinghouse for Bilingual Education.

Frank, A. R., & Brown, D. (1992). Self-monitoring strategies in arithmetic. *Teaching Exceptional Children, 24*(2), 52–53.

Franklin, E. A. (1992). Learning to read and write the natural way. *Teaching Exceptional Children, 24*(3), 45–48.

Franklin, M. E., James, J. R., & Watson, A. L. (1996). Using a cultural identity development model to plan culturally responsive reading and writing instruction. *Reading and Writing Quarterly: Overcoming Learning Difficulties, 12*(1), 41–58.

Frederico, M. A., Herrold, W. G., & Venn, J. (1999). Helpful tips for successful inclusion: A checklist for educators. *Teaching Exceptional Children, 32*(1), 76–82.

Freedman-Harvey, G., & Johnson, W. (1998). How it feels. *Teaching Tolerance, 7*(1), 29.

Freeman, D. E., & Freeman, Y. S. (1989). A road to success for language-minority high school students. In P. Rigg & V. G. Allen (Eds.), *When they don't all speak English: Integrating the ESL student into the regular classroom* (pp. 126–138). Urbana, IL: National Council of Teachers of English.

Freeman, S. F. N., Alkin, M. C., & Kasari, C. L. (1999). Satisfaction and desire for change in educational placement for children with Down syndrome: Perceptions of parents. *Remedial and Special Education, 20*(3), 143–151.

Freeman, Y. S., & Freeman, D. E. (1992). *Whole language for second language learners.* Portsmouth, NH: Heinemann.

Freire, P. (1970). *Pedagogy of the oppressed.* New York: Continuum.

French, N. K. (1999). Paraeducators and teachers: Shifting roles. *Teaching Exceptional Children, 32*(2), 69–73.

French, N. K., & Pickett, A. L. (1997). Paraprofessionals in special education: Issues for teacher educators. *Teacher Education and Special Education, 20*(1), 61–73.

Freschi, D. F. (1999). Guidelines for working with one-to-one aides. *Teaching Exceptional Children, 31*(4), 42–45.

Frieman, B. B. (1997). Two parents—two homes. *Educational Leadership, 54*(7), 23–25.

Friends of Project 10 (1993). *Project 10 handbook* (5th ed.) Los Angeles: Author.

Froschl, M., & Gropper, N. (1999). Fostering friendships, curbing bullying. *Educational Leadership, 56*(8), 72–75.

Fuchs, D., Deshler, D., & Zigmond, N. (1994, March). *How expendable is general education? How expendable is special education?* Paper presented at the meeting of the Learning Disabilities Association of America, Washington, DC.

Fuchs, D., Fernstrom, P., Scott, S., Fuchs, L., & Vandermeer, L. (1994). A process for mainstreaming: Classroom ecological inventory. *Teaching Exceptional Children, 26*(3), 11–15.

Fuchs, L. S., & Fuchs, D. (1998). Treatment validity: A unifying concept for reconceptualizing the identification of learning disabilities. *Learning Disabilities Research and Practice, 13*(4), 204–219.

Fuchs, L. S., Fuchs, D., & Kazdan, S. (1999). Effects of peer-assisted learning strategies on high school students with serious reading problems. *Remedial and Special Education, 20*(5), 309–318.

Fuchs, L. S., Karns, K. M., Eaton, S. B., & Hamlett, C. L. (1999, April). *Identifying fair, appropriate testing accommodations for students with learning disabilities.* Presentation at the annual meeting of the Council for Exceptional Children, Charlotte, NC.

Fueyo, V. (1997). Below the tip of the iceberg: Teaching language-minority students. *Teaching Exceptional Children, 30*(1), 61–65.

Fulk, B. M. (1997). Think while you spell: A cognitive motivational approach to spelling instruction. *Teaching Exceptional Children, 29*(4), 70–71.

Fulk, B. M., & Montgomery-Grymes, D. J. (1994). Strategies to improve student motivation. *Intervention in School and Clinic, 30*(1), 28–33.

Fulk, B. M., & Stormount-Spurgin, M. (1995). Fourteen spelling strategies for students with learning disabilities. *Intervention in School and Clinic, 31*(1), 16–20.

Gable, R. A., Arllen, N. L., Evans, W. H., & Whinnery, K. M. (1997). Strategies for evaluating collaborative mainstream instruction: "Let the data be our guide." *Preventing School Failure, 41*(4), 153–158.

Gajria, M. (1988). *Effects of a summarization technique on the text comprehension skills of learning disabled students.* Unpublished doctoral dissertation, Pennsylvania State University.

Gajria, M. (1995, November). *Preparing adolescents with learning disabilities to meet the demands of regular classrooms.* Presentation at the annual meeting of the New York State Federation of Chapters of the Council for Exceptional Children, Niagara Falls, NY.

Gajria, M., Giek, K., Hemrick, M., & Salend, S. J. (1992). *Teacher acceptability of testing modifications for mainstreamed students.* Paper presented at the meeting of the Council for Exceptional Children, Baltimore.

Gajria, M., & Salend, S. J. (1995). Increasing the homework completion rates of students with mild disabilities. *Remedial and Special Education, 16*(5), 271–278.

Gajria, M., & Salend, S. J. (1996). Treatment acceptability: A critical dimension for overcoming teacher resistance to implementing adaptations for mainstreamed students. *Reading and Writing Quarterly: Overcoming Learning Difficulties, 12*(1), 91–108.

Galda, L., Cullinan, B. E., & Strickland, D. S. (1997). *Language, literacy and the child* (2nd ed.). New York: Harcourt Brace.

Galvin, J. C., & Scherer, M. J. (1996). *Evaluating, selecting, and using appropriate assistive technology.* Gaithersburg, MD: Aspen.

Garcia, S. B., & Malkin, D. H. (1993). Toward defining programs and services for culturally and linguistically diverse learners in special education. *Teaching Exceptional Children, 26*(1), 52–58.

Garcia, S. B., & Ortiz, A. A. (1988). Preventing inappropriate referrals of language minority students to special education. *New Focus, 5,* 1–12.

Gardill, M. C., & Jitendra, A. K. (1999). Advanced story map instruction: Effects on the reading comprehension of students with learning disabilities. *The Journal of Special Education, 33*(1), 2–17, 28.

Gardner, H. (1993). *Multiple intelligences: The theory in practice.* New York: Basic Books.

Garey, M. E., & Wambold, C. (1994). Behavior management strategies for students with traumatic brain injury. *Beyond Behavior, 6*(1), 24–29.

Garmston, R., & Wellman, B. (1998). Teacher talk that makes a difference. *Educational Leadership, 55*(7), 30–34.

Garnett, K. (1989). Math learning disabilities. *The Forum, 14*(4), 11–15.

Garrick Duhaney, L. M., & Whittington-Couse, M. (1998, April). *Using learning styles and strategies to enhance academic learning for linguistically and culturally diverse students.* Presentation at the Conference on Providing Appropriate Instruction and Services to Culturally and Linguistically Diverse Learners, Fishkill, NY.

Garrity, C., Jens, K., Porter, W., Sager, N., & Short-Camilli, C. (1997). Bully-proofing your school: Creating a positive climate. *Intervention in School and Clinic, 32*(4), 235–243.

Gartland, D. (1994). Content area reading: Lessons from the specialists. *LD Forum, 19*(3), 19–22.

Gelfer, J. I., & Perkins, P. G. (1998). Portfolios: Focus on young children. *Teaching Exceptional Children, 31*(2), 44–47.

Gelzheiser, L. M., McLane, M., Meyers, J., & Pruzek, R. M. (1998). IEP-specified peer interaction needs: Accurate but ignored. *Exceptional Children, 65*(1), 51–65.

Genaux, M., Morgan, D. P., & Friedman, S. G. (1995). Substance use and its prevention: A survey of classroom practices. *Behavioral Disorders, 20*(4), 279–289.

Genesee, F., & Cloud, N. (1998). Multilingualism is basic. *Educational Leadership, 55*(6), 62–65.

George, M. P., Valore, T., Quinn, M. M., & Varisco, R. (1997). Preparing to go home: A collaborative approach to transition. *Preventing School Failure, 41*(4), 168–172.

George, N. L., & Lewis, T. J. (1991). EASE: Exit assistance for special educators—Helping students make the transition. *Teaching Exceptional Children, 23*(2), 34–39.

Gerber, P. J., & Popp, P. A. (1999). Consumer perspectives on the collaborative teaching model: Views of students with and without LD and their parents. *Remedial and Special Education, 20*(5), 288–296.

Gersten, R. (1999). The changing face of bilingual education. *Educational Leadership, 56*(7), 41–45.

Gersten, R., & Woodward, J. (1994). The language-minority student and special education: Issues, trends, and paradoxes. *Exceptional Children, 60*(4), 310–322.

Getch, Y. Q., & Neubarth-Pritchett, S. (1999). Children with asthma: Strategies for educators. *Teaching Exceptional Children, 31*(3), 30–36.

Giangreco, M. F., Baumgart, M. J., & Doyle, M. B. (1995). How inclusion can facilitate teaching and learning. *Intervention in School and Clinic, 30*(5), 273–278.

Giangreco, M. F., Cloninger, C. J., & Iverson, V. S. (1998). *Choosing options and accommodations for children: A guide to educational planning for students with disabilities* (2nd ed.). Baltimore: Paul H. Brookes.

Giangreco, M. F., Dennis, R., Cloninger, C., Edelman, S., & Schattman, R. (1993). "I've counted Jon": Transformational experiences of teachers educating students with disabilities. *Exceptional Children, 59,* 359–372.

Giangreco, M. F., Edelman, S. W., Luiselli, T. E., & McFarland, S. Z. C. (1997). Helping or hovering? Effects of instructional assistant proximity on student with disabilities. *Exceptional Children, 64*(1), 7–18.

Gibb, G. S., Young, J. R., Allred, K. W., Dyches, T. T., Egan, M. W., & Ingram, C. F. (1997). A team-based junior high inclusion program. Parent perceptions and feedback. *Remedial and Special Education, 18,* 243–249, 256.

Gibb, S. A., Allred, K., Ingram, G. F., Young, J. R., & Egan, W. M. (1999). Lessons learned from the inclusion of students with emotional and behavioral disorders in one junior high school. *Behavioral Disorders, 24*(2), 122–136.

Gibson, B. P., & Govendo, B. L. (1999). Encouraging constructive behavior in middle school classrooms: A multiple-intelligences approach. *Intervention in School and Clinic, 35*(1), 16–21.

Gilbert, S. E., & Gay, G. (1989). Improving the success in school of poor black children. In B. J. Shade (Ed.), *Culture, style and the educative process* (pp. 275–283). Springfield, IL: Charles C. Thomas.

Gillet, P. (1986). Mainstreaming techniques for LD students. *Academic Therapy, 21,* 389–399.

Gloeckler, T., & Simpson, C. (1988). *Exceptional students in regular classrooms: Challenges, services and methods.* Mountain View, CA: Mayfield.

Goddard, Y. L., & Heron, T. E. (1998). Pleaze, teacher, help me learn to spell better: Teach me self-correction. *Teaching Exceptional Children, 30*(6), 38–43.

Goforth, F. S. (1998). *Literature and the learner.* Belmont, CA: Wadsworth.

Goldman, S. R., & Hasselbring, T. S. (1997). Achieving meaningful mathematics literacy for students with learning disabilities. *Journal of Learning Disabilities, 30*(2), 198–208.

Goldsmith, L. T., & Mark, J. (1999). What is a standards-based mathematics curriculum? *Educational Leadership, 57*(3), 40–44.

Goleman, D. (1995). *Emotional intelligence.* New York: Bantam Books.

Gonzalez, L. A. (1992). Tapping their language—A bridge to success. *The Journal of Educational Issues of Language Minority Students, 10,* 27–39.

Gonzalez-Alvarez, L. I. (1998). A short course in sensitivity training. *Teaching Exceptional Children, 31*(1), 73–77.

Goodman, G. (1979). From residential treatment to community based education: A model for reintegration. *Education and Training of the Mentally Retarded, 14*(2), 95–100.

Goodman, K. (1986). *What's whole in whole language?* Portsmouth, NH: Heinemann.

Goodrich, H. (1997). Understanding rubrics. *Educational Leadership, 54*(4), 14–17.

Goodwin, M. W. (1999). Cooperative learning and social skills: What skills to teach and how to teach them. *Intervention in School and Clinic, 35*(1), 29–33.

Goor, M. B., & Schwenn, J. O. (1993). Accommodating diversity and disability with cooperative learning. *Intervention in School and Clinic, 29*(1), 6–16.

Gordon, T. (1974). *Teacher effectiveness training.* New York: Peter H. Wyden.

Gorman, J. C. (1999). Understanding children's hearts and minds: Emotional functioning and learning disabilities. *Teaching Exceptional Children, 31*(3), 72–77.

Gosselin, K. (1996a). *ZooAllergy.* Valley Park, MO: JayJo Books.

Gosselin, K. (1996b). *Taking epilepsy to school.* Valley Park, MO: JayJo Books.

Gosselin, K. (1998a). *Taking asthma to school.* Valley Park, MO: JayJo Books.

Gosselin, K. (1998b). *Taking diabetes to school.* Valley Park, MO: JayJo Books.

Graham, B. I., & Fahey, K. (1999). School leaders look at student work. *Educational Leadership, 56*(6), 25–27.

Graham, S. (1992). Helping students with LD progress as writers. *Intervention in School and Clinic, 27*(3), 134–144.

Graham, S., Harris, K. R., & Loynachan, C. (1996). The directed spelling thinking activity: Application with high-frequency words. *Learning Disabilities Research and Practice, 11*(1), 34–40.

Graham, S., Harris, K. R., & Sawyer, R. (1987). Composition instruction with learning disabled students: Self-instructional strategy training. *Focus on Exceptional Children, 20,* 1–11.

Grant, R. (1993). Strategic training for using text headings to improve students' processing of content. *Journal of Reading, 36,* 482–488.

Grant, S. H., Van Acker, R., Guerra, N., Duplechain, R., & Coen, M. (1998). A school classroom enhancement program to prevent the development of antisocial behavior in children from high-risk neighborhoods. *Preventing School Failure, 42*(3), 121–127.

Grasso-Ryan, A., & Price, L. (1992). Adults with LD in the 1990s. *Intervention in School and Clinic, 28*(1), 6–20.

Graves, A. (1995). Writing instruction for students with learning disabilities . . . The past five years. *LD Forum, 20*(3), 36–38.

Graves, D. H. (1994). *A fresh look at writing.* Portsmouth, NH: Heinemann.

Graves, D. H., & Hansen, J. (1983). The author's chair. *Language Arts, 60,* 176–183.

Green, A. L., & Stoneman, Z. (1989). Attitudes of mothers and fathers of nonhandicapped children. *Journal of Early Intervention, 13,* 292–304.

Green, S. K., & Shinn, M. R. (1995). Parent attitudes about special education and reintegration: What is the role of student outcomes? *Exceptional Children, 61*(3), 269–281.

Greene, G. (1994). The magic of mnemonics. *LD Forum, 19*(3), 34–35.

Greene, G. (1995). A spelling test for teachers of students with learning disabilities. *LD Forum, 20*(3), 15–17.

Greer v. Rome City School District, 950 f.2d, 699, 11th Circuit, 1991.

Griffin, C. C., & Tulbert, B. L. (1995). The effect of graphic organizers on students' comprehension and recall of expository text: A review of the research and implications for practice. *Reading and Writing Quarterly: Overcoming Learning Difficulties, 11*(1), 73–89.

Grigal, M. (1998). The time-space continuum: Using natural supports in inclusive classrooms. *Teaching Exceptional Children, 30*(6), 44–51.

Grigal, M., Test, D. W., Beattie, J., & Wood, W. (1997). An evaluation of transition components of individualized education programs. *Exceptional Children, 63*(3), 357–372.

Gronna, S. S., Jenkins, A. A., & Chin-Chance, S. A. (1998a). The performance of students with disabilities in a norm-referenced, statewide standardized testing program. *Journal of Learning Disabilities, 31*(5), 482–493.

Gronna, S. S., Jenkins, A. A., & Chin-Chance, S. A. (1998b). Who are we assessing? Determining state-wide participation rates for students with disabilities. *Exceptional Children, 64*(3), 407–418.

Grove, K. A., & Fisher, D. (1999). Entrepreneurs of meaning: Parents and the process of inclusive education. *Remedial and Special Education, 20*(4), 208–215, 256.

Guetzloe, E. (1989). *Youth suicide: What the educator should know.* Reston, VA: Council for Exceptional Children.

Guetzloe, E., & Ammer, J. (1995, April). *Addressing the needs of the hidden minority: Fostering a positive school climate for gay and lesbian youth.* Presentation at the annual meeting of the Council for Exceptional Children, Indianapolis.

Guillaume, A. M., Yopp, R. H., & Yopp, H. K. (1996). Accessible science. *The Journal of Educational Issues of Language Minority Students, 17,* 67–85.

Gullingsrud, M. (1998). I am the immigrant in my classroom. *Voices From the Middle, 6*(1), 30–35.

Gunter, P. L., Shores, R. E., Jack, S. L., Rasmussen, S. K., & Flowers, J. (1995). On the move: Using teacher/student proximity to improve students' behavior. *Teaching Exceptional Children, 28*(1), 12–14.

Guralnick, M. J., Connor, R. T., & Hammond, M. (1995). Parent perspectives of peer relationships and friendships in integrated and specialized programs. *American Journal on Mental Retardation, 99,* 457–476.

Gurganus, S., & Del Mastro, M. (1998). Mainstreaming kids with reading and writing problems: Special challenges of the mathematics classroom. *Reading and Writing Quarterly: Overcoming Learning Difficulties, 14*(1), 117–125.

Gurganus, S., Janas, M., & Schmitt, L. (1995). Science instruction: What special education teachers need to know and what roles they need to play. *Teaching Exceptional Children, 27*(4), 7–9.

Guterman, B. R. (1995). The validity of learning disabilities services: The consumer's view. *The Reading Teacher, 62*(2), 111–124.

Gutierrez, M. (1994, April). *Meeting the needs of bilingual migrant students.* Paper presented at the annual meeting of the New York State Chapter of the Association for Bilingual Education, Uniondale, NY.

Habel, J. C., & Bernard, J. A. (1999). School and educational psychologists: Creating new service models. *Intervention in School and Clinic, 34*(3), 156–162.

Hadden, S., & Fowler, S. A. (1997). Preschool: A new beginning for children and parents. *Teaching Exceptional Children, 30*(1), 36–39.

Hagiwara, T. (1998). Introduce multiculturalism in your classroom. *Intervention in School and Clinic, 34*(1), 43–44.

Hale-Benson, J. E. (1986). *Black children: Their roots, culture, and learning style* (2nd ed.). Baltimore: Johns Hopkins University Press.

Halford, J. M. (1996). How parents' liaisons connect families to school. *Educational Leadership, 53*(7), 34–36.

Hall, M., Kleinert, H. L., & Kearns, J. F. (2000). Going to college! Postsecondary programs for students with moderate and severe disabilities. *Teaching Exceptional Children, 32*(3), 58–65.

Hallenbeck, M. J. (1996). The cognitive strategy in writing: Welcome relief for adolescents with learning disabilities. *Learning Disabilities Research and Practice, 11*(2), 107–119.

Hallenbeck, M. J., & McMaster, D. (1991). Disability simulation for regular education students. *Teaching Exceptional Children, 24*(1), 12–15.

Hammond, H. (1999). Identifying best family-centered practices in early-intervention programs. *Teaching Exceptional Children, 31*(6), 42–46.

Hanson, M. J., & Carta, J. J. (1996). Addressing the challenges of families with multiple risks. *Exceptional Children, 62*(3), 201–212.

Hardman, E., & Smith, S. W. (1999). Promoting positive interactions in the classroom. *Intervention in School and Clinic, 34*(3), 178–180.

Haring, N. G., & Romer, L. T. (1995). *Welcoming students who are deaf-blind into typical classrooms.* Baltimore: Paul H. Brookes.

Harmon, J. M., Katims, D. S., & Whittington, D. (1999). Helping middle school students learn with social studies texts. *Teaching Exceptional Children, 32*(1), 70–75.

Harn, W. E., Bradshaw, M. L., & Ogletree, B. T. (1999). The speech-language pathologist in the schools: Changing roles. *Intervention in School and Clinic, 34*(3), 163–169.

Harniss, M. K., Hollenbeck, K. L., Crawford, D. B., & Carnine, D. (1994). Content organization and instructional design issues in the development of history texts. *Learning Disability Quarterly, 17*(3), 235–248.

Harris, A. J., & Sipay, E. R. (1985). *How to increase reading ability: A guide to developmental and remedial approaches* (8th ed.). New York: Longman.

Harris, C. R. (1991). Identifying and serving the gifted new immigrant. *Teaching Exceptional Children, 23,* 26–30.

Harris, K. R., Graham, S., & Freeman, S. (1988). Effects of strategy training on metamemory among learning disabled students. *Exceptional Children, 54,* 332–338.

Harry, B. (1995). African American families. In B. A. Ford, F. E. Obiakor, & J. M. Patton (Eds.), *Effective education of African American exceptional learners* (pp. 211–233). Austin, TX: PRO-ED.

Harry, B., Allen, N., & McLaughlin, M. (1995). Communication versus compliance: African-American parents' involvement in special education. *Exceptional Children, 61*(4), 364–377.

Harry, B., Rueda, R., & Kalyanpur, M. (1999). Cultural reciprocity in sociocultural perspective: Adapting the normalization principle for family collaboration. *Exceptional Children, 66*(1), 123–136.

Hartas, D., & Donahue, M. L. (1997). Conversational and social problem-solving skills in adolescents with learning disabilities. *Learning Disabilities Research and Practice, 12*(4), 213–220.

Hasazi, S. B., Furney, K. S., & Destefano, L. (1999). Implementing the IDEA transition mandates. *Exceptional Children, 65*(4), 555–566.

Hawley, R., & Hawley, I. (1975). *Human values in the classroom: A handbook for teachers.* New York: Hart.

Heal, L. W., Khoju, M., & Rusch, F. R. (1997). Predicting quality of life of youth after they leave special education high school programs. *Journal of Special Education, 31*(3), 279–299.

Healey, B. (1996). Helping parents deal with the fact that their child has a disability. *CEC Today, 3*(5), 12–13.

Heaton, S., & O'Shea, D. J. (1995). Using mnemonics to make mnemonics. *Teaching Exceptional Children, 28*(1), 34–36.

Heller, K. W., Fredrick, L. D., Best, S., Dykes, M. K., & Cohen, E. T. (2000). Specialized health care procedures in the schools: Training and service delivery. *Exceptional Children, 66*(2), 173–186.

Heller, K. W., Fredrick, L. D., Dykes, M. K., Best, S., & Cohen, E. T. (1999). A national perspective of competencies for teachers of individuals with physical and health disabilities. *Exceptional Children, 65*(2), 219–234.

Helmstetter, E., Curry, C. A., Brennan, M., & Sampson-Saul, M. (1998). Comparison of general and special education classrooms of students with severe disabilities. *Education and Training in Mental Retardation and Developmental Disabilities, 33*(3), 216–227.

Helmstetter, E., Peck, C. A., & Giangreco, M. F. (1994). Outcomes of interactions with peers with moderate or severe disabilities: A statewide survey of high school students. *Journal of the Association of Persons with Severe Handicaps, 19*(4), 263–276.

Hendrickson, J. M., & Gable, R. A. (1997). Collaborative assessment of students with diverse needs: Equitable, accountable, and effective grading. *Preventing School Failure, 41*(4), 159–163.

Hendrickson, J. M., Shokoohi-Yekta, M., Hamre-Nietupski, S., & Gable, R. A. (1996). Middle and high school students' perceptions on being friends with peers and severe disabilities. *Exceptional Children, 63*(1), 19–28.

Herbert, E. A., & Schultz, L. (1996). The power of portfolios. *Educational Leadership, 53*(7), 70–71.

Herdt, G., & Boxer, A. (1993). *Children of the horizons: How gay and lesbian teens are leading a new way out of the closet.* Boston: Beacon Press.

Herman, J. L., Aschbacher, P. R., & Winters, L. (1992). *A practical guide to alternative assessment.* Alexandria, VA: Association for Supervision and Curriculum Development.

Hertzog, N. B. (1998a). Gifted education specialist. *Teaching Exceptional Children, 30*(3), 39–43.

Hertzog, N. B. (1998b). Using open-ended learning activities to empower teachers and students. *Teaching Exceptional Children, 30*(6), 26–31.

Heumann, J. E., & Hehir, T. (1995). *Policy guidance on educating blind and visually impaired students.* Washington, DC: U.S. Department of Education.

Heuttig, C., & O'Connor, J. (1999). Wellness programming for preschoolers with disabilities. *Teaching Exceptional Children, 31*(3), 12–17.

Heward, W. L., Gardner, R., Cavanaugh, R. A., Courson, F. H., Grossi, T. A., & Barbetta, P. M. (1996). Everyone participates in this class: Using response cards to increase active student response. *Teaching Exceptional Children, 28*(2), 4–10.

Higgins, E. L., & Raskind, M. H. (1995). Compensatory effectiveness of speech recognition of the written composition performance of postsecondary students with learning disabilities. *Learning Disability Quarterly, 18*(2), 159–174.

Higgins, K., Boone, R., & Lovitt, T. C. (1996). Hypertext support for remedial students and students with learning disabilities. *Journal of Learning Disabilities, 29*(4), 402–412.

Hill, J. L. (1999). *Meeting the needs of students with special physical and health care needs.* Upper Saddle River, NJ: Prentice Hall.

Hilton, A., & Gerlach, K. (1997). Employment, preparation and management of paraeducators: Challenges to appropriate service for students with developmental disabilities. *Education and Training in Mental Retardation and Developmental Disabilities, 32*(2), 71–76.

Hobbs, R. J. (1995, April). *Inclusion + common sense = success.* Presentation at the annual meeting of the Council for Exceptional Children, Indianapolis.

Hobson v. Hansen, 269 F. Supp. 401 (1967) (D.C.C., 1967).

Hochman, B. (1979). *Simulation activities handout.* Bethlehem, PA: Project STREAM.

Hodgin, J., & Wooliscroft, C. (1997). Eric learns to read: Learning styles at work. *Educational Leadership, 54*(6), 43–45.

Hodgin, K. B., Levin, B., & Matthews. C. (1997). *Gender equity in the elementary school.* CD-ROM. Greensboro: University of North Carolina at Greensboro.

Hoener, A., Salend, S. J., & Kay, S. (1997). Creating readable handouts, worksheets, overheads, tests, review materials, study guides and homework assignments through effective typographic design. *Teaching Exceptional Children, 29*(3), 32–35.

Hoffman, J. V., Roser, N. L., & Battle, J. (1993). Reading aloud in classrooms: From the modal toward the "model." *The Reading Teacher, 46*(6), 496–503.

Hoge, G., & Dattilo, J. (1995). Recreation participation patterns of adults with and without mental retardation. *Education and Training in Mental Retardation and Developmental Disabilities, 30*(4), 283–298.

Hollingsworth, P. M., & Reutzel, D. R. (1988). Whole language with the LD child. *Academic Therapy, 23,* 477–488.

Holloway, J. H. (1999). Improving the reading skills of adolescents. *Educational Leadership, 57*(2), 80–81.

Hollowood, T. M., Salisbury, C. L., Rainforth, B., & Palombaro, M. M. (1994). Use of instructional time in classrooms serving students with and without severe disabilities. *Exceptional Children, 61*(3), 242–253.

Holmes, S. A. (1994, July 20). Birthrate for unwed women up 70% since '83, study says. *The New York Times,* A1, A8.

Holmes, S. A. (1998, August 7). Black populace nearly equaled by Hispanic. *The New York Times,* A15.

Hoover, J. J., & Collier, C. (1989). Methods and materials for bilingual special education. In L. M. Baca & H. T. Cervantes (Eds.), *The bilingual special education interface* (2nd ed., pp. 231–255). New York: Merrill/Macmillan.

Hopkins, M. H. (1993). Ideas. *Arithmetic Teacher, 40,* 512–519.

Horne, J. (1998). Rising to the challenge. *Teaching Tolerance, 7*(1), 26–31.

Horne, M. D. (1981). *Assessment of classroom status: Using the perception of social closeness scale.* (ERIC Document Reproduction Service No. 200 616).

Horney, M. A., & Anderson-Inman, L. (1999). Supported text in electronic reading environments. *Reading and Writing Quarterly: Overcoming Learning Difficulties, 15*(2), 127–168.

Horton, S. V., Lovitt, T. C., & White, O. R. (1992). Teaching mathematics to adolescents classified as educable mentally handicapped: Using calculators to remove the computational onus. *Remedial and Special Education, 13*(3), 36–60.

House of Representatives Report 103–208. (1993). Washington, DC: Author.

Howe, L., & Howe, M. M. (1975). *Personalizing education: Values clarification and beyond.* New York: Hart.

Howell, K. W., Evans, D., & Gardiner, J. (1997). Medications in the classroom: A hard pill to swallow? *Teaching Exceptional Children, 29*(6), 58–61.

Hoy, A. W. (1995). *Educational psychology* (6th ed.). Boston: Allyn & Bacon.

Hudson, P. (1996). Using a learning set to increase the test performance of students with learning disabilities in social studies classes. *Learning Disabilities Research and Practice, 11*(2), 78–85.

Hughes, C., Guth, C., Hall, S., Presley, J., Dye, M., & Byers, C. (1999). "They are my best friends": Peer buddies promote inclusion in high school. *Teaching Exceptional Children, 31*(5), 32–37.

Hughes, C., Pitkin, S. E., & Lorden, S. W. (1998). Assessing preferences and choices of persons with severe and profound mental retardation. *Education and Training in Mental Retardation and Developmental Disabilities, 33*(4), 299–316.

Hughes, C. A. (1996). Memory and test-taking strategies. In D. D. Deshler, E. S. Ellis, & B. K. Lenz (Eds.), *Teaching adolescents with learning disabilities: Strategies and methods* (2nd ed., pp. 209–266). Denver: Love.

Hughes, C. A., Deshler, D. D., Ruhl, K. L., & Schumaker, J. B. (1993). Test-taking strategy instruction for adolescents with emotional and behavioral disorders. *Journal of Emotional and Behavioral Disorders, 1*(3), 189–198.

Humphries, T. (1993). Deaf culture and cultures. In K. M. Chritensen & G. L. Delgado (Eds.), *Multicultural issues in deafness* (pp. 3–13). White Plains, NY: Longman.

Hunt, A. (1997, July 13). Young and gay: Coming out of the closet. *The Times Herald Record,* 3–5.

Hunt, P., Alwell, M., Farron-Davis, F., & Goetz, L. (1996). Creating socially supportive environments for fully included students who experience multiple disabilities. *Journal of the Association for Persons with Severe Handicaps, 21,* 53–71.

Hunt, P., Farron-Davis, F., Beckstead, S., Curtis, D., & Goetz, L. (1994). Evaluating the effects of placement of students with severe disabilities in general education versus special class. *Journal of the Association for Persons with Severe Handicaps, 19*(3), 200–214.

Hunt-Berg, M., Rankin, J. L., & Beukelman, D. R. (1994). Ponder the possibilities: Computer-supported writing for struggling writers. *Learning Disabilities Research and Practice, 9*(3), 169–178.

Hunter, M. (1981). *Increasing your teaching effectiveness.* Palo Alto, CA: Learning Institute.

Huntze, S. (1994). Does the chicken eat chop suey? Or how students with disabilities improve the quality of life for students in regular education. *Beyond Behavior, 5*(3), 4–7.

Hutchins, M. P., & Renzaglia, A. (1998). Interviewing families for effective transition to employment. *Teaching Exceptional Children, 30*(4), 72–78.

Hux, K., & Hacksley, C. (1996). Mild traumatic brain injury: Facilitating school success. *Intervention in School and Clinic, 31*(3), 158–165.

Hyun, J. K., & Fowler, S. A. (1995). Respect, cultural sensitivity, and communication. *Teaching Exceptional Children, 28*(1), 25–28.

Idol, L. (1987a). A critical thinking map to improve content area comprehension of poor readers. *Remedial and Special Education, 8*(4), 28–40.

Idol, L. (1987b). Group story mapping: A comprehension strategy for both skilled and unskilled readers. *Journal of Learning Disabilities, 20,* 196–205.

Idol, L. (1997). Key questions related to building collaborative and inclusive schools. *Journal of Learning Disabilities, 30*(4), 384–394.

Idol, L., Nevin, A., & Paolucci-Whitcomb, P. (1999). *Models for curriculum-based assessment: A blueprint for learning.* Austin, TX: PRO-ED.

Igoa, C. (1995). *The inner world of the immigrant child.* New York: St. Martin's Press.

Institute on Community Integration. (n.d.). *Integration checklist: A guide to full inclusion of students with disabilities.* Minneapolis: Author.

Inwald, R. (1994). *Cap it off with a smile: A guide for making and keeping friends.* Kew Gardens, NY: Hilson Press.

Irvine, J. J. (1991), May). *Multicultural education: The promises and obstacles.* Paper presented at the Sixth Annual Benjamin Matteson Invitational Conference of the State University of New York at New Paltz, New Paltz, NY.

Irving Independent School District v. Tatro, 104 S. Ct. 3371, 82 L.Ed. 2d 664 (1984).

Isaacson, S., & Gleason, M. M. (1997). Mechanical obstacles to writing: What can teachers do to help students with learning problems? *Learning Disabilities Research and Practice, 12*(3), 188–194.

Isaacson, S., & Gleason, M. M. (1998, April). *Practical writing instruction for students with learning problems.* Presentation at the annual meeting of the Council for Exceptional Children, Minneapolis.

Jairrels, V. (1999). Cultural diversity: Implications for collaboration. *Intervention in School and Clinic, 34*(4), 236–238.

Jairrels, V., Brazil, N., & Patton, J. R. (1999). Incorporating popular literature into the curriculum for diverse learners. *Intervention in School and Clinic, 34*(5), 303–306.

Janney, R. E., Snell, M. E., Beers, M. K., & Raynes, M. (1995). Integrating students with moderate and severe disabilities in general education classes. *Exceptional Children, 61,* 425–439.

Janover, C. (1997). *Zipper: The kid with ADHD.* Bethesda, MD: Woodbine House.

Jayanthi, M., Bursuck, W., Epstein, M. H., & Polloway, E. A. (1997). Strategies for successful homework. *Teaching Exceptional Children, 30*(1), 4–7.

Jenkins, J. R., & Heinen, A. (1989). Students' preferences for service delivery: Pull-out, in-class, or integrated models. *Exceptional Children, 55,* 516–523.

Jenkins, J. R., Heliotis, J. D., Stein, M. L., & Haynes, M. C. (1987). Improving reading comprehension by using paragraph restatements. *Exceptional Children, 54,* 54–59.

Jitendra, A. K., Cole, C. L., Hoppes, M. K., & Wilson, B. (1998). Effects of a direct instruction main idea summarization program and self-monitoring on reading comprehension of middle school students with learning disabilities. *Reading and Writing Quarterly, 14*(4), 379–396.

Jitendra, A. K., Hoff, K., & Beck, M. M. (1999). Teaching middle school students with learning disabilities to solve word problems using a schema-based approach. *Remedial and Special Education, 20*(1), 50–64.

Jitendra, A. K., & Kameenui, E. J. (1993). Dynamic assessment as a compensatory assessment approach: A description and analysis. *Remedial and Special Education, 14*(5), 6–18.

Jochum, J., Curran, C., & Reetz, L. (1998). Creating individual educational portfolios in written language. *Reading and Writing Quarterly, 14*(3), 283–306.

Johanneson, A. S. (1999, Spring). Follow the stream. *Teaching Tolerance, 15,* 32–39.

Johns, B. H., & Carr, V. G. (1995). *Techniques for managing verbally and physically aggressive students.* Denver: Love.

Johnson, D. E., Bullock, C. C., & Ashton-Shaeffer, C. (1999). Families and leisure: A context for learning. *Teaching Exceptional Children, 30*(2), 30–34.

Johnson, D. W. (1988). *The power of positive interdependence.* Paper presented at the conference on Designing the Future Together: Cooperative Learning, Team Building and Collaboration at Work, New Paltz, NY.

Johnson, D. W., & Johnson, R. T. (1986). Mainstreaming and cooperative learning strategies. *Exceptional Children, 52,* 553–561.

Johnson, D. W., & Johnson, R. T. (1996). Peacemakers: Teaching students to resolve their own and schoolmates' conflicts. In E. L. Meyen, G. A. Vergason, & R. J. Whelan (Eds.), *Strategies for teaching exceptional children in inclusive settings* (pp. 311–329). Denver: Love.

Johnson, L. R., & Johnson, C. E. (1999). Teaching students to regulate their own behavior. *Teaching Exceptional Children, 31*(4), 6–10.

Johnston, C. A. (1998). Using the learning combination inventory. *Educational Leadership, 55*(4), 78–82.

Johnston, P., Allington, R., & Afflerbach, P. (1985). The congruence of classroom and remedial reading instruction. *Elementary School Journal, 83,* 465–477.

Jones, B. E., Clark, G. M., & Soltz, D. F. (1997). Characteristics and practices of sign language interpreters in inclusive education programs. *Exceptional Children, 63*(2), 257–268.

Jones, E. D., Southern, W. T., & Brigham, F. J. (1998). Curriculum-based assessment: Testing what is taught and teaching what is tested. *Intervention in School and Clinic, 33*(4), 239–249.

Jones, G. A., Thornton, C. A., & Toohey, M. A. (1985). A multioption program for learning basic addition facts: Case studies and an experimental report. *Journal of Learning Disabilities, 18,* 319–325.

Jones, V., & Jones, L. (1998). *Comprehensive classroom management* (5th ed.). Boston: Allyn & Bacon.

Jordan, L., Reyes-Blanes, M. E., Peel, B. B., Peel, H. A., & Lane, H. B. (1998). Developing teacher–parent partnerships across cultures: Effective parent conferences. *Intervention in School and Clinic, 33*(3), 141–147.

Jorgensen, C. M. (1995). Essential questions—inclusive answers. *Educational Leadership, 52*(4), 52–55.

Juster, N. (1963). *The dot and the line.* New York: Random House.

Kagan, S. (1990). The structural approach to cooperative learning. *Educational Leadership, 47*(4), 12–15.

Kagan, S. (1992). *Cooperative learning.* San Juan Capistrano, CA: Resources for Teachers.

Kameenui, E. (1996). Shakespeare and beginning reading: The readiness is all. *Teaching Exceptional Children, 28*(2), 77–81.

Kameenui, E., & Carnine, D. (1998). *Effective teaching strategies that accommodate diverse learners.* Upper Saddle River, NJ: Prentice Hall.

Kamps, D. M., Ellis, C., Mancina, C., & Greene, L. (1995). Peer-inclusive social skills groups for young children with behavioral risks. *Preventing School Failure, 39*(4), 10–15.

Kampwirth, T. J. (1999). *Collaborative consultation in the schools: Effective practices for students with learning and behavior problems.* Upper Saddle River, NJ: Prentice Hall.

Kaplan, J. S. (1994). Using novels about contemporary Judaism to help understand issues in cultural diversity. *The School Counselor, 41*(4), 287–295.

Karl, D. (1992, November). *The special education needs of children treated for cancer.* Paper presented at the meeting of the New York State Federation of Chapters of the Council for Exceptional Children, Albany, NY.

Karnes, M., Collins, D., Maheady, L., Harper, G. F., & Mallette, B. (1997). Using cooperative learning strategies to improve literacy skills in social studies. *Reading and Writing Quarterly: Overcoming Learning Difficulties, 13*(1), 37–51.

Karrison, J., & Carroll, M. K. (1991). Solving word problems. *Teaching Exceptional Children, 23*(4), 55–56.

Katisyannis, A., Landrum, T. J., & Vinton, L. (1997). Practical guidelines for monitoring treatment of attention-deficit/hyperactivity disorder. *Preventing School Failure, 41*(3), 131–136.

Katz, C. A., & Johnson-Kuby, S. A. (1996). Like portfolios for assessment. *Journal of Adolescent and Adult Literacy, 39*(6), 508–511.

Kavale, K. A., Hirshoren, A., & Forness, S. R. (1998). Meta-analytic validation of the Dunn and Dunn model of learning style preferences: A critique of what was Dunn. *Learning Disabilities Research and Practice, 13*(2), 75–80.

Kea, C. D. (1998). Focus on ethnic and minority concerns. *Council for Children with Behavioral Disorders Newsletter, 11*(4), 4–6.

Kearns, J. F., Kleinert, H. L., Clayton, J., Brudge, M., & Williams, R. (1998). Principal supports for inclusive assessment: A Kentucky story. *Teaching Exceptional Children, 31*(2), 16–23.

Kearns, J. F., Kleinert, H. L., & Kennedy, S. (1999). We need not exclude anyone. *Educational Leadership, 56*(6), 33–38.

Keefe, C. H. (1995a). Literature circles: Invitation to a reading and writing community. *LD Forum, 21*(1), 20–22.

Keefe, C. H. (1995b). Portfolios: Mirrors of learning. *Teaching Exceptional Children, 27*(2), 66–67.

Kehle, T. J., Clark, E., & Jenson, W. R. (1996). Interventions for students with traumatic brain injury: Managing behavioral disturbances. *Journal of Learning Disabilities, 29*(6), 633–642.

Kelker, K., Hecimovic, A., & LeRoy, C. H. (1994). Designing a classroom and school environment for students with AIDS. *Teaching Exceptional Children, 26*(4), 52–55.

Kellermeier, J. (1996, March). *Teaching science and mathematics from a multicultural and feminist perspective.* Paper presented at the meeting of the 10 counties math educators, State University of New York at New Paltz, New Paltz, NY.

Kelly, E. (1997). Movies—A unique and effective tool for special educators. *CEC Today, 3*(8), 12.

Kemp, K., Fister, S., & McLaughlin, P. J. (1995). Academic strategies for children with ADD. *Intervention in School and Clinic, 30*(4), 203–210.

Kennedy, C. H., & Itkonen, T. (1994). Some effects of regular class participation on the social contacts and social networks of high school students with severe disabilities. *Journal of the Association for Persons with Severe Handicaps, 19*(1), 1–10.

Kennedy, C. H., Shukla, S., & Fryxell, D. (1997). Comparing the effects of educational placement on the social relationships of intermediate school students with severe disabilities. *Exceptional Children, 64,* 31–47.

Kern, L., Dunlap, G., Clarke, S., & Childs, K. E. (1994). Student-assisted functional assessment interview. *Diagnostique, 19*(2–3), 29–39.

Kerwin, C., & Ponterotto, J. G. (1994). Counseling multiracial individuals and their families—don't believe all myths. *Guidepost, 36*(11), 9–11.

Kerwin, C., Ponterotto, J. G., Jackson, B. L., & Harris, A. (1993). Racial identity in biracial children: A qualitative investigation. *Journal of Counseling Psychology, 40*(2), 221–231.

Kibler, J. M. (1996). Latino voices in children's literature: Instructional approaches for developing cultural understanding in the classroom. In J. L. Flores (Ed.), *Children of la frontera: Binational efforts to serve Mexican migrant and immigrant students* (pp. 239–268). Charleston, WV: Clearinghouse on Rural Education and Small Schools.

Kindler, A. L. (1995). *Education of migrant children in the United States.* Washington, DC: National Clearinghouse for Bilingual Education at George Washington University.

King-Sears, M. E. (1999). Teacher and researcher co-design self-management content for an inclusive setting: Research training, intervention, and generalization effects on student performance. *Education and Training in Mental Retardation and Developmental Disabilities 34*(2), 134–156.

King-Sears, M. E., & Bonfils, K. A. (2000). Self-management instruction for middle school students with LD and ED. *Intervention in School and Clinic, 35*(2), 96–107.

King-Sears, M. E., Burgess, M., & Lawson, T. L. (1999). Applying curriculum-based assessment in inclusive settings. *Teaching Exceptional Children, 32*(1), 30–38.

King-Sears, M. E., & Carpenter, S. L. (1997). Teaching self-management for elementary students with developmental disabilities. *Innovations.* Washington, DC: American Association on Mental Retardation.

Kinnison, L. R., Hayes, C., & Acord, J. (1981). Evaluating student progress in mainstream classes. *Teaching Exceptional Children, 13,* 97–99.

Kirby, K. M. (1997). A school counselor's guide to working with children adopted after infancy: Jason's story. *Elementary School Guidance and Counseling, 31*(3), 226–238.

Kirschbaum, G., & Flanders, S. (1995). Successful inclusion practices. *Intervention in School and Clinic, 30*(5), 309–312.

Kishi, G. S., & Meyer, L. H. (1994). What children report and remember: A six-year follow-up of the effects of social contact between peers with and without severe disabilities. *Journal of the Association for Persons with Severe Handicaps, 19*(4), 277–289.

Klemm, W. R. (1998). Eight ways to get students more engaged in online conferences. *Technological Horizons in Education Journal, 26*(1), 62–64.

Kling, B. (2000). ASSERT yourself: Helping students of all ages develop self-advocacy skills. *Teaching Exceptional Children, 32*(3), 66–70.

Klingner, J. K., Vaughn, S., Hughes, M. T., Schumm, J. S., & Elbaum, B. (1998b). Outcomes for students with and without learning disabilities in inclusive classrooms. *Learning Disabilities Research and Practice, 13*(3), 153–161.

Klingner, J. K., Vaughn, S., Schumm, J. S., Cohen, P., & Forgan, J. W. (1998a). Inclusion or pull-out: Which do students prefer? *Journal of Learning Disabilities, 31*(2), 148–158.

Kluwin, T. N. (1996). Getting hearing and deaf students to write to each other through dialogue journals. *Teaching Exceptional Children, 28*(2), 50–53.

Knight, D., & Wadsworth, D. (1993). Physically challenged students. *Childhood Education, 69*(4), 211–215.

Knowlton, E. (1998). Considerations in the design of personalized curricular supports for students with developmental disabilities. *Education and Training in Mental Retardation and Developmental Disabilities, 33*(2), 95–107.

Kolar, K. A. (1996). Seating and wheeled mobility aids. In J. C. Galvin & M. J. Scherer (Eds.), *Evaluating, selecting, and using appropriate assistive technology* (pp. 61–76). Gaithersburg, MD: Aspen.

Kortering, L. J., & Braziel, P. M. (1999). Staying in school: The perspective of ninth-grade students. *Remedial and Special Education, 20*(2), 106–113.

Kovaleski, J. F., Gickling, E. E., Morrow, H., & Swank, P. R. (1999). High versus low implementation of instructional support teams: A case for maintaining program fidelity. *Remedial and Special Education, 20*(3), 170–183.

Kozol, J. (1991). *Savage inequalities: Children in American schools.* New York: Crown.

Kroeger, S. D., Leibold, C. K., & Ryan, B. (1999). Creating a sense of ownership in the IEP process. *Teaching Exceptional Children, 32*(1), 4–9.

Krynock, K., & Robb, L. (1999). Problem solved: How to coach cognition. *Educational Leadership, 57*(3), 29–32.

Krystal, S., (1999). The nurturing potential of service learning. *Educational Leadership, 56*(4), 58–61.

Kubina, R. M., & Cooper, J. O. (2000). Changing learning channels: An efficient strategy to facilitate instruction and learning. *Intervention in School and Clinic, 35*(3), 161–166.

Kucera, T. J. (1993). *Teaching chemistry to students with disabilities.* Washington, DC: American Chemical Society.

Kuhn, B. R., Allen, K. D., & Shriver, M. D. (1995). Behavioral management of children's seizure activity: Intervention guidelines for primary-care providers. *Clinical Pediatrics, 34,* 570–575.

Kurtz, L. A. (1994). Helpful writing hints. *Teaching Exceptional Children, 27*(1), 58–59.

LaBlance, G. R., Steckol, K. F., & Smith, V. L. (1994). Stuttering: The role of the classroom teacher. *Teaching Exceptional Children, 26*(2), 10–12.

Lachat, M. A. (1997). *What policymakers and school administrators need to know about assessment reform and English language learners.* Providence, RI: Northeast and Islands Regional Educational Laboratory at Brown University.

LaFromboise, T. D., & Graff-Low, K. (1989). American Indian children and adolescents. In J. Taylor Gibbs & L. Nahme Huang (Eds.), *Children of color: Psychological interventions with minority youth* (pp. 114–147). San Francisco: Jossey-Bass.

Lago-Delello, E. (1998). Classroom dynamics and the development of serious emotional disturbance. *Exceptional Children, 64*(4), 479–492.

Lambert, M. A. (1996). Mathematics textbooks, materials, and manipulatives. *LD Forum, 21*(2), 41–45, 33.

Landau, E. D., Epstein, S. E., & Stone, A. P. (1978). *The exceptional child through literature.* Upper Saddle River, NJ: Prentice Hall.

Landau, S., Milich, R., & Diener, M. B. (1998). Peer relations of children with attention-deficit hyperactivity disorder. *Reading and Writing Quarterly: Overcoming Learning Difficulties, 14*(1), 83–105.

Landerholm, E. (1990). The transdisciplinary team approach in infant intervention programs. *Teaching Exceptional Children, 22*(2), 66–70.

Langan, J. (1982). *Reading and study skills* (2nd ed.). New York: McGraw-Hill.

Langdon, H. W. (1989). Language disorder or difference? Assessing the language skills of Hispanic students. *Exceptional Children, 56,* 160–167.

Larry P. v. Riles, 495 F. Supp. 926 (N.D. Cal. 1979).

Larson, P. J., & Maag, J. W. (1998). Applying functional assessment in general education classrooms: Issues and recommendations. *Remedial and Special Education, 19*(6), 338–349.

Lassman, K. A., Jolivette, K., & Wehby, J. H. (1999). Using collaborative behavioral contracting. *Teaching Exceptional Children, 31*(4), 12–18.

Lau v. Nichols, 414 U.S. 563 (1974).

Laufenberg, C., & Perry, M. (1993, April). *Dealing with staff and family: Establishing guidelines for bereavement procedures when working with children with special health care needs.* Presentation at the annual meeting of the Council for Exceptional Children, San Antonio, TX.

Lawrence, M. (1994). The use of video technology in science teaching: A vehicle for alternative assessment. *Teaching and Change, 2*(1), 14–30.

Lawry, J. R., Storey, K., & Danko, C. D. (1993). Analyzing problem behaviors in the classroom: A case study of functional analysis. *Intervention in School and Clinic, 20,* 96–100.

Lazarus, B. D. (1996). Flexible skeletons: Guided notes for adolescents. *Teaching Exceptional Children, 28*(3), 36–40.

Lazarus, B. D. (1998). Say cheese: Using personal photographs as prompts. *Teaching Exceptional Children, 30*(6), 4–7.

Learning Resource Center. (n.d.). *Study skills handouts.* New Paltz: Learning Resource Center State University of New York at New Paltz.

Leary, W. E. (1995a, April 21). Young people who try suicide may be succeeding more often. *The New York Times,* A15.

Lebzelter, S., & Nowacek, E. J. (1999). Reading strategies for secondary students with mild disabilities. *Intervention in School and Clinic, 34*(4), 212–219.

Lee, F. R. (1994, January 15). Grappling with how to teach young speakers of black dialect. *The New York Times,* A1, D22.

Lee, O., & Fradd, S. H. (1998). Science for all, including students from non-English language backgrounds. *Educational Researcher, 27*(4), 12–21.

Leigh, J. E., & Lamorey, S. (1996). Contemporary issues education: Beyond traditional special education curricula. *Intervention in School and Clinic, 32*(1), 26–33.

LeLoup, J. W., & Ponterio, R. (1998). Using the Internet for foreign language learning. *The ERIC Review, 6*(1), 60–62.

Lennon, J., & McCartney, P. (1967). A little help from my friends. On *Sgt. Peppers lonely hearts club band* [record]. Hollywood, CA: Capitol Records.

Leon, R. E. (1991, March). *Mathematical word problems.* Paper presented at the New York State Association for Bilingual Education Conference, Tarrytown, NY.

Leroy, C. H., Powell, T. H., & Kelker, P. H. (1994). Children with disabilities and AIDS: Meeting our responsibilities in special education. *Teaching Exceptional Children, 26*(4), 37–44.

Lerro, M. (1994). Teaching adolescents about AIDS. *Teaching Exceptional Children, 26*(4), 49–51.

Levine, K., & Wharton, R. H. (1993). *Children with Prader-Willi syndrome: Information for school staff.* Roslyn Heights, NY: Visible Ink.

Levine, P., & Nourse, S. W. (1998). What follow-up studies say about postschool life for young men and women with learning disabilities: A critical look at the literature. *Journal of Learning Disabilities, 31*(3), 212–233.

Levy, S. (1999). The end of the never-ending line. *Educational Leadership, 56*(6), 74–77.

Lewis, S. (1999). Blindness and low vision. In A. Turnbull, R. Turnbull, M. Shank, & D. Leal (Eds.) *Exceptional lives: Special education in today's schools* (2nd ed.) (pp. 662–709). Upper Saddle River, NJ: Prentice Hall.

Lewis, T. J., Scott, T. M., & Sugai, G. (1994). The Problem Behavior Questionnaire: A teacher-based instrument to develop functional hypotheses of problem behavior in general education classrooms. *Diagnostique, 19*(2–3), 103–115.

Leyva, C. (1998, November). *Increasing intercultural competence in students while celebrating diversity in the biracial child.* Paper presented at the Council for Exceptional Children/Division on Diverse Exceptional Learners Symposium on Culturally and Linguistically Diverse Exceptional Learners, Washington, D.C.

Li, A. K. F. (1992). Peer relations and social skill training: Implications for multicultural classrooms. *The Journal of Educational Issues of Language Minority Students, 10,* 67–78.

Lichtenstein, S. (1995). Gender differences in the education and employment of young adults: Implications for special education. *Remedial and Special Education, 17*(1), 4–20.

Linan-Thompson, S., & Jean, R. E. (1997). Completing the parent participation puzzle: Accepting diversity. *Teaching Exceptional Children, 30*(2), 46–50.

Lind, M. (1998, August 16). The beige and the black. *The New York Times,* 38–39.

Linhart, B., & Klingman, M. (1976). Friends. On *The best of Buzzy Linhart* [record]. New York: Buddah Records.

Lipkin, A. (1992). *Strategies for the teacher using gay/lesbian-related materials in the high school classroom.* Cambridge, MA: Harvard Graduate School of Education.

Lloyd, J. W., Saltzman, N. J., & Kauffman, J. M. (1981). Predictable generalization in academic learning as a result of preskills and strategy training. *Learning Disability Quarterly, 4,* 203–216.

Lock, R. H. (1996). Adapting mathematics instruction in the general education classroom for students with mathematics disabilities. *LD Forum, 21*(2), 19–23.

Locust, C. (1994). *The Piki maker: Disabled American Indians, cultural beliefs, and traditional behaviors.* Tucson: Native America Research and Training Center at the University of Arizona.

Loechler, K. (1999). Frequently asked questions about ADHD and the answers from the Internet. *Teaching Exceptional Children, 31*(6), 12–18.

Logan, K. R., & Malone, D. M. (1998). Comparing instructional contexts of students with and without severe disabilities in general education classrooms. *Exceptional Children, 64*(3), 343–358.

Lombardi, T. P. (1995). Teachers develop their own learning strategies. *Teaching Exceptional Children, 27*(3), 52–55.

Longmuir, P. E., & Axelson, P. (1996). Assistive technology for recreation. In J. C. Galvin & M. J. Scherer (Eds.), *Evaluating, selecting, and using appropriate assistive technology* (pp. 162–197). Gaithersburg, MD: Aspen.

Longwill, A. W., & Kleinert, H. L. (1998). The unexpected benefits of high school peer tutoring. *Teaching Exceptional Children, 30*(4), 60–65.

Lopez-Reyna, N. A. (1996). The importance of meaningful contexts in bilingual special education: Moving to whole language. *Learning Disabilities Research and Practice, 11*(2), 120–131.

Lorber, N. M. (1973). Measuring the character of children's peer relations using the Ohio Social Acceptance Scale. *California Journal of Educational Research, 24,* 71–77.

Lovitt, T. C., & Cushing, S. (1999). Parents of youth with disabilities: Their perceptions of school programs. *Remedial and Special Education, 20*(3), 134–142.

Lovitt, T. C., & Horton, S. V. (1994). Strategies for adapting science textbooks for youth with learning disabilities. *Remedial and Special Education, 15*(2), 105–116.

Lovitt, T. C., Plavins, M., & Cushing, S. (1999). What do pupils with disabilities have to say about their experience in high school? *Remedial and Special Education, 20*(2), 67–76, 83.

Lowenbraun, S., Madge, S., & Affleck, J. (1990). Parental satisfaction with integrated class placements of special education and general education students. *Remedial and Special Education, 11,* 37–40, 36.

Lowenthal, B. (1995). Naturalistic language intervention in inclusive environments. *Intervention in School and Clinic, 31*(2), 114–118.

Lucas, T., Henze, R., & Donato, R. (1990). Promoting the success of Latino language-minority students: An exploratory study of six high schools. *Harvard Educational Review, 60,* 315–340.

Ludi, D. C., & Martin, L. (1995). Self-determination: The road to personal freedom. *Intervention in School and Clinic, 30*(3), 164–169.

Lyon, C. S., & Lagarde, R. (1997). Tokens for success: Using the graduated reinforcement system. *Teaching Exceptional Children, 29*(6), 52–57.

Maag, J. W., & Reid, R. (1998). Attention-deficit hyperactivity disorder in schools: Introduction. *Reading and Writing Quarterly: Overcoming Learning Difficulties, 14*(1), 5–7.

Maag, J. W. (2000). Managing resistance. *Intervention in School and Clinic, 35*(3), 131–140.

Maag, J. W., & Webber, J. (1995). Promoting children's social development in general education classrooms. *Preventing School Failure, 39*(3), 13–19.

MacArthur, C. A. (1996). Using technology to enhance the writing process of students with learning disabilities. *Journal of Learning Disabilities, 29*(4), 344–354.

MacArthur, C. A. (1998). From illegible to understandable: How word recognition and speech synthesis can help. *Teaching Exceptional Children, 30*(6), 66–71.

MacArthur, C. A. (1999). Overcoming barriers to writing: Computer support for basic writing skills. *Reading and Writing Quarterly: Overcoming Learning Difficulties, 15*(2), 169–192.

MacArthur, C. A., Graham, S., Haynes, J. B., & De La Paz, S. (1996). Spelling checkers and students with learning disabilities: Performance comparisons and impact on spelling. *The Journal of Special Education, 30*(1), 35–37.

MacArthur, C. A., Schwartz, S. S., & Graham, S. (1991). A model for writing instruction: Integrating word processing and strategy instruction into a process approach to writing. *Learning Disabilities Research and Practice, 6*(4), 230–236.

Maccini, P., & Hughes, C. A. (1997). Mathematics interventions for adolescents with learning disabilities. *Learning Disabilities Research and Practice, 12*(3), 168–176.

Macciomei, N. R. (1996). Loss and grief awareness: A "class book" project. *Teaching Exceptional Children, 28*(2), 72–73.

MacMillan, D. L., Gresham, F. M., & Bocian, K. M. (1998). Discrepancy between definitions of learning disabilities and school practices: An empirical investigation. *Journal of Learning Disabilities, 31*(4), 314–326.

Maheady, L., Harper, G. F., & Mallette, B. (1991). Peer-mediated instruction: A review of potential applications for special education. *Reading, Writing, and Learning Disabilities International, 7*, 75–103.

Majsterek, D. J. (1990). Writing disabilities: Is word processing the answer? *Intervention in School and Clinic, 26*(2), 93–97.

Making Friends. (n.d.). *Making friends.* Vancouver, British Columbia: Author.

Maldonado-Colon, E. (1990, October). *Successful strategies for enhancing language arts instruction for exceptional second language learners.* Paper presented at the Symposium on Culturally Diverse Exceptional Children, Albuquerque, NM.

Maldonado-Colon, E. (1991). Development of second language learners' linguistic and cognitive abilities. *The Journal of Educational Issues of Language Minority Students, 9*, 37–48.

Maldonado-Colon, E. (1995, April). *Second language learners in special education: Language framework for inclusive classrooms.* Paper presented at the international meeting of the Council for Exceptional Children, Indianapolis.

Male, M. (1994). *Technology for inclusion: Meeting the special needs of all students.* Boston: Allyn & Bacon.

Malian, I. M., & Love, L. (1998). Leaving high school: An ongoing transition study. *Teaching Exceptional Children, 30*(3), 4–10.

Mallette, B., Pomerantz, D., & Sacca, D. (1991, November). *Getting mainstreamed students with special needs to perform as well as their peers: Peer-mediated instructional strategies.* Paper presented at the meeting of the New York State Federation of Chapters of the Council for Exceptional Children, Buffalo, NY.

Maloney, M. (1994). How to avoid the discipline trap. *The Special Educator, Winter Index,* 1–4

Mandlebaum, L. H., Thompson, L., & VandenBroek, J. (1995, April). *Choosing and using multicultural children's literature.* Presentation at the annual meeting of the Council for Exceptional Children, Indianapolis.

Mangiardi, A. J. (1993). *A child with a hearing loss in your classroom? Don't panic.* Washington, DC: Alexander Graham Bell Association for the Deaf.

Mannix, D. (1992). *Life skills activities for special children.* West Nyack, NY: Center for Applied Research in Education.

Mannix, D. (1995). *Life skills activities for secondary students with special needs.* Nyack, NY: Center for Applied Research in Education.

Manset, G., & Semmel, M. I. (1997). Are inclusive programs for students with mild disabilities effective? A comparative review of model programs. *The Journal of Special Education, 31,* 155–180.

Manzo, A. (1969). The request procedure. *Journal of Reading, 13,* 123–126.

Marable, M. A., & Raimondi, S. L. (1995). Managing surface behaviors. *LD Forum, 20*(2), 45–47.

Marcos, K. M. (1998). Second language learning: Everyone can benefit. *The ERIC Review, 6*(1), 2–5.

Margolis, H. (1999). Lack of student motivation: A problem solving focus. *Channels, 13,* 18–19.

Margolis, H., & McGettigan, J. (1988). Managing resistance to instructional modifications in mainstreamed environments. *Remedial and Special Education, 9*(4), 15–21.

Marks, S. U., Schrader, C., & Levine, M. (1999). Paraeducator experiences in inclusive settings: Helping, hovering, or holding their own? *Exceptional Children, 65*(3), 315–328.

Marks, S. U., Schrader, C., Levine, M., Hagie, C., Longaker, T., Morales, M., & Peters, I. (1999). Social skills for social ills: Supporting the social skills development of adolescents with Asperger's syndrome. *Teaching Exceptional Children, 32*(2), 56–61.

Marr, M. B. (1997). Cooperative learning: A brief review. *Reading and Writing Quarterly: Overcoming Learning Difficulties, 13*(1), 7–20.

Marshall, R. M., Hynd, G. W., Handwerk, M. J., & Hall, J. (1997). Academic underachievement in ADHD subtypes. *Journal of Learning Disabilities, 30*(6), 635–642.

Marson, J. W. (1995, November). *Understanding 504 and its educational implications.* Presentation at the annual meeting of the New York State Chapter of the Council for Exceptional Children, Niagara Falls, NY.

Marston, D. (1996). A comparison of inclusion only, pull-out only, and combined service model for students with mild disabilities. *The Journal of Special Education, 30*(2), 121–132.

Martin, D. (1997, June 1). Disability culture: Eager to bite the hands that would feed them. *The New York Times,* 1, 6.

Martin, D. S. (1987). Reducing ethnocentrism. *Teaching Exceptional Children, 20*(1), 5–8.

Martin, J. E., Marshall, L. H., Maxson, L., & Jerman, P. (1996a). *Self-directed IEP: Student workbook* (2nd ed.). Longmont, CO: Sopris West.

Martin, J. E., Marshall, L. H., Maxson, L., & Jerman, P. (1996b). *Self-directed IEP: Teacher's manual* (2nd ed.). Longmont, CO: Sopris West.

Marzola, E. S. (1987). Using manipulatives in math instruction. *Journal of Reading, Writing and Learning Disabilities, 3,* 9–20.

Mason, S. A., & Egel, A. L. (1995). What does Amy like? Using a mini-reinforcer to increase student participation in instructional activities. *Teaching Exceptional Children, 28*(1), 42–45.

Mastropieri, M. A. (1988). Using the keyword method. *Teaching Exceptional Children, 20,* 4–8.

Mastropieri, M. A., & Scruggs, T. E. (1998). Enhancing school success with mnemonic strategies. *Intervention in School and Clinic, 33*(4), 201–208.

Mateer, C. A., Kerns, K. A., & Eso, K. L. (1996). Management of attention and memory disorders following traumatic brain injury. *Journal of Learning Disabilities, 29*(6), 618–632.

Mathes, P. G., Grek, M. L., Howard, J. K., Babyak, A. E., & Allen, S. H. (1999). Peer-assisted learning strategies for first-grade readers: A tool for preventing early reading failure. *Learning Disabilities Research and Practice, 14*(1), 50–60.

Matte, R. R., & Bolaski, J. A. (1998). Nonverbal learning disabilities: An overview. *Intervention in School and Clinic, 34*(1), 39–42.

Maxim, G. W. (1995). *Social studies and the elementary school child* (5th ed.). Upper Saddle River, NJ: Prentice Hall.

McAlister, K. M., Nelson, N. W., & Bahr, C. M. (1999). Perceptions of students with language and learning disabilities about writing process instruction. *Learning Disabilities Research and Practice, 14*(3), 159–172.

McCarty, H., & Chalmers, L. (1997). Bibliotherapy: Intervention and prevention. *Teaching Exceptional Children, 29*(6), 12–17.

McCarty, L. L. (1998, November). *Examining prereferral as a means of examining disproportionate representation.* Presentation at the Council for Exceptional Children/Division of Diverse Exceptional Learners Symposium on Culturally and Linguistically Diverse Exceptional Learners, Washington, D.C.

McConnell, M. E. (1999). Self-monitoring cueing, recording, and managing: Teaching students to manage their own behavior. *Teaching Exceptional Children, 32*(2), 14–21.

McConnell, M. E., Hilvitz, P. B., & Cox, C. J. (1998). Functional assessment: A systematic process for assessment and intervention in general and special education classrooms. *Intervention in School and Clinic, 34*(1), 19–20.

McDonald, L., Kysela, G., Martin, C., & Wheaton, S. (1996). The Hazeldean project. *Teaching Exceptional Children, 29*(2), 28–32.

McDonnell, A. P. (1993). Ethical considerations in teaching compliance to individuals with mental retardation. *Education and Training in Mental Retardation, 28*(1), 3–12.

McDonnell, J. (1998). Instruction for students with severe disabilities in general education settings. *Education and Training in Mental Retardation and Developmental Disabilities, 33*(3), 199–215.

McDougall, D. (1998). Research on self-management techniques used by students with disabilities in general education settings: A descriptive review. *Remedial and Special Education, 19*(5), 310–320.

McDougall, D., & Brady, M. P. (1998). Initiating and fading self-management interventions to increase math fluency in general education class. *Exceptional Children, 64*(2), 151–166.

McFadyen, G. M. (1996). Aids for hearing impairment and deafness. In J. C. Galvin & M. J. Scherer (Eds.), *Evaluating, selecting, and using appropriate assistive technology* (pp. 144–161). Gaithersburg, MD: Aspen.

McKenna, M. C., Reinking, D., Labbo, L. D., & Kieffer, R. D. (1999). The electronic transformation of literacy and its implications for the struggling reader. *Reading and Writing Quarterly: Overcoming Learning Difficulties, 15*(2), 111–126.

McKenzie, R. G., & Houk, C. S. (1993). Across the great divide: Transition from elementary to secondary settings for students with mild disabilities. *Teaching Exceptional Children, 25*(2), 16–20.

McLeod, B. (1994). Linguistic diversity and academic achievement. In B. McLeod (Ed.), *Language and learning: Educating linguistically diverse students* (pp. 9–44). Albany: State University of New York Press.

McLeskey, J., Henry, D., & Hodges, D. (1998). Inclusion: Where is it happening? *Teaching Exceptional Children, 31*(1), 4–10.

McLeskey, J., Henry, D., & Hodges, D. (1999). Inclusion: What progress is being made across disability categories? *Teaching Exceptional Children, 31*(3), 60–64.

McLoughlin, J. A., & Nall, M. (1995). Allergies and learning/behavioral disorders. *Intervention in School and Clinic, 29*(4), 198–207.

McNamara, B. E. (1996, November). *Bullying: Implications for special educators.* Presentation at the annual meeting of the New York Federation of Chapters of the Council for Exceptional Children, Albany, NY.

McNaughton, D., Hughes, C. A., & Clark, K. (1997). The effects of five proofreading conditions on the spelling performance of college students with learning disabilities. *Journal of Learning Disabilities, 30*(6), 643–651.

McNaughton, D., Hughes, C. A., & Ofiesh, N. (1997). Proofreading for students with learning disabilities: Integrating computer with strategy use. *Learning Disabilities Research and Practice, 12*(1), 16–28.

McNeil, J. H., & Fowler, S. A. (1996). Using story reading to encourage children's conversations. *Teaching Exceptional Children, 28*(4), 43–47.

McTighe, J. (1997). What happens between assessments? *Educational Leadership, 54*(4), 6–12.

Meese, R. L. (1997). Student fights: Proactive strategies for preventing and managing student conflicts. *Intervention in School and Clinic, 33*(1), 26–29, 35.

Meese, R. L. (1999). Teaching adopted students with disabilities: What teachers need to know. *Intervention in School and Clinic, 34*(4), 232–235.

Meier, F. E. (1992). *Competency-based instruction for teachers of students with special learning needs.* Boston: Allyn & Bacon.

Meltzer, L. J., & Roditi, B. (1994). *The student observation system.* Chelmsford, MA: Research ILD.

Meltzer, L. J., Roditi, B., Houser, R. F., & Perlman, M. (1998). Perceptions of academic strategies and competence in students with learning disabilities. *Journal of Learning Disabilities, 31*(5), 437–451.

Menchaca, V., & Ruiz-Escalante, J. (1995). *Instructional strategies for migrant students.* (ERIC Document Reproduction Service No. 388 491).

Mendez, G. (1991). Constructive controversy: The bilingual dilemma. *Cooperative Learning, 12*(1), 22–23.

Menkart, D. J. (1999). Deepening the meaning of heritage months. *Educational Leadership, 56*(7), 19–21.

Mental Retardation Institution. (1991). *Assessment and educational planning for students with severe disabilities.* Valhalla, NY: Author.

Mercer, C. D. (1987). *Students with learning disabilities* (3rd ed.). Upper Saddle River, NJ: Merrill/Prentice Hall.

Mercer, C. D. (1997). *Students with learning disabilities* (5th ed.). Upper Saddle River, NJ: Merrill/Prentice Hall.

Mercer, C. D., & Mercer, A. R. (1993). *Teaching students with learning problems* (4th ed.). Upper Saddle River, NJ: Merrill/Prentice Hall.

Mercer, C. D., & Miller, S. P. (1992). Teaching students with learning problems in math to acquire, understand, and apply basic math facts. *Remedial and Special Education, 13*(3), 19–35, 61.

Meyer, D. J., & Vadasy, P. F. (1994). *Sibshops: Workshops for siblings of children with special needs.* Baltimore: Paul H. Brookes.

Meyer, D. J., Vadasy, P. F., & Fewell, R. (1996). *Living with a brother or sister with special needs: A book for sibs* (2nd ed) Seattle: University of Washington Press.

Michael, R. J. (1992). Seizures: Teacher observations and record keeping. *Intervention in School and Clinic, 27*(4), 211–214.

Michael, R. J. (1995). *The educators guide to students with epilepsy.* Springfield, IL: Charles C. Thomas.

Midkiff, R. B., & Cramer, M. M. (1993). Stepping stones to mathematical understanding. *Arithmetic Teacher, 40,* 303–305.

Milem, M., & Garcia, M. (1996). Student critics, teacher models: Introducing process writing to high school students with learning disabilities. *Teaching Exceptional Children, 28*(3), 46–47.

Miller, D. (1997). Mentoring structures: Building a protective community. *Preventing School Failure, 41*(3), 105–109.

Miller, M., Miller, S. R., Wheeler, J., & Selinger, J. (1989). Can a single-classroom treatment approach change academic performance and behavioral characteristics in severely behaviorally disordered adolescents? An experimental inquiry. *Behavioral Disorders, 14*(4), 215–225.

Miller, S. P., & Hudson, P. (1994). Using structured parent groups to provide parental support. *Intervention in School and Clinic, 29*(3), 151–155.

Miller, S. P., Strawser, S., & Mercer, C. D. (1996). Promoting strategic math performance among students with learning disabilities. *LD Forum, 21*(2), 34–40.

Miller-Lachmann, L., & Taylor, L. S. (1995). *School for all: Educating children in a diverse society.* Albany, NY: Delmar.

Millman, J., & Pauk, W. (1969). *How to take tests.* New York: McGraw-Hill.

Mills v. Board of Education of the District of Columbia, 348 F. Supp. 866 (D.D.C., 1972).

Mills, P. E., Cole, K. N., Jenkins, J. R., & Dale, P. S. (1998). Effects of differing levels of inclusion on preschoolers with disabilities. *Exceptional Children, 65*(1), 79–90.

Mills, R. P. (1998). *Least restrictive environment implementation policy paper.* Albany, NY: State Education Department.

Miner, C. A., & Bates, P. E. (1997). The effect of person centered planning activities on the IEP/transition planning process. *Education and Training in Mental Retardation and Developmental Disabilities, 32*(2), 105–112.

Mitchell, M., Baab, B., Campbell-LaVoie, F., & Prion, S. (1992). *An innovative approach to mathematics: Mathematics of the environment.* San Francisco: School of Education, University of San Francisco.

Mittag, K. C., & Van Reusen, A. K. (1999). Learning estimation and other advanced mathematics concepts in an inclusive class. *Teaching Exceptional Children, 31*(6), 66–72.

Moll, L. C. (1992). Bilingual classroom studies and community analysis. *Education Researcher, 21*(2), 20–24.

Monda-Amaya, L. E., Dieker, L., & Reed, F. (1998). Preparing students with learning disabilities to participate in inclusive classrooms. *Learning Disabilities Research and Practice, 13*(3), 171–182.

Montague, M. (1997). Cognitive strategy instruction in mathematics for students with learning disabilities. *Journal of Learning Disabilities, 30*(2), 164–177.

Montgomery, W. (in press). *Literature discussion in the elementary school classroom: Developing cultural understanding.* Multicultural education.

Morgan, K. B. (1995). Creative phonics: A meaning-oriented reading program. *Intervention in School and Clinic, 30*(5), 287–291.

Morningstar, M. E. (1997). Critical issues in career development and employment preparation for adolescents with disabilities. *Remedial and Special Education, 18*(5), 307–320.

Munk, D. D., Bruckert, J., Call, D. T., Stoehrmann, T., & Randandt, E. (1998). Strategies for enhancing the performance of students with LD in inclusive science classes. *Intervention in School and Clinic, 34*(2), 73–78.

Murdick, N. L., Gartin, B. C., & Yalowitz, S. J. (1995, April). *Enhancing the effective inclusion of students with violent behaviors in the public schools.* Presentation at the annual meeting of the Council for Exceptional Children, Indianapolis.

Murdick, N. L., & Petch-Hogan, B. (1996). Inclusive classroom management: Using preintervention strategies. *Intervention in School and Clinic, 31*(3), 172–176.

Murray, M. (1991). The role of the classroom teacher. In G. L. Porter & D. Richler (Eds.), *Changing Canadian schools: Perspectives on disability and inclusion* (pp. 173–189). Toronto: Roeher Institute.

Murray-Seegert, C. (1989). *Nasty girls, thugs, and humans like us: Social relations between severely disabled and nondisabled students in high school.* Baltimore: Paul H. Brookes.

Murrow, E. R. (1960). *Harvest of shame.* New York: McGraw-Hill Films.

Muth, K. D. (1997). Using cooperative learning to improve reading and writing in mathematical problem solving. *Reading and Writing Quarterly: Overcoming Learning Difficulties, 13*(1), 71–82.

Nabuzoka, D., & Smith, P. K. (1995). Identification of expressions of emotions by children with and without learning disabilities. *Learning Disabilities Research and Practice, 10*(2), 91–101.

Nagata, D. K. (1989). Japanese American children and adolescents. In J. Taylor Gibbs & L. Nahme Huang (Eds.), *Children of color: Psychological interventions with minority youth* (pp. 67–113). San Francisco: Jossey-Bass.

Nagel, D. R., Schumaker, J. B., & Deshler, D. D. (1986). *The FIRST-Letter mnemonic strategy.* Lawrence: University of Kansas Institute for Research in Learning Disabilities.

Nahme Huang, L. (1989). Southeast Asian refugee children and adolescents. In J. Taylor Gibbs and L. Nahme Huang (Eds.), *Children of color: Psychological interventions with minority youth* (pp. 278–321). San Francisco: Jossey-Bass.

Nahme Huang, L., & Ying, Y. (1989). Chinese American children and adolescents. In J. Taylor Gibbs and L. Nahme Huang (Eds.), *Children of color: Psychological interventions with minority youth* (pp. 30–68). San Francisco: Jossey-Bass.

Nahmias, M. L. (1995). Communication and collaboration between home and school for students with ADD. *Intervention in School and Clinic, 30*(4), 241–247.

National Center for Educational Restructuring and Inclusion. (1995). *National study of inclusion.* New York: Author.

National Coalition of Advocates for Students. (1991). *New voices: Immigrant students in U.S. public schools.* Boston: Author.

National Coalition of Advocates for Students. (1993). *Achieving the dream: How communities and schools can improve education for immigrant students.* Boston: Author.

Nesbit, C. R., & Rogers, C. A. (1997). Using cooperative learning to improve reading and writing in science. *Reading and Writing Quarterly: Overcoming Learning Difficulties, 13*(1), 53–70.

New York State Education Department. (n.d.). *Guidelines for educational interpreting.* Albany, NY: Author.

New York State Education Department. (n.d.). *The identification and reporting of child abuse and maltreatment.* Albany, NY: Author.

Newby, T. J., Stepich, D. A., Lehman, J. D., & Russell, J. D. (1996). *Instructional technology for teaching and learning: Designing instruction, integrating computers, and using media.* Upper Saddle River, NJ: Merrill/Prentice Hall.

Nickelsburg, R. T. (1995, April). *Racing to excellence—On track or derailed?: Better style—Better teaching, better learning.* Presentation at the annual meeting of the Council for Exceptional Children, Indianapolis.

Nieto, S. (1996). *Affirming diversity* (2nd ed.). New York: Longman.

Niguidula, D. (1997). Picturing performance with digital portfolios. *Educational Leadership, 55*(3), 26–29.

Noble, L. S. (1997). The face of foster care. *Educational Leadership, 54*(7), 26–28.

Nolan, E. E., Volpe, R. J., Gadow, K. D., & Sprafkin, J. (1999). Developmental, gender, and comorbidity differences in clinically referred children with ADHD. *Journal of Emotional and Behavioral Disorders, 7*(1), 11–20.

Oberti v. Board of Education of the Borough of Clementon School District, 995 F.2d, 1009, 3rd Circuit, 1993.

Obiakor, F. E. (1999). Teacher expectations of minority exceptional learners: Impact on accuracy of self-concepts. *Exceptional Children, 66*(1), 39–53.

Obiakor, F. E., & Utley, C. A. (1997). Rethinking preservice preparation for teachers in the learning disabilities field: Workable multicultural strategies. *Learning Disabilities Research and Practice, 12*(2), 100–106.

Ochoa, S. H., Rivera, B. D., & Powell, M. P. (1997). Factors used to comply with the exclusionary clause with bilingual and limited-English-proficient pupils: Initial guidelines. *Learning Disabilities Research and Practice, 12*(3), 161–167.

Ochoa, T. A., Vasquez, L. R., & Gerber, M. M. (1999). New generation of computer-assisted learning tools for students with disabilities. *Intervention in School and Clinic, 34*(4), 251–254.

Odean, K. (1997). *Great books for girls.* New York: Ballantine Books.

Odom, S., Ostrosky, M., Peterson, C., Akellenger, A., Spicuzza, R., Chandler, L., McEvoy, M., & Favazza, P. (1993). *Play time/social time: Organizing your classroom to build interaction skills.* Tucson, AZ: Communication Skill Builders.

Office of Diversity Concerns. (1999). *Multicultural book reviews for K–12 educators.* Reston, VA: Council for Exceptional Children.

Okolo, C. M., Bahr, C. M., & Gardner, J. E. (1995). Increasing achievement motivation of elementary school students with mild disabilities. *Intervention in School and Clinic, 30*(5), 279–286.

Oldrieve, R. M. (1997). Success with reading and spelling. *Teaching Exceptional Children, 29*(4), 57–61.

Olympia, D., Andrews, D., Valum, J. L., & Jenson, W. R. (1993). *Team homework: Cooperative student management of daily homework.* Longmont, CO: Sopris West.

O'Malley, J. M., & Valdez Pierce, L. (1996). *Authentic assessment for English language learners: Practical approaches for teachers.* New York: Addison-Wesley.

O'Neil, J. (1999, April 6). A syndrome with a mix of skills and deficits. *The New York Times,* F1, F4.

O'Neill, R. E., Horner, R. H., Albin, R. W., Sprague, J. R., Storey, K., & Newton, J. S. (1997). *Functional assessment and program development for problem behavior* (2nd ed.). Pacific Grove, CA: Brooks/Cole.

Ortiz, A. A. (1997). Learning disabilities occurring concomitantly with linguistic differences. *Journal of Learning Disabilities, 30*(3), 321–332.

Ortiz, A. A., & Wilkinson, C. Y. (1989). Adapting IEPs for limited English proficient students. *Academic Therapy, 24,* 555–568.

Ortiz, A. A., & Wilkinson, C. Y. (1991). Assessment and intervention model for bilingual exceptional student (Aim for the Best). *Teacher Education and Special Education, 14*(1), 35–42.

Ortiz, A. A., & Yates, J. R. (1989). Staffing and the development of individualized educational programs for the bilingual exceptional student. In L. M. Baca & H. T. Cervantes (Eds.), *The bilingual special education interface* (2nd ed., pp. 183–203). Upper Saddle River, NJ: Merrill/Prentice Hall.

O'Shea, D. J. (1994). Modifying daily practices to bridge transitions. *Teaching Exceptional Children, 26*(4), 29–34.

Ostrosky, M. M., & Kaiser, A. P. (1991). Preschool classroom environments that promote communication. *Teaching Exceptional Children, 23*(4), 6–10.

Ostrow, W., & Ostrow, V. (1989). *All about asthma.* Morton Grove, IL: Albert Whitman & Co.

Oswald, D. P., Coutinho, M. J., Best, A. M., & Singh, N. N. (1999). Ethnic representation in special education: The influence of school-related economic and demographic variables. *The Journal of Special Education, 32*(4), 194–206.

Oxer, T., & Klevit, M. (1995, April). *Cooperative discipline: A positive management approach.* Presentation at the annual meeting of the Council for Exceptional Children, Indianapolis.

Packer, L. E. (1995). *Educating children with Tourette syndrome: Understanding and educating children with a neurobiological disorder.* Bayside, NY: Tourette Syndrome Association.

Padeliadu, S., & Zigmond, N. (1996). Perspectives of students with learning disabilities about special education placement. *Learning Disabilities Research and Practice, 11*(1), 15–23.

Palinscar, A. S., & Klenk, L. J. (1991). Learning dialogues to promote text comprehension. In B. Means & M. S. Knapp (Eds.), *Teaching advanced skills to educationally disadvantaged students—Final report* (pp. 20–34). Washington, DC: U.S. Department of Education.

Palinscar, A. S., Parecki, A. D., & McPhail, J. C. (1995). Friendship and literacy through literature. *Journal of Learning Disabilities, 28*(2), 503–510, 522.

Palmer, D. S., Borthwick-Duffy, S. A., & Widaman, K. (1998). Parent perceptions of inclusive practices for their children with significant cognitive disabilities. *Exceptional Children, 64,* 271–282.

Pancheri, C., & Prater, M. A. (1999). What teachers and parents should know about Ritalin. *Teaching Exceptional Children, 31*(4), 20–26.

Panchyshym, R., & Monroe, E. E. (1986). *Developing key concepts for solving word problems.* Baldwin, NY: Barnell Loft.

Pang, O. (1991). Teaching children about social issues: Kidpower. In C. Sleeter (Ed.), *Empowerment through multicultural education* (pp. 179–197). Albany: State University of New York Press.

Panyan, M. V., Hillman, S. A., & Liggett, A. M. (1997). The role of focus groups in evaluating and revising teacher education programs. *Teacher Education and Special Education, 20*(1), 37–46.

Parette, H. P. (1997). Assistive technology devices and services. *Education and Training in Mental Retardation and Developmental Disabilities, 32*(4), 267–280.

Parette, H. P., & Hourcade, J. J. (1986). Management strategies for orthopedically handicapped students. *Teaching Exceptional Children, 18,* 282–286.

Parish, T. S., Ohlsen, R. L., & Parish, J. G. (1978). A look at mainstreaming in light of children's attitudes toward the handicapped. *Perceptual and Motor Skills, 46,* 1019–1021.

Parmar, R. S., & Cawley, J. F. (1991). Challenging the routines and passivity that characterize instruction for children with mild handicaps. *Remedial and Special Education, 12*(5), 23–32, 43.

Parmar, R. S., Cawley, J. F., & Frazita, R. R. (1996). Word problem-solving by students with and without mild disabilities. *Teaching Exceptional Children, 26*(4), 16–21.

Parsons, M. B., & Reid, D. H. (1999). Training basic teaching skills to paraeducators of students with severe disabilities: A one-day program. *Teaching Exceptional Children, 31*(4), 48–54.

Patton, J. R., Cronin, M. E., Bassett, D. S., & Koppel, A. E. (1997). A life skills approach to mathematics instruction: Preparing students with learning disabilities for the real-life math demands of adulthood. *Journal of Learning Disabilities, 30*(2), 178–187.

Patton, P. L., de la Garza, B., & Harmon, C. (1997). Successful employment. *Teaching Exceptional Children, 29*(3), 4–10.

Paulsen, K. J. (1997). Curriculum-based measurement: Translating research into school-based practice. *Intervention in School and Clinic, 32*(3), 162–167.

Pauk, W. (1984). *How to study in college.* Boston: Houghton Mifflin.

Payne, T., & Brown, W. (1994). Cooperative discipline. *Intervention in School and Clinic, 29*(3), 133.

Peacock, C. A., & Gregory, K. C. (1998). *Sugar was my best food: Diabetes and me.* Morton Grove, IL: Albert Whitman & Co.

Pear, R. (1998, September 25). Black and Hispanic poverty falls, reducing overall rate for nation. *The New York Times,* A1, A25.

Peck, C. A., Carlson, P., & Helmstetter, E. (1992). Parent and teacher perceptions of outcomes for typically developing children enrolled in integrated early childhood programs: A statewide survey. *Journal of Early Intervention, 16,* 53–63.

Peck, C. A., Donaldson, J., & Pezzoli, M. (1990). Some benefits non-handicapped adolescents perceive for themselves from their social relationships with peers who have severe disabilities. *Journal of the Association for Persons with Severe Handicaps, 15*(4), 241–249.

Peckham, V. C. (1993). Children with cancer in the classroom. *Teaching Exceptional Children, 25*(1), 27–32.

Pedrotty Bryant, D., Ugel, N., Thompson, S., & Hamff, A. (1999). Instructional strategies for content-area reading instruction. *Intervention in School and Clinic, 34*(5), 293–302.

Pennsylvania Association for Retarded Children v. *Commonwealth of Pennsylvania,* 343 F. Supp. 279 (E.D. Pa., 1972).

Perl, J. (1995). Improving relationship skills for parent conferences. *Teaching Exceptional Children, 28*(1), 29–31.

Perritt, D. C. (1997). Can technology increase opportunities for migrant students? *NASSP Bulletin, 81*(5), 15–18.

Perry, L. A. (1997). Using wordless picture books with beginning readers (of any age). *Teaching Exceptional Children, 29*(3), 68–69.

Peters-Walters, S. (1998). Accessible web site design. *Teaching Exceptional Children, 30*(5), 42–47.

Phelps, B. R. (1995, April). *Practical solutions for functional problems in transitioning students with traumatic brain injuries.* Paper presented at the annual meeting of the Council for Exceptional Children, Indianapolis.

Phillips, L., Sapona, R. H., & Lubic, B. L. (1995). Developing partnerships in inclusive education: One school's approach. *Intervention in School and Clinic, 30*(5), 262–272.

Phillips, N. B., Hamlett, C. L., Fuchs, L. S., & Fuchs, D. (1993). Combining classwide curriculum-based measurement and peer tutoring to help general educators provide adaptive education. *Learning Disabilities Research and Practice, 8*(3), 148–156.

Pike, K., Compain, R., & Mumper, J. (1994). *Passport to literacy: Becoming readers and writers.* New York: HarperCollins.

Plank, B. (1992). *Disabled doesn't mean immobile: Adaptive aids for transportation: Matching disability, vehicle, and equipment.* Tampa, FL: Becky's Treasures.

Plata, M. (1993). Using Spanish-speaking interpreters in special education. *Remedial and Special Education, 14*(5), 19–24.

Plyler v. *Doe,* 457 U.S. 202 (1982).

Poland, S. (1995). Suicide intervention. In A. Thomas & J. Grimes (Eds.), *Best practices in school psychology—3* (pp. 459–468). Washington, DC: National Association of School Psychologists.

Pollack, R., & Schwartz, C. (1995). *The journey out: A guide for and about lesbian, gay, and bisexual teens.* New York: Puffin Books.

Pomplun, M. (1996). Cooperative groups: Alternative assessment for students with disabilities? *Journal of Special Education, 30*(1), 1–17.

Poolaw v. *Bishop,* 23IDELR 406, 9th Circuit, 1995.

Poteet, J. A., Choate, J. S., & Stewart, S. C. (1996). Performance assessment and special education: Practices and prospects. In E. L. Meyen, G. A. Vergason, & R. J. Whelan (Eds.), *Strategies for teaching exceptional children in inclusive settings* (pp. 209–242). Denver: Love.

Powell, T. H., & Gallagher, P. A. (1993). *Brothers and sisters: A special part of exceptional families.* Baltimore: Paul H. Brookes.

Powers, L. E., Sowers, J., Turner, A., Nesbitt, N., Knowles, A., & Ellison, R. (1996). Take Charge: A model for promoting self-determination among adolescents with challenges. In L. E. Powers, G. H. S. Singer, & J. Sowers (Eds.), *On the road to autonomy: Promoting self-competence for children and youth with disabilities* (pp. 291–322). Baltimore: Paul H. Brookes.

Prater, M. A. (1993). Teaching concepts: Procedures for the design and delivery of instruction. *Remedial and Special Education, 14*(5), 51–62.

Prater, M. A. (1998, April). *Using children's literature to teach about disabilities.* Presentation at the annual meeting of the Council for Exceptional Children, Minneapolis.

Prater, M. A. (2000). Using juvenile literature with portrayals of disabilities in your classroom. *Intervention in School and Clinic, 35*(3), 167–176.

Prater, M. A., Bruhl, S., & Serna, L. A. (1998). Acquiring social skills through cooperative learning and teacher-directed instruction. *Remedial and Special Education, 19*(3), 160–172.

Premack, D. (1959). Toward empirical behavior laws. *Psychological Review, 66*(4), 219–233.

Prendergast, D. E. (1995). Preparing for children who are medically fragile in educational programs. *Teaching Exceptional Children, 27*(2), 37–41.

Prescott, C., Rinard, B., Cockerill, J., & Baker, N. (1996). Science through workplace lenses. *Educational Leadership, 53*(8), 10–13.

Program Development Associates. (1995). *I belong out there.* Cicero, NY: Author.

Prom, M. (1999). Measuring perceptions about inclusion. *Teaching Exceptional Children, 31*(5), 38–42.

Pugach, M. C., & Johnson, L. J. (1995a). *Collaborative practitioners, collaborative schools.* Denver: Love.

Pugach, M. C., & Johnson, L. J. (1995b). Unlocking expertise among classroom teachers through structured dialogue: Extending research on peer collaboration. *Exceptional Children, 62*(2), 101–110.

Putnam, M. L. (1992). Characteristics of questions on tests administered by mainstream secondary classroom teachers. *Learning Disabilities Research and Practice, 7,* 129–136.

Raborn, D. T., & Daniel, M. J. (1999). Oobleck: A scientific encounter of the special education kind. *Teaching Exceptional Children, 31*(6), 32–40.

Radabaugh, M. T., & Yukish, J. F. (1982). *Curriculum and methods for the mildly handicapped.* Boston: Allyn & Bacon.

Rademacher, J. A. (2000). Involving students in assignment evaluation. *Intervention in School and Clinic, 35*(3), 151–156.

Rademacher, J. A., Callahan, K., & Pederson-Seelye, V. A. (1998). How do your classroom rules measure up?: Guidelines for developing an effective rule management routine. *Intervention in School and Clinic, 33*(5), 284–289.

Rademacher, J. A., Cowart, M., Sparks, J., & Chism, V. (1997). Planning high-quality assignments for diverse learners. *Preventing School Failure, 42*(1), 12–18.

Rafferty, Y. (1998). Meeting the educational needs of homeless children. *Educational Leadership, 55*(4), 48–52.

Ramirez, J. D. (1992). Executive summary. *Bilingual Research Journal, 16*(1&2), 1–63.

Ramirez, O. (1989). Mexican American children and adolescents. In J. Taylor Gibbs & L. Nahme Huang (Eds.), *Children of color: Psychological interventions with minority youth* (pp. 224–250). San Francisco: Jossey-Bass.

Rapport, M. J. K. (1996). Legal guidelines for the delivery of special health care services in schools. *Exceptional Children, 62*(6), 537–549.

Raschke, D. (1981). Designing reinforcement surveys—Let the student choose the reward. *Teaching Exceptional Children, 14,* 92–96.

Raschke, D., & Dedrick, C. (1986). An experience in frustration: Simulations approximating learning difficulties. *Teaching Exceptional Children, 18,* 266–271.

Raskind, M. H., & Higgins, E. L. (1998). Assistive technology for postsecondary students with learning disabilities: An overview. *Journal of Learning Disabilities, 31*(1), 27–40.

Raths, L., Harmin, M., & Simon, S. (1978). *Values and teaching* (2nd ed.). Upper Saddle River, NJ: Merrill/Prentice Hall.

Ravosa, C., & Jones, M. (1981). Best friends. In *Silver Burdett music teacher's edition 2* (p. 184). Morristown, NJ: Silver Burdett.

Raymond, E. B. (1994). Teaching social competence to reduce behavior problems. *LD Forum, 19*(3), 42–45.

Raymond, E. B. (1997, November). *Accommodating diversity, combating homophobia.* Presentation at the annual meeting of the New York Federation of Chapters of the Council for Exceptional Children, New York.

Raza, S. Y. (1997). Enhance your chances for success with students with attention-deficit/hyperactivity disorder (ADHD). *Intervention in School and Clinic, 33*(1), 56–57.

Razeghi, J. A. (1998). A first step toward solving the problem of special education dropouts: Infusing career education into the curriculum. *Intervention in School and Clinic, 33*(2), 148–156.

Reetz, L. J. (1995, April). *Portfolio assessment in inclusion settings: A shared responsibility.* Presentation at the annual meeting of the Council for Exceptional Children, Indianapolis.

Reichart, D. C., Lynch, E. C., Anderson, B. C., Svobodny, L. A., Di Cola, J. M., & Mercury, M. G. (1989). Parental perspectives on integrated preschool opportunities for children with handicaps and children without handicaps. *Journal of Early Intervention, 13,* 6–13.

Reichel, H. (1997, November). *Now we can do worksheets on the computer.* Presentation at the meeting of the New York State Federation of Chapters of the Council for Exceptional Children, New York.

Reid, D. K., & Button, L. J. (1995). Anna's story: Narratives of personal experience about being labeled learning disabled. *Journal of Learning Disabilities, 28*(10), 602–614.

Reid, R., & Maag, J. W. (1998). Functional assessment: A method for developing classroom-based accommodations and interventions for children with ADHD. *Reading and Writing Quarterly: Overcoming Learning Difficulties, 14*(1), 9–42.

Reiff, H. B., Gerber, P. J., & Ginsberg, R. (1996). What successful adults with learning disabilities can tell us about teaching children. *Teaching Exceptional Children, 29*(2), 10–16.

Reilly, L. (1999). Leapin' lizards: The fun of fitness for kids. *Teaching Exceptional Children, 31*(3), 82–85.

Rein, R. P. (1995, April). *How to modify tests for students with learning disabilities: Elementary and secondary.* Presentation at the annual meeting of the Council for Exceptional Children, Indianapolis.

Reis, S. M., Neu, T. W., & McGuire, J. M. (1997). Case studies of high-ability students with learning disabilities who have achieved. *Exceptional Children, 63*(4), 463–479.

Renick, M. J., & Harter, S. (1989). Impact of social comparisons on the developing self-perceptions of learning disabled students. *Journal of Educational Psychology, 81,* 631–638.

Research Press. (1992). *I can problem solve: An interpersonal cognitive problem-solving program.* Champaign, IL: Author.

Reynolds, C. J., & Salend, S. J. (1990). Teacher-directed and student-mediated textbook comprehension strategies. *Academic Therapy, 25,* 417–427.

Rhodes, R. L. (1996). Beyond our borders: Spanish-dominant migrant parents and the IEP process. *Rural and Special Education Quarterly, 15*(2), 19–22.

Ricci-Balich, J., & Behm, J. A. (1996). Pediatric rehabilitation nursing. In S. P. Hoeman (Ed.), *Rehabilitation nursing: Process and application* (pp. 660–682). St. Louis: Mosby.

Riccio, C. A., & Jemison, S. J. (1998). ADHD and emergent literacy: Influence of language factors. *Reading and Writing Quarterly: Overcoming Learning Difficulties, 14*(1), 43–58.

Rice, L. S., & Ortiz, A. A. (1994). Second language difference or learning disability? *LD Forum, 19*(2), 11–13.

Richards, J. C., & Gipe, J. P. (1993). Spelling lessons for gifted language arts students. *Teaching Exceptional Children, 25*(2), 12–15.

Rikhye, C. H., Gothelf, C. R., & Appell, M. W. (1989). A classroom environment checklist of students with dual sensory impairments. *Teaching Exceptional Children, 22*(1), 44–46.

Rivera, D. P. (1996). Effective mathematics instruction for students with learning disabilities: Introduction to the two-part series. *LD Forum, 21*(2), 4–9.

Rivera, D. P., & Deutsch-Smith, D. (1988). Using a demonstration strategy to teach middle school students with learning disabilities how to compute long division. *Journal of Learning Disabilities, 21*, 77–81.

Roberts, C., & Zubrick, S. (1992). Factors influencing the social status of children with mild academic disabilities in regular classrooms. *Exceptional Children, 59*(3), 192–202.

Roberts, P. L., & Kellough, R. D. (1996). *A guide for developing an interdisciplinary thematic unit.* Upper Saddle River, NJ: Merrill/Prentice Hall.

Roberts, R., & Mather, N. (1997). Orthographic dyslexia: The neglected subtype. *Learning Disabilities Practice, 12*(4), 236–250.

Roberts, R. L., & Baumberger, J. P. (1999). T.R.E.A.T.: A model for constructing counseling goals and objectives for students with special needs. *Intervention in School and Clinic, 43*(4), 239–243.

Robinson, S. M. (1999). Meeting the needs of students who are gifted and have learning disabilities. *Intervention in School and Clinic, 34*(4), 195–204.

Rock, E. E., Fessler, M. A., & Church, R. P. (1997). The concomitance of learning and emotional/behavioral disorders: A conceptual model. *Journal of Learning Disabilities, 30*(3), 245–263.

Rojewski, J. W. (1996). Occupational aspirations and early-career choice patterns of adolescents with and without learning disabilities. *Learning Disability Quarterly, 19*(2), 99–116.

Rojewski, J. W., Pollard, R. R., & Meers, G. D. (1992). Grading secondary vocational special education students with disabilities: A national perspective. *Exceptional Children, 59*(1), 68–76.

Romero, M., & Parirno, A. (1994). Planned alternation of languages (PAL): Language use and distribution in bilingual classrooms. *The Journal of Educational Issues of Language Minority Students, 13,* 137–161.

Rooney, K. J. (1995). Dyslexia revisited: History, educational philosophy, and clinical assessment applications. *Intervention in School and Clinic, 31*(1), 6–15.

Rop, C. (1998). Breaking the gender barrier in the physical sciences. *Educational Leadership, 55*(4), 58–60.

Rose, T. D. (1999). Middle school teachers: Using individualized instruction strategies. *Intervention in School and Clinic, 34*(3), 137–142, 162.

Rosenshine, B. V. (1986). Synthesis of research on explicit teaching. *Educational Leadership, 43*(7), 60–69.

Rosenthal, R. C. (1998, November). *The rights of immigrant children in public schools.* Presentation at the annual meeting of the New York State Migrant Education Conference, Syracuse, NY.

Rosenthal-Malek, A. L. (1997). Stop and think. Using metacognitive strategies to teach students social skills. *Teaching Exceptional Children, 29*(3), 29–31.

Rosenthal-Malek, A. L., & Greenspan, J. (1999). A student with diabetes is in my class. *Teaching Exceptional Children, 31*(3), 38–43.

Rowley-Kelley, F. L., & Reigel, D. H. (1993). *Teaching the student with spina bifida.* Baltimore: Paul H. Brookes.

Rudo, Z. H., Powell, D. S., & Dunlap, G. (1998). The effects of violence in the home on children's emotional, behavioral, and social functioning: A review of the literature. *Journal of Emotional and Behavioral Disorders, 6*(2), 94–113.

Rueda, R., & Garcia, E. (1997). Do portfolios make a difference for diverse students? The influence of type of data on making instructional decisions. *Learning Disabilities Research and Practice, 12*(2), 114–122.

Ruef, M. B., Higgins, C., Glaeser, B. J. C., & Patnode, M. (1998). Positive behavioral support: Strategies for teachers. *Intervention in School and Clinic, 34*(1), 21–32.

Ruiz, N. T., Rueda, R., Figueroa, R. A., & Boothroyd, M. (1995). Bilingual special education teachers' shifting paradigms: Complex responses to educational reform. *Journal of Learning Disabilities, 28*(10), 622–635.

Russo, J. (1997, November). *The school's role in demystifying the stereotypes of gay/lesbian headed families.* Presentation at the annual meeting of the New York Federation of Chapters of the Council for Exceptional Children, New York.

Rutledge, M. (1997). Reading the subtext on gender. *Educational Leadership, 54*(7), 71–73.

Ryndak, D. L., Downing, J. E., Jacqueline, L. R., & Morrison, A. P. (1995). Parents' perceptions after inclusion of their child with moderate or severe disabilities in general education settings. *Journal of the Association for Persons with Severe Handicaps, 20,* 147–157.

Sabornie, E. J., & Beard, G. H. (1990). Teaching social skills to students with mild handicaps. *Teaching Exceptional Children, 22,* 35–38.

Sacramento City Unified School District, Board of Education v. Holland, 14F.3d, 1398, 9th Circuit, 1994.

Sadker, M. P., & Sadker, D. (1994). *Failing at fairness: How America's schools cheat girls.* New York: Scribner.

Safran, J. S., & Safran, S. P. (1985b). Organizing communication for the LD teacher. *Academic Therapy, 20,* 427–435.

Safran, S. P. (1998). Disability portrayal in film: Reflecting the past, directing the future. *Exceptional Children, 64*(2), 227–238.

Safran, S. P. (2000). Using movies to teach students about disabilities. *Teaching Exceptional Children, 32*(3), 44–47.

Saint-Laurent, L., Dionne, J., Giasson, J., Royer, E., Simard, C., & Pierard, B. (1998). Academic achievement effects of an in-class service model on students with and without disabilities. *Exceptional Children, 64,* 239–253.

Saint-Laurent, L., Giasson, J., & Couture, C. (1997). Parents + children + reading activities = emergent literacy. *Teaching Exceptional Children, 30*(2), 52–56.

Sale, P., & Carey, D. M. (1995). The sociometric status of students with disabilities in a full-inclusion school. *Exceptional Children, 62*(1), 6–19.

Salembier, G. B., & Cheng, L. C. (1997). SCUBA-DIVE into reading. *Teaching Exceptional Children, 29*(6), 68–70.

Salend, S. J. (1995). Using videocassette recorder technology in special education classrooms. *Teaching Exceptional Children, 27*(3), 4–9.

Salend, S. J. (1997). What about our schools, our languages. *Teaching Exceptional Children, 29*(4), 38–41.

Salend, S. J., & Allen, E. M. (1985). A comparison of self-managed response-cost systems on learning disabled children. *Journal of School Psychology, 23,* 59–67.

Salend, S. J., Dorney, J. A., & Mazo, M. (1997). The roles of bilingual special educators in creating inclusive classrooms. *Remedial and Special Education, 16*(5), 271–278.

Salend, S. J., & Duhaney, L. G. (1999). The impact of inclusion on students with and without disabilities and their educators. *Remedial and Special Education, 20*(2), 114–126.

Salend, S. J., Johansen, M., Mumper, J., Chase, A. S., Pike, K. M., & Dorney, J. A. (1997). Cooperative teaching: The voices of two teachers. *Remedial and Special Education, 18*(1), 3–11.

Salend, S. J., & Lamb, E. M. (1986). The effectiveness of a group-managed interdependent contingency system. *Learning Disability Quarterly, 9,* 268–274.

Salend, S. J., & Longo, M. (1994). The roles of the educational interpreter in mainstreaming. *Teaching Exceptional Children, 26*(4), 22–28.

Salend, S. J., Reeder, E., Katz, N., & Russell, T. (1992). The effects of a dependent group-evaluation system. *Education and Training of Children, 15*(1), 32–42.

Salend, S. J., & Schobel, J. (1981). Coping with name-calling in the mainstreamed setting. *Educational Unlimited, 3,* 36–37.

Salend, S. J., Whittaker, C. R., Raab, S., & Giek, K. (1991). Using a self-evaluation system as a group contingency. *Journal of School Psychology, 29,* 319–329.

Salisbury, C. L., Evans, I. M., & Palombaro, M. M. (1997). Collaborative problem-solving to promote the inclusion of young children with significant disabilities in primary grades. *Exceptional Children, 63*(2), 195–209.

Salisbury, C. L., Gallucci, C., Palombaro, M. M., & Peck, C. A. (1995). Strategies that promote social relations among elementary students with and without severe disabilities in inclusive schools. *Exceptional Children, 62*(2), 125–137.

Sanacore, J. (1999). Encouraging children to make choices about their literacy learning. *Intervention in School and Clinic, 35*(1), 38–42.

Sander, N. (1993). *So you have asthma too!* Research Triangle, NC: Allen & Hanburys.

Sandler, A. G. (1998). Grandparents of children with disabilities: A closer look. *Education and Training in Mental Retardation and Developmental Disabilities, 33*(4), 350–356.

Sands, D. J., Adams, L., & Stout, D. M. (1995). A statewide exploration of the nature and use of curriculum in special education. *Exceptional Children, 62*(1), 68–83.

Sanger, D. E. (1999, July 9). Big racial disparity persists in Internet use. *The New York Times,* A12.

Santos, K. E., & Rettig, M. D. (1999). Going on the block: Meeting the needs of students with disabilities in high schools with block scheduling. *Teaching Exceptional Children, 31*(3), 54–59.

Santos, R. M., Fowler, S. A., Corso, R. M., & Bruns, D. (2000). Acceptance, acknowledgment and adaptability: Selecting culturally and linguistically appropriate early childhood materials. *Teaching Exceptional Children, 32*(3), 30–37.

Sapon-Shevin, M. (1999). *Because we can change the world: A practical guide to building cooperative, inclusive, and classroom communities.* Boston: Allyn & Bacon.

Sarouphim, K. M. (1999). Discovering multiple intelligence through a performance based assessment: Consistency with independent ratings. *Exceptional Children, 65*(2), 151–161.

Sasso, G. M., Peck, J., & Garrison-Harrell, L. (1998). Social interaction setting events: Experimental analysis of contextual variables. *Behavioral Disorders, 24*(1), 34–43.

Savage, T. V., & Armstrong, D. G. (1996). *Effective teaching in elementary social studies* (3rd. ed.). Upper Saddle River, NJ: Merrill/Prentice Hall.

Scanlon, D. J., Deshler, D. D., & Schumaker, J. B. (1996). Can a strategy be taught and learned in secondary inclusive classrooms? *Learning Disabilities Research and Practice, 11*(1), 41–57.

Schaffner, C. B., & Buswell, B. E. (1992). *Connecting students: A guide to thoughtful friendship facilitation for educators and families.* Colorado Springs, CO: Peak Parent Center.

Schemo, D. J. (1994a, March 16). Facing big-city problems, LI suburbs try to adapt. *The New York Times,* A1, B4.

Schemo, D. J. (1994b, March 17). Persistent racial segregation mars suburbs' green dream. *The New York Times,* A1, B6.

Scheuermann, B., Jacobs, W. R., McCall, C., & Knies, W. C. (1994). The personal spelling dictionary: An adaptive approach to reducing the spelling hurdle in written language. *Intervention in School and Clinic, 29*(5), 292–299.

Scheuermann, B., & Webber, J. (1999, April). *Writing behavioral intervention plans that reflect positive behavioral supports.* Presentation at the annual meeting of the Council for Exceptional Children, Charlotte, NC.

Schiff-Meyers, N. B., Djukic, J., McGovern-Lawler, J., & Perez, J. (1993). Assessment considerations in the evaluation of second-language learners: A case study. *Exceptional Children, 60*(3), 237–248.

Schirmer, B. R. (1997). Boosting reading success. *Teaching Exceptional Children, 30*(1), 52–55.

Schirmer, B. R. (1999). Hearing loss. In A. Turnbull, R. Turnbull, M. Shank, & D. Leal (Eds.), *Exceptional lives: Special education in today's schools* (2nd ed., pp. 620–660). Upper Saddle River, NJ: Prentice Hall.

Schirmer, B. R., Bailey, J., & Fitzgerald, S. M. (1999). Using a writing assessment rubric for writing development of children who are deaf. *Exceptional Children, 65*(3), 383–397.

Schleien, S. J., Ray, M. T., & Green, F. P. (1997). *Community recreation and people with disabilities: Strategies for inclusion.* Baltimore: Paul H. Brookes.

Schloss, P. J. (1986). Sequential prompt instruction for mildly handicapped learners. *Teaching Exceptional Children, 18,* 181–184.

Schmid, R. E. (1998). Three steps to self-discipline. *Teaching Exceptional Children, 30*(4), 36–39.

Schniedewind, N., & Davidson, E. (1997). *Open minds to equality: A sourcebook of learning activities to affirm diversity and promote equity* (2nd ed.). Boston: Allyn & Bacon.

Schnur, B. (1999). A newcomer's high school. *Educational Leadership, 56*(7), 50–52.

Schoenbrodt, L., Kumin, L., & Sloan, J. M. (1997). Learning disabilities existing concomitantly with communication disorder. *Journal of Learning Disabilities, 30*(3), 264–281.

School Board of Nassau County, Florida et al. v. *Arline,* 480 U.S. 273 (1987).

Schorr, J. (1997, January 2). Give Oakland's schools a break. *The New York Times,* A19.

Schorr, L. B. (1988). *Within our reach.* New York: Doubleday.

Schrag, J., & Burnette, J. (1994). Inclusive schools. *Teaching Exceptional Children, 26*(3), 64–68.

Schroeder-Davis, S. (1994). Giftedness: A double-edged sword. *Book Links, 3*(4), 25–28.

Schrumpf, F., Crawford, D., & Usadel, H. C. (1991). *Peer mediation: Conflict resolution in schools.* Champaign, IL: Research Press.

Schulz, E. G., & Edwards, E. G. (1997). Stimulant medication management of students with attention deficit hyperactivity disorder: What educators need to know. *Teacher Education and Special Education, 20*(2), 170–178.

Schumaker, J. B., Denton, P. H., & Deshler, D. D. (1984). *The paraphrasing strategy.* Lawrence: University of Kansas Press.

Schumaker, J. B., Deshler, D. D., Alley, G. R., & Warner, M. M. (1983). Toward the development of an intervention model for learning disabled adolescents: The University of Kansas Institute. *Exceptional Education Quarterly, 4*, 45–74.

Schumaker, J. B., Deshler, D. D., Denton, P. H., Alley, G. R., Clark, F. L., & Warner, M. M. (1982). Multipass: A learning strategy for improving reading comprehension. *Learning Disability Quarterly, 5*, 295–304.

Schumaker, J. B., Deshler, D. D., Nolan, S. M., & Alley, G. R. (1994). *The self-questioning strategy.* Lawrence: University of Kansas.

Schumaker, J. B., Nolan, S. M., & Deshler, D. (1985). *Learning strategies curriculum: The error monitoring strategy.* Lawrence: University of Kansas Press.

Schwartz, B. (1995, December 19). American inequality: Its history and scary future. *The New York Times*, A25.

Schwartz, E. M. (1995, April). *Inclusion is not an illusion: Awareness leads to understanding.* Presentation at the annual meeting of the Council for Exceptional Children, Indianapolis.

Schwarz, S. P. (1995). *Dressing tips and clothing resources for making life easier.* Madison, WI: Author.

Schweinhart, L., & Weikart, D. (1993). *The High/Scope Perry preschool project.* Ypsilanti, MI: High/Scope Educational Research Foundation.

Scieszka, J. (1995). *Math curse.* New York: Viking Press.

Scott, B. J., Vitale, M. R., & Masten, W. G. (1998). Implementing instructional adaptations for students with disabilities in inclusive classrooms: A literature review. *Remedial and Special Education, 19*(2), 106–119.

Scott, P. B., & Raborn, D. T. (1996). Realizing the gifts of diversity among students with learning disabilities. *LD Forum, 21*(2), 10–18.

Searcy, S. (1996). Friendship interventions for the integration of children and youth with learning and behavior problems. *Preventing School Failure, 40*(3), 131–134.

Searcy, S., Lee-Lawson, C., & Trombino, B. (1995). Mentoring new leadership roles for parents of children with disabilities. *Remedial and Special Education, 16*(5), 307–314.

Seattle School District No 1 v. B. S., 82 F.3d 1493 (9th Cir. 1996).

Secada, W. G., & De La Cruz, Y. (1996). Teaching mathematics for understanding to bilingual students. In J. L. Flores (Ed.), *Children of la frontera: Binational efforts to serve Mexican migrant and immigrant students* (pp. 285–308). Charleston, WV: Clearinghouse on Rural Education and Small Schools.

Seidel, J., & Vaughn, S. (1991). Social alienation and the learning disabled school dropout. *Learning Disabilities Research and Practice, 6*, 152–157.

Seligman, M., Goodwin, G., Paschal, K., Applegate, A., & Lehman, L. (1997). Grandparents of children with disabilities: Perceived levels of support. *Education and Training in Mental Retardation and Developmental Disabilities, 32*(4), 293–303.

Semmel, M. I., Abernathy, T. V., Butera, G., & Lesar, S. (1991). Teacher perceptions of the regular education initiative. *Exceptional Children, 58*, 9–23.

Serna, L. A., & Lau-Smith, J. (1995). Learning with purpose: Self-determination skills for students who are at risk for school and community failure. *Intervention in School and Clinic, 30*(3), 142–146.

Sexton, M., Harris, K. R., & Graham, S. (1998). Self-regulated strategy development and the writing process: Effects on essay writing and attributions. *Exceptional Children, 64*(3), 295–311.

Shank, K. S., & Hooser, C. M. (1999, April). *Curriculum adaptations in general education settings: Creating effective learning environments for all students.* Presentation at the annual meeting of the Council for Exceptional Children, Charlotte, NC.

Sharpe, M. N., York, J. L., & Knight, J. (1994). Effects of inclusion on the academic performance of classmates without disabilities. *Remedial and Special Education, 15*(5), 281–287.

Shields, J. M., & Heron, T. E. (1989). Teaching organizational skills to students with learning disabilities. *Teaching Exceptional Children, 21*, 8–13.

Shinn, M. R., Powell-Smith, K. A., Good, R. H., & Baker, S. (1997). The effects of reintegration into general education reading instruction for students with mild disabilities. *Exceptional Children, 64*, 59–79.

Sicley, D. (1993). Effective methods of communication: Practical interventions for classroom teachers. *Intervention in School and Clinic, 29*(2), 105–108.

Siegel-Causey, E., & Allinder, R. M. (1998). Using alternative assessment for students with severe disabilities: Alignment with best practices. *Education and Training in Mental Retardation and Developmental Disabilities, 33*(2), 168–178.

Siegel-Causey, E., McMorris, C., McGowen, S., & Sands-Buss, S. (1998). In junior high you take science: Including a student with severe disabilities in an academic class. *Teaching Exceptional Children, 31*(1), 66–72.

Sileo, T. W., & Prater, M. A. (1998). Creating classroom environments that address the linguistic and cultural backgrounds of students with disabilities: An Asian Pacific American perspective. *Remedial and Special Education, 19*(6), 323–337.

Simon, S., Howe, L., & Kirschenbaum, H. (1972). *Values clarification: A handbook of practical strategies for teachers and students.* New York: Hart.

Sinclair, E. (1998). Head Start children at risk: Relationship of prenatal drug exposure to identification of special needs and subsequent special education kindergarten placement. *Behavioral Disorders, 23*(2), 125–133.

Sinclair, M. F., Christenson, S. L., Evelo, D. L., & Hurley, C. M. (1998). Dropout prevention for youth with disabilities: Efficacy of a sustained school engagement procedure. *Exceptional Children, 65*(1), 7–21.

Siperstein, G. N., & Leffert, J. S. (1999). Managing limited resources: Do children with learning problems share? *Exceptional Children, 65*(2), 187–199.

Sirvis, B. (1988). Students with special health care needs. *Teaching Exceptional Children, 20*, 40–44.

Skutch, R. (1995). *Who's in the family?* Berkeley, CA: Tricycle Press.

Slapin, B., Seale, D., & Gonzales, R. (1992). *How to tell the difference.* Philadelphia: New Society Publishers.

Slavin, R. E. (1990). *Cooperative learning: Theory, research, and practice.* Upper Saddle River, NJ: Prentice Hall.

Slavin, R. E. (1998). Can education reduce social inequity? *Educational Leadership, 55*(4), 6–10.

Slavin, R. E., Madden, N. A., & Leavey, M. (1984). Effects of cooperative learning and individualized instruction on mainstreamed students. *Exceptional Children, 50,* 434–443.

Slavin, R. E., Madden, N. A., & Stevens, R. J. (1990). Cooperative learning models for the 3 R's. *Educational Leadership, 47*(4), 22–28.

Sleeter, C. E., & Grant, C. A., (1994). *Making choices for multicultural education: Five approaches to race, class, and gender.* Upper Saddle River, NJ: Prentice Hall.

Smaile, C. (1998, April). *Multicultural summit.* Presentation at the meeting of the Council for Exceptional Children, Minneapolis.

Smead, V. S. (1999). Personal accounts of exceptionality: An untapped resource for child service professionals. *Intervention in School and Clinic, 35*(2), 79–86, 107.

Smith, D. D., & Lovitt, T. C. (1982). *The computational arithmetic program.* Austin, TX: PRO-ED.

Smith, D. J. (1997). Mental retardation as an educational construct: Time for a new shared view? *Education and Training in Mental Retardation and Developmental Disabilities, 32*(3), 167–173.

Smith, G. J., Edelen-Smith, P. J., & Stodden, R. A. (1995). How to avoid seven pitfalls of systematic planning: A school and community plan for transition. *Teaching Exceptional Children, 27*(4), 42–47.

Smith, S., Boone, R., & Higgins, K. (1998). Expanding the writing process to the Web. *Teaching Exceptional Children, 30*(5), 22–26.

Smithson, I. (1990). Introduction: Investigating gender, power, and pedagogy. In S. L. Gabriel & I. Smithson (Eds.), *Gender in the classroom: Power and pedagogy* (pp. 1–27). Chicago: University of Illinois Press.

Snyder, E. P., & Shapiro, E. S. (1997). Teaching students with emotional/behavioral disorders the skills to participate in the development of their own IEPs. *Behavioral Disorders, 22*(4), 246–259.

Soodak, L. C., Podell, D. M., & Lehman, L. R. (1998). Teacher, student, and school attributes as predictors of teachers' responses to inclusion. *The Journal of Special Education, 31,* 480–497.

Soska, M. (1994). Educational technology enhances the LEP classroom. *Forum, 17*(5), 1, 4–5.

Spector, S., Decker, K., & Shaw, S. F. (1991). Independence and responsibility: An LD resource room at South Windsor High School. *Intervention in School and Clinic, 26,* 238–245.

Spiegel, G. L., Cutler, S. K., & Yetter, C. E. (1996). What every teacher should know about epilepsy. *Intervention in School and Clinic, 32*(1), 34–38.

Sprague, J. R., & Horner, R. H. (1990). Easy does it: Preventing challenging behaviors. *Teaching Exceptional Children, 23*(1), 13–15.

SRI International. (1993). *Traversing the mainstream: Regular education and students with disabilities in secondary school.* A report from the National Longitudinal Transition Study of Special Education Students. Menlo Park, CA: SRI International.

Stahl, S. A. (1998). Teaching children with reading problems to decode: Phonics and 'not-phonics' instruction. *Reading and Writing Quarterly: Overcoming Learning Difficulties, 14*(2), 165–188.

Stainback, S., Stainback, W., East, K., & Sapon-Shevin, M. (1994). A commentary on inclusion and the development of a positive self-identity by people with disabilities. *Exceptional Children, 60*(6), 486–490.

Stainback, W., & Stainback, S., & Wilkinson, A. (1992). Encouraging peer supports and friendships. *Teaching Exceptional Children, 24*(2), 6–11.

Stanovich, P. J. (1999). Conversations about inclusion. *Teaching Exceptional Children, 31*(6), 54–58.

Staub, D., Schwartz, I. S., Galluci, C., & Peck, C. A. (1994). Four portraits of friendship at an inclusive school. *Journal of the Association for Persons with Severe Handicaps, 19*(4), 314–325.

Stein, M., Carnine, D., & Dixon, R. (1998). Direct instruction: Integrating curriculum design and effective teaching practice. *Intervention in School and Clinic, 33*(4), 227–234.

Stein, N., & Sjostrom, L. (1994). *Flirting or hurting? A teacher's guide to student sexual harassment in grades 6–12.* Washington, DC: National Education Association.

Steinberg, J. (1998, March 19). Reading experts suggest teachers mix 2 methods. *The New York Times,* A1, A17.

Stephens, K. R., & Karnes, F. A. (2000). State definitions for the gifted and talented revisited. *Exceptional Children, 66*(2), 219–238.

Stern, C. (1965). *Structural arithmetic.* Boston: Houghton Mifflin.

Sternberg, R. J. (1996). Investing in creativity: Many happy returns. *Educational Leadership, 53*(4), 80–84.

Stewart, R. A., & Cross, T. L. (1991). The effect of marginal gloss on reading comprehension and retention. *Journal of Reading, 35,* 4–12.

Stiggins, R. J. (1997). *Student-centered classroom assessment* (2nd ed.). Upper Saddle River, NJ: Merrill/Prentice Hall.

Stolberg, S. G. (1998, June 29). Eyes shut, black America is being ravaged by AIDS. *The New York Times,* A1, A12.

Stoll, C. (1995). *Silicon snakeoil.* New York: Doubleday.

Stormont-Spurgin, M. (1997). I lost my homework: Strategies for improving organization in students with ADHD. *Intervention in School and Clinic, 32*(5), 270–274.

Stough, L. M., & Baker, L. (1999). Identifying depression in students with mental retardation. *Teaching Exceptional Children, 31*(4), 62–66.

Strong, K., & Sandoval, J. (1999). Mainstreaming children with neuromuscular disease: A map of concerns. *Exceptional Children, 65*(3), 353–366.

Strong, M. F., & Maralani, V. J. (1998). *Farmworkers and disability: Results of a national survey.* Austin, TX: National Center for Farmworkers Health.

Stroud, J. E., Stroud, J. E., & Staley, L. M. (1997). Understanding and supporting adoptive families. *Early Childhood Education Journal, 24*(4), 229–234.

Stuart, J. L., & Goodsitt, J. L. (1996). From hospital to school: How a transition liaison can help. *Teaching Exceptional Children, 28*(2), 58–62.

Stuart, J. L., Markey, M., & Sweet, A. (1995, April). *Driving out myths and tracking resources concerning HIV and AIDS.* Presentation at the annual meeting of the Council for Exceptional Children, Indianapolis.

Students for Social Justice. (n.d.). Being gay at Greeley. *Left Is Right, 2*(1), 1–4.

Stump, C. S., & Wilson, C. (1996). Collaboration: Making it happen. *Intervention in School and Clinic, 31*(5), 310–312.

Sturm, J. M., Rankin, J. L., Beukelman, D. R., & Schutz-Muehling, L. (1997). How to select appropriate software for computer-assisted writing. *Intervention in School and Clinic, 32*(3), 148–161.

Sturomski, N. (1997, July). Teaching students with learning disabilities to use learning strategies. *NICHCY News Digest, 25,* 2–12.

Sugai, G. A., Horner, R. H., & Sprague, J. R. (1999). Functional-assessment-based behavior support planning: Research to practice to research. *Behavioral Disorders, 24*(3), 253–257.

Sugai, G. A., & Smith, P. (1986). The equal additions method of subtraction taught with a modeling technique. *Remedial and Special Education, 7,* 40–48.

Sumar, S. (1998). *Yoga for the special child: A therapeutic approach for infants and children with Down syndrome, cerebral palsy, and learning disabilities.* Buckingham, VA: Special Yoga Publications.

Summers, L., Mikell, S., Redmond, S., Roberts, D., & Hampton, J. (1997, April). *Educating the student with muscular dystrophy: A collaborative approach.* Presentation at the annual meeting of the Council for Exceptional Children, Salt Lake City, UT.

Suritsky, S. K., & Hughes, C. A. (1996). Notetaking strategy instruction. In D. D. Deshler, E. S. Ellis, & B. K. Lenz (Eds.), *Teaching adolescents with learning disabilities: Strategies and methods* (2nd ed, pp. 267–312). Denver: Love.

Suzuki, B. H. (1984). Curriculum transformation for multicultural education. *Education and Urban Society, 16,* 294–322.

Swaggart, B. L. (1998). Implementing a cognitive behavior management program. *Intervention in School and Clinic, 33*(4), 235–238.

Swanson, P. N., & De La Paz, S. (1998). Teaching effective comprehension strategies to students with learning and reading disabilities. *Intervention in School and Clinic, 33*(4), 209–218.

Sweeney, D. L., Clark, K. R., & Silva, D. (1995, April). *Meeting the challenges of HIV/AIDS prevention education for special education populations.* Presentation at the annual meeting of the Council for Exceptional Children, Indianapolis.

Sweeney, D. P., Forness, S. R., Kavale, K., & Levitt, J. G. (1997). An update on psychopharmacologic medication: What teachers, clinicians, and parents need to know. *Intervention in School and Clinic, 33*(1), 4–21, 25.

Swicegood, P. R. (1994). Portfolio-based assessment practices. *Intervention in School and Clinic, 30*(1), 6–15.

Swisher, K. G. (1997, Fall). Nations within. *Teaching Tolerance,* 11–15.

Synatschk, K. (1995). College-bound students with learning disabilities: Assessment of readiness for academic success. *LD Forum, 20*(4), 23–29.

Tankersley, M. (1995). A group-contingency management program: A review of research on the good behavior game and implications for teachers. *Preventing School Failure, 40*(1), 19–24.

Taylor, L. S. (1992). *Adult remedial mathematics: Diagnostic and teaching strategies.* Manuscript submitted for publication.

Taylor, L. S., Gutierrez, M. B., Whittaker, C., & Salend, S. J. (1995, April). *Adapting the curriculum to reflect the needs and experiences of migrant students.* Presentation at the annual meeting of the Council for Exceptional Children, Indianapolis.

Taylor, R. L. (1997). *Assessment of exceptional students: Educational and psychological procedures* (4th ed.). Boston: Allyn & Bacon.

Taylor, S. (2000). Multicultural is who we are: Literature as a reflection of ourselves. *Teaching Exceptional Children, 32*(3), 24–29.

Teicher, J. (1999). An action plan for smart Internet use. *Educational Leadership, 56*(5), 70–74.

The Governor's Commission on Gay and Lesbian Youth. (1993). *Making schools safe for gay and lesbian youth: Breaking the silence in schools and in families.* Boston: Author.

Thistlethwaite, L. L. (1991). Summarizing: It's more than just finding the main idea. *Intervention in School and Clinic, 27,* 25–30.

Thoma, C. A. (1999). Supporting student voice in transition planning. *Teaching Exceptional Children, 31*(5), 4–9.

Thomas, C., Correa, V. I., & Morsink, C. V. (1995). *Interactive teaming: Consultation and collaboration in special education programs* (2nd ed.). Upper Saddle River, NJ: Merrill/Prentice Hall.

Thomas, S. B., & Hawke, C. (1999). Health-care services for children with disabilities: Emerging standards and implications. *Journal of Special Education, 32*(4), 226–237.

Thomas, S. B., & Rapport, M. J. K. (1998). The least restrictive environment: Understanding the directions of the courts. *The Journal of Special Education, 32*(2), 66–78.

Thomas, W. P., & Collier, V. P. (1997). *School effectiveness for language minority students.* Washington, DC: National Clearinghouse for Bilingual Education.

Thomas, W. P., & Collier, V. P. (1998). Two languages are better than one. *Educational Leadership, 55*(4), 23–26.

Thompson, D. P. (1990). From "it easy" to "it is easy": Empowering the African-American student in the racially mixed classroom. *The Clearing House, 63,* 314–317.

Thompson, K. L., & Taymans, J. M. (1994). Development of a reading strategies program: Bridging the gaps among decoding, literature, and thinking skills. *Intervention in School and Clinic, 30*(1), 17–27.

Thoms, K. J. (1999). Teaching via ITV: Taking instructional design to the next level. *The Journal, 26*(9), 60–66.

Thornton, C., & Krajewski, J. (1993). Death education for teachers: A refocused concern relative to medically fragile children. *Intervention in School and Clinic, 29*(1), 31–35.

Thornton, C. A., Langrall, C. W., & Jones, G. A. (1997). Mathematics instruction for elementary students with learning disabilities. *Journal of Learning Disabilities, 30*(2), 142–150.

Thornton, C. A., & Toohey, M. A. (1985). Basic math facts: Guidelines for teaching and learning. *Learning Disabilities Focus, 1,* 44–57.

Thornton, C. A., Tucker, B. F., Dossey, J. A., & Brazik, E. F. (1983). *Teaching mathematics to children with special needs.* Menlo Park, CA: Addison-Wesley.

Thorp, E. K. (1997). Increasing opportunities for partnership with culturally and linguistically diverse families. *Intervention in School and Clinic, 32*(5), 261–269.

Thousand, J. S., Rosenberg, R. L., Bishop, K. D., & Villa, R. A. (1997). The evolution of secondary inclusion. *Remedial and Special Education, 18*(5), 270–284, 306.

Thurlow, M. L., Ysseldyke, J. E., & Reid, C. L. (1997). High school graduation requirements for students with disabilities. *Journal of Learning Disabilities, 30*(6), 608–616.

Thurlow, M. L., Ysseldyke, J. E., & Silverstein, B. (1995). Testing accommodations for students with disabilities. *Remedial and Special Education, 16*(5), 260–270.

Tiedt, P. L., & Tiedt, I. M. (1995). *Multicultural teaching: A handbook of activities, information, and resources* (4th ed.). Boston: Allyn & Bacon.

Tilley, W. D., Kovaleski, J., Dunlap, G., Knoster, T. P., Bambara, L., & Kincaid, D. (1998). *Functional behavioral assessment: Policy development in light of emerging research and practice.* Alexandria, VA: National Association of State Directors of Special Education.

Timothy W. v. Rochester, N.H. Sch. Dist., 875 F.2d 954 1st Circuit 1989.

Tindal, G., Heath, B., Hollenbeck, K., Almond, P., & Harniss, M. (1998). Accommodating students with disabilities on large-scale tests: An experimental study. *Exceptional Children, 64*(4), 439–450.

Tobias, T. (1977). *Easy or hard? That's a good question.* Chicago: Children's Press.

Tobin, T. J., & Sugai, G. M. (1999). Using sixth-grade school records to predict school violence, chronic discipline problems, and high school outcomes. *Journal of Emotional and Behavioral Disorders, 7*(1), 40–53.

Topping, K. J., & McKenna, M. C. (1999). Introduction to electronic literacy—Part 1. *Reading and Writing Quarterly: Overcoming Learning Difficulties, 15*(2), 107–110.

Torres, I., & Corn, A. L. (1990). *When you have a visually handicapped child in your classroom: Classroom suggestions for teachers.* New York: American Foundation for the Blind.

Trafton, P. R., & Claus, A. (1994). A changing curriculum for a changing age. In C. A. Thornton & N. S. Bley (Eds.), *Windows of opportunity: Mathematics for students with special needs* (pp. 19–39). Reston, VA: National Council of Teachers of Mathematics.

Trent, S. C. (1998). False starts and other dilemmas of a secondary general education collaborative teacher: A case study. *Journal of Learning Disabilities, 31*(5), 503–513.

Troia, G. A., Graham, S., & Harris, K. R. (1999). Teaching students with learning disabilities to mindfully plan when writing. *Exceptional Children, 65*(2), 235–252.

Trollinger, G., & Slavkin, R. (1999). Purposeful e-mail as stage 3 technology: IEP goals online. *Teaching Exceptional Children, 32*(1), 10–15.

Trowbridge, L. W., & Bybee, R. W. (1996). *Teaching secondary school science. Strategies for developing scientific literacy* (6th ed.). Upper Saddle River, NJ: Prentice Hall.

Tur-Kaspa, H., & Bryan, T. (1994). Social information-processing skills of students with learning disabilities. *Learning Disabilities Research and Practice, 9*(1), 12–23.

Turnbull, A. P., & Ruef, M. (1997). Family perceptives on inclusive lifestyle issues for people with problem behavior. *Exceptional Children, 63*(2), 211–227.

Turnbull, A. P., Turnbull, H. R., Shank, M., & Leal, D. (1999). *Exceptional lives: Special education in today's schools* (2nd ed.). Upper Saddle River, NJ: Prentice Hall.

Udell, T., Peters, J., & Templeman, T. P. (1998). From philosophy to practice in early childhood programs. *Teaching Exceptional Children, 30*(3), 44–49.

United States Department of Education. (1995). *Seventeenth annual report to Congress on the implementation of the Individuals with Disabilities Education Act.* Washington, DC: U.S. Government Printing Office.

United States Department of Education. (1996). *Eighteenth annual report to Congress on the implementation of the Individuals with Disabilities Education Act.* Washington, DC: U.S. Government Printing Office.

United States Department of Education. (1997). *Nineteenth annual report to Congress on the implementation of the Individuals with Disabilities Education Act.* Washington, DC: U.S. Government Printing Office.

United States Department of Education. (1998). *Twentieth annual report to Congress on the implementation of the Individuals with Disabilities Education Act.* Washington, DC: U.S. Government Printing Office.

United States Office of Special Programs (1999, Fall). Universal design: Ensuring access to the general education curriculum. *Research Connections in Special Education, 5,* 1–5.

Valente, R. (1994). *Law in the schools* (3rd ed.). Upper Saddle River, NJ: Merrill/Prentice Hall.

Vanderheiden, G. C. (1996). Computer access and use by people with disabilities. In J. C. Galvin & M. J. Scherer (Eds.), *Evaluating, selecting, and using appropriate assistive technology* (pp. 237–276). Gaithersburg, MD: Aspen.

Vargo, S. (1998). Consulting teacher-to-teacher. *Teaching Exceptional Children, 30*(3), 54–55.

Vasa, S. F. (1981). Alternative procedures for grading handicapped students in the secondary schools. *Education Unlimited, 3,* 16–23.

Vaughn, S., Bos, C. S., & Lund, K. A. (1986). . . . But they can do it in my room: Strategies for promoting generalization. *Teaching Exceptional Children, 18,* 176–180.

Vaughn, S., Elbaum, B. E., & Schumm, J. S. (1996). The effects of inclusion on the social functioning of students with learning disabilities. *Journal of Learning Disabilities, 29,* 598–608.

Vaughn, S., & Klingner, J. K. (1998). Students' perceptions of inclusion and resource room settings. *The Journal of Special Education, 32*(2), 79–88.

Vaughn, S., Schumm, J. S., & Kouzekanani, K. (1993). What do students with learning disabilities think when their general education teachers make adaptations? *Journal of Learning Disabilities, 26*(8), 545–555.

Vernon, D. S., Schumaker, J. B., & Deshler, D. D. (1995). Programs to teach cooperation and teamwork. *Intervention in School and Clinic, 31*(2), 121–125.

Villa, R. A., & Thousand, J. S. (1992). Student collaboration: An essential for curriculum delivery in the 21st century. In S. Stainback & W. Stainback (Eds.), *Curriculum considerations in inclusive classrooms: Facilitating learning for all students* (pp. 117–142). Baltimore: Paul H. Brookes.

Villa, R. A., Thousand, J. S., Meyers, H., & Nevin, A. (1996). Teacher and administrator perceptions of heterogeneous education. *Exceptional Children, 63*(1), 29–45.

Voltz, D. L. (1998). Cultural diversity and special education teacher preparation: Critical issues confronting the field. *Teacher Education and Special Education, 21,* 63–70.

Voltz, D. L., & Damiano-Lantz, M. (1993). Developing ownership in learning. *Teaching Exceptional Children, 25*(4), 18–22.

Wadsworth, D. E., & Knight, D. (1999). Preparing the inclusion classroom for students with special physical and health needs. *Intervention in School and Clinic, 34*(3), 170–175.

Wadsworth, D. E., Knight, D., & Balser, V. (1993). Children who are medically fragile or technology dependent: Guidelines. *Intervention in School and Clinic, 29*(2), 102–104.

Waldron, N. L. (1996). Child abuse and disability: The school's role in prevention and intervention. *Preventing School Failure, 40*(4), 164–168.

Waldron, N. L., & McLeskey, J. (1998). The effects of an inclusive school program on students with mild and severe learning disabilities. *Exceptional Children, 64,* 395–405.

Waldron, N. L., McLeskey, J., & Pacchiano, D. (1999). Giving teachers a voice: Teachers' perspectives regarding elementary inclusive school programs (ISP). *Teacher Education and Special Education, 22*(3), 141–153.

Walker, H. M., & Gresham, F. M. (1997). Making schools safer and violence free. *Intervention in School and Clinic, 32*(4), 199–204.

Wall, M. E., & Dattilo, J. (1995). Creating option-rich learning environments: Facilitating self-determination. *The Journal of Special Education, 29*(3), 276–294.

Wallerstein, J. S., & Blakeslee, S. (1989). *Second chances: Men, women and children a decade after divorce. Who wins, who loses—and why.* New York: Ticknor & Fields.

Walsh, R. (1994). Making the journey to communication with assistive technology. *Exceptional Parent, 24*(11), 37–41.

Walther-Thomas, C. (1997). Co-teaching experiences: The benefits and problems that teachers and principals report over time. *Journal of Learning Disabilities, 30*(4), 395–407.

Walther-Thomas, C., Bryant, M., & Land, S. (1996). Planning for effective co-teaching. The key to successful inclusion. *Remedial and Special Education, 17,* 255–265.

Wang, M. C., Reynolds, M. C., & Walberg, H. J. (1995). Serving students at the margins. *Educational Leadership, 52*(4), 12–17.

Webb, J. T. (1995). Nurturing the social-emotional development of gifted children. *Teaching Exceptional Children, 27*(2), 76–77.

Webb-Johnson, G. (1992, April). *Using cultural frameworks to educate African American youth who demonstrate educational/behavioral problems.* Paper presented at the meeting of the Council for Exceptional Children, Baltimore.

Webber, J. (1997) Comprehending youth violence: A practical perspective. *Remedial and Special Education, 18*(2), 94–104.

Wehman, P., West, M., & Kregel, J. (1999). Supported employment program development and research needs: Looking ahead to the year 2000. *Education and Training in Mental Retardation and Developmental Disabilities, 34*(1), 3–19.

Wehmeyer, M. L., & Schwartz, M. (1997). Self-determination and positive adult outcomes: A follow-up study of youth with mental retardation or learning disabilities. *Exceptional Children, 63*(2), 245–255.

Weishaar, M. K., & Boyle, J. R. (1997). Note taking for students with mild disabilities. *CEC Today, 4*(5), 12.

Welch, M. (1994). Ecological assessment: A collaborative approach to planning instructional interventions. *Intervention in School and Clinic, 29*(3), 160–164, 183.

Welton, E. N. (1999). How to help inattentive students find success in school. *Teaching Exceptional Children, 31*(6), 12–18.

Wenz-Gross, M., & Siperstein, G. N. (1997). Importance of social support in the adjustment of children with learning problems. *Exceptional Children, 63*(2), 183–193.

Werts, M. G., Wolery, M., Gast, D. L., & Holcombe, A. (1996). Sneak in some extra learning by using instructive feedback. *Teaching Exceptional Children, 28*(3), 70–71.

Werts, M. G., Wolery, M., Snyder, E. D., Caldwell, N. K., & Salisbury, C. L. (1996). Supports and resources associated with inclusive schooling: Perceptions of elementary school teachers about need and availability. *The Journal of Special Education, 30*(2), 187–203.

Wesson, C. L., & King, R. P. (1996). Portfolio assessment and special education students. *Teaching Exceptional Children, 28*(2), 44–48.

Wesson, C. L., & Mandell, C. (1989). Simulations promote understanding of handicapping conditions. *Teaching Exceptional Children, 21*(1), 32–35.

West, R. P., Young, K. R., Callahan, K., Fister, S., Kemp, K., Freston, J., & Lovitt, T. C. (1995). The musical clocklight: Encouraging positive classroom behavior. *Teaching Exceptional Children, 27*(2), 46–51.

Westby, C. E. (1992). Whole language and learners with mild handicaps. *Focus on Exceptional Children, 24*(8), 1–16.

Wetzel, K. (1996). Speech-recognizing computers: A written-communication tool for students with learning disabilities? *Journal of Learning Disabilities, 29*(4), 371–380.

Whittaker, C. R. (1991). *The cooperative learning planner.* Ann Arbor, MI: Exceptional Innovations.

Whittaker, C. R. (1996). Adapting cooperative learning structures for mainstreamed students. *Reading and Writing Quarterly. Overcoming Learning Difficulties, 12*(1), 23–39.

Whittaker, C. R., Salend, S. J., & Gutierrez, M. (1997). "Voices from the fields": Including migrant workers in the curriculum. *The Reading Teacher, 50*(6), 482–493.

Whitten, E., & Diecker, L. (1995). Intervention assistance teams: A broader vision. *Preventing School Failure, 40*(1), 41–45.

Wiener, J., & Sunohara, G., (1998). Parents' perceptions of the quality of friendships of their children with learning disabilities. *Learning Disabilities Research and Practice, 13*(4), 242–257.

Wiggins, G. (1997). Practicing what we preach in designing authentic assessments. *Educational Leadership, 54*(4), 18–25.

Wiig, E. H., Freedman, E., & Secord, W. A. (1992). Developing words and concepts in the classroom: A holistic-thematic approach. *Intervention in School and Clinic, 27*(5), 278–285.

Williams, V. I., & Cartledge, G. (1997). Passing notes—Parents. *Teaching Exceptional Children, 30*(1), 30–34.

Williams, W., & Fox, T. J. (1996). Planning for inclusion: A practical process. *Teaching Exceptional Children, 28*(3), 6–13.

Williamson, R. D. (1997). Help me organize. *Intervention in School and Clinic, 33*(1), 36–39.

Wilmore, E. L. (1995). When your child is special. *Educational Leadership, 52*(4), 60–62.

Wilson, B. A. (1999). Inclusion: Empirical guidelines and unanswered questions. *Education and Training in Mental Retardation and Developmental Disabilities, 34*(2), 119–133.

Wilson, C. L. (1995). Parents and teachers: Can we talk? *Learning Disabilities Forum, 20*(2), 31–33.

Winn, J. A., & Otis-Wilborn, A. (1999). Monitoring literacy learning. *Teaching Exceptional Children, 32*(1), 40–47.

Winsor, P. J. T. (1998). Talking-point: Books about children with learning disabilities. *Teaching Exceptional Children, 30*(3), 34–35.

Wissick, C. A. (1996). Multimedia: Enhancing instruction for students with disabilities. *Journal of Learning Disabilities, 29*(5), 494–503.

Witt, J. C., Elliott, S. N., Daly, E. J., Gresham, F. M., & Kramer, J. J. (1998). *Assessment of at-risk and special needs children* (2nd ed.). New York: McGraw-Hill.

Witte, R. (1998). Meet Bob a student with traumatic brain injury. *Teaching Exceptional Children, 30*(3), 56–60.

Wolery, M., & Schuster, J. W. (1997). Instructional methods with students who have significant disabilities. *The Journal of Special Education, 31*(1), 61–79.

Wolfensberger, W. (1972). *The principle of normalization in human services.* Toronto: National Institute on Mental Retardation.

Wong, B. Y. L. (1986). A cognitive approach to spelling. *Exceptional Children, 53,* 169–173.

Wong, B. Y. L., & Jones, W. (1982). Increasing metacomprehension in learning disabled and normally achieving students through self-questioning training. *Learning Disability Quarterly, 5,* 228–240.

Wood, J. W., & Wooley, J. A. (1986). Adapting textbooks. *The Clearing House, 59,* 332–335.

Wood, K. D. (1995). Guiding middle school students through expository text. *Reading and Writing Quarterly: Overcoming Learning Difficulties, 11*(2), 137–147.

Wood, M. (1998). Whose job is it anyway? Educational roles in inclusion. *Exceptional Children, 64*(2), 181–195.

Wood, M., & Long, N. (1990). *Life space intervention: Talking to children and youth in a crisis.* Austin, TX: PRO-ED.

Woodward, J. (1999). Redoing the numbers: Secondary math for a postsecondary work world. *Teaching Exceptional Children, 31*(4), 74–79.

Woodward, J., & Baxter, J. (1997). The effects of an innovative approach to mathematics on academically low-achieving students in inclusive settings. *Exceptional Children, 63*(3), 373–388.

Woodward, J., Baxter, J., & Robinson, R. (1999). Rules and reasons: Decimal instruction for academically low achieving students. *Remedial and Special Education, 14*(1), 15–24.

Worsley, L. (1995). All I need is a friend. In *Share the Music* (p. 362). New York: Macmillan/McGraw-Hill.

Wren, C. S. (1998, December 20). Alcohol and drug use by teen-agers declines some, report says. *The New York Times,* 45.

Wright, H. F. (1967). *Recording and analyzing child behavior.* New York: Harper & Row.

Wright-Strawderman, C., Lindsey, P., Navarette, L., & Flippo, J. R. (1996). Depression in students with disabilities: Recognition and intervention strategies. *Intervention in School and Clinic, 31*(5), 261–275.

Xin, Y. P., & Jitendra, A. K. (1999). The effects of instruction on solving mathematical word problems for students with learning problems: A meta-analysis. *Journal of Learning Disabilities, 32*(4), 207–225.

Yamaguchi, B. J., Strawser, S., & Higgins, K. (1997). Children who are homeless: Implications for educators. *Intervention in School and Clinic, 33*(2), 90–97.

Yasutake, D., Bryan, T., & Dohrn, E. (1996). The effects of combining peer tutoring and attribution training on students' perceived self-competence. *Remedial and Special Education, 17*(2), 83–91.

Yates, J. R. (1998, April). *The state of practice in the education of CLD students.* Presentation at the annual meeting of the Council for Exceptional Children, Minneapolis.

Yehle, A. K., & Wambold, C. (1998). An ADHD success story: Strategies for teachers and students. *Teaching Exceptional Children, 30*(6), 8–13.

Yell, M. L. (1997). Teacher liability for student injury and misconduct. *Beyond Behavior, 8*(1), 4–9.

Yell, M. L. (1998). *The law and special education.* Upper Saddle River, NJ: Merrill/Prentice Hall.

Yoder, D. I., Retish, E., & Wade, R. (1996). Service learning: Meeting student and community needs. *Teaching Exceptional Children, 28*(4), 14–18.

York, J., & Tundidor, M. (1995). Issues raised in the name of inclusion: Perspectives of educators, parents, and students. *Journal of the Association for Persons with Severe Handicaps, 20,* 31–44.

York, J., Vandercook, T., Macdonald, C., Heise-Neff, C., & Caughey, E. (1992). Feedback about integrating middle-school students with severe disabilities in general education classes. *Exceptional Children, 58*(3), 244–258.

Ysseldyke, J. E., & Olsen, K. (1999). Putting alternate assessments into practice: What to measure and possible sources of data. *Exceptional Children, 65*(2), 175–185.

Zetlin, A. G., Padron, M., & Wilson, S. (1996). The experience of five Latin American families with the special education system. *Education and Training in Mental Retardation and Developmental Disabilities, 31*(1), 22–28.

Zigmond, N., Jenkins, J., Fuchs, L. S., Deno, S., Fuchs, D., Baker, J. N., Jenkins, L., & Couthino, M. (1995). Special education in restructured schools. Findings from three multi-year studies. *Phi Delta Kappan, 76,* 531–540.

Zima, B. T., Forness, S. R., Bussing, R., & Benjamin, B. (1998). Homeless children in emergency shelters: Need for prereferral intervention and potential eligibility for special education. *Behavioral Disorders, 23*(2), 98–110.

Zurkowski, J. K., Kelly, P. S., & Griswold, D. E. (1998). Discipline and the IDEA 1997: Instituting a new balance. *Intervention in School and Clinic, 34*(1), 3–9.

Zvirin, S. (1994). Disabled kids: Challenges and choices. *Book Links, 3*(3), 44–49.

Zvirin, S. (1996). Disabled kids: Learning, feeling, and behaving. *Book Links, 5*(5), 15–20.

Author Index

Subject Index